Artists, Advertising, and the Borders of Art

Advertising,

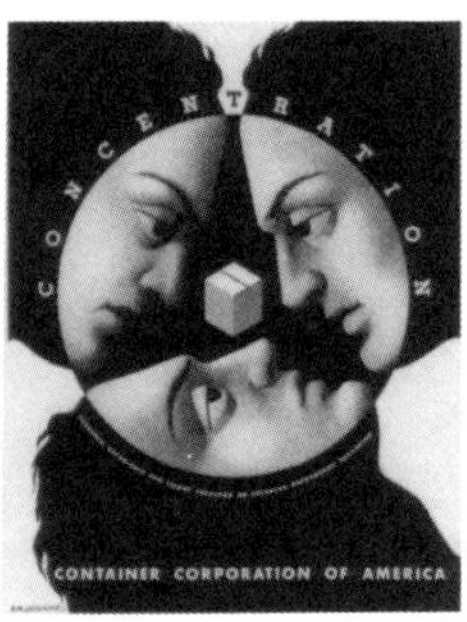

MICHELE H. BOGART

Artists,

and the Borders of Art

The University of Chicago Press
CHICAGO & LONDON

Michele H. Bogart is professor of art history at the State University of New York, Stony Brook. She is the author of *Public Sculpture and the Civic Ideal in New York City, 1890–1930,* also published by the University of Chicago Press.

The University of Chicago Press, Chicago 60637
The University of Chicago Press, Ltd., London

Printed in the United States of America
04 03 02 01 00 99 98 97 96 95 5 4 3 2 1

ISBN (cloth): 0-226-06307-0

This book has been supported by a grant from the National Endowment for the Humanities, an independent federal agency.

Library of Congress Cataloging-in-Publication Data

Bogart, Michele Helene, 1952–
Artists, advertising, and the borders of art / Michele H. Bogart.
p. cm.
Includes index.
ISBN 0-226-06307-0
1. Commercial art—United States. I. Title.
NC998.5.A1B63 1995
741.6′0973—dc20 94-43010
CIP

♾ The paper used in this publication meets the minimum requirements of the American National Standard for Information Sciences—Permanence of Paper for Printed Library Materials, ANSI Z39.48-1984.

Contents

List of Illustrations

Acknowledgments

ALTHOUGH I CANNOT BE SURE OF IT, I believe that this book was inspired by two experiences some twenty-odd years ago. When I was in high school I aspired to illustrate The Who's rock opera *Tommy;* this private project provided a glimmer of the challenges of illustration. At the same time, I worked during summers translating written responses to market research surveys into numerical codes for computer keypunchers. The experience sharpened my awareness of the craft, complexity, and especially the humor of advertising. These interests made their way into various undergraduate papers, but I then turned to other, seemingly more serious, aesthetic concerns.

I took up the project in earnest in 1988, when a Benno M. Forman Fellowship from the Winterthur Museum, Garden, and Library enabled me to begin research under ideal conditions. A Smithsonian Institution Senior Postdoctoral Fellowship at the National Museum of American Art, a Summer Fellowship from the State University of New York at Stony Brook, a publication subsidy from the Office of Seminars of Columbia University, and a National Endowment for the Humanities Fellowship provided assistance that made completion of the book possible. I am indebted to these institutions, and am particularly grateful for the hospitality provided by staff members at the Winterthur Museum and the National Museum of American Art. I also appreciate the efforts of Aaron Warner of Columbia University.

Thanks are due to the many people who helped me locate materials and generously shared their own ideas and research. I am especially grateful to Walt Reed, founder of Illustration House. I thank him for preserving the past, for sharing his knowledge of illustrators and their work, and for allowing me to consult unique books and archival materials in his possession. I also wish to express my appreciation to the following: Joshua Brown; Earl Davis; Robert Doherty; Elizabeth H. Hawkes; Kathleen Hulser; Patricia Johnston; Jackson Lears; Roland Marchand; James Morske; Carol Willis; Andrew Dolkart; Edward W. Warwick; Deborah Bershad and Peggy Hammerle, Art Commission of the City of New York; Greg Etchison, The Brownstone Gallery, Brooklyn; Bruce Weber, Berry-Hill Gallery; Barbara Dunlap, Archives, City College of New York; Fred Taraba, Illustration House; Nichole Friedler and Matilda McQuaid, Museum of Modern Art; the staff of the New York Public Library; Ruth Bassett, Brandywine River Museum; Rowland Elzea, Iris Snyder, and Helen

Farr Sloan, Delaware Art Museum; Neville Thompson and Catherine Hutchins, Winterthur Museum; Andrew Eskind, International Museum of Photography; Arthur Breton and Garnett McCoy, Archives of American Art; David Haberstich and Charles McGovern, National Museum of American History; Martin Kalfatovich, Patricia Lynagh, and the staff of the National Museum of Art/National Portrait Gallery Library; Ellen Miles, Lillian Miller, and Wendy Wick Reaves, National Portrait Gallery; Kimberley Cody, George Gurney, Richard Murray, and William Truettner, National Museum of American Art. NMAA fellows Elizabeth O'Leary, David McCarthy, Alex Nemerov, Michael Plante, Kathleen Pyne, and David Steinberg provided great ideas, excellent research leads, and good cheer. Lois M. Fink, Virginia M. Mecklenburg, Martina Roudabush Norelli, and Judith Throm deserve special thanks for their tremendously valuable guidance and support during my residency at NMAA. Amy K. Damin, Biederman Industries; Chris Jones, Pepsico; Carley R. Robison, Seymour Library, Knox College; Heidi Wanner, N. W. Ayer; Ellen G. Gartrell, John W. Hartman Center for Sales, Advertising, and Marketing History, Special Collections Library, Duke University, and Philip N. Cronenwett, Dartmouth College Library, were all exceedingly helpful.

My thinking about this book has benefited considerably from the thoughtful suggestions of other scholars. I would like to thank David Goldfield, Mark Weiss, and Leonard Wallock for providing me with opportunities to present my ideas at the American Historical Association and the City Seminar, Columbia University. Comments from Michael Leja, Donald Olsen, Karal Ann Marling, Susan Strasser, Sam Bass Warner, and Gwendolyn Wright helped me to refine sections of the manuscript. I am particularly grateful to Mary Panzer, for her thorough reading of my photography chapter, and to my anonymous readers for the University of Chicago Press, for their superbly incisive and constructive recommendations. I hope that all of these individuals will find the positive effects of their labors reflected in these pages. I would also like to express my appreciation to Ken Ames, Toby Appel, Greg Bogart, Sarah Burns, Vivien Green Fryd, Deborah Gardner, Katherine Jacob, Elizabeth Johns, John Maggiotto, Ann Smart Martin, Katharine Martinez, Catherine Mulhern, Roy Rosenzweig, Richard Shiff, and Wendy Katkin for all their help and support. I thank Norma Roche for her vigilance and sensitivity in copyediting the manuscript. I am also indebted to Karen Wilson, Maya Hoptman, and Candace Rossin at the University of Chicago Press for their encouragement and expert assistance throughout all phases of production.

My family deserves an ovation. I applaud Nicholas Bogart Pauly, who has lived with this book since his birth, for being such a kind, generous, and tolerant child. My husband Philip Pauly served on numerous occasions as sounding board, critic, and editor. I am truly grateful for all of his help on this book, but I am even more thankful for his remarkable optimism, courage, and strength. I dedicate this book to my parents, Agnes and Leo Bogart. Their experiences in the worlds of business and scholarship have contributed to this project in innumerable ways. Both offered encouragement and careful critical readings. They were there for me when I really needed them. Had it not been for them, this book would not now be complete.

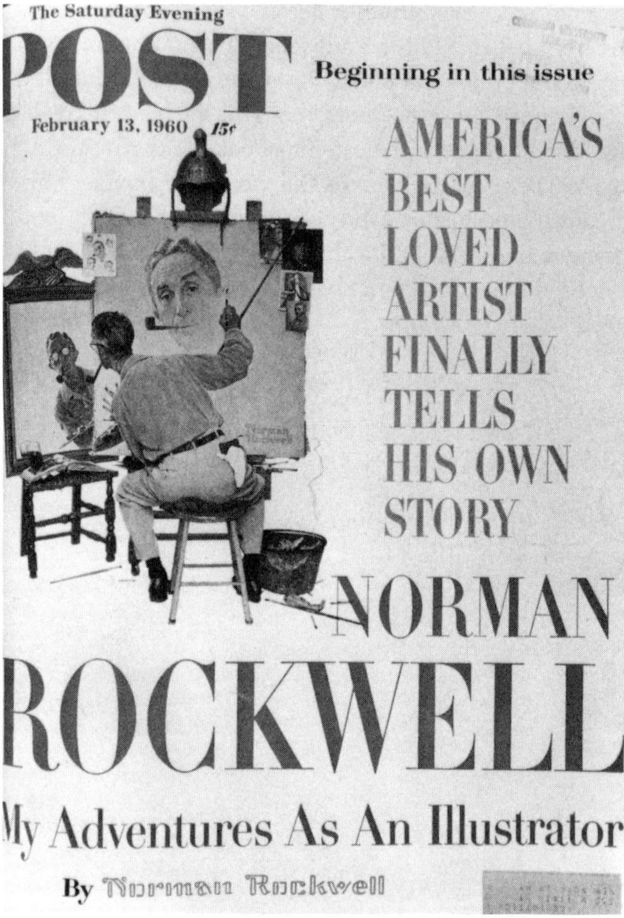

1. Cover, *Saturday Evening Post,* with *Triple Self-Portrait* by Norman Rockwell, 13 February 1960.

Introduction

Norman Rockwell's *Triple Self-Portrait* (fig. 1), the cover illustration of the 13 February 1960 *Saturday Evening Post,* depicted the popular artist at work at the vexing task of self-portrayal. Partly intentionally, but partly inadvertently, Rockwell represented both his own unique position and, more generally, the conflicting roles of the twentieth-century American artist in commerce. Literally and figuratively, several artists emerge.

The first Norman Rockwell is the one that "we all know," "the nation's favorite artist" and a "regular fellow." His very name conjures up images of Home, Family, Small Town Community, and the Common Man.[1] The self-portrait, through the emblem of the mirror with its eagle and stars-and-stripes crest, reinforces the linkage of Rockwell to patriotism and national identity. What the beholder sees is a picture of America, the America "mirrored" through Norman Rockwell's pictures. What Rockwell portrays *is* America. This confident public portrait is enhanced, yet simultaneously contradicted, as the poised, sophisticated, formal public portrait emerging from the artist's brush on canvas is contrasted with the bewildered face in the mirror. By juxtaposing this idealized portrayal and the mirrored "actuality," Rockwell self-assuredly mocks his own hifalutin pretensions, and thus reassures us that he knows he is really "just like us."

These familiar illusions of Rockwell as artist and person are strengthened further through his decision to focus on the act of self-portrayal. Rockwell's subject alludes to his lifelong, frequent practice of describing his working methods in articles, interviews, and autobiography.[2] These texts served several purposes: they reinforced the familiar persona of Rockwell as a real person, pleased to show the public how he did what he did. The descriptions also attested to Rockwell's artistic stature, to the fact that he was so successful that he could reveal the tricks of his trade without tarnishing his reputation. These explanations also expressed Rockwell's refusal to identify with fine artists. The technical revelations were his attempt to deflate and demystify the "artistes," whose actions were often presented by their interpreters as the inexplicable manifestations of genius. Rockwell's representation seemed to express his acceptance of his position as a conventional academic artist whose work could in theory be replicated by anyone.

The "other" Norman Rockwell to be found in *Triple Self-Portrait* is a more complex figure. This complexity is first suggested by the very choice of subject, for while artists' self-portraits have been commonplace, triple self-portraits are not. The decision to create a multiple portrait was itself an indication that Rockwell believed there was more than one side to himself, despite the familiar and beloved persona that he had helped to construct. Indeed, *Triple Self-Portrait* further suggests that there were aspects of his identity, and of illustrators more generally, that were uncertain and misunderstood.

These meanings were conveyed through the representation of the subject, Norman Rockwell. The painting depicts three Rockwells: the artist and beholder, the subject image he (and we) view, and the painted portrait, his representation. The "real" Norman Rockwell, the painter, is seated with his back turned to his loyal public, his viewers, who therefore get no visual "grasp" of him. In the image mirrored back to Rockwell, and to the viewer, the eyes that gaze (the windows to the soul, and emblem of their homonym "I,") are missing. The gaze that ordinarily has the power to represent identity is rendered nil. The picture of self is partial and incomplete.

This incompleteness is conveyed not only figuratively, but also literally, through the image of Rockwell's second self-portrait on canvas. That public and ideal image is presented as unfinished. It is also literally a self-effacement, a metaphor for the untemperamental temperament necessary for an artist to be successful in commerce. (Rockwell worked hard to project this unassuming manner in his autobiography.) And yet it still presents itself as the self-portrait of a confident professional—with upward-thrusting pipe—the patriotic, virtuoso technician who relies upon the real world for inspiration.

Triple Self-Portrait addresses the significance of Rockwell's working practices: in particular, the contingency of the connection between artistic purpose and meaning. As a self-portrait, *Triple Self-Portrait* presumably bore special significance for the creator, for, no matter what the stimulus for creation, self-portraits are always rendered for oneself. As such, certain significances of the image remained private. Yet this personal self-image was explicitly made for a mass audience: millions of *Saturday Evening Post* readers as represented by the art editor of the *Post*. *Triple Self-Portrait*'s subject matter was not determined by another, but it was done on order, and according to a deadline. It was displayed in a very public forum, and from the client's perspective was explicitly intended to sell the magazine. Yet the image's public and commercial purposes, in and of themselves, would not invalidate the picture's personal or more intimate expressive resonances, neither for the artist nor for the many individuals who enjoyed viewing *Triple Self-Portrait* in their homes. If anything, the picture's very presence on the *Post* cover was a demonstration of the centrality of Rockwell's work as a truly popular art existing within the frame of mass media and national advertising.

That meaning is underscored by the reproductions of famous self-portraits that Rockwell displayed attached to his canvas. These features induce the viewer to address the perplexing issues regarding relationships of practice, style, talent, public, and artistic reputation (the complexity of which would be sufficient cause for the puzzled look on the mirrored Rockwell face). The Dürer, Rembrandt, Picasso, and Van Gogh self-portraits indicate that Rockwell judged his art and his artistic identity in relation to a tradition of old and modern master painters. Rockwell's own formal self-portrait is itself an "easel picture" (a term that since the mid-nineteenth century had connoted painting meant to be appreciated in the original), a factor that connects his practice with that of the masters. Whether he considered his work to be the true legacy of these artists, or simply inspired by them, is uncertain. What linked all of these artists by the 1960s, however, was the fame they had as a result of mass reproduction of their images. By juxtaposing his own art and the Old Master pictures, Rockwell asserted that the relationship between fine art painting and commercial culture was an intimate one, integral to the identity of any famous and popular artistic practitioner of the twentieth century.

As this preceding reading of *Triple Self-Portrait* suggests, when it comes to the relationships between art and life, painting and illustration, fine art and popular culture, art and advertising, and the identity of the artist, there is clearly more than meets the eye. Indeed, Rockwell's work—both as image and as productive activity—raises important issues that are central to the definition of art in this century. It highlights questions—still unresolved—about the status of the artist, the nature of artistic work, the relationship between artist and public, and the relationship between fine art, popular culture, and commerce in a society shaped by national advertising and mass media.

Despite some recent artistic and historical efforts to level "high/low" distinctions in art, debates continue and distinctions persist.[3] Many scholars regard artwork like Rockwell's, commissioned to sell products or appeal to a popular audience, as unworthy of serious study and even beneath contempt. Commercial art still occupies a marginal place in modern American art's history, if not society at large. This study seeks to alter that state of affairs, and to uncover the circumstances that will shed light on how and why it has occurred. The meanings and ambiguities of *Triple Self-Portrait,* as I have interpreted them, are thus the concerns of this book.

Artists, Advertising, and the Borders of Art investigates the fluctuations of status among illustrators, poster producers, art directors, photographers, and painters in relationship to conceptions and practices of fine art and commercial art in the United States during the first half of the twentieth century. It examines the emergence and organization of artistic activities and products promoting commerce. And it explores the real and perceived changes in practice and purpose accompanying these new configurations of art for publicity. The histories recounted here are intended to illuminate the mechanisms and effects of what scholars describe as the culture of consumption, linked closely to the rise of mass culture.[4] The accounts track shifting notions of artistic and professional identity as they developed within the culture of corporate commerce that characterizes this distinctly modern period of American cultural history, whose parameters are set by the rise of mass-market periodicals and the saturation of the public market by television.

The book explores how late-nineteenth-century developments in publishing and advertising widened the confines of art to include illustration and posters. Initially, practitioners in these fields met with a favorable reception. Enthusiasm faded in the second decade of the twentieth century; many observers perceived the forces of commerce to be adversely affecting the intents and practices of artists and to be encroaching inappropriately into realms of experience once deemed private. The standing of illustration and billboards was diminished.

United States involvement in World War I helped advertisers attain greater respect and influence; during the 1920s, advertising art directors maneuvered, relatively successfully, to make the circles of art and advertising intersect. Also in this decade, photographers gained new favor with advertisers by challenging the validity of art as a claim to visual or professional authority in the world of advertising. The effects of the Great Depression induced a skittish advertising industry to embrace commercial photographers' rhetoric of indifference toward art, at the very point when some painters were trying to forge new links between art and business. Even so, in the late 1930s and early 1940s, collaborations between unusual clients and art directors, painters and graphic designers led to speculations that fine art and commercial art were converging.

Scholars have followed this line of thinking. Art historians, focusing on developments of the 1950s and 1960s with eyes trained on masters like Pollock, De Kooning, and Warhol, have regarded corporate business and art as increasingly intertwined, the boundaries between them as (threateningly) permeable.[5] This book, which builds from the premise that our picture of art's history is skewed by overemphasis on major artists, offers different conclusions. It shows that with the emergence of television, the terrain of art practice expanded and became more stratified, but the ideological borders of fine art narrowed and rigidified. This last point is crucial. In many ways, the ideological parameters of art established four decades ago still inform many people's conceptions of what is art and fuels their prejudices against what is "not."

THE ASCENDANCY OF the mass print media in the late nineteenth century produced crucial changes for artists, both positive and negative. The 1890s saw the introduction of numerous new general interest and specialty magazines, including *Ladies' Home Journal, Collier's, Saturday Evening Post, Life, Cosmopolitan, Pearson's,* and *Everybody's.* Seeking to capitalize on the increased literacy and leisure time enjoyed by a broad sector of the American populace, and hoping to expand the market for books, publishers targeted audiences of unprecedented size, and they now especially courted women. From publishers' perspectives, women were important not only as readers but as purchasers of the goods publicized in the advertisements in the new magazines. Pictures became a major part of the strategy for luring and keeping new readers.[6]

The proliferation of illustrated magazines was possible in part because of the rise of national advertising. Advertising itself was of course not new. In the United States, signs, broadsides, and newspaper advertisements flourished throughout the nineteenth century. A few advertising agencies, space brokers who mediated between advertiser and publishers, existed in 1865. More of them emerged in the 1870s and 1880s, and increasingly the agencies became involved with the design and production of advertisements.[7]

The role of advertising and the identity of advertising agents changed dramatically in response to the transformations from local to national markets and from a producer economy (one in which the goods produced were essential and served primarily as a means of survival) to a consumer economy (one in which production exceeded consumption, so that advertising became necessary to ensure continued production and profit). Advertising agencies expanded and became more bureaucratic. Instead of just selling space to the advertiser, they began to advise clients where to place their advertisements and then to produce advertisements themselves.[8] At the turn of the century, publishers began to depend on high-circulation magazines whose income derived from advertisers, who used them to reach as many people as possible and to increase consumption. The relationship between publishers and advertisers became one of mutual dependence, although power increasingly gravitated into the hands of the advertisers, who had a multitude of options and outlets.

Other aspects of mass-market magazines and national advertising would affect artists. Standardized national products (like Uneeda Biscuits) were made possible by the transcontinental railroad and other systems of communication and management. These brands lent themselves to advertising in nationally oriented print media. Transformations in color printing methods and photomechanical reproduction technologies were also crucial. The screen halftone process enabled a major expansion in the amount of printed pictorial matter and vastly improved the quality of reproductions. In the words of historian Neil Harris, it transformed "the whole system of packaging visual information" by making pictorial matter more prevalent, appealing, and persuasive.[9]

All of these circumstances created work possibilities for a new generation of image makers. By the turn of the century, new opportunities opened up in magazine and book illustration, print advertising, poster design, art direction, and photography. The new print technologies enabled artists to disseminate their images in the form of reproductions to huge numbers of people. The new commercial modes of patronage offered artists the opportunity to achieve much greater visibility and influence. Not least appealing was the fact that these enterprises offered artists the possibility of earning real money. Yet the ascendancy of these same print media also introduced new problems and challenges. As the field of artistic practice widened, older, familiar categories of art and aesthetic hierarchies underwent adjustment. Broader audiences complicated the already complex economies of power among artists, critical supporters, and patrons and produced new debates about the nature and purposes of representation. The sheer numbers of artistic practitioners created new kinds of professional uncertainties. These instabilities, combined with disagreements about the relationship of means to ends in art, resulted in charges of "commercialism" against some artists. This unflattering but highly fluid term became a repository for all of the ambivalent feelings that artists had about the new technical and marketing possibilities.

FINE ART AND commercial art have never coexisted happily, but their differences have never been fixed; commercial art never had an essential or inherent identity any more than did fine art. There is a long tradition of illustrations rendered by painters. And, of course, artists since antiquity have worked on commission. American painters were no exception. In the United States, moreover, illustration as a distinctive, professional enterprise emerged in the late nineteenth century as a form of fine art, as did poster design. The artistic status of photography was consistently problematic. The term commercial art itself dates back only to the turn of the century. From that point on, its borders were constantly shifting. The growth and concurrent artistic marginalization of advertising and magazine illustration were not inevitable.[10]

Since careers and attitudes toward work were not static, we need to consider how, through the course of various artists' careers, their education, expectations, reputation, and previous experience and clients operated to classify them, and how they resisted or adapted to such representations of themselves.[11] This task makes it especially important to focus on particulars—to consider the individuals, groups, organizations, and activities that shaped the identity and enterprises of art in commerce. To this end, each chapter in this book focuses on crucial moments at which a given medium or group of actors played an active role in marking the borders. The story moves back and forth chronologically, but each chapter pushes the narrative focus forward in time.

The dichotomy between fine and commercial art has been linked with a tendency to conceive of American art as the history of major painters and their works, rather than as an activity. This book, like *Triple Self-Portrait,* will consider art from the latter perspective. From this standpoint, "art" is a function of particular but shifting groups of producers, work practices, organizational frameworks, and publics, in relation to larger social networks, and even to urban politics. These social networks and processes were unstable because they were the products and loci of struggles for control over definitions of artistic status and artistic work, definitions that were themselves affected by the influence of art on society.[12]

The key argument of this book is that the changing boundaries of fine and commercial art resulted from efforts on the part of painters, illustrators, advertisers, advertising artists, art directors, photographers, and assorted elite groups to claim jurisdiction over "art" as a means of acquiring authority and influence in their fields and in the broader culture. A great deal was at stake for all involved. Control of the discourses of art meant more than just management of day-to-day activities. It meant the power to assert class and self-legitimacy in a society in which shifting economies, technologies, and social demographics were rapidly calling old ways of life and power relations into question. Power was a crucial variable.[13] Three issues in particular help to highlight these changing relations of authority: the tension between romantic ideals and commercial activity; the vacillating attitudes toward art's relation to commodities; and changing interpretations of the relationship of art and audience.

Art (capital A), with its varied and conflicting connotations of expressivity, sensuousness, spirituality, freedom, and order, wielded tremendous cultural weight. That influence extended far beyond the immediate sphere of its creators to business and society at large. Art and aesthetic discourse penetrated the representations and organizational worlds of commerce, and were privileged to a remarkable degree in advertising practice. Romantic ideals of individualism and freedom proved to be especially pervasive—underscoring growing fears about diminishing autonomy in the context of urban industrial transformation.[14] Successful image makers for magazines and advertising maintained a strong devotion to those values even through they did not consistently adhere to them. In many cases, they found support from art directors, who often shared many of the artists' convictions about artistic goals, methods, and standards.

But, as we shall see, the cultural influence of Art (especially romantic values) did not necessarily translate into personal, occupational, or organizational power for artists. There was a tension between artistic ideals and commercial practices that persisted throughout the period, even under changing conditions and among different actors.

The conflicts between ideals and practices, between romanticism and commercialism, were mediated by shifting attitudes about the uses of art for selling. The clash between the commodity status of art and the status of commodities is a second concern of this book. Imagery was problematic in advertising because it forced artists, publishers, advertising people, and businessmen to contend with art's duality as both valued, marketable property and intangible truth. In the late twentieth century, Andy Warhol and pop artists helped to make such discussions a commonplace, but in fact they had already emerged at the start of the century with the rise of illustrated mass-market magazines, billboard posters, and print advertising. Together, the disagreements over art and commodities raised basic questions about the nature and purpose of artistic representation. Among the crucial questions at the heart of the debate were the following: should images be used to sell goods at all? Was it morally appropriate to do so? If so, should such images be described as art, and what were the ramifications of doing so? What kinds of art and artists ought to be enlisted? What did the term "art" mean in this commercial context? What should such images do and how should they function? Was visual form merely a means of attracting attention to the copy or to the product illustration, or was its purpose to convey the meaning of the product in some more fundamental way? Also at issue was the matter of how aesthetically arranged visual imagery—which might be prized in its own right—could create a desire for a distinct and seemingly unrelated product. Some believed that an image should resemble the product and not highlight its creator. Others believed that advertising artists should evoke interest and desire by indulging their own creative expressiveness and sensuousness, assuming that viewers would connect their responses positively to the product in question.

The questions raised were often similar for artists, art directors, other advertising practitioners, and their clients. As we shall see, however, the answers they gave varied depending on the circumstances, and within any one group or constellation there were often numerous divisions. Consequently, the characterizations of art in advertising fluctuated considerably. From about 1900 through the 1920s, for example, many writers referred to any handcrafted illustration as art, but still distinguished art (or "fine" art) from art done for fiction or advertisements. An additional notion gained currency in the 1920s: an art for advertising could be stylistically modernistic, idiosyncratic, expressive and personal in its rendering. In contrast, illustration was more anecdotal, more transparently "illusionistic." During the depression, certain art directors and writers began to distinguish fine art in advertising from illustration. For some this difference boiled down to a distinction between work by "art-artists" (a term used in the 1920s)—rendered as if painted totally independently, for self-expressive purposes—and painted illustration, created with a concern for reproduction and emphasizing the human form and legible content.[15]

Certain camps of business clients and advertising men (for indeed, nearly all people in high-level advertising jobs were men) were skeptical about using "art-art" in advertising, arguing that it drew attention to itself, but not to the product. Others, however, especially art directors, were enthusiastic about using "art-art," for the very reasons that made it unattractive to others. They believed that the cultural status associated with fine art would rub off on the product. Defenders of fine art in advertising contended that art had always been bound up with commerce. Commercial commissions gave artists opportunities to reach huge audiences and even to advance public taste.

Discussions of the merits of art for advertising were often linked with the question of audience. Thus a third major issue I shall address is the status of commercial art as popular art. As a group, artists formed part of the professional managerial nexus bound up with the emergence of mass markets and national advertising.[16] One task, then, is to explore artists' and advertisers' responses to the new linkages between cultural production and mass distribution. What happened to the borders of art when "public" no longer connoted a relatively well educated and wealthy elite, but rather a mass of millions of people, with varied income, education, ethnicity, and class, whose ideals and concerns could not be readily gauged? Each chapter explores from a different angle how changing conceptions of audience and market governed the relationship between art and publicity from the point of view of the producer. The lens through which artists and advertisers focused on art and public often distorted the interests, opinions, experiences, and lifestyles of the people to whom they ostensibly directed their images. An assessment of art and consumer publics and the latter's responses to painting, illustration, and advertising more generally must, however, await further study. My concern here is with professional artists', advertisers', and businessmen's (mis)perceptions of those publics and how such representations articulated the borders of artistic and commercial status and work. In the cases of art posters, portrait photography, and Maxfield Parrish art prints, however, we shall examine how popular response—in the form of consumption of images—could have consequences for the construction of artistic identity. In general, I concentrate on myths of a "media public" rather than on the actual constitution and cultural practices of such groupings.

AMERICAN PAINTERS AND engravers had always, on one level at least, looked upon their works as commodities, had always sought a market. Mid-nineteenth-century painters like Thomas Cole, George Caleb Bingham, and William Sidney Mount worked on speculation, in search of patrons. Once they had obtained support, from individual collectors (like Luman Reed) or from collectives like the American Art Union, the artists gladly worked on commission. So far as we know, they generally did not regard such practices as problematic. They catered to a large but relatively limited audience. Creative activity was premised on the assumption that artists and their patrons shared a common culture and ideals. It was assumed that the product of the artist's work would be seen either in its original form or as a masterfully crafted translation of it.

The artists who entered the field of illustration in the late nineteenth century regarded themselves as working within the framework of this older system of values and expectations, even as the circumstances of production were changing. They envisioned themselves creating inspiring images for a wider but still cultivated audience. They saw the new technologies and modes of production as means to extend their reach and to create demand for more and better art, in the form of reproductions as well as originals. Broad distribution of art would advance public taste and enlightenment; it would help to realize the democratic ideals of the nation.

Many artists experienced something different from what they had expected. Mid-nineteenth-century artists believed that they could control the uses and signification of their images. With mass-market magazines and national advertising, an artist could no longer be certain that his audience's reactions would correspond to his own concerns. He found that his work might be used for purposes that he did not anticipate and could not oversee. In some societies the artists' interests had been irrelevant. But in democratic America, artists, swayed by bourgeois ideals of individualism, felt it was their prerogative to disseminate representations to a free yet receptive public. Tensions emerged when selfhood became so intimately linked to livelihood and when the artist's public seemed (from the artist's point of view) erratic and uncontrollable. Artists had hoped to create an art that was popular among ordinary people, but not necessarily a popular art. While many were imbued with a traditional ideal of service that committed them to more than just personal creative satisfaction, many balked at the idea, as interpreted by publishers and advertisers, that serving a popular audience meant not edifying but pleasing, and that pleasing in many instances meant acquiescence to publishers' demands regarding values, practices, schedules, subject matter, and modes of production. Matters became worse when service no longer meant producing a work that would stimulate and challenge both artist and public, but rather creating a facile image that catered to some client's perception of the lowest common denominator. The intimacy and trust that many artists assumed would constitute the artist's relationship with his public was too often not present. In the view of a growing number of artists, the creator seemed to be creating in a void, for a public of phantoms.

Throughout the twentieth century, artists and their advocates tried to establish some common ground that encompassed a popular public art and commercial practice. The most successful popular artists, like Maxfield Parrish and Norman Rockwell, forged uneasy but workable solutions. One way they did so was by consciously taking a populist stance: they affirmed that both their publics and themselves were ordinary individuals engaged with life and with pictures, and denied that their fans were lumpish and ignorant masses and themselves, superior.

Several factors, however, thwarted an easy resolution of the tensions between artists' ideals and the practices of advertising and illustration, and also between art and popular commercial culture. On one level, artistic and commercial interests seemed to connect. Commercial culture's obsession with the "consumer" meshed with the older ideologies of public service at the heart of the kind of artistic training that artists like Rockwell and Parrish would have experienced. The left-wing political concerns of many Depression era artists also led them, like Rockwell, to share advertisers' and publishers' concerns with reaching a broad audience, although their views of means and ends clearly diverged. Ultimately, however, the commercial interests gained the upper hand. They could corner the market on popular art because of their huge financial resources, their control of mass media, their ability to finesse complex aesthetic and ethical issues, their eagerness to employ favored artists like Rockwell to give consumers pleasure, and their willingness to experiment with a wide range of artists and styles. Industry's commitment to "fine-art painting" as a means of reaching consumers was short-lived, however. By the

1950s, art directors and their clients were rapidly abandoning painting in favor of photography, thus affirming "fine-art painting" as a narrow category, separate and distinct from advertising.

A FEW WORDS about the scope of this book are in order at this juncture. First, my earlier use of the inclusive term "modern" to describe a chronological moment needs explanation. It is meant to connote the explosive social changes of modernization, such as the rise of new print media, mass markets, managerial capitalism, leisure time, immigration, and urbanization.[17] It also refers to the shifting modes of the experience of modernity: the concurrent efforts by individuals and groups to cope psychologically with the effects of modernization.[18] Throughout the book, moreover, the term "modern" will refer to certain pervasive and self-conscious modes of artistic expression generated during this period. It is meant to connote both those modernist styles derived from consciously avant-garde forms innovated by European contemporaries, and those self-described efforts to express a spirit of contemporary life, the experience of modernity.[19] In the United States, as in Europe, the development of modern art in all of its aspects was inextricably bound up in the same social frameworks that produced mass-market periodicals, and hence illustration and advertising art. Yet modernism also describes ideologies and attitudes that posited a schism between so-called easel painting and art for print media and advertising. I shall explore the negotiation of these contradictions.

My account of the relationship between art and advertising is, of course, selective. I have chosen to concentrate on two-dimensional advertising. Although several scholars have convincingly shown the ways in which the emergence of packaging and industrial design were central to the marriage of modern commerce and art, these developments are less germane to the larger concerns of this study, which focuses more on the negotiation of artistic occupational boundaries than on the structuring and marketing of modernism. Moreover, although there were artists in print advertising who became pioneers in the field of industrial design (most notably Walter Dorwin Teague), commentators of the period differentiated packaging and product design as categories and occupations distinct from print media advertising.[20]

Finally, it should be noted that those who seek a restatement of the critique of consumer or corporate culture will not find it here. My argument is informed by much of this literature, but I believe it more illuminating to take a less Whiggish stance that gives credence to individual aspirations, actions, and responses without being seduced by them. I seek to avoid an attitude that holds advertising and corporate commerce as the source of the world's evils, and that dismisses art produced for commerce or for a popular audience as tainted and inauthentic.[21] My concern is not to celebrate or scorn the activities of artists in commerce or the quality of their images, but to understand who these individuals were, how they operated, and how they responded to pressures from art and business spheres. By taking commercial artists seriously, I hope to encourage the reader to regard them not as stereotypes, but as historical actors who shape the course of history as much as more esteemed artists.

To A REMARKABLE extent, matters of art shaped interests and actions within even the most crassly materialistic sectors of American society. Whether the motives of people in advertising were truly sincere, whether these spokesmen misrepresented the true meanings and purposes of art, and whether their use of art was a good thing were subjects of much disagreement. For art-in-advertising advocates, the commercial man's engagement with art would do nothing but good. It would help business by improving sales, but it would also help artists more generally by providing patronage for new and innovative creative work, and by exposing such art to an audience of millions who might otherwise never enter a museum. Yet the very strength of such romantic artistic ideals as integrity, self-expression, independence, and truth, tenets instilled as an inherent part of cultural education, led other camps of artists and businessmen to insist that art and advertising were incompatible. These values were the primary motivating forces underlying their gut conception of "true art." The persistence of such convictions prevented even some of the most popular commercial artists from coming to terms with their publics, their work, and themselves.

Recognition of the pervasiveness of ideologies of artistic freedom and individualism will help to explain how, on one level at least, business and commercial interests succeeded in claiming jurisdiction over art, and why debates about art were initially central to the production and process of advertising and later marginal to them. It will reveal the extent and limitation of artists' and art directors' influence in culture and business spheres and suggest how artists and others could resist the commercialization of culture, with both positive and negative professional consequences. To acknowledge art as a powerful political discourse is to highlight the dilemmas that Rockwell pictured in *Triple Self-Portrait*, the unresolved problems of the artist in commerce.

chapter I

The Problem of Status for American Illustrators

American illustration occupies an anomalous position in art history. Its proponents celebrate its brief but glorious history, a "Golden Age" lasting roughly from 1880 to 1930. It is a history with a definite, limited chronology, determined by issues of quality and stylistic development, focused on the achievements of a few individuals. Detractors regard American illustration as a minor episode in the history of art. Illustrators, publishers, and advertisers of this period themselves reinforced this perspective. Regarding illustrators' activities as ephemeral, part of a throwaway culture, they often disposed of artwork and correspondence, and displayed little concern for building a historical legacy.

Yet illustration was crucial. As an element in the rise of the mass media and in the shift from a production-driven economy to a consumerist one, illustration extended modes of visual representation into entirely new realms. Illustration furnished new artistic and professional opportunities, new audiences, and new, widely disseminated images of American life. It was also an enterprise that generated some of the era's most fundamental artistic struggles and contradictions. For some artists and observers, these conflicts played a central role in crystallizing the boundaries within which fine art was defined and practiced. For others, the emergence of illustration as a form of expression thoroughly complicated the nature and significance of aesthetic experience. For just as much as, if not more than, with the process of independent painting, the production of illustration resulted in a clash of interests—between freedom and compromise, inspiration and accommodation, challenging self-expression and accessibility, individual and group identity—all fundamental tensions in the larger history of twentieth-century art and culture.[1] Why, then, has illustration been considered so marginal? Why has such a large portion of its history been lost or ignored?

The dichotomy of opinion has resulted in part from the dominance in scholarship of modernist perspectives that construed art as a self-sufficient expressive entity. Differences have also arisen because of a more general suspicion that illustration was commercial, whereas fine art was not. This schism between fine and commercial art is notable, not only because it has been an ongoing theme in the discourse on American illustration throughout this century, but also because the boundaries between what was "fine art" and what was "commercial" in illustration were constantly shifting. In the 1890s, for example, painter-illustrators like Edwin Austin Abbey drew strong distinctions between book and magazine illustration (which they sought to establish as a fine art) and advertising art. Twenty years later, Maxfield Parrish was creating frameable prints as advertisements for General Electric Mazda Lamps. By 1936, the art director for the magazine *Redbook* referred to book, magazine, advertising, and billboard illustration together as commercial art, "one of the country's foremost industries."[2] Given these differences in attitude, it is clear that we need to pay closer attention to the matter of who defined the relationship between artistic and commercial illustration and under what conditions they did so; we need to know what their motivations might have been, whether or not they succeeded in controlling such definitions, and the larger significance of those successes and failures in shaping the reputation of illustrators and illustration.

This chapter will investigate the significance of the "Golden Age" of illustration as the history of a new vocation structurally bound up on the one side with fine art, and on the other side with the development of national advertising and mass-market publishing. Specifically, I explore how illustrators of this period sought to develop personal and group strategies to control their self-images as fine artists within this new market framework. As we shall see, this task meant surmounting the overly feminine image of the field, a goal that illustrators accomplished. Other challenges confounded them. Illustrators had difficulties bridging the gap between the successes of individual illustrators and the artistic identity of the group. The chapter will examine the relationship between that tension and the social and artistic status of illustration vis à vis painting. It will show how the competitive framework and the market conditions in which illustrators worked enabled certain individuals to achieve renown as artists, but hindered illustrators collectively from achieving a comparable position. In turn, these circumstances prevented individual illustrators from attaining either stable identities or artistic reputations comparable to those of painters of "easel pictures."[3] Their troubled group reputation deterred them from realizing their high artistic goals.[4]

The problem of "commercialism," which exacerbated tensions between the individual and the group and gradually widened divisions between illustrators and independent painters, will also be tracked throughout this chapter. Illustrators attempted to avoid the taint of commercialism that many increasingly associated with their practice, beginning in the early years of the twentieth century. They sought to do so by forming professional schools and societies as well as alliances with the Metropolitan Museum of Art, and by public service during World War I. In all three cases, however, they lost the struggle. Part of the problem was that the notion of commercialism, while always an opprobrious term, varied from person to person and from time to time. One individual associated commercialism with advertisements, another with magazine illustration or covers, and yet a third with mass-produced calendars and art reproductions.

The concept of commercialism remained too broad and unfixed for illustrators to overcome negative associations on all artistic fronts. At any given point they could find allies among their artist peers, critics, or the market, but they could rarely win over all three. By the 1920s, illustrators' ultimate inability to attain clear-cut artistic status within the world of urban culture produced a shift in their ideals and practices: they recognized that publishers and advertising clients would remain their primary patrons, and that these people and the market they served (not museums, galleries, or art critics) would ultimately determine illustrators' artistic stature. Instead of aspiring to be accepted as fine artists, on a par with easel and mural painters, illustrators became reconciled to shuttling between the magazine and advertising arts. By the time of the depression, the broad distinctions once drawn between illustration and commercial art had virtually disintegrated. Many in the worlds of art, advertising, and publishing now regarded illustration as a form of commercial art. Even so, a review of the structure of the field of advertising illustration will reveal the limitations of equating commercial art activity with crass commercialism on the part of the artist-producers. Illustrators, many of whom came from "fine arts" backgrounds, remained strongly influenced by the romantic aesthetic ideals with which they had been inculcated through schooling and peer contact. As the case of Norman Rockwell, which concludes this chapter, will indicate, these values continued to shape their beliefs, expectations, and even their business practices.

Chapter One

The Rise of Illustrators and Uncertain Identities

Painting and illustration have always been related in Western culture, although the status of the illustrator has of course changed over time. Medieval manuscript illuminators who crafted elaborate, unique illustrations of Scripture were generally regarded as artisans or master craftsmen, admired for their ability to give material form to God's word. Their images, although revered, were nevertheless considered secondary in importance to the written text. The idea of an independent "creative" artist arose only during the transition from medieval to early Renaissance culture, with the rise of the independent easel painter.[5] Even then, works of art from Leonardo's *Last Supper* to Jacques-Louis David's *Oath of the Horatii* had an illustrative component in that they depicted narratives that preceded the painting itself. The subordination of painting to text, moreover, went hand in hand with the subordination of painter to patron. When Peter Paul Rubens painted paeans to the life of Maria de Medici, it mattered little whether or not he believed what he portrayed. Most active painters worked on commission, conformed to their patrons' demands, and suffered no loss of reputation for doing so.

The idea that works of fine art might be unique, direct, nonanecdotal expressions of an artist's emotional experience arose in the late eighteenth and early nineteenth centuries. The romantic ideal of art as the expression of the self came to favor the artistic process over anecdotal subjects at about the same time that photography liberated painters from the obligation to depict the world illusionistically. Although painting remained referential, there was growing debate about the nature of the reality it should represent, and a growing belief that narrative representation alone no longer admitted the same immediate access to the painting's truth, to meaning, as composition and artistic process. For some late-nineteenth-century artists (such as Maurice Denis and Paul Serusier), form, color, and composition—as expressions of feeling—became the artist's primary subject.

Romantic conceptions of art, which developed in Europe, were often incompatible with illustration for reasons that went beyond the latter's illusionism. From the romantic perspective, art had to flow directly from the wellspring of the individual soul. By contrast, an illustrator had to stick to a predetermined text.[6] His freedom of expression was limited. The processes of mass reproduction also placed restrictions on illustrators. Romantic theory prized originality, but reproductions of drawings often lost, in translation, the appearance and aesthetic impact of the original. Engravers and lithographers seemed inevitably to distort the artist's prototype. Illustration would not allow for the expression of personal vision.

Further artistic limitations were placed on the illustrator by the nature of the audience and by the context in which he or she was now working. With the rise of mass-market magazines, illustrators were no longer working for small groups of like-minded connoisseurs. Instead, they were under pressure to appeal to a large, faceless public. In England, affiliates of the Pre-Raphaelite, Arts and Crafts, and Aesthetic movements sought to offset these dilemmas. Attempting to reconcile traditional high standards of craftsmanship with modern mechanisms of broad distribution, they envisioned a society in which producer and public were one and the same, and in which all fruits of production were equal. Nevertheless, all of the tendencies mentioned above, which accompanied the development of the mass press in Europe, contributed to a growing ambivalence toward anecdotal narrative in art on the Continent, especially on the part of progressive and avant-garde artists.

Avant-garde European aesthetics notwithstanding, most nineteenth-century American painters conceived of their work in connection with some kind of narrative content. The creation of both paintings and print illustrations did not pose aesthetic inconsistencies, and a young person's decision to pursue illustration as part of a fine arts career did not cause conflict, and in fact seemed quite sensible.

Indeed, in the last third of the nineteenth century artists had notable success in elevating the reputation of illustration from the level of a craft to that of a fine art. The activities of Winslow Homer (1836–1910), Edwin Austin Abbey (1852–1911), John La Farge (1835–1910), and Howard Pyle (1853–1911) were representative of the enhanced artistic status of illustration and illustrators during this period. These men were among a growing coterie of art school-trained individuals who became involved with illustration in the late 1860s and 1870s. Homer, an artist-correspondent, designed wood engravings for *Harper's Illustrated Weekly* during and after the Civil War. La Farge created a highly innovative series of book and magazine illustrations for children in the late 1860s. Abbey became a staff artist for the publishing house of Harper and Brothers in 1871. Pyle, working freelance, created many drawings for *Harper's New Monthly Magazine* and *Scribner's* beginning in the late 1870s.[7] Yet all four men identified themselves as fine artists and were accepted as such among their peers in genteel art and literary circles of the late 1870s and 1880s (those in the New York City artists' group the Tile Club, for example)—men who themselves attained high reputations by the late 1880s and 1890s.[8] Homer and La Farge (in the 1860s) and Abbey (in the late 1880s, along with others like Frank Millet, Kenyon Cox, and Childe Hassam) moved back and forth between illustration for publications and painting for its own sake. Mastery of both enterprises was consistent with the ideals of the English Pre-Raphaelite and Aesthetic movements, which they and Pyle admired. Proponents of both movements believed, for example, that the so-called minor arts—illustration, decorative arts, and other crafts—should be accorded the same artistic status as painting and sculpture. They advocated collaboration on the production of elegant illustrated books and journals as a valuable means of achieving this unification of the arts.[9]

Thus, for Abbey, Homer, La Farge, Pyle, and others, illustration of texts was compatible with their self-images and aspirations as artists. It represented a lucrative, challenging blend of fine art and high-level popular culture, more broadly accessible than easel or mural painting but still geared toward an upper-middle-class audience. Success required both high standards of excellence and popularity.

High standards plus broad appeal still seemed feasible goals in the late 1880s, when illustration, despite its growing prevalence, remained a limited enterprise. Circumstances and possibilities began to change drastically in the 1890s with the emergence of numerous new general interest and specialty magazines supported by advertising. A closer view of these conditions will enable us to begin to chart the reconfiguration of the relationship between art, illustration, and advertising. To this end we shall focus on Curtis Publications, whose magazines *Saturday Evening Post* and *Ladies' Home Journal* were central to the emergence of illustration as a mass-market art.

Mass-Market Magazines and the Emergence of Curtis Publications

The expansion of the publishing industry in the 1890s created new markets and opportunities for American illustrators. The passage of the International Copyright bill in 1891 helped indirectly by providing both political and financial incentives for publishers to print the works of American authors (and artists), rather than those of foreigners.[10] At the same time, improvements in printing technology, such as the halftone process, also cut costs, making it possible to produce both expensive illustrated gift books and bargain editions with fewer pictures.[11]

The explosive growth of newspapers and illustrated mass-market periodicals in the late 1880s and 1890s was another contributing element. In the larger cities, illustrators found work at daily newspapers like the *New York World* and the *Philadelphia Inquirer.* Initially their task was simply to collaborate with several other artists to make pen and ink drawings

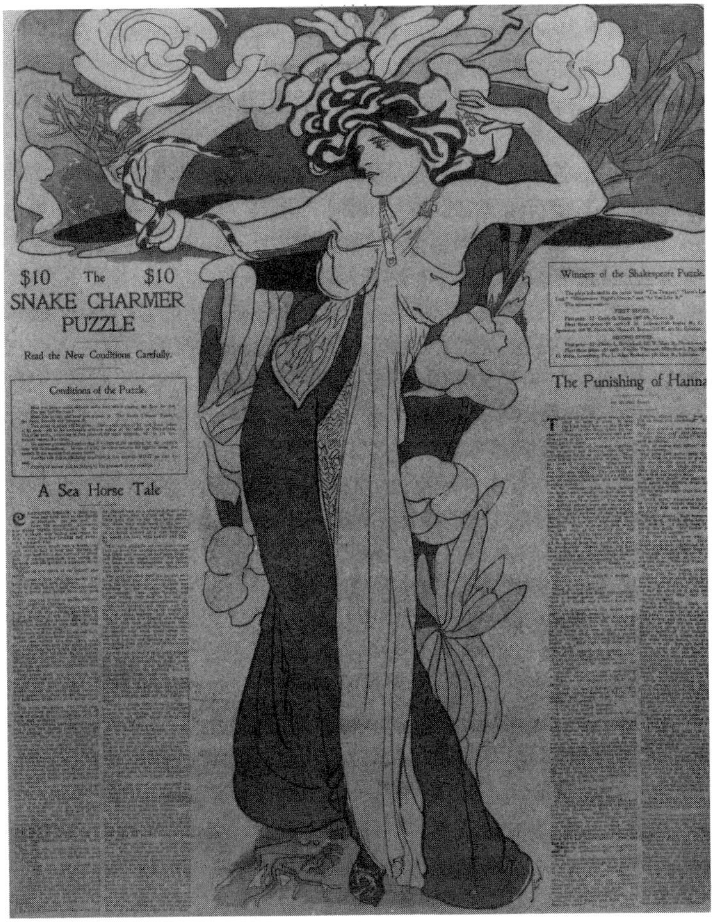
$10 The $10
SNAKE CHARMER
PUZZLE
Read the New Conditions Carefully.
Conditions of the Puzzle.
A Sea Horse Tale
Winners of the Shakespeare Puzzle.
The Punishing of Hanna

1.1. John Sloan, *Snake Charmer Puzzle,* 1901, from *Philadelphia Press.*

over photographic images. But some, like George Luks, became artist-reporters, dispatched to the scene of an event; others, like John Sloan, illustrated stories, society events, and picture puzzles (fig. 1.1).[12] Eugene Witla, the artist-hero of Theodore Dreiser's autobiographical novel *The "Genius"* (1915), began his career with such a newspaper job. "They did not pay very much," noted the authorial narrator, "twenty five dollars to beginners."[13]

As in the 1860s and 1870s, high-toned publishing houses such as Harper, Century, and Scribner hired illustrators on a freelance basis to create pictorial accompaniments for their magazine essays and fiction and their books. But now in the 1890s, an entirely new group of inexpensive popular publications became available: magazines such as *Collier's Weekly* (1888), *Ladies' Home Journal* (1884), *McClure's* (1893), and *Saturday Evening Post* (purchased by Cyrus Curtis in 1897). According to art historian Rowland Elzea, by 1905, 85 percent of magazine circulation was for periodicals costing ten cents or less.[14] Many of the newer magazines were business ventures whose revenues were based on advertising as much as on subscriptions. The key to these magazines' survival was high circulation.[15] Publishers quickly learned that pictures sold magazines. By 1900, most of the major publications were profusely illustrated. The halftone process facilitated this development, making it technically possible to reproduce the bravura brushstrokes of paintings, as well as refined line drawings, without the intervention of an engraver (although engraving continued to be used to touch up some images). Such circumstances to a certain extent solved the problem of mistranslation; they enabled a larger pool of talented artists to enter illustration, and imparted a greater artistic range and aura of fantasy to the medium. In contrast to the situation in the 1860s and 1870s, when magazines like *Harper's Weekly* had staff artists working on salary, most of these artists worked freelance. Besides being more economical, this arrangement helped art editors (the men who decided what should be illustrated and who selected the artists), providing them with a greater freedom of choice; it also opened up the job market to more illustrators.

The *Ladies' Home Journal* and the *Saturday Evening Post,* both published by Cyrus H. K. Curtis (1850–1933), were especially important in shaping the contours of illustrators' identities and of commercial art practices at the turn of the century. Together these two general interest magazines contributed significantly to the shift from limited to mass circulations. Curtis gave substantial independence to editors Edward William Bok (1863–1930) of the *Ladies' Home Journal* and George Horace Lorimer (1868–1937) of the *Saturday Evening Post,* and built up a publishing empire of staggering proportions. As part of this effort, the two magazines carried an unprecedented amount of pictorial illustration.[16] In so doing, they helped to establish illustration as both a prestigious high-profile form of art and an attractive career option.

Illustrators' practice and identity became closely linked to the visualization of fiction, which had been a key factor in the rise in circulation for both magazines.[17] For many readers, the meaning of stories was contingent upon pictorial representation. Some critics found this trend unsettling, arguing that such dependency on pictures distorted the stories, stifled readers' imaginations, and manipulated their thinking.[18] Such criticisms mattered little to Bok and Lorimer. From their perspective, good illustration contributed to the popularity, circulation, high standards, and uplifting aims of their magazines.[19]

Bok's and Lorimer's intention to obtain the best for the general interest reader (with women especially in mind) led them to search for illustrators of the highest order. To this end they established procedures to attract good artists: they kept the turnaround time on decisions to publish to a minimum, paid on acceptance, and rewarded artists for loyalty.[20] The magazines provided opportunities for a multitude of new talent. Moreover, once the editors had found illustrators whom they especially liked, they helped to promote the latter as unique artists. Repeated exposures, signatures, covers, and special promotions made certain illustrators into big names. In 1901, for example, Bok offered reprints of *Ladies' Home Journal* illustrations (without text) for sale to the public. The notice stated that the reproductions (by W. I. Taylor), if framed, were "works of art fit to hang beside any painting."[21] Indeed, both Bok and Lorimer were instrumental in making the careers of a new generation of illustrators, and ultimately in boosting the reputation of some, like Maxfield Parrish, Joseph Leyendecker, Jessie Willcox Smith, and (later) Norman Rockwell, to the level of nationally acclaimed "media stars."[22]

Art in color on magazine covers also enhanced the reputations of *Post* and *Ladies' Home Journal* illustrators. Bok helped to pioneer the enterprise by changing cover images from month to month.[23] The artists who rendered such covers conformed to the standards of representation generally expected of illustrators; although their images did not illustrate a text, they often conveyed (or implied) anecdotal content. Covers were usually done by artists whose principal identity at the time was as illustrators rather than as independent painters, although a few, like Albert Herter, (fig. 1.2) straddled both fields. Artists and editors were conscious of vocational differences between illustrators and career painters. Nevertheless, the practices of Curtis, Bok, and Lorimer contributed to a blurring of borders between art and illustration on the part of the general public, who framed the pictures and for whom such covers signified "art."[24]

These cover images—of children, old people, and especially pretty young women—were targeted primarily at women. Those depicted were always financially comfortable, always Caucasian. Together they presented heartwarming, affirmative views of a pre–World War I world of shared values and experiences touted as American. However mystifying and unconfrontational that perspective, it was one with which many readers could identify and one that—judging by circulation and reader re-

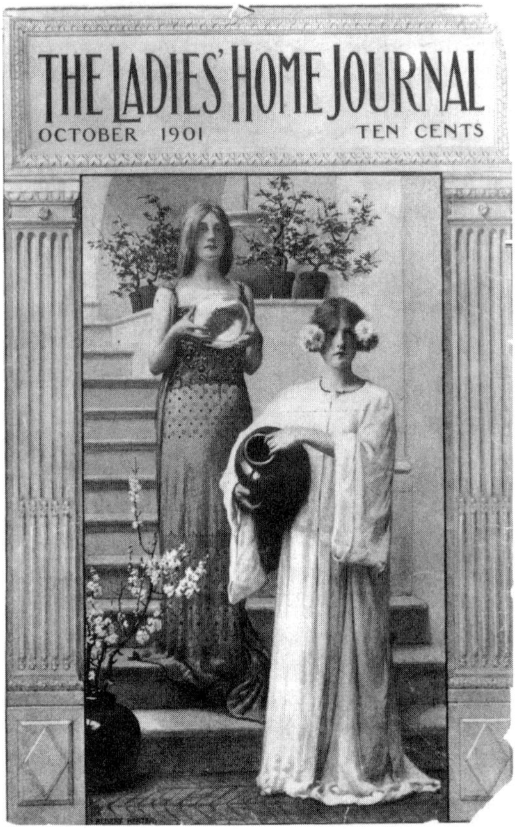

1.2. Albert Herter, cover for *Ladies' Home Journal,* October 1901. Herter, winner of a 1895 magazine cover competition sponsored by *Scribner's* and an accomplished illustrator, was a holdout for the older Aesthetic movement's aims. He illustrated three covers for *Ladies' Home Journal* in 1901 and 1902, but also gained renown as a painter, and soon after, as a decorative artist. In 1911 he founded The Herter Looms, which made fabrics, tapestries, and other designs.

sponse—they clearly enjoyed. (It was thanks to Lorimer's patronage, after all, that Rockwell came to be regarded as the premier American artist.) And reader approval was crucial in selling the magazine. Cover illustrations as pioneered by Curtis publications (among others like *McClure's* and *Collier's*) thus came to set an important precedent as art and as advertisements for the magazines themselves.[25] As such, they represented a crucial shift from an older ideal of illustration as purely artistic medium to its newer purpose as instrument and expression of consumerist commercial values.[26]

The link between illustration and advertising established in the Curtis publications (and others) was very calculated, and connected with another element that Curtis publications would help to innovate: the relationship between editorial features and advertising. Here, too, Curtis, Lorimer, and Bok sought to maintain consistency between the upright tenor of their magazines' editorial content and the advertising on which it depended. To this end, publisher and editors exercised strict controls over what could be advertised in their magazines.[27] Illustration became bound up in this larger enterprise. The editors' selection policies for editorial illustration and the rising circulations of the magazines provided a strong incentive for clients to improve advertising design. The majority of advertisements at this point were clustered together. They were small (one to two inches) and cluttered with text; images, if present, were tiny drawn or photographed objects or faces, based on retouched halftones. From the perspective of Curtis, Bok, and Lorimer, as well as some advertisers, the best way to insure quality and linkage between illustration in advertising and in editorial content was to have better-known illustrators do both. Some illustrators, like Maxfield Parrish, were already making advertising posters for publishing houses at the turn of the century. By 1910, as we shall see, many illustrators would follow a comparable path. Advertisements would become bigger, bolder, and more calculatedly artistic.

By 1900, then, illustration had developed into an artistic vocation sui generis for hundreds of practitioners. Artists, critics, and publishers defined the field not only in terms of "painter-illustrators" who created illustrations and painted independent pictures; illustration also encompassed book illustrators, poster and newspaper artists, and "magazine men," whose activities might overlap with one another but who remained identified as illustrators.[28] Theodore Dreiser, for example, writing from experience, distinguished between the New York "painting world" and the "illustrating world."[29] Particular individuals were now also identified with specialized genres: Charles Dana Gibson with social satire, Abbey and Pyle with medieval subjects, Frederic Remington with Western scenes, Parrish with fantasy, and Smith with mothers and babies. Critical assessments included evaluation of a work's appropriateness as an illustration, with particular concern for its relationship to the accompanying text. More often than not, however, these issues were indistinguishable from considerations of aesthetic merit. The question was not simply whether an individual's works were "dainty in execution" or well composed, but whether these aspects contributed to an effective presentation of the author's idea.[30] Thus, although critics used similar aesthetic rhetoric to evaluate illustration and painting, they made additional demands that were specific to illustration.

Money and contracts also began to differentiate illustrators from painters. Relative to remuneration linked to painting, sculpture, etching, and other professional pursuits such as teaching, illustrators' fees were on the average quite high. The top illustrators made extraordinary sums. In 1886, his first year as an illustrator, Frederic Remington earned about $1,200. In two years his earnings skyrocketed to $8,000. At this time the average yearly pay was $256 for a schoolteacher, $794 for a minister, and $354 for someone in a bakery. Judy L. Larson has estimated that the average active illustrator in the 1890s earned approximately $4,000 a year (enough to buy a nice home and employ a servant).[31] Illustrators began to sign contracts for which they received money up front. Charles Dana Gibson stunned the art world in 1903 when he accepted an offer to switch from *Life* to *Collier's*. He struck a deal that paid him $100,000 for one hundred drawings over a four-year period.[32] Howard Chandler Christy, Harrison Fisher, James Montgomery Flagg, Joseph C. Leyendecker, and Maxfield Parrish were among the others who commanded high prices.[33] A few women illustrators, especially former Pyle students such as Elizabeth Shippen Green, Alice Barber Stephens, and Jessie Willcox Smith, also found a ready market and good earnings for their work, primarily commissions for images of women and children (fig. 1.3).[34] Illustrators who met the aesthetic and pragmatic demands of publishers were amply rewarded.

Education

Attainment of high standards and success in illustration was possible because its practitioners had had the necessary technical training. Few art schools offered specialized illustration courses before the turn of the century. From the standpoint of school officials, illustration was just another aspect of the artistic enterprise. Students had to learn the fundamentals first. They had to become artists before deciding upon a vocation. Those who wished to become illustrators were expected to do so on the basis of the practical experience they gleaned on the job through applying the knowledge that they learned in their painting and drawing courses. Students aspiring to a career would attend schools like the Art Students League, the National Academy of Design, the Pennsylvania Academy of Fine Arts, and the Art Institute of Chicago, where they would receive

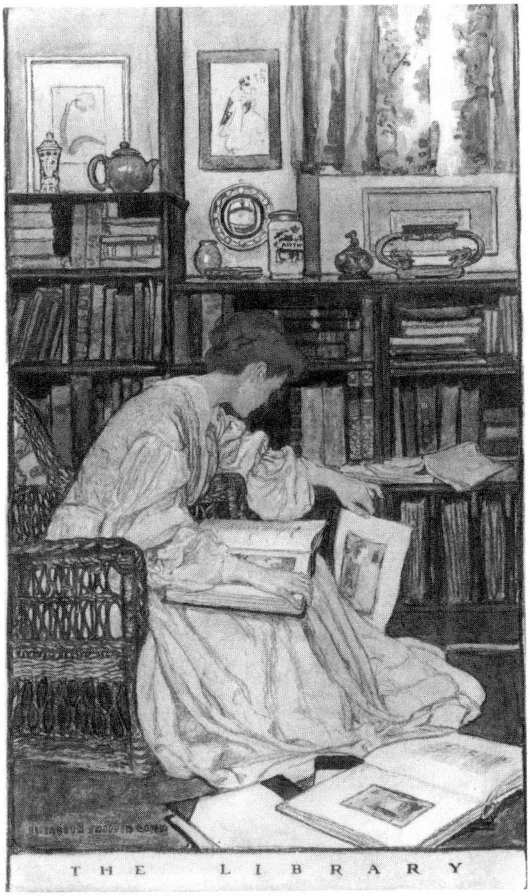

1.3. Elizabeth Shippen Green, *The Library,* 1905.

thorough grounding in painting, drawing, anatomy, and composition. John Sloan (see fig. 1.6), George Luks, and Everett Shinn, for example, attended the Pennsylvania Academy; Gibson and Pyle studied at the Art Students League; Dreiser's Eugene Witla, at the Art Institute of Chicago.

The League, in particular, encouraged students to go into illustration as early as the 1880s. Its teachers and students were the generation involved in the Aestheticist effort to break down artistic boundaries between the so-called minor arts—illustration, decorative arts, and other crafts—and painting and sculpture. Moreover, one of the League's early presidents, William St. John Harper, was both an illustrator and head of the art department of the *New York Daily Graphic;* it is thus not surprising that he encouraged the training of illustrators. This advocacy became explicit when in 1883 Harper and Brothers offered a $3,000 prize through the League for the best illustration by an American student of Alfred Domett's *Christmas Hymn;* the winning entry was to be published in *Harper's Monthly*. In an Art Students League lecture on illustration in 1891, W. Lewis Frazer provided students with additional incentives; illustrators, he told them, made lots of money.[35] To enable art students to take advantage of the new career options, a range of different art schools responded by implementing courses in illustration. Cooper Union established a course in pen and ink illustration in its art school for women during the 1889–1890 academic year. The New York School of Applied Design for Women instituted an illustration department in 1894.[36] That same year, Drexel Institute of Art, Science, and Industry in Philadelphia began to offer illustration classes. In addition to these reputable institutions, there were other, less high-flown enterprises. For example, in 1895 advertisements for a correspondence school drawing course used Remington's supposed "$50,000" a year salary as an enticement to students.[37]

Aspiring illustrators, then, had reason to be optimistic. They could obtain a thorough grounding in fine art techniques, and new opportunities for a variety of well-paying jobs and a receptive public appeared to await them. The stage seemed set for illustration to be not only a career, but a legitimate fine art. The question remained, however, whether such an ideal could be realized.

Howard Pyle certainly seemed to think so. Whereas Abbey, La Farge, and other members of his generation traveled abroad and focused increasingly on easel and mural painting, Pyle remained identified with illustration.[38] In 1878 he returned to his hometown of Wilmington, Delaware, and continued to work full-time within the framework of publishing. Instead of following the path of becoming a painter, Pyle branched out by turning to writing. During the 1880s, he wrote and illustrated works such as *The Merry Adventures of Robin Hood* (1883), *Pepper and Salt* (1886), *The Wonder Clock* (1888) (fig. 1.4), *Otto of the Silver Hand* (1888), and *Modern Aladdin* (1892). These children's books achieved the status of popular classics.[39] His work was in demand among a range of popular magazines (including *Collier's, Harper's Monthly, Harper's Weekly,* and *St. Nicholas*).

Publishers, on the other hand, though optimistic about illustrators' newfound cachet and its ability to help boost circulation, were not about to take chances with artistic and public attitudes. In the early 1890s, they became involved with promotional efforts to champion illustration as a noble art, and thus to enhance the appeal of the work they commissioned.

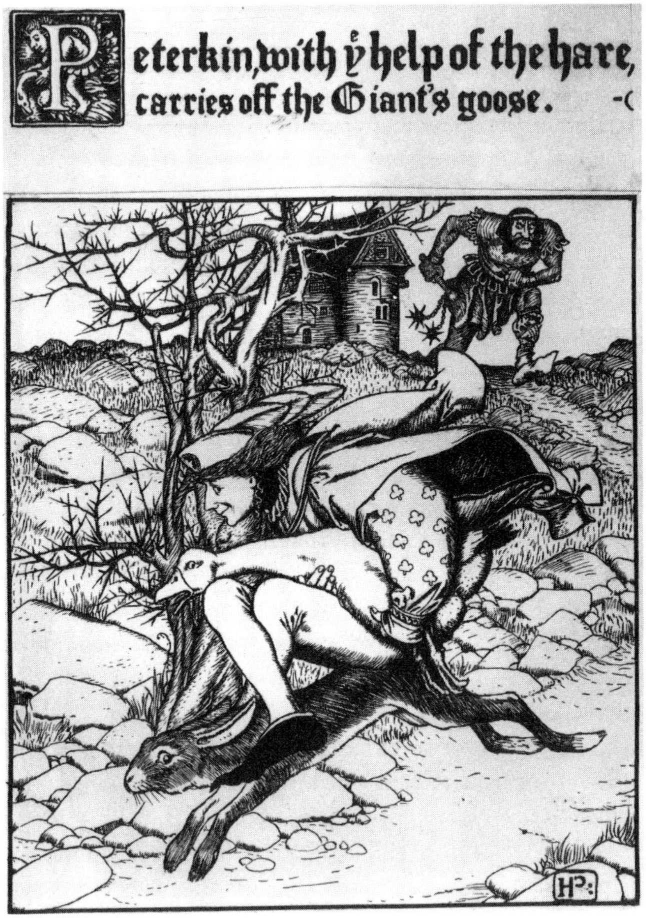

1.4. Howard Pyle, "Peterkin, with ye help of the Hare, carries off the Giant's goose," ca. 1885, for "Peterkin and the Little Gray Hare," *Harper's Young People.*

The mid-1890s saw the publication of sumptuous gift books on illustration, such as *American Illustrators* by Francis Hopkinson Smith, issued by Charles Scribner's Sons. Articles in *Bookman, Scribner's Magazine* (both with ties to publishing houses), *The Independent,* and *Contemporary Review* plugged illustration. Several of these were histories of American illustration, assertions designed to legitimize the existence of a field and to delimit what was relevant. In her series on "New Leaders in American Illustration" in *Bookman,* for example, Regina Armstrong implicitly asserted the standing of illustration by celebrating individual masters of the art. Other articles served similar purposes.[40] Such promotions often worked. For future illustrators Wanda Gág *(Millions of Cats)* and Norman Rockwell, for example, the leading magazine illustrators represented their earliest paragons of the true artist.

Yet despite the publicity, illustrators as a group still had substantial obstacles to overcome to establish illustration as a distinguished activity. One problem was the perceived feminization of the field—a matter linked to the organization of artistic training. In spite of the growing popularity of illustration as a career for young male artists, it was dominated by women. Indeed, illustration's very popularity among women became a factor in the initial resistance on the part of some professional art schools to taking illustration seriously and to implementing specific illustration courses.[41] Despite the British Henry Blackburn's call in 1873 for courses in illustration, for example, the National Academy of Design did not establish one until 1901. The Pennsylvania Academy also resisted attempts to teach illustration. The Cooper Union, School of Applied Design for Women, and Drexel Institute courses of the early 1890s catered primarily to unmarried women seeking vocational training. The course at the New York School of Applied Design for Women was explicitly for women, as was the class at Cooper Union.[42]

Many of these women went on to successful careers as schoolteachers and as magazine, newspaper, and children's book illustrators. Yet women's work tended to be stereotyped; for the most part, their subjects were women (see fig. 1.3), children, and fashions. Their images, however, played a crucial role in the popular market, where the readership was largely female.[43] Yet from the standpoint of male artists, the prevalence of women in the field was an indicator that illustration was not fully established as a profession; it lacked the image of masculine strength considered requisite for any truly professional enterprise.[44] Women stigmatized the field as unserious and created competition for attention and jobs during a period in which the economy was weak. The fact that easel painters were experiencing comparable "problems" underscored all the more the need to take immediate action to secure the prestige and influence of this less established endeavor.[45]

Howard Pyle's schools of illustration—first at the Drexel Institute of Art, Science, and Industry in Philadelphia, then at Chadds Ford—demonstrate both the problem and a partial solution. These classes represented Pyle's efforts not only to promote the creation of American art but also to legitimate the art of illustration as a male and professional endeavor. Pyle, who had been dissatisfied with the availability of training for illustrators, had initially proposed to the Pennsylvania Academy of Fine Arts that he teach a course in the subject. The Academy refused, on the grounds that illustration was not a fine art like painting or sculpture. However, Drexel Institute was pleased to have his services, and beginning in 1894, Pyle began to teach illustration to a group of thirty-nine students. By 1896 the class had expanded into a school, but despite its success and popularity, Pyle became increasingly frustrated. The school did not sufficiently advance his cause; with so many students, he could not give those who deserved help the proper attention.[46] There were too many mediocre and unserious students, and too many leisured women. "The great majority of the class is hopelessly lacking in all possibility of artistic attainment," he wrote James McAlister, Drexel's president. "I can't stand those damned women in the front row who placidly knit while I try to strike sparks from an imagination they don't have."[47] Whereas Pyle did not object to individual women as illustrators (indeed, he had quite a few successful protégées), he did not want to contribute to the feminine identity of the field any more than necessary. He clearly discouraged women; whereas 84 percent of his students were female in 1897, only 66 percent were in 1898; that percentage dropped to 49 in 1899.[48]

In addition to discouraging these undesirables, Pyle found a means of evasion when, in 1898 and 1899, McAlister raised a fund of $1,000 that allowed him to set up a small and exclusive summer school of illustration at his home in Chadds Ford (for which he received no remuneration).[49] The positive experience of these two summers convinced Pyle all the more that his Drexel arrangements for the rest of the year were unsatisfactory. In 1900 he resigned from Drexel altogether and established his own school. There the proportion of men to women was very different from Drexel. When Pyle had weeded out all but the most select, talented, and "dedicated" students, the men were clearly the majority (fig. 1.5): Pyle biographer Henry Pitz mentions two females and twelve males as students during the first year. Rowland Elzea listed three women and thirteen men as students for the year 1901–1902. By 1904 there were three women and seventeen men.[50]

The new sex ratio served as a signal: illustration had gained ground as a serious artistic enterprise, and was no longer to be regarded as an idle pastime or as simply a means of earning a livelihood. This strategy in the realm of education helped illustrators to shore up their image of independence and mastery, but only to a limited degree: they remained sufficiently insecure about the status of their endeavor to feel an ongoing need to assert its strength, in both subtle and not-so-subtle ways. For some illustrators, clarification of work procedures and construction of an organizational hierarchy seemed like viable goals and methods of professional self-assertion.

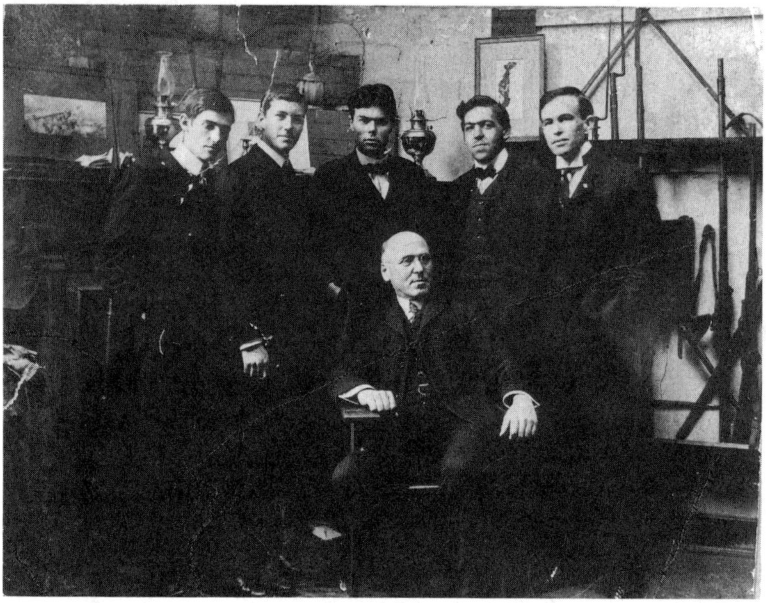

1.5. Howard Pyle with his students in studio, ca. 1903 (shows George Harding, Gordon McConik, Thornton Oakley, N. C. Wyeth, and Allen True).

Work and Organization

Illustrators' doubts were linked to other factors that intersected with, and were compounded by, the matter of a feminine identity. In spite of the success of specific individuals in establishing renown as artists, illustrators' market position and their lack of power within that framework compromised their group status as fine artists over the long run. The organization of the illustrators' artistic practice in the 1890s put many of them in a weak and subordinate position. First, there was the uncertainty of the commissioning process. Prior to 1900, many illustrators had little conception of what rights or payments to expect from publishers. Apart from illustrators who had major reputations and who could negotiate from positions of strength, most illustrators did not know how far they could assert themselves. As freelancers, anxious for work, they were easily exploited. Hiring illustrators on a freelance basis gave publishers and editors a greater number of aesthetic choices and fewer long-term financial and personal commitments. While freelance arrangements gave illustrators the freedom to pursue varied assignments and to work on their own schedules, they offered little assurance of regular income.[51]

Securing commissions, especially from magazines, could be an unnerving and humiliating experience. Unlike the situation forty years later, when many illustrators hired agents, turn-of-the-century illustrators were their own publicists. They had to reach the art editor (also known as the art director) who had primary authority over the artwork in a magazine. The art editor selected the illustrators, doled out assignments, enforced deadlines, and approved or disapproved the submissions. Prior to about 1900 he often selected the subject to be depicted. After that time the illustrator had more leeway to decide, an indication both of art directors' regard for illustrators' judgment and of their own diminished time for such tasks.[52]

Encounters with the art editor were by no means guaranteed. Part of an illustrator's "initiation rite" consisted of seeking out appointments with the magazines' art editors to show them work samples. Since not all art directors would commit their time in advance, an illustrator often had to shuttle from one office to another, usually carrying a heavy portfolio. The illustrator could only hope that an art director would agree to see him (or her), and that an assignment might be available. John Sloan's experiences were typical (fig. 1.6). "I decided to go out in search of work today," he wrote in 1908,

> so with my packet of proofs under arm, I went first to F. Stokes where a young Mr. O'Connor treated me decently but told me that I'd best see Mr. Stokes who was, at present, away. Went to McClure's, then to see Willing at the Associated Sunday Magazine. He was affable and talked but no work was produced. From there I went to 17th St. and for the first time went into Baker, Taylor Co. Here I talked with a Mr. Hackett. . . . Went to the Century where Miss Jackson was very kindly. . . . Called at Everybody's saw young Mr. Campbell, Brown was away. Then to Bobbs, Merrill where Mr. Baker was decent but the work they produce is of an awful popular grade. Came home feeling rather blue—the usual effect of these trips on me.[53]

Artistic success and financial survival seemed less a function of talent and vision than of persistence and sheer luck. Such excursions were not what artists had in mind when they decided to pursue careers in illustration.

Even after accepting a drawing or assigning a commission, the art director might demand substantial changes, some of which could alter the finished composition entirely.[54] Moreover, despite contemporary commentary that ascribed artistic value to works by specific, *named,* people,

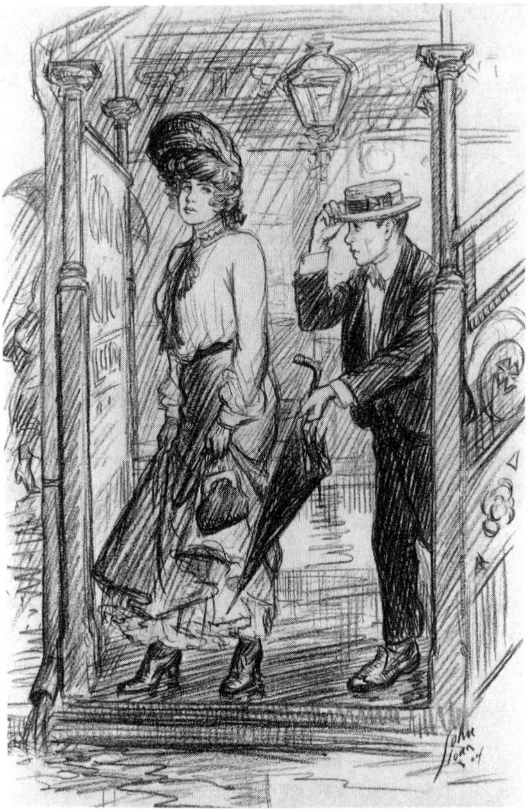

1.6. John Sloan, *"Don't you want—th'umbrella?"* 1904. Sloan's loose rendering reflects the romantic conviction that the idiosyncratic marks of the hand are expressions of the artist's individuality and sincerity.

art directors of some magazines were either wary of well-regarded, highly paid illustrators or could not always afford to employ them. While this meant that they were receptive to new and younger talents, both the younger and more seasoned artists could end up feeling cheated.[55] Because they were powerless newcomers, the younger artists were strung along waiting for assignments, called on short notice to complete assignments with imminent deadlines, and paid less than the art directors themselves felt they deserved. Illustrators felt frustrated, yet they could do little about this state of affairs. The art director had total control. He (and most art directors at the time were men) was the buyer who determined the production of the illustrator's wares and fixed the terms.

Illustrators were clearly aware of their lack of power. Irritation with their vulnerability became a common subject of shop talk at their informal dinners and meetings. In 1901, a group of ten New York-based illustrators and one businessman decided to take ameliorative action. Following in the footsteps of sculptors, mural painters, and watercolorists, they formed an organization, the Society of Illustrators, to try to resolve their problems.[56] Charter members, the majority of which were respected illustrators, were Otto Bacher, Reginald Birch, Henry Hutt, Frank Vincent Du Mond, Henry Fleming, Louis Loeb, Albert Sterner, Alfred Beck Wenzell, Frederick Coffay Yohn, and William Thomas Smedley, who became the organization's president. In 1901 this body elected fourteen additional fellows, including such top names as Howard Pyle and Charles Dana Gibson. Almost all members lived in the New York City area and illustrated regularly for the major magazines.[57]

According to its constitution, the society's goal was "to promote generally the art of illustration" and to hold periodic exhibitions.[58] This rhetoric deliberately downplayed the commercial aspects of the organization's purpose, which was to protect the rights and royalties of illustrators by establishing proper procedures for their "business dealings" with publishers and art directors. To accomplish this, it was necessary first to convince art directors that illustrators were not falling victim to organized labor—that the society would not turn into "a sort of labor union" that might "hold them up." To assuage any such fears, the illustrators held a series of monthly dinners to which art editors were invited "to find out and approve what was going on." In the words of a 1928 history, "the fine spirit of these meetings," combined with the "frank discussions and the friendliness promoted by them, soon convinced the editors that no desperate measures were contemplated."[59] The mention of "labor union," written retrospectively at the height of a business boom, served as a reminder that the illustrators' actions took place within the context of larger antagonisms between union labor and managers at the turn of the century—struggles that from the business perspective had been successfully overcome. At the same time, the tone of the rhetoric impressed upon readers that illustrators, despite their pragmatic concerns, had never regarded themselves as class-conscious "troublemakers," but as upright professionals who actually identified with art directors.

To assert and reinforce their credentials as artists, the illustrators decided to hold annual exhibitions of their works, "drawings which shall have been made for the purposes of illustration," but "original drawings only."[60] In demanding original drawings (as opposed to the published reproductions), the illustrators sought to highlight the unique and autographic aspects of their pictures as autonomous works of fine art that would stand on their own without accompanying text. The society devoted a great deal of energy to these exhibits. They became a crucial means of drawing attention to illustrators and their activities, and were thus one of the major events of the illustrators' year.

There remained the ongoing matter of establishing illustration as a male profession—of overcoming the perception of it as a woman's field. Like many artistic and scientific societies, the Society of Illustrators controlled its self-image as a professional group by controlling its membership. Initially it did not admit women. After a period of struggling to enlist male members, however, the society acknowledged in 1903 that a small group of women were as active and renowned in the field as many male illustrators, and decided to accept women "who have attained prominence in the art of illustration" to the category of associate membership. These associate members would have the right to exhibit their work and to attend special, select meetings. Since membership was controlled by vote (by committees on which women could not serve), the society could keep a cap on the number of women to keep the ranks of membership from being flooded by them. Elizabeth Shippen Green and Florence Scovell Shinn, who were elected the first year, and Violet Oakley, May Wilson Preston, and Jessie Willcox Smith, who became members in 1904, contributed as regularly to the leading magazines as any of their male counterparts. No women were admitted in 1905–1906. In 1906 the society consisted of seventy-three fellows, five honorary members, and five corresponding members—all male—and five female associate members.[61] As with Pyle's school, selectivity helped to ensure the public image of illustration as a high-class masculine endeavor.

The society's activities reinforced this conception. Monthly dinners, held in select restaurants and often accompanied by entertainment, provided opportunities for illustrators and art directors to meet in an informal atmosphere that temporarily deflected the tensions of the marketplace. These affairs also provided introductions to art directors whom illustrators might otherwise not meet. Like the yearly shows and smokers, however, most dinners were "stag" affairs. Such affairs served much the same business purposes as male social and literary clubs like the Century: not only did they provide an additional bond between (male) illustrators and art directors, but they also contributed to the desired association between illustration, professionalization, and masculine identity (fig. 1.7).

The society clearly nurtured new acquaintances and business relationships, and thus helped to advance illustrators' commercial interests. More generally, it promoted a new awareness of illustrators as "good old boys," businessmen, and serious workers. To outsiders it projected the semblance of professional unity and strength—an intelligent strategy at

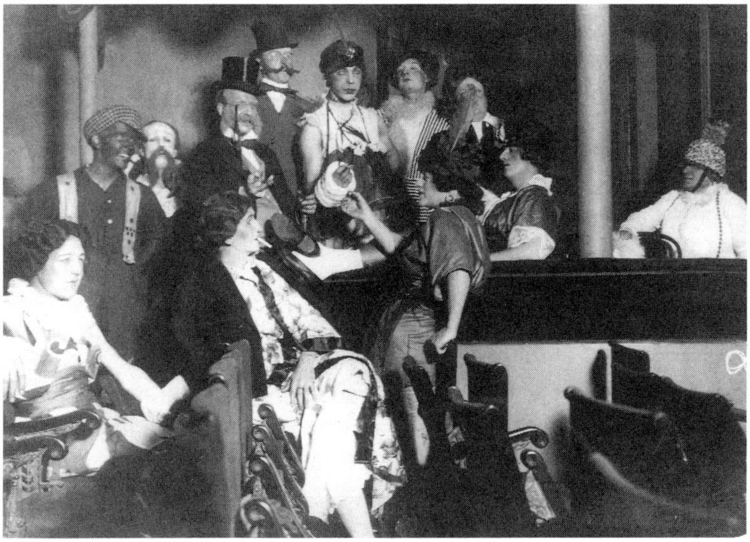

1.7. Illustrators at Play, 19 February 1914. Costume parties and revues helped to break the ice between illustrators and art directors. This photograph of illustrators in drag and blackface is a telling record of their conficted attitudes toward their profession. Illustrators here assert their authority in gendered, class, and racial terms, through the power to parody other, different people. Yet through such performance, the illustrators also revealed (through displacement) their own sense of marginality.

a point when most illustrators were in demand collectively but individually weak.[62]

Despite these positive developments, however, the society's efforts failed to secure illustrators' long-term artistic stature among painters, museum curators, cultivated intellectuals, elite patrons and collectors, art directors, and even the illustrators themselves. Part of the problem arose from a lack of commitment to the Society of Illustrators on the part of its members.[63] The very proposal to form the organization had come from an outsider, coal importer and construction engineer Henry S. Fleming; his business capabilities and his friendship with the group's founding members resulted in his becoming the society's treasurer for fifteen years. It was Fleming who proposed a constitution and proper membership rules and procedures. While such assistance and support from non-illustrators had obvious benefits, it also had the effect of diminishing some illustrators' determination to assert an independent position from the very beginning. Lack of cooperation and goodwill among many of the illustrators led the founding members to lobby hard to recruit members. Moreover, while the founding members were all reputable and successful illustrators, the top-flight illustrators—with the exception of Charles Dana Gibson—did not become actively involved in administration or committees. In this sense the illustrators' experience paralleled that of New York sculptors, who encountered difficulty in trying to enlist big-name artists as members of their National Sculpture Society.[64]

Many successful illustrators resisted association with the society. Some, like Maxfield Parrish, evidently felt no need for affiliations to legitimate their work. Others, especially those who aspired to become full-time painters, considered membership in a society of mostly career illustrators to be plebeian and demeaning. Frederic Remington wrote illustrator Daniel Beard in 1902, for example: "The Society of Ills—is a nigger baby and it ain't worth saving—at least that is my opinion. . . . I don't want to discourage you but since you put it up to me—there is no good in shuffling."[65] John Sloan, on the other hand, was put off by the society's disorganization and what he perceived as its commercialism, his sense that it kowtowed to the advertising and publishing industry. Elected to the Society in 1907, Sloan joylessly sent in his five-dollar dues.[66] Within a month he was complaining that he had been put on an entertainment committee, and that he did not "expect much from the bunch, they are so various in their absence of ideals (that's not a good word, 'forces' better)."[67] In other words, all that the group did was party; they were ineffective in advancing the art and the profession of illustration. The next January he characterized the group ironically as "young fossils" and "nice commercial gentlemen." By the end of the month he had tendered his resignation, with no regrets.[68]

Indeed, such changes of heart on the part of artists like Sloan, who identified themselves chiefly as painters (whether they also illustrated or not), did not help illustrators' efforts at organization building. In fact, many painters, in the midst of their own battles for cultural influence and clearly concerned about professional standing, increasingly wondered whether their ties with illustration, so recently forged, were threatening their claims to expertise and independence. Illustration seemed to impose uncertainties, constraints, and artistic concessions that were weakening the ideological foundations of the painters' very claims to professional authority and distinction. It was all right to compromise under certain conditions, but the decision had to be the artist's. Hence numerous painters concluded that in theory, for the sake of their status, freedom, and integrity, they should break from the Aestheticist ideals of the earlier generation and disavow the view that illustration was a genre comparable to painting.[69]

Thus, according to the Society of Illustrators' 1928 history, the organization had "a good deal of a struggle during its early years." Meeting attendance was "meager," members brought up "impractical proposals" (not elaborated), and finances were "strained." "Sometimes the little band of faithful ones came near to giving up in despair," the history admitted, "but there were always a few who would not allow this to happen. . . ."[70] At least at some times and to some degree, illustrators achieved some group solidarity, especially later during World War I, when their service to the government enabled them to achieve greater professional stature. For the most part, however, illustrators were too uncertain of the purpose and significance of their field—of who defined and controlled it, and whether it was art or something else—to set clear-cut professional priorities and to forge a unified image of themselves as serious, confident, and committed artists of vision.

The illustrators' lack of solidarity and unresolved identity arose from the clash of their socioeconomic and artistic aspirations and the instabilities and setbacks of their actual careers. Painters and other artists faced similar problems, but income and competition became issues for illustrators in ways they were not for painters, at least not so overtly. The dilemmas facing illustrators were in part a function of their patronage. Galleries and dealers provided some control in regulating supply and demand in painting and in shielding the reputation of the artist from associations with the marketplace.[71] Illustrators had no such middlemen; they confronted fewer controls and a less organized market. Like painters, they hoped for a big break, a boost in artistic reputation. But the bottom line was business and jobs. For an illustrator, regular work was the key to financial and professional survival.

The dream of a steady income led many artists to illustration in the early years of the twentieth century. But despite the many work opportunities constantly becoming available, only a select and limited group received assignments fairly regularly. During the first two decades of the century, the most popular magazines often included the work of as many as fifteen illustrators per issue, and there was strong competition among the illustrators. Art directors found it preferable to keep their talent pool as large as possible. However, they either tended to use the same artists each time or to commission work from such a wide range of people that most individuals received an assignment only periodically.[72]

The Society of Illustrators in fact reinforced this two-tier system. The society devoted to raising the stature of illustrators elected to membership only the already accomplished. The artists who needed the connections most were those portrayed by Sloan and Dreiser, who made the rounds and were rejected. The struggles of Dreiser's "genius" Eugene Witla were based on Dreiser's own experiences as an editor, as well as those of such illustrator acquaintances as W. L. Sonntag, William Glackens, and Earl Shinn. Dreiser observed: "It takes quite a number of drawings at seventy-five and one hundred dollars each to make a living income, and artists were too numerous [estimates range from several hundred to several thousand] to make anyone's opportunity for immediate distinction easy."[73] A letter to the *New York Times* in 1910 addressed the issue even more poignantly:

> What is to become of the illustrator? I see advertisements in the magazines, "Learn to be an illustrator," "Be an artist," "Artists receive from $25 to $100 a week," &c. . . . This occupation or profession is crowded and boiling over: every month sees two or three more new names signed to the illustrations that are published in the magazines. What becomes of the illustrators who had a story to "picture" in a magazine last year?[74]

The dramatic rise in the number of practitioners and the need to hustle for business made the situation seem overwhelming at times, especially for those on the margins. The nature of the market was such that one illustrator's work might be in the spotlight one month and forgotten the next. For most illustrators, work was hard to come by and fame was ephemeral.

The competition for jobs was made worse by resentment over the issue of money. Illustration had the reputation of being a well-paying profession, but the big money earners like Gibson, Christy, Leyendecker, and Flagg were atypical. Newcomers and less regular contributors had to be happy with what was offered them, usually on a piecemeal basis. Charles Robert Knight reminisced with enthusiasm about being offered $25 per drawing by the American Book Company for two "small" children's book illustrations, "very good pay" in 1893.[75] Dreiser's Eugene Witla, on the other hand, a personification of craving and careerism, complained that he was "not making money" as an illustrator (working in the 1890s). "He had been able to earn $1200 the first year, the second he made a little over two thousand," and "a little better" the third year. But this amount seemed insufficient by comparison with the incomes of his more successful peers. In the context of a burgeoning consumerist culture of desire, the drive for more money was unavoidable. Two thousand dollars (worth approximately $29,000 today) was not enough to live the life to which he hoped to become accustomed.[76]

The nature of good pay and the good life were matters of perception. An illustrator might earn good money on a single assignment, but if he or she had no contract, the future was uncertain. Unquestionably, incomes varied considerably, and depended very much upon the whims of the publisher and art director. Most art directors offered less than many illustrators would have preferred. Indeed, responding to a query in a 1911 *Ladies' Home Journal,* one art director wrote:

> Adequate drawings for average stories in a magazine bring from $25 dollars to one hundred and fifty dollars each, but where special research for data is required, and the picture is intended for reproduction in large size, two hundred dollars may be obtained. These prices apply only to the work of artists who are thoroughly experienced and who are considered safe—that is to say, dependable to turn out satisfactory drawings on time. You will not get much for your first efforts, even if they show ability. Better let the publishers have the pictures at their own prices until you have become independently busy, then put up your charges.[77]

Myths and rumors about illustrators' incomes abounded nevertheless. Along with such matters arose a new concern about "commercialism"—the idea that the illustrator was not truly dedicated to artistic self-expression, but was merely trading his talents for money.

Earnings became a highly publicized issue. Many articles began to focus as much on illustrators' incomes as on their talents or their works. "Illustration in America is a Fine Art and more," observed a *New York Times* article:

> For while art of a certain sort is like much fine gold, twentieth century illustration in this country gives more princely emoluments than Fortunatus would have dreamed of. Not so many years ago, as art goes, Henry Murger, in his "les Bohemians des Paris [*sic*]," wrote of the impecunious devotees of the palette and brush, who on occasion broke up the furniture to make fuel for a post-prandial séance. Such happenings may still obtain even in Manhattan among those disciples of the artistic muse who live and paint for their ideals alone, but not so with the successful illustrator—and his name goes into two score and ten. In this day and generation the chug-chug of a $15,000 motor car clipping its mile-a-minute rush toward a luxurious country home is best in keeping with the man or woman whose genius has concentrated upon a certain type, preferably a girl and emphasized in colors, to be spread country wide through the medium of the big magazines, calendars, gift books, and even postal cards.
>
> Commercialism with a big C has entered the lists of illustrative art as opposed to old fashioned and out of date idealism.[78]

Leading illustrators were not the only artists with substantial incomes. Daniel Chester French, one of the foremost American sculptors of the early twentieth century, recorded his net income from his studio alone as averaging $36,621 a year between 1903 and 1906.[79] Yet neither his earnings nor those of painters were the subject of public discussion. Rather, the concern with illustrators' finances reflected a larger public fascination with and envy of their particular social and professional circumstances. For one thing, illustrators' reputed high incomes seemed to disavow the myth, as the *Times* put it, of "disciples of the artistic muse who live and paint for their ideals alone"—the idea that artistic activity alone should be its own remuneration. The practice of illustration belied the fantasy that the value of art could be gauged only when the work was completed. Illustrators like Gibson received contracts before work had even started. For illustrators to demand high pay up front, then, especially for work that took them little time or effort, seemed a clear signal of greed. That perception was heightened by the penchant of several illustrators for conspicuous consumption and high living, epitomized by the "$15,000 motor car."[80] Indeed, some critics implied, the talents of many of these illustrators were vastly overrated. By 1905, in fact, the perception was mounting that illustrators were but mediocre commercial artists, churning out vapid, repetitious images for the mass print media.[81] Their connections to mass-market business clearly did not help illustrators' reputations. Art had always been perceived as uplifting, the antithesis of Mammon, not an extension of it. For the first time, visual artists seemed to be reaping inordinate benefits from modernization, mechanization, growth of big business, and national markets. In the wake of Gilded Age exploits and excesses, an art that somehow seemed to feed off the public aroused a certain suspicion and resentment. Indeed, for some intellectuals, like Max Eastman, illustration itself became an emblem of the deleterious consequences of modernization.[82]

Whereas earlier the development of the art of illustration had been the dominant concern, by 1910 the connection of illustration with commercial interests had become a significant issue both within and outside the profession. This disrepute began to take its toll, both internally and externally. The negative aspects of the connection increasingly became a problem because illustrators could not establish clear distinctions between what kinds of work were artistic and what kinds were commercial. The debates over illustration galleries in the Metropolitan Museum of Art represent one example of the impact of illustrators' uncertain status at the institutional level.

ILLUSTRATION GALLERIES FOR THE METROPOLITAN MUSEUM

In 1907, illustrators began a campaign to try to convince the Metropolitan Museum to set up a department of illustration. Speaking at a Society of Illustrators dinner, the museum's director, Caspar Purdon Clarke, made some remarks that led his listeners to expect that the museum planned to follow up on the suggestions. Perhaps trying to exert additional pressure, the *New York Herald* published two long articles on whether illustration should be exhibited in museum galleries. Around this issue, illustrators and their supporters found a momentous opportunity to map out more definitively the boundaries between fine art and commercial illustration. They hoped this would result in the creation of galleries of American illustration that would firmly ground the artistic status of eminent illustrators and their work. Yet the nature of both the negotiations and the players made these efforts unsuccessful. The illustrators' cause was not helped by the fact that a key player was a commercial publisher, thus linked with the very values that museum officials and illustrators were trying to avoid.

The *Herald* articles consisted of interviews with Clarke, Joseph Chapin (art director of *Scribner's*), and several prominent painters and illustrators, including Remington, Maxfield Parrish, and N. C. Wyeth. (Significantly, the most highly paid illustrators, such as Charles Dana Gibson, Harrison Fisher, and J. C. Leyendecker, were not among those interviewed.) Most of them favored the idea of galleries. Nevertheless, the discussion brought out the ambivalence about the status of illustration even within the field. Chapin and several illustrators argued for the educational value of an exhibit, so long as high standards prevailed. Indeed, they contended, selectivity was crucial to distinguish art from illustrative work executed from a "purely commercial point of view." "Commercial" work presumably referred to poorly designed, made-to-order illustrations for popular magazines or advertising (and possibly even to the work of some of the "five figure" illustrators). Nevertheless—and in all likelihood, deliberately—these men never really defined what they meant by the term.[83] Yet much of the discussion centered around how to keep out of the galleries "the mass of commercial trash that under the name of art is daily being dished up to an unsuspecting public."[84] Wyeth argued that a collection at the Metropolitan would lend "moral support" to illustration; it would encourage quality and reduce the "tendency toward commercialism." Remington pooh-poohed the idea, as did illustrator and painter William Glackens, who dismissed the entire field as too commercial.[85] The next article tried to downplay Glackens's negative remarks. Parrish, also aware of the commercial connotations of illustration, argued another way.

He tried to downplay distinctions between illustrations and other pictures by remarking that easel painting could be illustration, and that the crucial consideration was the work's artistic impact, not its original purpose.[86] Even advertising illustrations could then presumably merit inclusion. Parrish thus offered a rationale for considering all forms of illustration while he circumvented the issue of commercialism that so disturbed Wyeth, Glackens, and others.

Clarke, as the *Herald* noted one week later, was now more circumspect, pointing to the fact that the New York Public Library was involved in collecting and promoting illustration as an art form.[87] While he agreed that the "place for exhibition of illustrations is in a museum of art," and that perhaps arrangements could be made for purchasing originals from publishers, he left the issue of the Metropolitan's establishing a gallery open and unaddressed.

Clarke had an immediate reason to be cautious. Only a day earlier, Arthur W. Little, art editor at the popular magazine *Pearson's,* had written trustees of the Metropolitan, citing Clarke's earlier statements at the Society of Illustrators dinner. The Metropolitan, he had heard, was contemplating setting up a collection of drawings "representing the best types of illustrative art," and he assured them that such a collection would be of great educational value (thus alluding to the museum's stated mission of educating the public). Little stated that such a collection could be easily assembled through donations by artists and publishers.[88] The latter had much to gain from such an arrangement, for it was in the interest of art directors to raise the artistic estimation of the work they commissioned. Distinct promotional advantages might be gained from the claim that artists working for their magazine had work displayed in the Metropolitan Museum.

To assist in the inauguration of such a gallery, Little offered the museum a drawing, *Wee Annie* (fig. 1.8), drawn for a recent issue of his magazine by Thomas Fogarty. Little also suggested in passing that the Metropolitan consider establishing a department devoted to American illustration.[89] The museum's trustees were not happy. It appears that trustee Robert de Forest asked Clarke how *Pearson's* had gotten the idea that the museum was contemplating such a venture. On 6 December, five days after the first published *Herald* interview, Clarke informed de Forest that his comments had been made as part of an interview. But he also added that his comments, which appeared in the newspaper, never suggested that the museum was establishing such a collection.[90]

Clarke obviously realized that he had initially spoken too precipitously and enthusiastically concerning the possibility of a collection. The museum was open to perhaps acquiring a limited number of outstanding

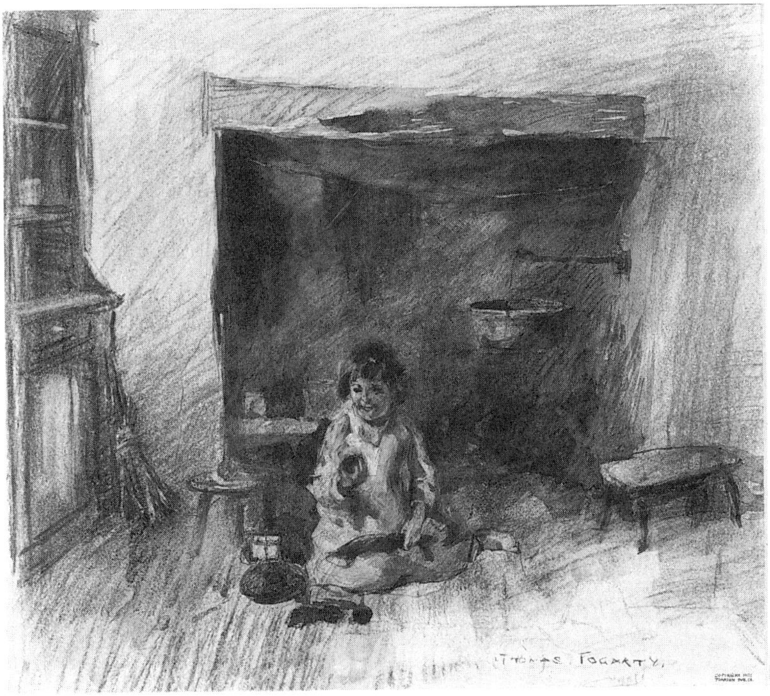

1. 8. Thomas Fogarty, *Wee Annie,* 1907.

works, but, its officials insisted, quality of expression and execution had to take priority. Clearly not all Clarke's colleagues were as positive about American illustration as he was. In fact, painting curator Roger Fry (an English historian, painter, and art critic, later renowned for his theories of formalism) objected vigorously to both the idea of such a department and to the acceptance of the *Wee Annie* offer. He contended that the illustration had to be considered purely on its aesthetic merits as a drawing (as opposed to an illustration for a text). This argument then became his excuse for turning it down. "The drawing offered by Messrs. Pearsons," Fry wrote, "is not one that approaches our standard [left unspecified] when judged as a drawing. . . ."[91] Perhaps he feared that this case would set a bad precedent.

These responses are best understood in light of the particular history and internal politics of the Metropolitan Museum. The museum itself had initially been modeled after the South Kensington Museum in London. The latter was established explicitly to raise the quality of British manufactures and put the country's industries on a better competitive footing. With similar commercial prospects in mind, the Metropolitan's founders planned displays of the best examples of industrial and practical arts, alongside the fine arts, to inspire artisans. Within such a framework, illustration would certainly have been an appropriate aspect of the museum's educational mission.[92] This was clearly the attitude of Caspar Purdon Clarke, and not surprisingly. Prior to becoming director of the Metropolitan in 1905, he had been director of the South Kensington Museum.[93]

Clarke, however, had to answer to the Metropolitan's trustees, whose recently elected president, financier J. P. Morgan, had initiated dramatic shifts in the museum's goals and acquisition policies. Turning its back on the South Kensington model, the Metropolitan adopted a more exclusivist policy. The museum would serve as a force of social uplift by assembling a collection of "the masterpieces of the history of art." The museum's trustees institutionalized as "high" art a narrowly classified realm of artistic production, defined in opposition to other, more vulgar forms of expression by educated experts like Fry.[94]

American book and magazine illustration's place in this new cultural hierarchy was uncertain at best. Fry and the trustees may have sought to curb Clarke's enthusiasm on the basis of "pure" aesthetic principles. But they may well have been motivated by additional, unconscious concerns that pertained to the insecurity of their larger cultural enterprise. Acceptance of art directors' self-serving gifts might throw into question the motives of the museum's other donors, mostly businessmen or their wives. The trustees had to act precipitously to protect the notion of "fine art" itself from being undermined. The disagreements over *Wee Annie* only underscored the fragility of the category and the ideological premises underlying their own cultural authority.[95]

In an action reflecting intensifying tensions between Fry and Morgan (Fry considered Morgan to be a self-important boor who undercut his curatorial authority), the trustees ultimately ignored Fry's evaluation and accepted *Wee Annie;* nevertheless, they made it clear that this gift was not the beginning of a new collecting policy. Instead, they used the fact that the New York Public Library was assembling its own collection of American prints and drawings as justification for avoiding the issue of a gallery of illustrative art at the Metropolitan.[96] Nevertheless, magazines continued to press the idea. The art director of *Ladies' Home Journal* wrote to Clarke, suggesting that they might also make a contribution.[97] This offer signaled to other publishers that they, too, might have the opportunity to ally with the prestigious forces of the museum and its trustees. The trustees received several queries and offers from other art editors, who were trying to coax museum officials to shift their position—to no avail.[98]

Thus the illustrators did not achieve the crucial stamp of approval that broad representation of illustration in the Metropolitan Museum of Art might have offered. They did not succeed in attaining support within the institutional framework of this major institution, whose backing at that juncture might have helped to establish clearer distinctions between the artistic and the commercial in illustration.

Individual images might defy categorization. Cultural experts might even deem a select few magazine pictures works of art. But illustrators' conspicuous efforts to earn a living, usually from publishing and other businesses, made it hard for them to shake the mounting belief that their work was merely art for profit. Such perceptions, which gathered momentum during the first two decades of the century, were responses not only to the changing structure of the magazine industry but to another "avenue of advancement" that was to attract the attention of artists like Dreiser's Eugene Witla: "art in advertising."[99]

Advertising Illustration

Illustrators' dilemmas regarding the nature and status of their work were compounded by the growing strength and lure of the advertising industry. Advertising before 1900 had been a shaky and unstable enterprise. Unscrupulous claims on behalf of patent medicines had tarnished the credibility of advertisers in general. The marginality of advertising was reflected in its design and imagery. Early advertisers rarely commissioned drawings or paintings, but tended to use crude lithographs by anonymous individuals, largely because of the limitations of printing technologies.[100]

In conjunction with the emergence of popular magazines and national markets before the end of the century, however, individual companies and advertising agencies began to make concerted efforts to boost their standing and to establish credentials as honest professionals. Illustration became a crucial means of enhancing both the products' and advertisers' reputations. A number of advertising men argued that good illustration could be invaluable in attracting the public's attention, in obtaining its sympathy, and in improving their own credibility. Quality illustration would be an indicator of the refinement and good taste of the advertiser, the product, and the purchasing public. These arguments proved effective. Advertisers established art departments to produce eye-catching publicity. Increasing numbers of them also began to commission independent illustrators at high fees to create designs for magazine displays, streetcar signs, and posters (fig. 1.9).[101] In 1902, the advertising trade journal *Printer's Ink* began a series of monthly columns by George Ethridge, with "before and after" drawings that demonstrated how to im-

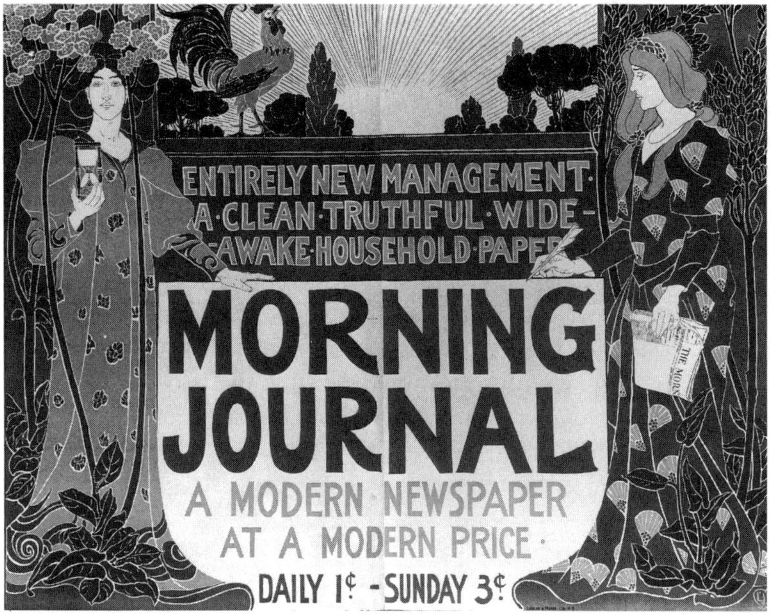

1.9. Louis Rhead, Poster for the *Morning Journal*, 1895.

prove "commercial art." This column, which became a regular feature in the journal, signaled advertisers' commitment to high artistic standards.[102] Metropolitan Museum officials might not consider illustration a prestigious artistic enterprise, but some advertisers were determined to differ.

Certain illustrators saw the creation of advertising in print and posters as a new opportunity. Maxfield Parrish, Will Bradley, Louis Rhead, Jessie Willcox Smith, and J. C. Leyendecker, for example, created advertising posters for clothing, bicycles, toilet soap, and food products (figs. 1.10, 2.3, 5.1), as well as for the more respectable publishing houses. "The thought of ad creation" (and its ten-thousand-dollar income possibilities) quickly caught Eugene Witla's "fancy."[103] But more often than not, turn-of-the-century illustrators resisted offers from advertisers, who were still viewed with suspicion. Concern about their tactics was at a height around 1906, with the passage of the Pure Food and Drug Act and emergence of the Truth in Advertising movement, which clamped down on advertisers making false claims. Many illustrators were apparently concerned that their artistic reputations might be tarnished by association with advertis-

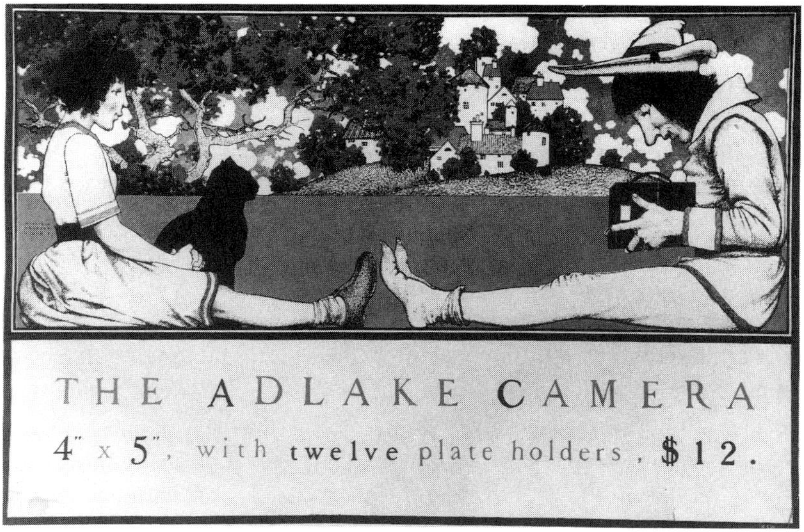

1.10. Advertisement for *The Adlake Camera,* illustration by Maxfield Parrish, 1897.

ing men. They also feared embarrassment if they were found to have made too many aesthetic compromises in pursuit of sales. The problem of aesthetic compromise had also been an issue in the *New York Herald* discussions about the commercialization of magazine illustration. But whereas many illustrators could rationalize their need to modify their artistic vision to reach the reading public, they found such accommodations harder to justify when it came to selling products. They viewed such changes as "selling out," and dissociated themselves from advertising—the one artistic activity unquestionably identified as commercial. Yet the fact remained that most illustrators created advertisements at one point or another. They simply avoided publicizing the fact.[104]

The challenges faced by Earnest Elmo Calkins in his early efforts to promote advertising art reflect illustrators' resistance to such work. Calkins (1868–1964), founder and president of the agency of Calkins and Holden, became a self-appointed proselytizer for advertising art. His activities represented advertisers' counterpart to the illustrators' efforts with the Metropolitan Museum. Unlike the illustrators, however, who labored to distinguish "art" from "commercial trash" in book and magazine illustration, Calkins sought to position commercial art firmly within the larger spectrum of art. Like the illustrators lobbying the Metropolitan Museum, however, Calkins encountered obstacles. As a young man, he had taken art courses at Pratt Institute. While working for ad man Charles Bates, Calkins worked to create the first art department in an advertising agency, and tried his own hand at advertising designs. An astute publicist (whose activities will be discussed in more detail in chapters 2 and 5), Calkins also recognized that efforts to improve the standing of advertising art would not succeed unless artists themselves were convinced of the value of such work; the problem, he later wrote, was that "in those days no artist with any self respect would dream of making a commercial design."[105]

In about 1905, determined to overturn the negative image of advertising art, Calkins set out to woo talented illustrators and to prove that commercial artists were indeed artists. He sought to paint a bright picture of the possibilities in artistic advertising, and insisted that there was nothing wrong with creating art for commercial purposes. Contrasting the situation with that in the late nineteenth century, Calkins contended that artists were now pleased and honored to be doing advertising art. To a great extent, however, his words reflected wishful thinking, as may be surmised from his experience with the Art in Advertising exhibition—one of the first American exhibitions to link art and advertising.

Calkins organized the show in 1908, at the National Arts Club in New York City. "The idea was to segregate what was really good, so that it could be seen by itself," he wrote. The exhibition would show "that not only is the standard of art in advertising high, but also that this work bears the names of many men already famous in other lines of work."[106] The submissions, however, did not live up to Calkins's expectations or claims.[107] In addition, the best entries were for magazine cover art rather than for what Calkins considered to be "advertising designs in a stricter sense."[108] He thus had to solicit directly suitable top illustrators such as Parrish, Leyendecker, Penfield, and Wyeth. Calkins, ever conscious of public relations, would not admit that artists were hesitant to submit their advertising work. Instead, he explained the prevalence of cover designs (submitted mostly by publishers and not by illustrators) by claiming that just as the publisher "was first to appreciate the work of the best designers," so too was he the "first to appreciate the importance of exhibiting it."[109] In other words, Calkins downplayed what he perceived as the relative absence of first-rate advertising art by emphasizing the positive contributions of the publishing industry. The exhibition gained little critical notice; the *New York Times* published a small, unfavorable review. To ensure that the exhibition would receive at least some attention, Calkins himself wrote a publicity piece in the form of a review, published in *International Studio;* there he proclaimed the overall success of the show and the high level of achievement in advertising work.[110]

Such claims regarding publishers were reasonable. As we shall see, publishers did in fact play a major role in shaping the contours of art for commerce. Mindful of the need to attract the attention of passersby, publishers and outdoor advertisers were receptive to artistic images earlier than many print advertisers. The latter were generally more concerned with showing what was available than with trying to lure people into impulse buying. Widespread use of large, technically proficient and artistic magazine ads would lag close to a decade behind that of posters.[111]

Calkins, who had worked his way to the top in the very difficult world of advertising, was nonetheless not easily discouraged. He persisted in his efforts to use exhibitions to promote and improve advertising art, organizing similar shows in 1909 and 1910.[112] Just as in 1908, these exhibitions received minimal press coverage, suggesting that editors did not take seriously Calkins's assertions about the artistic merits of advertising. Again, Calkins wrote a glowing account of the 1909 show for *International Studio,* but a year later in the same journal, art critic John Nilsen Laurvik wrote a very critical review, especially of the American contributions. Paradoxically, he berated the submissions for being too artistic. The American artists, he argued, had failed to consider properly the ultimate mission of this art, namely, advertisement. They focused too hard on making attractive, self-sufficient pictures, rather than on creating designs that would draw attention to the copy and the product. "With rare exceptions they are too intent on picture making, too conscious of their exalted positions as artists, and thus they fail of their purpose."[113] In other words, consciously or unconsciously, artists continued to resist association of their work with commercial aims, even when they actually accepted advertising assignments. The tensions highlighted by Laurvik, between the romantic ideal of a "pure" art experience and the need to sell, would become the source of a central and ongoing debate in advertising circles over the coming years.

More immediately, these conflicts forced Calkins to realize that he had so far failed to find a supportive constituency, and he gave up on the exhibitions, at least for a time. Again minimizing his setbacks, he later wrote, "the [National Arts Club] committee grew tired of [holding these advertising art exhibits] and [they were] allowed to lapse. . . ."[114] Calkins's inability to dispel negative preconceptions about the quality and status of art in advertising was symptomatic of the unresolved questions regarding the relationships of magazine and advertising illustration and the nature of commercialism. Not even the most highly esteemed illustrators could escape the effects of such uncertainties.

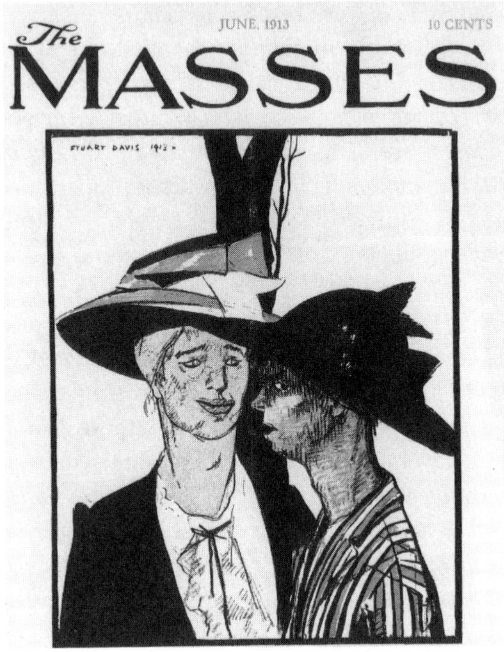

1.11. Stuart Davis, *"Gee Mag, Think of Us Bein' on a Magazine Cover,"* cover illustration for *The Masses* 4 (June 1913).

Critiques of Commercialism

The disappointments of Calkins's Art in Advertising exhibitions indicate the extent to which magazine covers were linked with advertising art and how illustrators hoped to dissociate their work from the taint of commercialism. But critics refused to allow them that detachment. A letter in *Collier's Weekly,* for example, intimated that some cover illustrations and advertisements were by and large indistinguishable.[115] Max Eastman, editor of the radical magazine *The Masses,* also implied as much in his attack on illustration. In his 1916 tract *Journalism versus Art,* Eastman denounced illustrators and editors as commercial hacks who had sacrificed all freedom and artistic integrity because they were at the mercy of mass-market publishers who cared only about circulation. His argument, as well as *The Masses'* editorial policy, made explicit the problems regarding illustrators' artistic reputations that they had faced since the 1890s.[116]

That Eastman should condemn the popular press and its illustrators is not surprising. From its very outset in 1911, *The Masses* had countered the organizational, editorial, and artistic policies of large-circulation magazines and the capitalist enterprise they represented. Artists and writers ran it collectively, the majority of the staff worked without pay, and the magazine accepted very little advertising. Most of *The Masses'* contributing artists (who included John Sloan) had had first-hand experience with the mass-market press, and a number of their drawings deliberately parodied such journals' illustrational work. Stuart Davis's June 1913 cover, for example, (fig. 1.11) attacked the exploitative, exclusionary, and commercial aspects of magazine art. In so doing it meshed with associations drawn between cover art and advertising that had surfaced with the Art in Advertising exhibit of five years earlier. As art historian Rebecca Zurier has shown, Davis's two working-class women, representing the Real in American life, ironically parodied the ideal (or unreal), but more pervasive, imagery of the patrician WASP beauties who attracted buyers to the popular magazines (fig. 1.12).[117] This picture was the visual counterpart to East-

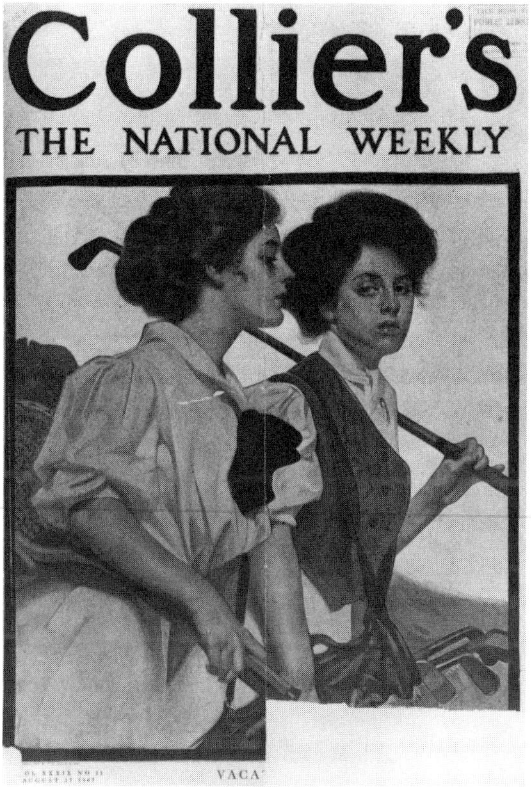

1.12. Joseph C. Leyendecker, *Vacation*, cover for *Collier's*, 17 August 1907.

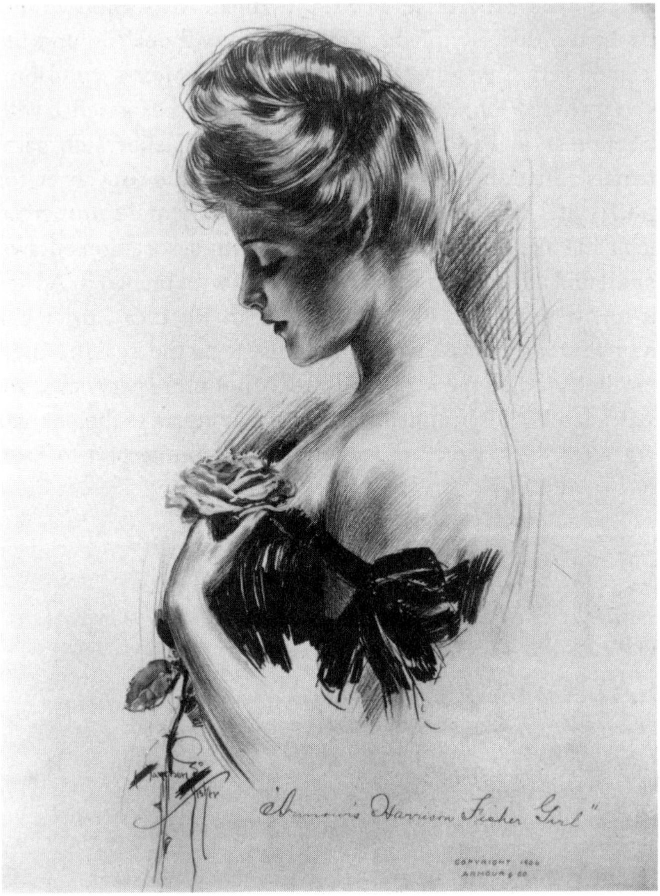

1.13. Harrison Fisher, *Armour's Harrison Fisher Girl,* 1906.

man's denouncement of name-brand illustrators and their generic subjects: "'The Gibson Girl,' 'The Christy Girl,' 'The Stanlaws Girl,' 'The Harrison Fisher Girl' (fig. 1.13)—These are features to be advertised on the front cover. And yet what is the advertisement, but an obituary notice of these men as artists? It certifies that they have given up their profession of realizing in line the varieties of life's experience, and gone into the manufacturing business."[118] Eastman and Davis admittedly were extreme cases, but the objections they raised influenced many painters and intellectuals, especially those in sympathy with progressive art and political causes. Others echoed their criticisms of illustrators' commercialism—their lack of sincerity and their overriding interest in profit, their willingness to dishonor themselves.[119]

In the face of such varying and negative attitudes in the first two decades of the twentieth century, illustrators faced an uphill struggle to maintain their artistic reputations—to combat associations between their work and market values. They waged this battle on both personal and institutional grounds, but ultimately unsuccessfully. To understand how and why, let us look briefly at three leading illustrators of the pre-World War I period, all of whom succeeded in meeting the demands of their clients and in achieving popular artistic reputations in their own times and beyond. These individuals represented different points of view and different responses to the range of problems already discussed regarding commercialism.

Individual Responses: The Cases of Howard Pyle, N. C. Wyeth, and Charles Dana Gibson

Howard Pyle (1853–1911) never needed to turn to advertising. He could choose whatever kinds of assignments he wanted. But by 1906 he had become unhappy with his career as an illustrator, feeling increasingly dissatisfied with the conventionality and repetitiveness of the work he was doing.[120] Moreover, expenses had caught up with him. He was supporting his wife, six children, his invalid mother-in-law, and a seven-member household staff; he also liked to throw dinner parties. His finances had become strained, and he did not feel in a position to cut back on assignments. Just at that point, Pyle received an offer of $36,000 a year to become art director of the popular magazine *McClure's*.[121] He agreed to work half-time at $18,000, but found he was not temperamentally suited for such a demanding administrative position. Alienating former students by pressuring them to sign contracts, and unable to sign up the talent he or his publishers wanted, Pyle resigned after only five months on the job. His cash reserves low, he resumed illustration. In 1906 he made an about-face and set his sights on mural painting—far less lucrative, but, in his mind, unquestionably a fine art. He hoped that continued illustration assignments would keep him afloat financially.[122] Thus, in the last five years of his life, Pyle attempted to surmount the artistic constraints that he felt his career as an illustrator had placed on him by embarking on a civic enterprise (mural painting) divorced from publishing and other businesses, but that still demanded accommodation and compromise. He did so, however, only after first attempting and failing to go the more profitable route of being art director for a large magazine publisher. For Pyle, the quest for artistic identity could never be divorced from the practice of illustration or the support of the print media.

Unlike his teacher Pyle, who at least started out satisfied with his career, Newell Convers Wyeth (1882–1945) was never able to come to terms with his work as an illustrator. Steeped in the romantic ideal of the artist as independent visionary, Wyeth was tormented from the beginning by doubts about the value of illustration; he remained deeply ambivalent about illustration in general and its relation to commerce.[123] Wyeth found it impossible to dissociate illustration from the idea of artistic compromise and commercialism, especially when it was compared with easel painting. Painting enabled freedom of subject matter, technique, composition, and expression; illustration was too formulaic. Art directors and publishers placed too many restrictions on the illustrator, but he had to conform because he had to make money. "I want to be a painter," he wrote in 1907.

> I respect illustration but now realize keener than ever before the terrible rut I'm in. A dangerous one too. I shall continue illustrating by all means, that has its commercial value, my bread and butter. But I want to be *able* to *paint* a *picture* and that is as far from the realms of illustration as black is from white. Illustration is built up on superficial technique, pet receipts of effect and *everything* that's artificial, besides always containing a literary meaning and expressing some melodramatic incident.[124]

Wyeth vowed on numerous occasions that he would give up illustration for painting just as soon as he had greater financial security and confidence in his talents. But with an ever-growing family (with five children) and ongoing frustrations with his own painterly abilities, Wyeth continually avoided making the break. Seven years later he would write:

> I *know,* that with my intense love of life, my emotional sense of things about me and the power to sustain enthusiasm would have carried me well into the nobler realms of interpretation had I not *bitched* myself with the accursed success in *skin*-deep pictures and illustrations. I *know* this is so—and all the passive talk about being content with the really-noble-art-of-illustration-if-you-are-doing-your-best, etc., etc., is emphatically wrong.[125]

An issue for Wyeth, and for other illustrators as well, was the matter of contracts. For Wyeth, they were "a blight on my artistic ardour," turning him "into too much of a machine."[126] Easel painters ostensibly worked for themselves, and on their own schedules. Like other easel painters, Wyeth believed that an illustration had to have a value independent of what it illustrated and that to produce the finished work, the illustrator could not be bound by deadlines or time constraints. The contract system provided money up front, but demanded that an illustrator produce images within a specified time period. In Wyeth's view, this setup effectively

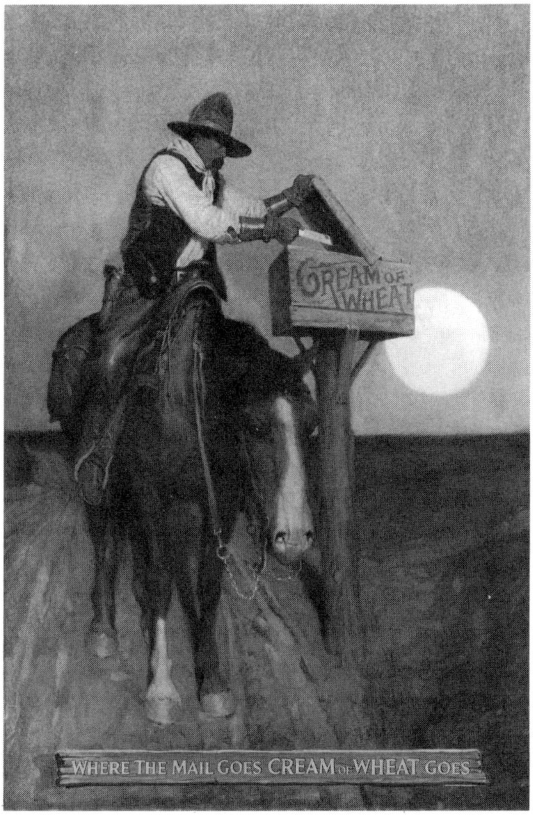

1.14. N. C. Wyeth, *Where the Mail Goes, Cream of Wheat Goes,* 1906. Wyeth's image manifests the new corporate strategy of packaging and mass marketing goods as national brands. Cereals, durable yet processed, were among the earliest products to be sold in distinctively designed individual packages. They were promoted as modern breakfast food, convenient to store and prepare. This advertisement communicated the message that Cream of Wheat was part of this modern phenomenon of national standardization, and was available to those living even in remote regions of the country. At the same time, Wyeth's image of a manly cowboy conjured up the same nostalgic associations of a lost, authentic West that he imparted to his independent paintings. In the advertising context, however, such a representation was meant to reflect on the product: notwithstanding its refined name, Cream of Wheat had rugged, old-fashioned goodness, and was a real man's food.

denied the individual value of the artist's work. There was also the fact, as Wyeth described it, that "a picture to the publisher is essentially a commercial asset. Its principal function is to attract attention. It is, in short, a form of advertisement. . . . And so to be practical for the publisher the true function of a picture [to express the truth, the artist's "inner feeling"] is distorted." The illustrator was charged with conveying an idea, in the most direct manner, and with merely repeating the incidents of the text, rather than with submitting the idea to his own emotions and interpretations.[127] Moreover, he had noted earlier, the requirements of modern reproduction were also inhibiting.

> An illustration must be made practical, not only in its dramatic statement, but it must be a thing that will adapt itself to the engravers' and printers' limitations. This fact alone *kills* that underlying inspiration to create a thought. Instead of expressing that inner feeling you express the outward thought or imitation of that feeling, because a feeling is told by subtleties and an engraver cannot handle such delicate matter.[128]

Thus for Wyeth, to be an illustrator was to succumb to the practicalities and commercial concerns of the magazine industry. To create a work for reproduction was, in itself, a commercial activity. Wyeth's notion of commercialism was even more broadly defined than Eastman's or Sloan's. By Wyeth's definition, there could be no art of illustration. Yet he continually accepted both illustration and advertising assignments (fig. 1.14), painting landscapes on the side; partly for financial reasons, partly for reasons of personality, Wyeth never followed the logic of his convictions to break from illustration. As late as 1943, two years before his death, he was reiterating the same sorts of dismissive statements about illustration that he had made thirty years before; whereas earlier these outbursts might have served as incitements to change, they now had become means of releasing his feelings of guilt and self-hatred.[129] For Wyeth, fine art ideals and early-twentieth-century illustration were incompatible.

The famous image of *The Weaker Sex* (fig. 1.15), published in *Collier's* in 1903, represents well the situation faced by its creator, Charles Dana Gibson (1867–1944, fig. 1.16). Like its handsome hero, Gibson was torn between two attractions: fine art, especially painting, and popular illustration. Unlike Wyeth, however, Gibson was able to reconcile the two realms successfully. He did so through professional service, and later, through activism. Like Pyle, he took on administrative work. But whereas Pyle's role as art director and his forays into mural painting were attempts to escape illustration, Gibson's public activities were part of his larger effort to attain artistic respectability for illustrators and their work, as well as for himself.

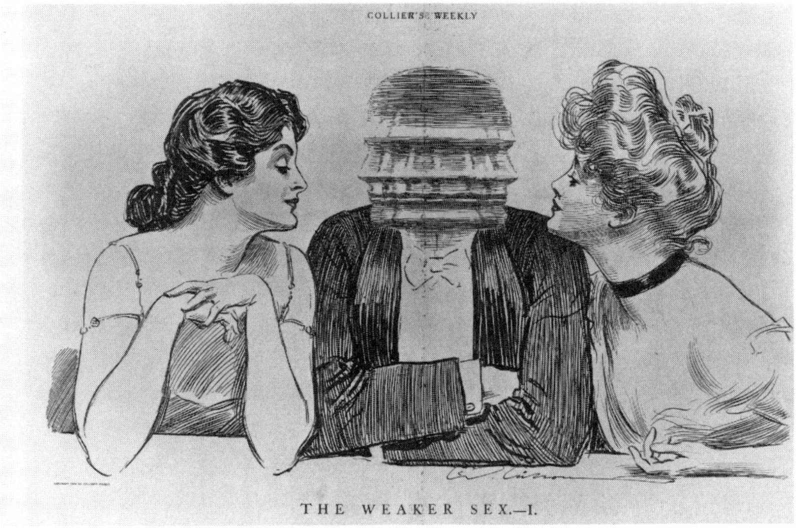

1.15. Charles Dana Gibson, *The Weaker Sex I, Collier's,* 27 June 1903.

Gibson came from a formerly wealthy New England family of old stock. With his patrician confidence, good taste, and aloofness, he parodied in virtuoso pen-and-ink drawings the aspirations and antics of nouveau riche Gilded Age parvenues. These images, published in the pages of *Life, Harper's, Scribner's,* and later, *Collier's,* were tremendously popular. "He ruled through the power of pictures," wrote his biographer, "pictures with a simple message needing no interpreter, pen strokes which seldom really required written words as captions."[130] Indeed, one of the significant aspects of Gibson's work early on was that his satirical drawings were independent. Whereas Gibson sometimes illustrated texts, his most popular work did not accompany other authors' writings.

Gibson became best known for his Gibson Girl, the image of ideal white Anglo-Saxon American womanhood, whose looks and fashions were widely emulated and copied. Indeed, the Gibson Girl became an important early example of a "media image" whose legacy remains with us today. Gibson by no means resisted the commercial dissemination of his creation; on the contrary, when appropriately compensated, he gave his blessing and lent his name and image to manufacturers of such items as Gibson Girl plates, wallpaper, and souvenir spoons. His popularity

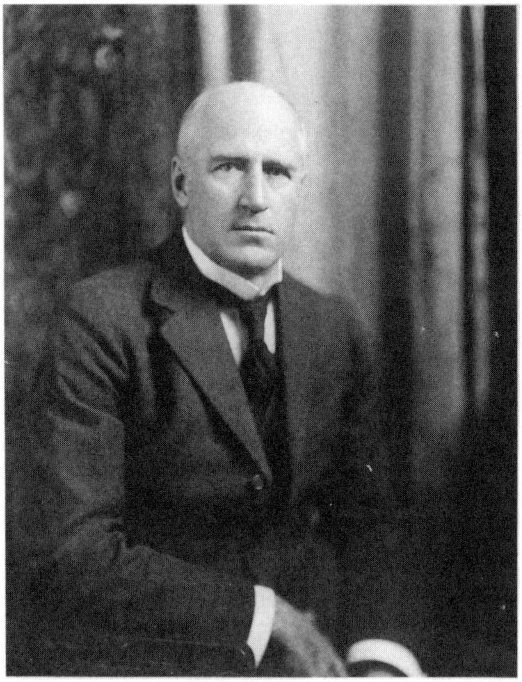

1.16. Charles Dana Gibson, 1916.

among the middle classes did little to diminish his standing among the social elites he satirized. With his debonair manner, good looks, and debutante wife, Gibson mingled quite happily with the society set; fame only added to his appeal.[131]

Indeed, high-society America became both his subjects and his patrons. It was they who promoted his drawings as fine art and convinced him to hold exhibitions of his work. In the early 1890s, purchasers paid up to $3,000 for an original Gibson. His works stood on their own as independent pictures in wealthy and middle-class circles alike; these drawings held their own as a unique form of self-sufficient, storytelling picture.[132] By 1900 Gibson was renowned both as a creator of commodified images and as an artist. Yet despite this popularity and social acceptance, Gibson aspired to more: he longed for respectability.

He sought respect in two ways: through painting and through professional service. In 1905, at the height of his career, Gibson dropped his satirical illustrations and his $65,000-a-year income and left for Europe to pursue oil painting. His hopes were quickly dashed. His paintings received only a lukewarm reception, and he himself was not pleased with them. And in 1907, a financial panic wiped out a substantial part of the fortune on which he had planned to live. No longer able to afford an aristocratic painter's life abroad, Gibson returned home and to his work as an illustrator.[133] He also resumed the active professional service that he had begun to take on before leaving. If he could not be an independent painter, Gibson resolved, he would work to assure the place of illustration as an art. To this end, he served as president of the Society of Illustrators from 1909 to 1921. His presence helped to boost membership and draw press attention to the society, a feat that the group might not have accomplished on its own. In 1920 Gibson helped to purchase the faltering humor magazine *Life*.[134] And, as we shall see, between 1917 and 1919, Gibson, roused by the atrocities of the Great War, also took on a new role as propagandist and activist. Service enabled Gibson to combine his activity as a popular illustrator with responsible public contribution. Until his retirement, when he resumed painting, these activities provided Gibson with the upright reputation and the emotional satisfaction he failed to attain as a painter or as an illustrator alone.

World War I

America's entry into World War I offered the opportunity for a new shift in illustrators' activities, reputations, and self-perceptions. It became an inducement for them to change and to organize effectively. And it provided the impetus for some illustrators to work aggressively to improve their artistic standing among other groups and to acquire greater autonomy. The war helped to revitalize the illustrators' enterprise through an act of public service: their selling of patriotism, the war effort, and the United States government. Along the way, it helped to imprint upon the minds of advertisers the potential value of art as a method of persuasion.

On the United States home front, one of the significant aspects of World War I was the way in which government sought to shape mass opinion. The Committee on Public Information, America's "propaganda ministry," was largely responsible for undertaking this task. The committee, headed by George Creel, was "charged with encouraging and then consolidating the revolution of opinion which changed the United States from an anti-militaristic democracy to an organized war machine."[135] In April 1917 Creel asked Charles Dana Gibson, then president of the Society of Illustrators, to solicit help from his colleagues in the propaganda effort; together they launched the Division of Pictorial Publicity, to which Gibson and members of the society enthusiastically volunteered their services in making war posters that would counter those produced by the Germans.[136] While Creel recognized the value of propaganda posters, not every government department was so convinced in the beginning. Indeed, the initial response of the heads of several of the "war-making branches" typified the distrust and negative perception with which illustrators as a group had long had to contend. Government officials expected the artists to be incapable of organizing and to spend their time squabbling. And, according to Creel, the illustrators would have to rectify "the current Washington idea that imagined art as a sort of slot machine," an enterprise that swallowed up dollars but with minimal payoff.[137] From the standpoint of government officials, illustrators were not sufficiently pragmatic, efficient, or businesslike. Illustrators, previously chided for being too market-oriented, were now criticized by government bureaucrats for being too artistic.

Having convinced government officials that commissioning posters would be an asset, not an unpredictable risk, a large group of illustrators and a smattering of painters created over 700 posters (figs. 1.17, 1.18, 1.19), 122 placards for cars, stores, and buses, 310 advertising illustra-

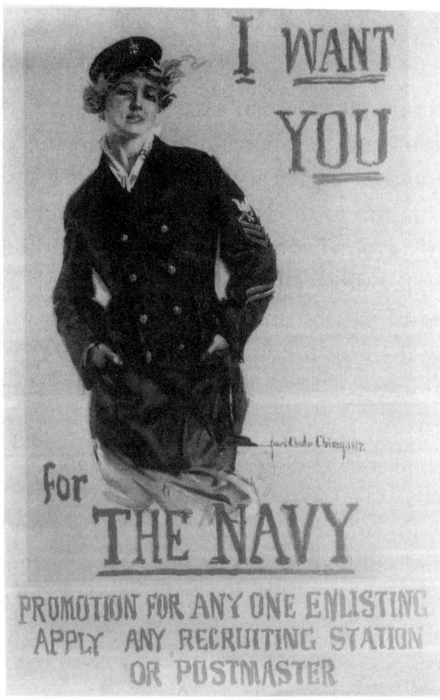

1.17. Howard Chandler Christy, *I Want You for the Navy*, 1917.

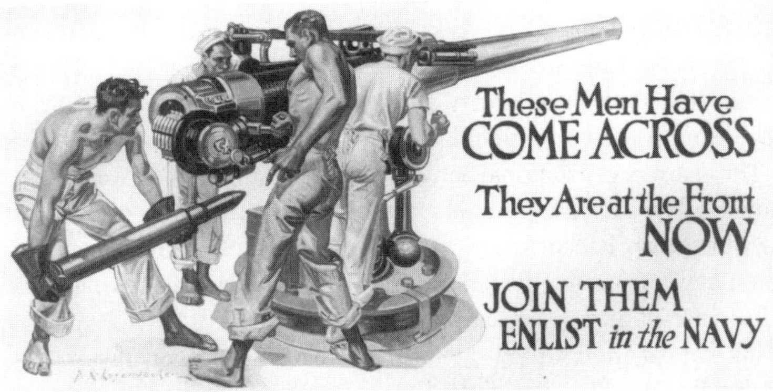

1.18. Francis Xavier Leyendecker, *These Men have Come Across,* 1917.

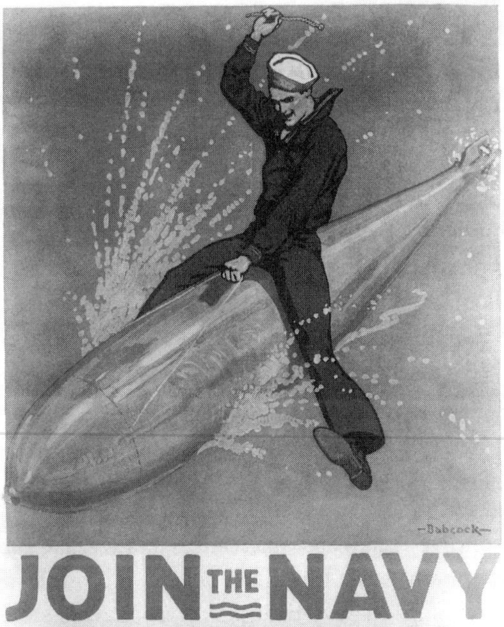

1.19. R. F. Babcock, *Join the Navy,* 1917.

tions, and 287 cartoons. They worked on behalf of such causes as recruitment, the Food Commission, the Red Cross, American Ambulance, American Relief, and the Liberty Loans.[138] To enlist illustrators, Gibson traveled around the country and established local branches of the division. The main organizational activity took place in New York at weekly meetings, followed by stag dinners of the type that members of the Society of Illustrators had held for years. At the meetings, illustrators and representatives from the designated division mapped out plans; Gibson and his assistant then selected appropriate volunteers.[139]

This war experience proved to be a positive one for many illustrators. The belief that they had contributed significantly to American society and to a just cause clearly boosted their self-esteem. The memorable images by such men as Gibson, Flagg, and Christy enhanced illustrators' artistic reputations, and generated much positive commentary. In some cases the creative process itself became a publicity event, as when a group of illustrators set up shop and painted a 90 by 25 foot canvas for Liberty Bonds in front of the U.S. Subtreasury Building (fig. 1.20).[140] The strength of their convictions and the vibrancy of their posters seemed to reinforce many illustrators' sense of confidence. On another level, however, the posters tell a different story. From one perspective, of course, they are expressions of the general masculine attitudes and outlooks of the time, highlighting the glamorous female to express her subordination to men. From another, their prevalent imagery of seduction and phallic dominance also represents some illustrators' attempts to displace and deny their lingering doubts about the true manliness of their profession.

At the same time, illustrators' collaborations with advertising men strengthened their professional and social ties with this group. During wartime and after, many illustrators' aspirations and standing remained structured by their relationship to publishing and business. The Division of Pictorial Publicity worked closely with the Division of Advertising, whose members, all leaders in the agencies, conceived publicity campaigns for the various government branches involved with the war effort and prepared copy for the posters.[141] The illustrators' work for the Division of Pictorial Publicity brought them together with advertisers, but now on behalf of an "appropriate" and reputable cause: to advertise for the federal government.[142] In many ways, this effort helped to promote a greater acceptance of the value of art in advertising. By 1920, having seen Liberty Bonds sold masterfully by leading illustrators, younger men and women would have much less difficulty with the idea of advertising cars, tomato soup, cigarettes, or life insurance. Advertising copy would help to reassure them that these products, like the war effort, could contribute to the progress, protection, and happiness of the American family. These

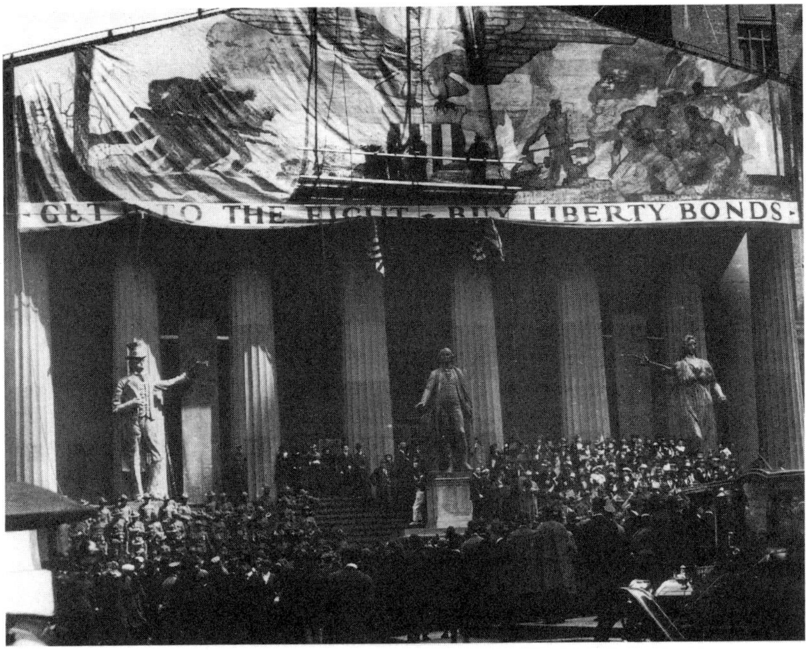

1.20. Henry Reuterdahl and N. C. Wyeth putting last touches on giant battle picture at the Subtreasury Building, Third Liberty Loan Campaign, April 1918, Paul Thompson, photographer.

were good causes on behalf of which a new generation of illustrators might work. Thus increasing numbers of them were drawn into advertising.

Art on Demand

Advertising's visibility and dominance in United States society in the 1920s altered the attitudes, practices, and identities of many illustrators. These changes were both signaled by and an outgrowth of the crystallization of a highly structured art world of advertising work with its own expectations, demands, procedures, products, and relationships. Many of the variables, processes, and complications were comparable to those mentioned earlier regarding magazine illustration. However, there were also differences worth elaborating upon, not only between advertising art and magazine illustration, but also between the practices of illustrators and of easel painters, with whom illustrators were often invidiously contrasted.

On one level, the working practices of advertising artists from the 1920s through the 1940s seem rote and predictable. The art director or his representative would solicit an artist and offer him a price. After negotiating the size of the fee, the artist would embark on the assignment, whose conception, basic design, and subject matter would usually be supplied by the art director. The artist would execute the project within the time allotted in his contract. During this period he might consult with the art director to insure that he was carrying out his assignment appropriately. After completion, the artist would submit the work, make modifications in accordance with the art director's specifications, and submit it again. Only after the art director and client had accepted the project would the artist receive payment. Most freelance assignments were handled in this fashion. For many artists, such projects entailed a friendly but short-term relationship between illustrator and art director. The average artist rarely had contact with the client or with other personnel of the advertising agency. Prominent artists like Rockwell Kent and Norman Rockwell were the exceptions.[143]

From a sociological perspective, however, the activities within this rigid system were subject to a great deal of variability. However mechanical the enterprise, the circumstances were always contingent upon an artist's social background, past experiences, expectations, artistic style, reputation, connections, geographic location, client, and budget.[144]

For one thing, an illustrator could take other paths besides freelancing. The field of advertising art offered several modes of practice and occupational hierarchies, which were determined both by circumstantial variables and by a system of values specific to art. Many advertising agencies (and department stores) established their own specialized commercial art departments, in which salaried artists worked under the supervision of the art director in developing sketches and layouts. Another outlet was the art service, "an aggregation of artists under business management" that offered entire production packages to advertisers and publishers. According to J. Walter Thompson art director Gordon Aymar, the service usually covered "the various phases of commercial illustration—figure painters, decorative men, retouchers, photographers, fashion artists. They are usually on a salary basis, but in certain instances share in the profits. Salesmen do all the contact work and acquire new business."[145] In addition to obtaining assignments for member artists, the service would take care of "models, photography, research, mechanical details, shipping, and billing."[146]

The nature of the work depended on a host of contingencies, including client, medium, constraints of technology, time expectations, purpose, and budget. Requirements for advertisements for national brands, placed principally and regularly in magazines (although sometimes also in newspapers) differed considerably from those for a one-week sales promotion for a local department store placed in daily newspapers. Depending on the size of the budget, national advertisers might commission different advertisements with renderings appropriate to different media. Newspaper advertisements were likely to be black-and-white line drawings, for example, because they reproduced well.[147]

Working for an art service enabled a young artist to break into the field and served as a form of apprenticeship, offering the security of a steady income. Many advertising agencies preferred art services because of their reliability and expertise in working for reproduction. A drawback for the artist employee, however, was that art services often became associated with a particular, distinctive "look," to which the artists then had to conform. In addition, the artist worked anonymously, and thus received little credit for his accomplishments. His contributions, often highly specialized, constituted just one part of the larger design. Indeed, wrote Ernest Watson, "in such studios illustration functions on an assembly-line basis."[148] An artist who began working for a service might find that such specialization made it harder to break away and go freelance. Nevertheless, for many of these individuals, work for an art service was a perfectly satisfying creative challenge and a respectable, well-paying occupation. Those with higher artistic ambitions and expectations were more likely to chafe at the compromises and the specialization demanded of them in the advertising field. These were the men and women who were most likely to rely on the freelance system or who sought to break out of commercial work altogether.

This third form of practice, freelancing, at the top of the commercial artistic occupational pyramid, was subject to the same insecurities and tensions as magazine illustration. The freelance artist usually had training from a fine arts school. He did not get his technical training on the job, as might art service, in-house retail, or agency artists. An art school background inculcated in the freelancer the romantic artistic ideals of freedom and authentic self-expression that were often at odds with the practicalities of actual advertising work. Some freelancers thus found it hard to balance what sociologist Robert Faulkner described (with reference to Hollywood composers) as the "dual tendencies" of "business versus art, routine versus innovation, equivocal versus unequivocal demands, recurrent versus nonrecurrent ties, and altruistic versus selfish motives."[149] Those like Rockwell, Leyendecker, and McClelland Barclay

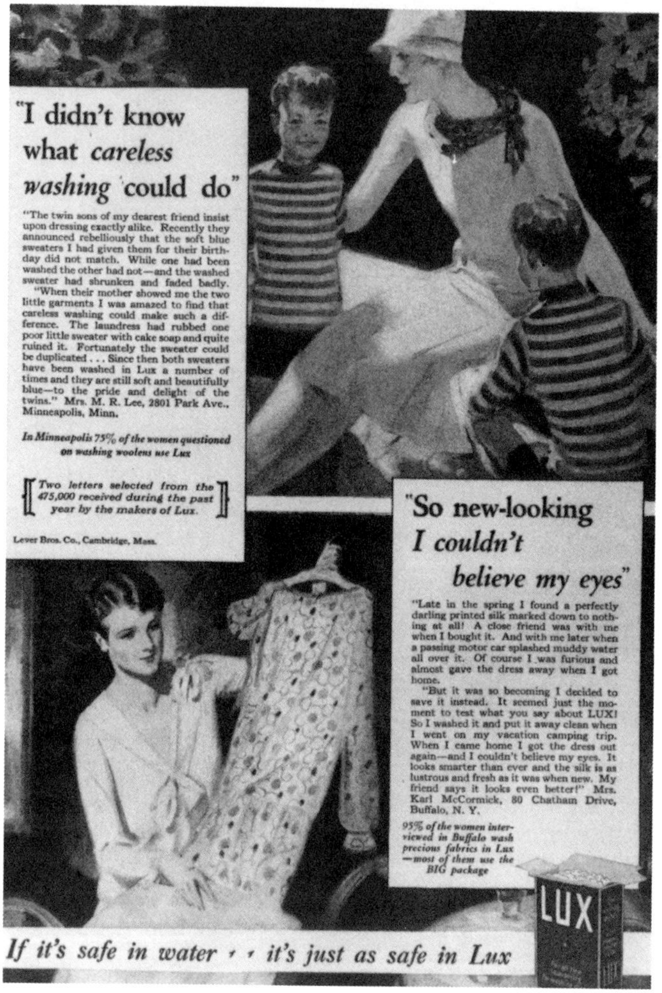

1.21. Advertisement for Lux, illustration by McClelland Barclay, 1927.

(1891–1943, renowned for his advertisements for Fisher Body, Lux [fig. 1.21], and other products), who could do so with a minimum of professional disruption, were generally the most successful.

The occupational structure of freelance work had its own specific hierarchy that paralleled those of other artistic professions. As with magazine illustration, at the bottom were the majority: the large circle of newcomers trying to break in and the more experienced artists on the outer fringes, who together eked out a living. Over the course of their careers, some of these individuals might receive a number of advertising assignments from major agencies, but they were hardly the regulars.[150] In the middle were those who represented the core of the occupation, a large secondary tier of competent, prominent illustrators whose signatures became familiar in advertisements and who received numerous commissions over a period of a decade or two. These included artists like Barclay, John LaGatta (1894–1977), Andrew Loomis (1892–1959), Frederick Mizen (1888–1965), Coles Phillips (1880–1927), Howard Scott (1902–1983), and Haddon Sundblom (1895–1976).[151] At the top were the inner circle, artists who maintained their name recognition over a long period of time: Norman Rockwell, Maxfield Parrish, and Rockwell Kent, for example. These individuals did not necessarily take on more advertising assignments than those in the second tier, partly because their strong reputations for excellence and reliability allowed them to be more discriminating and to be paid more for the work they did do. In turn, the commissions they did accept were valued all the more highly. At the same time, the options of the top tier could be limited. Not every client wanted to deal with a demanding "artistic temperament."[152]

In part, what determined the top status of these commercial artists was their success in forging reputations as fine artists, picture-makers, among a certain sector of the middle-class public (an issue to be examined at greater length in chapter 5). Their ability to do so hinged upon their self-promotional skills, political savvy, and networking efforts as well as design talent. Those like Rockwell, Leyendecker, Kent, and Parrish, who could juggle their conflicting interests, often prospered. In turn, such success provided them with a greater degree of artistic autonomy than some of their peers enjoyed. Those at the top had greater authority in dictating the limits of what they would do for an advertiser.[153] Yet even the big names had to control their egos and balance conflicting aesthetic and practical interests.[154] These artists also knew that their stature was contingent on ongoing big commissions. Thus even the established artists sometimes took on more work than they might have liked in order to maintain their ties and an active presence. These artists' decisions to take on lots of work were not necessarily the result of greed. Maintaining ongoing commissions was an important business strategy. With no long-term contracts and no salary, topflight artists occasionally saw fit to work for smaller companies (if they could afford sufficient payment) as a way to maintain their presence and broaden their professional networks.[155]

Men dominated this multitiered world of work, but women functioned within it, both as freelancers and as agency artists at the middle and lower levels. Art directors frequently selected women such as Jessie

Willcox Smith (1863–1935) or Gladys Rockmore Davis (1901–1971) to illustrate advertisements for "women's products": babies' and children's items, women's fashions, and bathroom furnishings such as towels (Davis, Cannon Towels) and soaps (Smith, Ivory Soap). Women illustrators operated according to strategies similar to those of their male counterparts, but had to contend with fewer opportunities, lower pay, paternalism, and other social restrictions that made it harder to build up professional contacts through networking. Thus for both female and male illustrators, work in advertising offered possibilities for economic and professional advancement, but it also entailed artistic and personal challenges.

The Changing Image of Illustrators

Where did these new conditions leave illustrators as a group? With the temporary boost of the war now over, illustrators were again confronted with their old uncertainties about their identities. By the mid-1920s, they had come to a professional impasse. Apart from its annual exhibitions, the Society of Illustrators was neither a forceful promoter nor a highly visible public enterprise. A sign of this weakness was the society's 1919 decision to admit women as full Fellows, now defined as "the professional producers of art works intended for reproduction."[156] On one level this gesture was a concession to the power of the movement for equality of the sexes, signaled by the passage of the Nineteenth Amendment. On another level, however, it represented an implicit acknowledgment that earlier attempts to identify illustration with fine art and socially acceptable male professionalism could not be sustained. Some Society of Illustrators members, such as the prominent illustrator Thornton Oakley, had become disillusioned with the organization because of its failure to address serious professional matters. Although he did not name such issues, they might have included business ethics, the rising use of agents, the impact of photography, and artistic education. In a letter to the society, Oakley complained that he rarely received notice of any meaningful activity—that the group spent too much time focusing on smokers and entertainment.[157]

Indeed, while the annual exhibition remained a major focus of the society's efforts and provided essential publicity for its members and their work, the annual stag fund-raisers occupied an increasingly important place on its agenda.[158] By the mid-1920s the society's girlie shows had become glittery social events that brought together illustrators, art directors, and other patrons, as well as New York's social, political, theatrical, and literary set. The shows certainly drew attention to the illustrators—for example, one of them was raided by police in 1935—but as satirists and personalities rather than as creators.[159] Girlie shows brought in crucial funds that allowed the Society to operate, but did little to increase respect or support for the art of illustration per se.[160] Not convinced of the merits of their enterprise, illustrators again expressed their professional and artistic aspirations symbolically: they asserted themselves through theatrical parodies of their professional plight and bawdy expressions of sexual prowess and command rather than through practical maneuvers in the "real" worlds of culture and business.

Illustrators' roles changed because the market for illustration was shifting. There were few choice opportunities for book illustration compared with those at the turn of the century. Illustrators continued to do book illustration, especially of children's books, but the enterprise lost much of its previous distinction and became a much more specialized activity. Publishers of high-toned magazines either cut down on illustration or turned to photography for nonfiction, both because they wanted to economize and because they perceived their audience to be less interested in elaborately illustrated texts. In the elite journals, images could not reverse a serious decline in circulation.[161]

By the 1920s, the mass-market magazines and advertisers became the primary patrons for illustrators; increasingly, they controlled definitions of artistic worth. Advertising in particular took on more prominence. Advertisers had more money for salaries, fees, and color pictures. Advertising copy now assumed roles that had once been the domain of books and magazines—providing human interest stories, for example (fig. 1.21). Advertisements became little dramas of consumerism. Likewise, the advertising work of such artists as McClelland Barclay and Norman Rockwell was indistinguishable from their magazine illustration.[162]

These circumstances marked a dramatic expansion of the parameters of "commercialism" in illustration. Indeed, for many illustrators, it was no longer feasible to distinguish the two realms of magazine and advertising illustration. Whereas earlier illustrators like Abbey sought to ally their work with painting as a fine art, by the late 1920s illustration was linked closely with commercial art, a fact illustrators now accepted, if sometimes ruefully.[163] The new typing of illustrators as commercial artists had consequences even for exceptional individuals like Norman Rockwell. Rockwell succeeded tremendously within the professional framework of illustration, and even managed to elude some of the restrictions and negative associations that affected the group. Nevertheless, he had trouble transcending the categorizations imposed upon him by virtue of his work for mass-market magazines and advertising. Rockwell's career, at its height between the Great War and the Cold War, further articulates the conflicts among group identities, self-representations, and individual actions that remained inherent aspects of the identity of the illustrator, the commercial artist. His example offers a fitting conclusion to this chapter.

Norman Rockwell, Illustrator

Like Pyle, Wyeth, and Gibson, the art school–trained Norman Rockwell (who dropped out of high school to become a full-time student, first at the National Academy of Design, then at the Art Students League), was raised on romantic artistic ideals. Born in 1894, he was of a generation that still believed that high art and illustration were compatible.[164] Determined to become an illustrator on the order of Pyle, part of an "ennobling profession," the young Rockwell vowed "in blood . . . never to prostitute our art, never to do advertising jobs, never to make more than fifty dollars a week."[165]

The vow was soon broken. By 1915 the money-conscious Rockwell had succumbed to the allure of the expanding worlds of publishing and business, and was pursuing successful careers in both magazine illustration and advertising (fig. 1.22). The dual activities and the competition seemed to pose little problem for him. His popular reputation soon became such that he could readily choose whatever jobs he wanted.[166] He also maintained more artistic control than many of his peers. Rockwell's achievement was to find common ground between the ideals of consumption and leisure propagated by his clients—publishers and advertisers—and the visions of humanity that his middle-class public aspired to and enjoyed.

Always overlooked by the work worlds of museum curators, scholars, and independent painters, Rockwell was lionized by editors, publishers, and readers of popular magazines, who identified him principally with his ingenious covers for the *Saturday Evening Post*. Rockwell was widely admired for his heartwarming idealizations of "common Americans" (who, in keeping with prevailing assumptions about appropriate modes of representation, were mostly white Anglo-Saxons). He capitalized on this success by projecting a comparably "wholesome" persona, "transparently sincere," as Arthur Guptill described him, "honestly earnest."[167] For over half a century, Rockwell rendered myths of modern Americans engaged in the little dramas and comedies of everyday life.

Yet Rockwell's art and career also appear to have been propelled by a desperation to stay one step ahead of a debilitating sense of inadequacy. The myths and sentimental idealizations of Rockwell's art and personal-

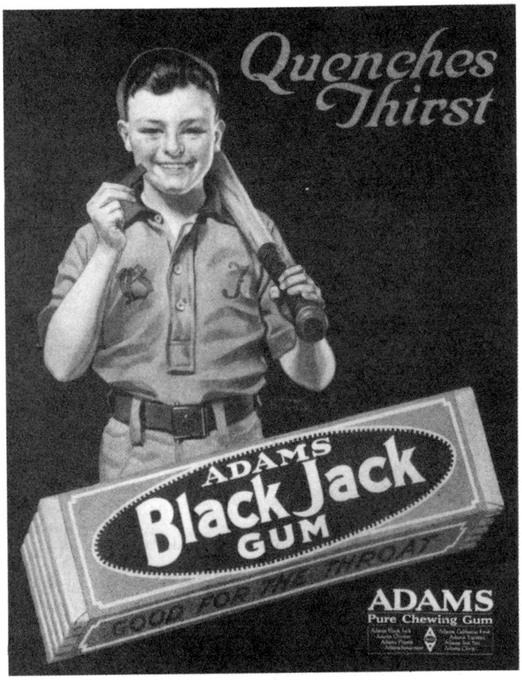

1.22. Advertisement for Adams® Black Jack Gum®, illustration by Norman Rockwell, 1920.

ity, his conventionalism and superficiality, represented the artist's constructive alternative to what on one level, at least, was a basic inability to come to terms with his life and modernity more generally. He resolved the conflicts arising from his practice as a very public illustrator by adapting an older ideology (which linked the productive contributions of virtuous, independent individual workers to the growth and virtues of the American republic) to the demands of a growing culture of consumerism (in which work was regarded not as an end in itself but as a means toward consumption).[168] Throughout his career, Rockwell threw himself into his work and avoided painful public self-analysis.

The young Rockwell was no country-boy provincial; he was the quintessential class-conscious and ethnically sensitive urbanite, coming from a tough neighborhood in upper Manhattan. ("On election nights the Third Avenue gang and the Amsterdam Avenue crowd would meet in a pitched battle on 147th Street and St. Nicholas Avenue," he reminisced. "We used to watch from our roof.")[169] Rockwell's parents, religious people, were determined to keep their son above and away from it all; Rockwell served as a choirboy in New York and later in suburban Mamaroneck. From there, Rockwell commuted to art school.

Rockwell's father, who worked for a New York textile firm, rose from office boy to office manager. The family lived modestly. Although not "desperately poor," Rockwell admitted to being conscious of needing money.[170] In his autobiography, Rockwell recalled that the family did things together but was hardly "close knit."[171] Among his most positive childhood memories were those of summers spent with his family in the country. "Those summers seemed blissful," he later wrote, "sort of a happy dream."[172] It was in the country that urbanism had its greatest impact on Rockwell's future art. The country experience became everything that city life and Rockwell's own reality were not. ". . . I wasn't a country boy. I didn't really live that kind of life. Except . . . in my paintings."[173]

Rockwell channeled his negative feelings about urban and family life and their inadequacies into ambition and idealized images. From the earliest stages of his career, Rockwell focused on making accessible, upbeat "universal" stereotypes to which any white middle-class American could ostensibly relate. His images froze "significant" mundane moments in time. They confirmed the shared humanity of players and audience and never depicted a darker side of life. This part of the equation had to be bracketed.

Rockwell's illustrations thus represented the epitome of modern "antimodernism," denial, and escape from the ills of modernization, and, later in life at least, he was the first to admit it.

> The view of life I communicate in my pictures excludes the sordid and ugly. I paint life as I would like it to be. . . . Maybe as I grew up and found that the world wasn't the perfectly pleasant place I had thought it to be I unconsciously decided that, even if it wasn't an ideal world, it should be and so painted only the ideal aspects of it—pictures in which there were no drunken slatterns or self centered mothers. . . . If there was sadness in this created world of mine, it was a pleasant sadness. If there were problems, they were humorous problems. The people in my pictures aren't mentally ill or deformed. The situations they get into are commonplace, everyday situations, not the agonizing crises and tangles of life.[174]

Rockwell's pictures touched a common chord among members of the public and helped sell millions of copies of the *Saturday Evening Post,* as well as consumer goods. Rockwell's desires to have "everybody like my work" and to avoid anxiety, coupled with his clients' demands and the excellent money, were sufficient motivation for him to continue to work in the same vein.[175] But this solution did not prove to be as satisfying as

Rockwell would have liked. Throughout his career, Rockwell's concerns about his reputation and his life's work were heightened by three factors: a sense of inferiority about his gawky, ungainly, un-macho appearance; self-consciousness about his family heritage; and the force of the romantic ideologies with which he and his peers had been inculcated through artistic training. As he put it, one side of his family (his father's) was staid, upright, "substantial," and Victorian; his father's father was "in the coal business." But Rockwell's grandfather on his mother's side was a "poverty ridden" immigrant who made his living painting detailed pictures of people's favorite pets. When business was slow, he painted "potboilers." "Three subjects—the Indian maiden, the grieving mother, *Homeward Bound,* a picture of a clipper ship clearing the white waves toward its (dimly seen) home port—were repeated over and over without variation or embellishment."[176] Still desperate for money, he painted houses. In Rockwell's eyes, this "impoverished painter of animals, potboilers, and houses" was clearly the "black sheep" of the family.[177]

Rockwell sought to remove himself from this legacy, yet his own career represented a certain continuation of it, as he himself admitted. Seeing himself as a "queer mixture" of both family traditions, Rockwell struggled to maintain self-respect by exaggerating the respectable side, by never challenging convention or breaking loose.[178] Unlike his maternal grandfather, he would succeed in supporting his family through art-making. But he nevertheless could not fully convince himself of the adequacy of his work. His respectability bothered him.

Like Wyeth, Rockwell was driven by romantic fine art ideals of originality, freedom, sincerity, and experimentation.[179] Hence, he too had misgivings about his art, despite his enormous success. Rockwell's standards of aesthetic value were influenced by the commentators and artists whose views dominated the art press and were reflected in the taste of upper-crust circles (the very people who ignored or condemned Rockwell's work). The academic conventionalism of his illustration veiled his actual interest and sympathy toward modernist ideals and investigations, especially those of Pablo Picasso. On numerous occasions, Rockwell sought to explore other subjects and approaches to representation: when young, he tried Gibson Girl types; later, in the 1920s, he experimented with more "modern styles," but noted that his efforts "weren't very good."[180] Frustrated with the results of his self-searching explorations, Rockwell heeded the advice of *Post* editor Lorimer, and of others on whom he depended, to fall back on the same good old work.[181]

Like Wyeth, then, Rockwell was driven by a belief that he should move on—if not beyond illustration, at least beyond his standard repertoire of subject-predicaments and styles. Unlike Wyeth, however, Rockwell felt he was not up to the challenge. It was easier simply to continue to do what fans already liked. Thus Rockwell, unlike Pyle, Wyeth, or Gibson, never really sought actively to distance himself from his corporate clients. He never made claims to be anything other than an "illustrator."[182] But the consequences were ongoing crises of purpose and bouts of depression (exacerbated when his first wife, whom he claimed not to love, left him for another man).[183] These culminated in the 1950s, when the very modern Rockwell became a client of psychoanalyst Erik Erikson, the man most closely associated with the concept of "identity crisis."[184]

Rockwell did find a workable solution, however.[185] Always exercising restraint, he channeled his personal anxieties about his life's meaning into work. Production, solving immediate creative problems for magazine covers and advertisements, became Rockwell's outlet, a source of personal strength and professional success. His credo: "If you fall on your face, don't lie there and moan, *get up*."[186] Rockwell also channeled his reticence and fears into his public persona. Through articles and interviews, he built up an image that hinged upon the revelation of process, not meaning. According to commentators like publisher Arthur Guptill, Rockwell was "sincere," "modest," and had no "pretense."[187] In other words, what was on the surface was truly there, and was all that existed. This myth of comforting superficiality was sustained by Rockwell in his autobiography, an informal, dictated narrative that purported to reveal more of the "true" man than it actually did (fig. 1.23). Throwaway comments about Rockwell's depressions, for example, were followed not by introspection about their causes or significances, but by evasive statements about not knowing why they occurred. "Even now I don't understand, really, what caused the trouble or how I gradually worked through it," he wrote of one incident. "Since then I've had other difficult periods. Each time, as I reached the point where I felt I was finished, at the end of my rope, I've managed to right myself. Always by simply sticking to it, continuing to work though everything seemed hopeless and I was scared silly."[188] Rockwell's key to survival required that he avoid painful introspection. Psychologically and artistically, he had to be a highly self-controlled worker, an artist of surface who depended upon the tactics of expediency. The postscript to his book, accompanied by a line drawing of the artist at work, his back to his audience, was "Still going strong." Only through the unspeakable bouts of despair, and through later images like *Triple Self-Portrait* (fig. 1), could Rockwell's conflicts emerge.[189]

In the late 1880s and early 1890s, many illustrators self-confidently sought to set their own agendas. They did not expect that the structure of their patronage would fundamentally alter the image of autonomous fine

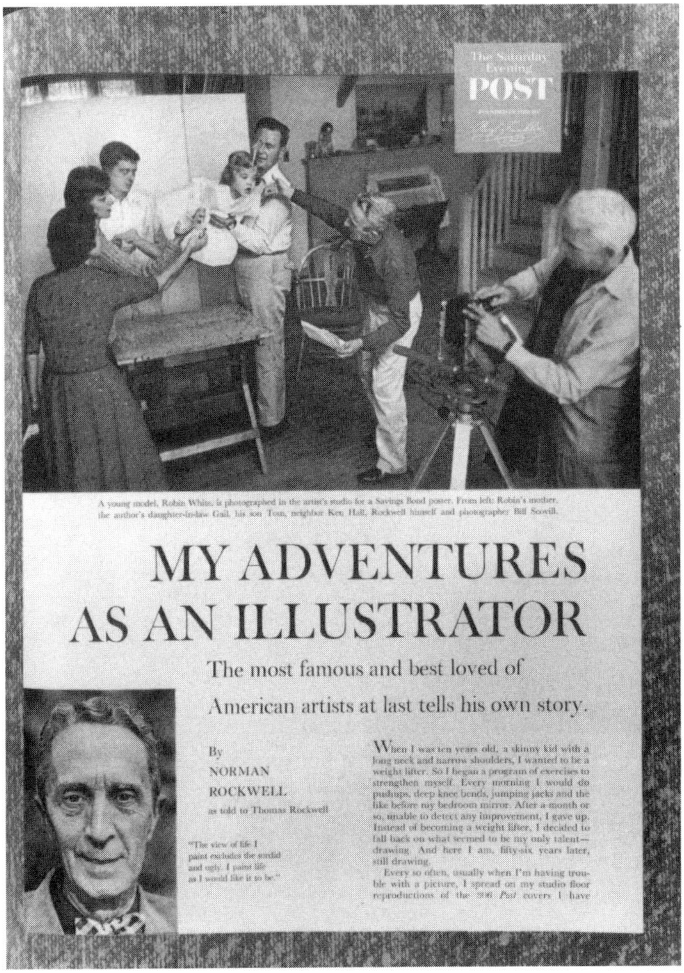

The Saturday Evening POST

A young model, Robin White, is photographed in the artist's studio for a Savings Bond poster. From left: Robin's mother, the author's daughter-in-law Gail, his son Tom, neighbor Ken Hall, Rockwell himself and photographer Bill Scovill.

MY ADVENTURES AS AN ILLUSTRATOR

The most famous and best loved of American artists at last tells his own story.

By NORMAN ROCKWELL as told to Thomas Rockwell

"The view of life I paint excludes the sordid and ugly. I paint life as I would like it to be."

When I was ten years old, a skinny kid with a long neck and narrow shoulders, I wanted to be a weight lifter. So I began a program of exercises to strengthen myself. Every morning I would do pushups, deep knee bends, jumping jacks and the like before my bedroom mirror. After a month or so, unable to detect any improvement, I gave up. Instead of becoming a weight lifter, I decided to fall back on what seemed to be my only talent—drawing. And here I am, fifty-six years later, still drawing.

Every so often, usually when I'm having trouble with a picture, I spread on my studio floor reproductions of the 306 *Post* covers I have

1.23. Page from Norman Rockwell, "My Adventures as an Illustrator," *Saturday Evening Post*, 13 February 1960, 19.

artists that most envisioned for themselves when they decided to illustrate. Their identity would be comparable to that of easel painters and etchers: illustrators would create works of power and vision that would then be used by book and magazine publishers.

This ideal began to change by the turn of the century with the growing authority of mass-market publishing and national advertising. The nature and demands of this patronage created new conditions and restraints for illustrators, and compromised their expectations about both artistic identity and practice. But many illustrators and critics attempted to ignore these realities. The shifting conceptions of identity that resulted were a function of the extent to which individual illustrators and commentators accepted or resisted the conditions imposed by the framework of publishing and advertising within which they now operated. Some, as we have seen, attempted to deny their sense of subordination and weakness through overblown representations of masculinity; some did so by ostensibly distancing themselves from some vague notion of commercialism. In the end, none of these strategies produced the widespread cultural authority and respectability illustrators had hoped for.

By the end of World War I, many illustrators were resigned to the idea that their art was intimately connected to commercial concerns; in other words, they acknowledged the authority of their patrons, not only in controlling their work activities but in defining the very art of illustration as well. With this concession, their struggle for autonomy and respectability as "fine" artists had effectively ended. All illustration was now commercial art. Its creators' ideals and practices were finally consistent.

Yet, while illustration might be commercial art, to be an advertising artist meant different things. Painters, critics, and even illustrators might condemn the commercialism of illustration, especially for advertisers. Yet their attitudes were based in part on conceptions rooted in a certain misapprehension. For while the 1920s were a boom time for advertising illustration, only rarely did such work offer a steady and substantial income and an enduring reputation. In fact, for the majority, a freelance career in commercial art was as insecure and uncertain as one in painting. Misconceptions continued, in part because the press emphasized the positive, lucrative side and tended to cover the success stories. Misinterpretation also persisted because an ideology of romanticism continued to shape many illustrators' own expectations, aspirations, and perceptions of accomplishment. Illustration remained marginal, in large part because illustrators themselves regarded it as such. Swayed by the ideals of painters and intellectuals, illustrators continued to evaluate their activities in terms of standards whereby they could not win.

chapter 2

Posters versus Billboards

Like illustration, the advertising poster was widely regarded as an exciting new art form at the turn of the century. In the view of many artists, writers, and businessmen, good posters would oil the machinery of economic progress; the harmonious conjunction of art and commerce would also help society to reach its full potential. Strategically placed, artistically rendered posters would draw attention to advertisers' products; they would also provide opportunities for the broader public to experience advanced American art and to learn the principles of good design. Posters would help people become more discriminating consumers and more refined citizens.

This "promise" of the poster faded within ten years, in good part as a consequence of the rise of billboard advertising (fig. 2.1).[1] From the standpoint of the cultured viewer, billboards were excrescences. It would not be difficult to argue that such images were reviled because the majority of them were tasteless, crudely rendered, and unattractive. But such an assertion would beg the question. Aesthetic status depended on the agencies or individuals who made the images and who had the power to decide whether "art" should be a priority in their creation. Such authority was not preordained, and as circumstances developed, artists in fact played a rather marginal role in the resolution of this question. In this respect, the enterprise of advertising poster design differed considerably from illustration.

Indeed, by contrast with illustration, the question of identity and significance in the case of advertising posters was fought out first and foremost in the realms of urban politics and the institutional frameworks of

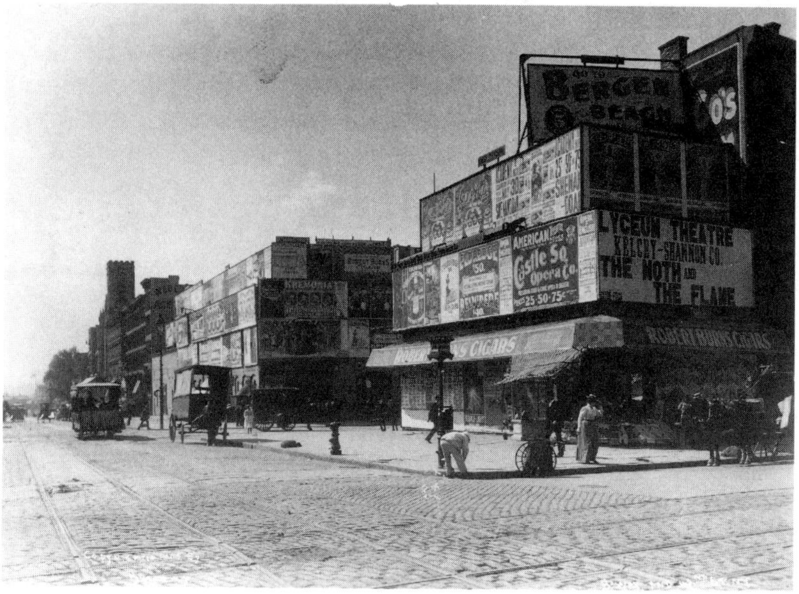

2.1. Billboards, Broadway at Forty-second Street, 1905.

culture, rather than in the sphere of occupational politics. This occurred because of the distinctive characteristics of posters and billboards as very public signs. In one sense, of course, illustrations and posters were both public forms of imagery. Both were assumed to communicate desirable, "shared" values, both presumed a community of viewers, and both employed many of the same rendering techniques. But for the most part, illustration was experienced in the home, with the viewer's consent. Posters, on the other hand, intruded upon the pedestrian or commuter in public urban spaces, in conjunction with other visual and physical distractions. The rise of posters and billboards thus forced a broad range of groups to consider the significance of outdoor advertising, especially as an invasion of privacy. More broadly, this phenomenon forced people to confront the question of the limits of the free enterprise system in an urban context: how to reconcile the interests of businessmen with the social welfare of the citizenry at large.

These issues were at the core of the disagreements over the design, purpose, and artistic status of posters and billboards. But the meaning of the debates also turned upon irreconcilable differences among artists, publishers, advertisers, politicians, museum curators, and big and small businessmen over the definitions and aims of art. Was art meant to beautify the environment or to promote sales? And who had authority to make such decisions with regard to art in outdoor advertising?

The Rise of the Fine Art Poster in America

Colored posters for advertising purposes had been commonplace in the United States since the early nineteenth century. The first posters were woodblock-printed in one or two colors. This technique remained in use well into the 1880s, although color lithography, perfected by firms established by immigrants, such as the German-American Strobridge Company of Cincinnati, had superseded it some twenty years earlier. Mid-nineteenth-century posters by anonymous draftsmen hawked patent medicines, circuses, and theatrical events. Produced not as part of a national campaign but on an ad hoc basis through contracts between advertising agents and billposters, these posters adhered to no particular standard of size or quality.[2]

A shift in attitude and production occurred in the late nineteenth century. The development of large businesses, national brands, and an expanded advertising trade resulted in more complex systems of commercial publicity, such as zoned advertising (in which particular types of goods were advertised to specific publics in specially designated regions), which could be adapted to either national or local conditions. Improvements in lithographic and photographic technologies allowed production of billboards and posters in large quantities at lower cost. Following broader trends toward centralization and specialization, advertisers, lithographers, and billposters formed the Associated Billposters Association of the United States and Canada in 1891, thus joining the many trades and professions that founded organizations and societies during this period. The association, the second of several in the field, sought limits on franchises and competition as well as standardization of billboard size, cost, and placement.[3] According to one turn-of-the-century trade publication, approximately twenty establishments in the United States specialized in posters. They represented a capital investment of $3 million and employed close to 100 designers and draftsmen and 500 "artists" to reproduce the originals.[4] Thus a powerful and highly organized billboard industry, heavily controlled by German- and Irish-Americans, emerged.

One offshoot of the billposting phenomenon was the rise of the "art" poster (see fig. 1.9). Its sponsors, mostly high-class book and magazine publishers and some newspaper publishers, regarded it as separate and distinct from the billboard. Yet the art poster's very distinctiveness would quickly prove to be its downfall.

To a certain extent both the billboard and publishing industries took their cues from Europe, where recent poster trends suggested new design possibilities. In the 1880s, artists like Jules Cheret, Theophile-Alexandre Steinlen, and Henri Toulouse-Lautrec had made names for themselves as poster designers and had upgraded the reputations of such signs. They offered eye-catching, decorative images, primarily of women, rendered with heavy outlines, asymmetrical, cropped composition, bird's-eye perspectives, and bold, flat tints. Their images were influenced by impressionist and symbolist painting and especially by Japanese prints. These new art posters, commissioned for publishers, theaters and cabarets, and assorted manufacturers of consumer goods (such as bicycles), were displayed on specially designated and elegantly designed poster boards and kiosks. They received widespread publicity in Europe, and became the rage to collect.[5] Some cognoscenti bought posters legitimately from book publishers and sellers; others ripped them from the kiosks.

Interest in French posters soon spread to the United States. The billposting industry took note of the new design trends but rarely adopted them. Their posters remained mostly written text, which was cheaper to produce than images.[6] New York publishers, on the other hand, were quick to embrace the European art poster. Publishers were kept well apprised of the activities of their European counterparts; many undoubtedly viewed French posters at an 1890 exhibit at New York's Grolier Club, as well as on trips abroad.

Inspired by French publishers' success in luring new audiences through posters, and ever conscious of the sophisticated tastes and aspirations of their reading public, American publishers began to use art posters to advertise their magazines and books, and promoted such posters as a new art form, as collectibles, and as a means to beautify cities. *Harper's New Monthly Magazine* began the process in 1893, commissioning the magazine's art director, Edward Penfield, to create a series of strikingly simple, stylistically up-to-date posters, signed (but not individually). Their quality of design and technical execution stood on a par with the book and magazine illustrations produced for publishing houses. Charles Scribner's Sons, J. B. Lippincott, Century (fig. 2.2), and others quickly followed suit.[7]

Thus the growth of elite-sector national publishing was largely responsible for the emergence of the commercial fine art poster. The creation of posters for magazines, newspapers, and books introduced new working arrangements and aesthetic attitudes. Whereas most billposter designers remained anonymous, publishers encouraged their poster creators to sign the plates for images, an act that lent new prestige to the works and asserted their stature as art. A signature, the mark of self-

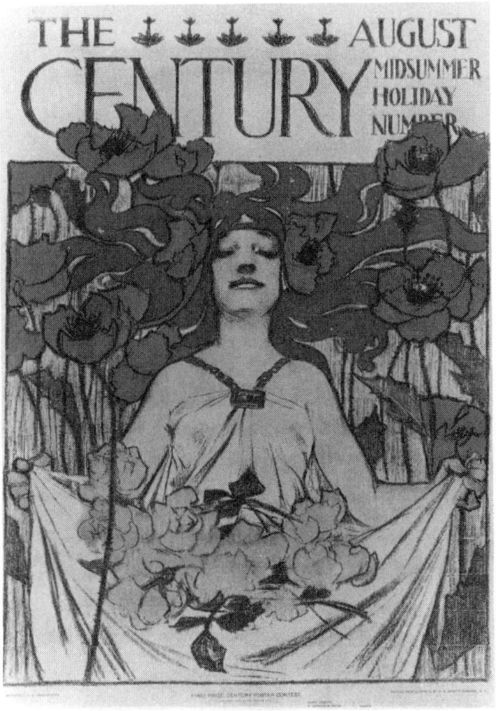

2.2. Joseph Christian Leyendecker, poster for the August *Century* Midsummer Holiday Number, 1896. This winning entry for the *Century* Poster Cover competition evoked the art nouveau style of Czech artist Mucha.

expressivity, labeled the work as the product of a sincere creator.[8] The artists, who included Will Bradley (1868–1962), Edward Penfield (1866–1925), Ethel Reed (1874–after 1900), and Louis Rhead (1857–1926), worked in sophisticated, conventional styles (fig. 2.3) whose asymmetry, flat color, and simplified forms, influenced by the English Aesthetic movement, French avant-garde painting and posters, and Japanese prints, signified uniqueness, "refinement," sophistication, "daring invention," and cachet.[9] These were the indices of art.[10] The fine art status of these advertising posters was further underscored by their small size (on average 19 by 14 inches, which made them ideal collectors' items), and also by their imagery: for the most part idealized, beautiful, but—in contrast to European posters—rather unsensuous women. In general, women

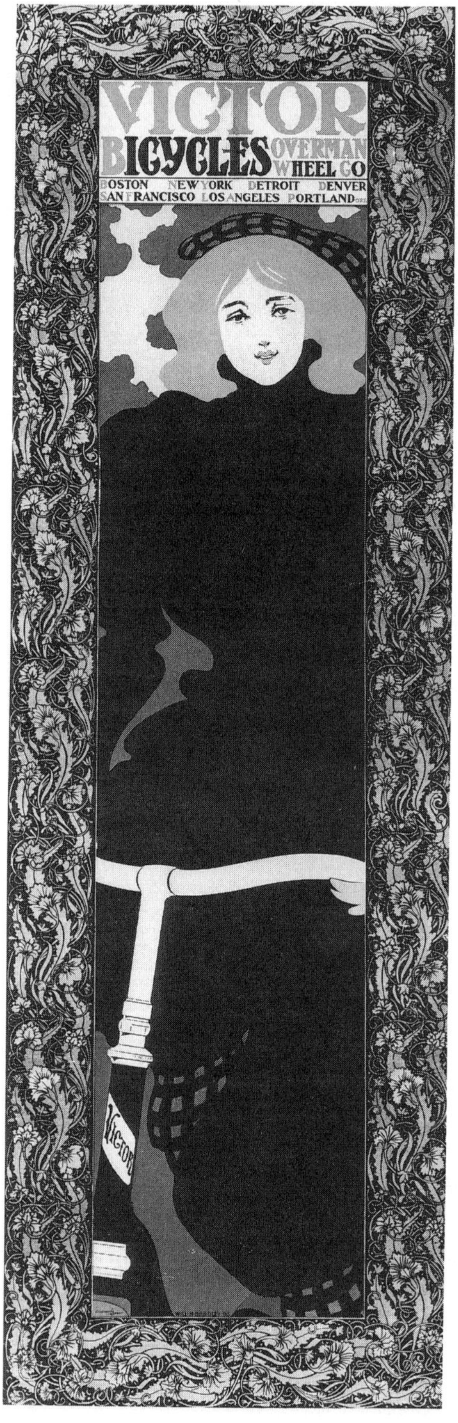

2.3. Will H. Bradley, poster for Victor Bicycles, 1896.

were rendered as purely decorative forms rather than as thinking, acting individuals. (Edward Penfield's images of women holding magazines [the goods] or dreamily reading were about as active as such images tended to be. Bicycle posters depicted women on bicycles, but never exerting themselves.) This imaging of feminine passivity was itself not new, but when done in a style that rendered both the human figure and other ornamental elements in the same schematized manner, such images signaled a new artistic departure for American advertising. Such representations were to connote beauty and to stimulate a "healthy" form of desire (based on pure visual attraction). Any inappropriate erotic urges evoked by the picturing of women had to be displaced and channeled into consumer desire for the product advertised.[11]

Cheaper than paintings, art posters also became coveted collectors' items in the United States. Publishers initially encouraged this craze, supplying posters to booksellers and newsstands for display as advertisements for current publications. But collectors quickly snapped up the signs. Before long, some booksellers simply hoarded the posters to sell to collectors without ever displaying them in the store.[12] Self-promotional articles in *The Chapbook,* a magazine published by printer and poster artist Will Bradley, helped to reinforce this trend by plugging the value of posters and the necessity of acquiring a complete collection. In addition, Scribner published *The Modern Poster* in 1895. Designed to appeal to collectors, it included a limited edition of 1,000 posters with a series of signed and numbered Bradley compositions. The Century Company inaugurated a series of cash-prize poster competitions in 1896 (see fig. 2.2); that same year two specialty magazines—*Poster* and *Poster-Lore*—began (and ceased) publication.[13]

The new poster fad was neither universal nor entirely successful. Its chief promoters were high-class publishers, along with some who produced for the mass market, who felt an affinity with things foreign, urbane, and stylistically progressive. As with illustration, they hoped that associating their enterprises with art, and not with posted signs, could be very good business because art appealed to their sophisticated, well-to-do clients and collectors. On the other hand, members of the billposting industry rarely embraced the new design trends. Lithographers and billposters resented publishers' introduction of new, costlier processes and standards; they were also put off by the air of snobbery surrounding the art poster. Printers and lithographers who had usually relied on in-house draftsmen for their poster designs (fig. 2.4) could not have applauded the new standing of the more independent poster artists. After all, these individuals now moved into territory previously controlled by lithographers. Moreover, publishers and designers had to be more dis-

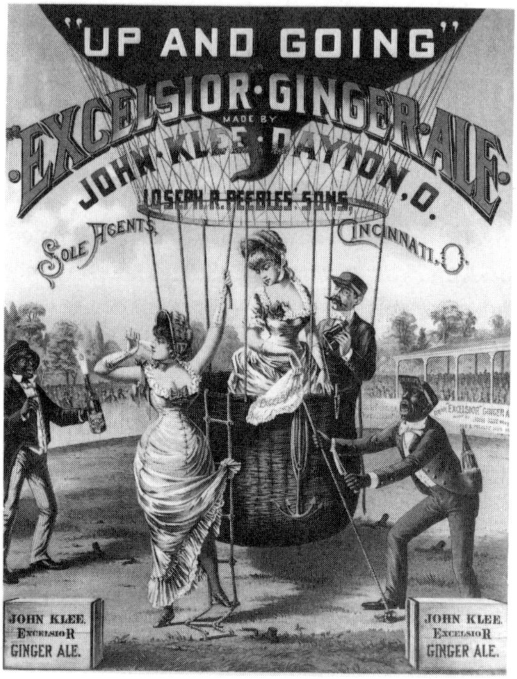

2.4. "Up and Going," Excelsior Ginger Ale poster, late nineteenth century. Grotesque caricatures of African-American men were often used as attention-getting devices in American advertising. Here, the advertiser draws a peculiar analogy between the light, airy soda and the anticipated "high" of air balloon travel. The knowing glance of the monocled white man with binoculars, combined with the glimpse of leg and the popping cork, offers risqué implications, late-nineteenth-century style.

cerning to attain the high technical quality demanded by the new poster artists, and thus intervened more in printers' and lithographers' work. Images (as opposed to text) also increased costs and added workers and procedural complications for lithographers and their clients. Some in the billposting trades accepted the freelance arrangements to advance their business; some readily embraced the idea. A few select companies like Victor Bicycles, Procter and Gamble, Adlake Camera, and the Springfield Brewing Company commissioned designs from Will Bradley, the young Maxfield Parrish, and others (see figs. 1.10, 2.3).[14] But many lithographers, billposters, and clients resisted the transformation of their advertising work into an artistic enterprise.

The tensions among lithographers, artists, publishers, advertisers, and billposters were to some extent functions of class, ethnicity, and concerns about turf. Such matters were never discussed openly in billboard and advertising trade journals, but indirectly, through aesthetic attacks and through gender stereotyping. Frequent articles in billboard and advertising trade journals railed against the "weird and multicolored barbarities in the way of 'art.'" *Billboard Advertising* singled out Penfield and Bradley (the latter in particular had appropriated multiple roles as artist-printer-publisher) for special attack. Satirizing the pretensions of artists and publishers, with their penchant for things French, the magazine accused the artists of "producing results far more hideous and soul disturbing than anything their transatlantique confreres ever dreamed of." Suggesting that what was really at issue was territory and decision-making authority, but never acknowledging such concerns, the author concluded that "the time is at hand when its [the art poster's] further encroachment upon the domain of legitimate art should be promptly and effectually terminated. It is no longer original, no longer effective, no longer anything but utterly wearisome and monotonous."[15] Such images, they insisted, in other words, were not art at all. Producers of art posters could thus hardly claim themselves to be arbiters of taste or, by extension, authorities on advertising.

Indeed, some in the advertising trades saw the new pictorial posters less as advertising than as a dilettantish, feminine trend associated with passivity and weakness. Writing retrospectively in 1912, for example, Herbert Cecil Duce clearly linked more recent developments with masculinity, strength, and directness, in contrast to the amateurishness, gentleness, and femininity he saw in earlier developments. "Before poster advertising was established as one of the more important industries, poster art was one of the fads that greatly interested the art amateurs and the host of gentle societies and women's clubs. When it developed into a great advertising force and became the greatest and most successful of all advertising media, its vogue was somewhat less dilettante and more strenuous. It eliminated the jobber, the commission man, the drummer and a host of middle men, and became the direct connecting link between the manufacturer and the consumer."[16] Like women, such aesthetes had best stay removed from the affairs of real working men. (Publishers and others who supported art posters as a mode of advertising might now be branded as foppish, but fifteen years later it would be the anti-billboard campaigners, linked with women's groups, who would be branded as elitist, effeminate, and threatening.)

By the late 1890s, publishers themselves began to reassess the merits of their posters. As Nancy Finlay and Jacqueline Serwer have observed, fancy art posters were not serving publishers' primary purpose of advertising books and magazines. Few dealers could display all the many large posters they received at any one time, and so sold them off to collectors, who did not purchase magazines or books. Once publishers acknowledged that posters were not selling their wares, they stopped commissioning them. The small lithographic publishing houses who had made posters their primary product went out of business.[17]

Publishers sought to market their goods, in effect creating categorical distinctions between art and non-art posters and billboards. They failed because their claims over art had been too successful; their posters had been transformed from advertising media into art commodities. Yet publishers by no means gave up efforts to identify their larger enterprise with art. Rather, they extended the possibilities and ambitions of art by hiring illustrators to create posterlike cover and editorial designs and by actively promoting these images as fine art, collectible on purchase of the magazines.[18] The decline of art posters as advertisements was thus accompanied by more extensive efforts by publishers and editors to identify their books and magazines with art, in order to enhance their own prestige and to build new markets. Recasting failure into advantage, they sought to reclassify the notion of art as commodity in order to sell their merchandise instead of just their advertisements.

By 1900, however, the reputation of the poster was ambiguous. Publishers' experiences suggested that it was problematic to identify posters as art, not only because art—as idea—meant pure design, removed from the "real" world and divorced from commercial connotations of service, but also because art—as object, bound up with social experience—was so integrally linked to commodity status. Commodities could not easily sell other commodities. They had their own special meanings, bound up with form and medium, that had little to do with the poster's overt advertising message: buy magazines. Lithographers, billposters, and advertisers could feel vindicated; they had suspected this early on. Over the years they would resist outside pressures to reduce the size of their images and to conform to any but self-imposed standards. The billboard trades' determination to evade categorization as an "art" field produced tensions that came into full play in the New York billboard debates.

The Billboard Debates in New York City: Commercial Culture as Urban Art

At the same time that publishers were involved in their art poster promotional efforts, advertisers were augmenting their use of large billboards and painted and electric signs. Such outdoor advertisements were employed to remind people of the product brand name; their visual imagery functioned differently than that of magazine advertisements, whose purpose was to attract the reader to the textual message. Multisheet lithographed billboards, on average ten feet high, became especially prevalent in large cities like New York (see fig. 2.1), where such advertisements could reach wide and diverse audiences. These developments produced ambivalent responses. Advertisers and small property owners welcomed billboards as a vibrant new expression of free enterprise and business progress and as a source of profit. For some in business, law, and art, the new developments still held possibilities for the advancement of the poster as a new art form. Controversies, however, soon overshadowed these optimistic visions. For many people, billboards, however artistic, spelled nothing but trouble.

As some artists, architects, lawyers, and businessmen saw it, the most immediate problem was that billboard advertisements in American cities did not follow Europe, either in terms of artistic level or of standards regarding location. Throughout northern Europe, state and local governments had successfully controlled the placement, size, and even aesthetics of billboards through legal regulation.[19] Several cities, such as Paris and Berlin, utilized specially designed advertising kiosks, often furnished and maintained by private companies that held municipal franchises. Hence government worked in partnership with private enterprise, but government maintained the ultimate authority.

The power of the government in American urban politics was less well defined, partly because mercantile interests were such a forceful influence in legislative negotiations. Some American cities had passed ordinances restricting billboards. The New York City Building Code, for example, regulated the size and height of billboard frames (called hoardings) on the grounds of fire prevention. But typically the law went unenforced, and there were no other substantial restrictions.[20] The consolidation of the boroughs into Greater New York had occurred in 1896, and citywide ordinances involving matters of private property rights were still being ironed out in 1901. It was at this time that the idea of the billboard as an important artistic and urban problem began to take hold in New York City. Anti-billboard campaigns were in step with developments nationwide.

A thorough examination of the debates over billboards in New York provides a specific case of how local civic and business groups used "art" as an expandable and contractible weapon to control commercial development and the destiny of the city. It reveals how class identities shaped conceptions and parameters of urban art, space, and place. It nonetheless shows that no single group occupied a dominant position in these negotiations. New York mercantile and real estate interests were not monolithic. The outcome of the billboard debates was the consequence of the parties' varied occupational and economic stakes and their differing access to ideological resources and political power.

Convinced that a viable policy on billboards and signs was necessary to steer the new metropolis in the direction of beauty and livability, groups of civic activists—especially members of the Municipal Art Society and the City Club of New York—embarked on an effort to establish controls and parameters. Both groups formed committees to address the problem of the increasing numbers of large signs in commercial and residential areas. The City Club of New York, founded in 1892, sought better government and civic improvements. Its members, mostly prominent lawyers and businessmen, studied and proposed legislation, prepared briefs, and lobbied state and municipal politicians. The Municipal Art Society (MAS) was founded in 1893 "to provide adequate sculptural and pictorial decorations for the public buildings and parks in the City of New York and to promote in every way the beautifying of its streets and public spaces."[21] Its membership roster included some of the city's most eminent artists, architects, and, soon after, lawyers and businessmen. Important civic activists like lawyer Albert Sprague Bard belonged to both groups. Initially the MAS sought to raise money for works of art to be donated to the city. By 1900 it abandoned the focus on philanthropy and turned its attention to the broader question of the urban landscape. By 1902 the society was planning competitions for street furnishings and other forms of civic art, and had joined with other organizations to lobby for a comprehensive City Beautiful plan. It had also allied with other groups like the City Club in serving as watchdogs, hoping to prevent abuses of New York's built environment.[22]

Author and city planner Charles Mulford Robinson (1869–1917) provided an intellectual basis for the civic organization's efforts. Robinson, a journalist and later a founding member of the American Civic Association (1904), began writing on municipal improvement in articles for *Atlantic Monthly* and *Harper's Monthly,* material he subsequently published as *The Improvement of Towns and Cities* (1901) and *Modern Civic Art*

(1908). Widely regarded as a primary spokesman for the burgeoning City Beautiful movement, Robinson touted the ideal of the city as an aesthetically unified entity. His models were the great cities of Europe: Paris, Rome, and Vienna. Robinson argued that buildings, streets, parks, statues, monuments, street furnishings, and even advertising should be designed with an eye to their effects on the whole. Such planning presupposed both an artistic and a political ideal. To achieve such unity, collaboration and authority was necessary, not just among artists, architects, landscape architects, and engineers, but also politicians, lawyers, and merchants. Public and private interests would meet in a marriage of mutual benefit.[23]

This ideal of free enterprise conjoined with a cooperative civic-spiritedness was at the heart of Robinson's view of the urban billboard. His concern was to improve the billboard, to transform it into civic art. For Robinson, advertising was inevitable, even "indispensable."[24] He wanted restraint, not suppression. There could be no excuses for lewd imagery—the community would see to that. But a meeting of minds was necessary on matters of size, location, and aesthetics. Robinson acknowledged the growing organizational, financial, and political strength of the billboard interests. But, he argued, the rights of others had to be accommodated; concessions were necessary. The solution was to regard billboards not as nuisances to be eradicated (at least not in cities) but as "splendid" opportunities for developing new, artistic advertising for the modern cityscape.[25]

In Robinson's view, all sides would benefit if advertisers spent more for more artistic work, and produced less of it. The advertising artist would have

> plenty of subjects, generous pay, and the inspiration of an immense public,—aside from the consciousness that his is truly a civic art, that he works not merely for his own glory, for his employers' sake, or for the pleasure and profit of the public; but for the beauty of his town. . . . There opens the vista of a great opportunity, of our streets freed from shrieking letters, and made picturesque and attractive by innumerable announcements, beautiful in design, workmanship, or color. The old rivalry is transferred to a worthier field. Commercial architecture, no longer disfigured with signs, assumes the importance that it ought to have.[26]

Robinson's ideal street would have posters, each "an artistic study that is strengthened, not ruined by its distinctly separated neighbor." Each would be attached to "well designed fixtures," each in its own place and protected from rain and decay. "Dull streets" would be "brightened with colors, and with colors that harmonize."[27] Posters would exhibit "grace of line" and "careful design" as well as "care of color." In addition, Robinson recommended a revival of rebus signs and heraldry, spare and attractive visual symbols instead of cluttery verbal texts.[28]

The MAS, following Robinson's lead, initially took the tack of trying to get better, smaller signs. They asked a group of 500 advertisers to help fund and promote a competition and exhibition of artistic signs that could be posted on kiosks, much as in Europe. In effect, the society sought to overlook publishers' failures. They had to convince billboard advertisers that artistic advertising posters had several kinds of value: that they would improve sales if they were art objects, and might possibly have an independent value of their own. When advertisers did not respond, the MAS's advertising committee mounted its own 1905 exhibition of "Artistic and Commercial Posters and Advertising Signs" at the National Arts Club. The show's purpose was to "stimulate improvements" and to "show that such work is commercially profitable" and that good design was possible.[29]

Advertisers, unwilling to allow civic groups to dictate their actions, took little notice, and the exhibition had little immediate effect. Deciding that efforts to reach out to advertisers were futile, the MAS and other civic groups began to assume an adversarial stance toward them. Instead of trying to improve the designs of individual posters, they shifted their focus to regulation of billboards. In so doing, they became part of a larger effort on the part of the city's cultural, mercantile, and real estate interests to shape the face of the municipal landscape: to determine the appropriate place for commerce and the proper use of urban space.[30]

Public debate over sign regulation originated in about 1905 and centered not on billboards, but on electric signs. Appropriately, the earliest discussions focused on the area of Times Square. Times Square, the controversial "epicenter" of the city's entertainment, promotion, and display, represented the leading development in commercially organized public space and experience.[31] The *New York Herald* and the MAS mounted a campaign to control the height and number of electric signs on Broadway and in the Times Square vicinity. Allying with the fire department, they contended that such signs were unaesthetic and unsafe.[32]

By 1910 the debates centered on the area from Broadway to Fifth Avenue and focused on billboards as much as on electric signs. The MAS now joined forces with civic reform and mercantile groups—the Fifth Avenue Association, the American Civic Association (a national organization dedicated to the City Beautiful ideal), the City Club, the Twenty-third Street Association, the Manhattan Central Improvement Association, and the Woman's Municipal League—to try to find a workable means to regulate signs and billboards through legislation.[33] They determined that it was time to protect not only midtown, but also other sections of the city. They argued that there were too many signs and billboards on building roofs; many, they noted, violated the height restrictions set by the building code. Signs blocked views and desecrated the architecture and surrounding landscape (see fig. 2.1). Moreover, too many rows of double- and triple-decker billboards stood alongside scenic vistas near Central and Riverside Parks (figs. 2.5, 2.6, 2.7). Most of the signs were badly de-

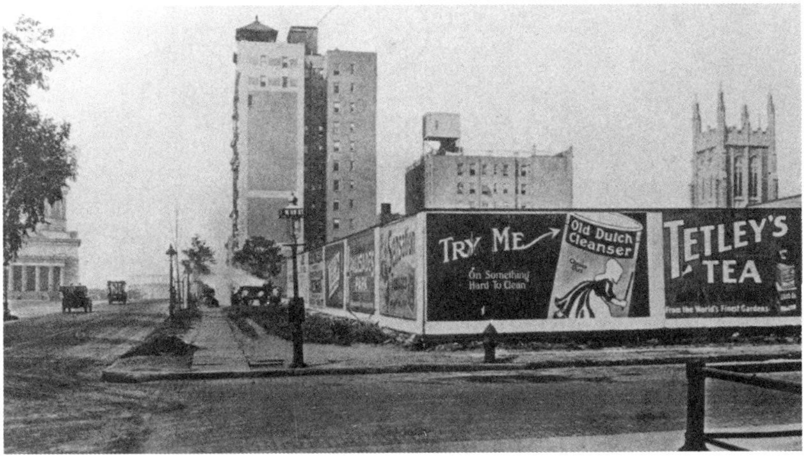

2.5. Riverside Drive at 119th Street, ca. 1912. Notice Grant's Tomb in the left background.

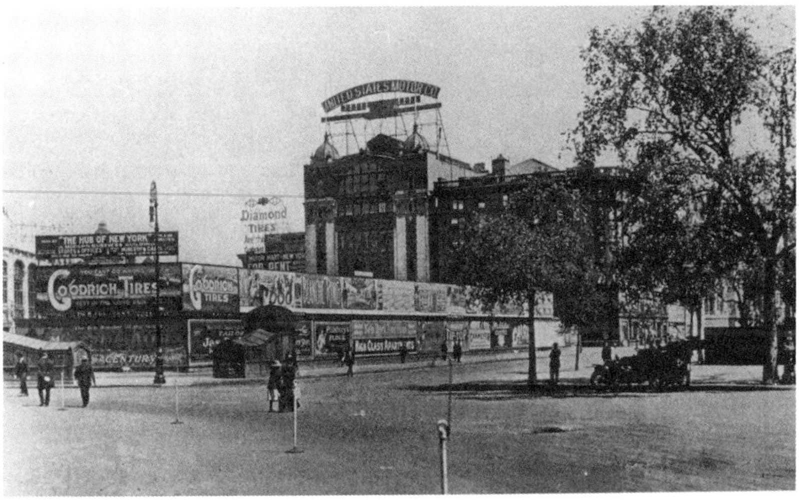

2.6. Central Park West, 60th Street and Broadway, ca. 1912.

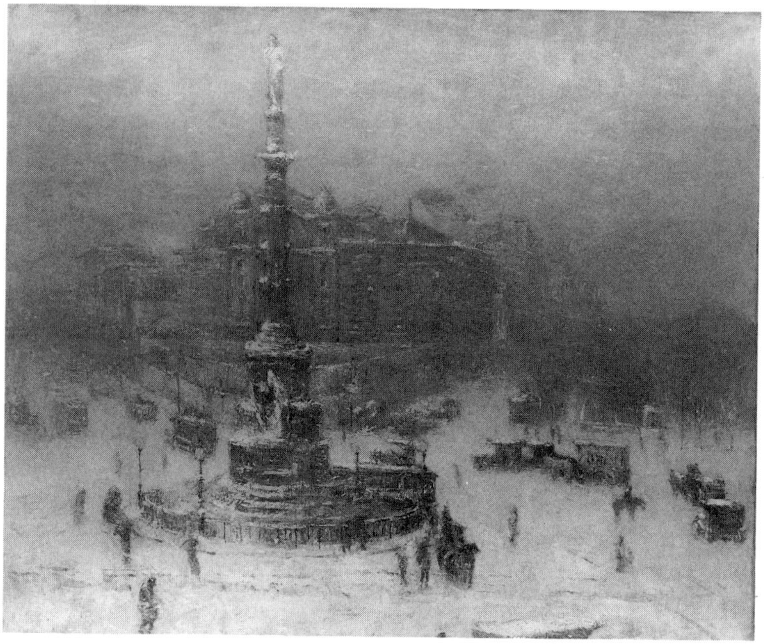

2.7. Guy Carlton Wiggins, *Columbus Circle,* 1911. Guy Wiggins commemorated the pervasiveness of billboards in his dreamily romantic rendering of Columbus Circle. Wiggins's response, unlike that of the civic activists, was to accept the billboard. Aestheticizing the billboards, Wiggins makes them an integral part of the cityscape.

signed, they argued; too many were cheap and tawdry. In their view, the emphasis of advertising had shifted from fulfillment of immediate individual desires and needs to mere stimulation. The public was being subjected to an overabundance of sensory bombardment, and by companies whose signs had no connection to the buildings they adorned.[34] The organizations also tried to convince advertisers on economic grounds, arguing that optic nerves would be so deadened by constant stimulation from billboards that people would fail to notice the messages.[35] These efforts were to no avail, and the civic groups were forced to consider new strategies through the police power to regulate "nuisances."

The MAS committee on advertising, made up mostly of lawyers, played a central role in the lobbying effort. Arguing, along with lawyers for the Citizens' Union, that appealing to "public sentiment" had so far been ineffective, MAS officials contended that some kind of regulatory legislation or tax was necessary.[36] If advertisers had to pay through the nose to erect signs and billboards, especially if they were taxed on the basis of size, then the number and size of signs might be substantially reduced. In turn, advertisers might come to recognize that a few smaller but more artistic posters would attract more attention and thus be more effective advertising.

Central to the committee's argument, then, was the idea that aesthetics could be a source of immediate cash value for advertisers. Civic beauty could only be enhanced by a policy of "special burden" taxation that would single out advertisers because billboard disfigurements so affected an entity described as the public welfare.[37] Nevertheless, whereas some MAS officials favored such an idea in theory, some lawyer members were wary of promoting taxation, especially on private property, because the courts tended to strike down legislation that interfered with "private economic rights."[38] They also knew that efforts to push for restrictive legislation on this basis would not pass muster with one of the MAS's principal allies in this endeavor, the Fifth Avenue Association.

The Fifth Avenue Association (FAA), a group with more direct interest in the matter and greater power than the MAS, became a leading force in the citywide anti-billboard campaign. Founded in 1907 to promote the interests of residents and merchants, the association's primary reason for involvement in the debate was to eliminate signage from Fifth Avenue. Their concerns and tactics were not just local, however. The association represented many of the city's leading businesses and its most powerful real estate agents, property owners, and merchants, some of whom lived on Fifth Avenue. The organization's concerns were thus those of New York's most prominent and influential citizens.[39]

FAA members certainly agreed with the MAS that there was a direct relationship between aesthetics and cash value. They claimed that large, ugly signs, most of which did not advertise local businesses, threatened to downgrade the street's beauty and refined atmosphere and reduce property values. Fifth Avenue merchants contended that the street was a "high-class thoroughfare," the "walking and driving place of the cultured and prosperous" (fig. 2.8). Crass billboards and huge painted signs like those on the old Levi Morton mansion at the northeast corner of Forty-second Street and Fifth Avenue made a mockery of important new civic structures like the New York Public Library (diagonally across the street from the mansion). Indeed, the proliferation of signs threatened to turn the avenue into a "Midway," with all of its associations with immigrants and other rabble.[40]

Being businessmen themselves, however, FAA members generally

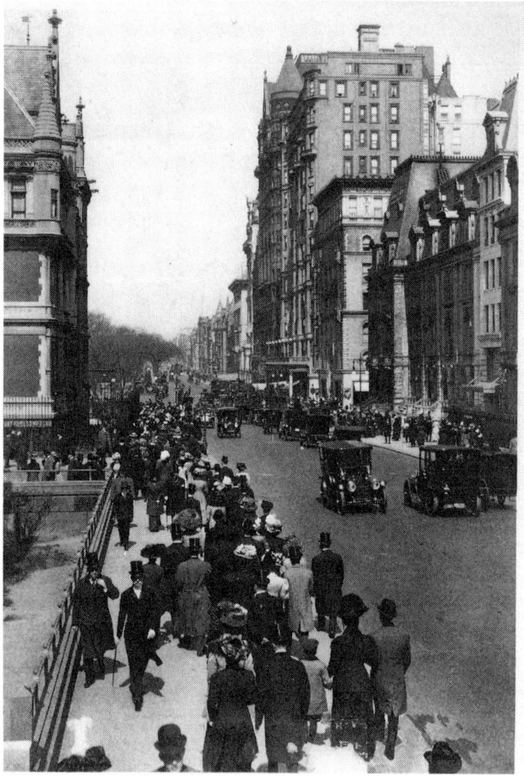

2.8. Fifth Avenue, ca. 1910–1915.

did not favor legal precedents that might constrict their own practices. Their members preferred to pursue "silent persuasion" as a solution to the billboard situation.[41]

The anti-billboard cause was advanced significantly by municipal government intervention. In October 1911, Manhattan Borough President George McAneny (1869–1953) and municipal Commissioner of Accounts Raymond B. Fosdick (1882–1972) began investigations that culminated in a 1912 report by Fosdick, proposing height and other limitations on billboards and signs.[42] In November 1912 Mayor William J. Gaynor added the weight of his office, appointing an official Mayor's Billboard Advertising Commission to follow up on the earlier report. Gaynor appointed anti-billboard activists Robert Grier Cooke of the FAA as chair and Alfred Sprague Bard of the MAS as secretary, thus signaling his support for their cause, which put urban aesthetics and public welfare above private interests. The commission's subsequent report would make this position abundantly clear.[43]

The commission's report, published in August 1913, assailed the billboard posters as public "nuisances" on a variety of grounds. These are worth elaborating because they show how far the activists' positions had shifted from their original emphasis on poster improvement toward one on regulation as a means of preserving the aesthetic integrity of the city, maintaining the well-being of its citizens, and promoting upscale commerce. The poster, which had flowered as art twenty years earlier, had become a social evil, a target of urban planners, Progressive reformers, and even some merchants and developers.

The commission had to convince the courts that aesthetic considerations were as "legitimate a basis for social regulations as are sanitary conditions," and hence just as reasonable to regulate by law.[44] The courts had rarely been willing to accept aesthetic considerations as viable reasons for exercising the police power, arguing that aesthetics were a "matter of luxury and indulgence rather than of necessity, and it is necessity alone which justifies the exercise of the police power" to restrict private property "without compensation." Several state supreme and U.S. circuit courts had ruled that exhibition of billboards on private property was a property right that could not be taken away for public benefit. The commission wanted such precedents overruled. They insisted that the sense of sight was entitled to protection.[45]

The commission report began by pointing to the intrusiveness and depravity of billboards, stating that outdoor advertising "so intimately affects the public welfare" that government regulation was warranted "in the interest of the greatest good to the greatest number." Not to take action was to "abandon our communities to serious evils."[46] Indeed, ideologically and rhetorically, the report dovetailed with the anti-vice and anti-prostitution campaigns being waged in New York at the same time. This fact is not surprising, especially because Raymond B. Fosdick, whose report formed the backbone of the 1913 billboard investigation, was by 1912 an employee of John D. Rockefeller's Bureau of Social Hygiene, one of the reform groups centrally involved in those crusades. From this particular reform perspective, government intervention, even use of the police power, was necessary to protect the citizenry from the unsafe and degrading forces of the billboard, just as it was necessary to eliminate crime and prostitution.[47] The rationale for such actions was bound up with an ideal of masculine strength, the capacity to resist evil, and the desire to protect the weak through police and legislative muscle.

To highlight the threat, the report utilized a rhetoric of aggression and depravity. Billboards "are no respecters of place," the report argued:

> They are thrust into the finest vistas which our public spaces present. Beautiful churches, fine public buildings, monumental private structures, park spaces upon which the wealth of generations has been lavished, superb river views, are confronted and environed by enormous, unsightly and at times disgusting billboard advertisements, which neutralize the effects produced by the exercise of our finest genius and the expenditure of vast sums of money, and rob the people of their rightful heritage of natural beauty.[48]

On top of their being intrusive and ugly, the majority of signs contributed in no way to the local welfare or economy. Most were "huge, crude, tasteless, and disfiguring," and advertised sinful products—wines, beers, gin, tobacco, cigarettes, patent medicine, gum, and tea (fig. 2.9).[49] The courts, in protecting the rights of property owners to allow erection of billboards, were "putting the cart before the horse." It was property owners of the *surrounding* areas who needed protection from billboard aggression, for in order to be effective, the experience of billboards had to take place in someone else's space.[50] In essence, billboard owners were taking others' property without compensation. Furthermore, billboard structures were themselves wind and fire hazards (fig. 2.10). The posters also gave cover for "immoral practices, encourage the commission of unclean nuisances, afford concealment for the collection of rubbish, filth, and garbage, and promote the propagation of flies and the spread of disease."[51]

An additional argument centered on tactics and appropriate audience. According to the commission, the majority of the "unsuspecting" targets of billboards were not the sophisticated, but those who, "if not actually illiterate . . . are of the generally unthinking class and who are

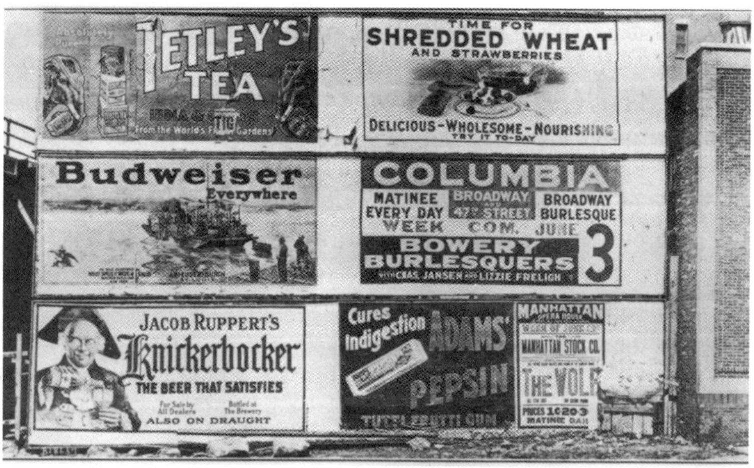

2.9. Ninety-sixth Street and Riverside Drive, ca. 1913.

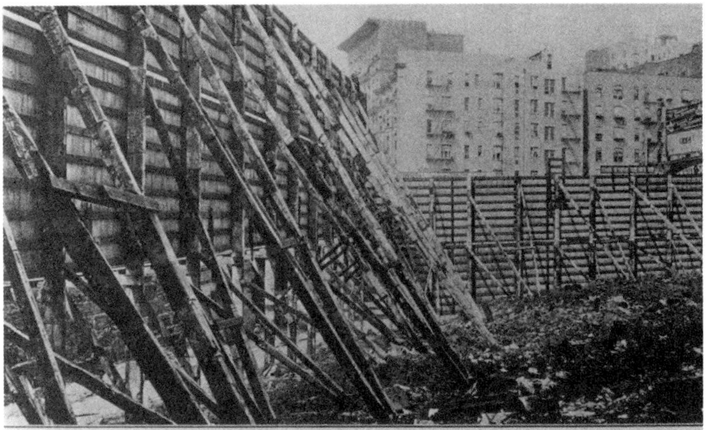

2.10. Rear of sign on Riverside Drive, ca. 1912.

caught by a bold and glaring appeal to their senses rather than to their intelligence."[52] Commission members asked advertisers rhetorically whether these people, even though they might be gullible viewers and consumers, should be given as much consideration as those who "revolt against the unrestrained riot of outdoor advertising." Might it not be more effective to "appeal to the intelligent" (presumably Americans with higher incomes) by making more artistic posters and signs?[53]

Issues of race and class were certainly at the heart of the commissioners' argument, but were not expressed explicitly. What the report highlighted was aesthetics. Urban "beauty and the happiness it gives are as legitimate objects of recognition in the law as more material things," the report insisted, and thus could be legitimately protected.[54] But artistic value also had monetary value. It was inconsistent and foolhardy for the city to be able to spend millions in tax dollars for public buildings, monuments, and parks (valued for their beauty and thereby benefiting owners of private property financially), but not to be able to protect this beauty by preventing owners from using their property to "despoil that beauty" for their own purposes. Referring to the City Beautiful movement and efforts by New York's art organizations to promote civic art, the report asked how the city could spend thousands on educating its citizens to appreciate beautiful things, then stand helpless as unscrupulous advertisers violated the taste it promoted (fig. 2.11). How was it that a "city may spend millions for art in a glass case, but cannot protect itself against the flagrant violations of art in its daily life."[55] Indeed, contended the commissioners,

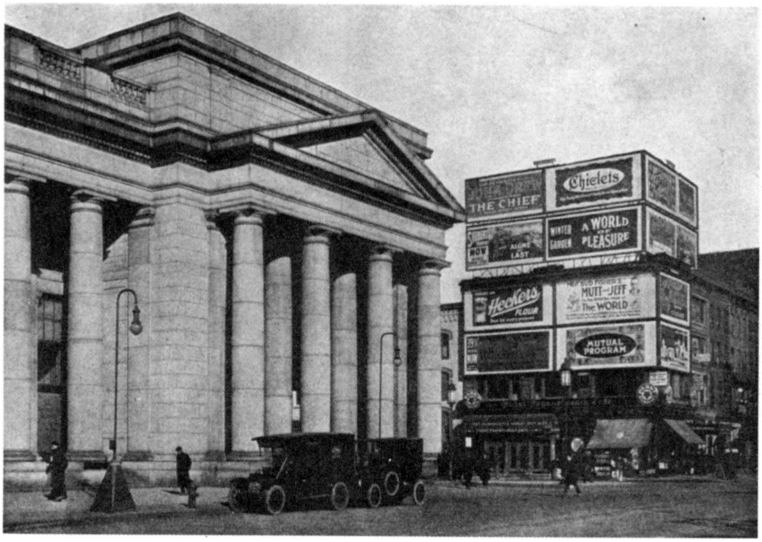

2.11. View of Pennsylvania Station and Eighth Avenue at Thirty-fourth Street, ca. 1916.

the matter of outdoor advertising was "one of *many* municipal and public matters demanding regulation . . . from the point of view of aesthetics and municipal beauty."[56]

With its rhetoric of aesthetic value, the billboard commission's report implicitly pictured the streets as uncluttered, uncongested, and refined traffic arteries, promoting free circulation "of people and store bought commodities" and augmenting the property values of the city's wealthiest merchants and cultivated residents. Like the concurrent efforts to determine the placement of monuments, to control heights of buildings, and to ban peddlers and pushcarts, the commissioners aimed at realizing a distinctly middle-class vision of modern urbanity as attractive, rational, efficient, uplifting, and discreetly lucrative.[57]

The commission made recommendations that clearly represented a compromise between the commercial interests of the FAA and the civic concerns of the MAS. The commissioners called for size limitations on signs and for taxes on advertisers and property owners. They also recommended that the state constitution be amended to make aesthetics a legitimate basis for regulation by statute or ordinance, which it presently was not. And they demanded that the city prohibit billboards on or near parks, squares, public buildings, and "streets of exceptional character and in other places of special beauty or sentiment" (e.g., Fifth Avenue).[58]

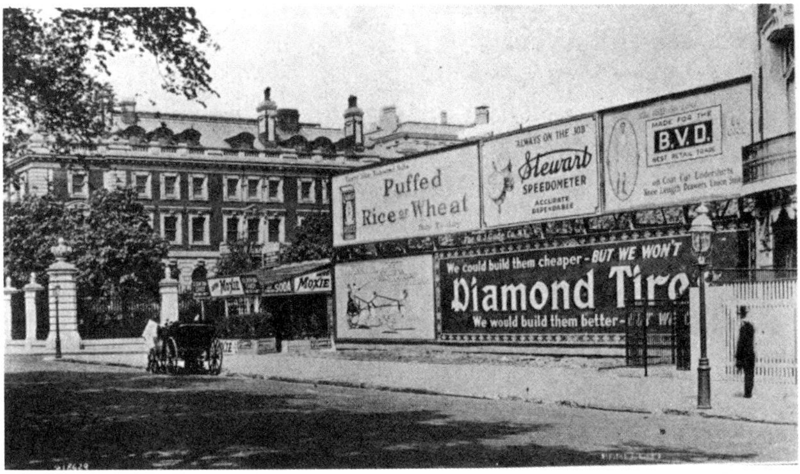

2.12. Fifth Avenue at Eighty-ninth Street and Nintieth Street opposite the Carnegie Mansion, ca. 1913.

Maintaining the aesthetic character of those select locales—those inhabited by wealthier New Yorkers—was clearly a high priority for the commission. These concerns had become evident in the commission's pre-report public hearings, when commissioner Henry Sackett caustically grilled developer Walter Salomon on how exactly the billboards on the lot next to the Andrew Carnegie mansion on upper Fifth Avenue could be made to harmonize with their surroundings (fig. 2.12); or when MAS president Laurel Harris stated that regulation should focus on Riverside Drive and Fifth Avenue because the situation of Sixth Avenue was already hopeless. (The tracks of the Sixth Avenue El shrouded the streets in shadow. Signs lined midtown buildings, and many structures were crowned with billboards, aimed at elevated-train passengers.)[59]

Thus, in contrast to the earlier desire to improve the aesthetic merits of the individual poster, the pragmatics of New York politics necessitated a larger goal: active preservation, through legislative protections, of the aesthetic integrity of the urban built environment by focusing on the harmony of the whole rather than on individual works. The ideal of the city as a valuable work of art had taken priority over single artistic images. Whereas civic groups earlier sought to convince advertisers to abide by stringent regulations governed by placement and size considerations, the Mayor's Billboard Advertising Commission now narrowed aesthetic definitions to exclude billboards. Under the political systems in New York City and State at that time, only regulation through taxation and ordinance additions to the building code seemed feasible ways of negotiating the boundaries of public and private rights and of art and commerce.

The MAS actively lobbied the Board of Aldermen and the state legislature to follow up on the commission's recommendations.[60] Together with the mayor's commission, the Real Estate Board, and the City Club, the MAS drafted an ordinance for the city's Board of Aldermen. The proposed law, applicable to the entire city, would set height limits, prohibit outdoor advertisements in major public areas, prohibit flashing signs in residential districts, and prohibit signs across windows and doors and on roofs of tenement dwellings.[61] Like the report, it emphasized aesthetic factors, arguing that billboards, as eyesores, negated the beauty of architectural monuments and parks and threatened property values and the quality of life.

The civic groups insisted that the purpose of such legislation was not to eradicate billboards but to discourage the worst offenders and thus to make the remaining signs all the more valuable. To this end they had consulted prominent members of the industry. But members of the Real Estate Board (representing some developers and property owners), not convinced that the ordinance was legitimate, called for additional hearings to allow local property owners to voice dissent.[62] Real estate owners, lithographers, labor unionists, and others expressed strong opposition, contending that the bill would effectively eliminate billboards and thus harm them financially.[63] Indeed, newspaper reports of the growing resistance to the reformers brought into the open class and ethnic tensions between Anglo-Saxon lawyers and businessmen and German, Irish, and Eastern European merchants, developers, and workers, tensions that were at the core of the debate but that heretofore had been only hinted at in the press, as in the earlier reference to midways. Faced with the impending threat of the ordinance, the small businessmen, property owners, and advertising companies on the other end now spoke out against the cultural and political authority they believed that civic activists ("Art Leaguers") had unfairly appropriated.[64] The president of the Lithographers Apprentice Union contended, for example, that the ordinance would create great hardships for "labor men." Outdoor advertising representative Alphonse Koeble linked aesthetics and class issues more explicitly to a lack of manhood, referring to the men behind the ordinance as namby-pamby, untanned "aesthetic, lily white boys." Thus the connections drawn by the billboard industry at the turn of the century between an interest in the aesthetics of the poster and effete dilettantism emerged once again. Now, however, the tables were turned: whereas at the turn of the century the unmanly types were the aesthetically minded poster collectors, now, from the standpoint of the billboard men, the "feminine" ones were those who *opposed* posters on aesthetic grounds.[65] Such perceived associations between aesthetics and femininity were undoubtedly heightened by the increased involvement in the anti-billboard movement of women's organizations like the Woman's Municipal League and the Garden Club of America.[66] At stake for the outdoor advertisers was the image of (masculine) strength bound up with the expression of individualism in the form of free enterprise and the assertion of private property rights. As earlier, and like the reformers, the outdoor advertising interests framed the economic threat posed by political and class conflict in terms of gender stereotypes. As with the illustrators, gender constructs were part and parcel of the discourse of cultural power in the efforts to assert difference and influence in urban politics.

The growing force of the opposition resulted in the preparation of a revised bill that addressed fire and safety hazards but omitted the aesthetic issues that had been central to the Mayor's Billboard Advertising Commission report.[67] Recognizing that legislation involving aesthetics had no way of passing, the City Club agreed to go along with the revised bill if the advertising and real estate interests would agree to the formation of a voluntary Outdoor Advertising Commission to regulate aesthetic matters. They proposed that the group be composed of the presidents of the MAS, the Mural Painters of America, the Architectural League, and the Real Estate Board, representatives of the New York Edison Company, and representatives of the O. J. Gude Company and the Van Beuren and New York Billposting Company (the two major New York outdoor advertising firms). The commission would work explicitly to eliminate billboards where they literally hit home: in designated "special neighborhoods," such as those areas near parks and Riverside Drive, where some of the city's wealthiest residents had built elegant mansions.[68]

Such a "Commission of Censorship" was formed after the Board of Aldermen passed the revised sign ordinance in May 1914. Yet despite the talk of collaboration, neither side was willing to compromise on the matter of aesthetics. The commission never really got off the ground. The two outdoor advertising companies were willing to cooperate only on the condition that "these efforts progress along lines not merely of pure aestheticism but of aestheticism coupled with the essential needs and rights of the large real estate, labor, and business interests involved."[69] The Architectural League claimed it could not collaborate as long as the commission included members with economic interests in outdoor advertising.[70] The commission was never heard from.

Thus, after twelve years of work, the MAS was still unsuccessful in using aesthetic discourse to force billboard advertisers to conform to its standards. Beauty was a politically loaded issue that New York's advertisers, real estate developers, and small businessmen regarded as a smokescreen for control by wealthy businessmen and effete upper-class professionals. Opponents of regulation were also concerned about aesthetic matters. O. J. Gude (1862–1925), president of the country's preeminent outdoor advertising firm (fig. 2.13), had offered to cooperate with the MAS, and even served briefly on its advertising committee. But his involvement had little effect. He and his colleagues in outdoor advertising backed off when they perceived that aesthetic issues might be used to destroy their livelihood.[71] These business groups had sufficient political clout to demand significant compromises. In the resulting 1914 ordi-

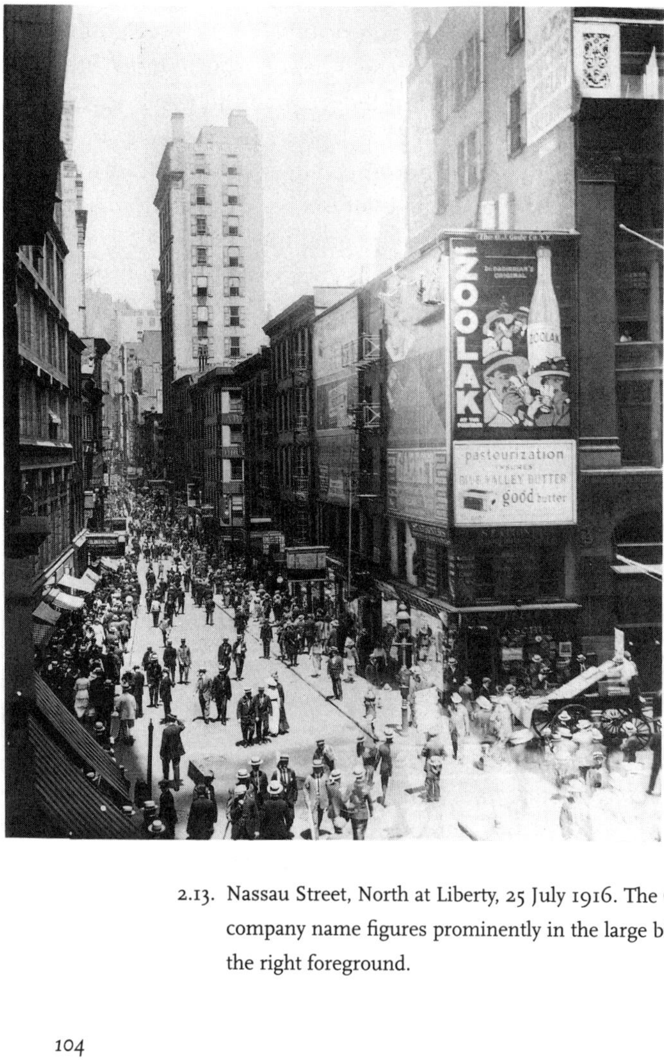

2.13. Nassau Street, North at Liberty, 25 July 1916. The O. J. Gude company name figures prominently in the large billboard in the right foreground.

nance, aesthetics remained marginalized, and advertisers and property owners remained untaxed and essentially free to continue posting bills, with minimal restraints. From a political and legal standpoint, the relationship between art and the billboard remained unresolved. The artistic camp claimed authority to deal with the aesthetics of billboard publicity, but such assertions meant little in the New York political arena. The tensions between the art societies and the outdoor advertising and real estate interests continued to increase, and the MAS joined with other local and national groups like the National Highways Association to wage an all-out war on billboards.[72]

Reformers had found it economically and politically impossible to control individual billboards. But it was possible to regulate them in the broader context of planning and development, a process in which the Fifth Avenue Association and other groups were already involved. Specifically, the urban war against billboards was bolstered by the passage of the zoning ordinance of 1916. Zoning helped the reformers' anti-billboard cause because developers had a strong financial interest in its passage and were willing to compromise to attain its approval. While no one stated outright that control of billboards was one aim of the zoning commission, such considerations undoubtedly came into play, given the involvement of the FAA and Manhattan borough president McAneny in the passage of the ordinance. The zoning ordinance of July 1916 supplemented and strengthened the 1914 sign ordinance by limiting heights of buildings and establishing specific commercial, industrial, and residential districts.[73] Eliminating congestion in major fashionable districts was a primary concern, but the law had the additional effect of cutting down the number of billboards by relegating them to industrial and business areas: all billboard restrictions remained in place, and billboards were forbidden in residential areas.[74] Thus it was zoning that ultimately made the New York City billboard problem manageable from the standpoint of the civic groups, predominantly concerned with the city's elegant park, residential, and shopping neighborhoods, and with ensuring order and solid middle-class values in the expanding outer boroughs.

World War I

With the 1914 ordinance and the 1916 zoning laws in place, the MAS and other civic groups had won a limited victory. With World War I they suffered a setback. First, at the onset of the war, the MAS pressured Treasury Secretary William McAdoo to include a tax on outdoor advertising in war revenue bills before Congress.[75] Government agencies instead decided that posters would be effective forms of propaganda. For example, Herbert Hoover, director of the wartime Food Administration, proposed having large electric signs placed on public buildings to urge the public to save food—an idea that the MAS did manage to quash in the public spaces of New York.[76]

The MAS could not, however, prevent the proliferation of the billboards and posters of the Division of Pictorial Publicity, which was headed, as mentioned in chapter 1, by prominent illustrator Charles Dana Gibson. The Division helped to coordinate the volunteer production of images, rendered both as small (averaging 20 by 30 inches) and as billboard-size posters and painted signs (fig. 2.14). Along with the obvious gendered equation of torpedoes and muscles, these images also constructed ideals of femininity different from the passive nonentities of turn-of-the-century art posters. Howard Chandler Christy, James Montgomery Flagg, and others created fantasies of worldliness, sensuousness, and physical vitality, sometimes aggressively enticing, sometimes threateningly domineering, larger than life.[77] The signs, designed by illustrators like Christy and Flagg (see figs. 1.17, 1.18, 1.19), were tremendously well received. In fact, World War I represented a turning point, garnering unprecedented public support for outdoor advertising.

What has rarely been highlighted is the extent to which the billboard industry itself engineered the shift in public opinion in favor of outdoor advertising. According to outdoor advertising historian James Fraser, it was members of the industry who actually initiated the idea of public service posters for the United States government. Outdoor advertiser O. J. Gude had urged the industry as early as 1913 to enhance its reputation through public service billboards.[78] The threat of war in 1915 offered an occasion to seize the moment. Thus in April of that year, the presidents of the Poster Advertising Association and the Associated Advertising Clubs of the World called a meeting of poster industry leaders to discuss ways to "stir the art, design, and advertising communities to help mobilize industry." In addition, to help pique widespread interest, the outdoor advertisers invited select painters and well-known, popular illustrators (who themselves were looking for ways to improve the stature of their profession) to join with industry leaders to create designs promoting war preparedness.[79] Poster Advertising Association president Barney Link told artists, "If you will give us now a store of war posters calling the nation to arms we will, on a possible outbreak of war, put them on 50,000 poster boards in this country in twenty four hours, shipping allowed for."[80] It was an offer the artists did not refuse. Together, association officials and their new collaborators, the illustrators and painters, then successfully convinced officials of the Navy's Publicity Bureau that modern

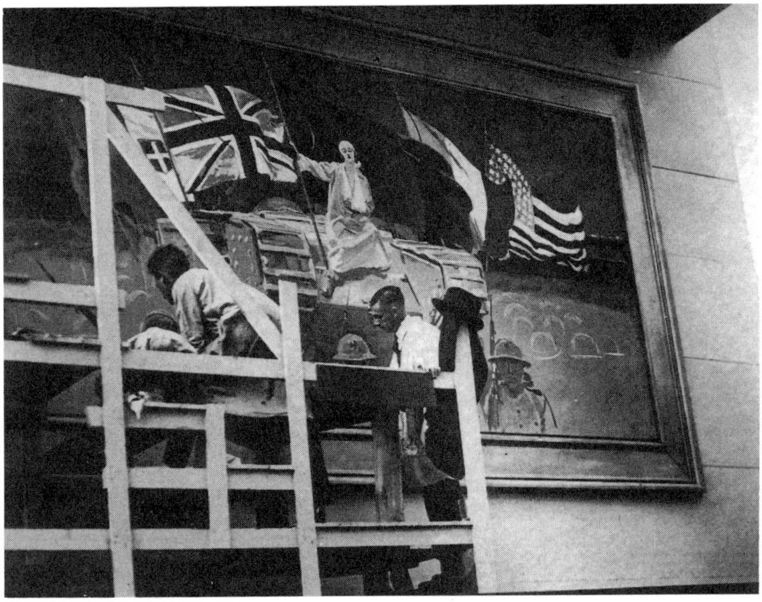

2.14. James Montgomery Flagg painting Belgium at New York Public Library for Fourth Liberty Loan Campaign, Underwood & Underwood, photographers. The original caption of this picture stated that Belgium was "wounded and bleeding, but ever leading onward in the struggle for democracy."

methods of billboard advertising were just the thing for recruitment and other modes of preparedness.[81]

Thus poster industry leaders were fully prepared by the time the United States actually entered the war in 1917. During the war the outdoor advertising industry forged full speed ahead, sponsoring prize competitions for well-designed propaganda posters and donating $1.5 million worth of billboard space for Pictorial Publicity posters and painted showings. (A showing is an outdoor advertising display, mounted for a particular length of time and directed toward a specific audience in a given locale.) The industry was thus able to show its public-spiritedness and its sensitivity to aesthetic values. Along the way, such activities enabled it to snub civic reformers and to circumvent legalized restrictions on billboards.

Produced by admired illustrators like Christy and Leyendecker, the virtuoso designs for the Division of Pictorial Publicity must have seemed

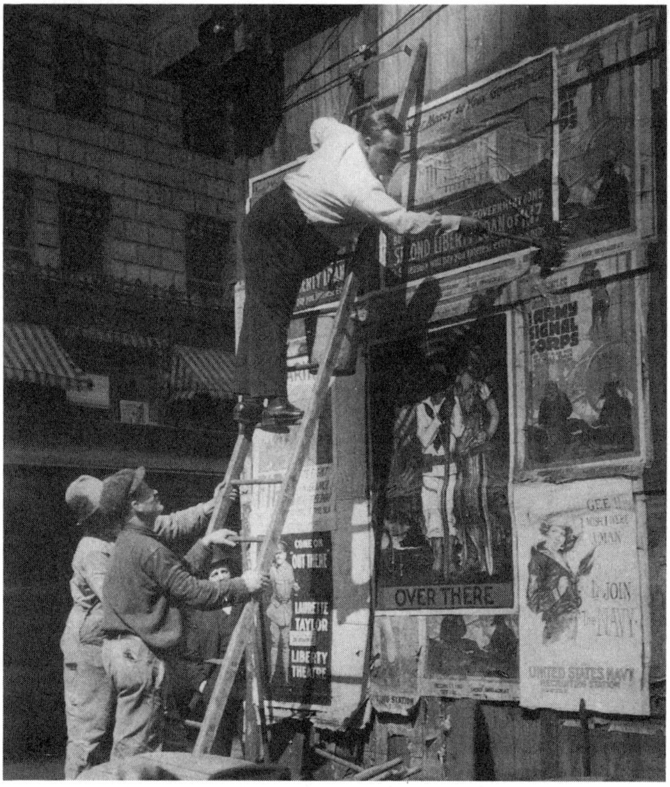

2.15. "Fatty Arbuckle, the movie star, putting up a Liberty Loan poster at Times Square," n.d. [1918], Paul Thompson, photographer.

exactly the kind of solution that the MAS had been calling for fifteen years earlier. But the ubiquity and inharmonious placement of the posters however small or artistically composed, threatened to unravel all the civic groups' efforts to control signs (fig. 2.15). The MAS complained to Gibson that the federal government was setting a bad precedent in overriding local restrictions, even for the war effort. While sympathizing, Gibson responded that "just at this time any action on the part of any person or organization or any objection to the placing of posters at particular sites, might be misunderstood by those not particularly interested in civic beauty."[82] In other words, anyone objecting to patriotic signs ran the risk of being dubbed a German sympathizer. MAS members thus decided to refrain from voicing disapproval and to take advantage of the widespread interest in the war posters to renew their old efforts to promote *good* outdoor advertising.[83]

In the meantime, the realms of illustration, art, propaganda, and commercial culture were moving closer together. The modern men and women depicted on war posters were the updated legacies of types seen in magazine illustrations—models pioneered by artists like Gibson, Christy, and Flagg. The war posters were clearly hits. Movie stars like Fatty Arbuckle jumped into the picture, posing for photos while pasting yet another sign upon a wall of peeling Christies at Forty-second Street (see fig. 2.15). The public structures whose aesthetic integrity and environmental harmony the MAS had worked so hard to protect were themselves turned into giant billboards for display of posters for the Liberty Loan and other campaigns by eminent illustrators like Henry Reuterdahl and N. C. Wyeth (see fig. 1.20). The illustrators' billboard-size images were proof positive—at least for some—that such signs could be tasteful and purposeful.

Advertisers, lithographers, billposters, and property owners had displayed their patriotism. In some sectors, at least, the shift from a commercial to a patriotic cause helped to shift public opinion and power relations in advertisers' favor.[84] Some observers argued that advertising artists and illustrators were uniquely qualified to perform the significant public service of mobilizing America through billboards. As Lee Simonson wrote for the *New Republic:*

> Publicity committees . . . have failed to realize the qualities essential to posters if they are to become effective substitutes for heralds' banners, or town-criers' bells. A poster is an advertisement made beautiful in order to be more convincing, a mural decoration that successfully harangues the crowd. Its beauty is a sudden and unexpected simplicity, violent juxtaposition of silhouettes, vivid patterns of light and shade that hold the eye spellbound. . . . A poster's meaning should be latent in every image it uses so that, at its first words, they become militant symbols. And for that reason a poster designer's understanding of human psychology must equal his skill as a designer. . . . Without graphic gifts he will produce nothing more potent than an ugly advertisement. Without a genuine sense of what advertising means he will create decorations, beautiful, but irrelevant.[85]

The MAS was hard-pressed to dispel this new positive image of advertising posters and billboards. After the Armistice, Charles Lamb of the MAS vigorously implored the U.S. government to remove all posters in a "clean-up campaign." With restrictions on billboards lifted during the war, the society felt that enforcement of local sign ordinances had slackened, and that it needed to renew its educational campaign begun before the war.[86] By the mid-1920s the anti-billboard crusade was again being waged on a national scale, with organizations like the National Roadside Council, the Garden Club of America, and the Federation of Women's Clubs now fanning the fires of public outrage. Now, however, the campaigns centered on highways and rural landscapes. These were increasingly favored by outdoor advertisers as a result of the rise in interurban automobile traffic spurred on by the 1921 passage of the Federal Highway Act, which created a national road system.[87]

The fights in New York City continued, but seemed less immediate and spirited now that existing zoning ordinances had banished billboards from most of the city's more exclusive sections.[88] Businesses and civic reformers established an uneasy truce. The latter seemed resigned to defeat on the issue of aesthetics and had abandoned their critiques of poster designs. In 1918 the Woman's Municipal League had held a 24-sheet poster competition to raise artistic standards. In 1922 it decided to refrain from commenting too much on aesthetic issues, because such matters would require too much "education" on the part of the public.[89] The *New York Times*'s own promotional advertising benefited from the use of billboards, but its editors had usually sided with the civic associations. Now they backed away from the idea of banning billboards on the basis of aesthetic judgments handed down by municipal art groups claiming cultural expertise. Their editorials stated that "professional esthetes" might just be blind to the "expressive art quality" of billboards or electric signs. In making this argument, they in effect accepted the primacy of the billboard industry, which developed the billboard according to its own priorities.

The Outdoor Advertising Industry

The outdoor advertising industry gained momentum after the war, both locally and nationally, although it had always been healthy. Its members had successfully stood up to detractors for decades because of the strong organizational identity, loyalty, and lobbying power of the men in the trade (women are rarely mentioned).[90] As its house organs constantly reiterated, organization was the "watchword" in the billposting business, which required collaboration among many groups of people: clients, lithographers, printers, designers, billposters, plant owners, and by the 1920s, selling agents and advertising agencies. But autonomy was just as crucial as cohesion.[91] The entire procedural thrust of the Outdoor Advertising Association was self-management, to be attained by adhering to standards of voluntary censorship and other regulations established *internally*. According to one spokesman, the key to the industry's success was in its fierce determination to protect its authority and to regulate itself.[92]

Despite their concern for autonomy, outdoor advertisers recognized that their ability to profit depended upon achieving a good reputation, and that this required good relations with community influentials and ordinary people. Their efforts in this direction, begun before the war, intensified afterward. Hence, as one of the industry's promotional publications remarked, its policies were specifically geared toward harmonizing "advertising practice with progressive community development." Active cooperation with "civic representatives and local officials" was necessary "to place the medium above criticism" and to make it "worthy of praise."[93] To maintain the public's goodwill, the industry had to uphold high moral standards and ensure that none of its billboards would be too vulgar or risqué (like some of the earlier French art posters). In addition, industry leaders resolved, outdoor advertisers had to develop the highest standards of excellence for poster design, whether for 24-sheets, car cards, or bus signs. To that end, outdoor advertisers had to formulate policies on advertising and art. The industry's definition and conception of "art," like those of the 1913 Mayor's Billboard Advertising Commission, would turn on its dual value.

Like its concern for moral propriety, the industry's desire to establish aesthetic standards had arisen before World War I in response to pressures from civic activists. Billboard advertiser Cecil Duce had, as early as 1912, defensively called for improvement of the art of the billboard in his book *Poster Advertising*. Prior to America's entry into the war, the magazine *The Poster* ran a few articles on modern poster design, with special focus on Germany. There, artists such as Lucien Bernhard worked with a strong emphasis on bold and flat color, using schematically rendered imagery that contrasted sharply with the American proclivity for highly detailed pictures and "reason-why" text (fig. 2.16).[94] The industry rarely followed up on such propositions for product advertising, however, and the articles ceased as soon as Germany became the war enemy.

Leading men in the poster industry also appropriated art as an instrument of public relations. For example, lithographer M. Rusling Wood mounted an active campaign to "elevate the billboard," enlisting Maxfield Parrish and even N. C. Wyeth to raise the artistic status of the 24-sheet poster through their ads for Fisk Tire (see fig. 5.8).[95] O. J. Gude, the publicity-conscious president of the eponymous outdoor advertising company, one of the biggest in the trade, served briefly in 1913 on the MAS's committee on advertising. At the time when the society was seeking legal restrictions, Gude pressed for aesthetic improvements. He recommended a design competition funded by his company and the society, to be judged by a jury of "distinguished artists."[96] He initiated a series of

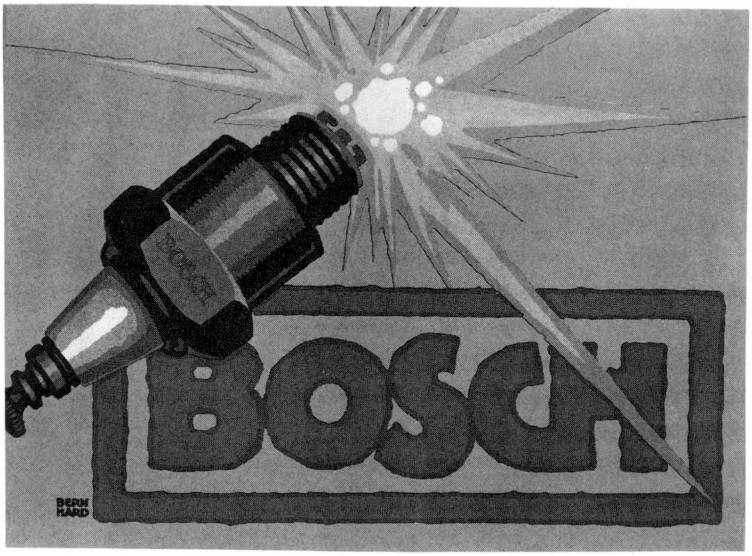

2.16. Lucien Bernhard, poster for Bosch, 1914. Bernhard's image literally energizes an otherwise nondescript spark plug.

lectures for his numerous employees by "artists of standing in New York City [such as Edwin Blashfield], on the possibilities of making advertising displays less offensive, and more artistic."[97] He also proposed temporary displays of billboards "reproducing famous paintings and great masterpieces, which would illustrate the history of the country, and tend to inculcate lessons of patriotism, and thus make the billboards a magnificent auxiliary to the work in the public schools and a power for good in the land."[98] As civic groups stepped up the pressure to pass legislation, Gude evidently decided not to bother with compromise and instead to lobby for the industry's position of keeping aesthetics from being a viable legal issue.[99] For a time, however, Gude championed billboards as nothing less than a valuable new civic commercial art.

Earnest Elmo Calkins, determined as ever to bridge the cultural gaps between art and advertising, had a similar vision, which he proposed to Fifth Avenue Association chairman Robert Grier Cooke in 1917. Like Wood, Calkins hoped to get more of the independent artists involved in the poster advertising enterprise. Hire real artists, he suggested—mural painters and illustrators—instead of in-house designers. Have architects create the billboard frames in harmonious relation to their surroundings. Works of excellence would stand out, give advertisers more for their money, provide them with a greater incentive to hire more good artists, and thus transform billboards into "the poor man's picture gallery."[100] Like Charles Mulford Robinson, Gude and Calkins sought to place billboards back into the earlier City Beautiful framework, one in which the best artists would join civic-minded business professionals in creating a new urban art—advertising.

These men's arguments, though largely expedient, were also partially sincere. Both Gude and Calkins, aficionados of high culture, made some efforts to identify with the cultivated tastes and class values of the civic activists, however indirectly. After World War I, outdoor advertising men were more overtly self-serving. They continued to use a rhetoric of accommodation with reference to the artistic standards of posters, but they now employed such a discourse much more confidently and aggressively, and among themselves. With the defeats of the reformers and the rise of the highways as advertising territory, outdoor advertisers were flexing their muscles and asserting influence. By means of statements on standards and articles on poster art and artists in house organs like *The Poster,* outdoor advertisers took an active role in educating clients about the value of art, as they defined it. In so doing, the trade publicizers sought to convince such clients to pay for more and better artwork.[101]

Assertions about art became assertions of self-control. Thus a promotional book, *Outdoor Advertising: The Modern Marketing Force,* published by the Outdoor Advertising Association included a chapter on outdoor advertising and art. It began by acknowledging that "Art enters inevitably into the problem of outdoor design," but also stated forthrightly that the primary purpose of a poster or painted bulletin was to sell goods or services. Having said that, it continued: "It is everywhere accepted that good Art is necessary to good advertising." In fact, the "degree of art excellence" would determine how acceptable an advertisement would be.[102] What good art meant and who should define it was, of course, open to question. From the outdoor advertisers' perspective, however, there was no uncertainty. Their conception turned on the dual value of "art" as something both aesthetically meritorious and economically advantageous. It also hinged on subsuming "posters," "billboards," "car cards" and "bus signs" under the common rubric of "posters." Unlike the situation at the turn of the century, billboard advertisers agreed that posters could be art so long as they could sell products and services. However, good poster art—its design—was not the same as a good "art" poster, of the sort produced by publishers at the turn of the century. From outdoor advertisers' perspective, good billboard art was not itself a commodity; good art was defined in terms of what outdoor advertisers would buy and of what they thought would help them sell.[103]

The promotional apparatus of the outdoor advertising industry bolstered its claim that art was what would sell by casting outdoor advertising men and their clients as the new patrons of a great new democratic and modern public art. Outdoor advertisers would commission pictorial images for the multitudes. In fact, the billboard industry would demonstrate the marginality of museums in the age of mass media. As the author of the Outdoor Advertising Association's promotional book wrote in 1928:

> Posters, [painted] Bulletins, and flashing electric signs were not primarily devised to purvey "free art" to the people; nevertheless, one feels that this aspect cannot be overlooked. We have our beautiful museums and Art Galleries, but the people will not go to them—at least, not in great numbers. The attendance at the Metropolitan Museum of Art is small when compared to the ten million souls who live in greater New York. While the Posters and Bulletins cannot rightly be called an Art Gallery, they do provide a means of bringing Art to the people. . . . Most of the "80%" who read little and derive their amusement and recreation from the radio and "movies" obtain more genuine joy and satisfaction from a first rate Poster than they would from an old masterpiece.[104]

Capitalizing on the rhetoric of democracy, outdoor advertisers proclaimed that posters would be art and entertainment for the majority, the "great mass of people." Privately, among colleagues, some jettisoned that rhetoric, revealing the same class and cultural biases as the professionals. As an advertising representative for J. Walter Thompson admitted, for example, billboard images had to reach the lowest common denominator, not just "the big public" but also "the dim thinkers."[105] All such accomplishments necessitated that the billboard industry control the look of their posters as well as the rhetoric of description.

Just as outdoor advertisers would not allow critics to impose their theories of reform upon the sign business through legislation or taxation, so too did they insist upon controlling their own methods of billboard presentation and placement. The industry had earlier devised its own size standards for posters as well as regulation hoardings, usually painted green with latticework (fig. 2.17). (The standard size was eight feet, ten inches by nineteen feet.) On the West Coast, one leading company, Foster and Kleiser, fashioned its own form of commercial "civic art," placing its billboards in lighted structures framed by art nouveau style female herms (pillars, narrower at the base than at the top, surmounted by heads or upper bodies of human figures.)[106] Billboards now tended to be "exhibited" individually rather than shown in long or double-decker rows. M. Rusling Wood, the lithographer who commissioned the Fisk Tire posters from Maxfield Parrish, added the subtitle "Mural Advertising" to the name of his firm in 1922.[107]

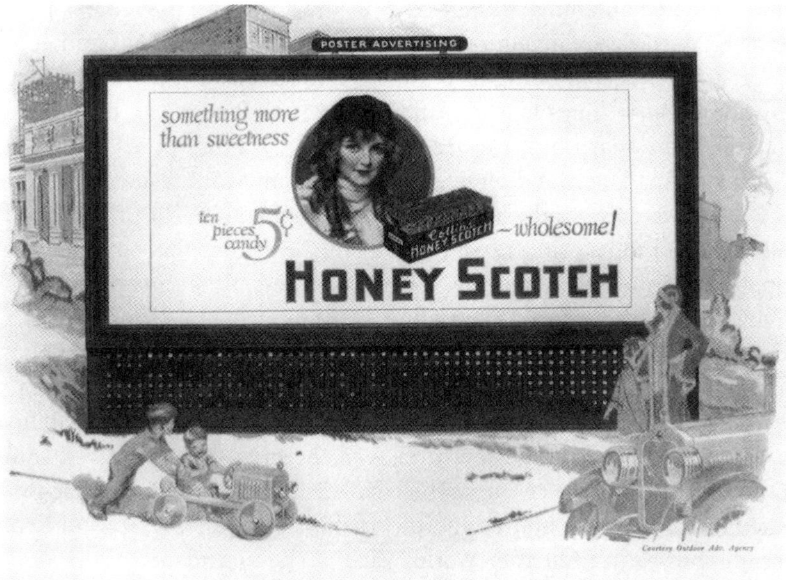

2.17. Advertisement for poster advertising, featuring billboard for Honey Scotch Candy, 1926. Note the juxtaposition of billboard and latticed hoarding with the elegant Beaux-Arts civic structures in the background. This arrangement is meant to suggest the edifying potential of artistic outdoor advertising, especially for the nation's young people.

Similarly, industry experts and clients insisted on formulating their own channels for showcasing their products and their aesthetic ideals. Billboards were illustrated in journals like *The Poster,* the official organ of the Poster Advertising Association. The magazine was originally geared toward plant owners and advertisers, but by the 1920s it had broadened its focus and format to appeal to designers and teachers as well. *The Poster* thus kept readers informed of art school doings. In 1925, the PAA published its own primer, *The Essentials of Poster Design*. The Outdoor Advertising Association became a member of the National Poster Alliance. Composed of artists, students, and teachers, and especially lithographers, printers, and advertising agencies, the alliance sought the development of a "distinctively American Poster Art," principally through competitions in the schools, sponsored by the outdoor advertising industry.[108] *The*

Poster initiated an annual design issue in 1925. In 1929 the Outdoor Advertising Association inaugurated a series of yearly exhibitions of outdoor advertising "art." Beginning in 1938, the exhibition was accompanied by an annual, *Advertising Outdoors.* Later entitled *100 Best Posters,* the annual illustrated the year's best images, as selected by a jury of art directors, advertising managers and directors, and company vice presidents.[109]

What was "art," as the billboard industry defined it? The art of a good billboard had to be "sincere and convincing," qualities that could not be "applied to a mediocre painting." Effective posters, they argued, required highly specialized, exacting measures of craftsmanship. In particular, a poster artist had to know how to attract attention through striking color, bold silhouette, simplified composition, and dramatic action that conveyed one central idea with immediacy. He or she had to have an "ability to convey largeness with a few strokes of the brush."[110] Compared with those at the turn of the century, which gave priority to text, later billboards relied much more on figures and pictorial images. (Photography did not become prevalent until after World War II.) The ascendancy of the automobile was crucial in this regard. Advertisers sought to grab the automobile riders' short attention span, and found that pictures worked more efficiently than text.[111]

The notions of "artistic" images held by the outdoor advertising industry remained highly conservative. Unlike their European counterparts, American outdoor advertisers tended to be unreceptive to the vanguard stylistic developments pioneered by such designers as Lucien Bernhard (see fig. 2.16), Ludwig Hohlwein, Lucien-Achille Mauzan, and El Lissitzky—this despite the fact that these artists used many of the very compositional methods American designers deemed most effective.[112] Designers like Bernhard and McKnight Kauffer used simplified, bold color images and symbols to evoke abstract associations with or feelings about the product in question.

American outdoor advertisers did not generally use such abstraction. There emerged a distinct difference between billboard designs on the East Coast and on the West, where Foster and Kleiser commissioned more stylistically innovative images, but the more conservative trends of the East Coast remained predominant. Despite the growing prevalence of European-influenced "modernistic" styles in 1920s print advertising, the billboard industry resisted such infiltrations. Otis Shepard's distinctive, summarily modeled designs for the William Wrigley Company (fig. 2.18), mildly indebted to cubism and constructivism, were about as "modern" as American outdoor advertisers were willing to get.[113] Industry members preferred "iconicity," the apparently transparent and obvious; they sought more detail and allusion to spatial depth. They wanted greater anecdotal

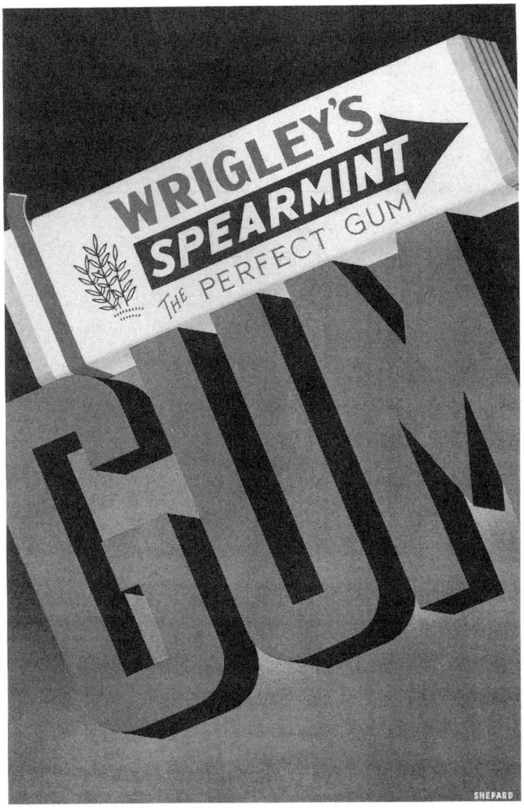

2.18. Otis Shepard, poster for Wrigley's Spearmint Gum, 1936.

emphasis, with "reason-why copy," and images with erotic or sentimental appeal—the pretty girl, the dashing young man, the cute child.

There were two main reasons for this conservatism. The first was pragmatic. Turn-of-the-century posters had been planned to catch the eye of pedestrians, who could then stop and read the copy. Billboard advertisers had to make an immediate, positive impression on passengers looking out from moving trains, buses, and especially automobiles. Outdoor advertisers believed that avant-garde abstractions drew too much attention to the image (like painting) but not enough to the product, especially during a short time span.

The second reason for conservatism was clients' and designers' perceptions of the targeted consumers as a relatively uneducated, uncultured, and tradition-minded group to whom they had to condescend. According to the outdoor advertising expert at J. Walter Thompson, "our public does not take to the German type of flat color poster, preferring more realistic pictures such as those used by Camel or Palmolive."[114] Modern design may not have caught on in part because of postwar mistrust of Russians, Germans, and "foreign influences" in general. Like their predecessors and contemporaries in the civic groups (and in print advertising), many outdoor advertisers saw their publics as socially inferior and acted on this basis.

This conservative outlook continued strong during the depression (fig. 2.19), when outdoor advertisers were under even greater pressure from clients to post images that would *work:* risky experiments in modern or idiosyncratic poster design were roundly discouraged. Thus the majority of advertising posters commissioned remained in the "realistic" Rockwellian or photographic vein—with cropped blowups of men, women, and children engaged in an activity connected to snappy copy.[115]

Despite some receptivity to European avant-garde styles, then, bill-

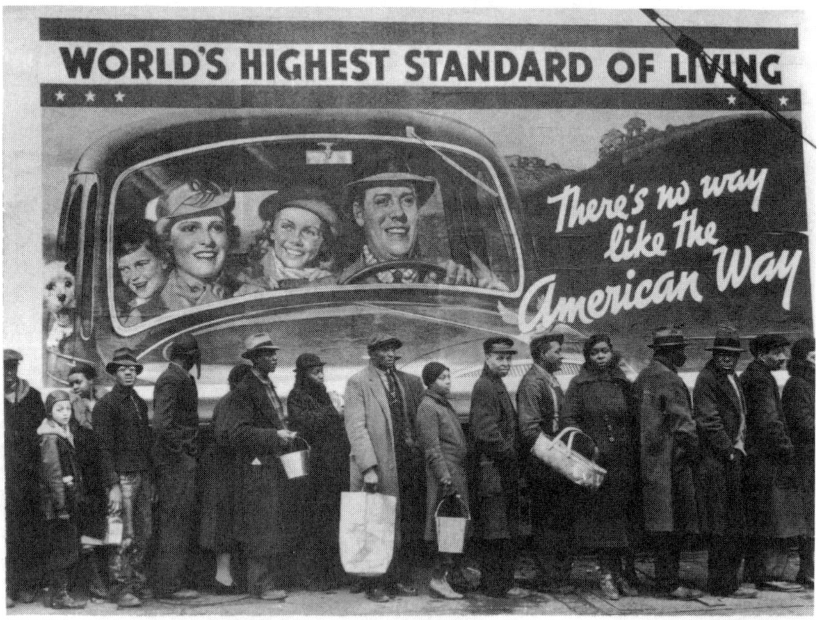

2.19. Margaret Bourke-White, *At the Time of the Louisville Flood,* 1937. Bourke-White used formal hierarchy and contrast of color, scale, and facial expression to underscore the blindness and hypocrisy of government and corporate business, represented here by the billboard.

board advertisers articulated their own discrete notion of billboard art, a vision linked much more closely to traditional print illustration than to contemporary painting. Such trends discouraged those designers and art directors who were anxious to innovate in the field of outdoor advertising. From their perspective, the billboard was just another mode of imaging, its artistic qualifications dubious at best. In the view of J. Walter Thompson art director Elwood Whitney, "there is no such thing as an American poster art. This is a complete myth."[116] Along with poster artist Lucien Bernhard, Whitney felt that modern techniques needed "a fair trial." To accomplish this it would be necessary to give *creators* more authority; advertisers relegated too much design responsibility to the lithographer, whose primary concern was completion of reliable work at minimal cost—little wonder they stuck with a predictable, pretty girl image, instead of allowing artists to create new, more daring images.[117]

The size, location, and production process of the 24-sheet billboard would never allow its fundamental commercial character to be overlooked or downplayed. Try as it did to bring the two realms together, the outdoor advertising industry became separated from the authoritative but narrowly focused institutional structures of art. The paths of billboards and art had diverged. The introduction to the catalog of the Outdoor Advertising Association's 1946 Poster Annual, a display of the year's best billboards, made this abundantly clear. That year's exhibit, held under the auspices of the Art Directors Club, signaled artistic legitimacy within the framework of the world of advertising. Following the strategies of advertising agency art directors, the outdoor advertisers defined the best billboard posters as art according to their own terms. But now more than ever, these criteria hinged explicitly on a given billboard's success in pitching the "sales message."[118]

Outdoor advertisers refused to allow the production process to become subservient to art. In the opinion of Whitney and Bernhard, billboard posters were thus doomed to remain merely superficial and to contribute only to the cultivation of banality. There were several factors that prevented billboards from attaining stature as art in modern American society: client unwillingness to relegate authority over artistic work to artists; the low priority and fragmentation of the creative process; and the interest in signs solely as a service rather than as ends in themselves.

The Modern Poster versus the Billboard

The division between art and outdoor advertising, evident by the late 1920s, became further institutionalized over the next two decades. The activities of the poster division of the Works Progress Administration and of the Museum of Modern Art exemplify these developments. With varying degrees of influence and success, both operations promoted the poster as a distinctly modern art form, differentiated from other product advertising.

The WPA poster represented an early, brief, but widespread experiment in using "modern," avant-garde designs for outdoor, civic, noncommercial publicity purposes. In 1934 New York City Mayor Fiorello LaGuardia initiated the Mayor's Poster Project, through which the city, in conjunction with the Federal Civilian Works Administration, sponsored public service posters. The Works Progress Administration/Federal Art Project absorbed the New York City poster division in 1935, and the project expanded, now producing silkscreened posters for whatever government agency requested them. By 1938 there were poster divisions in 38 states. Staff artists, many of whom had worked in advertising and industry, designed images for civic activities, band concerts, transportation, and public health (fig. 2.20). Designated for local use and for close-range viewing (for example, on walls of community centers), the majority of posters were small.[119] Certainly the designs were simpler, more schematic, and more symbolic than those of advertising posters, relying more on the bold flat patterns, rapid shifts in scale, and strong color contrasts of modernist painting and European design of the past twenty years.

The WPA poster could thrive because the work was meant to serve civic purposes. Government officials, unconcerned about making profits and desiring to encourage self-expression, allowed designers freedom to try new approaches. In addition, WPA/FAP officials were consciously trying to discourage associations between their artistic productions and the imagery of advertising.[120]

A variety of commentators pointed to the WPA posters' high level of artistic excellence as a sign of progress in the field of poster design. But the same independence that made the project successful from the designers' point of view also led to its demise. Design innovation became a political football. With the decline of the New Deal and a rise in union activism, Congress became increasingly wary of the poster projects—as it did of the WPA art programs more generally—fearing that such ventures offered too ready a outlet for Communist and other anti-American activities. As in other artistic sections of the WPA, many of the artists in the Poster Division were leftists and Artists' Union members, though not necessarily members of the Communist Party. The Dies Committee on UnAmerican Activities (chaired by Senator Martin Dies) began investigations of the artists' political affiliations. Some conservative politicians were therefore prone to read left-wing ideological connotations into the

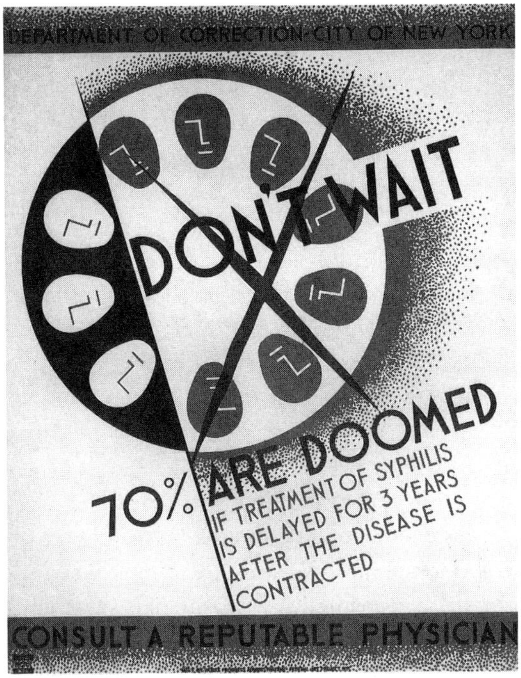

2.20. Anonymous, *Don't Wait,* WPA poster, ca. 1936, 22 by 28 inches.

images' stylistic progressivism. The WPA posters' smaller size and self-consciously modernist modes of representation may have signified art in the minds of some creators and viewers, but unlike Museum of Modern Art officials, the United States government bureaucracy did not allow the posters to become "art," either by reputation or through commodification.[121]

The WPA civic poster succumbed to the fate of the WPA art projects in general. Unable to stand up to the growing conservative backlash, and rendered superfluous by the strong wartime economy, the entire venture was phased out by 1943. The government made no provisions to preserve the posters. In New York, for example, most of them were sold off by the pound to a Long Island salvage dealer.[122]

The federal government's relative unreceptivity toward posters as art continued during World War II. The Office of Civilian Defense and the Office of War Information commissioned numerous propaganda billboards and posters, again working closely with the outdoor advertising industry, just as the United States government had done during World War I.[123] But despite concerted efforts by artists' groups and art institutions to sell the federal government on the idea of artistically adventuresome work, the government preferred to take its cues primarily (though not exclusively) from the imagery of magazine advertising. Hence the government's activities during World War II ultimately did little to enhance the reputation of billboards as anything other than visual propaganda. Neither did events at the Museum of Modern Art (MoMA).

The museum was at the forefront of efforts to forge an alternative vision of posters as art by defining art in terms incompatible with those put forth by the outdoor advertising industry. Alfred Barr, director of the new museum, sought to incorporate the poster into a new canon of modern art, which would include design, partly by transforming it back into an object of smaller scale.[124]

The museum's poster collection was in fact begun as a private collection (which Barr and his associate Jere Abbott had amassed while traveling in Europe and then donated to the new museum), and the museum's idea of poster art hinged primarily on aesthetics.[125] Its officials saw themselves as aesthetic advocates, and made several efforts to improve poster design. The Department of Architecture and Design held a competition for high school students in 1933, and mounted exhibitions of advertising posters by the French A. M. Cassandre (1936) and the American (living in England) E. MacKnight Kauffer (1937). In his catalog essay on Kauffer, author Aldous Huxley enumerated the principles that made such work "modern": directness and immediacy of symbolic expression; unconventional design; and an emphasis on qualities, not specifics, with reference to the product.[126]

In many ways, these exhibitions resuscitated the turn-of-the-century notion of the art poster as collectible commodity—an idea that put the artist, his design, and the poster itself above the product advertised. Within the framework of the exhibition, posters-as-art were divorced from the products they advertised.[127] Unlike the earlier publishers' posters, which were purchased at bookstores and newsstands, and hence at least initially would have been associated with a commercial context, the posters in MoMA exhibitions were totally protected from any commercial "taint." The majority of posters were by Europeans, and thus many museum-goers had probably never seen the images functioning as advertisements. Moreover, they were smaller, not the 24-sheet posters seen on hoardings. (The Cassandre poster reproduced here [fig. 2.21], one of the few oversized images, was a gift from the artist.) In contrast to the Outdoor Advertising Association posters, they were in no way linked with billboards.[128]

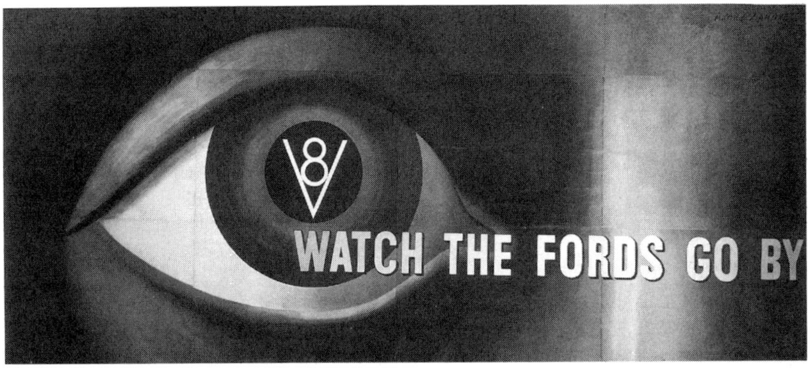

2.21. A. M. Cassandre, *Watch the Fords Go By,* 1937. Judgment Day for all those souls whose old, underpowered cars are unworthy.

The museum's promotion of civic posters underscored the seriousness and authenticity of its enterprise. In November 1937, for example, the institution displayed United States government posters and others produced for the Republican side of the Spanish Civil War that was then raging. During World War II, the museum, along with the organization Artists for Victory, sponsored another poster competition, this time to encourage first-rate artists to create propaganda for wartime government agencies, as well as to instruct a broader audience about the benefits of modern design. Museum officials' desire to contribute to the war effort motivated them temporarily to regard the poster as a purveyor of patriotic service through the artistic representation of a message. The federal government did not accept many of these designs; neither, it appears, did the museum.[129] Of the 25 percent of the museum's posters accessioned between 1930 and 1947, the majority were World War I posters. Judging from the derisive comments written about one of Christy's World War I posters in a 1941 *Bulletin of the Museum of Modern Art,* the museum appears to have acquired such images primarily for their historic significance. Curators were much more discriminating when it came to collecting more contemporary work, civic or otherwise. Most of the civic posters acquisitioned during this period were by artists with acknowledged modernist credentials, such as Lester Beall and Ben Shahn. Artistic desirability hinged on the aesthetic force of the visual message, not on the posters' actual ideological persuasiveness.[130]

MoMA stayed on its modernist course. During the post–World War

II period, the idea of the art poster promulgated by art institutions like MoMA became culturally prevalent, even dominant. Legacies of the late nineteenth century, posters, but not billboards, functioned as art within a highly circumscribed context: as the property of the art museum, high-toned gallery, or private homeowner. By 1950 this narrower conception of the poster as property, as aesthetic experience, and as an object performing no work or service would win out as art.

The MoMA ideal of poster art represented a victory for the museum and a defeat for advertising agency art directors. The re-aestheticization of advertising posters was an affirmation of the value many art directors placed upon bringing art to advertising. At the same time, the museum's activities marginalized art directors professionally. The outdoor advertisers' recent decision to put sponsorship of their "100 Best Posters" exhibitions into the hands of the art directors had bestowed an additional artistic pedigree upon the latter group. This presumed that art directors were especially qualified to strike an appropriate balance between art and advertising. But art directors achieved such license on a false assumption—that they would put the commercial interests of their clients ahead of everything else. The museum's aesthetic criteria, antithetical to the commercial priorities of outdoor advertisers, thus implicitly threw the art directors' influence and expertise into question. Such professional uncertainties were nothing new, however. While art directors played central roles as designers, managers, sellers, and gatekeepers during the interwar years, it was not always clear, even to themselves, for whom they were working, and to what end. To understand these circumstances, let us turn to art directors and their efforts to contend with their own tug-of-war between art and business.

chapter 3

Art Directors and the Art of Commerce

The inability of illustrators to achieve professional leadership must be seen alongside the rise of the advertising agency art director, who acquired new prominence in the 1920s.[1] Although production of images certainly involved visual artists, art directors were the central players in the day-to-day work of advertising and in the resulting struggles of art versus commerce. As crucial figures in the organizational structure of advertising, art directors shaped the relations among art, publicity, work, representation, and audience. Illustrated advertising increased markedly after World War I, but the new influence of art directors depended upon more than just the business boom and growing corporate appreciation of images and attractive layouts. Their authority hinged upon their ability to disseminate their standards among artists, agency colleagues, and most of all, advertisers. Even more than illustrators, art directors had to reconcile the ideologies of romanticism and commercialism, not only for themselves but for their clients and employees. It was a task at which they only partially succeeded. Nevertheless, their efforts had a tangible effect in the work worlds of advertising, if not always on the advertisements themselves.

While many art directors shared the romantic artistic ideals of their illustrator colleagues, no practicing and effective art director could maintain a stance that true art, free and autonomous, was incompatible with commercial practices. As many of them saw it, the art director's task was to improve advertising by bringing art and commerce together—to use art as a vehicle for attracting attention and generating desire. The key to this accomplishment was the art director's ability to lay claim to fine art as part of his professional domain. Art directors had to convince clients that art could be an appropriate selling tool. They also had to convince artists that art directors shared their values, yet still controlled standards and procedures for advertising illustration.

Here, however, art directors faced resistance from within the advertising trade as well as from outside. Artists, advertising managers, clients, and art directors themselves differed about what art was and whether it belonged in advertising in the first place. There were two basic camps with many variations. One camp included art directors and ad men who sought to link the notion of art with the representations created for selling purposes. The other camp contended that art had little to do with advertising because the form and content of advertising images could never be distinguished from the activity of commercial persuasion. Such debates stemmed from differences in opinion about the relations both between word and image and between art and business. They were also bound up with broader uncertainties about class and power relations between advertisers and audiences. These irresolutions were grounded largely in gender issues precipitated by the changing status of women and symbolized by their right to vote.

Women had been the primary purchasers for the household since the mid-nineteenth century. Late-nineteenth-century merchants, especially department store owners, made special efforts to advertise to women and, according to historian William Leach, to establish shopping as "a female activity." With the passage of woman's suffrage (1919), the expansion in the number of women in the workforce, and the growing influence of the "New Woman" persona after World War I, advertisers increasingly regarded women not just as providers of necessary goods, but as liberated, active, and desiring "consumers." The efforts to reach these coveted purchasers intensified.[2] The political and purchasing power of women represented both an opportunity and a threat to the business and advertising men who catered to this expanding female market. Art directors, like other business executives, were overwhelmingly male, and therefore had to convince clients and other ad men that they could speak both to and for middle- and upper-middle-class women, their main targets. Thus, like illustrators, civic reformers, and outdoor advertisers, art directors sought actively to shape and control relations between art, commerce, gender identity, and professional expertise. Much advertising was addressed to both sexes, or only to men. Nevertheless, the tensions arising from advertisers' typically gendered construction of audience motivated many of the attitudes discussed in this chapter, both explicitly and implicitly.

Art directors had to strike a delicate balance between their own artistic interests and the demands of their clients. Through involvement with the Art Directors Club, they found a creative outlet that enabled them to override their ambivalence about having to put pragmatic business concerns above artistic excellence. Some derived personal satisfaction from achieving authority and influence within social and artistic organizations like the Art Center—related to, but outside of, the immediate occupational sphere of advertising. Exhibitions of advertising art enabled art directors to communicate the message that they were seriously engaged with art patronage and practice. Exhibits also helped art directors in their relations with illustrators, whose esteem and cooperation were vital. Many art directors worked out their uncertainties through internal debates about the appropriate aesthetics of advertising. Some, like Nathaniel Pousette-Dart, sought compromise by treating their work as an artistic contribution in its own right. Others, like Charles T. Coiner, who utilized high modern painting in advertising during the depression, established a new ideological divide between fine and commercial art. For the majority of art directors, however, concerns about fine art were already outside professional bounds. Business success required a greater concession: deference to a construct called "the consumer" rather than to one designated as "art." Art directors' strategies for maintaining self-respect thus involved complex psychosocial juggling; still, competent practitioners performed this act routinely.

The Art Directors Club

Efforts by Earnest Elmo Calkins and others to upgrade the effectiveness and quality of visual imagery in advertising during the early years of the century had mixed success. Both illustrators and clients had resisted the idea of aestheticizing the sales pitch. Clients and advertising men were not especially interested in making art. Concerned with communicating their message, they were suspicious of artists and apprehensive that artwork would not produce results. Illustrators feared losing their artistic autonomy and selling out to advertisers.

Attitudes changed over the second decade of the twentieth century: advertisers, though still wary, increasingly saw art (as opposed to just "images") as an asset, and the art director took on a more significant and visible role. These developments, like so many other aspects of artistic culture of the day, were dramatized by Theodore Dreiser in his scathing *The "Genius."* After suffering a nervous breakdown and working in menial jobs, illustrator-painter Eugene Witla suddenly moves effortlessly into a position as art director at an advertising agency. Although his boss voices great skepticism about "these regular high-brow artists" working as illustrators and art directors, Witla has just the blend of impudence, managerial know-how, and artistic talent to defy expectations and thrive in the advertising world.[3] Through Dreiser's deadpan irony, Witla the art director personifies the inevitable alliance between art and commerce in consumer society. Neither art nor commerce are pure in Dreiser's eyes; both are congenial, mutually exploitative bedfellows.

Dreiser's Witla, of course, was just a fiction, but the "art values" he represented did in fact make their way into the worlds of advertising. World War I helped the cause of the pro-art camp of advertising men—not only those who opted for handcrafted images to illustrate texts, but also those who valued creativity and stylistic idiosyncracy as design features in their own right. Illustrators' experiences with war posters indicated that quality was certainly possible in publicity. The collaborations of illustrators, mural painters, and advertisers on the posters for the federal government and Red Cross raised the public's opinion of pictorial publicity. Advertisers took notice; encouraged by their perception of growing markets, increasing numbers jumped on the bandwagon. Coincidently, a new generation of artists was entering the job market. Unlike many of their predecessors, these illustrators drew few status distinctions between magazine illustration and advertising, and were glad to take on advertising assignments. To advertising men like Calkins, committed to integrating good art and publicity, these changes were promising. The future would lie in the hands of the art director.

The Art Directors Club symbolized the new prominence of advertising, as well as art directors' determination to establish its commercial and artistic parameters. Founded in 1920 by Louis Pedlar, the club, with about twenty incorporating members, was the organizational expression of advertisers' new importance both as patrons and as artistic practitioners. The club in effect capitalized on artists' ongoing lack of organizational unity, highlighting art directors' greater opportunity for controlling quality and procedures in illustrational practice. Its purpose was "to show forcefully that good art and good advertising are consistent and that successful advertisers are using as high a standard of art as that used in illustration or shown in the average exhibition of studio painting."[4] Although the art directors' use of the phrase "average exhibition" may have unwittingly divulged some mixed feelings about the quality of the work they commissioned (if their standards were as high as those of the average exhibition, they were, in essence, mediocre), they did not intend this reading. To the contrary, art directors aimed to prove that advertising art could be as meritorious as easel painting, and indeed far surpassed the crude renderings so prevalent five years earlier.

The group, guided by member Earnest Elmo Calkins (who had mounted the 1908 show discussed in chapter 2), initiated an annual exhibition of art in advertising in 1921. In so doing, the club provided the organizational framework within which works commissioned by its members would be acknowledged as art. It now offered to place its own stamp of approval on the aesthetic claims of commercial illustration, whose reputation had been so suspect. To lend additional artistic legitimacy to the enterprise, the club brought in a jury of distinguished painters, illustrators, and art directors, including Edwin Blashfield, Robert Henri, and Charles Dana Gibson. This group judged the entries, divorced from their accompanying texts, on the basis of their aesthetic merits rather than their effectiveness as instruments of persuasion.[5] The club's decision to mount an exhibition as an initial activity was an important statement about art directors' sensibilities; their work might serve commerce, but their ambition was to make art. The exhibition venue implicitly put advertising images and easel painting on an equal plane.

The content of the first (1921) exhibition was geared toward showing this correspondence. The styles and imagery of the works drew heavily upon older, tried-and-true traditions in illustration, such as the Pyle school (not surprising, since Charles Dana Gibson was a member of the jury), and on more progressive but dated tendencies in painting, especially the "Ashcan" school (undoubtedly favored by jurist Robert Henri). For example, F. R. Gruger's rendering for the deodorant Odorono—an anxious woman at a party hiding behind a partition and pressing her upper arms to her body—was strongly reminiscent of the work of John Sloan and Everett Shinn. The first-prize winner for paintings and colored drawings, W. Heitland's boldly patterned, summarily treated painting of a Spanish dancer commissioned by the George Batten agency for the Columbia Company (fig. 3.1), was inspired both by turn-of-the-century art posters and by the paintings of Shinn, Sloan, and Henri. A few designs, like those of René Clarke, were more consciously up-to-date. His paintings of Wesson Oil cans effortlessly pouring their contents into starkly rendered frying pans (fig. 3.2) aestheticized labor in elegant compositions indebted to more experimental, modernist modes of representation.[6]

The decision to display the art divorced from its larger advertising context was also important for highlighting art directors' artistic sympathies. Club members had debated whether or not to do so. Those who chose to regard the images as autonomous works of art contended that they had already served their function and proved their worth as advertisements.[7] They argued that art directors should emphasize their accomplishments as arbiters of aesthetic merit, not their business successes. By highlighting the talents of artists in advertising, art directors would

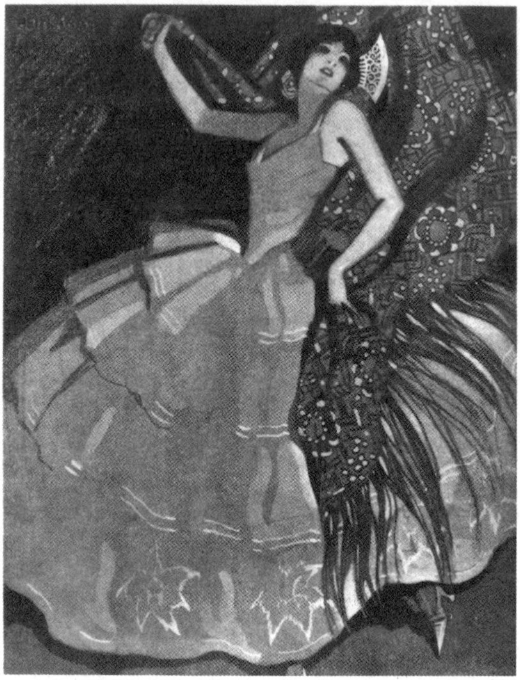

3.1. *Carmen*, advertisement for Columbia Graphophone Company, 1920–1921.

demonstrate that the capacity to evoke an aesthetic experience of any sort was worthy of acknowledgment and celebration, regardless of its purpose.[8] In asserting this, the art directors were making a plea for the dissenters to take artistic contributions seriously and promote them more actively.

This view prevailed and had manifold implications. The decision showed the extent to which art directors identified with romantic artistic ideals and felt uncomfortable with mere business roles. Such a display, emphasizing formal creativity, served as a form of self-justification: art directors were in fact not merely crass commercial men, but sensitive and aesthetically minded people for whom endeavors of the spirit were a high priority. The exhibition also represented a power play, an assertion of professional strength and command. As a straightforward assertion that good art was important to advertising, it insisted both that art directors had the expertise to designate what art meant and that commerce could be the basis for producing art. Art directors would serve as the nurturing patrons and, in some cases, even as the artists.

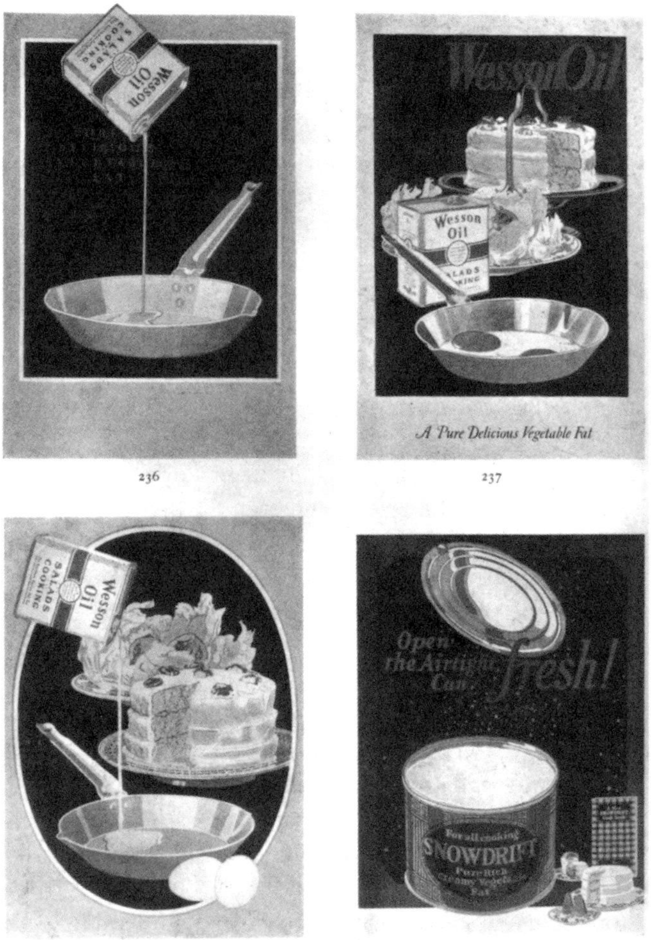

3.2. Advertisements for Snowdrift and Wesson Oil, 1920–1921.

The exhibit was not only a display of the expertise of art directors, but also an assertion of the power of art as a cultural and educational force. As good art, advertising illustration would familiarize viewers with fine design, set high standards for future endeavors, and improve the level of public taste. This goal was especially important given the fact that women were the designated audience for many advertisements. Indeed, art directors' appropriation of Art may also have represented an attempt to counteract their uncertainties, and even a certain embarrassment, arising from the widespread perception that women were the primary consumers to whom any such images had to be geared.[9] The display of works divorced from their texts betrayed the art directors' concern that there was actually a fundamental difference in aesthetic status between an image employed in advertising and one viewed alone. With its interdependent picture and text, the female-oriented advertisement compromised the freedom, purity, and strength of the isolated image. The art directors' exhibition, then, underscored the gendered nature of the advertising enterprise by ignoring the [female] audience. In the context of advertising, true art was possible only by stripping the image of its original purpose and meaning, for in most cases the isolated image was, paradoxically, created expressly to communicate an advertising message. Within the framework of this exhibition, an image's aesthetic value was contingent on its merits as incomplete—hence ineffective—advertising.[10]

Significantly, the extreme approach taken in the first exhibition lasted only one year. The majority of art directors and even the first-year exhibition jury implicitly acknowledged that their procedures had been mistakenly impractical. Thus, in a reversal of policy, the second annual show exhibited not only the image but also a proof of the entire advertisement. The first year's jury had concluded that too many artists were not sufficiently mindful of the demands of reproduction. Art directors needed to acknowledge their role as mediators between artists and clients. They were obliged to use their exhibitions to educate as well as to honor artists. Art directors had to provide artists with models of work that had proved itself adequate for mass reproduction.[11] This mandate was followed in the second exhibition, which emphasized not only the image's "worthiness as an art expression but as a commercial tool." Display of the advertisement in its totality would show "in practical aspect the part played by the art director in collaboration with the artist."[12] Such actions downplayed the artist, but if anything, stressed the art director's role and influence even more overtly than before. The art director was a co-creator of art for the print media. "The prominence given proofs this year," wrote art director Gordon Aymar in 1923, "helps to emphasize the fact that the real exhibition for artist and art director is the daily one in magazines and newspapers and billboards."[13]

However, residues of the art values emphasized in 1921 continued to make themselves felt. In its published annuals commemorating the exhibitions, the club offered to posterity an alternative that asserted art directors' own leverage and their continued commitment to the ideal of art. For the next decade and a half, the main portion of the annuals offered large illustrations of the submissions, separated from their advertisements. A short, later section provided minuscule views of complete layouts, but only a sampling.

The club's exhibitions and annuals enabled art directors to celebrate both their artistic and business successes, and to claim their central place in both worlds. The clash of artistic and commercial priorities—articulated in the difference of approach between the first and subsequent exhibitions—continued, however. As we shall see, this tension between art, selling methods, and audience became the source of ongoing and unresolved debate among art directors, other advertising personnel, and businessmen.

The Art Center

The Art Directors Club exhibits clearly worked to art directors' personal benefit, helping to counter the conflicting feelings that some experienced as "art men" in advertising. But art directors also sought to be taken seriously in broader advertising spheres. In declaring that advertising images had aesthetic significance and that art directors could successfully employ current styles for promotional purposes, the Art Directors Club annual exhibition was a first and positive step toward gaining advertisers' support. Art directors' involvement with the New York Art Center also worked to their advantage, further highlighting their importance and presence in the urban art scene. With its broad-based artistic membership and its elite supporters, the center lent social and cultural power to art directors' activities.

The Art Center, founded in 1920 by "social welfare and art worker" Helen Sargent Hitchcock (1870–1958), was both a corporation and a building at 65–67 East Fifty-sixth Street in Manhattan. Established "to advance the Decorative Crafts and the Industrial and Graphic Arts of America," it linked seven constituent societies: the Art Alliance of America, the American Institute of Graphic Art, the New York Society of Craftsmen, Pictorial Photographers of America, the Society of Illustrators, the Stowaways (a small art and social club), and the Art Directors Club. Its members organized lectures, exhibitions, classes, and "practical demonstrations . . . for educational purposes fostering the arts of design."[14] Displays included textiles, packaging, greeting cards, pottery, toys, glassware, graphics, posters, painting, sculpture, photography, and advertisements. The Art Directors Club held its annual exhibitions and numerous other shows at the Art Center.[15] One of the more outlandish shows was undoubtedly that mounted with the help of publicist Edward Bernays as part of a promotional campaign for a new type of salad oil manufactured by Best Foods Company. The exhibition, which Bernays dubbed "A

Tribute to the Palate and to the Palette," combined paintings of salads by "modern French masters" from the Reinhardt and Ferargil Galleries and "the pet salad recipes" of a "host of VIPs." A committee headed by Henry B. DeV. Schwab of Best Foods and composed of Brooklyn Museum curator Stuart Culin, New York School of Fine and Applied Arts director Frank Alvah Parsons, and artist Mary McKinnon curated the show. "Salads were dedicated to Governor Alfred E. Smith, Mayor James J. Walker, and Mrs. Calvin Coolidge," recalled Bernays.

Like the other groups, the Art Directors Club held open lectures on subjects like "Making Artistic Talent Profitable," "The Use of Industrial Material in Modern Design," "Adventures in Book Collecting," "The Opportunity for Commercial Art," and "How Art Directors Work with Artists."[16] Through such activities art directors served as expert guidance counselors, imparting their knowledge to advance art, business, and individual careers.

Art directors' newfound roles as professional exemplars made a certain sense in light of the Art Center's history and development. The Center had grown out of the Art Alliance (1914) and the Art Workers Club for Women (1898), both founded by Hitchcock. These organizations, dedicated to helping craftswomen and models find jobs, were outgrowths of a distinctly female political culture organized around social welfare work and voluntarism to alleviate women's problems.[17] The Art Center represented a transmutation of this older woman-oriented reform enterprise into a corporate, male-dominated operation in which women artists now competed with male practitioners.[18] Indeed, on a day-to-day basis the center appeared less like a placement bureau than like an elite men's club that melded business with social life. Women were behind the inception and operation of the center, but their actual power and presence, and to some extent their priorities, were eclipsed.[19] Art directors now took on the advising roles formerly handled by patrician women; they also dispensed patronage. Thus the reform impulse deferred to the interests of business.

Within the context of the Art Center, art directors were able to position themselves in situations where they would have the upper hand. They became patriarchs of a new "corporate" family, with Hitchcock, the social welfare mother figure, at the symbolic helm as president. An art director like Condé Nast's Heyworth Campbell (a founder and crucial supporter of the center) could play the patronizing, protective father to doting female art workers, the stern yet magnanimous big brother to rivalrous male illustrators, and the attentive, dutiful husband (or suitor) to the patrons of the center—the wealthy society women who represented the ideal consumer.[20]

The Art Center thus offered crucial benefits to art directors. It provided opportunities to forge important alliances with artists, socialites, wealthy businessmen, and high-class advertisers. It gave them occasions to hobnob with graphic artists and illustrators and to view the latest new and potentially usable artwork in a leisurely, unpressured, informal manner. Art directors could "slum" with the artists, and even play "artists" themselves by holding exhibitions of their own work. Yet as a place specifically dedicated to selling art directors and businessmen on the talents of illustrators, photographers, and craftsmen, the Art Center permitted the art director to operate in a context where he remained professionally in command. As a meeting ground and source for information, gossip, and new talent, the center thus institutionalized the involvement and authority of the art director within that sector of the art world geared toward commerce and publishing.

Balancing Personal Goals and Professional Demands: The Work of the Art Director

The Art Directors Club and the Art Center helped art directors strengthen their positions among elite consumers, patrons, and potential employees, but contemporary accounts also indicate frustrations, doubts, and disunity.[21] Art directors recognized that beyond the immediate spheres of commercial art their influence was limited. They had much less authority among advertising executives and their clients. Thus, like illustrators, art directors had to resolve tensions arising from uncertain identities and frustrated expectations. Their problems arose as a result of their necessary efforts to combine administration and creation.

In the 1920s, as earlier, a majority of successful art directors had trained at established art schools. For example, Vaughn Flannery (1895–1955), chief art director at N. W. Ayer, Inc. from 1923 to 1930 (and later art director at Young and Rubicam), attended the Chicago Academy of Fine Arts, as did Charles Coiner, his successor at Ayer; Guy G. Clark (1882–1945), who worked at Blackman Ross, Calkins and Holden, and Street and Finney, attended both Pratt Institute and the New York School of Art; Gordon Aymar (1893–1989), art director at J. Walter Thompson, had been a student at the Boston Museum School of Fine Arts; René Clarke (1886–1969) of Calkins and Holden studied at the Connecticut League of Art Students in Hartford; Nathaniel Pousette-Dart, art director at Barton, Durstine, and Osborne and the George Dyer agency, studied at the Chase School, the St. Paul Art School, and the Pennsylvania Academy.

Given these educational backgrounds, art directors often arrived on the scene with many of the same expectations and aspirations as illustrators and painters.[22] Many of these individuals tended to view advertising in artistic terms, as an aesthetic challenge; they preferred to focus on the means of advertising rather than on its ends. Yet the demands made upon them often seemed antithetical to their artistic ideals. Attracted by what Dreiser called a "probably never before experienced salary," art directors were willing to sell themselves "into bondage."[23] Yet try as they might to sell out, some art directors were so indoctrinated with romantic ideals that they had difficulty embracing commercial priorities wholeheartedly. The strength of art ideologies within the world of advertising gave rise to internal conflicts.

Unlike artists, art directors could not avoid the fact that their work depended on business, and that their job was to sell, not create. As Earnest Elmo Calkins reminded his advertisers, the art director could not be "so much an artist as a man who has a knowledge of art, especially applied to the purposes of advertising."[24] In this capacity, art directors' day-to-day activities were less visionary than mundane in focus. As a brief description of the work of the average art director will illustrate, his tasks had their creative aspects but also involved a good deal of rote administrative work.

Presented with a given product and client and with themes, priorities, and copy (worked out in collaboration with the client's advertising manager, the agency's account representative, and the copywriters—then cleared with the client), the art director embarked on a multistage task. First came the initial "generative" phase—from the art director's perspective, the truly creative portion of the work. Depending upon the client and the size of the agency staff, the art director or his assistants would develop rough sketches of illustrations and layouts, indicating the arrangement of headlines, text, and displays. When it came to developing variations on a given theme, the designs might also be based on the copywriters' suggestions for visualization. If the production manager or agency head okayed them, these designs would be submitted to the client for approval. If the client gave his blessing, the art director would proceed to work with his in-house staff or to hire an art service or freelance artist through the process described in chapter 1.[25]

From this point on, the "executive" portion of the project, the art director's job turned more administrative. Having chosen an artist, the art director wrote or called that individual. The art director negotiated a contract and provided the artist with the rough sketches. (Rarely did the artist have any say about the amount of the fee.) When the artist completed the assignment, there would often be additional exchanges, some quite lengthy, in which the art director would goad the artist into making appropriate changes.[26] Once the art director approved the artist's finished design, it would be returned to the agency, where production would be completed under the art director's supervision.

This combination of routine and unpredictability was as stressful for art directors as it was for any other manager. Like his peers in the agency, the art director had responsibility for organizing others under tremendous time pressures, knowing that the future success of the agency, as well as his job, was at stake. Coordinating the activities of many illustrators required special talents. Art directors had to reassure touchy artists that they were basically sympathetic to their interests and concerns. To a certain extent, art directors undoubtedly envied the relative autonomy and creative talent of the artists with whom they collaborated. At the same time, getting the job done meant showing who was in control.[27] The tensions resulting from this combination of managerial demands and personal resentment sometimes emerged in art directors' writings in the trade press and in instruction manuals, especially those directed toward artists. A recurring theme of these often paternalistic discussions was the necessity of being a team player. The artist had to make personal sacrifices and suppress his temperament—in effect, just as the art director did.[28] (The difference, of course, was that the art director was a salaried manager.)

Art directors also faced hurdles in the other direction. They believed that success in their tasks was contingent upon maintaining artistic control. Yet many advertising executives, clients, and even some art directors themselves questioned their competence and the legitimacy of their professional and personal priorities. Many were convinced that art directors were too caught up with artists and artistic concerns rather than being concerned with selling and the consumer. Debates often focused on issues of audience and representation. They centered on several specific disagreements over the nature and appropriateness of advertising art, one of which was over modernism and another over signature.

Modernism and Advertising Art

Beginning in the second decade of the twentieth century, but especially during the 1920s, art directors sought to link the discourses of fine art to advertising. In particular they attempted to integrate vanguard imagery and commercial activity. Art directors themselves were attempting to transgress the boundaries of artistic acceptability by experimenting with new styles and techniques, especially those derived from European avant-garde movements like cubism or futurism. Indeed, art directors played an important role in introducing large numbers of Americans to these

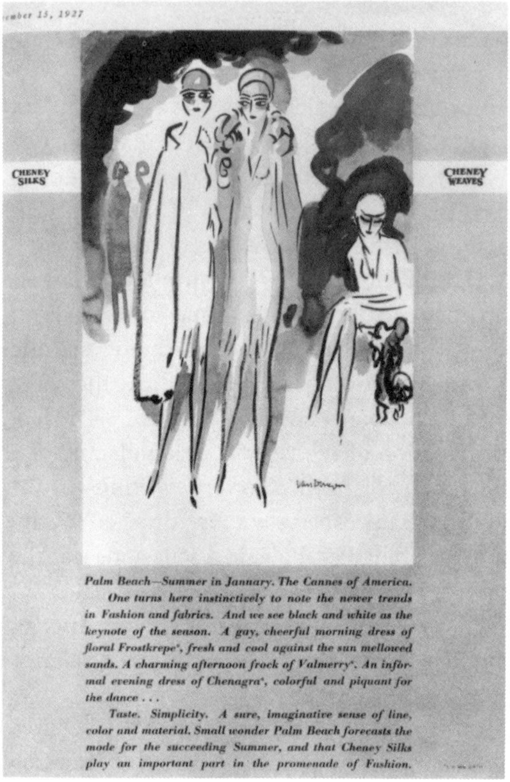

3.3. Advertisement for Cheney Silks, illustration by Kees Van Dongen, 1927.

modern styles.[29] Discussion of these experiments brought into the open crucial disagreements about the relationships of advertising illustration, clients, and consumers to the larger meanings and purposes of both art and advertising. The advertising press took on a key role in spotlighting the issues. Trade publications functioned as the sober voice of "reality," reminding art directors and illustrators that their ultimate responsibilities and priorities had to be promotion of sales. In the view of many advertising men, such reminders were necessary. Art directors' statements and actions regarding modernism suggested that they were not always sufficiently convinced of the primacy of selling over creating. Modernism raised too many disturbing questions, not only about art but also about advertising.

Historian Roland Marchand has noted several characteristics of mod-

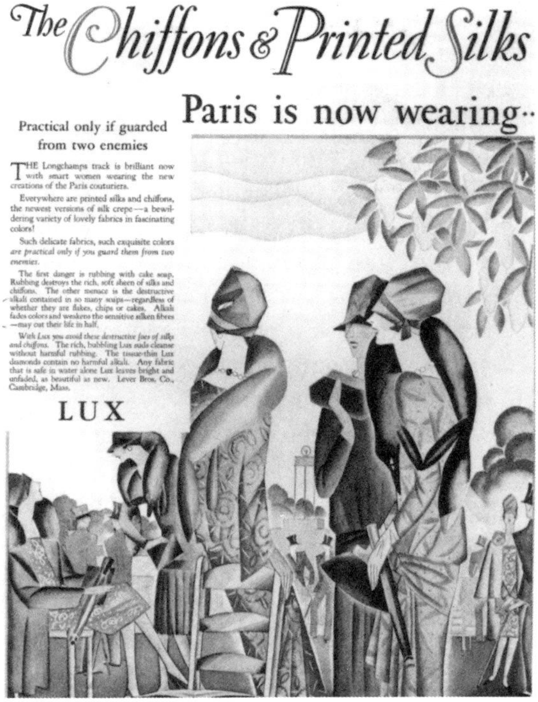

3.4. Advertisement for Lux, 1927.

ern styles that art directors especially favored for advertising illustration in the mid- to late 1920s: the sweeping diagonal line and asymmetrical "off-center layout" that evoked a sense of movement and caught the attention of the beholder (see fig. 3.2); a sense of unresolved tension, achieved through juxtaposition of familiar forms in unexpected ways and through fragmentation of form and spacial discontinuities; and "expressive distortion," rejection of more traditional mimetic or academic conventions of representation in favor of images that connoted subjective experience and a "feeling" for the product (fig. 3.3). Such distortions could include montage, a seemingly arbitrary use of chiaroscuro, radiating and zig-zagging "cubo-futurist" lines, and exaggerated, elongated renderings of human proportions, especially in depictions of the female (fig. 3.4). In addition, advertisers favored modernist simplifications of form and composition to convey nonverbally the idea of simplicity, purity, directness, and honesty. By paring form down to its barest essentials, advertisers could also direct the viewer's attention more selectively.[30] Indeed, all these methods supposedly attracted the viewer by lending new excitement to ordinary objects.

Art directors appropriated modern styles for advertising purposes because they thought these techniques would succeed in drawing attention. Indeed, many undoubtedly had personal motives for their experimentations. The artist and art lover in them believed that modernist styles were a more authentic mode of representation. Many art directors may have unconsciously identified modern art with an autonomy that they felt they themselves did not have. Use of such imagery served as a form of personal liberation, enabling them to partake vicariously in a movement that incarnated freedom. Yet a belief in the sincerity of modern art would also have forced art directors to confront the discrepancies between their romantic ideals and the commercial ends to which they applied modernist imagery.

Some art directors were clearly aware of such problems. Others repressed the dilemma and rationalized these contradictions in ways that seemed personally and professionally more constructive. They preferred to construe modernism as a means of validating art directors' work and artistic interests to themselves as well as to others. Thus some art directors conceived of modernism as a way to assert symbolically the importance of Art in a field in which cultural concerns were too often trivialized. To this end, art directors' arguments for modernism in advertising were directed in part toward achieving more professional influence. The legitimacy of their work hinged on their power to discriminate and set aesthetic standards.

For some art directors this objective was best achieved by expanding the definitional boundaries of art to include commercial work, and then going on from there to distinguish art from non-art. They argued that it was necessary to distinguish between art and non-art in advertising, just as it was in painting and other, non-art endeavors. "Modernistic" easel painting and advertising imagery were, in theory at least, equally legitimate forms of artistic activity; nevertheless, not every painting or advertising image could rightfully be described as art. The highest aesthetic standards had to apply to both practices.[31]

Such assertions, however, begged the question: Should art directors serve as artistic gatekeepers? Was this part of their job? To be sure, in the mid- to late 1920s, the use of "modernistic" advertising images increased markedly, suggesting that clients endorsed art directors' standards and found such images effective.[32] But within the industry there was in fact much debate about the appropriateness of such borrowings from avant-garde painting. Underlying the conflict was the issue of whether and to what extent Art—especially modern art—should be part of the enterprise of advertisers and art directors. The controversies were motivated explicitly, however, by differing conceptions of audience and attitudes toward it. Divisions also centered on the relative merits of intelligibility versus intellectual challenge in art and advertising.

For some advertising pundits, modern art and "modernistic" advertising were two separate entities whose status was determined by matters of gender. One group of detractors felt that the use of modernist imagery in advertising violated the sanctity and purity of art because advertising was created for women. Modernism in advertising watered down the codes and messages of modern art to make the image intelligible to "simple minded" female consumers, who, critics insisted, were less concerned than men with hard facts and more easily swayed by "emotional" qualities evoked through distortions of style.[33] Thus, in contrast to the field of "art-art," in which—as feminist historians have shown—modernism and maleness were intimately linked, in the commercial context modernism was—often negatively—associated with the feminine.[34]

From another perspective, the central issue involved modes of representation more generally. This viewpoint highlighted distinctions of education and class, not only between art directors and audiences, but also among different consumers. From this perspective, modern art was inappropriate for advertising because it was often unintelligible to beholders and received with hostility. Modernist imagery in advertising risked failing to communicate. At the very least it might distract viewers' attention from the goods. "Modern Art may be *modern*," read a headline from a J. Walter Thompson Company in-house newsletter, "but is it art? Whether art or no, does it sell?"[35]

Responding to a series of exhibits of modern art on the J. Walter Thompson agency's bulletin boards, one member of the creative staff, William Day, was prompted to editorialize in 1927, "Is Art Always Advertising Art?" For Day, the answer hinged upon who the audience was. He drew an analogy between advertising and magazine covers. Each, he argued, was "chosen with an eye to the breadth of its appeal rather than in a desire to hew out new art trails for the public." Modernism might work for the "sophisticated, bizarre and *small* class circulation field represented by Vogue and Harper's Bazar [*sic*]," but it was illustrators like Norman Rockwell, J. C. Leyendecker, and Jessie Willcox Smith that exerted the most pulling power for the "millyuns."[36] For Day, the issue boiled down to "mass versus class."[37] There could certainly be modern art in advertising, but it would remain a limited enterprise.

Art Deerson, another member of the Thompson staff, disagreed. His response set out explicitly the themes and terms of the debate: the role of art in advertising, the responsibility and relationship of advertiser to public, elitism versus populism, knowledge versus emotion, and attraction versus desire. Implicit, too, was the ongoing tension between male professional and cultural authority and female purchasing power.

Deerson wrote:

> Reactions to beautiful things whether they are pictures or utilitarian objects are emotional and not visual or part of our knowledge; as for instance, we know that leaves are green and yet a picture of a forest painted in green would be entirely inadequate. Still we persist in giving our "millyuns" commonplace art where the burden of creating beauty is placed on the beholder.[38]

"The possibility of stimulating emotion with such truth," Deerson continued, was "out of the question." Art directors and artists had to take a more active hand. "Is our American peasantry less susceptible to beautiful things—less emotional artistically than the peasantry of Europe?" No, he insisted, like so many turn-of-the-century art critics, they deserve to have beauty, and will respond by demanding more. Drawing upon popularized theories of psychophysics that contended that particular visual configurations had specific psychological resonances, Deerson stated that a painting of an "orange panel with nothing but an upward movement of white lines" may be much more successful in creating a feeling of joy in the spectator than a "commonplace picture" with a high degree of technical finish. "The principles of Cezanne have been put to use admirably in the advertising of Snowdrift and Wesson Oil [commissioned by Calkins and Holden]—with nothing but admiration from our supposedly moron public. If this type of illustration had been poor business, it would have been discarded long ago." "Since emotion is the essence of modern art," Deerson insisted, "is there not a special field for its adaptation in American advertising of today?[39]

Numerous publications extended the arguments of the Thompson staffers. Many, like Day, argued that modern art was both distasteful and incomprehensible to the average viewer; it was folly to foist such imagery (which represented art directors' own aesthetic preferences more than anyone else's) upon the public, and assume that it would attract attention and that people would eventually come to accept it. Advertising could not work eventually; it had to succeed then and there. From this point of view, the art director could not be both advertiser and art educator. Consumers' well-tested preferences for transparently "realistic" and anecdotal images had to take priority over some nebulous "modernistic" appeal to the senses grounded in unreliable psychology. Besides, the eccentricities of modernism were likely to backfire in advertising by drawing more attention to the art than to the product. Straightforward, attention-getting, informative pictures had to prevail over idiosyncratic art. In fact, noted several observers, this overriding concern for favorable consumer response meant that advertising art and fine art were ultimately incompatible.[40]

Advocates and even some critics of modernism disagreed. Supporters of advertising modernism argued that impressionism, cubism, futurism, and Ashcan school styles could work both as art and as advertising. They reiterated Deerson's view that the use of self-consciously artistic techniques attracted notice and gave allure to the product in ways that eluded more iconic forms of representation. For some, a taste for modernism represented a new worldliness on the part of a public jaded by the experience of world war. As the director of service at Frank Seaman, Inc., speculated in 1928: "Possibly it means that America is coming of age—and that a generation fed on War-Radio-Movies-Wells-Shaw-Lewis-Dreiser-O'Neill-Will Durant-Van Loon-Anita Loos, *et al.* will respond to something less naive in advertising pictures than the sweet inanities of the days before the war."[41] Others claimed that modern art in advertising would help to raise public taste by exposing the masses to imagery they might not otherwise experience.[42] More snobbish commentators argued that the public did not know any better, but since "futuristic monstrosities" appealed to these people, advertisers had to "pander" to them.[43] Others, while acknowledging as positive the trend toward modernism, warned against merely appropriating its superficial stylistic features without proper concern for the epistemological issues that had motivated its use in avant-garde painting.[44]

The efforts to enlist the self-reflexive art of modernism to further the causes of advertising led to a variety of perspectives and rationalizations. Such irresolutions reflected the fact that for art directors, modernism was more than just a technique, a device for selling. It was a site of conflict over the meanings of art and the meaning of art directors' work—matters about which they cared a great deal. The modernism question forced art directors to probe the relationship between art and authenticity, raising issues of aesthetics and ethics that—despite the assertions of some advertising men—were essential to the advertising process. Similar concerns about art, advertising, and values were implicit in concurrent discussions regarding the artist's signature.

Signature

The matter of whether to allow advertising artists to sign their images was less controversial than the modernism question. Yet it was a subject discussed in the trade press, and implicitly was an issue by virtue of the fact that some images bore signatures and others did not. Like modernism, the question of signature raised the larger issues of the artistic status of advertising work and of the position of the artist. Although the signing of an illustration clearly had to have the consent of the artist, the art director was ultimately in the position of defending or opposing the practice. Here, as in the case of modernist influence, art directors were not always the primary discussants on the issue in the trade press; nor could they always determine the outcome of the debates, since any agency or client company executive could overturn their decisions. Nevertheless, practices and disputes with regard to signature had an important bearing on art directors' ability to work in a manner that was consistent with their artistic convictions—to set and regulate advertising art standards.[45] For in any given case, the outcome of the debate reflected the degree to which clients and agency executives were willing to acknowledge art as an important element in advertising, and to let the production of images be governed by a romantic ideology of authenticity connoted by signature but at odds with the fundamental purposes of advertising.

J. Walter Thompson president Stanley Resor had grappled with such issues as early as 1917. Unless the client specifically requested otherwise, declared Resor, signatures would not be included. "Anything which tends to draw the attention from illustration itself lessens the strength of the advertisement," he stated. "We want the readers to be conscious only of the ideas expressed in the illustration, not of the artist who executed the drawing." In Resor's opinion, signature also augmented the name recognition of the artist, his reputation, and hence his price. It let other agencies know who was doing the work and thus gave the competition unnecessary access to the artist. The more advertisers using a given artist's work, he insisted, the less its originality, impact, and selling power.[46]

For a time at least, Resor's policy was standard at many advertising agencies. Many advertisers simply continued to omit the artist's name. Such a tack served to underscore the factuality rather than the expressivity of the representation, and clearly communicated that the advertiser's priority was the product, not art.

But many other advertising illustrations during the 1920s and onward bore their creators' names. Clients like Texaco, Lux, R. J. Reynolds, Edison Mazda, and Marcus Jewelers found that the indexical trace of the artist's hand lent prestige to the images, and less directly, to the product, especially when the signature was that of a leading illustrator like Norman Rockwell, McClelland Barclay, Andrew Loomis, or Frederick Mizen. For indeed, inscription was a statement that the advertiser did prize art both as creative expression, the ideal as opposed to the real, and as property. Signature, then, implicitly commodified the advertising representation as well as the product. This strategy had failed with turn-of-the-century art posters when collectors hoarded the image as object rather than as an expression of the advertised goods. But the tactic could evidently succeed with print advertising, perhaps because the image was usually acquired as an incidental part of a prior purchase, that of a magazine. Signature implied that anyone who could afford a magazine could have the pleasure of "owning" the work of a prominent artist. Advertisers may have banked on the idea that anyone attracted to the image on that basis would also be likely to give some notice to the product if they could be lured into paying attention to the advertisement as a whole. Signature would also serve as an indication that the agency did "high-class" work. It would also function as a sign of credibility, of the fact that client and artist stood behind the product they promoted. As such, the signature served as a subliminal form of testimonial.

The advertisements for Kelly-Springfield Tires of the mid-1920s indicate that the conventions of signed advertisements had become so familiar that they could be parodied. In one 1923 image, for example (fig. 3.5), the "handwritten" words "Lotta Miles" stand both as and in place of the artist's signature. The signature was a sendup of the artist-worship it symbolized. Dissatisfied with a practice that did not seem to contribute directly to the selling message, Kelly Tire advertisers instead put an advertising message in the signature. This copy-as-signature thus seemed to acknowledge the effectiveness of signature for advertising purposes. In this instance, the "pretty girl" used a pointer, itself an index, to direct attention to the signature, another index, and visually to link the message "Lotta Miles" to the tire, to which the signature really referred. The copy underscored the idea of signature as a signifier of credibility, noting that "there is ample justification for the absolute confidence which the owner of Kelly Cords places in them." What really counted, asserted the advertisement, was not art values or the artist, but the image-cum-copy as message—and, of course, the product, Kelly Cord Tires.

The Kelly-Springfield Tire advertisement was an ingenious but one-time solution. In its own peculiar way it highlighted ambiguity about the value of signature, which continued to be debated behind the scenes. Differences of opinion were rooted in the same uncertainties about the role of art in advertising that were at play in the conflicts over modernism. In one instance in 1930, notable for its nuanced array of arguments, disagreement over signature arose in the context of a protest mounted by copywriters over perceived inequities of treatment, privilege, and pay.[47] The circumstances reveal that the stature of visual art in advertising was by no means certain, but that successful freelancers, creators of pictures, were in a higher artistic position than writers in the institutional hierar-

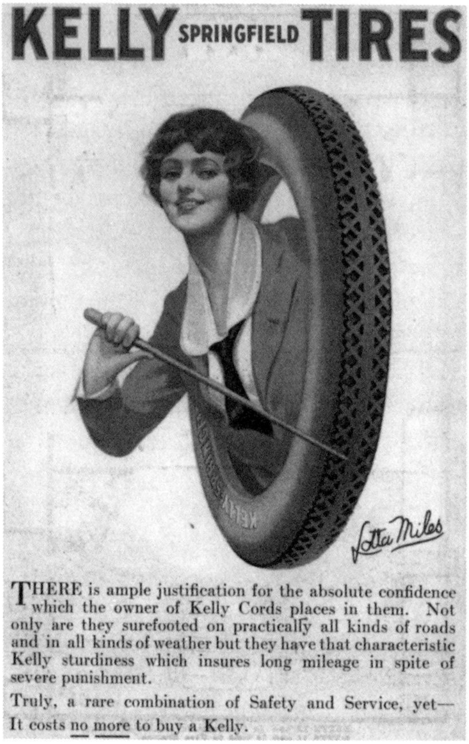

3.5. Advertisement for Kelly-Springfield Tires, 1923.

chies of advertising. The romantic view of art as an authentic expression of the artist's vision held sway, even among art directors and ad men who did not support art in advertising. One Edward Prager, for example, justified signature as a mark of the artist's privileged place. Responding to copywriters' complaints that freelance illustrators were paid more than copywriters, Prager contended that this was the case because the visual artists had to be more specialized, less versatile, than copywriters on staff. These illustrators' signatures were the mark of their uniqueness; they should have the right to sign their work precisely because no staff artist could duplicate their work.[48]

Although John F. Arndt disagreed with Prager, he implicitly embraced the romantic view of art as an expression of the artist's sincerity. He stated that since pictures used in advertisements could no longer be considered art, they should not be expected to bear a signature, the signifier of individuality, artistry, and authenticity. Like advertising copy, the images in advertising formed part of a larger whole not of the artist's creation, an entity dedicated to a wholly different end than expression of an individual artist's feeling.[49]

G. W. Freeman of the Conklin-Mann agency met the other two commentators halfway, contending that freedom, not sincerity, was at issue. The purpose of the advertising image was to get people to "look," not to "believe." Its purpose was to attract, not to signify the truth. Thus, if an artist wished to sign his name there was no reason he should not. The decision to sign or not should be that of the artist, not the art director or client, for aesthetic concerns (such as the relationship of art to truth) were not the issue at all.[50]

Coming in 1930, as the Great Depression deepened, Freeman's bracketing of art took on new meaning. It indicated a shifting climate in the creative departments of advertising agencies, whose effects we shall soon explore. In the late 1920s, however, the prevalence of artists' signatures suggested that many clients and advertising people otherwise wary of claims for promotional "art" were willing to accommodate art directors' efforts to transform advertising into an artistic enterprise. The presence of modern styles in advertisements alongside the more academic and conservative renderings was further indication that art directors were gaining additional professional ground.

But ongoing respect and professional influence was no foregone conclusion; it took a great deal of work and persuasion on the part of art directors and their supporters to keep ideologies of Art at the forefront of advertising practice. Much of the credit for their success can be attributed to the perseverance of a few individuals. One of them was Nathaniel Pousette-Dart.

The Art Director as Artist

The artistic aspirations of many of the art directors in the larger agencies were both exemplified and championed in the 1920s and 1930s by Nathaniel Pousette-Dart (1886–1965). Pousette-Dart's career has been overshadowed by that of his more famous son, the painter Richard Pousette-Dart (1916–1992), but for two decades, Nathaniel Pousette-Dart was a prominent figure in the organizational worlds of both easel art and advertising. His activities typified the effort to spotlight art directors' artistic concerns and to situate the art director in a position of influence and eminence. At the same time, they represented an attempt to harmonize commercial and fine art in a manner that would reconcile the personal conflicts arising from his own dual activities as painter and advertising man.

Born Nathaniel Pousette in Saint Paul, Minnesota, Pousette-Dart studied at the Saint Paul Art School, the Chase School in New York (under Robert Henri), the Art Students League, and the Pennsylvania Academy of Art. He taught at Saint Catherine's College in Saint Paul and at the Minnesota College of Art between 1919 and 1924. On marrying the poet, musician, and suffragette Flora Louise Dart in 1913, he changed his name to Pousette-Dart as an expression of "mutual respect for each other's integrity."[51] The couple had three children.

Moving to New York in 1918, Pousette-Dart worked on murals with Ezra Winter (possibly those for the ceiling of the Cunard Building at 25 Broadway, which were completed in 1921).[52] He also began to take on freelance assignments. He worked for a short period as assistant to J. Walter Thompson art director John De Vries. In 1921 Pousette-Dart became art director at the agency Barton, Durstine, and Osborne. He also served briefly as art director at the George L. Dyer Agency, but he sought greater freedom to implement his ideas, and founded his own freelance art directing service in 1923. According to *New York Times* art critic Edwin Alden Jewell, Pousette-Dart dedicated his time to the advancement of modern art in advertising. (Unfortunately, there is no available evidence of which campaigns he worked on.)[53] Throughout the 1920s and indeed, his entire career, Pousette-Dart painted on his own, in a style clearly inspired by Cézanne, Picasso, Braque, and Marsden Hartley. He exhibited paintings in the Anderson Gallery in New York in 1928, and succeeded in having himself identified as an easel painter as well as an art director.[54]

As a freelancer in a highly competitive commercial art market, Pousette-Dart was well aware of the importance of visibility. But his concerns went beyond his personal desire to promote his agency and feed his family. He was committed to uplifting both the art director's profession and commercial art more generally. To that end, he also sought to maintain an autonomy that would enable him to keep his artistic priorities at the forefront of advertising practice. He served as the third president of the Art Directors Club of New York in 1924, and was an associate editor for the Art Center's bulletin in the late 1920s. In these capacities he lobbied to give the art director more of what he envisioned as "an official professional standing in the commercial field."[55] More importantly, he campaigned vigorously, through personal contacts and through the printed word, to position art and advertising as equivalent aesthetic enterprises.

As a key spokesman for art directors beginning in the late 1920s, Pousette-Dart sought not merely to appropriate art rhetoric and imagery for advertising purposes, but to break down distinctions altogether between art for advertising and art for personal enjoyment. Son Richard recalled his father as someone engaged in an "acrobatics of survival," who tried to separate and distinguish his breadwinning activities from his true and uncompromising love, painting.[56] While this memory undoubtedly has some validity, Pousette-Dart's public activities and writings suggest that he was also an optimistic pragmatist, determined to overcome the contradictions between his personal and professional commitments and between commercial activity and art.

"I believe that in the next few years we shall see a much finer type of art used in advertising," he told a class in art appreciation. "The artist will be able to express himself *sincerely* [and] . . . not be forced, as he is today, to work within the scope of a bag of tricks."

> Many artists feel that commercial art is a bad influence on their more serious work. I believe this view erroneous. Commercial Art, properly approached, can improve, rather than injure, the ability to create pure art.
>
> A man's art can only be as great as he is himself. If his commercial art helps him to broaden and deepen, his pure art should benefit.[57]

Adhering staunchly to the romantic ideology of art, Pousette-Dart insisted that commercial art, if rendered with intensity and vision, could be as positive and legitimate an artistic influence as any "pure art." Distinctive style alone would not suffice as the "hallmark of individuality" and truth. The artist's work had to be the expression of a "unique inner self," even in advertising.[58]

For Pousette-Dart, advancement of modern advertising art did not mean wholesale appropriation of "modernistic" devices, "making tricky and clever arrangements of shapes and portrayals of people who are merely dummies, lack [*sic*] in truth, and life." It meant "an advertising art that is beautifully organized in line, color, structure, and form and that will have balance, harmony and rhythm of such a high order that it will hold its place beside the fine art of all time."[59] Art, advertising or otherwise, could not consist of useless embellishment, but must have a concern for "fundamentals." "Every created thing must have a meaning and purpose," he insisted. Above all, it had to be sincere.[60]

To help young artists achieve this end, Pousette-Dart had proposed that the Art Directors Club establish an art school, which would provide "first a fundamental art training, then a thorough practical training. . . . to enable [students] to make places for themselves in a comparatively short time after leaving school."[61] He envisioned such classes as a logical and important strategic step in raising the artistic quality of advertising. The school never materialized, but Pousette-Dart persisted, suggesting that the club at least sponsor a class for the "serious study of art" and an annual exhibition of the "serious art efforts" of Art Directors Club members.[62]

Lack of support from colleagues and then the depression prevented Pousette-Dart from bringing his ideas to fruition. But this spokesman for advertising art used another strategy to try to bridge the art-commerce gap: art criticism. Although trade press commentators (most notably W. Livingston Larned of *Printer's Ink*) wrote "criticism" of art in advertising during this period, they mostly focused on the merits of certain styles for advertising purposes. Pousette-Dart reviewed exhibitions of advertising images with the same discriminating attention usually lavished on easel painting, applying similar critical vocabulary and turns of phrase. Haddon Sundblom's painting for Maxwell House Coffee was "an ambitious composition somewhat in the English tradition . . . not carried through altogether successfully." James Daugherty's work for the Vacuum Oil Company had "qualities of real painting. Not only has the artist been interested in telling a story, but he has tried for organic structural composition in which the form has vitality and power." Luza's drawing for Martex towels was "charming and decorative, having a delicately balanced color harmony and arrangement."[63] Such rhetoric legitimized the commercial artistic enterprise, implying that the artist had serious and important interests and intentions no matter what the ultimate purpose of the picture.

During World War II Pousette-Dart continued to link art-making, business, and professional activity. He served on the publicity committee of Artists for Victory (the organization devoted to helping the war effort, which cosponsored the 1942 poster competition at the Museum of Modern Art). He also chaired a committee planning for postwar programs that would keep artists employed and highly visible as consultants and teachers.[64] Next to Earnest Elmo Calkins, no individual sought more energetically to convince advertisers and artists alike of the aesthetic validity of art in advertising. But unlike Calkins, who always regarded himself as a businessman, Pousette-Dart continually identified himself as an artist. He continued to paint, and at the time of his death was preparing a book called "Art—Its Creation and Appreciation."[65] Yet he left as his primary legacy neither his paintings nor his accomplishments as an art director, but rather his contributions as critic, activist, and promoter of advertising art.

Depression

Pousette-Dart had his work cut out for him during the depression. As the economic slump worsened, clients became increasingly unwilling to take risks. They demanded dependability, not experimentation. Consequently, advertising trends shifted away from the "modernistic" styles that imitated fine art toward a more tried-and-true "realism" and another type of highly popular imagery derived from the comics.[66] In the 1920s, as I noted earlier, many advertising executives had been willing to accept art directors' arguments that an emotionally malleable female public would be especially receptive to the messages of modernism. In the 1930s, many of the same executives insisted that the public wanted legibility, real people, and "lifelikeness." From the standpoint of many businessmen, dramatic, clearly focused photographs or the fantasy of comic strips were the only acceptable pictorial alternatives. Both types of imagery could be found in the tremendously popular big city tabloids. Use of the comic strip became so widespread in both tabloid and broadsheet newspapers that one advertising executive commented ironically that "possibly the present period in advertising art will be remembered as the 'balloon talk period.'" (fig. 3.6)[67]

If art directors earlier had used "class" imagery to attract the "masses," this practice declined as agencies lost major accounts and advertising executives their jobs. Art directors, under fire for their perceived self-indulgence and lack of concern for real selling, were forced to abandon aesthetics and artistic posturing for a more concentrated focus on their public, no longer the "peasant" but (the ironically labeled) "Mr. and Mrs. John Citizen."[68] As advertisers retreated from art, art directors quickly lost credibility.

Existing tensions between art directors and businessmen were heightened as art directors came under increasing attack in the trade press. "Finnegan is a fine chap," wrote a vice president of Picard-Sohn.

> An able art director is Finnegan . . . deft, imaginative, and earnest. He has a quick sympathy for the message of a product. He reads text and lends to the discussion of visuals a most practical intelligence. But once a month, Finnegan and I have a row. It is when he wants to go modern.[69]

"The art director has been going along on the theory that his trade is art," protested a Young and Rubicam executive in 1932, "advertising being merely the vehicle. As a consequence his work has lacked that shrewd understanding of the interests and tastes of the majority of readers which is advertising's most valuable tool." The art director, he continued, "under

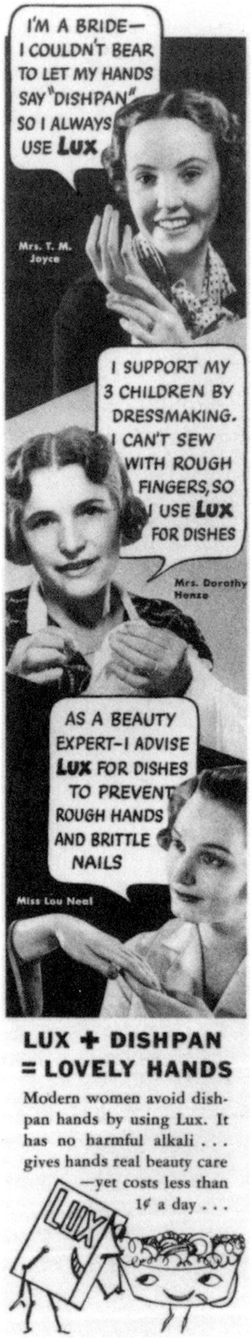

3.6. Advertisement for Lux, 1936.

that mysterious cloak of good advertising art of his, has been giving free rein to his own likes and fancies with money that is not his, and without permission." The art director, he proclaimed, had turned "disloyal."[70] Like an artist, the art director was following his own temperament too much. He was not acting as a good team man should. And he was too out of tune with the tastes of his public.

In the view of this and many other advertising executives, it was now essential to maintain distinctions between art and advertising images. Art directors had to dedicate themselves to creating the most effective pictures for merchandising. They should not be attempting—like Pousette-Dart—to make advertising images for the aesthetic enjoyment of men like themselves.

Advertising executives' denunciations of art directors were partly a survival tactic. Yet their arguments also revealed the extent to which romantic ideologies of art had influenced their thinking. "Art-art" was one thing, pure and autonomous. Advertising imagery was another: explicitly commercial, it catered to the lowest common denominator, not to "a group made up of those who are somewhat lamely described as 'artistically inclined,'" but to "that conglomerate public which, God bless 'em, buy merchandise."[71] As Young and Rubicam's William K. Nield put it:

> There is, or should be, as much difference between fine art and advertising pictures as there is between literature and copy. Fine Art is the expression of the artist's ideas and emotions. It is sufficient if he is satisfied. It needs no mass approval or interest to show its worth. Advertising pictures are the artist's expression of someone else's ideas or emotion, and if they do not attract and interest the majority of possible buyers quite obviously it would have been better to use a different picture. These two are separate and distinct.[72]

A decade later, two other writers reiterated the argument. "This point would probably not be worth elaborating if there were not so many art directors who appraise themselves inaccurately: men to whom it does not occur that the ability to portray a two door sedan is not the ability that painted the ceiling of the Sistine Chapel."[73]

In making such assertions, advertising executives insisted that they knew what they were talking about—that they had scientific evidence for their claims. For now, more than ever, the need for sensitivity to the nature and tastes of the consumer led to increased reliance on marketing research and opinion polling.[74] In the United States, market research into consumer tastes dated back to the 1890s, and focused on obtaining responses to products and to the advertising itself. Extensive use of scientifically derived consumer research, based upon statistical sampling and panels (in which the same respondents were questioned over intervals of time), gained momentum in the 1920s. Businesses sought to anticipate and shape consumer preferences to suit the new mass production industries of cars and other goods. In the 1930s, market research served businesses under greater pressure to make their advertising and sales methods as cost-efficient and effective as possible. Several leading firms conducted opinion research using systematic survey sampling techniques. In 1932, psychologist Daniel Starch inaugurated the influential Starch Readership Service, which measured the effectiveness of advertisements based upon the number of readers who could recall having seen specific advertisements. Following the successful initiatives of Batten, Barton, Durstine, and Osborne copywriter and mail order specialist John Caples, advertisers also refined and augmented their use of copy testing and split-run testing. (In split-run testing, two different advertisements for the same product were divided between alternate copies of a newspaper or magazine. Both advertisements used coded coupons; advertisers gauged readers' responses by measuring the number of coupons returned.) By the middle of the decade, pollsters like Archibald Crossley, Elmo Roper, and George Gallup were routinely measuring public opinion on social, economic, and political matters. Social scientists like Paul Lazarsfeld and W. Lloyd Warner bridged the realms of business, government, and academia, using survey data from public opinion research to gauge less tangible dimensions of human experience: the motives and meanings of consumer behavior.[75]

Drawing upon the precedents and scientific authority of opinion pollsters without necessarily applying their rigorous methods, art directors and other advertising men took measures during the depression to quantify consumer attitudes toward art in advertising. In 1935, for example, the Art Directors Club held its annual exhibition in Macy's department store, "where typical consumers would naturally see it." They asked viewers to vote on their preferences. Viewers could choose among images by Edward Steichen, Margaret Bourke-White, Albert Dorne, Virginia Huget, Norman Rockwell, Otto Soglow, and James Thurber, among others. Not everyone voted, yet according to Deane Uptegrove, art director for Richardson, Alley, and Richards, those who did were "divided between 48 percent men; 52 percent women," with ages ranging from 7 to 65, but mostly 16 to 37. Voters included mostly "housewives and juveniles," but also

> secretaries and machinists, doctors, dressmakers, lawyers, hairdressers, electricians, waiters, newsboys, bankers, dancers, actors, chemists and engineers, to say nothing of a priest, an army officer and a member of the Parole Board. An almost perfect slice through O. Henry's Four Million.[76]

The poll results verified what many advertising executives had been insisting all along: this unrepresentative selection of the public preferred old-fashioned sentimentality and readable illustration. The majority of voters in the "survey" selected the Winemiller and Miller studio's retouched photograph of a "quaint" but sly little old lady in a rocking chair, looking over her shoulder while coyly reaching for a Chesterfield cigarette. As ad man C. B. Larrabee put it, "The public plucked for grandma." "It is a picture of grandmother to end all pictures of grandmothers," quipped Deane Uptegrove of the Richardson, Alley, and Richards agency.[77] (A Norman Rockwell came in in second place.)

From the advertising man's perspective, the lesson was clear. While there was "no doubt that artistically the public is wrong," Larrabee assured his peers, it was evident that the "public still pretty generally" liked a story-telling picture, and admittedly it was "the public that must be attracted by the advertisements." When art directors tried to be aesthetes and to educate the public, they lost sight of the primary purpose of the advertisement and became a "real danger."[78] Art directors who wanted to keep their jobs had best give up their mission and keep art out of the picture.

The depression, then, in heightening advertisers' concerns about public response, considerably constricted the aesthetic parameters of many art directors' work. Organizationally, there were other signs of art directors' diminished prestige and influence. The Art Center and its bulletin folded in 1931. The capital stock of the center and its constituents was shifted to a new organization, the National Alliance of Art and Industry, which essentially reverted to the old Art Alliance. By 1940, it no longer played an ambitious or prominent role in connecting clients, art directors, and artists. Its goals had become merely to promote "good artistic standards in industrial products."[79] Art directors no longer played any galvanizing role. Their concern had become simple survival.

Art directors, as business executives, attempted to respond pragmatically to the attacks on their professional judgment. First, many who were already receptive to photography as a mechanism for representing "reality" began to commission even more of it. In so doing, they accepted the arguments of photographers and photographic advocates who, as we shall see in the next chapter, had themselves engaged in campaigns to attain greater recognition and more jobs, insisting that the photograph offered just the realism the public demanded. Increasing numbers of art directors combined photography with the comic strip serial format and speech balloons, or commissioned more comics.[80] In addition, art directors now took pains to emphasize the diversity of their publics and claimed to cater to viewers' tastes rather than trying to change them. Among themselves, art directors acknowledged the schism between their ideals and work practices, but resisted the demands of clients and superiors that they modify their own sensibilities and priorities.[81]

In discussing the 1935 Art Directors Club exhibition at Macy's, for example, Uptegrove defended the discrepancies between the preferences of art directors and those of most of the survey respondents by reminding his trade press readers that the show's purpose was not to show the advertising imagery geared to the majority public; it was to celebrate art made for advertising, creative expressions deemed aesthetically compelling by those in the know. He admitted the necessity of appealing to the consumer under ordinary circumstances, but the art directors' exhibition was, of course, not real life. The show represented a tribute to the art director's work on behalf of Art. It was also necessary to keep in mind, Uptegrove averred, that different products and media were geared toward different markets with varying tastes in art. To use a uniform yardstick "in preparing advertising for a class magazine would be as ridiculous as to bind an editorial insert from True Story into Harper's Bazaar."[82] For champions of the exhibition, its stylistic variety simply reflected the heterogeneity of publics. Hence the show insisted that diversity could be desirable and profitable.

To emphasize the heightened concern for diversity in markets and taste cultures, the art directors initiated a new set of award categories in the annual exhibition. No longer did they note only the creative medium (such as color painting and color drawing, black-and-white illustration, color or black-and-white photography); they also created a new set of overarching categories. The new classifications referred to categories of print media, and included "Advertising Art Work" for mass-market magazines, class magazines, trade publications, newspapers, posters, and comic strips. In addition, the art directors added another award category, devoted primarily to themselves, honoring the design for a complete advertisement. They also began to list the art director for each of the projects.[83] These changes reflected a recognition that different types of publications had different characteristics and technical requirements, but they also served to assert that art and the work of the art director indeed had its proper place in advertising.

To this end, art directors increasingly sought to downplay the tabloid trend and the comic strip type of advertisement (directed explicitly at those whom advertisers regarded as "Lowbrows"), despite their current popularity. The exhibition committees included small selections of such works, but also tried to highlight the "quality and the diversity of the art work" done for advertising. Hence, noted a reviewer of the 1937 exhibition, that year's Art Directors Club annual was actually "somewhat less than representative of the advertising industry as a whole."[84] What the exhibitions represented instead was art directors' "special Art Ideology, according to which their particular brand of Art really should have no other existence, except a purely utilitarian role of an element (and not always an important one) in an advertising message."[85]

The club annuals remained a crucial forum for art directors to air their views. Yet while previously they had served as a public showcase for the artistic achievements of art directors and artists, now they functioned as a symbolic stage on which art directors could act out their defiance of the cultural philistinism foisted upon them by edgy executives. Under siege, art directors had turned inward. They rallied support from the already converted, and accented the exceptional rather than the typical in advertising.

The Art Directors' Art Director

The Art Directors Club celebrations of the 1930s were mostly symbolic. At the same time, however, there were individuals whose activities really made a difference within the larger organizational worlds of art and advertising. Charles T. Coiner (1898–1989), art director at N. W. Ayer and Sons from 1929 to 1964, was a crucial figure in this regard.[86] Whereas most art directors could only posture about the importance of uniting art and advertising, Coiner was in a position to act and to resist the vulgarity and high-pressure sales tactics of Depression era advertising. His career underscores the fact that there is no fully valid generalization about the relationship between art and advertising at any given point.

Coiner reclaimed "Art with a Capital 'A'" for art directors as a legitimate advertising concern at a time when the gap between fine art and commercial art seemed to be widening.[87] He did so through several innovative and highly successful campaigns that used European graphic design and modernist painting as the primary sales pitch. Instead of hiring commercial illustrators to mimic current European trends, as many art directors in the 1920s had done, Coiner went directly to the sources themselves, the "art-artists." During the 1930s and early 1940s he and his staff commissioned paintings and drawings for advertisements from such luminaries as Pablo Picasso, Man Ray, László Moholy-Nagy, Salvador Dali, Raoul Dufy, Marie Laurencin, Aristide Maillol, Georges Rouault, Herbert Bayer, Adolphe Mouron Cassandre, and Bernard Lamotte, among others (figs. 3.7, 3.8). Coiner's success hinged on more than just his advertisements' stylistic originality and "artiness." It depended upon the mystique and cachet of avant-garde "Art with a Capital 'A'" and "art-

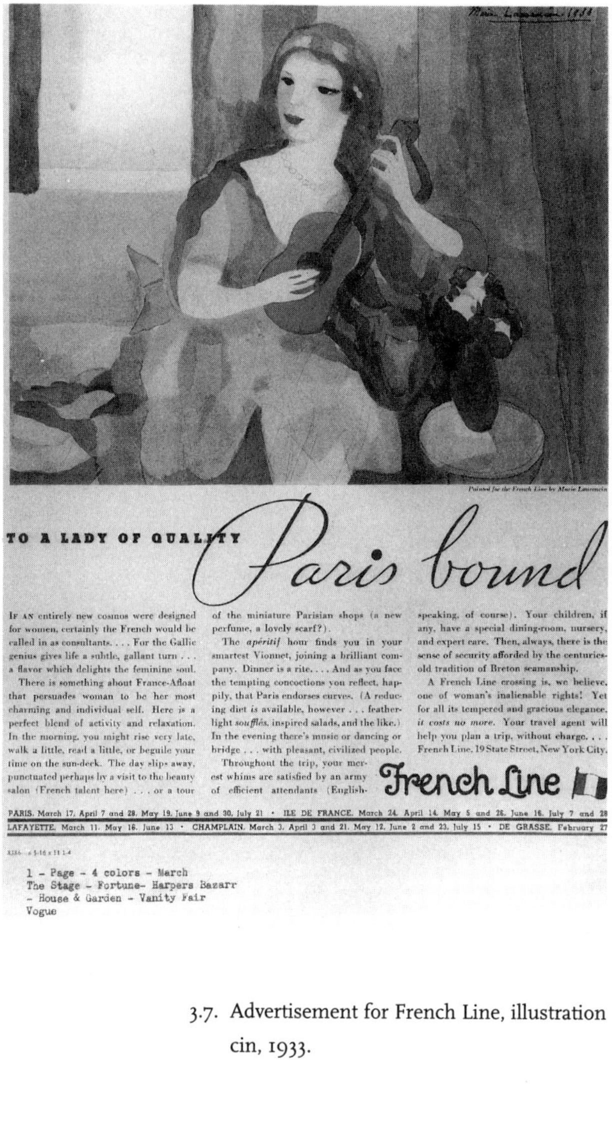

3.7. Advertisement for French Line, illustration by Marie Laurencin, 1933.

artists." If Coiner agreed with Nathaniel Pousette-Dart about the value of bringing art to advertising, they had different opinions about methods and goals.

Pousette-Dart had urged art directors and advertising artists to work together to improve the quality, significance, and stature of art in advertising. By uplifting themselves and their work, he insisted, art directors could reconcile commercial activity and aesthetic values. Art and advertising could be reformed from within the profession. Coiner took a somewhat different path in the late 1930s and 1940s. Bypassing career com-

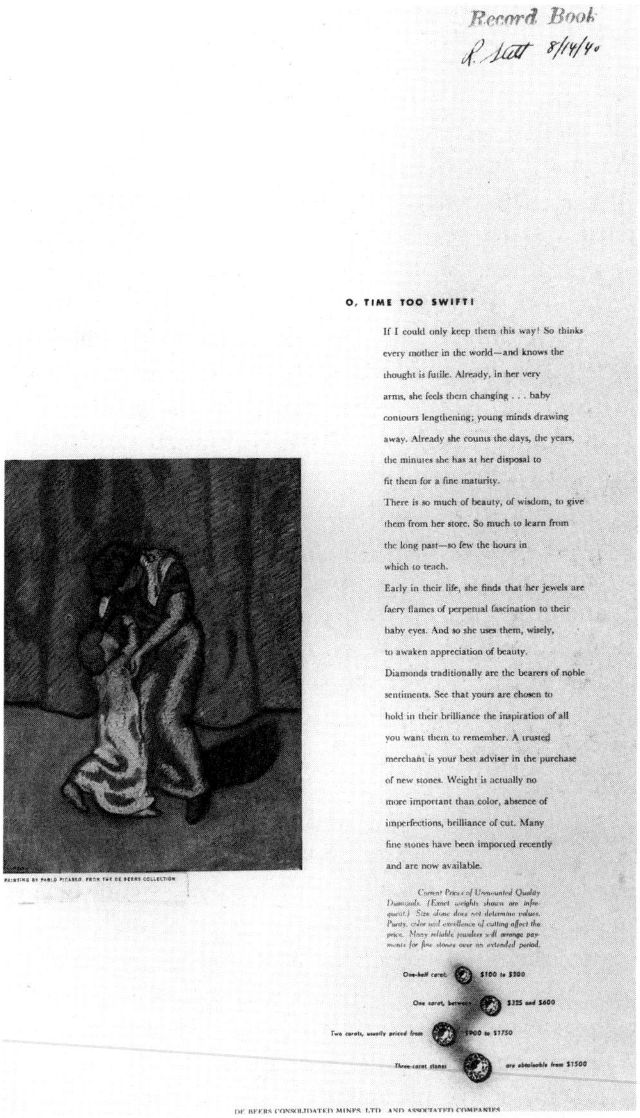

3.8. Advertisement for De Beers Consolidated Mines, Ltd., illustration by Pablo Picasso, 1940.

mercial artists, he shifted artistic authority from the realm of the commercial illustrator to that of "art-artists." Instead of highlighting fine art and commercial art as potentially integrated practices, Coiner emphasized the distinctiveness of "art-art." He exploited that separateness to emphasize the Art in advertising. This process in turn promoted clients' goods through an appeal to consumers' sense of class distinction. Coiner's approach succeeded because markets were becoming increasingly differentiated. His projects received much attention. Over the long term, however, Coiner's imbrication of Art and advertising did not bridge the divide between the two enterprises within the industry as a whole.

Coiner's strategy was not new. N. W. Ayer and Sons had set the precedent of using famous artists twenty years earlier, commissioning paintings by N. C. Wyeth, Rockwell Kent (fig. 3.9), Miguel Covarrubias, Ernest Blumenschein, Sergei Soudeikin, and Ignacio Zoalaga, among others, for piano manufacturers Steinway and Sons. Unlike most advertising of the day, the Steinway paintings rarely referred directly to the product or to the advertising copy, although many were inspired by the theme of music. In addition, the advertisements capitalized on the cultural cachet of art as a commodity by referring to the images as part of the Steinway "collection," evoking exclusiveness, refinement, and value. "By this strategy," wrote Ayer historian Ralph M. Hower, "the Steinway Company was able to provide a rich and distinguished atmosphere for piano advertising as well as to tap a new source of sales—people who had not previously been actively interested in music."[88] Over the years, the Philadelphia-based Ayer agency, outside of the Madison Avenue mainstream, built a reputation for its effective advertising art, winning numerous honors.[89]

But during the depression mere precedent was insufficient to justify artistic adventuresomeness. In the context of the 1930s, other factors had to come into play to make advertising campaigns effective and worthwhile. Innovation required a confluence of circumstances: a distinctive type of client and product, and a common perception of audience and purpose on the part of client and advertiser. Clients and agency executives had to be willing to take risks. They had to be willing to believe that the esoteric could both stand out and sell; and they had to be absolutely confident about the advertising know-how of their art director.

Coiner had certainly proved his ability to draw attention to himself and his products. In 1933 he had been the National Recovery Administration's choice to design its emblem. The famous blue NRA eagle, symbol of federal government efforts to put Americans back to work, displayed Coiner's skill at attracting publicity through eye-catching conjunctions of words and pictures.[90]

French Lines, Hawaiian Pineapple, De Beers Consolidated Mines, Cannon Towels, and Container Corporation of America, for whom Coiner and his staff created some of N. W. Ayer's most celebrated campaigns, were just the right sort of clients. Many of these companies were extensive, tightly managed corporations, controlled by old families with

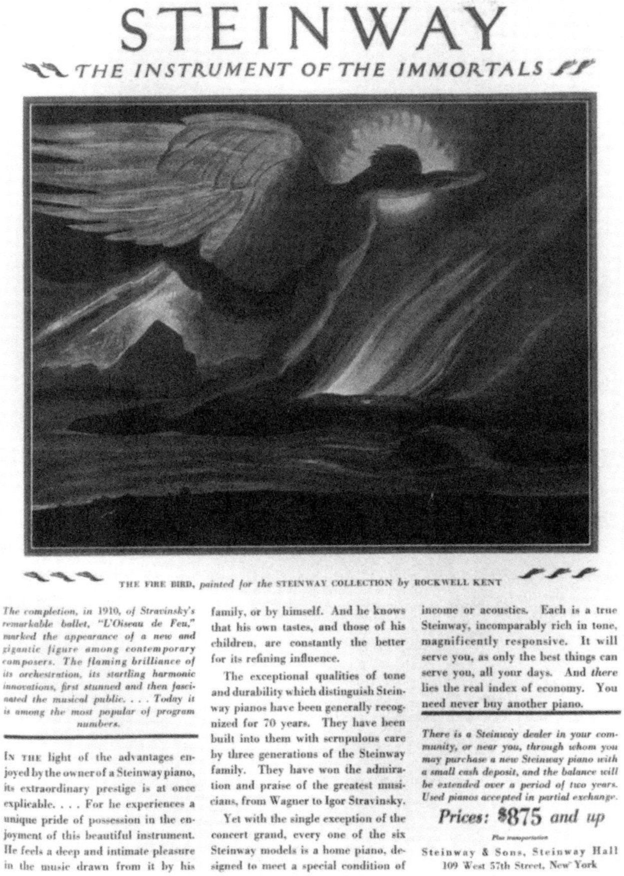

3.9. Advertisement for Steinway Piano, illustration by Rockwell Kent, 1927.

long-standing colonialist and highbrow cultural interests. Such clients clearly saw advantages in advertising campaigns marked by the urbane refinement and social distinction of Art rather than by the appeal to base emotions so characteristic of ads produced for the "masses" in the context of 1930s desperation.[91] For company executives, a high-status, high-profile "class" image communicated through advertisements had personal as well as professional implications.

Clients were a key consideration, but the advertisements' singularity was another. In the 1920s, advertising inspired by modernist trends in painting had become commonplace; in the 1930s, as we have seen, it was often considered iconoclastic. In one sense, these developments followed concurrent trends in painting, where social realism had become the order of the day, thanks in part to government art projects. Many of Ayer's campaigns bucked the realist trends—linked with low-brow, populist, and working-class tastes—found in different ways both in art-art and in advertising. The projects appealed to clients' and consumers' sense of cultural distinction through images whose complexity and exclusivity connoted the importance of both economic and cultural "capital."[92] "What could be more effective than a series of illustrations by such famous French artists?" Coiner wrote of the campaign for French Line.

> The advertisements which reproduce their work appear, of course, only in the class publications. The readers of these magazines are, by and large, an informed and civilized group. If they are not already familiar with the artists, they suspect that they should be.[93]

As with art posters, "Art with a Capital 'A'" would symbolize the cosmopolitanism and prestige of the product to consumers who, depending upon their social, educational, or economic status, might wish to distinguish themselves from the hoi polloi.

Coiner used this approach most consistently with luxury products like French Line and De Beers Diamonds. In the case of Dole Pineapple Juice or Container Corporation of America, the enterprise was less conspicuous. In the case of Dole, for example, Coiner hired famed caricaturist Miguel Covarrubias, poster designer A. M. Cassandre, and painter Georgia O'Keeffe (figs. 3.10, 3.11, 3.12) to evoke exoticism and the "tropical romance" of pineapple juice in popular middle-class magazines like the *Saturday Evening Post.* The hiring of well-known artists was part of a $1,500,000 national advertising campaign designed to lead Hawaiian Pineapple out of a fiscal crisis that had put it on the brink of bankruptcy in 1932. The campaign centered on a new product, pineapple juice. In a new departure, the company marketed the product under the Dole family name, in order to associate it with the "quality, quality, and quality" on which the company saw itself built.[94] Crucial to this campaign was the linking and contrast of modernism and primitivism, of naturalness and exotic romance. Such connections were undoubtedly familiar to better-educated readers; they were very much au courant. For example, Robert Goldwater's study of the influence of primitive art on turn-of-the-century European avant-garde artists was published in 1938, the same year Cassandre's image appeared.[95] In addition, these advertisements played upon mainstream stereotypes of obsequious natives and paradisiacal landscapes, encouraged by Hawaiian industrialists themselves to develop

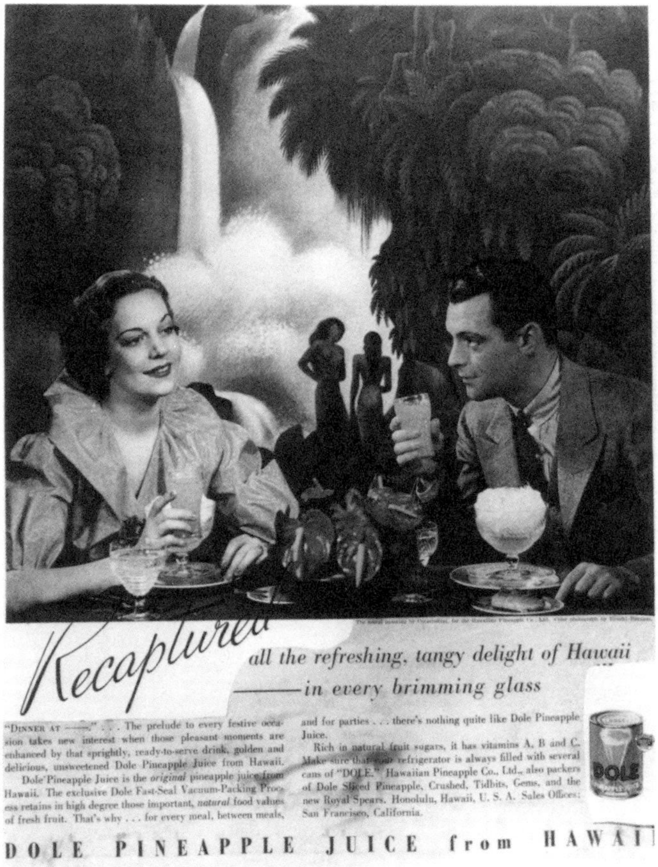

3.10. Advertisement for Dole Pineapple Juice, illustration by Miguel Covarrubias and Anton Bruehl, 1937.

tourism.[96] Indeed, an important aspect of Coiner's success with the Hawaiian pineapple campaign was the ingenious way in which he self-consciously conjoined the stereotypical (representations of the exotic) and the ineffable (signified by modern art).

Advertisers, following magazine publishers, had long tried to associate themselves with the cachet of artists, mostly the popular illustrators, but also some painters. Coiner was no exception, but he, more than his predecessors, capitalized on the romantic myth of the mysterious modern art-artist and his authentic, independent, and intellectually challenging work. But Coiner went further and exposed the myth, at least partially;

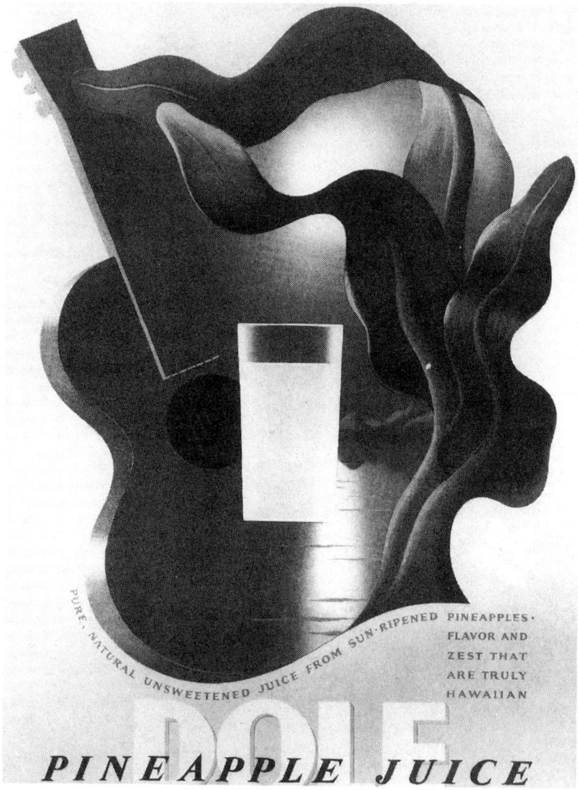

3.11. Advertisement for Dole Pineapple Juice, illustration by A. M. Cassandre, 1938.

this was part of the advertisements' impact. His work became proof that Coiner could make the visually inaccessible accessible and could tame even the most temperamental artist normally accommodating to no vision but his or her own. This popularization of highbrow modern art extended trends of the 1920s, but it was also in keeping with the cultural trends of the moment; Coiner's efforts were consistent with the activities of those at both extremes of the cultural spectrum—erudite leftists and Walt Disney. Coiner's experiences with Georgia O'Keeffe were a good example. The process of bringing such an individual into the fold was often arduous, but from the perspective of Coiner, his staff, and his clients, the results were well worth the trouble.

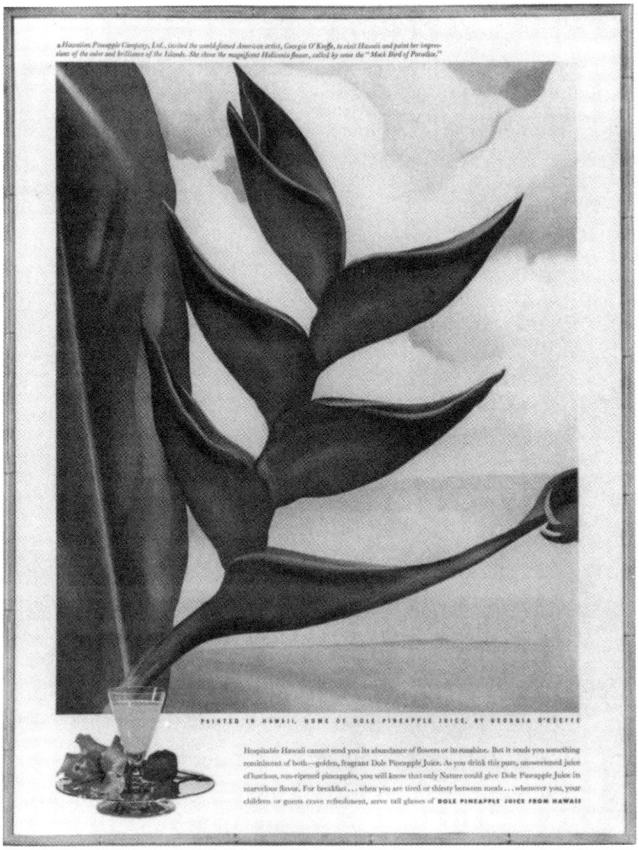

3.12. Advertisement for Hawaiian Pineapple, illustration by Georgia O'Keeffe, 1940.

In the summer of 1938, the Ayer agency asked O'Keeffe (already a highly regarded painter) if she would be willing to travel to Hawaii to do a series of paintings for Hawaiian Pineapple. The agency dictated no terms in order not to annoy the artist, who was notoriously unwilling to take on commercial assignments. The hope was, however, that O'Keeffe would naturally end up painting some pineapples, which would then be used to promote pineapple juice. Attracted by the money and the all-expenses-paid trip to Hawaii, O'Keeffe did agree to undertake the assignment. An Ayer representative shepherded her around while she studied local flora. However, when he finally broached the issue of her painting pineapples, O'Keeffe insisted on staying in the village where the pineapple workers lived, to avoid making the long round-trip drive there every day. Taken aback, the representative tried to explain that local custom would not permit such a close association between an upper-class white woman and native workers. Incensed, O'Keeffe refused to paint a pineapple during her entire stay in Hawaii. Instead she painted papaya trees and ginger flowers, and Ayer had to make do with one of these (fig. 3.12). The Dole company still demanded a pineapple painting, however. Undaunted, Coiner telephoned Honolulu and had an enormous pineapple plant shipped air express to O'Keeffe's New York penthouse at the Shelton Hotel. According to contemporary published accounts (which Coiner or a close associate may well have planted), this action evidently convinced the artist to fulfill her end of the bargain. *Art Digest* declared, undoubtedly exaggerating, that, having "found it [the pineapple plant] amazingly appealing," O'Keeffe "completed its portrait in a day."[97] In other words, press accounts gleefully highlighted the agency's skills in roping this unapproachable artist. O'Keeffe, for her part, disputed this unflattering picture, but N. W. Ayer had won its "O'Keeffe" pineapple and publicity to boot.[98]

From Coiner's perspective, this episode implicitly demonstrated two important, if paradoxical, lessons. Even great modern artists like O'Keeffe were not *so* different from everybody else. Even they would "stoop" to commerce. This, and the fact that their advertisements worked, were proof that art and advertising were perfectly compatible. Yet precisely because art could contribute so much to advertising, advertisers should cultivate art and especially excellence in art as something special and important. Art created by painters like Georgia O'Keeffe was different from run-of-the mill commercial imagery. Coiner and his creative staff had proved as much. Advertisers should thus listen to art directors like himself and take their art expertise seriously.[99]

Coiner's claims on behalf of the art director were made most forcefully and effectively with his work for the Container Corporation of America, a campaign whose significance I will elaborate upon in chapter 6. As with the Hawaiian Pineapple and De Beers accounts, this campaign was dependent on a client, Walter Paepcke, who, with a firm hand on his business, personally aspired to make a mark on American culture. The campaign also hinged upon the support and encouragement of Paepcke's socialite wife, Elizabeth. The Container Corporation advertisements arose from Coiner's and the Paepckes' mutual interest in modern European graphic design and painting as a communicative force.[100]

Like the advertising for Hawaiian Pineapple and De Beers, but even more so, the Container Corporation ads exalted art. In the earliest of a series of campaigns (begun in 1937), Coiner, his staff, and Container Corporation art director Egbert Jacobson incorporated the latest in avant-garde European design, especially the Bauhaus and constructivist aesthetics, into American advertising (a move partly made possible by the recent immigration of important members of the Bauhaus faculty like Herbert Bayer and Gyorgy Kepes).[101] The copy was absorbed into the image; typography became part of its composition. Art literally absorbed advertising; the two became one (see fig. 6.2). Through these ads, Coiner (along with his counterparts at Condé Nast and *Harper's Bazaar,* Mehemed Fehmy Agha and Alexey Brodovich) effectively broadened conceptions of Art to include graphic design.[102] The symbolic, nonanecdotal advertising art asserted the value of the image in its own right. This emphasis on image was good for business. Coiner's solution, using minimal copy and pictures by some of the most prominent names in contemporary painting and design, received national attention. That publicity, achieved by cultivation of reputation and high modernism, served advertising purposes as greatly as the images themselves.

These developments also appeared to be good for art, at least as conceived by a synthesizer like Nathaniel Pousette-Dart. The approach taken in the initial series was certainly consistent with his vision of artistic advancement and professional integration. The aesthetic of modern design, especially as espoused by Bauhaus practitioners, advocated art as a force of uplift and as gratifying, meaningful *work.* From this perspective, no one *type* of art was better than another.

The Container Corporation advertisements also highlighted the artist. Unlike the usual practice, in which the art director or assistants designed an advertisement's composition and layout, in this and other Container Corporation ad campaigns, the artist became much more involved with both conceptualization and execution. For example, in Coiner's third campaign for Container Corporation, he and his art buyer, Edward W. Warwick, provided each artist with the general subject and left him or her to interpret the theme in sketch form.[103] Artist became designer. The artist's signature was an important and inherent part of the image; advertising and art were now inextricable, but it was art, expression of individual vision, that was emphasized. This concern for the art-artist became increasingly evident in the early to mid-1940s in the second and third advertising series for the Container Corporation (the United Nations and United States series). In these two campaigns, Coiner and Jacobson shifted from the black-and-white graphic design images of the early series—many of which relied heavily on typography and photographic montage—to the full color range of modern painting (see fig. 6.4).

Such procedures reflected Coiner's (and Paepcke's) respect for individual creativity; from the perspective of a Pousette-Dart, this was all to the good. At the same time, Coiner's activities were also consistent with efforts on the part of important institutions like the Museum of Modern Art to transmit the idea that the visions of modern art could actively shape the contemporary world; as long as the designs were of the right style, aesthetic distinctions between fine and applied art were theoretically irrelevant.[104] In practice, such an outlook, premised upon stylistic hierarchies, translated into artistic and typological distinctions. Certain types of production by certain types of artists were art; other forms of imaging were not. The effectiveness of Coiner's advertising enterprise thus rested as much on distinctions of reputation and artistic ideology as on straight aesthetic impact. The advertisements that he and his staff commissioned worked not only because they were good and unusual art and design, but also because they were pitched to an audience that was conscious of the status value attributed to cultivated high modernism. This emphasis on the prestige of modern art—made by Artists—diverged from the ideal of integrated professional practice envisioned by Pousette-Dart and Bauhaus theoreticians.

Although Coiner's well-known campaigns of the 1930s and 1940s helped bolster a perception that distinctions between fine art and commercial art were diminishing, he was able to succeed as he did because his practices celebrated and reinforced traditional romantic ideologies of art, and because the gap between fine and commercial art was so large. Art advocates, pleased to see what they regarded as art in advertising, admired Coiner for not succumbing to the pressures of public opinion. But Coiner's pioneering independence was as much a function of his clients and clientele as of courage and conviction. Art and the high culture associated with it were indisputably effective strategies for making box and pineapple advertisements truly notable during depression and wartime. Businessmen and advertisers alike took notice of Coiner's and N. W. Ayer's embrace of art-art as advertising. Some permitted their art directors to follow in Coiner's footsteps, as we shall see in chapter 6. In actuality, Coiner, along with a handful of other art directors, remained a highly visible exception. The received wisdom—demonstrating the continued strength of the romantic ideology of art—was that commercial art and art-art were mutually exclusive, and that the latter was inappropriate for advertising. In general, recalled photographer Ralph Steiner, the art director was a "disappointed" artist, "part way between the money people, the word people, and the sales people."[105] Most businessmen still refused to support art, and believed that an art director should aspire to be nothing more than a "master strategist" who constructed effective advertising images. Quite a few believed that Coiner and his Container Corporation campaign were eccentrics, and that the artistic pretensions of art directors were liabilities.[106]

Art direction became linked less with the production of Art than with graphic design. Art directors like Agha and Brodovich and designers like Paul Rand would invigorate the design of class magazines, corporate public relations material, and other products, including advertising. Their approach to graphic representation attained greater visibility and influence by the 1950s, especially in "class" advertising. (Indeed, the last major Container Corporation Series, "The Great Ideas of Western Man," returned to using the work of self-identified "graphic artists" as well as that of painters and sculptors.) Yet outside the immediate circles of those with vested interests, few people associated graphic design with art-art. Graphic design was generally regarded as a visual language with manifold applications, as a commercially oriented enterprise separate from painting, but one that could also subsume it. Fine art as advertising would have its moment in the 1940s, as we shall see in chapter 6; however, it could not prevail.[107]

Even the most bitter opponents in the "advertising wars" of the 1950s and 1960s—Rosser Reeves and David Ogilvy—could agree on this score. Both men were firm believers in the power of representations: Reeves contended that an effective advertisement had to make a "Unique Selling Proposition," a catchy statement attesting to the distinctiveness of the product, whether or not it really was warranted; Ogilvy, chairman of Ogilvy and Mather, insisted that the key to successful advertising was "brand image," a representation (like the aristocratic, eye-patched Hathaway Shirt Man) that gave the product an individualized "personality." Both men disapproved of the Container Corporation's advertisements.[108] Reeves cited a study of a Container Corporation advertisement with a William Baziotes painting (part of the Great Ideas series), which demonstrated that 100 percent of the respondents did not understand the picture and 85 percent did not understand what the advertisement was trying to say. He criticized this "advertising designed as art, without reference to its business function."[109] Ogilvy stated that Walter Paepcke alone had succeeded in using nonrepresentational advertising, "but it takes more than one swallow to make a summer. Reader, beware of eccentricity when you advertise to people who are not eccentric."[110]

Ogilvy's outlook was rooted in a faith in words and the power of photography. His influential aphorisms translated into action. For by 1960, questions of painterly aesthetics played second fiddle to debates about the semiotics of mass communication: the selling power of iconic media like photography and television and of symbolic devices like animation.[111]

These events were not surprising. The typical art director's inability to lay claim to "art-art" for advertising coincided with the rise of photography as an accepted code for communicating "reality in advertising"—a coincidence for which art directors themselves were partly responsible.

chapter 4

The Rise of Photography

Prior to the depression, the activities of illustrators and conceptions of art in advertising were discussed independently from photography. From the 1930s onward, however, this was no longer the case, for photography became the dominant form of pictorial advertising. The standard explanation for why this occurred is that advertisers preferred photographs because they were more realistic than drawn or painted illustrations. But, as recent scholarship suggests, this explanation presents only part of the picture; in fact it begs the question.[1] To delve deeper into the circumstances in which photographers managed to claim authority over representation in advertising, this chapter examines some of the conditions under which this shift took place. It focuses on the organization and identity of the photographer's work.

Camera Worlds

To explore these issues, it is necessary to know something about what sociologists dealing with "social worlds" might define as the "camera world"—the concerns, activities, and production systems that resulted in those things called photographs.[2] At the turn of the century there were several groups active in the American camera world. First, there were people trying to earn a living by taking pictures, then called "professionals." Dominant among these practitioners were the portrait photographers. They distinguished themselves from so-called "commercial" photographers, who pictured landscapes, factories, and goods. Within the portrait world, however, there were gradations. There were upper-crust portraitists like Edward Steichen (1879–1973) and Pirie MacDonald (1867–1942, fig. 4.1), who catered primarily to national figures.[3] And there were more mass-market photographers who practiced locally among a broad middle-class clientele. In addition, there were a large number of amateur photographers, who did not photograph for a living. Distinctions between the amateurs and professionals had long been hazy, since amateurs sometimes did sell their work.[4]

At the turn of the century, tensions arose between these two groups, not because amateurs differed from professionals in working for pleasure rather than profit, but from the fact that—from the standpoint of profes-

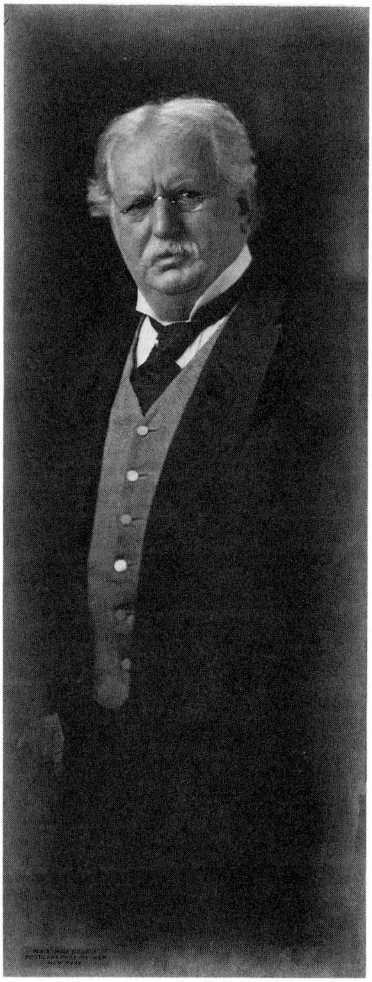

4.1. Pirie MacDonald, portrait of Theodore Vail.

sionals—the amateurs were both worse and better. "Amateurs" included "Kodaker" types—snapshot enthusiasts using cheap box cameras, who, from the vantage point of "serious" practitioners, reduced the craft and art of photography to a low level. They also included the exclusive and elitist "pictorialist" photographers, devoted to making photography a fine art akin to painting or sculpture. Their most notable advocate was the charismatic and domineering Alfred Stieglitz (1864–1946).[5]

Tense relationships prevailed among all these elements. There were disputes among the serious amateurs, especially the pictorialists. One faction, led by Stieglitz, sought not only to distance themselves from hobbyist snapshooters but also from other—from his perspective, less serious—pictorialists. As vice president of the New York Camera Club and as editor of its official publication *Camera Notes,* Stieglitz insisted that too many enthusiasts interpreted pictorialism simply as superficial technique and consequently produced trite results. For him, technique was the means to an aesthetic end whose success only he and an exclusive few were capable of judging. Stieglitz's elitist views alienated him from other metropolitan amateurs, and the New York Camera Club members forced him out of his editorship—a move that prompted him to found the Photo-Secession and his own magazine, *Camera Work.*[6] As photography historian Ulrich Keller has observed, the birth of the Photo-Secession marked the failure of Stieglitz's previous campaign to transform amateur photography into a narrowly "high art" enterprise; nevertheless, it laid the foundations for an institutional framework in which certain types of pictures by certain select individuals would and could be characterized as art.[7] The existence of such a framework and the influence of Stieglitz's views would indirectly have a bearing on the emergence and success of advertising photography.

The professionals also had problems. For example, portraitists, the mainstay of the photography business (fig. 4.2), had no cohesive national organization.[8] A national association with a constitution did exist—the Photographers' Association of America (PA of A), founded in 1879; however, its members were only a small fraction of the photographers in business. Poor attendance at annual conventions was a constant source of contention for PA of A organizers. To the extent that group activities existed, they centered around local clubs like the Professional Photographers' Societies of New York City and Philadelphia.[9]

In particular, portraitists were unresolved about the meaning of their identity as "professionals." For example, Juan Abel, editor of *Abel's Photographic Weekly,* the official house organ for professional portrait photographers and the PA of A, conceived of the professional in idealistic terms as an expert who provided essential services and thus engaged the com-

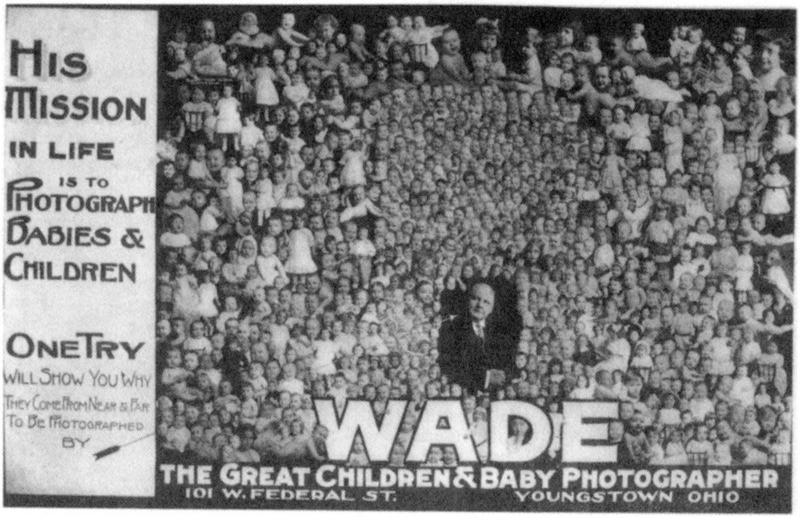

4.2. Advertisement for Wade photographic studio, 1915.

munity's trust. Abel insisted that portraitists could not really call themselves professionals (as many of them did) because, as businessmen engaged in commerce, they had to advertise—something Abel insisted that professionals were not supposed to do.[10] Some spokesmen took more of a unionist stance. They hoped to advance professionalism by controlling standards and procedures, establishing schools and a photographic academy (on a par with the National Academy of Design, a ceremonial body composed of practicing artists), licensing photographers, abolishing apprenticeships, and supervising practitioners, especially those permitted to sell photographic work.[11] Abel urged portraitists to stop worrying about professional status and instead to push for greater occupational unity. He argued that business was ailing because of photographers' lack of discrimination, organizational commitment, and skills in self-promotion. Only these factors would upgrade the reputation of photographers.[12]

Tensions also existed between professionals and pictorialists. The independently wealthy Stieglitz, for example, regarded any form of personal compromise to please a client as a sellout that distorted the nature and substance of photographic truth. He sought to make opposition to "professional" photography one of the basic operating premises of pictorial photography, and was reasonably successful in theory, if not always in practice.[13] The differences here were partly class-related, representing the interests of leisured pictorialists versus middle- and working-class working photographers. To a lesser extent, the differences reflected an antagonism between metropolitans and provincials.[14] While the amateur/professional dichotomy was well established, the identities of the two groups changed their meanings. This fluidity was an important element in the rise and ultimate success of photography as an advertising medium.

The uncertainty of photographers' identities and activities became increasingly important in the context of the rise of mass-market magazines and related developments in print technology at the turn of the century. The perfection of the halftone screen facilitated mass replication of photographic images integrated with printed text, just at the time when magazine publishers, seeking to cater to a broader market, became more dependent on advertising.[15] These changes seemed to set the stage for the full-blown emergence of photography as a vehicle for advertising. Some magazine publishers were quick to employ photography as a medium within editorial matter, and some small advertisers employed isolated elements in minuscule (1 by 2 inch) ads, but relatively few major clients used photography for large-scale, visually compelling advertisements until after World War I. Studio photography still cost more than illustration, for it required special lighting, models, and props on top of all the other expenses for chemicals and materials. Although the halftone process had greatly facilitated the reproduction of photographic or drawn originals, retouching by an engraver or draftsman was usually still necessary to ensure appropriate contrast and detail in reproduction. Most of the tiny faces, shoes, corsets, typewriters, houses, and cars seen in the average halftone advertisement lacked tonal contrast and looked gray and two-dimensional. Even the crude black-and-white engravings in small illustrations looked bold by contrast.[16] Although lavish, self-consciously artistic illustrated advertisements were also the exception rather than the rule prior to 1910, noticeable changes did occur after that time. Once advertisers enlisted more illustrators, many of the images expanded in size. By 1915, the illustrated pictures, often full-page and in color, were much more commanding than the majority of photographic advertisements, whose size and design changed relatively little in appearance; photographic images seemed dated and much less significant. In fact, from about 1915 to 1920, as illustrated advertisements became larger, multicolored, and more noticeably arty, photographic illustrations diminished in number in some magazines. Their flat, mechanical look could not compare with the vibrant line drawing and color of a J. C. Leyendecker or Coles Phillips. "The camera," recalled Earnest Elmo Calkins, was "contemptuously cast aside as soon as pencil and brush artists began to make good."[17] In other words, use of photography in magazines was not necessarily a foregone conclusion even after the perfection of the halftone screen.

There were attempts to make photography more attractive to advertising clients. As early as 1903, at the point when advertisers were trying to woo illustrators into their service, amateur photography journals began promoting photography as suitable for advertising. The apparent truthfulness of a realistic camera image, they argued, could be readily exploited to produce symbolic meanings that would trigger consumer demand.[18] Film and camera manufacturer Eastman Kodak established a $1,500 prize contest to demonstrate the "possibilities of photography in advertising" and at the same time to secure a series of fine pictures that Kodak could use in its own advertising. The company (one of the few to utilize technically superior reproductions of entire photographs in their prewar advertising) asserted that some men could make photographs "that are better from an advertising standpoint than anything that can be drawn." While such photographs might cost more than good paintings, they would be worth it. "[T]he pictures are pictures of real people," exclaimed *American Photography*. "Here is endless possibility for art and technique for creative genius and for profit."[19] Some others agreed, insisting that the photograph was far superior to paintings or wash drawings in its "power of conviction" and human interest.[20] However, numerous publishers and advertisers were unconvinced of the value of photography for advertising purposes. Many still preferred the pictorial conventions and the artistry of handcrafted illustration. As late as 1915 it was contended that the camera image was a mere "statement of fact," accurate, to be sure, but lacking dimension. The painted or drawn illustration could at once evoke the fullness, the totality, of an object perceived and endow it with an aura of lifelikeness, of spirit. "Wherever the stimulation of human interest is part of the purpose," stated a writer for *Abel's*, "we find the photographer cold-shouldered and the graphic artist commissioned in his stead."[21]

Indeed, even photographers themselves did not consider photography in advertising particularly significant. Magazine advertising was not even mentioned as a category in a 1909 volume in the *Self Instructing Library of Practical Photography* (heavily promoted in *Abel's Photographic Weekly*). The volume discussed "commercial photography," a term that had been in use since the turn of the century to refer primarily to architectural and industrial photography—representations of commercial power and substance rather than products. The commercial photographer was "the man who specializes in everything but portraiture." His (or her) work included "news-pictures; photographs of buildings, machinery, manufactures of every nature . . . pretty posings for advertisers, interiors of workshops or palaces. . . ." Subjects could be store windows, fruits and vegetables (for seed catalogs), and factory workers. In 1909 commercial photographs could be used for postcards, summer resorts, studios, book covers, illustrations, sheet music, and novels.[22] Given the inclusiveness of the definition of "commercial photographer" in this volume, the omission of photography for print advertising is an indication of how marginal it was still considered to be.

Uncertainties about the worthiness of advertising photography were reinforced by the fact that photographers were also divided as to who was qualified to produce such images. On the one hand, the amateurs' journal, *American Photography*, could assert that it would be perfectly feasible to produce an "impressionistic" "art picture" for pleasure, but then use it in an advertising campaign. *Abel's*, geared toward the professional, insisted, on the other hand, that advertising photography was "no job for amateurs." The "right rendering of texture," "correct lighting," "emphasis adroitly placed," and "suppression of details" demanded "skill and experience" and "nine-and-ninety other details which only a camera man who is also a business specialist would consider worth while."[23] The professionals, however, stood on shaky ground. The quality of the images in *Collier's* and *Ladies' Home Journal* certainly did not provide compelling evidence of professionals' superior skill. As many professionals were aware, the pictures produced by amateurs often surpassed their own in technical merit.

Prior to the early 1920s, photographers were not a major presence in the organizational framework of advertising. These circumstances were due to the above-mentioned internal divisions within the camera world, and to the fact that professionals were unable and unwilling to advance beyond limited identities, roles, and techniques. The rise of advertising photography occurred when people at the hub were able to rally around a common cause and overcome certain differences—when the occupational worlds and values of the portraitists and pictorialists converged. A limited number of influential individuals working at the center paved the way for this change. They included Edward Steichen and Clarence White, whose own identities and practices had always straddled the borders of amateurism/professionalism, pictorialism/portraiture, and art/commerce.

Edward Steichen

Steichen began his career by meshing art and commerce at the regional periphery. As a young man in Milwaukee, Wisconsin, a painter as well as a photographer, he became involved with local art groups and exhibited his work. At the same time he worked as an apprentice for a local advertising lithographer. Into that commercial framework Steichen introduced his photographic art. According to his memoir, he suggested to his supervisor that photographs would serve well as models for designs. The lithographer responded favorably, and Steichen provided him with pictures of wheat and wheat fields to serve as the basis of beer advertisements. "My crowning achievement was to make some portraits of pigs that were much admired by the pork packers," he reminisced. "Usefulness," Steichen claimed in hindsight, has always been attractive in the art of photography.[24] Thus, even at the outset of Steichen's work life, utility was directly linked to the issue of profit.

In about 1900, Steichen experienced a change in identity and status. He moved to New York, where he became a member of the Stieglitz inner circle and a founder of the Photo-Secession. During that period, circa 1900–1905, he cultivated an image as a painter and photographer "artiste" who would elevate photography, including portraiture, to an art form. Traveling to Europe, he calculatingly exalted the status of the portrait photograph by seeking out artists and intellectuals as subjects (and clients) for his highly manipulated portrait images. His sitters included painters Frederick Watts, Franz von Lenbach, and Fritz Thaulow, poster designer Alphonse Mucha, *chanteuse* Yvette Guilbert, author Maurice Maeterlinck, and his greatest coup, sculptor Auguste Rodin.[25] Through Steichen, artistic portrait photographs of cultivated people, now invested with cultural prestige, became regarded by those very subjects as a high art. Steichen embarked upon a "professional" career on this basis, shooting the famous and wealthy (like actress Eleanor Duse and financier J. P. Morgan) for large sums of money.[26] Steichen's self-promotional efforts had thus worked beyond his highest expectations. By 1905, having one's portrait taken by Steichen had become, as he later put it, quite "the thing to do."[27] Steichen the artist was also the consummate professional photographer.

Steichen was certainly not the only photographer of the day working in this vein. His friend and fellow Photo-Secessioner colleague Gertrude Käsebier, for example, was a successful professional portrait photographer prior to and during her involvement with the group. Since 1899 she had promoted her business by displaying her portraits in "art" photography exhibitions, and she too had used her artistic credentials to court prominent clients. Käsebier, however, always maintained her closest ties with the institutional frameworks of professional portrait photography. Steichen cast a wider net.[28]

Steichen's professional career attained an added dimension through his association with Condé Nast, the new publisher of *Vogue*. The alliance began in 1907, when Steichen photographed Nast's first wife Clarisse. Nast was already attuned to linkages among "fine art" images, high fashion, high status, and selling power through his work at *Collier's Weekly*, where he had masterminded the use of Charles Dana Gibson covers and drawings as a strategy for augmenting sales of the magazine. By the middle of the next decade Nast would capitalize on the use of fine photographers in his own new magazine, *Vanity Fair*, and, a bit later, in *Vogue*. In 1923, the earlier Nast/Steichen connection was lucratively renewed when Nast hired Steichen as a society portraitist and fashion photographer for Condé Nast Publications.[29]

Given Steichen's reputation, outlook, and work, the move to Condé Nast seemed logical. Steichen was a virtuoso technician and a camera worker of unusual vision, but he was not, after all, starry-eyed about the life of a fine artist. He had dabbled in that life during the years of his close association with his mentor Steiglitz.[30] However, he would not be cowed by Steiglitz, or by Steiglitz's highly idealistic and romantic artistic scruples and demands. Stieglitz worked hard to establish photography as a truly modern art and to assert that the market played no role in determining aesthetic value. Steichen was of a different generation and sensibility. He could build upon the aesthetic and institutional foundations Stieglitz helped to create, but was always more at home in the worlds of commerce and consumption.[31] Steichen always maintained his independence.

Yet Steichen's postwar attitudes and practices must be understood not only in light of his prewar outlook and activities, but also in light of the war experience itself. For certainly whatever commitment Steichen had to the Stieglitz ideal of living as a poor but committed fine artist died in 1914 with the onset of World War I. Living at the time in Crécy-la-Chapelle, France (he would return to the United States later that year), the 34-year-old Steichen wrote despairingly to Stieglitz about Germany:

> "What a *sham* she has been—during these past years all this pretense of *culture* and civilized progress—on paper—theories and down at the bottom only one serious real intend [*sic*]—making ready for this war—and then going at it without anything but a mash of pretense at civilization—ruthless. If Germany comes out a victor—we are all in the same boat—I can't foresee any point for reestablishing my interest in life. . . . What a joke is human intelligence."[32]

Steichen's disillusionment was underscored by the fact that Stieglitz himself staunchly supported Germany at the time. Their political differences wrenched the two men apart, and Steichen appears to have experienced a period of personal crisis. He rejected Stieglitz and the art identity Stieglitz represented. Steichen gave up painting and distanced himself from the enterprises pursued under Stieglitz's aegis. Such activities, Steichen believed, no longer seemed useful, just self-indulgent.[33]

Steichen did continue with photography. Volunteering for war service, he became a first lieutenant in the United States Army Signal Corps and helped in the development of aerial photography. This experience revitalized him, and gave him new appreciation for the possibilities of photographic representation and applications. The experience also converted him to the objective of useful, "straight" photography, as opposed to the manipulations and distortions of pictorialism.[34]

After the war, having come to terms with himself, Steichen (now Colonel Steichen) determined to do something purposeful. He jumped enthusiastically back into the realm of glamour, money, and status. Thus in 1923, the same year he joined Condé Nast, Inc., the man dubbed "the greatest of all living portrait photographers" also began making photographs for the J. Walter Thompson advertising agency. His hiring was part of a larger strategy to bring eminence and expertise to the agency, which had also led to the recruitment of the psychologist John Broadus Watson as a vice president three years earlier.[35] Like Watson, Steichen had a public reputation that transcended both advertising and his immediate field of proficiency. Indeed, Steichen was hired less because of his standing in the photographic industry than because of his artistic credentials. Like Watson, Steichen was brought in by agency president Stanley Resor and his codirector and wife Helen Landsdowne Resor, a former copywriter, who offered him yearly contracts between 1924 and 1931.[36] Steichen's jobs included portraits of women like Mrs. William K. Vanderbilt (fig. 4.3), which were often indistinguishable from his society portraits for *Vogue* but which served as celebrity endorsements for Pond's Cold Cream and Vanishing Cream. They also included elegant images of women's hands ironing clothes and dusting to sell Jergens Lotion (fig. 4.4).[37]

These images, although comparable in style to the work being produced by some of the leading commercial studios, presented a notable contrast to earlier advertising photographs. Instead of representing a face, figure, or object isolated from a background or visual context, Steichen's photographs were entire compositions, albeit sometimes cropped. In the Pond's advertisements, for example, they often depicted celebrities in their sumptuously decorated homes. The image formed a discrete, self-sufficient formal unit within the advertisement and often had equal

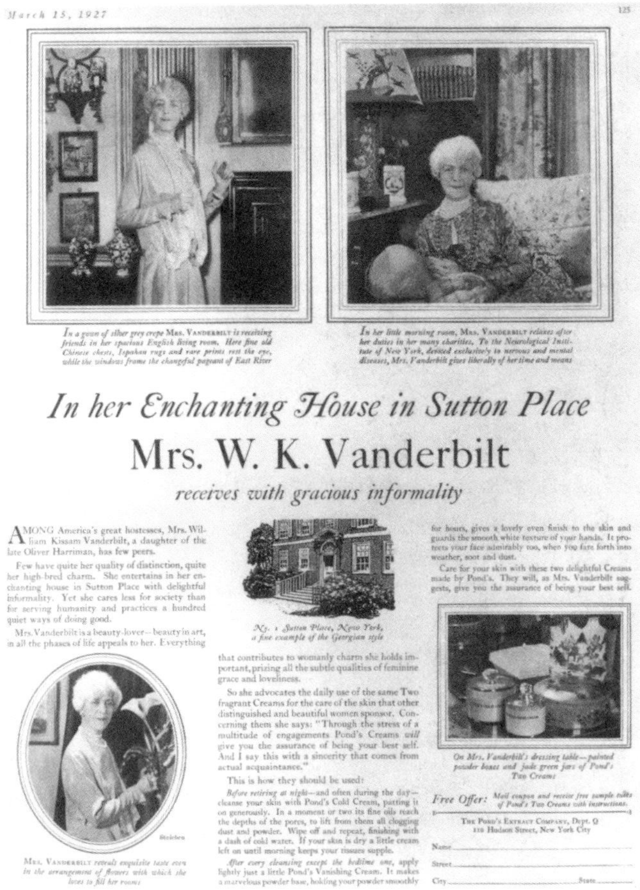

4.3. Advertisement for Pond's® Extract Company, Edward Steichen, photographer, 1927.

standing with the text. The pictures had a wide and rich gradation of tones and were much more three-dimensional in appearance than the majority of advertising photographs. Forms might be crisply defined or softer in focus, depending on the product, but the appearance was clearly a function of the photographer's artistic and technical decisions.

Through these photographs, along with his fashion pictures, Steichen meshed the practices of artistic, portrait, and commercial photography. His achievement resulted not only from his superior artistry, but also from his ability to capitalize on his reputation.[38] At the same time, his success was also a function of his irreverent attitude toward art

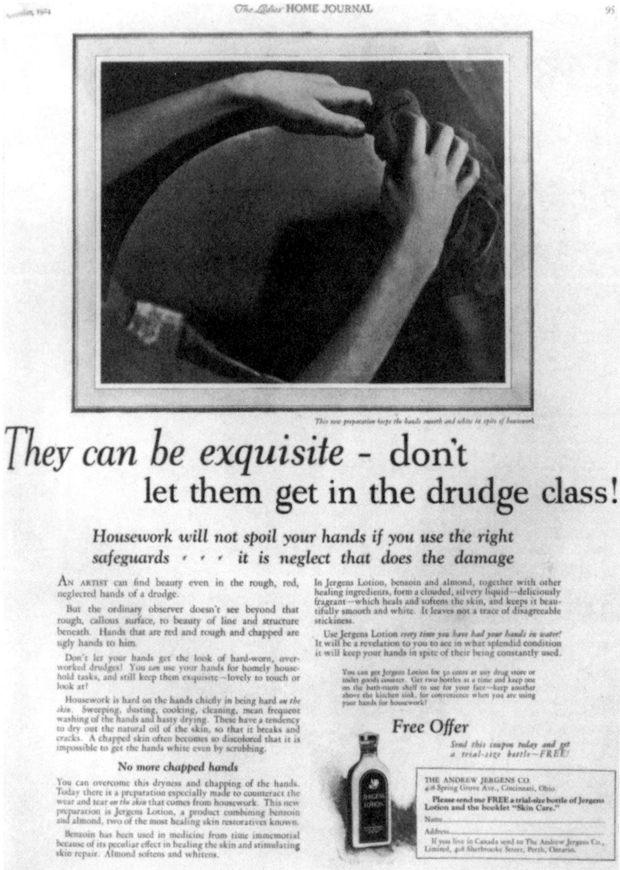

4.4. Advertisement for Jergens Lotion, Edward Steichen, photographer, 1924. This elegant and deceptively simple composition evoked (quite intentionally) an ideal of leisured beauty not normally associated with the "drudgery" of dusting.

and his receptive stance toward advertising, positions that jibed with the concerns of many clients and advertising people. They knew that for the right sum of money, this photographer could provide them with masterful images to help sell their products.

Steichen's own reputation within the framework of advertising might be secure, but, he believed, his situation was still exceptional. Advertisers and art directors remained too tentative about the worthiness of photography, and did not take photographers seriously enough. Unaware of its potential, too many believed photography to be literal and mundane. They were inadequately informed about the complexity of photographic representation and about what photography might mean in the context of advertising.

In a series of published and unpublished talks and interviews, Steichen took it upon himself to set the record straight. He did so by engaging with the aesthetic issues currently being debated in-house at J. Walter Thompson and in the advertising trade press. Banking on the authority of his art reputation, he aimed to show the centrality of photography as a paradigmatic mode of representation in advertising.

Steichen presented his case in a most belabored fashion to representatives of the creative staff at J. Walter Thompson. Its people were at the cutting edge of discussions about photography, illustration, modern art, and their role in advertising. Steichen's strategy for upgrading the work of photographers was to turn the relationship between art and advertising on its head. In the first place, he told the Thompson creative staff, the very notion of art itself was ambiguous. Given this condition, it was misguided to draw a hard-and-fast aesthetic distinction between fine art and commercial art. Indeed, Steichen suggested, any artist working on commission was really a commercial artist. Even the Old Masters were like advertising artists, insofar as neither group of artists was entirely free and independent. "There has never been a period that the best thing we had was not commercial art. If there ever was a poor harassed artist, more so than Michelangelo," he mused tongue-in-cheek, "I never heard of him, thrown on this kind of work and never being able to do what he thought he wanted to do himself."[39] So much for the romantic myth of the isolated, autonomous fine artist.

Having debunked the ideal of the artist, Steichen then went on to position photography on an equal aesthetic plane with painting by seemingly dismissing the importance of art. Given this confusion about the nature of art, he continued, who could say for certain whether photography was or was not an art form? "I have often been asked whether photography is an art. If 90% of the paintings in the Metropolitan Museum are art, then photography is an art." But, he went on, deliberately muddying the issue, "I don't feel that way about things in the Metropolitan Museum." Thus, it appeared, much museum art was not art, and therefore, neither was photography—or did it really matter? "Why worry?" Steichen had stated earlier, in 1923.[40]

In Steichen's view, advertisers and artists needed to get their priorities straight. It was irrelevant whether his or anyone else's photographs or paintings were art. Instead of worrying about matters of typology, or romantic ideologies of aesthetic autonomy, advertisers and art directors should concern themselves with whether process effectively served purpose. "Setting down and getting the thing whether with paint and brush or with the camera cannot be called creation," Steichen insisted (in a generalized invocation of the rhetoric of Deweyan pragmatism). The engineer, after all, was "a creator—he does not create for aesthetic purposes but for utilitarian purposes. . . . Just because a man happens to be very good as a painter once in a while does not make him a creator."[41] Advertisers should value creative excellence. Work created for utilitarian purposes could be creative, whereas freely produced work created for purely aesthetic purposes might not necessarily be truly artistic. Very little artistic production was actually art, and conversely, just because a work was fashioned for commercial purposes did not disqualify it as art. This was as true for photography as it was for painting. Both could be artistic and serve the purposes of advertising, if properly conceived.[42]

Steichen set out to make his case for using photographs in advertising and for treating the photographer as an expert professional. In fact, he acknowledged, one of his goals was to find a way of "worming" photography into the choice advertising accounts and "worming the art fellows out."[43]

Steichen's method of shutting out the "art fellows" was to link the photographic image with a notion of superior objectivity, one that effectively collapsed the categories of realism and idealism. Insofar as advertisers wanted objective representation, he stated, photography was the best means of achieving such an end. Insofar as "we paint and imitate and copy, why not use the means which does that logically?"—the camera. At the same time, Steichen insisted, advertisers should not take the realism of the photograph for granted, for "you can have objectivity in many ways."[44] Objectivity could be rendered by a variety of visual methods and it could mean different things. It could be construed in expressive and psychological, as well as visual, terms. Hence the goal of the advertising photographer was not just to freeze an arbitrary slice of life but to fashion a highly selective (idealized) representation of life and endow it with "aliveness"—a quality Steichen evoked through a vignette of mundane existence as advertising men often construed it: "To show the difference between a young lady coming home from work, says she has a headache, is bored, mother wants her to do something, maybe wash dishes, so tired—telephone rings and it's Bill, wants to go to movies—and it's all gone. That's the quality of aliveness." Advertisers should think not in terms of pictures but "in terms of reality."[45]

In the particular example just cited, "reality" was not just an image but also an emotion, a feeling of innervation. The iconicity of the photograph—its resemblance to external appearances—made it the most suitable medium for representing this reality, this gendered fantasy of life as man's invigorating presence. Such challenging objectives could be achieved only by creative means, and not just by anybody. Advertisers should thus commission more photographs and delegate full responsibility to the photographer. Only the photographer had the expertise to endow the image with life. That task involved skillful arrangement of objects and light. The earlier photographic practice of retouching images to make them look better or more realistic was out of the question; so too was the process of heavily retouching and recombining images, still being used to acclaim, for example, by Lejaren à Hiller.

> The photographic way of doing an ad is not the easy way to do it. It is the most complicated way. You have to do a great deal of work. It's objective and don't think you can fake it. Photographs patched and pasted together won't work. They may get by the elevator man, but the result is flat. And don't—don't ever pay me $500 for a picture and then pay someone $10 to touch it up. The air brush spells ruin.[46]

Despite Steichen's insistence upon creative autonomy and the uniqueness of his craft, he presented himself as the quintessential commercial artist and professional photographer, ready and willing to carry out his tasks. "It is my business," he stated, "to get enthusiastic about everything I do."

> If you come to me with a proposition of some kind and I can get enthusiastic about it, I am off. Someone comes in to me to be photographed. Unless I get enthusiastic about it, I cannot do anything with the person. . . .
>
> In portraiture, I have to use extreme measures sometimes—occasionally make a fool of myself, which works well, and sometimes make a fool of the person by making him angry. . . .
>
> When I am doing something for you, I have got to consider myself and the person in charge of the account, and the entire background behind the account.[47]

In discussing his identity and his relationships with clients, Steichen again sought to dissociate himself from the idea of art; he claimed that such a notion was too closely associated with a tradition of producing useless, expensive goods for an limited, elite few. Instead, Steichen presented an image of himself as a picture-maker for a new mass audience, made possible by the print media's expansion.

> When I was putting my soul on to canvas, and wrapping it up in a gold frame, and selling it to a few snob millionaires, who could afford it—after I got to thinking about it, I did not feel quite clean. But now I have an exhibi-

> tion every month that reaches hundreds of thousands of people through editorial and advertising pages.[48]

"What I'm trained for is making pictures," he told an interviewer in 1932. "At least I belong to my period."[49] Steichen conceived of his era as one marked by the cultural ascension of photographers and the diminished influence of rarified, romanticized, elitist artistic practices, knowing at the same time that art was the source of his leverage.[50]

Certainly Steichen made no apologies for what he was doing. "The greatest thing I've done for photography," he boasted in 1932, was to raise prices. Steichen had transformed photographs into high-priced commodities, much like coveted works of art.[51] For many photographers, then, Steichen's accomplishments were far more than just aesthetic. He had succeeded in convincing top advertising executives that his pictures were as effective vehicles of persuasion as advertising paintings, if not actually more so. Yet he also won over advertisers to the idea that photography was equally creative and inspired, and thus worth top dollar. Other photographers had also made headway in these areas, but Steichen's endeavors altered the very identity of photography and the photographer. By virtue of his special position he was able to insert photography unequivocally into discussions of advertising representation. His career collapsed the discrepancies between amateur and professional, portrait and commercial photographer, and photographer and artist. In leveling such occupational and identity differences, Steichen enabled advertising photographers to attain greater prestige and visibility.

Clarence White

The J. Walter Thompson agency was one of the leaders in advertising photography in the 1920s. In addition to their work for Pond's and Jergens, the agency was behind the highly successful campaigns for Fleischmann's yeast, which also used photography.[52] The agency's interest in photography was no doubt spurred in the first place by the promotional and educational activities of photographer Clarence H. White (fig. 4.5) in the late 1910s and early 1920s.[53] White, like Steichen, started at the periphery, as a grocery clerk and amateur photographer in Newark, Ohio. He too moved into pictorialism and was a founding member of the Photo-Secession in 1902.[54] White became a professional photographer in 1904. For a time he, like Steichen, fluctuated between amateur pictorialist and professional portraitist values, between high- and middle-class cultural activity and aspirations. Unlike Steichen, however, he also oscil-

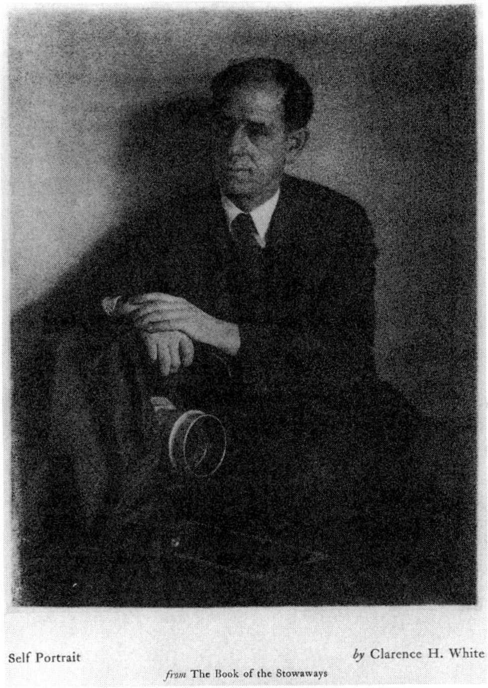

4.5. Clarence White, *Self Portrait,* n.d.

lated between the social and geographic periphery and the center. In fact, White helped to bridge them, both as a photographer and as an educator, but perhaps even more as an organizer.

Quitting his job as a bookkeeper in 1904, he traveled through the central Midwest, Pennsylvania, and West Virginia, doing mostly portraiture. A move to New York City in 1906 enabled him to interact more regularly with the Photo-Secessionists. At the same time, he continued to work as a professional photographer, and in 1907 (after the birth of his third child), as a commercial photographer who shot the homes of rich Newporters for the mass-market magazine *Everybody's.* He also taught courses at Teachers College. In 1910, White broke with Stieglitz over the latter's artistic policies.[55]

In 1914, White opened his own school of photography at 230 East Eleventh Street in New York City, an expansion of a summer school he began earlier in Maine, the first of its kind. The school's innovative curriculum bore the imprint not only of White, but also of Teachers College art professor Arthur Wesley Dow (who had hired White as a lecturer in 1907 and who himself was an amateur photographer) and painter and school cofounder Max Weber, a former Dow student. Their art and aesthetic theories emphasized the emotional force of formal principles of design—space, texture, and tone—over the rendering of specific motifs, narratives, or feelings. White and Weber transposed their interests into a pedagogy of photographic experimentation: students were assigned problems that encouraged them to seek solutions through varied modes of composition, lighting, or printing. In addition, students in the 1920s could attend lectures on aesthetics, the psychology of art, and the art of the cinema.[56]

Influenced by Dow's teachings, the White curriculum also espoused the application of artistic principles to utilitarian objects and the breakdown of distinctions between arts fine and applied. Students were thus not discouraged from applying their talents to commercial ends. Many of White's students became leaders in the field of advertising photography. This core group included Anton Bruehl, Margaret Bourke-White, Paul Outerbridge, Ralph Steiner, and Margaret Watkins.[57] As several of these photographers later acknowledged, the White school prepared them to branch out in different creative directions; it gave them freedom to break away from soft-focus pictorialism and to explore new modes of imaging objects. The positive outcome of this experimentation was a factor that attracted postwar advertisers to the work of these individuals.[58]

But it was through White's activities as organizer and promoter that art directors and advertisers became aware of these photographers' works in the first place. Specifically, White's involvement with Pictorialist Photographers of America and with the Art Center helped form an institutional framework that further narrowed the gaps separating amateur, professional, portraitist, commercial, and advertising photographers. The Pictorialist Photographers of America, founded in 1916 as a spinoff from the New York–based Photo-Secession and the Los Angeles Camera Pictorialists, promoted the art of photography. It was a nationwide group admitting both amateurs and professionals and ostensibly uniting photographers in metropolitan and regional locales. The organization had chapters in seventeen states and published a yearbook.[59] White was a cofounder and the first president.

In 1921, the Pictorialist Photographers established headquarters at the Art Center. This base in New York gave their members the advantage of direct social and professional proximity to art directors, their sources of patronage. As early as 1917, the Pictorialist Photographers plugged advertising as an area offering many opportunities, especially for producers of "the very best kind of photographs." Through their exhibitions at the

Art Center, the Pictorialist Photographers continued these efforts, playing up the potential of artistic advertising photography, by White students in particular.[60] For example, the group devoted one-man exhibitions to former White students Paul Outerbridge (March 1924) and Anton Bruehl (December 1926), thus presenting their work as especially suitable for commercial purposes. With *Vogue* art director Heyworth Campbell (a close friend of White's) serving as president of the Art Directors Club at that point, it is not surprising that the work of these photographers increasingly showed up in the advertising pages of such magazines as *Vanity Fair, Vogue,* and *The New Yorker* (figs. 4.6, 4.7).[61]

If these White students succeeded as a consequence of their creative techniques, they also flourished because of White's and their own promotional skills. As Ralph Steiner recalled, he was driven to advertising and commercial work by the need to survive. Unlike many of the earlier pictorialists, women and men like Bourke-White, Watkins, Steiner, and Steichen were neither amateurs nor independently wealthy. For this generation, Stieglitz's fine art ideal of leisured creativity seemed unfeasible.

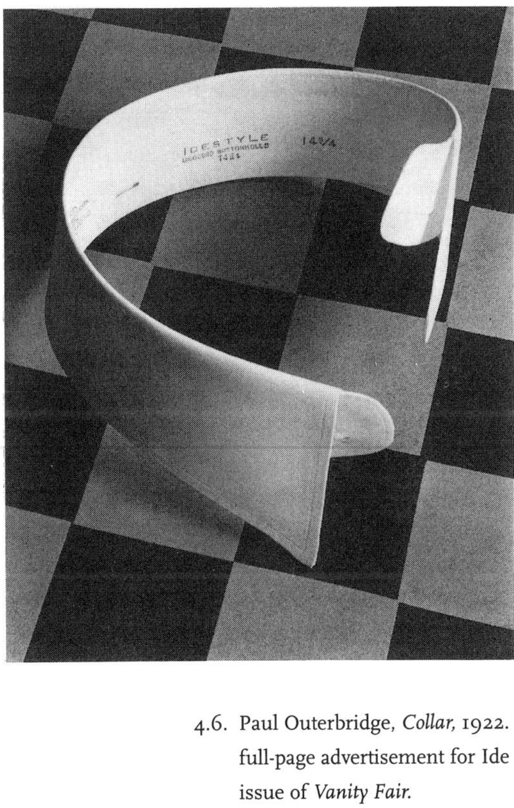

4.6. Paul Outerbridge, *Collar,* 1922. This photograph dominated a full-page advertisement for Ide Collars in the November 1922 issue of *Vanity Fair.*

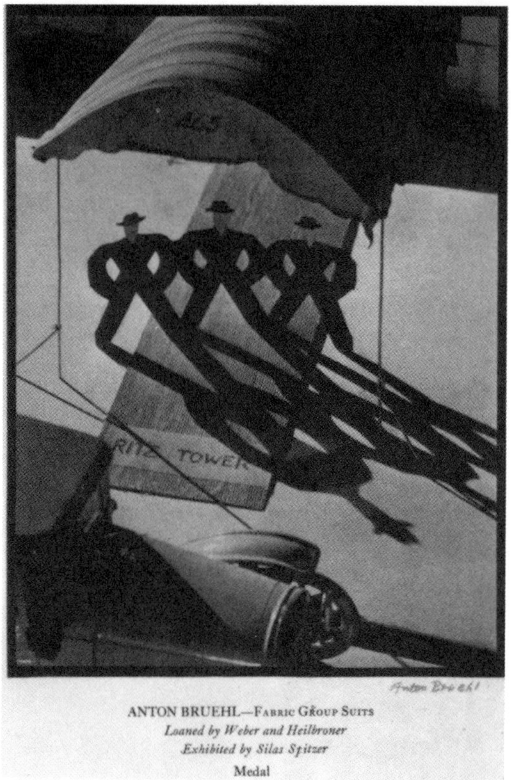

4.7. "Fabric Group Suits," advertisement for Weber and Heilbroner, Anton Bruehl, photographer, 1927.

These were practical people who needed to do well.[62] Talent and innovation helped, but their connections with artists, socialites, and business people in New York inner circles also did not hurt.

The New Advertising Photography: Bending the Truth

Advertisers were attracted to the modernist and consciously artistic devices pioneered by Steichen and this new young group. Their methods included sharply angled views and closeups, bird's-eye perspectives, dramatic plays of light and shade, careful arrangement of objects in patterns, and "painstakingly staged" miniature props (or people) to create illusionistic tableaux (fig. 4.8).[63]

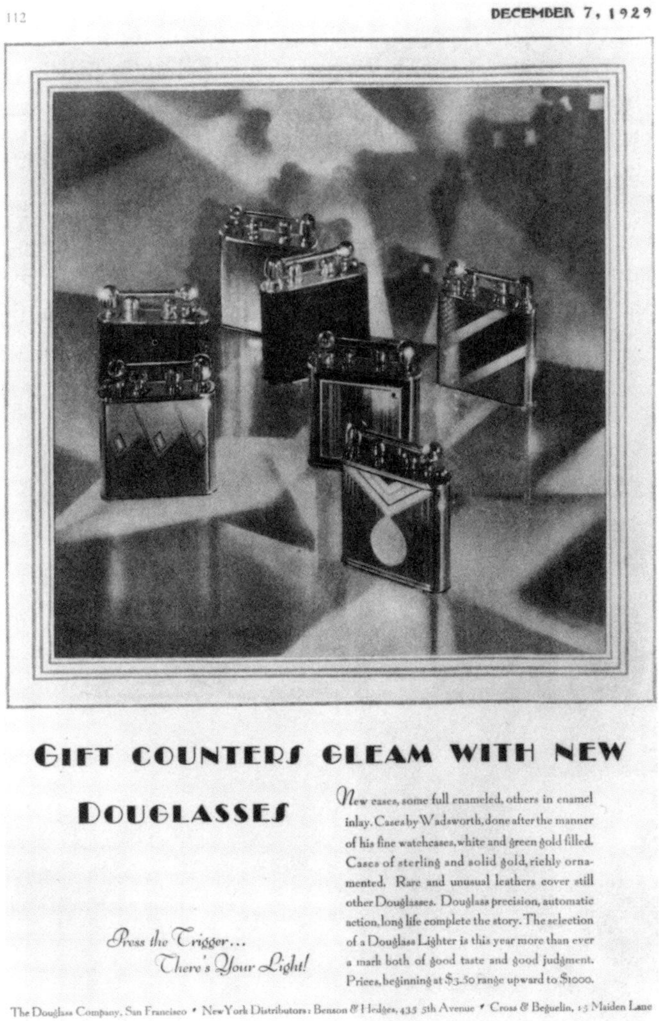

4.8. Advertisement for Douglass Lighters, Edward Steichen, photographer, 1929. For all Steichen's anti-art posturing, he remained committed to the sophisticated, modernist photographic styles that he helped to pioneer. In this advertisement, objects, light, and shadow are ingeniously arranged in a cubist composition, in which the "gleam" of reflection and play of surface patterns conjure up the "light" of the Douglass product and its flickering fire.

The counterpart to these avant-garde–influenced visions was the range of highly stylized and deceptive realisms conjured up by Steichen, Bruehl, Outerbridge, and others like Lejaren à Hiller, William Shewell Ellis, and Horace W. Scandlin; they used close-ups, deft manipulations of light and shade, and, often, posed models to achieve their effects.[64] In some cases, the image referred only obliquely or metaphorically to the commodity itself, as with Steichen's disembodied image of hands dusting or peeling potatoes, or Bruehl's tableau of artists and model (fig. 4.9; see note 65 on page 364 for an extended discussion of this illustration). In

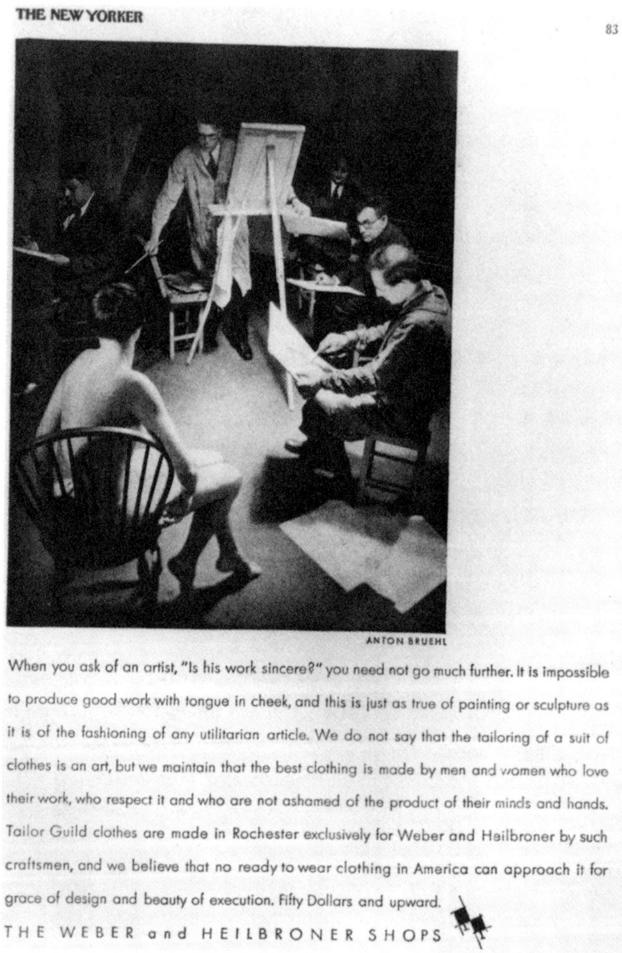

4.9. Advertisement for Weber and Heilbroner Shops, Anton Bruehl, photographer, 1929.

these cases, the transparent "realistic" signifiers of truth and "sincerity" directed beholders' attention and complemented the explanatory copy. Indeed, Bruehl's image for Weber and Heilbroner alluded quite explicitly, if tongue in cheek, to the dialectic between sincerity and artifice, both in the case of photography versus painting and that of art versus advertising—a tension of which Bruehl was clearly conscious.[65] Such realisms, in the words of historian Jackson Lears, "sanitized" the "messy actualities of human experience," or animated "the inanimate commodity with the appearance of life" (Steichen's "aliveness"), and even endowed the goods with "magical powers." In turn, these methods seemed to suggest that, as critic Miles Orvell has stated, "there was some defect in everyday reality that had to be remedied by the more authentic reality," the commodity.[66]

Bruehl, Hiller, and Ellis, among others, often employed such strategies in photographs of food, which, according to consumer marketing studies, people preferred to resemble the real thing. Even here, however, appearances were deceptive: ice cubes could be glass; water, cellophane; beer foam, soap bubbles.[67] The camera did lie, as its spokesmen constantly acknowledged. Nevertheless, as Steichen predicted and as present-day scholars have confirmed, the "truth of surface" and sincerity of effect connoted by photography proved to be "one of advertising's most effective stratagems."[68] Many photographers followed Steichen in using "straight" photography to connote believable, if contrived, appearances.

Periphery

The work that resulted as a consequence of these photographers' metropolitan ties provided inspiration to those on the margins. For the activities of Steichen, White and his former students, and other leading practitioners like Ellis and Grancel Fitz (fig. 4.10) were not lost on the spokesmen for the photographic industry at large, most of whom were not New York City–based, but had been experimenting with new approaches and organizational structures. As a result of these developments, which brought about altered relations between portrait and commercial photographers, more professionals were becoming actively involved in the field of advertising photography. Understanding the structures and individual enterprises of the industry at large will provide insight into how photography superseded illustration. These circumstances highlight the role of organizational as well as individual action in shaping ideologies and practices of representation. Moreover, once photography had "taken the lead," so to speak, it raised new questions about the interrelated discourses of art and persuasion, and about ongoing efforts to

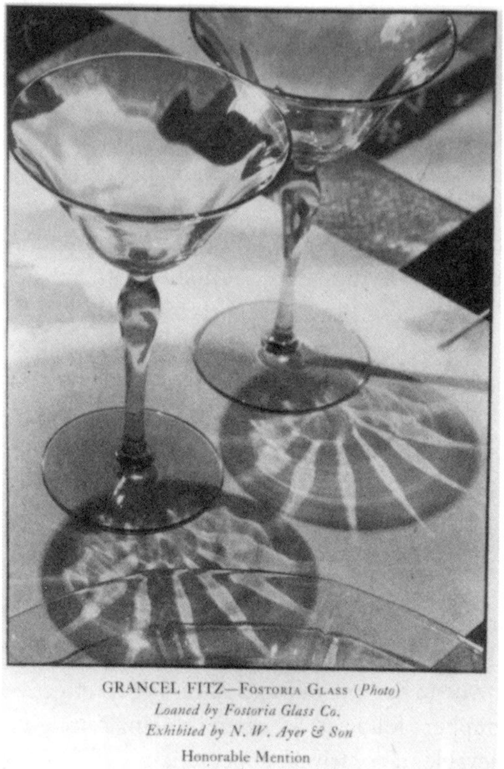

4.10. Advertisement for Fostoria Glass, Grancel Fitz, photographer, 1927.

demarcate artistic identity within the spheres of easel painting and commercial illustration. In particular, photography further confused the complex and contradictory impulses of realism and artifice, imitation and authenticity, that were already such debated descriptive and experiential categories in high art and drawn or painted publicity.

Even before World War I, the portrait industry was in considerable disarray, suffering from a glut of practitioners, too much competition, and wildly fluctuating prices.[69] The sphere of commercial photography, on the other hand, was coming into its own. These trends continued after the war. After a brief depression in the early 1920s, industrial output and national wealth rose considerably, largely as a result of increased production of cars and other consumer goods. These conditions contributed to an expanded field of commercial photography. Advertising for the print media now formed one segment of this enterprise.

These changes were reflected in the structure of the Photographers' Association of America. By 1920 the commercial members of the PA of A were numerous enough to form a separate commercial section. The group was originally subordinate to the portrait section. However, because of its breadth of scope and the activism of its leadership, the commercial photographers' group gradually acquired considerable clout within the organization, and even its own magazine, *Commercial Photographer,* published by Juan Abel's son Charles.[70] *Abel's Photographic Weekly,* which remained devoted to portraiture, maintained the primary link to the national organization. But both *Commercial Photographer* and *Abel's Photographic Weekly* continued the crusade Abel had begun to demonstrate to art directors and advertisers the advantages of photography.[71]

Photographers had worked in magazine advertising prior to the war with little fanfare. In the early 1920s, professionals were becoming more attuned to the possibilities at hand in advertising photography. In part motivated by old rivalries, they quickly became concerned with staking a claim to this field of endeavor. As earlier, some professionals perceived amateurs as a primary obstacle.

Amateurs also saw possibilities for doing advertising photography. At war's end, professionals, especially portrait photographers hurting for business, noted that more amateurs were getting into commercial photography and even turning boldly entrepreneurial. Spokesmen for the amateur journals encouraged these activities. As one commentator observed, "Many amateurs doubtless have pictures in their possession that possess distinct advertising value for, very often, an experienced advertising agent can see possibilities in a picture made without any thought of its being used as an advertisement."[72] This writer recommended that amateurs work through an agent; another suggested selling photographs directly to manufacturers.[73] Amateurs were reassured that this new shift by no means implied deserting the cause of art. "Perhaps I have failed to acquire the true artist's spirit, which requires that one think only of 'Art for Art's sake,'" wrote one spokesman in *American Photography,* "but to me art and making money are not incompatible. On the contrary, one's art may help to make money, and the making of money through it gives a better impetus to the study of art."[74]

Indeed, amateurs, some of whom may have tapped into White's Pictorialist Photographers of America network, saw advertising photography as a potentially lucrative venture. The success of Steichen, Outerbridge, Scandlin, Watkins, and others provided one impetus. Articles in amateur journals like *American Photographer* also pushed the possibilities, telling readers that the advertising pages offered a highly specialized field that "demanded original and telling ideas" and paid well—$25–$1,000 per picture, if "at all good."[75] The emergence of commercial photography as a field ensconced between amateur and professional practices added a new twist to the contest between them. Previously, the competition was mostly for status. Now there was a financial component.

Professionals were not pleased to see this development. Amateur incursions in the early 1920s prompted them to move more actively into the commercial arena and to become more vocal about their expertise. Commercial photographers were not the only ones to promote their services. The achievements of men like Steichen indicated that advertising was a growth field that could accommodate portraitists. Meanwhile, the portrait business slackened further.[76] Responding to these circumstances, Juan Abel, still primary advocate for the portraitists, now downplayed his earlier emphasis on organizational unity in favor of self-promotion and sales. Greater column space was devoted to the concerns of the "commercial man," and Abel's editorial columns urged portraitists to retool and move into areas like advertising. Many followed his advice.[77]

The task for the Abels and the PA of A was to attain for the rank and file a centrality comparable to what Steichen and White's students were already achieving among the art directors of the leading advertising agencies. Such goals required varied tactics, which both diverged from and intersected with those of Steichen.

Steichen's accomplishments were predicated on complicating the distinctions between amateur, pictorialist, portraitist, and commercial photographer. The average photographer, on the other hand, sought to maintain distinctions between amateurs and professionals, and between portraitists and commercial people. This division allowed the portrait and commercial sectors to mount publicity campaigns on their separate behalfs. Portraitists maintained their old anti-art stance, claiming that theirs was a business of capturing likeness, not an interpretative artistic act. Commercial photographers sought to imitate Steichen and break down the boundaries between art and life, commerce and art.[78] Such methods, they hoped, would enable them to attain higher status and more work outside as well as inside the major cities.

Advertising Photography

In the mid- to late 1920s, commercial photographers affiliated with the PA of A were in a position to begin a crusade to supplant advertising illustration. They did so as part of a larger effort to expand photographic occupations. Their efforts included a new summer class for commercial photographers that helped broaden PA of A influence among photographic businesses.[79] Commercial photographers' self-promotional enterprise culminated in 1927, when the PA of A launched a national service bureau and advertising campaign.[80] In conjunction with this project, advocates of photography joined Steichen to insist that photography offered both novelty and effectiveness in selling.

Spokesmen for photography used several strategies to push photography's advantages over illustration. First, they touted the medium's supposed new prominence in advertising as a fait accompli, even while admitting a need to "create a greater interest" in its use. "No longer an innovation or a novelty," proclaimed George Winemiller (a partner in the successful commercial New York studio Winemiller and Miller), "the studio which produces photographic illustrations for advertising has established itself as an institution of singular interest in achievement and latitude of service."[81] Once having "acknowledged" photography's preeminence, articles explained why it had come to the fore, providing the rationales to contest illustration's capability to represent both art and reality.

Commercial photographers lay claim to both these aspects of representation. Articles on the photograph in advertising now highlighted the art of photography, the very concern that professionals had disdained in the past.[82] While photography had once seemed an impersonal, mechanical medium, they observed, now it bore the stamp of individual personality. "The trouble with the commercial photograph of yesterday was its absolute lack of individuality," stated an unsigned article in *Abel's* in 1922. But "in the face of harsh criticism and the stubborn refusal of advertising to take it seriously, the art was progressing."[83] Today's photographers, both men and women, have "high spirit and genuine, deeply rooted convictions," wrote the observer in *Abel's*. "They are not mere photographers; they are indeed 'artists,' with the souls of artists and the artist's sensitiveness to subtlety, so essential to big things."[84]

The new photographers "react to light and shade, composition, the pulse beat of a picture-story, 'good drawing' as applied to models, form, sentimental values, proportion, perspective, as does the most serious painter in his studio. They literally 'paint' with the lens. The mere mechanical processes of 'taking a picture' are quite incidental."[85] It was the actions before and after that mattered. But for the absence of brush marks, these photographs could "easily be mistaken for original paintings." Indeed, the author noted, rhetorically appropriating the older amateur artistic enterprise, "although not gifted, perhaps, with the ability to draw, these experts are in every respect true professional idealists."[86] The photograph readily combined idealism and realism, with no apparent contradiction.

Moreover, it was not merely photography's aesthetic qualities that made it superior to drawn and painted illustration. The photograph, argued its advocates, was not just artistic, it was more realistic; it seemed more truthful and believable. As Temple Scott put it in a commercial supplement to *Abel's*, "a pictorial advertisement must be realism with just that touch of idealism in it that will make it arresting and pleasurable, and . . . this kind of realism can best be produced by a photographer who knows how to use his camera."[87] For the advertisers' purposes, Scott insisted, the photograph far excelled text in informing the consumer about the product. Copywriters might get carried away with their rhetoric and thereby distract or mislead. "The photographer is not so liable to ensnare you on the horns of this dilemma—his camera will not permit him to lie."[88]

When it came to advertising, moreover, the photograph's unique mode of figuration had significant additional advantages over illustration. It could express individual feelings and bear the imprint of a creative process. Yet unlike drawn or painted imagery, it was not so personal as to draw attention away from the advertised product. As Scott described it:

> You have a piano player [player piano] to sell, and you desire to present that commodity so that people will be moved to buy it. All piano players are much alike in appearance, and the same story can be said of all. Well, you commission an artist to paint or draw something that will attract attention. Now, the best artist who will lend himself for that work is but a mediocre craftsman. You may explain to him the fine idea it has taken you months to elaborate, and his embodiment of it will fall woefully short of your vision. It must necessarily fall short. Were he even a genius, he has not your enthusiasm, and it is the enthusiasm that makes the thing 'go.' He may, if he be a genius, produce a beautiful and striking picture, and it will then serve as an end for itself, and not for you and your piano player.[89]

Even the best advertising artist was not good enough when compared with a photographer. Like Steichen, Scott argued that photographers could rouse more enthusiasm and produce more effective pictures. Referring back to the publishers' art poster dilemmas at the turn of the century, Scott reminded readers that too artistic an image might become commodified and fail as advertisement. Such photographs would be "like the exquisite posters by Cheret and Steinlen, a work of art for collectors to hoard, and for no one, who might want a piano player, to look at again. In other words, the journeyman artist fails because he has not done what you want, and the genuine artist fails because he has done what he himself wants."[90] Illustration was not the answer.

For Scott, the photograph, with its superior claim upon both art and reality, was the perfect amalgam of aesthetics and commerce for advertisers. The PA of A itself ultimately adopted a similar argument. "Sparkling," announced a 1929 PA of A advertisement in the trade journal *Printer's Ink.*

> "That is the story this photograph tells. . . . To even prosaic products they lend new beauty and allure. Photographs mingle romance and reality; present your wares exactly as they are; yet with a captivating charm that leads to bigger, quicker sales. Photographs are not discounted as the fanciful dream of the artist. They tell your story as an unprejudiced eyewitness."[91]

Illustrators, organizationally weak, did not seek to counter such claims to their territory. At least in the 1920s, they did not need to. Full-color illustrations by prominent illustrators still dominated the magazines.

For although photography had made great inroads into advertising during the decade, those in the center more than those on the sidelines experienced the successes. A limited number of big-name metropolitan photographers and studios still had a corner on the advertising market, especially among advertising agencies like J. Walter Thompson and Newell-Emmett.[92] Even in the late 1920s and early 1930s, the burden remained on those on the periphery to persuade advertisers and art directors to use their work.[93]

The relative marginality of the rank and file was confirmed by a nationwide survey of the entire photographic profession conducted by the advertising agency Erwin, Wasey, and Company and the research council of the Photographers Association, International. Their findings showed one-half of all photographers doing one-seventh of the "entire annual photographic business," while at the other extreme, one-seventeenth of the photographers accounted for one-fourth of the business. One-fourth of all photographers acquired six-tenths of the business.[94] The situation in photography clearly paralleled that in illustration: a core group of leaders still dominated both fields. Nevertheless, photographers' struggles to promote themselves did have some effect.

The depression, arriving soon after the Photographers' Association campaign, helped turn the tide of interest toward photography. With the economic collapse placing pressure on art directors not to take the risks of subtlety, but to sell bluntly, the "literalness" of straight photography became increasingly attractive (figs. 4.11, 4.12). Some photographers and art directors continued to use modernist devices such as montage, soft focus, and double exposure. Straight photography also became a crucial design element in the boldly modern, asymmetrical editorial layouts and bleed-edge pages (in which the image extended to the edge of the page) of class magazines *Vogue* and *Harper's Bazaar.* Such visual devices became increasingly common in advertising aimed at the higher end of the mar-

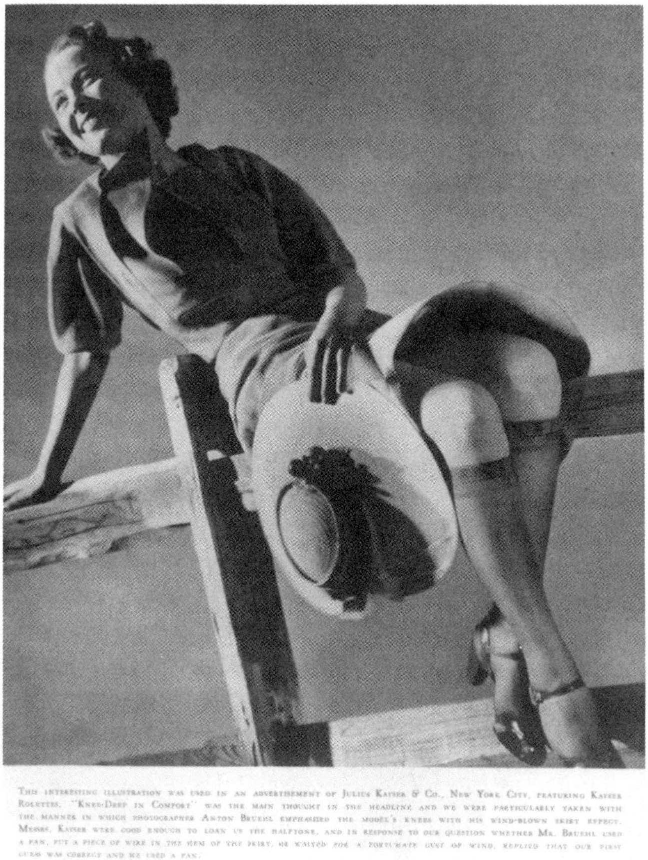

4.11. Advertisement for Julius Keyser and Company, Anton Bruehl, photographer, 1936.

ket in the 1950s and 1960s, by which time photography in advertising was commonplace. They were not, however, typical during the 1930s.[95] At the height of the depression, with clients anxious to produce immediate sales results, advertising photographers were cautioned to forgo being "arty" and to "evidence some return to sanity if the public, who do the judging in the final analysis, are not to lose entirely their fond impression that 'Photographs have Believability.'"[96] Whereas in the 1920s photographers and their spokesmen championed advertising photographs as works of craft and vision, in the 1930s many preferred transparent "sincerity," "realism," and drama (fig. 4.13).[97] One writer, Edwin Buxbaum,

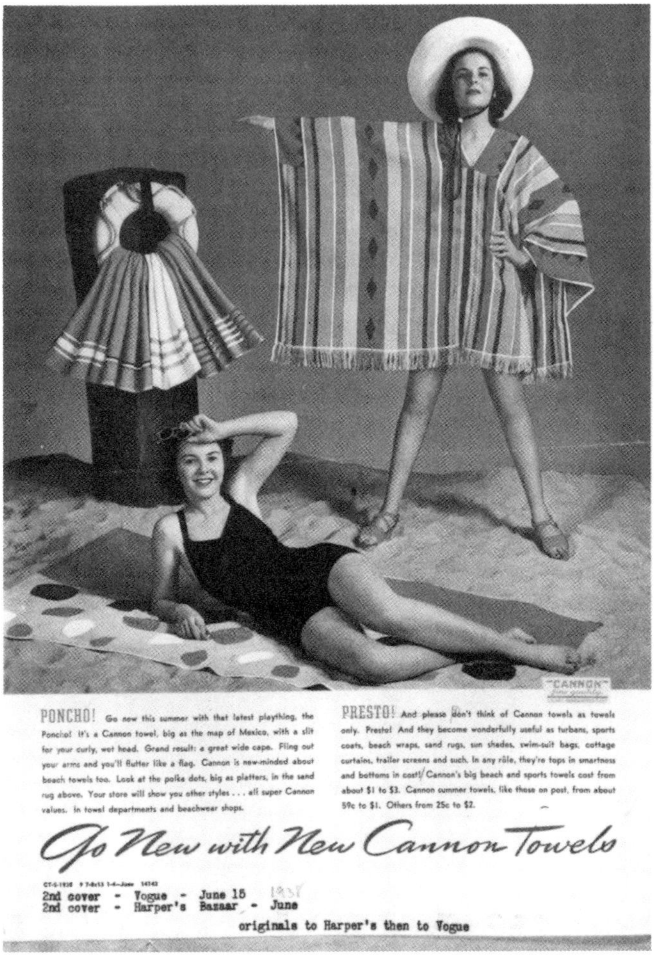

4.12. Advertisement for Cannon Towels, 1938.

described straight photography as part of the "new school of modernism," but in general, advertisers and their art directors played up realism and downplayed the associations with art.[98] Photographers, who had haggled for years to establish prices at a level high enough for them to survive, also managed to persuade advertisers that photographs were more convenient and cheaper than paintings.[99] Figures are hard to come by, but even leading photographers like Steichen, who insisted upon fees of $500 to $1,000 per picture, still received less per image than comparably prominent illustrators and painters.[100]

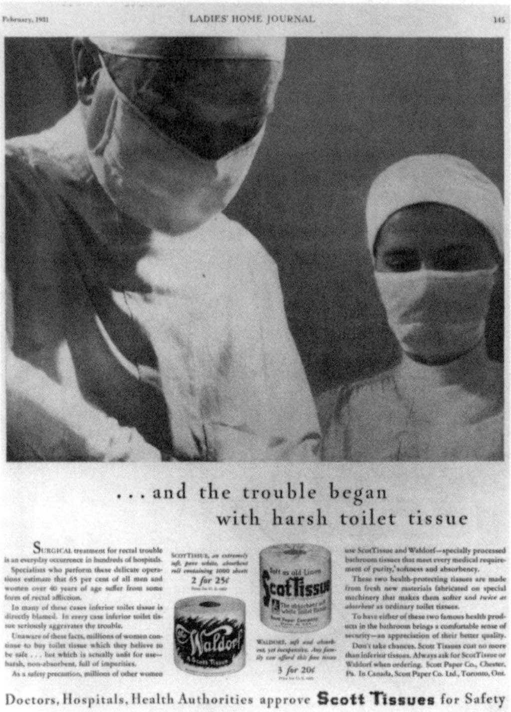

4.13. Advertisement for Scott Tissue, 1931.

Photographers' strategies worked. A 1932 Gallup survey of 4,000 magazine readers showed that most considered photography to be more effective than other forms of illustration. Cost-cutting improvements in production technology enhanced the quality of detail, tonal variation, and overall appearance.[101] Photography increasingly overtook illustration on the advertising pages of mass-market magazines. Roland Marchand has noted that photographs dominated the advertising pages of *Ladies' Home Journal* in 1932. According to other sources (unnamed), one out of four advertisements in one large-circulation magazine were illustrated by photography in July 1927, although only 5 percent of commercial photography was used for magazine advertising at that time. By October 1932, 80 percent of all printed page advertising was photography. The percentage had risen to 90 by 1935, and in the words of one smug spokesman in *Commercial Photographer*, "the life of the commercial artist and illustrator today is full of woe."[102]

If photographers superseded illustrators by successfully asserting their medium's virtue as a business *art,* they maintained their position by carving out a new, explicitly commercial niche that highlighted imitation over authenticity, realism over creation. Photographers excelled not by underscoring their works' stylistic idiosyncracies as forms of personal expression, but by positioning photographs as accessible, compelling, impersonally rendered pictures uniquely capable of capturing life. These circumstances were precipitated by the depression, but they soon converged with the new strategies of press and documentary photography, as seen in the magazines *Life,* begun in 1936, and *Look,* begun in 1937. With photojournalism the photographer was glorified as a "reporter."[103] Photojournalism exploited the instantaneousness of the photograph to represent the immediacy of an event and to create a myth of larger humanistic significance (see fig. 2.19). The picture would bear the primary meaning, with text being ancillary.

Documentary photography also received widespread attention during the depression through the government-sponsored Farm Resettlement Administration (later Farm Security Administration) programs and other New Deal projects already mentioned, which supplied thousands of pictures to publications like *Time, Fortune, Look, Literary Digest,* and the *New York Times.*[104] Documentary photography utilized the photographic image, seemingly in opposition to the enterprise of commercial photography, to represent "objectively" the myths of the American experience. Yet as recent scholars have shown, documentary photographers did not rely on the camera's impersonal mechanism. They relied upon specific photographic codes and devices (cropping, for example) to persuade viewers of the truthfulness of their representations. The social reconfirmation of photography as "factual truth" provided further incentive for advertisers to use it for public relations as well as advertising purposes.[105]

Amidst all of these changes, Edward Steichen continued to play a pivotal role in shaping the identity and stature of photography. He continued to promote a functional photography, withstanding attacks from the likes of Walker Evans, Lincoln Kirstein, Paul Rosenfeld, and Paul Strand, who carried Stieglitz's torch in seeking to enforce stringent boundaries between artistic and commercial photography.[106] Steichen had always maintained links both with the worlds of the art, advertising, and fashion establishment and with those of portrait and commercial photographers, giving technical talks and interviews, for example, to the PA of A, for whom he represented a high-status exemplar.[107]

Steichen continued his advertising work on into the 1930s. In the 1940s, however, he began a new career as Director of Photography at the Museum of Modern Art, where he replaced Beaumont Newhall, who, like Evans, Kirstein, and Strand, was a staunch advocate of a separate and exclusive realm of fine art photography. Many photographers and other advocates of the medium did not concur with attempts to ascribe greater value to some photographic enterprises than to others, and accused MoMA's Department of Photography of snobbism and elitism.[108] Top officials on the board of trustees, seeking a broader constituency and more funding for expansions, believed that Steichen was a better man to help them accomplish their goals.

At MoMA, Steichen continued to trace the contours of the photographic art. Yet Steichen's earlier disinterest in promoting photography as art had, if anything, become stronger. If he had once admonished photographers to avoid being too affected and "arty" and to cut down on the "drivel about art effects," he now claimed not to give "a hoot in hell" about photography as a fine art.[109] Instead, as Christopher Phillips has shown, Steichen concerned himself with photography's role as a medium of mass communication and persuasion. His curatorial work thus remained in keeping with his priorities and activities of the previous twenty years, and helped the museum gain the support of the photographic industry, which it had not enjoyed under Newhall.[110] With Steichen at the helm, the disparate segments of the institutional worlds of photography came together in agreement, at least until Steichen retired in 1962.

That consensus was reinforced at a rank-and-file level as well. The pages of *Commercial Photographer* and *Professional Photographer* (the former *Abel's Photographic Weekly*) concentrated on assertions of professionalism, expertise, and service, and dispensed with self-absorbed ruminations about artistic status or identity in general.[111] In 1950 the journals re-merged because, according to Abel, studios specializing exclusively in either portrait or commercial work had become a rarity.[112] Now that photography had displaced illustration, the means and ends of the portrait/commercial realms could be interchangeable. The categories of artist, commercial, and professional had for all intents and purposes collapsed as useful descriptions of identity for photographers in advertising.

chapter 5

Promotion and Painting

Painting and commerce have always been connected. Yet painting has conventionally been regarded as a bastion of artistic purity. Painters had little connection with advertising until the late nineteenth century. Then the situation changed markedly, and the two enterprises began to become aligned.

The same social factors that had broadened access to images in general—the growth of cities, the changing organization of work, the rise of commercial entertainment, the perfection of the halftone screen, and the growth of national advertising—produced shifts in career options, styles, and identity among artists who saw themselves primarily as easel painters. All the elements that precipitated the rise of the illustrator also modified painters' and advertisers' perceptions of their relations to a potential audience. Conditions were ripe, as never before, for interaction among painters and advertisers.

This chapter addresses the consequences of those changes. It examines painters' efforts to come to terms with the rising force of advertising under circumstances that offered a new range of career and aesthetic alternatives for many of them, but that also required dramatic shifts in ideology, aspirations, and practices. We shall explore these issues by focusing on individuals: in particular, we shall see how one ad man, Earnest Elmo Calkins (to whom I have already referred in chapters 1 and 2) articulated the cultural contribution of art in advertising, and how six painters reacted to the formidable commercial presence his ideas and activities represented. The artists selected all worked in a manner bound up in some way with advertising, either through career trajectory, modes of depiction and signification, or aesthetic principles. Taken together, their cases reveal a range of responses to the conflicts arising from the commercial presence, at a given moment or over time. The fragility and contingency of the historical category called "painting" is apparent when we examine artists' activities as formulations of commercial culture and as reactions to it. As this chapter will demonstrate, the persistence and ideological cohesion of the ideal of painting-as-ennobling-art itself owed much to the ascendancy of corporate business and of men like Calkins. The impact of corporate enterprise to which I am referring is not, however, primarily a matter of advertisers' appropriation of modern art and artists. Rather, in a very real sense, self-proclaimed painters framed their identities, activities, goals, and perceptions of their audience in terms of the expectations, practices, and publics defined by commercial discourses.

Initially, as we shall see in a comparison of advertising agency president Earnest Elmo Calkins and establishment mural painter Edwin Howland Blashfield, the ideals of advertisers and painters, previously distinct, began to converge; discursive asymmetries were not terribly pronounced. Advertising men like Calkins claimed to lift up the lives of ordinary people through consumerism; painters like Blashfield were reaching down to broad new constituencies. Furthermore, as I shall indicate through a discussion of Walt Kuhn and the Armory Show, the linkages and parallels between painting and publicity remained strong, even with the emergence of new artistic groups, styles, and attitudes whose modernist interests seemed at odds with those of Blashfield's generation. By the second decade of the twentieth century, however, advertisers and businessmen were increasingly setting the pace, and they were generally more flexible in outlook but socially more stable than painters. Painters, sometimes despite themselves, were following business's lead, but rarely enjoyed the same successes. Responding to conditions in the 1920s, artists like Walter Pach challenged the Calkins vision. Like some of the advertising men mentioned in chapter 3, who were unsympathetic to art directors' efforts to lay claim to art, Pach insisted that art and advertising could not be on familiar terms. His statements were indicative of a gap opening between artistic and commercial pursuits. The gap widened further, from Pach's standpoint, when business clients like Marcus and Company and Hupmobile, following up on Calkins's suggestions for improving art in advertising, joined forces with well-regarded painters like Rockwell Kent. Disputing Calkins's belief that, practically speaking, distinctions between fine art and commercial art often did not exist, Pach attempted to constrict conceptual boundaries in order to widen the differences.

To some degree, artists' perceptions were a consequence of ideological incompatibilities that the actors themselves often envisioned in aesthetic terms: as the clash between sincerity, freedom, and self-expression on the one side and false consciousness and crass commercialism on the other. Divisions also occurred because of paradoxes that emerged in the process of experiencing the numerous social and aesthetic convergences between art and commerce that we shall track throughout this chapter.

For painters like Stuart Davis (whose tobacco paintings confirmed with irony the Calkins vision of an interdependent art and advertising), Maxfield Parrish, and Rockwell Kent, such distinctions between fine art and commercial art seemed at times very real, at other moments inconsequential. Davis and Parrish had no problem reconciling these differences. They ultimately utilized them to personal advantage, although in divergent ways. Kent exploited the mechanisms of the commercial world, but in order to promote categorical distinctions that did have a certain minor effect on the relationship between painters and advertisers. Kent's usage of the category "commercial art" was inconsistent, and ultimately trapped him. One thing was clear, however: In contrast to the late nineteenth century, by the time of the 1929 Crash many easel painters identified their aesthetic interests as antithetical to those of business. Those who maintained this stance painted themselves into a corner with the arrival of the depression.

Earnest Elmo Calkins and the Confluence of Art and Advertising

At the turn of the century, as we have seen, the field of advertising was being reconfigured. In the world of commerce, advertising agencies were taking on the responsibility of producing their clients' advertisements, as they had done since the 1880s. Challenges awaited them. The immediate task was to create more effective advertising. This entailed improving advertising design. It also meant enhancing the reputations of advertising and advertisers. The new generation of advertising men had to make concerted efforts to rid the vocation of the questionable reputation it had acquired as a result of numerous misleading patent medicine promotions. By forming local clubs like the Sphinx Club (1898) and, later, national groups like the Associated Advertising Clubs of America (1904) (whose work culminated in the "Truth in Advertising" movement mentioned earlier), advertising men sought to establish standards of propriety in their work and to forge an image of advertising as an upright service profession managed by honest, self-regulating experts, responsible citizens. A number of them adopted the high-minded rhetoric of other professionals in order to protect themselves and to stave off attacks.[1] Art was enlisted as part of this process. Earnest Elmo Calkins (1868–1964) was at the center of it.

Calkins's appreciation of art and advertising evolved early in his career. It stemmed from a personal tragedy: his deafness, caused by a bout of measles at the age of six. Advertising and its visual images offered the bookish young man the challenge of communicating without hearing or speech. Advertising was a creative activity, yet it demanded business skills and an aptitude for personal interaction and politics. In short, advertising offered Calkins opportunities to test his capacities to overcome his disability. Advertising art, like copywriting, represented a crucial part of the communication process.[2] Calkins's insistence on the importance of art in advertising was more than crass puffery. His concerns with art enabled him to uplift himself and the reputation of advertising and, indeed, to make a real mark. Thus his activities were motivated by both commercial interests and personal convictions.

Calkins began putting his ideas into practice in about 1900. While working as a copywriter at the Charles Austin Bates advertising agency, he enrolled in a night course in applied design at Pratt Institute. The experience convinced him that good design was the key to effective advertising.[3] "Here was what advertising needed and lacked:" he later reminisced, "form, visualization, the attractiveness of color and design to strengthen its appeal to the eye."[4] If advertising could effectively adopt some of the bold renderings and technical expertise of contemporary illustration, posters, and painting, Calkins surmised, it might produce a real triumph for commerce. He proceeded to convince art manager George Ethridge (author of the column "Commercial Art" in *Printer's Ink*) to introduce "the poster idea, the eye-catching quality, into advertising art."[5]

Calkins continued the campaign after founding his own agency, Calkins and Holden (with Ralph Holden, who handled the managerial side of the business). First he brought in a staff of experienced designers to develop spare, tasteful, but compelling compositions. His team included Earl Horter (who had done lettering for Wanamakers), Walter Fawcett (known for his silhouette drawings), Walter Dorwin Teague (later famous as an industrial designer), and wood engraver Rudolph Ruzicka.[6] Then Calkins worked to lure "name" talent from magazine illustration to enhance the quality and status of the advertising image further. The 1908–1911 Art in Advertising exhibitions were part of this venture. Such efforts had questionable success, as we saw in chapter 1. Over the years, however, Calkins did secure the services of such prominent illustrators as Joseph C. Leyendecker, N. C. Wyeth, and Maxfield Parrish. The big, boldly designed advertisements produced by Calkins and Holden between 1905 and 1917 played an important role in changing the look of advertising: their style of imagery increasingly resembled that of academic illustration and painting. These affinities were most conspicuous in one of advertising's most famous early trade images, the Arrow Collar Man (fig. 5.1), created by Joseph C. Leyendecker for Cluett-Peabody and Company beginning about 1907.[7]

Highlighting image over copy, the Arrow Collar advertisements portrayed the vision of an ideal American, whose clean-cut features bore a noticeable resemblance to the young men rendered by such academic mural painters as Edwin Howland Blashfield. The similarities are not surprising, given the fact that Leyendecker and Blashfield had comparable artistic training in Parisian ateliers (Leyendecker at the Académie Julian with Bouguereau and Blashfield with Léon Bonnat). Moreover,

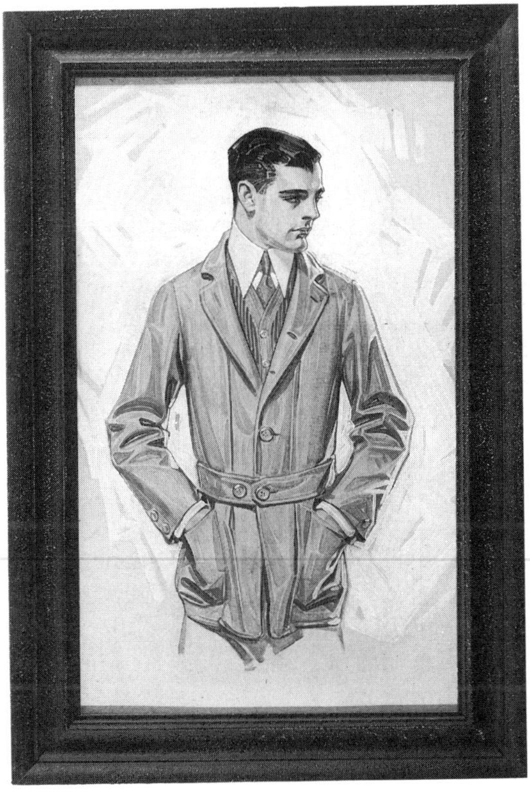

5.1. Advertisement for Arrow shirt, ca. 1912, illustration by Joseph C. Leyendecker.

Leyendecker himself had been invited to paint murals for the Boston Public Library and the New York Public Library; he declined in favor of advertising.[8] Suave, passionless, square-jawed, handsome, Anglo-Saxon, wealthy, and virile, the Arrow Collar Man was not necessarily supposed to appeal to everyone. Nor did he purport to represent all classes of people, or even his viewing audience. By definition, the advertised product was targeted at white-collar workers. Leyendecker's image was an accessible symbol of sophistication. For even the lowliest of clerks, it elevated the dignity of nonmanual work into an illusion of snobbish superiority. The Arrow Collar Man's attraction derived as much from his remoteness from the lives of ordinary people as from his stiffly starched collar. The Arrow Collar Man was an escapist fantasy; in his ideal perfection and psychological disengagement, he expressed the spirit of the modern and at the same time warded off its uncertainties. The image appealed to individual tastes and sensibilities, rather than trying to shape the collective moral will of the people like its counterpart in mural painting, which stressed nonmaterial social values. Yet Leyendecker's image suggested possibilities within its audience's actual reach. The artfully rendered Arrow Collar Man touched a chord, and sold many collars.

Art, as the consummate method of communication, became a critical element in Calkins's vision of advertising. In this he differed from contemporaries like ad man Claude Hopkins, who argued that fancy advertising images were elitist distractions, unattuned to the interests and tastes of the ordinary reader, and doomed to fail. Calkins vehemently disagreed. He felt that artistic advertising could be a democratizing force.[9] At the same time, he kept his sights within reasonable expectations, and focused on reaching a predominantly middle-class audience.

Calkins believed that high-quality images, like good copy, could make a big difference in sales (and, if the Arrow Collar advertisements were any indication, he certainly proved Hopkins wrong). Striking visual campaigns like the Arrow ads and other memorable ads for the Pierce-Arrow Motor Car Company and Wesson Oil (see fig. 3.2) won Calkins and his firm ongoing praise from other advertising people, especially art directors. Calkins and Holden became a frequent award winner after the Art Directors Club exhibits were initiated in 1921, and Calkins became widely respected as an important art advocate.[10]

For Calkins, such accolades were satisfying confirmations of his beliefs, but he never stopped proselytizing for the idea that art was central to modern society and to the commercial practices that shaped it. He continually attempted to impress upon artists and advertisers that their common and compatible interests constituted important aspects of a modern public culture.[11] Art was part of advertising's mission to inform consumers about products, to give assurances of quality, and to improve people's lives. But advertising could also serve as part of art's larger mission to enhance spiritual well-being.[12] Advertising, Calkins argued, provided an unprecedented opportunity to expose millions of people to fine works of art. Advertising art, reaching millions of people, was in effect the poor man's picture gallery. In showing the best, advertising served as an educational force. Art and advertising, in Calkins's view, were mutually reinforcing forces of uplift.[13]

Indeed, Calkins, more than just a copywriter and administrator, served as a cheerleader and publicist throughout his career. Although he articulated his values most vociferously and in greatest depth after World War I, he hinted at them earlier, as in his book *Modern Advertising,* coauthored with his partner Ralph Holden in 1905. Calkins and Holden advertisements were visible manifestations of Calkins's beliefs. On one level, to be sure, his efforts were self-serving and manipulative—as in the articles in which he praised his own art director (René Clarke) for his pioneering artistic innovations, insisted that business was a force in stimulating art, and proclaimed that the distinctions between commercial and fine art had dissolved.[14] On the other hand, Calkins was a pragmatist. His attitude was that advertising was here to stay, and that it might as well be good. His correspondence suggests that he truly believed that art for advertising was a genuinely meaningful form of expression, and that an advertising artist pushed to do his best made as worthy a contribution as any other type of artist. "Commercialism," he contended, had less to do with the ends to which art was to be put or the fact that the artist made money than with the creative *spirit* an artist brought to his work.[15]

Calkins could write in good conscience because he also subscribed to romantic beliefs. Like many artists, he held the view that artistic techniques (color, composition, and brushwork) were signifiers of individuality and sincerity. He regarded modern art as an expression of contemporary life, one that offered self-fulfillment for the artist and effective new modes of persuasion for the advertiser. Thus he wholeheartedly embraced the innovativeness and stylistic diversity of modernism.

In Calkins's view, the self-referential aspects of painting, especially modernist painting, could be used to advantage by advertisers. Images no longer necessarily had to illustrate copy anecdotally or hawk the product explicitly. Advertising could be more subtle and refined, less dependent on copy, because the image itself could be the primary mode of communication.[16] Like all art, art in advertising, when commissioned by supportive patrons (clients and art directors), would ostensibly be the expression of an individual creator. In theory at least, the means of expression alone, with its connotations of sincerity, could stand as a self-evident, self-sufficient statement of fact about the product.[17] The presence of art intimated that artist and client stood behind the product. Artists could enjoy the pleasures and challenges of creation, maintain their integrity, and still serve others through their work. Advertisers could not only minister to their clients but also contribute to art and society by using clients' money to commission fine works of art that might raise consumers' standards of taste and the quality of their lives. Advertisers would carry out their jobs with the knowledge that they were not vulgar and materialistic, and that their activity served a much higher cause than mere selling.[18]

In claiming to appeal to the best in his audience, Calkins kept his goals limited. He never denied the commercial motivation for his arguments. His target was middle-class "people of taste," and he was candid about it.[19] Calkins was not out to create unattainable desires among the have-nots, but to create a "favorable state of mind" in the consumer already inclined "toward the advertisers' goods."[20] Calkins's goals, limited and exclusionist from the outset, were thus more realistic than those of many of his artistic contemporaries.

Calkins set forth a transformed notion of art that responded directly to the new twentieth-century commercial structures. For better or worse, his ideas permeated the cultural fabric of American society as greatly as those of artists or art critics. To understand fully the values, activities, and images of American painters, we need to examine them in relation to the emerging commercial influence on art in general.

Edwin Howland Blashfield and Mural Publicity

In essence, Calkins regarded advertising imagery as a new form of public art. However, he was by no means the only one thinking about the subject. During the same period, at the turn of the century, a group of American painters were developing new career paths and new ideals for fine art in the form of large public murals. Many established critics and painters argued that murals, a truly public art, could express and advertise the ideals of the "race" more effectively than smaller-scale easel paintings. Part of the tendency self-consciously dubbed the "American Renaissance," the mural movement took off after the 1893 World's Columbian Exposition in Chicago, when large-scale murals were commissioned nationwide for federal, state, and municipal government buildings and schools.[21] At the core of the enterprise was a vision of murals as a force of social improvement, premised upon an ideal of professional service.[22] Mural art would stand as truthful, compelling renderings of the nation's vision of its past and ideals of its present and future. More than merely educating, they would inspire. "It is then on wall paintings, public and accessible to all," wrote muralist Charles M. Shean, "that we may most hopefully look for the development of a national art." "They tell to the people the story of the people," declared another commentator.[23] Mural painting, like billboards, was premised on the assumption that there was a broad new public of viewers.[24]

Comparisons between turn-of-the-century American mural painters and advertisers may seem outlandish. In fact, the ideals of the two groups converged in their common desire to reach an expansive new audience. Ultimately, however, advertisers were in a better position to make good on their promises. They could act more consistently in accord with their ideals of public service because of the particular audiences they targeted. The development of mural painting starts to look very different from the way it is usually conceived when it is examined in relation to new developments in advertising. We shall explore the affinities and disjunctions between the two fields concretely in the career of Edwin Howland Blashfield.

Blashfield was the ultimate establishment artist. Born in Brooklyn in 1848, he had studied for two years at the Boston Institute of Technology before traveling to France to study in the painting atelier of Léon Bonnat.[25] Blashfield had been elected an associate of the National Academy of Design and the Society of American Artists in the early 1880s. He had become a full member of the National Academy in 1888. In addition, Blashfield served on the National Commission of Fine Arts (appointed by President Taft in 1912), and as president of the Society of American Artists (1895–1896) and of the National Institute of Arts and Letters (1915–1916). He was awarded honorary degrees by Yale (M.A., 1914), Columbia (Litt.D., 1916), and New York University (D.F.A., 1926). By 1920, when he became president of the National Academy of Design (a post he held for six years), he had become one of the most powerful and venerable figures on the New York cultural scene.[26] He was the epitome of the patrician and genteel artist: "Charm was a characteristic of Mr. Blashfield in his personal relationships," noted the *New York Times* ruefully in his obituary. "A gallant gentleman," Harry W. Watrous eulogized him. "Tall, slender, aristocratic, he was quiet and modest, the soul of courtesy."[27]

Blashfield won the honors that he did largely as the result of his achievements in mural painting, an activity with which he had been involved since the early 1880s. The dome of George B. Post's Manufactures and Liberal Arts Building at the World's Columbian Exposition, Blashfield's first major commission, established his reputation as a muralist. From that point on, he spent much of his career working on civic mural projects. They included pictures for the Library of Congress, the Detroit

Public Library, and the courthouses of Newark, Jersey City, Madison, Youngstown, Rapid City, Baltimore, and Wilkes-Barre. Blashfield's experience with these projects strengthened his already strong position within the worlds of culture, business, and politics in New York and nationwide. This helped him to secure numerous private decorative commissions: panels for the Bank of Pittsburgh; the Lawyers' Club in New York; the library in the Philadelphia townhouse of G. W. C. Drexel; the supper room in the New York home of W. K. Vanderbilt; a room in the home of financier Adolph Lewisohn.

By mid-career, Blashfield had also become the nation's foremost spokesman and publicist for American mural painting. He set forth his ideals most comprehensively in his Scammon lecture series, delivered at the Art Institute of Chicago in 1912. Published in 1913 as *Mural Painting in America,* the talks highlighted the themes of accessibility, education, and accommodation, concerns that also set the standard for the illustrator and artist in advertising. Just as advertising men like Calkins saw themselves as striving to upgrade the consumer's taste and lifestyle, the muralists regarded themselves as reaching down to raise up the public. Like the artist in advertising, the mural artist had to "repress," even "sacrifice," himself to ensure the success of his project. If one "collaborator" tried to "make himself conspicuous by the display of a more forcible personality than that of his fellow," he became "dangerous—virtuosity, a quality desirable *per se,* may swell into a disturbing note."[28] The artist had to experience this personal and professional hardship in order to serve his public; the public, after all, was "as essential to the creation of art as is handle to blade; it drives and enforces the purpose of the artist."[29] The results would be worth the trouble. They would serve as valuable educational forces that would enhance not only the life of the individual but also the well-being of the nation as a whole.[30]

If such virtuous principles failed to convince his readers of the merits of murals, Blashfield was willing to appeal to other, more "corrupt" interests, assuring his readers that there were good pragmatic reasons for such works. Mural art (like advertising) might serve financial interests as well. Art, Blashfield reminded readers, encouraged tourism, and thus brought in revenues. "[V]isiting pilgrims bring throughout the ages, in wallet or toga, bosom or breeches pocket, obolus and denarius and dollar, which go into the market to keep things stirring." Murals in public places, like other types of cultural treasures, were sources of economic as well as spiritual benefit.

> It is perhaps a low plane, this of the consideration of the money value to hotel keeper and shopman and railway of the visiting tourist; but its corollary

is up on a higher plane, and is a better support to our contention which is for the stimulus and education returned to that same visitor as a thousandfold the equivalent of his money.[31]

Blashfield's theories, like Calkins's, purported to reconcile idealism and commercial self-interest.

In contrast to Calkins, however, there was a clear disjunction between Blashfield's artistic aspirations and his practice, one that becomes evident when we relate his statements to one of his actual enterprises—the mural *The Graduate*. Notable in its own right, the discrepancy also has ramifications within the broader context of our discussion. At this juncture, a brief examination of *The Graduate* will help shed light on why Calkins's ideal of commercial art attained cultural longevity, while murals did not. Another important aspect of *The Graduate*—the way that it highlighted affinities between murals and advertising—will be addressed later, when we turn to Walter Pach.

The Graduate (fig. 5.2), a work that gave concrete form to Blashfield's high-art beliefs and aspirations, was contracted in 1906 and completed in 1907 for the Great Hall of Shepard Hall, a new building at City College of New York, designed by George B. Post. A 41 by 22 foot lunette on

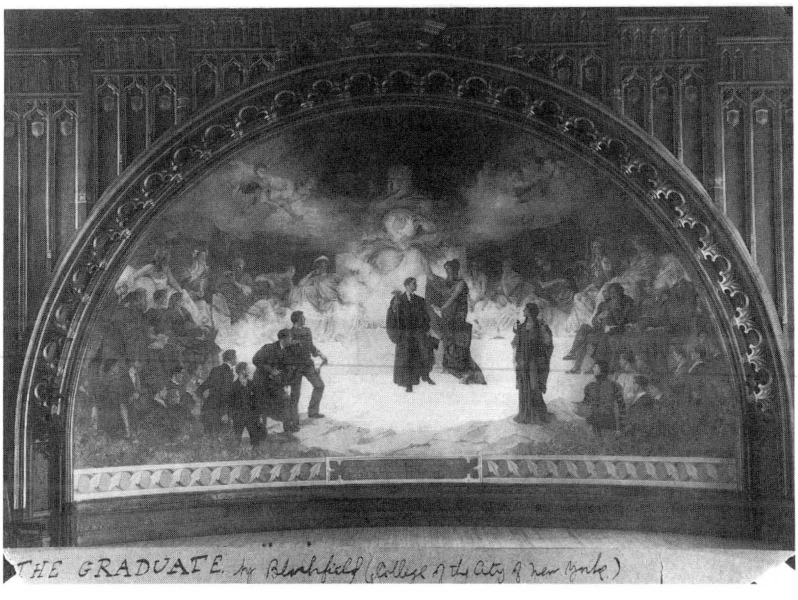

5.2. Edwin Howland Blashfield, *The Graduate*, 1907–1908, College of the City of New York.

canvas, it still adorns the speakers' platform at the western end of the Collegiate Gothic–style hall on St. Nicholas Terrace. Painted by Blashfield and assistants Vincent Aderante and Alonzo E. Foringer, the mural was funded by the city of New York at a cost of $25,000.[32]

According to Blashfield's official description, the mural depicts the graduate, who has just lit "his torch at the altar of learning," and is about to embark upon "his voyage of life." To his right stands Alma Mater with the "Phrygian Cap of Liberty" and a coat of arms of the college. She points toward an enormous statue of benign Wisdom "holding the earth in her hands." On either side of Wisdom sit ten female personifications "typifying great Universities or educational centres of the past": Alexandria, Rome, Cordova, Bologna, and Athens on the left; Uppsala, Leyden, Paris, Heidelberg, and Oxford on the right. Below them are seated male figures representing the arts and sciences. Looking from left to right, they are Lavoisier (chemistry), Democritus (philosophy), Harvey (medicine), Augustus Caesar (law), Sir Isaac Newton (mathematics "for physics"), Shakespeare ("poetical literature"), Beethoven (music), Michelangelo (art), Petrarch (human letters), and Galileo (astronomy). Missing from Blashfield's written description was the last figure, Lord Kelvin (William Thompson), who according to another account, represented "modern forces."[33]

Blashfield's description continued:

> At the right of Alma Mater stands a female figure of Discipline waiting to accompany the Graduate and to prepare him for the Battle of Life with the Scourge for himself and the sword for others. Below and in the foreground are, at the left, the *people,* the Aspirants, men of all classes. At the right are the students with gown and cap or in their costumes of football or baseball team.
>
> In the upper part of the Decoration at right and left of the head of Wisdom and riding upon the smoke clouds from the altar are two groups of children holding respectively, at left an open volume, at right a glass retort, as symbolizing the two great divisions of education: education by the printed page and education by experiment.[34]

Blashfield's academic Parnassus represented a grand civic allegory, a positive, confident image of white Western humanity—the high-art version of the vision presented by advertisers. From another perspective, however, *The Graduate* was even less true to social "reality" than advertising images like the Arrow Collar Man. Blashfield's assertive images of European-American types bracketed the large urban audience of new immigrants, especially Irish, Italians, and eastern European Jews, that he and other artists claimed that they wanted to reach. In fact, the mural resolutely avoided the ethnic reality of City College's student body, which was 75 percent Jewish in 1910, two years after Blashfield completed *The Graduate*.[35] There is no question that Blashfield, like Calkins, genuinely desired to serve a broad public, to forge a common American culture, and to improve the lives of middle-class white natives as well as immigrants. Yet Blashfield's rhetoric and imagery (which were representative of his peers') suggests that muralists' methods could succeed only through avoidance and denial. The painter had to repress the actual cultural backgrounds and pragmatic needs and concerns of the real public, whom he held at arm's length. Such strategies were necessary because the muralists' goals were premised upon an ideal of Americanness that demanded that other ethnic and racial groups assimilate to the value systems of white, upper-middle-class Anglo-Saxon Protestant society. Hence appearances insinuated certain wishful assumptions about behavior: "maybe if the ideal for a Jew is to look like a WASP, he will think and act like one." Like many of his artist contemporaries, Blashfield, in spite of his virtuous intentions to serve humanity, was fundamentally ambivalent about and patronizing toward the "indifferent" public whom he claimed to want to educate.[36]

Blashfield's correspondence reveals that he was quite conscious of his omissions. In late 1907, Blashfield received a letter from an attorney, Lewis Sayre Burchard, an alumnus of City College. Burchard had seen an article on the mural in a campus newspaper, which stated that the seated figures were to represent countries that had been centers of education (as opposed to the universities themselves—which Blashfield represented in the finished mural). Burchard wrote to complain about Blashfield's [earlier] inclusion of Russia and Islam [both later omitted]. Why not Switzerland, Japan, or even "Israel"? he asked. Blashfield's response is no longer extant, but it is possible to glean some insights from Burchard's second letter. "As for the rival claims of the two I's," Burchard wrote, "Islam and Israel, it's hard to decide, and I don't pretend to insist. I suppose if the students of the present day—the undergraduates—had to decide it, the Hebrews would swing 'considerable of a majority—,' but perhaps the very fact that there are so many Jewish boys in the college might lead some cynical critic to say you were making an easy bid for popularity."[37] Israel might be "illustrious in philanthropy, education, the freeing of thought, the breaking down of barriers."[38] Nevertheless, Israel had to be excluded because to include it would appear to be "selling out" to special interests. Blashfield ultimately solved the problem posed by Burchard by depicting just the great universities and by not representing Jews or Russians. The decision-making process continued to be a controversial one, however. According to City College professor Alfred N. Goldsmith of the

Department of Physics, at least half of the time involved in the production of the mural was taken up in "thoughtful criticism and recasting of almost completed details."[39]

Making the common argument that he would not kowtow to special interests, Blashfield refused to capitulate to those he considered to represent new forces of political and financial power in the metropolis. In so doing, however, he merely submitted to other social pressures; the resulting painting was hardly disinterested or detached. *The Graduate* typified various efforts to provide a constructive response to the problems posed by immigration and urbanization. Blashfield and his counterparts in actuality spoke primarily to their own favored group—a public conceived as an enlightened civic body of upright men and women, people like themselves. Their images were visualizations of the mythical way life should be ordered, and of the social structures and processes needed to produce that result. Sculptor William Couper wrote to Blashfield of *The Graduate* that it was "great in the influence it must have on every young man who sees it, that has the slightest spark of ambition for the future."[40] Rhapsodized Couper's wife, Elizabeth:

> The richness and delicacy of the coloring, the luminous, ethereal quality of the light which poured down upon the figure of the young student—the great charm of the figure and face which represent all that is finest and noblest in the young manhood of our country—the attention of all the other youths centered upon him as he steps down to join the one who wants to lead him out into the world to work, struggle and win. The meaning and beauty of it all gave us a thrill and brought tears to our eyes.[41]

Perhaps significantly, the Coupers' letters are among the only extant responses to the mural in the artist's papers. To a certain extent, of course, works like *The Graduate* did speak to other, socially marginalized groups of Americans. To those young men and women who yearned to belong, to assimilate, such mural images could mean a great deal. Indeed, college officials made didactic use of the mural as an inspirational and ideological model.[42] No contemporary student responses survive, however. Moreover, as we shall see, the assumed power relations depicted by muralists like Blashfield met with considerable resistance on some crucial artistic fronts. By hindsight, the rhetoric of mural imagery and its criticism accentuates the social uncertainties that the proponents of mural painting sought to deny. In representing his clean, white, idealized world of "high aspirations," Blashfield's *The Graduate,* like so many Progressive era American murals, advertised a highly restrictive vision of American life. Blashfield could go only partway to reach an enlarged and diversified urban public. Indeed, despite the efforts and the successes of professional groups like the National Society of Mural Painters, even they themselves were never fully convinced that their mission had been accomplished. Like artists in the commercial sphere, the muralists were financially dependent upon others. Their projects entailed political haggling. But their failure came because they were unable to perform as consistently as their counterparts in the sphere of advertising, who were more forthright about their commercial interests and more realistic in their expectations about publics.

The activities of Calkins suggested that the advertising man might be public-spirited, rely on academic styles, and yet be more effective than the mural painter in achieving his goals. Indeed, Blashfield appeared to be increasingly conscious that advertisers might have something to offer. Calkins's ideas and practices represented a way for muralists to use their skills toward more realizable ends: to serve a public through business. If advertisers and muralists shared certain aims at the turn of the century, in the years around World War I their enterprises actually converged in an explicitly commercial activity, the production of advertising billboards.

Billboards would offer experienced muralists a valuable opportunity to extend their authority and broaden their work options. Billboard designers, after all, shared many of their essential concerns. Like a mural, a billboard depended for its success upon the clarity of its composition, the silhouette of its forms, and the force of its color and drama. Although billboard iconography had to be simpler than that of complex allegorical murals, such a task was no problem for any experienced muralist. In Blashfield's eyes, it made sense for the muralist to lend his expertise to the outdoor advertiser, who was interested in ways to maximize sales.

In 1913 Blashfield did just that. At the behest of O. J. Gude, a fellow member of the Municipal Art Society's Committee on Advertising, Blashfield delivered a lecture to the Art, Sales, and Promotion departments of the O. J. Gude Outdoor Advertising Company.[43] The lecture is no longer extant, but according to MAS records, it addressed "the possible co-relating of art with publicity . . . the instruction of the artists and designers in the best methods of color harmonies along with forceful display, and . . . the engendering of an art spirit between the man that spends the money for an Advertising Campaign and those who executed the work."[44] Blashfield undoubtedly saw himself as one who could contribute to that art spirit in advertising. Indeed, Calkins himself recalled some years later that Blashfield confided to him that "were he a young man beginning his artistic career he would certainly devote his attention to this stimulating field."[45]

Calkins had a similar agenda in mind for uniting art and billboard advertising, and his plans included Blashfield. In 1917, Calkins wrote

Fifth Avenue Association president Robert Grier Cooke to suggest that a campaign for art, not for abolishing signs, would be both the most intelligent answer to the billboard problem and the path to better business. "I am an advertising man," Calkins declared, "and have many times used this method in advertising. I, like you, have a certain civic pride. I do not like to see my sense of beauty and taste affronted each day by things so badly done as these forms of advertising." But the solution, he emphasized, was not to eradicate the billboard. Such a goal was unfeasible. A more satisfactory alternative would be to encourage advertisers to secure "the services of the greatest mural artists until our street corners and vacant lots were enriched by the works of such artists as Blashfield, Violet Oakley, Sargeant, Ludwig Hohlwein, Kenyon Cox, Frank Brangwyn, George Covey, John Massell." This might "sound like a fantastic dream," Calkins admitted, but "I happen to know that Maxfield Parrish accepted the commission for the Fisk Tire Company entirely on this ground—that it was his duty to do his bit toward raising the standard of billboard advertising." In fact, he added, "This same Fisk Tire Maxfield Parrish caused one woman to erect a billboard on her beautiful estate near Los Angeles for the purpose of showing it (and it alone)."[46] From Calkins's perspective, Parrish billboards were mural art.

Calkins maintained that fewer but more artistically designed posters would work better as advertisements. Moreover, "when all the posters are the works of artists, when the billboards have become in truth the poor man's picture gallery, their individuality and contrast would be obtained by the judicious 'hanging' which would place side by side designs which mutually enhanced and displayed each other."[47] This would solve all the problems of the double-decker billboards about which the civic activists had been complaining. If advertising artists like Leyendecker could not be solicited to improve civic architecture, one could at least seek out prominent civic artists to enhance the commercial cityscape.

Although Calkins's ideas were never implemented over the long haul, his conception of billboards as mural art did resonate in the immediate setting of World War I. Calkins's letter to Cooke coincided with the early poster productions of the Division of Pictorial Publicity (see fig. 1.18)—an enterprise supported by the outdoor advertising industry, some of whose clients (like Fisk Tire, see fig. 5.8) were also clients of Calkins. Blashfield was one of the painters who donated work to the war poster program, which, as we have seen, helped pave the way for the improved status of billboards. (See, for example, his *Carry On!* [1918], a 76 by 36 inch poster in the collection of the Museum of Modern Art.) Blashfield's activities in these circumstances succeeded in ways his earlier works could not. Here, he accommodated to the recommendations made by the advertising men—his fellows in persuasion in the Division. The division's poster artists utilized personifications similar to the images in *The Graduate.* But the posters were meant to appeal, not to the best in the best of men and women, but to the gut emotions of people of all class and ethnic backgrounds. The poster enterprise succeeded, in other words, because at least in this instance, the painters were willing to reach down, to do work like Calkins and colleagues in illustration and advertising. Such adjustments helped these artists maintain a certain credibility within the postwar social and institutional realms of art and business—at least until the mid-1920s, when other, more progressive artistic groups increasingly began to challenge the influence of enterprises like those of Blashfield. These efforts, initiated during the previous decade, paradoxically also relied on crass commercial tactics that conjoined advertising and art.

Advertising and the Avant Garde

Painters on the margins of the New York art world were highly conscious of the affinities between established artists like Blashfield and ad men like Calkins. While young artists were struggling to exhibit their work, Blashfield was thriving; indeed, as a well-connected National Academician and as an active member of organizations like the National Society of Mural Painters, Blashfield exerted substantial influence on the kinds of images deemed suitable for public consumption. As a result of such influences, proponents of newer artistic trends were usually excluded.[48] Those shut out (mostly younger artists) sought to set up an alternative, framed explicitly in relation to the institutions, values, and alliances represented by artists like Blashfield.

The Armory Show was at the center of this effort to circulate alternative conceptions of fine art identity and practice and to loosen academic painters' hold on what little market existed for American art. Subsequently mythified as the event at which modern styles in American art emerged publicly, the Armory Show was actually one moment in a larger struggle for artistic authority, of which debates over style were just one manifestation. Yet the exhibition was a critical occurrence because of the way its organizers, like their nemesis Blashfield, embraced the mechanisms of the commercial world to advertise, validate, and commodify a body of diverse practices they called modern art.

Like the mural painters, Walt Kuhn (1880–1949), Arthur Davies (1862–1928), and Walter Pach (1853–1938) went into their careers with the expectation of reaching a wide audience. However, in contrast to artists like Blashfield, these nonacademic painters were full proponents of an ideology of romantic individualism. In theory, this stance discouraged artistic accommodation or compromise, thereby placing the artists' careers in something of a bind. In contrast to those of mural painters and illustrators, their identities hinged on artistic independence, on refusing to pander to the external demands of making money. Nevertheless, many of these artistically moderate painters actively sought a broader audience and market for their art, if only to give themselves a greater opportunity to pursue their own individual interests.

Such pragmatic concerns were understandable, given the artists' backgrounds and circumstances. Walter Pach, for example, was the son of a New York commercial photographer. He studied art as a youth, but it was assumed that he would also receive a "real" education that would prepare him for the world. His German Jewish father, concerned about the low-status, unremunerative nature of the painter's profession, sought to discourage Pach from becoming an artist. Pach worked as a journalist to "earn a livelihood until painting should support him." Unlike most artists of his generation (Pach was born only three years after Blashfield), he went on to a higher education, graduating from City College of New York in 1903.[49]

Walt Kuhn began his artistic career in 1899 as a cartoonist. For the next ten years he drew for *Life, Puck, Judge,* the *New York Sunday Sun,* and *New York World,* painting in his spare time. Kuhn was a strong-willed and ambitious artist, but in 1911, at the age of 34, he could hardly be called a successful painter in a world where success was defined in terms of sales of easel pictures and positions of influence. Kuhn's drive for financial and professional security intensified when his wife became pregnant. He determined to create his own organization and forum for display.[50] Drawing on his experience with mass publishing, he worked to exploit the modern phenomenon of press publicity to draw attention to the ideals he championed.

Kuhn contacted other struggling painters—Jerome Myers (1867–1940), Elmer MacRae (1875–1953), and Henry Fitch Taylor (1853–1925). In December 1911, they formed the Association of American Painters and Sculptors (AAPS), an alternative organizational framework that they hoped would challenge the authority of the National Academy of Design, provide an opportunity for exposing new artistic trends, and thereby place progressive artists in a more competitive position in the marketplace.[51] Henry Fitch Taylor told fellow organizers that the association would consist of "live and progressive men and women" who would "lead the public taste in art rather than follow it. The National Academy of Design is not expected to lead the public taste," he stated. "It never did and it never will. . . . And as no such organization as the one contemplated exists in this country today, we must all, I think, admit the very positive need of forming one."[52]

In spite of its plans, however, the Association was never a cohesive organization.[53] In fact, its first and only enterprise was the organization of the Armory Show. Over the next year, Kuhn, Davies, Pach, and their associates embarked on an unprecedented fund-raising, publicity, and curatorial enterprise. They assembled a formidable array of American and European modernist painting and sculpture, and rented the new home of the Sixty-ninth Regiment of the National Guard to house the International Exhibition of Modern Art (as the Armory Show was called). The exhibition opened for one month on 15 February 1913. It was the first show to bring together the latest developments in European and American art on a large scale.[54]

Whatever their ultimate aesthetics of spiritual transcendence, the Association members were as much engaged in the emerging commercial culture as anyone in business or advertising. Much like advertisers, the Armory Show organizers sought to promote their clients' products. The International Exhibition of Modern Art was geared toward selling new art trends to the public, and its organizers were not above using manipulative tactics to do so. The exhibition was sponsored through financial support provided mainly by one "client," Association president Arthur B. Davies, who, it was claimed jokingly, "knew a lot of rich old ladies."[55]

The Armory Show was a public relations success, if not a commercial one, thanks to association members' ability to band together on the crucial matter of publicity. Taking full advantage of the expansion of the modern press media and the apparatus of press agentry, they promoted modern art as a more vital, sincere expression of true contemporary experience than academic art, and countered the negative view of it fostered by National Academicians and their supporters. On this score, association members' efforts bore affinity to other emerging publicity enterprises, which sought free press publicity for their clients by planting "news" rather than through paid advertising.[56] Even before the formation of the AAPS, Kuhn, the mastermind of the operation, was clearly thinking of the venture in terms of promotion.[57] The AAPS hired Frederick James Gregg (an editorial writer for the *Evening Sun*) as its "Publicity Man" (fig. 5.3), and the promotional effort became a major component of the show's organization.[58]

Such tactics were not entirely new. Kuhn was following predecessors like James MacNeil Whistler, who had masterfully kept his name in the press to construct an image that became integrally linked with the reputation of his work.[59] Kuhn was also building upon the successes of The Eight, a group of painters that included four active newspaper and maga-

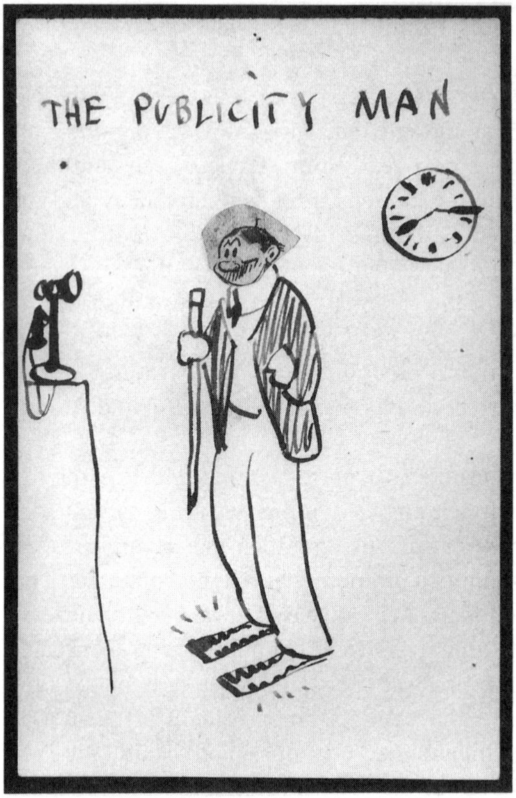

5.3. Walt Kuhn, *The Publicity Man* (Frederick James Gregg), 1912–1913.

zine illustrators (William Glackens, George Luks, Everett Shinn, and John Sloan) as well as future AAPS president Arthur Davies. As art historian Elizabeth Milroy has shown, these artists used their savvy and connections as commercial-press insiders effectively to promote their February 1908 exhibition at New York's MacBeth Gallery. The show was greeted by a barrage of headlines and extensive press coverage in major New York newspapers like the *Herald* and the *World*.[60]

The Armory Show was unprecedented in the size, scope, and ingenuity of the publicity enterprise. Its organizers' strategies amounted to a new form of national advertising for art. Publicity man Gregg sent out posters, postcards, and letters to newspapers, art schools, libraries, museums, and art dealers across the country. The association printed 50,000 catalogs, 5,000 copies each of four different pamphlets, and thousands of postcards of the works of art.[61] Kuhn himself wrote his numerous acquaintances—artists, newspaper and magazine editors, and critics—pushing them to spread the word and to write articles on the upcoming exhibition. Writing to his friend Edward Goewy of the *Kansas City Post,* for example, Kuhn explicitly highlighted the crucial connection between modern American commercial strategies and his efforts to get individuals and institutions literally and figuratively to "buy" progressive fine art.

> As I was looking over our book of advance press clippings regarding our coming exhibition, it has occurred to me that you might be able to use some stuff for your paper. . . .
>
> Could you let me know as soon as possible whether your people would care to take this up? I could furnish you with a fine selection of photos, and in fact a story if you require it, which would make a very attractive Sunday. *We are doing this according to American methods and have already spent a good deal on advertising.*[62]

In speaking of "American methods," Kuhn was referring to a set of distinctive techniques geared toward promoting a consumerist ethos and expanding productive capacity; foremost among those means was high-powered national advertising.[63] By claiming to use such "American methods," Kuhn sought to position art alongside other key modern developments. Art had to become visibly and commercially competitive with other goods and services. It had to acquire national recognition.

To this end, Kuhn's publicity tactics extended beyond the print media. Contacting a representative of the O. J. Gude Company, Kuhn also explored the possibility of placing an electric sign on Broadway for six weeks. The representative quoted a price of $900, noting that Gude himself was very "much interested in this enterprise of such radical departure from established convention." Ever the cultural iconoclast, Gude expressed a possible willingness "to be enrolled as a patron in promoting publicity."[64] However, for reasons unknown (probably financial), no sign went up.

In using these promotional strategies, the AAPS deliberately set itself apart ideologically and procedurally, as well as aesthetically, from established artists' organizations like the National Academy of Design.[65] Drawing in the press, artists like Kuhn, Pach, and Davies spurned the academicians' ideal of "disinterested" public enlightenment and improvement in favor of a hard-sell appeal to individual emotions and appetites. Like the publicity and advertising people, they sought to capture public attention and stir up discussion. They differed from the commercial men, however, because they did not worry about whether they made a positive impression. In contrast to both Blashfield and the advertisers, the AAPS did not target any particular group as its audience.[66] From the perspective of AAPS members, exposure was the crucial factor. It was a necessary prelude to breaking down entrenched attitudes and wresting status and customers away from the more established artists. Publicity tactics worked for business; the same devices might be suitable for selling modern art. At the very least, they might start an opinion conversion that could gradually result in institutionalizing modern art and turning its works into salable commodities.

Kuhn and Gregg's strategies worked. The exhibition received massive newspaper coverage (over 3,000 columns' worth) both before and during the event.[67] As with advertising, the responses (as recorded in and by the press) were often incredulous and indignant, proving that Kuhn, Pach, and Gregg had accomplished their primary goal of drawing attention to the art. About 300,000 people attended the exhibition in New York and the smaller version that traveled to Chicago. Kuhn estimated that 40 percent of the New York attendees were people who had never been to any kind of art exhibition, proving that "American methods" certainly had the capacity to attract the attention of potential new consumers.[68]

Yet the Armory show publicity was ineffective advertising. The exhibit did not produce a significant market for avant-garde American painting and sculpture. Still uncertain of the merits and status of American painting, collectors continued to buy mostly European art until years after World War I.[69] Moreover, the AAPS failed from an institutional standpoint. Members did not maintain organizational cohesion after the close of the Armory Show. Their cooperative spirit, always tenuous, collapsed under the strain of producing the exhibition, the higher cause that had initially drawn them together.[70] Art could serve as the crux of advertising for consumables, but art was less successful when used to advertise itself.

Walter Pach

Although the academic ideology of serving and edifying a public still predominated among businessmen and government officials (those involved in commissioning murals, for example), the Armory Show was sufficiently threatening that some academicians went on the offensive, expressing their disdain for the work of the exhibited artists and maintaining their politics of exclusion.[71] The artistic conservatives further bolstered their positions during World War I, at least temporarily, through their service as war artists. Whereas the Armory Show organizers engaged in more personal, expressive, less visible pursuits, the poster and mural campaigns seemed to reclaim the righteousness and artistic expertise of academic painters and illustrators.

Several of the more progressive painters of the early to mid-1920s sought to respond to these activities and the political alliances they engendered. Walter Pach was one of them. Pach, whose own painting had a loosely rendered figurative approach, spent the war years and the 1920s painting, traveling, writing, and lecturing. Very much engaged with modern art and the New York art world, he was well aware that Blashfield and his cohort still controlled institutional and popular perceptions of art; this displeased him immensely. Attempting to turn Blashfield's highbrow stand on the virtues of mural painting on end, Pach accused him and his sympathizers of lowbrow vulgarity and outright corruption. To make his point, Pach drew evidence directly from the flourishing commercial culture of 1920s America, and sought to position his interests above that level.

In 1928, in his book *Ananais, or the False Artist,* Pach mounted an attack on the values and organizational structure of the New York art world. Pach defined modern art—elite, but sincere and independent—explicitly in contradistinction to academic painting, especially mural painting, which he linked with advertising illustration and posters and with postwar mass commercial culture. Pach denounced what he considered the false values that prevailed on the contemporary art scene, exacerbated by museums and other institutions' underhanded connections with academic insiders.[72] Such corruption and deceit resulted in a superficial art that merely pandered to a crass, faceless mob. This academic art, he contended, shared much in common with advertising, or as Pach dubbed it disdainfully, referring to car cards (the small advertising posters placed in public transportation), the "Art of the Subways." Reminding readers of the degree to which advertising art derived from academic methods, Pach implied that poster advertising, with its mimetic, conservative, academic-style images repeated ad nauseam, had cheapened academic art. "The conception of practically all the paintings in the Academies and Salons is due to the mind that expresses itself most openly in the Subway Pictures."[73] Academic and subway art were both vulgar and lower-class.

"Subway Art does more than sell face powder and cigarettes to the crowd," Pach warned. "It 'sells' the art-conception of its makers to the vast majority of people, and in every rank of society."[74] That conception included a disregard for the expressive skill of the artist's hand and a dependence upon superficial appearances. "Naturalness and always more naturalness is the demand," Pach insisted (ignoring the fact that contemporary advertisers were tapping "modernism" as extensively as academic

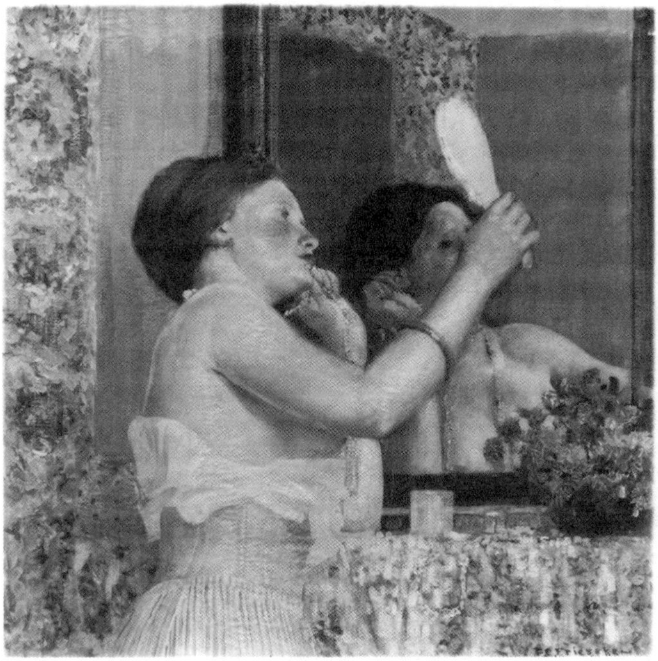

5.4. Frederick Carl Frieseke, *The Toilet.*

"realism"). That "naturalism" was "supplied as the Subway Artists, attracted to their profession by its high wages, train themselves for it more intensively. The reproductive processes, always based on photography, have been perfected and now seem to be at a maximum of efficiency."[75] "Subway Art" pictures narrated brief and superficial incident, avoiding any hint of real conflict, either visual or emotional. Its images encouraged stupor and discouraged any effort to provide insight into life's complexities.[76]

Among the paintings Pach singled out for ridicule were several in the Metropolitan Museum of Art's collection. They included *The Toilet* by Frederick Carl Frieseke (1874–1939) (fig. 5.4), which Pach likened to a corset advertisement, and *The Passing of Summer* (fig. 5.5) by Harry W. Watrous (1857–1940), a National Academician and prominent donor.[77] In the latter, the "cocktail glass was probably intended, like the more carnal allurements offered by Mr. Frieseke, to suggest surcease from the monotony of existence . . . [W]ith this picture," he wrote sardonically, "we get back to the art of the Subway, hear again the clatter of its turnstiles, and feel that all's well with the world."[78]

Pach bestowed some of his most severe criticism upon Blashfield and *The Graduate* (see fig. 5.2).[79] There was a distinct "identity of type," he observed, between Blashfield's type of Ivy League Anglo-Saxon graduate and "those 'ideal American youths,' the wearer of a much advertised collar" (J. C. Leyendecker's "Arrow Collar Man" [see fig. 5.1]).

> . . . what effect would be produced if some of the Subway advertisements were placed beside the painting? Would their resemblance cause the observer to condemn the work of the well-known decorator? Or would the "touch of vulgarity that makes the whole world kin" (to use Whistler's paraphrase) react in the other direction, and lead the Subway rider to see in his daily art exhibit a higher value than he had imagined it to possess? I am sure that the latter result would be the one produced. The enormous effect of Subway Art is to be observed everywhere.[80]

In Pach's opinion, Blashfield's strong-jawed model of male perfection

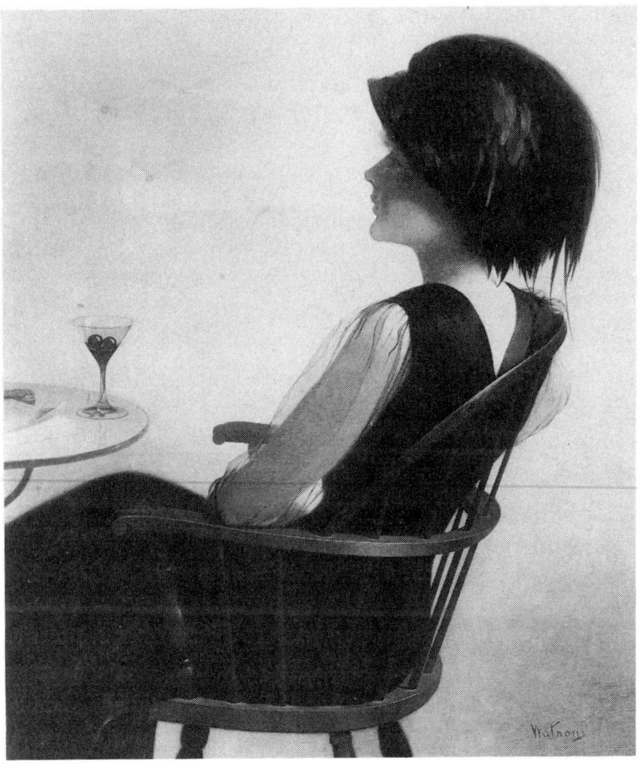

5.5. Harry W. Watrous, *The Passing of Summer,* 1912.

typified the deceptions of contemporary academic artists and middlebrow advertisers, whose images sanitized and trivialized the deep meanings in the reality of modern life; in *The Graduate* and "Subway Art," signs promised more than the meanings actually delivered. Pach seemed keenly aware of the contradictions between Blashfield's rhetoric and practice. Portraying the typically Eastern European Jewish City College graduate as the quintessential WASP seemed the ultimate travesty. For Pach, the Arrow Collar Man-*Graduate* ideal of American manhood was a mask, an expression of the simplemindedness of the painterly legacy of the late nineteenth century, and a denial of the urban presence of the immigrant on the part of the genteel representatives of the New York social establishment. Pach, of all people, would have been sensitive to, and possibly ambivalent about, these very issues.[81]

With Pach, just as with his nemesis Blashfield, issues of ethnicity and especially of class continued to inform the discourse of artistic identity in relation to commerce. For Pach, the representations of academic painters—especially public muralists—were linked to a dominant but outdated conception of American society in which ideals of ethnic assimilation were at once touted and thwarted. Lumped together with advertising and mass culture as commercial configurations, such images threatened to consume art in general. From Pach's standpoint these artistic boundaries had to be challenged.

Thanks in part to his numerous writings on modern art, the exhibitions he organized, and the collections he helped to build, Pach laid the groundwork that helped modernist viewpoints gradually achieve cultural dominance.[82] Yet even he could not realize the ideals that he set forth. Pach claimed that academic painting represented an inappropriate equation of old ideas and new institutions and beliefs. Such art pandered to ignorant public taste instead of "imparting *its* mood to the beholder."[83] Pach sought to reverse the priorities, to give the advantage to elite self-expression and to originality of conception while confirming a longstanding notion of art as essential truth. Yet Pach's own 1935 mural for the City College campus, a fresco titled *Respice, Adspice, Prospice,* itself moved little beyond the conventions he decried in academic painting. It consisted of a group of classically garbed allegorical personifications. It received minimal press coverage, and was criticized by Edward Alden Jewell as "drearily static," and by another commentator as "disappointing," "halting if not niggly" in drawing and brushwork. Indeed, in contrast to his contemporaries Blashfield and Leyendecker, Pach always remained better known as a writer than as an artist.[84]

Stuart Davis

Diametrically opposed to the values of Earnest Elmo Calkins and Edwin Blashfield, Pach believed that the true painter could not respond to popular interests and tastes and also maintain respect and integrity. Not all modernist spokesmen were such purists. Stuart Davis (1894–1964), for example, rejected what he described as the sentimental, "romantic" aspects of academic art, but unlike Pach, he did not lump advertising art and academic painting together.[85] He never did product advertising, but at one level he shared Calkins's conviction that art and advertising could converge to express and enhance contemporary life. In contrast to Calkins, however, Davis saw little commonality of purpose between the professions of painting and advertising art. Fluid boundaries between art and advertising could exist at certain expressive and aesthetic levels and in some aspects of distribution, but this did not extend to the ideological or vocational realms.

Davis found the commercial culture of the 1920s frustrating, but also exciting and liberating. During the immediate postwar period, he was deeply involved with exploring the formal potential of painting. Yet he was determined to bring to his work something expressive of contemporary life. "I want direct simple pictures of classic beauty expressing the immediate life of the day," he wrote in a personal journal in 1921. "I conceive of pictures which while having all the Rembrandt-Cezanne structure will at the same time be more sociable," nonesoteric, and that would treat such "popular subjects" as Scott Joplin, Fatima cigarettes, pretty girl illustrator Harrison Fisher, and Uneeda Biscuits.[86] Davis's investigations resulted in a series of "Cigarette" pictures (1921–1924), which, as art historian Barbara Zabel has shown, brilliantly evoked the vitality of product marketing (including car cards) and the transformation of the social habitat in the wake of World War I.[87] Davis's synthetic cubist *Lucky Strike* (1924, fig. 5.6), for example, complete with a newspaper "billboard" (or subway car card), presented a commercial "landscape" that contrasted tradition with modernity and high culture with popular culture. He achieved this by evoking the shift from pipe smoking to rolled cigarettes, a change induced by packaging and marketing pressures, and by contrasting the exclusivity and elitism of painting with the infinite replicability of popular mass media. Davis's use of an avant-garde style suggested that contemporary painting shared sociocultural roots with other modes of contemporary imaging. All were responses to modernity. Less explicitly, the painting revealed the extent to which Davis framed modernity in masculine terms, by depicting male habits and symbols.[88]

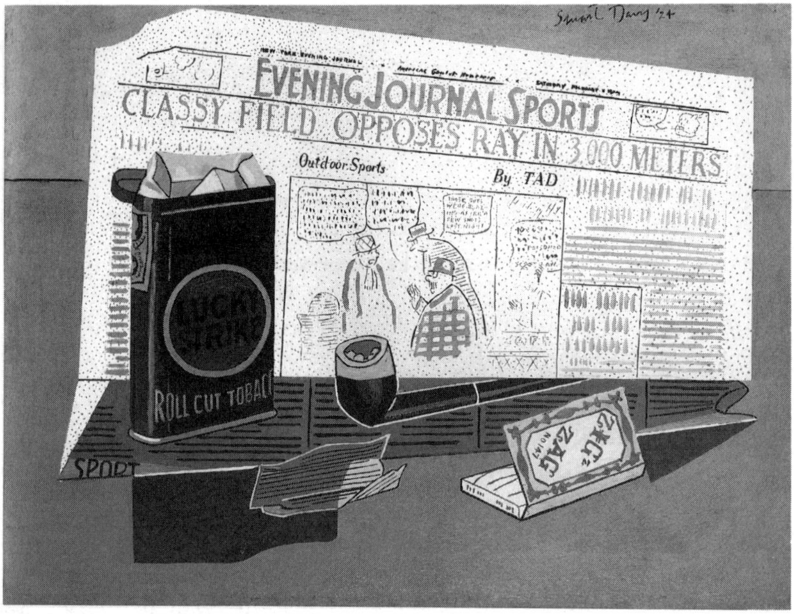

5.6. Stuart Davis, *Lucky Strike,* 1924.

In painting such pictures, Davis dreamed not only of creating a new kind of American art but also of making the meaning of art accessible. The impact of national advertising and mass print media did not threaten him as it did Pach. Davis had grown up quite familiar with the spheres of magazines, newspapers, and advertising. Son of a newspaper art editor, Davis had himself worked as an illustrator to earn bread and butter. His experience as a contributor to *The Masses* made him highly conscious of what it meant to draw for a less profitable socialist enterprise rather than for the commercial press. He was also well aware of the potential of the print media and national advertising for shaping contemporary consciousness, especially his own. In 1921 he wrote in his notebook the aphorism "I do not belong to the human race but am a product made by the American Can Co and the N.Y. Evening Journal."[89]

Eight years earlier, in *The Masses,* as we have seen in chapter 1, the young Davis had pilloried the commercialized visual constructs found on the covers of popular magazines (see fig. 1.11). In 1921, he continued to find inspiration in the commercial presence. He mulled over how to take advantage of his own position as a product of commercial culture to create authentic works that would deviate from the paths of that culture yet still appeal to the mass public. He mused about how to apply his approach to illustration or advertising pictures, and very briefly his searches meshed with those of Calkins.[90]

The new modern pictures would have

> nothing in common with the trade in art of the galleries. They should be sold in stores like newspapers and magazines. That is to say large colored reproductions to sell for 5 or 10 dollars. Black and white would be cheaper of course but the idea is that they would be looked forward to as entertainment by a number of people just like the Saturday Eve. Post and have no holy art about them. It should develop into a business just as painting and engraving was in its big days. Of course the logical thing seems to be their publication in a magazine which increases distribution.[91]

Commercial culture offered new ways to reach an audience by providing new channels of mass dissemination.

Davis ultimately decided that the sorts of images he had in mind would probably be judged "too unorthodox" by magazine editors. Indeed, his thoughts about advertising appear to have been mostly theoretical. He seems not to have given serious consideration to jumping on the Calkins bandwagon and applying his expertise to advertising. He continued to illustrate for literary and political magazines *(Dial, Transitions, Liberator, New Masses, Little Review)*, which had a relatively small readership compared with mass publications like the *Saturday Evening Post*. However, he did not endeavor to adapt his theories of painting to commercial enterprises.[92] Instead, Davis continued doggedly to channel his energy into developing his formal theories of "popular picture" making.[93] He ultimately chose to renegotiate the boundaries between advertising and painting iconographically, drawing inspiration from the activities and products of corporate America.

Like Walter Pach's, Davis's identity as a painter hinged upon his ideological distancing from the commercial domain. Davis reached many people through his magazine illustrations and sought to reach a larger public through mural commissions. Yet in the 1920s he invested more in fashioning "popular pictures" than in acquiring a popular audience of the sort garnered by new forms of mass entertainment like radio and film. Davis chose to travel an artistically more conservative and less lucrative route. Unlike his contemporaries Maxfield Parrish and Rockwell Kent, he ultimately did not try to reconfigure the notion of painting to include work for advertising or for mass reproduction.

MAXFIELD PARRISH AND ROCKWELL KENT

Davis and Pach, struggling New Yorkers whose family backgrounds gave them an insider's knowledge of commercial art businesses, embraced romantic ideals that insisted on the autonomy and privileged place of the artist in society. Maxfield Parrish (1870–1966) and Rockwell Kent (1882–1961), college-educated descendants of old-stock, solidly middle-class families, came to art as outsiders with fewer preconceptions.[94] They were therefore less committed to narrowly framed art values that would distinguish their interests from those of a mass audience. Much in the same spirit as Calkins, both were committed to the popularization and democratization of art. Both created art for advertising; in fact, Parrish worked for Calkins at one time. The careers of Parrish and Kent highlight the varying ways in which prominent painters began to insert themselves into the broadening organizational nexus of art production and commodification—how they both responded to and influenced the development of commercially structured art-making. Together they provide intriguing studies in likeness and contrast, accommodation and conflict. For this reason, we need to examine their attitudes and activities in detail.

Maxfield Parrish

Maxfield Parrish (fig. 5.7) found the mass audience that Stuart Davis had once dreamed of for his "modern pictures." This broad constituency was a key to Parrish's celebrity and prosperity and distinguished his artistic identity from that of his colleagues. Blashfield's accomplishments were contingent for the most part on the support of a narrow group of politicians and urban elites. Kuhn's and Pach's endeavors with the Armory Show depended on press publicity. Davis relied on moral support from dealers and fellow artists. By contrast, Parrish's artistic reputation did not depend on promotion by the press or exclusive art galleries or on purchases of individual work by wealthy patrons for display in the home. Instead, his success hinged on his willingness to work within a expansive new institutional framework of art that included small companies, large corporations, print and lithography businesses, and artists' agents. These groups were Parrish's immediate clients, but they also operated as intermediaries, marketing Parrish's work to ordinary people, the nation's art consumers. While Blashfield's art was part of a social effort to build a shared public culture, Parrish's art acquired its identity as a product intended to satisfy individual consumer desire. Parrish constructed images to please audiences who would appreciate and purchase his work, rather than to challenge or dictate ideals or to set didactic standards. At the

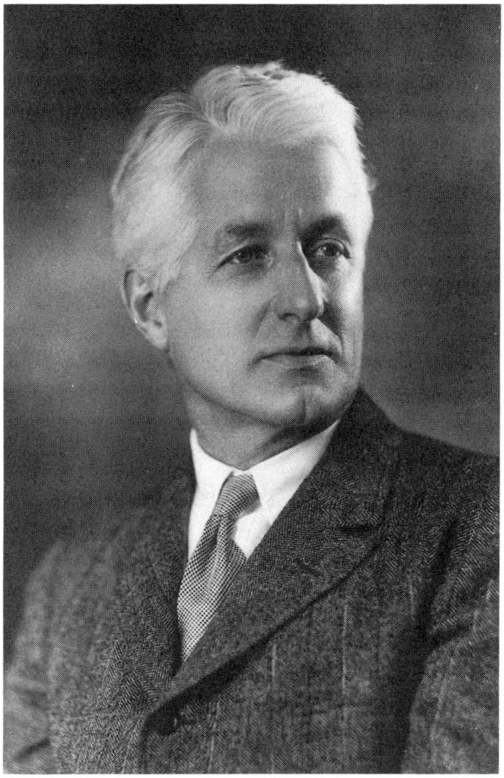

5.7. Maxfield Parrish.

height of his career, in the 1920s, Parrish was phenomenally successful, both popularly and financially. In 1925 he reported an income (before taxes) of over $92,000 (equivalent to approximately $713,650 in present-day purchasing power).[95]

Like Davis and Pach, Parrish was influenced by creator-oriented art values that led him occasionally to doubt his own activities and status. Nevertheless, he suppressed these highbrow, personal artistic aspirations, which were inconsistent with his artistic practice. Instead, Parrish narrowed his professional goals and focused on pleasing people whose tastes in art often differed from his own. Serving middle- and lower-middle-class consumers, Parrish forged a reputation as an artist who generated publicity by creating images shaped for reproduction and a popular market. Within that commercial framework Parrish found a niche that allowed him to maintain a sense of artistic self-assurance, autonomy, and integrity.

Parrish began his postcollege career as both a muralist and an illustrator. After Haverford, he attended the Pennsylvania Academy of Fine Arts (1892–1894), where he studied under painters Robert W. Vonnoh and Thomas Anschutz. He also sat in on Howard Pyle's classes at Drexel University.[96] His first commission, executed in 1894 when he was 24, was a mural of Old King Cole for the University of Pennsylvania's Mask and Wig Club. Studies for the mural, exhibited in the Pennsylvania Academy of Fine Arts, drew the attention of Harper and Brothers art director Thomas Ball, who invited Parrish to submit a design for a special 1895 Easter cover. The picture's success led to additional commissions for magazine covers and story illustrations. In 1897 Parrish illustrated his first book, *Mother Goose in Prose* by L. Frank Baum. Such children's stories became the keystone of Parrish's career, the inspiration for many of his illustrations for stories and advertisements.[97]

Parrish's earliest illustration work also included advertising. Indeed, he was one of the first successful illustrators to take up Calkins's call to improve advertising art. In 1896 he won competitions for posters for H. O. Oatmeal and Columbia Bicycle.[98] He took on commissions to produce magazine advertisements for such products as Sterling Bicycle, Royal Baking Powder, Dutch Boy Cleanser, and Adlake Camera (see fig. 1.10). He became one of the "name" artists whose work was prominently displayed in Calkins's 1908 "Art in Advertising" exhibition. In 1914 he worked for Calkins and advertising lithographer M. Rusling Wood to produce a prominent series of five paintings (one not used) for the Fisk Tire Company (fig. 5.8). Variations on themes from Mother Goose rhymes, these images were reproduced as car cards and 24-sheet posters. Parrish earned up to $2,000 for each painting, each of which he completed in roughly six months (while also working on other projects). It was these images to which Calkins was alluding when he spoke to the Municipal Art Society about bringing artists into billboard production. Such posters, Wood had also predicted optimistically, would help to "elevate the billboard" in the court of public opinion.[99]

From Ads to Art Prints

Whether Parrish's work enhanced the long-term artistic reputation of billboards is debatable. What is certain, however, is that his visibility, first as an illustrator, then as an advertising artist, enabled him to forge a reputation as a popular artist. Finding the work of advertising illustration increasingly disruptive because of the effort and time expended in negotiations, Parrish began to bank upon his celebrity status to pursue an equally lucrative alternative, painting pictures for calendars and art prints that

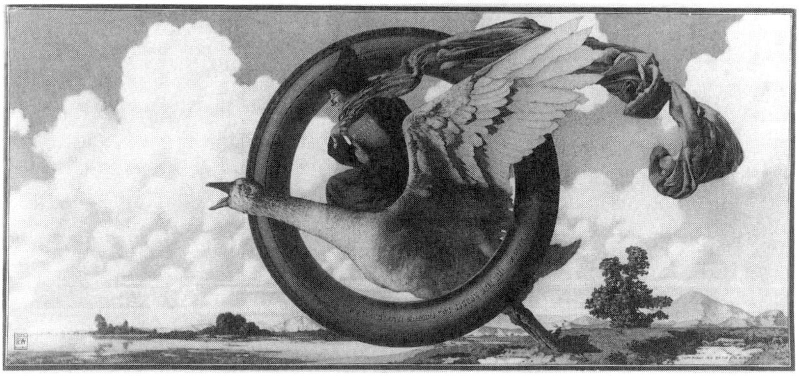

5.8. Advertisement for Fisk Tire, illustration by Maxfield Parrish, 1920. In this poster, Parrish used a Fisk Tire to encircle a highly illusionistic Mother Goose "flying through the air on a very fine gander," thus freezing the action and riveting the eye on the center and the product. Parrish employed a familiar subject to attract initial attention. In linking a novel product to a well-known theme through simply designed yet technically adept composition, he innovated a mnemonic device that advertisers have exploited ever since, most recently, with rock 'n' roll music. Parrish's speciality, variations on the Mother Goose themes, undoubtedly attracted notice and appealed because they triggered positive memories of the experience of young childhood for many Americans.

millions of people mounted on their walls.[100] For him, at least, this work bridged the gap between fine and commercial art, permitting him to create paintings that could also be used for selling purposes. In doing such work, Parrish was able to capitalize on improvements in print technologies that made cheap color prints a truly viable option. Parrish produced paintings for full-color calendars—advertisements for Edison-Mazda Lamps—that sold in the hundreds of thousands, and even the millions; owners often framed the prints at the end of the year. General Electric selected the themes of the early calendars, but by 1923 Parrish had arranged not only to choose his own subjects but also to market his original designs as art prints at year's end. Parrish received $5,000 for his 1922 calendar painting *Venetian Lamp Lighter.* By the late 1920s, his fee for calendar paintings was $10,000.[101]

The art print route was not a new one for Parrish, or for other artists, for that matter. Art prints had their genesis in the mid-nineteenth century with such firms as Currier and Ives, whose artists created original designs for lithographic reproduction. Art unions and printmakers like John Sartain and Goupil marketed lavishly engraved renditions of celebrated English and American paintings by such artists as William Sidney Mount, George Caleb Bingham, and Lily Martin Spencer. Lithographic companies like Prang followed suit. We already saw, in chapter 2, that turn-of-the-century publishers of popular magazines offered reproductions of famous paintings and of illustrations from their pages as art, ready for framing.[102] Reproductions of Parrish paintings, originally produced for *Ladies' Home Journal,* had been sold since 1904. (Other magazines had also sold reproductions but Parrish no longer had claim to their copyrights.) But Parrish became one of the first major artists to become involved in transforming advertisements into a substantial art print enterprise. Retaining his copyright over the original paintings, he was also one of the first actually to make real money from such reproductions.

In 1916, candy manufacturer Clarence Crane began marketing art prints based on a design that Parrish had initially created as a package decoration. By 1920, having made almost $50,000 in royalties from the sale of prints of three subjects for Crane's Chocolates, Parrish entered into an agreement with a New York–based publishing and distribution firm, the House of Art, run by publishers Reinthal and Newman.[103] He would create pictures of his own choosing, and House of Art would distribute them as color reproductions, suitable for framing. In turn, Parrish was requested to make paintings of a size, shape, and subject that would prove salable.[104] Parrish's activities thus were part and parcel of the broadening consumer culture of the 1920s. His task was both to cater to popular demands for art and to convince average Americans, especially women, that art was an aesthetically and economically accessible commodity. Through his arrangements with House of Art and other businesses, Parrish produced a reliable, reproducible "national brand" of standardized art with wide appeal.

Parrish's most popular subjects were variations of his most successful Edison-Mazda calendar, *Daybreak* (fig. 5.9), a work that sold 78,118 copies in 1925 alone. Whether intentionally or unintentionally on the artist's part, *Daybreak* was a metaphor for budding sexuality. It was a postwar expression of middle-class captivation with the culture of youth and the freedom and lost innocence it represented.[105] Bathed in peaceful aquamarine-tinted early morning light, a prepubescent girl, clothed in classically styled dress, lies recumbent, like an odalisque, with arms over head, as if just awakening. She peers into the eyes of a second girl, who,

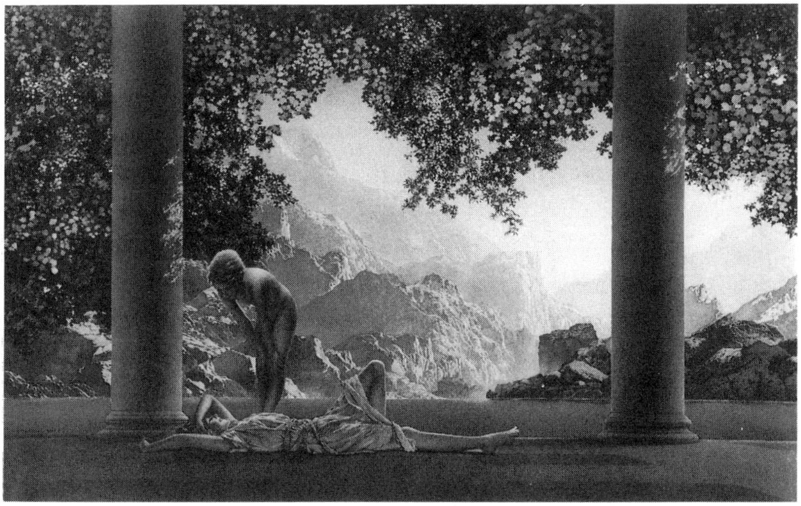

5.9. Maxfield Parrish, *Daybreak,* 1923, Reinthal and Newman lithograph.

although nude, stands conveniently posed in a gesture of modesty and thus remains unviolated by the gaze of the beholder. The appeal of the image was undoubtedly partly erotic. Viewers could experience the pleasure of desire through voyeurism, yet remain free from guilt because the subject seemed so ostentatiously virginal. Not surprisingly, for just such reasons, Parrish's images found an enthusiastic audience among adolescents. Somewhat self-deprecatingly, Parrish himself alluded to the interest in his work among college boys and "young ladies" in seminaries.[106]

The fame of *Daybreak* and works like it offered Parrish satisfactions but also problems and a sense of ambivalence. He was forced to preimpose standards of propriety. Although he himself never actually acknowledged in writing the erotic undertones of his paintings, he was clearly conscious that this element constituted their appeal. Aware that nudity was controversial (especially after his teenage daughter and other local girls began resisting his efforts to use them as models), Parrish knew that he had to watch what he painted, and to avoid seeming prurient. He had to accommodate to the idea of depicting uncontroversial subjects.[107] These considerations led him (in contrast to Norman Rockwell) to resist anecdotal description: he refused to discuss the meaning of his works. For example, when asked by his print dealer to write a little story about *Daybreak,* Parrish responded:

> I could do almost anything in the world for you but that. I know full well the public want a story, always want to know more about a picture than the picture tells them, but to my mind if the picture does not tell its own story, it's better to have the story without the picture. I couldn't tell a single thing about *DAYBREAK* because there isn't a single thing to tell: the picture tells all there is, there is nothing more. . . . *DAYBREAK* is just daybreak, and if it doesn't mean enough to the observer, it's unfortunate, that's all.[108]

Much like his modernist counterparts, Parrish contended that the meaning of the picture was there, right on the surface of the canvas.

Parrish's unwillingness to tell a story was not just a matter of prudence. Demands for explication also conflicted with his own artistic sensibilities. Parrish's insistence on the self-sufficiency of the artist's expression was indicative of a romantic strain in his thinking that—as with N. C. Wyeth in chapter 1—periodically produced conflict whenever he began to compare his actual practices with his vision of true art.

Success did have drawbacks. Like advertising copywriters and art directors, Parrish was pressured by his clients to continue his accomplishments. At times he was manipulated. House of Art owners Reinthal and Newman urged him to work in a formulaic manner, in the same vein as *Daybreak*. "[A] full composition picture with plenty of opportunity for reflective thoughts, is the order of the day."[109] Yet two years later they were demanding that he do "something radically new and different" and as soon as possible.[110]

Parrish was sometimes confounded about how to respond to the whims of his clients and the shifting tastes of his public—how to reconcile his own interests with theirs. "This whole question of pictures made to order is a darn peculiar form of merchandise," he wrote Reinthal.

> As a gamble, poetry and music and literature are not far off. A man makes a great hit, a best seller, with a novel. His publishers are frantic for him to repeat, and the chances are his first success will be his last. You may order another best seller from me, and God knows *I'm* willing enough, but—can I deliver the goods? I have given the matter no end of thought and analysis, for I am just as keen as the next one to make money and not one bit ashamed to own it. I think I know more than I did, but there are a lot of things to consider in making a picture that is as good a work of art as you know how to produce and at the same time be popular to the public at large. I have gone about, in this connection, and kept my ears open, proposing mild questionnaires, and I confess to being somewhat at sea still. They all seem to like the tiresome M[axfield]. P[arrish]. blue, for one thing, and girls having a pleasant chat, for another. They must look pleasant, like GARDEN OF ALLAH [another popular painting]

> and DAYBREAK. The contemplative kind, such as HILLTOP, not so popular. . . .
>
> You know, and I know that what people like is a beautiful setting with charmed figures, clothed or otherwise, and probably no one special feature. Whatever it is, it's elusive.[111]

Parrish could not fathom what exactly his audience wanted and why, but of one thing he seemed convinced: "Needless to say the good art quality has no particular appeal: that is only for those who know."[112] Only well-educated people with sophisticated tastes like himself could appreciate the true art quality to which he aspired but felt unable to achieve. Acknowledging his predicament, he figuratively threw up his hands. "The question of judgement is a puzzling one," he concluded. "I am beginning to doubt my own. I'd rather have the cook's opinion concerning popularity than my own."[113] The cook presumably would offer more realizable, less convoluted recipes for success.

Parrish became increasingly frustrated with the compromises he felt obliged to make to ensure continued commercial success. His audience-oriented aesthetic strategies periodically clashed with his personal goals, which continued to be governed by traditional creator-oriented conceptions of artistic freedom and expressivity, shaped by his own art school background. He basically respected his audiences' individual taste preferences and sincerely longed to maintain popular approval, just as he also feared the consequences of forfeiting his income. Yet he was clearly torn, knowing that his work appealed primarily not to cultured intellectuals but to middlebrow housewives and teenagers. The repercussions periodically frustrated him. His work of the 1920s did not bring self-fulfillment. He felt unable to take risks, and (like Wyeth) he blamed himself. In commenting on the matter, he referred to yet another interpretation of "commercial art"—as the mass-produced art prints. "I'm done with girls on rocks," he told the Associated Press. "I've painted them for thirteen years and I could paint them and sell them for thirteen more. That's the peril of the commercial art game. It tempts a man to repeat himself."[114]

Yet compromise brought flexibility. By 1930, Parrish was in a position to pick and choose his work. He broke ties with Edison-Mazda and moved away from explicit product advertisements (whose tight deadlines were as much the problem as anything else). He maintained his business relations with House of Art, but also entered into a long-term arrangement to paint landscapes for the Minnesota firm Brown and Bigelow, publishers of art prints, calendars, and greeting cards. Brown and Bigelow allowed Parrish to do the type of picture he had long hoped to paint—landscapes. Since the mid-nineteenth century, landscapes had been considered the genre most conducive to self-expression; hence, to Parrish, landscapes represented artistic freedom.[115] Brown and Bigelow had the choice of reproducing these paintings as calendars, greeting cards, or prints (but only as long as Reinthal and Newman did not plan to use them as prints). Parrish received a 10 percent royalty on the sale price of each item.[116] Parrish had long-standing disagreements with Reinthal and Newman over an exclusivity clause that stated that only House of Art could reproduce his paintings as art prints. Parrish insisted that the distinction between art prints, calendars, and magazine pictures was ultimately arbitrary, since anyone who wanted the picture would simply mount it on the wall. House of Art was especially concerned about the problem during the depression, when they were forced to cut prices because people were not buying.[117]

From Parrish's perspective, it was all the same. Artistic freedom and popular interest were what mattered. Now in his sixties, he painted what he wished, knowing that he still enjoyed a visible, if uncertain, standing as an artist among thousands of people who also did not (or could not afford to) distinguish between pictures, art prints, and calendar pictures.[118] In Mark Sandrich's 1935 movie *Top Hat,* Jerry Travers (Fred Astaire) characterizes Horace's (Edward Everett Horton) black eye as looking "like a sunrise by Maxfield Parrish." "Ohhh. Oh," responds Horace, "Jerry, that's *terrible.*" The line reveals the extent to which the work of Parrish had become a commonplace, the subject of jokes. Yet the point is ambiguous (is what's terrible the eye or its resemblance to a Parrish?), suggesting the uncertainty of Parrish's reputation among Hollywood scriptwriters themselves struggling to slough off reputations as hacks.

In downplaying differences, Parrish's interests again seemed to intersect with those of Calkins. Referring to advertising, Calkins had argued that the status of a work hinged not on the uses to which it was put, but rather on the creative sincerity and quality that the artist brought to it. Calkins made this argument to challenge perceived hierarchies and distinctions drawn between "fine" and "commercial" art. Parrish, by contrast, held up such distinctions. In painting to serve a mass public of consumers of art reproductions, he harbored no illusions. He freely admitted himself to be a "commercial artist, who, ever since his beginning, has made his living by having his work reproduced"—a man who, for all his independence, lacked a certain control and confidence.[119] Although like Davis a painter of "popular pictures" (albeit without a comparable irony), Parrish made no claims to make "works of art." Writing in 1930, he instructed his son:

> . . . whenever you ever do me the honor to talk over the undersigned with anybody, tell them the truth, that I never was supposed to be any more

> than an illustrator, or even a commercial artist, and that at times I entered realms that were beyond me. I don't mind that artists make potboilers, but I do mind their claiming they are works of art. And it's funny, there are some doubtful specimens up in the sacred realms too.

"I would still like to paint just the subjects I have painted and have them right and not pretty and sentimental," he continued, "but I am not up to it. Maybe it is something like the ancient ones who tried to paint divinity and religious feeling; they inevitably ended up with piety and malnutrition."[120]

Parrish's success did not endear him to art critics or to his more progressive artistic counterparts, who regarded his ubiquitous images as insipid clichés. His practices also were antithetical to the romantic concern for individuality, sincerity, autonomy, and uniqueness guarded by modernists like Pach, and even, to some extent, by Parrish himself, as the comments I have cited above suggest.[121] Yet as long as his art prints and calendars were adequately reproduced, and as long as people enjoyed them as art, it did not matter to Parrish if they served commercial purposes along the way. He justified his activity to himself and others as he had always done. He acknowledged that he was a product of the new commercial print technologies and marketing systems, but he also stressed that these commercial mechanisms were what ultimately provided him with artistic independence and financial security. His concerns were quite straightforward. He wanted to enjoy the freedom to paint what he wanted and to provide for his family. He regarded the successful completion of his commissions as a satisfying creative challenge that demanded a synchronization of taste and craft, not originality.[122] Such pragmatism, combined with tenacity, unpretentiousness, and a shrewd business sense, enabled Parrish to find a satisfactory middle ground between his artistic objectives and his profit-making practices for over four decades. Although not a modernist like Rockwell Kent, Parrish was, like Kent, an artist of modernity.

Rockwell Kent

Like Parrish, Rockwell Kent (fig. 5.10) was socially independent, sometimes reclusive, yet extremely prolific and artistically successful. He shared with Parrish a fascination with exoticism, fantasy, and primitivism. Their means of expression, however, varied significantly, as did their cultural ideologies and politics.

Compared with Parrish, Kent had a firmer place in the elite institutional realms that defined the boundaries of fine art in relatively narrow terms. In the early 1900s the young Columbia University graduate

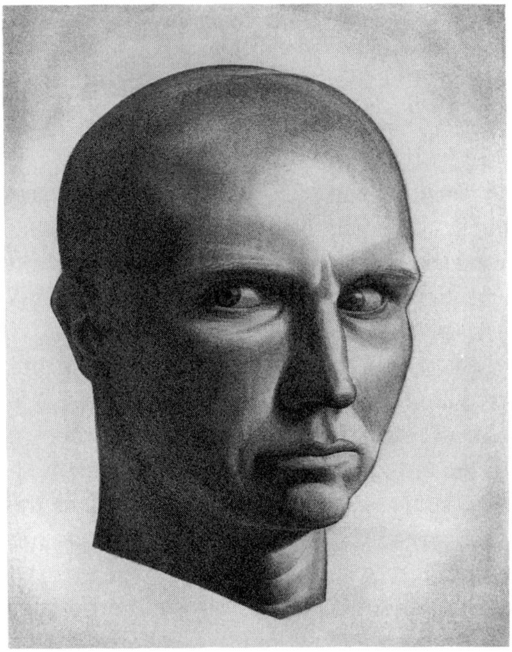

5.10. Rockwell Kent, *Self Portrait (It's Me O Lord)*, 1934.

worked as a draftsman for the new, yet well connected, architectural firm of Ewing and Chappell.[123] On the side he pursued his strong interest in art, enrolling in Robert Henri's (1865–1929) life class at the New York School of Art on a scholarship offered him by the school's founder William Merritt Chase (1849–1916). In addition to his classes with Henri, Kent began to study with Kenneth Hayes Miller (1876–1952).

Although Parrish, like Kent, studied painting with painters (Parrish's teacher Anschutz had also taught Kent's mentor Henri), Kent, more than Parrish, was imbued with an appreciation for romantic notions about originality, the uniqueness of the artist, and the sanctity of individual expression. In further contrast to Parrish, Kent achieved a reputation as an easel painter, graphic artist, and master book illustrator.[124] He capitalized on these media as unique or limited-edition expressions of quality and conviction. In 1907, early in his career, Kent sold paintings to the Metropolitan Museum of Art and the less notable New Britain Museum of Art.

A charismatic personality, Kent also developed connections to many of the art world's leading figures.[125]

Talented, refined, and well educated, Kent had all the makings of a successful artistic or architectural career in establishment circles, had he wished for it. In art he embraced the ideals of expertise and professionalism espoused by his Progressive contemporaries like Blashfield. Like them, Kent believed that artistic activity entailed obligations of service to the public at large. His conception of that public was more sympathetic and moderate than that of avant-garde colleagues like Pach.[126] But, like Pach, Kent rejected the ethnocentrism and institutional exclusionism underlying the ideology of service espoused by painters like Blashfield. Kent rebelled against the social order that he believed produced such attitudes and inequities. Challenging what his Columbia professor A. D. F. Hamlin termed the "habits of respectable society," Kent joined the Socialist party in 1904.[127] A political and artistic nonconformist, he made the search for independence a theme of his life's work.[128]

Yet Kent was also a vocal organization man who believed in acting to achieve his goals. He believed that a strong organized labor movement would be the driving force that would pave the way to socialism, and he fervently embraced Communism after 1917. He denied ever being a member of the Communist Party of the United States, but maintained close ties to party members and party-controlled organizations and crusaded for their causes from the mid-1930s onward.[129] Long prior to this, however, Kent's commitment to socialism, romanticism, and activism led him to be an engaged, important participant in efforts to reshape the institutional frameworks that defined the nature of art. For Kent, as for Calkins, that process entailed a reconfiguration of art to embrace advertising and print media, especially reproductions. Unlike Pach and Davis, who tried to draw distinctions between painting and commercial art, Kent often acted as if such distinctions were nonexistent. Yet he was not consistent on this score.

Much more than Parrish, Kent brought his traditionalist aesthetic priorities to bear on his practices as a commercial artist. Parrish, despite his more conservative style and personal concerns, was usually willing to play by advertisers' and printmakers' rules. Kent sought to change the procedures in order to serve the expressive concerns of the fine artist in advertising. His challenge was to convince advertisers, art directors, and other powers to defer to ideologies that respected the artist and the new, highly personal and stylistically progressive modes of expression. He only partially succeeded. Like painters, business clients and advertising executives faced constraints that permitted them to be flexible only up to a point.

Kent's commercial art activities must be understood in the context of his earlier efforts to broaden artistic participation in the more narrowly defined sphere of "fine art" painting. Early on, Kent, like Pach, had contested the authority of influential but stylistically conservative artists like Blashfield and of established institutions like the National Academy of Design. Kent began this campaign in 1910, helping to mount an exhibition of paintings by such progressive artists as Maurice Prendergast, Alfred Maurer, George Luks, and Marsden Hartley. In 1916 he joined the new Society of Independent Artists, who called for an unjuried exhibition.[130] Kent continued to take on the art establishment in the 1920s. Now, however, he took off in two new directions that exploited the mechanisms of contemporary media culture. First, taking his cue from individuals like Kuhn and the precedent of the Armory Show, Kent mounted a publicity campaign against the National Academy by writing letters to newspaper editors. Second, he challenged the elitism of many fellow artists by actively promoting the mass dissemination and consumption of art through advertising and print reproductions.

A consummate rhetorician (much like Calkins), Kent demonstrated his publicity savvy on many occasions. In 1927 he took several opportunities to broadcast his interests. Acting as his own press agent, he launched a vigorous assault upon the academic establishment. With exhibitions at Wildenstein and Weyhe Gallery, he was by now a successful and well-regarded painter by American standards, and his articulate and passionate statements were taken seriously and often published. Writing to the magazine *New Masses* and to the *New York World, New York Herald Tribune, New York Times,* and other newspapers, he assailed the hegemony of the National Academy of Design over the institutional structures of art in New York City. He condemned its too-exclusive exhibitions, its members' ties to municipal and federal authorities, and their monopoly on public commissions.[131]

Kent's protests came despite the fact that the 1927 exhibition of the National Academy of Design included a section devoted to an unprecedented number of "modernist" artists, including Guy Pène du Bois, Joseph Stella, Robert Winthrop Chanler, Charles Burchfield, and Raphael Soyer. (Their work was selected by a three-man committee and accepted without going through the academy's jury review process.)[132] Kent's efforts to alter the public's perception of the academy's claims to authority fell on deaf ears. After many attacks but few victories, he abandoned the direct assault. Instead, he attempted to organize a gallery of contemporary art in order to broaden definitions of legitimate artistic activity to give younger and more progressive artists more control. This project came to naught. However, Kent would continue to seek out press publicity for his causes on behalf of artists' liberation, actions that—combined with his other political agendas—would severely damage his reputation among political moderates and conservatives from the depression on into the McCarthy era.[133]

Having made little headway working within the framework of established art institutions, Kent broadened his focus and concentrated on other art worlds with which he was involved. Among other things, he turned to advertising. For Maxfield Parrish, advertising offered certain artistic challenges and a way to meet financial obligations. For Kent, advertising had additional personal, artistic, and political advantages. It gave him the opportunity to reach a broad audience. Also, significantly, it provided him with a method of reducing his financial obligations and domestic worries. An inveterate womanizer, Kent could lighten his conscience by supporting his three wives and five children.[134] Hence Kent cultivated advertising jobs in the 1920s, taking on commissions for clients like Steinway, Hupmobile, and Marcus and Company.

Kent had a certain ambivalence toward advertising, just as he did toward painting. Advertising was low in his esteem, less because it sought to whet consumer desire for unnecessary products than because advertisers did not conform to his ideal of artistic practice. In Kent's view, advertising procedures unnecessarily denied artists the freedom of inspiration that made them artists and that was integral to their identity.[135] He thought that similar problems, arising from similarly oppressive circumstances, also afflicted easel painters. Artists were obliged to exhibit their work as a form of public entertainment, with little remuneration. Like other workers, they needed to earn a living. Both advertising art and fine art forced artists to sell their souls.[136]

Kent's concerns were consistent with his larger belief that the artist was marginal in American society. To change this situation, he sought to blur distinctions between easel painters, printmakers, and other artists, including those working in advertising. He aspired to achieve common ethics and professional standards that would give artists more autonomy and free them from exploitation by dealers, museums, patrons, and business clients. He thus fought on behalf of easel painting and advertising art as equally valid forms of artistic work.[137]

During the same period as his newspaper campaigns against the National Academy, Kent became involved in a strategy to better the lot of the artist in advertising. His efforts coincided with those of both Calkins and the art directors. As we saw in chapter 3, art directors claimed jurisdiction over art in order to consolidate their professional control within the spheres of both art and advertising. Kent, on the other hand, wanted to help artists acquire more power to shape business practices. He demanded that even art directors defer to artists. Advertisers could borrow from fine art, but only by allowing art and artistic interests to supersede and even subsume commercial activity. The priorities could not be reversed.

In other words, fine art had to shape the parameters of commercial practice, not the other way around. "Art is imagination," Kent stated in a solicited, but then unpublished, introduction to the Art Directors Club Annual. "On the appreciation of that distinction [art as imagination] by the men who plan advertising depends both the development of advertising as an art and the progress of art in advertising." Progress meant the "flowering of whatever freedom has been accorded the artist to think for himself and to do his work as it may please him." Advertising art would lose its "stigma" only when "the *appreciation* of art shall have finally supplanted the 'directing' of it." Only under these circumstances could advertising art "bring to merchandising . . . the persuasive power of unhampered eloquence."[138]

Kent achieved a qualified success in consciousness-raising. He had several advantages: he had a knack for attracting press publicity, his aesthetic views jibed with those of many art directors, and yet he had a firm footing in the more exclusive "nonprofit" sector of the American art world. All of these factors helped Kent in his battles with Marcus and Company jewelers. This case enabled Kent to showcase his demands to improve artists' rights, but it also revealed the limits of his artistic and political power. The incident is thus worth reviewing fully.

The Case of Marcus and Company

In 1926, N. W. Ayer art director Vaughn Flannery hired Kent to do a series of pen-and-ink illustrations for advertisements for the jewelry firm of Marcus and Company. The advertisements were published in elite magazines like *Vogue, Vanity Fair, Town and Country,* and *The New Yorker.*[139] Stylistically and iconographically, the black-and-white pictures were comparable to Kent's easel and graphic art and book illustrations, and to other advertisements he had designed. They were crisply linear depictions of figures (either in classical garb or in a highly simplified version of contemporary dress) in a manner influenced by Michelangelo, Flaxman, Blake, and Rococoesque renderings of elegant eighteenth-century women, exotic Arabs, and other orientalisms. Ayer paid Kent $400 for each of the drawings. Marcus and Company, in collaboration with Flannery and Kent, determined the subject matter, although the artist was accorded the final judgment and occasionally objected to Ayer's suggestions.[140]

Relations between artist and client were cordial until early 1929, when Kent learned the outcome of that year's Harvard advertising awards. Begun in 1923 by *Ladies' Home Journal* editor Edward W. Bok and administered by the Harvard Business School, the Harvard Awards were meant to educate advertisers and promote high standards of quality. Awards of $1,000 each were conferred for the best work in such categories as "the advertisement most effective in its use of text as the chief means of delivering its message," and "the advertisement most effective in its use of pictorial illustration as the chief means of delivering its message."[141] The 1929 award for the latter category (illustration) went to Marcus and Company, "with recognition to Charles A. Hammarstrom" (an advertising manager and publicity director for Marcus and Company), for an illustrated advertisement titled "The Delectable Crescent" (fig. 5.11). Kent had rendered the award-winning drawing, but to his chagrin, his name was not mentioned. Chagrin turned to anger when Kent learned that "in naming Mr. Hammarstrom, the Harvard School of Business Administration had followed its usual custom of asking the winner of the prize [i.e., the winning organization] to suggest the individual most worthy of honorable mention, and Marcus & Co. had named Mr. Hammarstrom, had ignored Mr. Kent." Hammarstrom made the decision to nominate himself.[142] When the awards jury and the dean of the Harvard Business School protested the omission of Kent's name, Marcus and Company split the award, sending $500 to Kent and the remainder to Hammarstrom. Yet according to Kent, Hammarstrom had played no part whatsoever in the production of the "Delectable Crescent" advertisement, apart from approving Kent's suggestions.[143] The litigious Kent returned his check and "took steps toward legal action."[144]

While preparing for judicial battle, Kent also readied himself for a fight in the court of public opinion. "The way that I can best retaliate for such an abominable trick," he wrote his lawyer, "is through publicity."[145] To that end, he sent another barrage of letters to editors and other influential individuals (although only some were published), and banked on his connections and his artistic reputation to help him win sympathy.[146]

Kent's promotional efforts enabled him to air the grievances he hoped to take into court. He had to use his advertising work to gain recognition as an artist. At stake was not money, but his "professional reputation and the very important principle as to who, in all first class and what I may call stellar advertising art, deserves credit for the pictures."[147] Kent was willing to submerge his interests on behalf of the client within certain limits, but he would sacrifice only so much. He refused to have his contribution ignored completely, especially when someone else took credit for it. To make this case, Kent had to prove the value of his name "as a mark of the honest workmanship and the integrity" of his art.[148] The

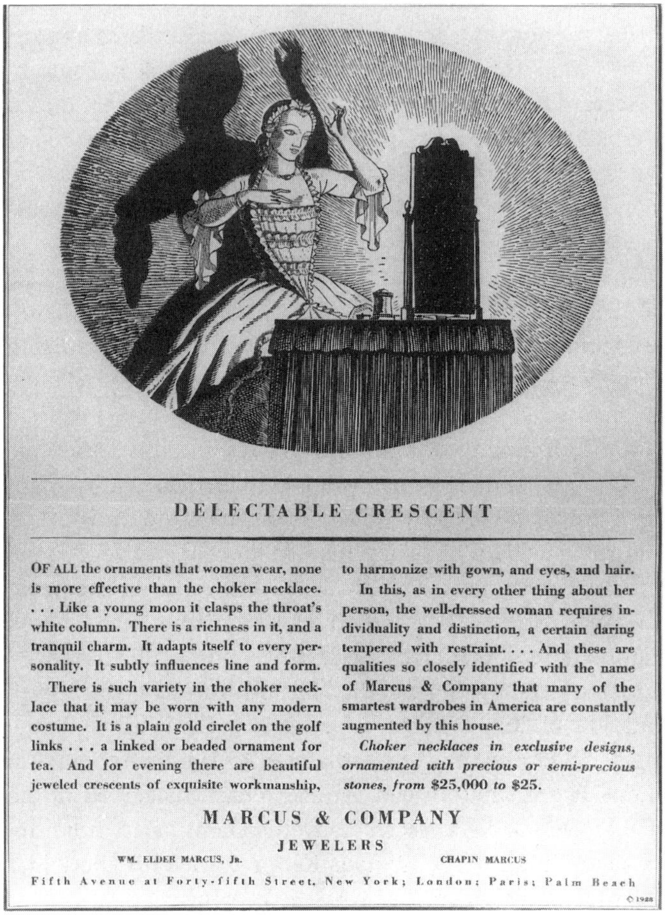

5.11. "Delectable Crescent," advertisement for Marcus and Company Jewelers, 1928, illustration by Rockwell Kent.

artist's work was unique and irreproducible. It was this individual mark of the artist's hand that lent cachet to an advertisement, that made it visually effective, and hence helped produce sales. Signature thus became a central issue for Kent, just as it had been for the art directors.

The matter of signature had already been a bone of contention between Kent and Marcus. N. W. Ayer, it will be recalled, was one of the agencies that often relied on prominent artists for its advertising, and hence it encouraged the signature. Initially, when Ayer's art directors had sent him ideas in the form of sketches, Kent had refused to sign his name. "I took the stand that my name was my guarantee of the personal integrity of my work, and that, although the manner, style, and general appearance of the drawings were my own . . . unless I was allowed great liberty in the interpretation of these ideas I would not sign my name."[149] Freedom meant adhering to standards "determined by work that I had previously done for myself." Kent insisted that "I should be in no way dictated to in my work, and that the drawings were not to be, in the conventional sense, illustrative of the text."[150] Only when Ayer stopped sending him sketches did Kent sign his pictures. "The Delectable Crescent" bore Kent's name; from Kent's perspective, that signature marked the illustration in the ad as his authentic creation. Moreover, he argued (correctly), Marcus and Company were well aware of the advertising cachet of the Rockwell Kent name. Kent had been specifically hired because advertiser and client deemed his work especially appropriate for their needs. Furthermore, Kent claimed, the firm even hung his originals (still Kent's property) in their office hallways—an indication of the company's pride in Kent's drawings (minus the copy) as art. They were commodities with a value independent of their relation to the text and to the ads as a whole. Since the award for the advertising was based upon the excellence of the illustration that contributed to it, Kent concluded, the award should have gone to him. Marcus and Company had done Kent a moral and legal wrong in deliberately suppressing credit to the artist for his work.[151]

In making these claims, Kent fully expected to have to reassure a jury that he was not trying to act like a prima donna, an aesthete who put a premium on art for art's sake. Rather, Kent insisted, he was defending the right of artists to respect for their work. He was trying to protect artists as "workmen," and (as Kent intended to tell the jury) he had always stood on the "side of labor."[152] Indeed, in this as in other instances, Kent hoped to highlight class as fundamental to debates over artistic identity and authority. For Kent, the issue was not merely aesthetic freedom and accountability, but power relations between workers and employers as well as between artists and businessmen. In theory, the craft of the artist in advertising was equal to that of a painter or any other laborer. In Kent's view, however, the practice of advertising cheapened his work by forcing him to pander to others' demands. Even when this did not happen, such as in Kent's case with Marcus, the businessman still exploited artists. The battle would not be won until artists were truly accepted as professionals—until their standards governed artistic practice in all areas of application like advertising, and not the other way around.[153]

Kent and his client could not reconcile their differences of opinion concerning the priority of art within an advertising hierarchy, and this situation sheds light on art directors' problems as well. Unlike Earnest

Elmo Calkins and many art directors, the players on the Marcus team were unwilling to concede to the demands of the individual creator. Kent and his lawyers got an inkling of the troubles they would encounter, were they to go to court, when they discovered that even the Harvard Business School officials administering the award were prepared to defend the rights of the advertiser over those of the artist. Ever since the Harvard Awards had first been implemented, but especially in recent years, advertising executives had criticized them for seeming to measure abstract aesthetic qualities rather than the effectiveness of various features of the advertisement in selling the product. The Harvard Business School administrators hardly wanted to alienate business leaders. Clearly responding to these pressures, the assistant dean wrote Kent that the award was "given *not for art* but for an advertisement distinguished for its effective use of illustration as the chief means of delivering its message." The Harvard Awards jury, he claimed, considered other parts of the advertisement in making their decision.[154] The Business School dean admitted that the school preferred to have the award go to an individual—as was the current practice with the Art Directors Club exhibition—but noted that the effectiveness of an advertisement and its illustration was often the end result of the work of more than one person, who could be the advertising manager or art director as well as the artist. Although hedging on the issues at the heart of Kent's argument, the Harvard dean thus refused to agree with the idea that the artist was the appropriate and obvious recipient.[155] Chapin Marcus, the head of the firm, himself insisted that as advertising manager, Hammarstrom had supervised the winning advertisement and in that capacity was designated to go and receive the award.[156] Yet this action went against precedent. With the exception of the first year's prizes, the Harvard Awards had always been given to the artists who had illustrated the advertisements.[157] Thus the response from the Marcus and Harvard people indicated that a meeting of minds would not occur.

Kent and his lawyers prepared to take the case to court in the spring of 1929, but ultimately did not. Kent's correspondence provides no explanation, but he hinted at the reason in his autobiography: "Harvard, Marcus, and Ayer were prepared for such mutual support and buck passing as would make a suit too costly for my means." Not one to shrink from court battles, Kent probably became convinced that he had been pinned to the wall by representatives of powerful corporate and academic institutions. He could not afford to fight.[158]

Kent's animus toward Marcus and Company did not deter him from accepting other advertising commissions. Swayed by artistic interest and financial concerns, he went on to do designs for Hupmobile, American

Car and Foundry, National Brazilian Coffee, and, in the 1940s, American Export Lines (fig. 5.12). Like Wyeth, Parrish, and others, he wanted the income that he could not make from painting alone. Frustrated by his continued financial dependence on business clients, Kent increasingly sought to draw rhetorical distinctions between his true art and his "low-

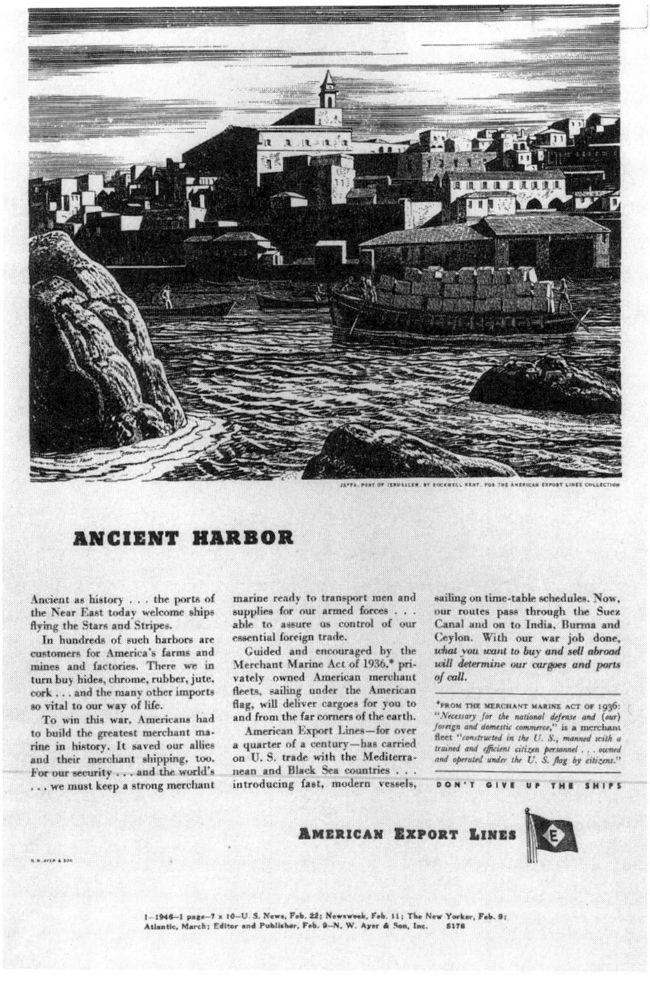

5.12. Advertisement for American Export Lines, illustration by Rockwell Kent, 1946.

down" commercial activity, especially during the depression. Writing to photographer Margaret Bourke-White in 1936 (a point when anticapitalist, pro-labor sentiments were at new heights and Kent's own involvement with Communist Party–sponsored causes intensified), he commented, "We are workmen. We make with our hands things that are meant to sell. . . . I support myself by turning my hand to the production of almost every lowdown job that commerce, the great prostituting patron of the arts demands. . . . Art is the enshrinement of the best in heart and soul that men have in them," he insisted. "I have never supported myself by any of those products of my heart and soul that may make some things I do worth while."[159]

But Kent's rhetorical distinctions between fine art and commercial art were just that. His differentiations were especially questionable in the light of his insistence that all artists were laborers and craftsmen. Whatever the theoretical distinctions he drew between the products of his heart and soul and those other "lowdown jobs," in practice the two were virtually identical in style and subject. Moreover, as art historian Alan Wallach has observed, Kent's artwork was curiously devoid of the energy and political fervor that were so integral to other aspects of his life. From the standpoint of artists, art directors, and many businessmen, the boldly linear style of Kent's art, as well as its idealism and strength, contributed a great deal to the advancement of art in advertising. By contrast, his painting style was rather conservative. It did not attempt to change the world or cure injustices; it was not politically oriented in any overt way.[160] That transformative role was reserved for service and organizational activism, an outgrowth of the artist's commitment to Marxism and professionalism. In this latter sense, Kent paradoxically shared some common ground with his old antagonist Blashfield. Both believed that, in the modern era, the artist had to enhance his own stature and that of art to enrich the lives of a broadening public.

But Kent's view of that public and his marketing practices had more in common with that of Maxfield Parrish. Like Parrish, Kent took advantage of opportunities offered by the many new businesses that contributed to the mass commodification of art. Art as a form of public service might not be consistent with art in service to advertising. Nonetheless, from Kent's perspective, artistic activity could entail commercial and political practices and serve a broad public too. The same year in which he wrote to Bourke-White, Kent also joined forces with his old friend Carl Zigrosser on a plan to "buck the print racket" by mass-marketing large editions of unsigned prints at two dollars each.[161] Paradoxically, the idea was to downplay valuation based on artist's name or signature and to broaden public interest in owning art, all the while providing the artist freedom of expression and a chance to make money.[162] This was only one of several money-making and popularizing ventures with which Kent became involved.[163]

Aware that his own work made it difficult to claim consistently that fine art was inherently different from commercial art, Kent insisted on maintaining a psychological dichotomy. He distinguished between the artist in advertising, who produced freely inspired pictures that did not necessarily illustrate a text, and commercial practices, in which craftsmen conformed to "every horrible contrivance for reducing art to that low level of standardized perfection which it must reach to sell."[164] In distinguishing free creativity from conformity, Kent's views coalesced with those of Calkins. Both contended that differences between true art and hack work existed in all spheres of artistic activity, for profit or not.

In drawing these contrasts, Kent tried to provide an argument that would give painters and printmakers new financial opportunities and professional leverage. His dichotomy "free creativity vs. conformity" justified commercial work to fellow painters wary of taking on such commissions. For independent painters and artists in advertising, Kent's claims offered a reassuring rationale for drawing aesthetic distinctions between "real" art and commercial work, but without the concomitant need to establish social or professional hierarchies between "pure" easel painting and art for advertising or mass-produced prints.

Championing romantic ideals of creative freedom and sincerity, Kent acknowledged, as had Calkins, Blashfield, Kuhn, Pach, Davis, and Parrish, the growing cultural preeminence of commercial and corporate interests. Like them, he resisted the implications of such business incursions. He challenged advertisers and other patrons to accept artists' nonnegotiable claims over the terrain of all artistic work. His efforts helped the interests of artists in advertising, if only by making clients more conscious of artists' expectations. This took place at a time when some advertisers were experimenting with work by "fine art" easel painters. But as Kent's experiences suggest, and as the next chapter will make clear, painters' growing involvement with advertising and corporate public relations did not in fact result in much greater influence for them. Uncertain of their audience and preoccupied with the mundane problems of employment, painters were forced to grapple with new articulations of identity, practice, and status during the period between the depression and the end of World War II.

chapter 6

Artists and Organizations

From the beginning of the twentieth century, painters had struggled to connect with business clients, reach broad audiences, and earn good money without compromising their ideals. Artists' identities were shaped in relation to business activities even more during and after the 1930s, when thousands of them sought regular work and corporations emerged as important sources of art patronage. As we shall see in the following pages, companies like Container Corporation of America, American Tobacco Company, IBM, Standard Oil (New Jersey), The Upjohn Company, and Pepsi-Cola utilized the work of career painters for product advertising and public relations to an unprecedented degree—some more appropriately than others, from the standpoints of artists and critics. Painters' new involvement with corporate advertisers kindled more debates about the relation of fine art to commercial art. For all the loud proclamations about business's new contributions to art and vice versa, art critics, industrialists, advertisers, and artists themselves remained ambivalent about the merits and meanings of this activity. Although painters' expectations for (and suspicions of) corporate beneficence increased during World War II, the following years in fact saw a substantial weakening of painters' ties with advertising agencies and corporations. In the mid-1950s, the emergence of another commercial presence, television, further confounded painters' anticipations by undermining their claims to artistic expertise. Recent discussions of the art of this period have highlighted ways in which corporate culture co-opted avant-garde painting. This chapter, by contrast, will argue that in some crucial respects, corporate management and advertising agencies abandoned fine art during this period.

These developments had important ramifications for conceptions of and the status of art and the artist from the 1950s to this day.

IN SEARCH OF WORK

Rockwell Kent's 1929 encounters with Marcus and Company demonstrated that painters' associations with advertisers were often tenuous even before the crash on Wall Street changed bargaining positions. During the depression painters became more dependent on businessmen, and their relationship was laden with even more problems. As I mentioned earlier in discussing art directors, advertising agencies during the depression shunned experiments with modernist styles except in photography, which they generally favored for its apparent realism. Advertisers were being forced to cut back on all advertising just at the point when painters were searching for work and new patrons.[1]

The relative prosperity of the 1920s, combined with the rise of an organized nexus of art institutions and dealers, had expanded the numbers of American painters. The majority experienced difficulties in exhibiting and selling their art, and earned their living through occupations other than pure painting, but most were at least able to eke out some kind of living. The depression threw many of these artists, along with millions of other Americans, out of work and into desperate straits. The federal government provided artists with some support, first through the Emergency Work Bureau (1932) and then through the unprecedented ventures into federal art patronage implemented by the New Deal.[2] The New Deal art projects, however, were meant to be temporary. Congress was reluctant to allocate any more funding than absolutely necessary, and few artists found the programs sufficiently comprehensive to alleviate their financial and emotional distress.[3]

For many artists, the disappearance of jobs in the commercial sector coincided with the moment when they were experiencing a crisis of confidence and purpose. Some painters attempted, through the labor movement and the Popular Front, to take action to become more influential and artistically productive both in the short run and over the long term. Groups like the Artists' Union (1934–1938) and the American Artists' Congress (1936–1942) sought both to expand government programs and to contact new publics.[4] Echoing the broader reverberations of radical and labor politics during this period, these artists (many of whom were Communist Party members or had close ties to the Party through affiliations with the John Reed Clubs, and later, the Popular Front) identified with workers and sought to reach out to workers.[5] But they became increasingly divided on ideological and aesthetic grounds as both the American labor movement and leftist politics were shaken by the shifts in Soviet foreign policy and by the Hitler-Stalin pact. Radical stances ultimately placed these artists at odds with strong and well-organized conservative forces, and with publics toward which many of them had been ambivalent in the first place.[6]

During World War II, through more politically centrist organizations like Artists for Victory—an alliance of artists' groups working on behalf of the war effort—some artists continued to try to secure government patronage, but with minimal success.[7] The failure of Artists for Victory underscored their predicament: the war cut unemployment, but numerous contemporary painters who saw creative work as the only desirable means of earning a living still faced a significant dearth of employment and support.[8] Yet, as painters were becoming increasingly aware, alternative possibilities for patronage were actually available.

Not-for-profit activities managed by artists ultimately foundered. Commercially run organizations, on the other hand, proved to be considerably more successful, although only a relatively small number of enterprises provided artists with jobs in any significant way. One of the most successful and prosperous of the new commercial art ventures, Associated American Artists, actually originated during the depression. As Erika Doss has noted, "in the depressed economy of the 1930s, the AAA acted as an agent of economic salvation for American scene artists." Its appeal to the public sprang from the ideology of "democratic culture" already popularized through the New Deal.[9] Founded in 1934 by former *Chicago Tribune* reporter and artists' agent and public relations expert Reeves Lewenthal, Associated American Artists was dedicated to the popularization and sale of American art, especially of regionalism. To that end, Lewenthal tapped into the expanding networks of mass art production and marketing of which Maxfield Parrish was already taking advantage. Lewenthal commissioned well-known American scene painters (such as Thomas Hart Benton, John Steuart Curry, Raphael Soyer, and Grant Wood), whose politics were generally, though not exclusively, more to the center than to the left, to create designs for prints, which he then marketed in department stores for five dollars and through mail-order coupons in magazines. Like Reinthal and Newman's House of Art, with which it now competed, AAA was geared toward putting art into the hands of "ordinary" people. AAA, however, pushed art considered to be of higher quality and more progressive artistically than that of Parrish, the House of Art's star. According to Doss, Lewenthal's choice of American scene painters was motivated by the recognition that such art had an enormous popular following and also by a personal distaste for European culture. "Their art, like the politics of the New Deal, aspired to cultural democracy and forecast an American utopia based on the revitalization of the country's earlier republican values: community and productivity. In the midst of Depression anxiety, regionalist art—like New Deal rhetoric and product advertising—took on a broadly therapeutic role through which Americans believed they could regain psychic and social well-being."[10]

The practices of the regionalist artists and the openly commercial strategies of the AAA had their detractors, especially among painters and intellectuals pursuing a critique of mass culture; the latter tendency emerged after the end of the Popular Front in the late 1930s and continued during the postwar period.[11] Nonetheless, Lewenthal's ingenious merchandising scheme made AAA a $500,000-a-year business by 1941 and provided royalties to more than 35 artists.[12] The success of the plan inspired him to open an "Art for Advertising" department in 1938, dedicated to supplying the work of AAA artists to business clients.[13] In its capacity as broker, the AAA soon played a crucial role in bringing together art-art and advertising. As we shall see, Lewenthal convinced several corporations to take the lead in commissioning paintings for advertising and public relations purposes during World War II. Let us now examine the motives of these companies that engaged in "fine art" ventures.

Container Corporation of America

We saw in chapter 3 that the Depression era advertising campaigns of N. W. Ayer's Charles Coiner, working on behalf of clients like French Line, Hawaiian Pineapple, and De Beers diamonds, established productive and mutually advantageous alliances between painters and businessmen. The success of these advertisements lay in the fact that they utilized avowedly modern painting at a time when most advertisers considered it imprudent to do so. Of the several N. W. Ayer "fine art" advertising campaigns, those of Container Corporation of America made the most profound impression on businessmen, advertisers, and painters alike. This company's remarkable series of advertisements reflected the particular configuration of people at the helm. Although few other companies followed Container Corporation's lead, the series represented a new way of using art for advertising and in business generally.[14]

The Chicago-based Container Corporation of America (CCA) produced paperboard containers and cartons essential for packaging (for clients like Campbell's Soup, Hunt's Foods, and Scott Tissues). Like many businesses, it experienced substantial losses by 1934. By 1936 profits returned to earlier highs, and the company seemed to be recovering.[15] Owner and company president Walter Paepcke (1896–1960) made a concerted and successful effort to improve his relationships with both workers and stockholders. He believed it important to boost consumer awareness of CCA and to restore public confidence in corporate activity generally. Following the example of other companies, he embarked on an institutional advertising campaign to promote the company's reputation. Paepcke made the management decision, but it was his wife, Elizabeth Nitze Paepcke, who evidently instructed him how exactly to implement the process. The solution, she insisted, was to use art metaphorically to "package" the company.[16]

Daughter of an eminent University of Chicago professor of romance languages, Elizabeth Nitze Paepcke had grown up in a socially prominent and cultured family. Like many young leisured women, she studied painting and music and became a devotee of avant-garde European art. Although it took some doing, Elizabeth Paepcke persuaded her husband, a somber second-generation German-American with conservative bourgeois tastes, that the path to success was to burnish CCA's image by associating it with design excellence.[17] For Mrs. Paepcke, this meant modernism, especially the montage, the bold type, the bright color, and the simplified asymmetrical composition pioneered by French, Swiss, and German designers (especially by members of the German Bauhaus) and seen in such European journals as *Graphis* and *Gebrauchsgraphik*. Paepcke reportedly suggested to his wife that she become company art director. She refused, preferring to remain in an advisory position and insisting that Paepcke stick with male "professionals."[18]

Following his wife's counsel, Paepcke hired former J. Walter Thompson art director Egbert Jacobson as company art director. Jacobson redesigned the CCA logo and created an all-encompassing, uniform design image for the corporation's factory, offices, letterhead, and trucks, thus reinforcing the impression of a quality product produced by a dedicated, unified labor force (a significant gesture at the height of the industrial union movement).[19] The company then launched its ambitious new print advertising campaign, masterminded by Coiner and Jacobson.[20]

As we saw in chapter 3, CCA's advertisements used highbrow, up-to-the-minute images to sell its notably mundane and plebian cardboard boxes to stockholders, businessmen, and mid-level managers in offices and plants. The first series, begun in 1937, included twelve black-and-white designs by famed poster artist Adolphe Mouron Cassandre, for which he was paid $500 each. Additional work was done by Toni Zepf,

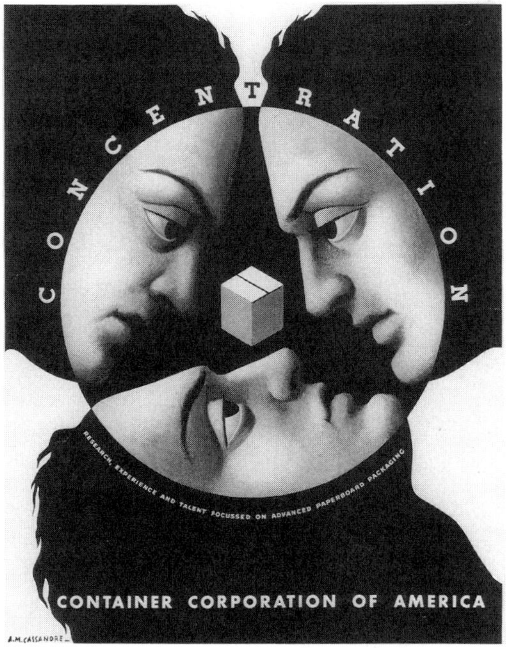

6.1. "Concentration," advertisement for Container Corporation of America, illustration by A. M. Cassandre, 1938. Cassandre depicts three identical male heads, with profiles modeled upon ancient Greek sculpture. Their gazes converge on a cubelike cardboard box. They thus metaphorically represent the copy, "Research, experience and talent focused on advanced paperboard packaging," a phrase that in the complete advertisement ran parallel to the lowermost arc of the circle that binds the faces together compositionally and psychologically. The circle, with its highlightened faces and centered cube, thus represents concentration both literally (iconically), through composition and through depiction of three concentrated stares, and symbolically, through allegory. Cassandre's image departed from the stereotyped expression of desire, typically evoked in advertisements via images of white middle-class women. Concentration is nonetheless constructed in subtly gendered terms, with worldly and intellectual/spiritual activity represented in terms of male strength and directness.

Jean Carlu, Herbert Bayer, Gyorgy Kepes, and others. A number of the artists, including Bayer, were former members of the Bauhaus who had fled Europe to escape the Nazis.[21] These artists created visual analogues for abstract attributes of the paperboard industry (such as "concentration" and "diversification") that served both as composition and as copy (figs. 6.1, 6.2).[22] The differences between these works and the average advertisement were considerable, reflecting the gap in outlook and praxis be-

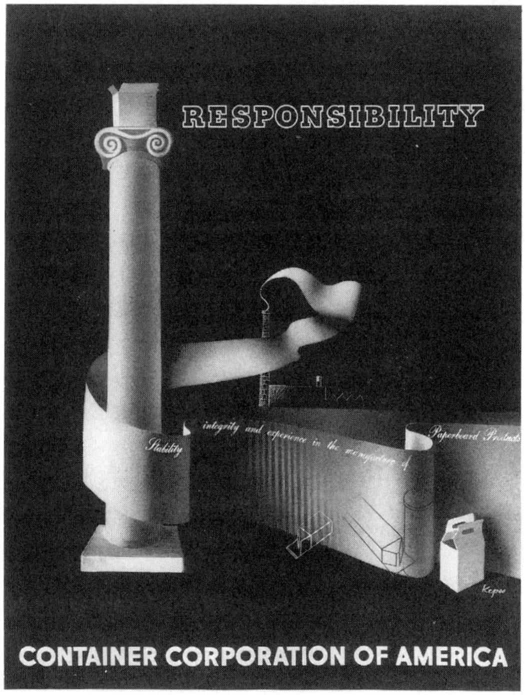

6.2. "Responsibility," advertisement for Container Corporation of America, illustration by Gyorgy Kepes, 1938. An Ionic column, signifying the stability, integrity, and experience of a universal classical tradition, is linked with paperboard both visually and metaphorically. Visual continuity is established through the resemblance between the prominent column and the factory smokestack in the "distance," and through the "smoke." The smoke encircles the column, is transformed into paperboard, and intersects and envelops other paperboard representations. The connection between the stability of the process and the product is further suggested through the carton as abacus atop the volute of the column.

tween Americans and avant-garde Europeans. The CCA images were nonanecdotal; they did not, strictly speaking, illustrate. Meanings were intended to be suggestive, not definitive. Symbolic associations between images and text, between design, paperboard, and the Container Corporation, were metaphorical, poetic, and comparatively subtle.[23] Several of the artists favored montage, a device that did not employ clear, sequential narratives. Each advertisement, as a whole, privileged art, complexity, authenticity, and class, contrasting sharply with the hysterical, hard-sell, direct approach seen in the comic book and photographic advertisements pitched to the less affluent and educated. At the root of avant-garde design, especially that of the Bauhaus, was a concern for creating harmonious visual relationships, compositions that could have a transformative effect in broader spheres of life. The entire curriculum of the Bauhaus was formulated around the idea of the unity of the arts. Artists like Bayer believed in universal design principles ostensibly applicable to any form of creative production, whether painting, sculpture, or furniture design. Unlike many American artists, he felt no need to relegate painting and advertising to separate spheres. The requirements might vary from product to product, but identical spiritual and compositional laws underlay the different modes of activity.[24]

This Bauhaus-influenced design philosophy remained visible in CCA advertising on into the 1940s. During this period some of the advertisements became more overtly propagandistic, emphasizing the patriotic contributions of the paperboard industry to the war effort (fig. 6.3). CCA's motivations at this time were the same as those of other large businesses. Many continued to advertise even though goods were in short supply and demand was strong, in the belief that institutional promotion would keep the company name in the public eye and thus maintain client loyalty until the war was over and markets returned to normal. They also hoped to raise public esteem by demonstrating that they were doing their share to help the war effort.[25] CCA advertisements continued to be distinctive visually, but the actions and ideologies they set forth were very much in step with the broader trend. To this end, by 1944 the early series of advertisements identified CCA as a service industry through the theme of the "worldwide impact of paperboard packaging."[26]

This new emphasis on the company's role as an international industry was consistent thematically with a second group of advertisements, the United Nations series. Published between 1941 and 1946, these ads served as war propaganda by honoring the Allied nations fighting the Axis.[27] They touted the ideal of cooperation and harmony among nations while confirming the growing international presence of CCA as a worldwide supplier of packaging for war materiel and as an employer in Mex-

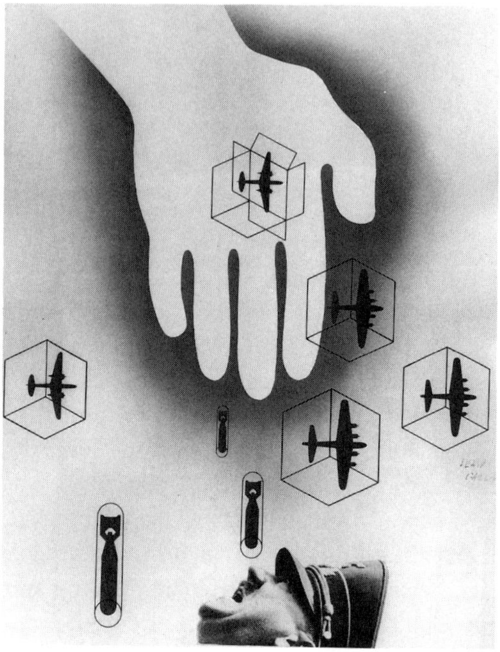

6.3. Jean Carlu, *Gift Packages for Hitler,* 1943. "Bomb and bomber parts by the thousand start their journey in protective paperboard packages." The fears evoked by an all-too-familiar image of fighter bombers releasing their cargo are defused through humor. Through montage, Carlu encased planes and bombs in schematic line drawing "packages" that incorporate the box-like form that was the corporate trademark.

ico, Panama, and Colombia. Contributors to the series included some of the century's most eminent artists, including Henry Moore, Fernand Léger, Rufino Tamayo, and the young (then-unknown) Willem de Kooning (fig. 6.4).[28]

In 1946 CCA launched a third campaign, the United States series, which, in keeping with the growing attention given to domestic matters after the war, stressed the corporation's expansion nationally. The creators of the United States and United Nations series were not associated with the Bauhaus, unlike those who designed the early series. Hence, while CCA's early work showed the effect of the integrative aesthetic of modern German and Russian graphic design, the series that followed gave prior-

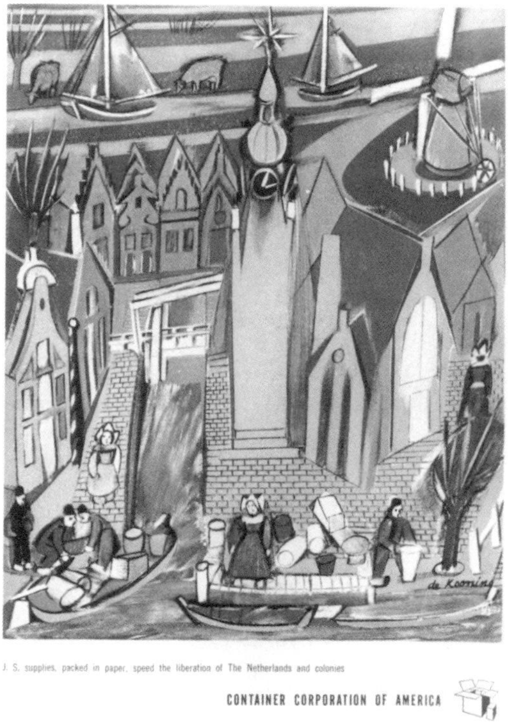

6.4. "The Netherlands," advertisement for Container Corporation of America, United Nations series, illustration by Willem de Kooning, 1944. "The Netherlands" was hardly de Kooning's sole foray into advertising, but it was unusual for being rendered in his "signature" style. Only one year earlier, De Kooning was drawing crude "illustrator-style" pictures of servicemen for Model smoking tobacco advertisements. (An example can be seen in *Life*, 1 February 1943, 97.)

ity to modern painting, reflecting the particular strengths of the artists chosen. N. W. Ayer's art buyer searched the art galleries for appropriate artists.[29] Selection criteria were by no means fixed or predetermined, but interest in the cosmopolitan modern clearly prevailed over the narrower, nationalistic category "American." CCA commissioned artists as stylistically diverse as Stuart Davis, Charlotte Sternberg, and Jacob Lawrence (figs. 6.5, 6.6). The inclusion of Lawrence, an African-American, notably challenged (but did not break down) the long-standing racial barrier in American advertising.

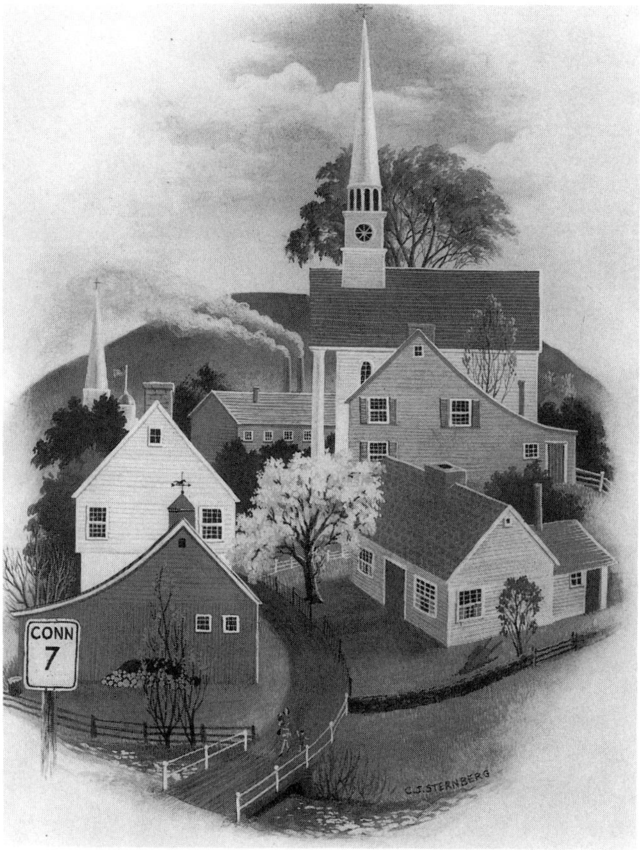

6.5. Charlotte J. Sternberg, *Connecticut,* 1946.

Although many painters were wary of advertisers and corporate business, the nature of the CCA product and the creative terms offered were attractive enough to enable the invited artists to disregard their prejudices. Cardboard boxes, totally unembellished and utilitarian, were goods that artists could promote without embarrassment. Painters still struggling to earn a living, find a public, and come to terms with the meaning and purpose of their art could pride themselves on contributing to useful "industry," not corporate enrichment. Furthermore, the singular characteristics of the paperboard container were such that the client could afford to encourage creative freedom and variety. The artist did not have to glorify the product specifically, nor was he or she obliged to tap into the

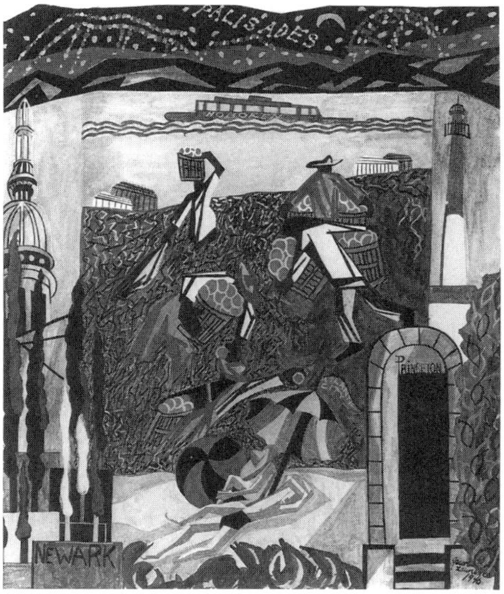

6.6. Jacob Lawrence, *New Jersey*, 1946. The selection of Lawrence was consistent with Container Corporation of America's and N. W. Ayer's emphasis on high-quality art. Although African-American artists still faced de facto discrimination within the elite art world, Lawrence personally was enjoying success within that framework in 1946. He had been given a one-man exhibition at the Downtown Gallery in 1941, and the Museum of Modern Art and Phillips Collection had purchased his paintings. Still, Lawrence's sense of self as a modern artist was very much bound up with his identity as a "Negro," and this consciousness made its way into his work for Container Corporation. "New Jersey," a pepped-up modern version of a tourist poster, depicted the state's diverse identities as a center of factories, government, elite education (signified by the Princeton arch), agriculture, and amusement. Within the positive, promotional message of the painting, however, Lawrence also placed a somber reminder of racial difference and inequity by juxtaposing white bathers prone and slumped over in blissful relaxation with black farm laborers erect or hunched over in work. Lawrence placed the laboring figures in the center of the composition, as if to assert their centrality to the state's economy and identity. At the same time, their difference and their labor would allow them little time or opportunity to enjoy the pleasures of Atlantic City beaches, like their white counterparts.

representational traditions of commercial design or to be identified with it. Artists could depict whatever they wanted (as long as the image did not transgress obvious rules of propriety); the box was like a three-dimensional frame for their expressions. Their images, well reproduced in color, dominated the page. The soft-sell text, in small print at the bottom, looked like a mere caption, like a label on the frame of a painting. Hence, not surprisingly, painters considered the CCA commissions attractive. In both the United Nations and United States series, artists were supposed to be native to the region depicted.

CCA's unusual approach continued through its last and most ambitious and controversial advertising series, "Great Ideas of Western Man." Begun in 1950 (and continuing until 1980), the "Great Ideas" series was Walter Paepcke's own brainchild, resulting from his involvement, and his wife's, in a Chicago Great Books Club. Initiated by University of Chicago president Robert M. Hutchins and philosophy professor Mortimer J. Adler, the Great Books Clubs were devoted to the study and discussion of the canon of classic literary and philosophical texts from Homer to Freud.[30] Deeply committed to the humanistic values such books represented, Paepcke hired Adler to select quotations from the latter's *Synopticon,* an index to the ideas of the 54 books of the Great Books series. N. W. Ayer's staff once again selected the artists. Among those who worked on the project prior to 1960 were Herbert Bayer, Leonard Baskin, Joseph Cornell, William Baziotes, Philip Guston, Leo Leonni, René Magritte, and Ben Shahn. With the "Great Ideas" series, CCA transcended paperboard. Embracing what James Sloan Allen termed the "entire Western intellectual tradition" as its rightful domain, the company posited the Great Ideas as the authentic spiritual core of all humanity, including corporate industry. Art and ideas, which Paepcke sincerely considered to be beyond "material gain," were nonetheless put to the service of corporate enrichment.[31] A 1966 article in *American Artist* claimed that "from a business viewpoint (perhaps surprisingly to some), at least two studies suggest that the 'great ideas' series outsells, dollar for dollar, all other competitive campaigns."[32]

Although CCA's bold move into modern art initially met with mixed reviews, the ads, many of which were placed in the elegantly designed business magazine *Fortune,* succeeded in achieving Paepcke's primary goal of attracting the attention of the businessmen who—rather than ordinary consumers—were the packaging industry's main customers.[33] Artists, critics, curators, and art dealers applauded CCA's commitment to an advertising art that appeared to value the interests of painters as much as those of the client. The campaign represented a determination on the part of sympathetic businessmen to commission the highest-quality art with few strings attached, and on behalf of an innocuous and necessary product. As early as 1943, art educator and painter Ralph M. Pearson (a former member of the American Artists' Congress) wrote that CCA ads represented a "coming of age of American advertising."[34] For many artists and critics, CCA seemed a dream come true.

Yet, as we shall see, the Container Corporation of America was an anomaly. From the standpoint of some advertisers and businessmen, the effectiveness of its advertisements may well have hinged on the perception that its specific strategies were unrepeatable.[35] CCA's success with art was a function of a variety of factors, including the particular nature of the product, the boldness and uniqueness of the advertisements, and especially the strong cultural commitments of Walter and Elizabeth Paepcke. In fact, relatively few clients proved willing to support artists in advertising in a comparable fashion.

AMERICAN TOBACCO COMPANY

In the 1940s, however, some other corporate executives, perhaps inspired by the example of CCA, attempted to use painting for public relations and product advertising (fig. 6.7). A few were sufficiently committed to the concerns of stylistically progressive artists to be adventuresome: they broadened the pool of artists they used and gave them a fair amount of autonomy regarding subject matter and technique. The majority of clients insisted that painting serve their interests—both iconographically and procedurally. Unlike Paepcke, moreover, most corporations opted not for the avant-garde but for the stylistic and ideological middle of the road; some of them utilized the services of Associated American Artists. Many major companies notable for their use of painting in advertising during this period were concerned with their public image and used art-art as a form of damage control in the wake of conflicts with the government.

American Tobacco Company advertisements were one example. As the likelihood of American involvement in World War II increased, tobacco companies anticipated, and sought to stimulate, a rise in demand for cigarettes (especially among soldiers, as had occurred in World War I). In 1940 R. J. Reynolds and Liggett and Myers began preparing war-related campaigns. American Tobacco Company president George Washington Hill took an alternative route. He conceived a new publicity campaign to distinguish Lucky Strikes from R. J. Reynolds's Camels and Liggett and Myers's Chesterfields and catapult them into first place in the market.[36] The goals of the campaign soon expanded, however, when the Justice Department charged the three companies with price-fixing and

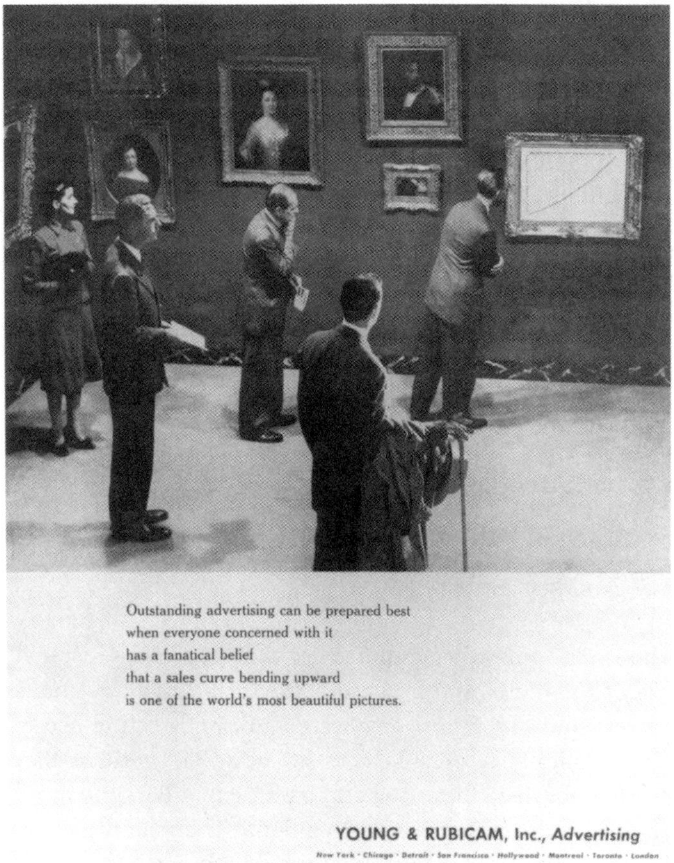

6.7. Corporate advertisement for Young and Rubicam, 1945. The appropriation of "fine art" by advertising is rendered literal in this corporate advertisement for the advertising agency Young and Rubicam, one of a series run in the mid-1940s. Yet in depicting how sales take priority over aesthetic quality, expression of sincerity (inner character), and artistic tradition (all signified by the elegant gold-framed portraits—ignored), this advertisement conveys advertising executives' growing ambivalence toward "art-art" as advertising.

monopoly. In the wake of these government efforts to regulate the industry's business practices, the advertisements had to boost public approval of American Tobacco as well as cigarette sales and brand loyalty. Given these exigencies, it is not surprising that Hill and his advertising agency, Lord and Thomas, turned to the "Art for Advertising" department of Associated American Artists. Hill commissioned seventeen highly popular regionalist painters, including Thomas Hart Benton, John Steuart Curry, and Peter Hurd, to paint pictures for Lucky Strike cigarette advertisements. The full-page ads were placed in mass-market magazines like *Time, Life,* and *Saturday Evening Post,* as well as *Fortune.*[37]

These paintings of what the advertising copy called "tobacco country," such as that reproduced in *Time,* 20 July 1942, depicted complacent, congenial, rugged, hardworking tobacco farmers, evoking the ideal of a company whose identity was synonymous with its suppliers. (American Tobacco Company declined my request to reproduce this image.) Image and copy highlighted American Tobacco's commitment to obtaining the highest-quality tobacco on the auction block, despite uncertainties of price and supply. Accompanied by text that emphasized the independence and impartiality of the tobacco experts who, as Erika Doss points out, the company had just recently been convicted of bribing, the advertisement courted public support by backing "their objectivity (and hence innocence) with the equally impartial realism" of regionalist art.[38] Whether or not they achieved their public relations goals, the advertisements served their marketing purpose. Lucky Strikes, which had run second in popularity to Camels in 1941, moved into first place by 1943.[39]

From the perspective of the artists involved, however, the Lucky Strike campaign was another story altogether. While Paepcke, Coiner, and Jacobson had gone out of their way to reconcile corporate needs with artistic expectations and expertise, Hill regarded the artists as hired hands, whose representations had to conform to his wishes. The advertiser sought out prominent painters, but autonomy was not part of the bargain. Thus the tobacco country paintings had to be carefully edited to avoid any sensitive political issues. Thomas Hart Benton, for example, found one of his paintings rejected because a little white girl he rendered looked sickly; another, because it depicted black sharecroppers. "Don't you know you cannot show Negroes doing what looks like slave work," he recalled the Lord and Thomas executives admonishing him.

> Yes, yes, of course we want realism. That's why we quit the conventional model stuff and hired you artists, but we don't want realism that will foul up our sales. The Negro institutions would boycott our products and cost us hundreds of thousands of dollars if we showed pictures of this sort. They want Negroes presented as well-dressed and respectable members of society. If we did this, of course, the whole of the white South would boycott us. So the only thing to do is to avoid the representation of Negroes entirely in tobacco advertising.[40]

Manufacturers could sell to blacks, but advertising could not represent them, if this risked displeasing those who despised them. The result, to Benton's chagrin, was a form of whitewashed regionalism. The regionalists' readable style and "realist" content were desirable, but not the critical and sometimes melancholy edge that was also characteristic of American scene painting. From the standpoint of the client, artists, to be artists in advertising, had to censor themselves.[41] Commissioned as modern fine art, the Lucky Strike pictures actually harked back to the practices of illustration.

In demanding that Benton rework his image to ensure that Lucky Strikes would be viewed in a positive light, George Washington Hill was, of course, behaving no differently than any other advertising client. Nor was he an unknown quantity. A shrewd and aggressive promoter, Hill had made news in 1928 when he launched a notorious and controversial campaign in which celebrities attributed their slender figures to their intake of Luckies. ("Reach for a *Lucky* instead of a sweet," went the phrase.)[42] It seems unlikely, then, that the artists on the Lucky Strike account, especially the astute Benton, would have naively taken on the assignment, unaware of the sort of businessman with whom they would be dealing. Yet Benton at least brought to this assignment the apparent unrealistic expectation that as a painter, he would somehow be treated differently, that Hill would defer to his artistic vision and expertise.

Hill disappointed him. An exasperated Benton and other art supporters condemned the campaign, not, it should be noted, on the issue of race, but for stifling self-expression. American Tobacco might be a "big Money sponsor," noted Frank Caspers in the widely read, middle-of-the-road *Art Digest,* but it "so restricts the artists that their work, reduced to a standardized formula, is utterly lacking in the particular qualities that earned them their national reputations." In the view of *Art Digest* editor Peyton Boswell, the campaign produced a "pseudo-commercial monstrosity . . . the 'Lucky Strike School.'" Even Reeves Lewenthal admitted that the campaign was an artistic failure because Hill had insisted that every image include large yellow tobacco leaves, the unofficial trademark and symbol of product quality.[43] "Product advertising," commented Benton, "is not a field for fine art. . . . The commercial artist who specializes in dressing up commercial ideas is a better hand at this than the fine artist who must either represent himself and his ideas or blunder into ineptitude."[44]

Art for Industry in Wartime

Other major industry leaders of the 1940s, also hoping to use painting as a way of bolstering public goodwill and of acquiring cultural authority for big business, tried to find a middle ground between Paepcke's accommodating attitude and Hill's authoritarian practices. One approach, comparable to that of CCA but without its aesthetic innovativeness, was to use art indirectly, for public relations, as well as for product advertising. Instead of using advertising agencies to commission art for advertising goods, some corporate managements looked to art dealers and to Associated American Artists for assistance in forming corporate art collections. These pictures, reproduced in catalogs, calendars, and booklets, were intended to boost the corporation's image and employee morale, with the expectation that this would also help sales.

International Business Machines (IBM) set an early precedent. IBM thrived during the depression as a result of strong demand for its tabulating services—based upon leases of punch card counter-sorter machines—especially by the federal government. In 1937, IBM president Thomas J. Watson decided to start a company art collection. IBM would purchase a contemporary painting to represent each of the countries in which the corporation operated its business. Juries of local art experts would make the selection, and the works would be purchased "outright at the artist's asking price."[45] The corporation assembled two collections of contemporary art from seventy-nine countries and displayed them, along with business machines, at the 1939 World's Fairs in New York and San Francisco as a way to "promote better understanding between business and art as well as between nations then on the brink of war."[46] In 1940, six years before Container Corporation of America launched its United States series, IBM established a collection of contemporary American art representing an artist from each of the forty-eight states.[47] Such actions were clearly calculated, coming precisely at the moment when artists' antagonisms toward business and their involvement with the left were having a notable effect on the cultural scene. Artists—both nationals and foreigners (Diego Rivera, for example)—had played a key role in shaping the public image of business.[48] By extending a hand through art patronage, IBM undoubtedly hoped to lure artists over to their side, to convince them to see business more favorably. Ongoing support for artists, which the American Artists' Congress and Artists' Union had been demanding from the federal government, might well be one of the fruits of corporate activity. The exhibits would reveal the beneficence, authority, and multinational scope of IBM.

Though well aware that art collecting served such public relations purposes, Watson minimized this function. Instead he insisted that IBM's patronage was dedicated to the edification and enjoyment of employees and the public, and that it reflected the corporation's sense of cultural responsibility. Such attitudes were consistent with Roosevelt supporter Watson's larger and successful efforts to insure good employee relations and to avoid the labor unrest that many other corporations were experiencing.[49] To reinforce this commitment to art and high cultural values, Watson decreed that the works in the collection were not permitted to be reproduced for institutional advertising, and, according to a company spokesman, "None were ever to be used to sell a company product or ever resold."[50]

In drawing sharp distinctions between fine art as individual artistic expression and "sponsor-related interests," Watson typified the outlook of post–World War II industrialists.[51] During the war, however, the situation was different, as big corporations became interested in experimenting with fine art painting explicitly as institutional publicity and as a means to circumvent high wartime excess-profits taxes. These taxes, along with a 1935 congressional ruling allowing corporations to deduct up to 5 percent of before-tax income for charitable gifts, created strong incentives for businesses to become patrons of the arts.[52] To these ends, three large and controversial companies, Standard Oil of New Jersey (today's Exxon), Abbott Laboratories, and The Upjohn Company, bought or commissioned paintings and used them for public relations and product advertising. Their particular solutions, like those of the Container Corporation of America, enabled them to utilize the paintings for enhancing profits and the corporate image while also providing work and creative freedom for painters. Significantly, all three, like American Tobacco, were trying to recover either from scandals or from bad press arising from conflicts with the federal government.[53]

Standard Oil of New Jersey (SONJ), for example, was under fire from a number of directions. A 1929 cartel agreement with the German petrochemical company I. G. Farbenindustrie was later alleged to have helped the Nazi military by delaying American development of synthetic rubber. The company and some of its competitors were accused of overcharging the Navy for fuel oil. To fight these allegations, SONJ established a public relations department in 1943. In consultation with the public relations firm Earl Newsom and Company, and in particular, Edward Stanley, a vice president, SONJ embarked on a campaign to reverse negative public opinion, especially among white-collar professionals (or as pollster Elmo Roper characterized them, "thought leaders").[54] The public relations department commissioned through the AAA a large series of paintings by artists such as Benton, Robert Benney, Adolf Dehn, Ernest Fiene, Kerr Eby, Carlos Lopez, Lawrence Beall Smith, and Frederic Taubes. Together, these paintings were to constitute a "pictorial record of the development and distribution of oil during the war years."[55] Stanley also brought in former Farm Security Administration head Roy Stryker to run a documentary project, comparable to the FSA's photographic program and to the SONJ paintings, showing all aspects of the production and consumption of oil. Many of the images were published in the company magazine *The Lamp*. The original paintings were sent around the country in traveling exhibitions.[56]

Benton's SONJ experiences were clearly more satisfying than those with American Tobacco, for he later insisted that although the more subtle approach of documenting the "going concerns of business" still provided plenty of possibilities for "corrupting the artist," such practices theoretically enabled him also to "argue and fight for his right to perform as an artist rather than a commercial functionary." Constructive debates with patrons over interpretation had their precedent in disagreements between Michelangelo and the popes, Benton noted, and "the intelligent, socially alert artist should be able to win most of his points here."[57]

Like SONJ, pharmaceutical companies were also on the defensive in the late 1930s and early 1940s. The Pure Food and Drug Act of 1906 had been passed to control production standards and stop misleading promotions of patent medicines. Federal regulators' efforts to enforce it had proved inadequate. Under the New Deal, Food and Drug Administration chief Walter Campbell and Assistant Secretary of Agriculture Rexford G. Tugwell began a campaign—backed by the American Medical Association—to control substance labeling, advertising, and sales. Their efforts provoked angry opposition from businessmen who objected to unwarranted federal government intrusions into private enterprise.[58] The culmination of negotiations between these groups, the Wheeler-Lea Act of 1938, sought to place new, more stringent restrictions upon the food, drug, and cosmetics industries, especially with regard to ingredients and directions for use. The law drew sharper distinctions between self-administered drugs that could be purchased over the counter and those for which doctors' prescriptions were required. The act also regulated advertising, so that certain kinds of drugs could be promoted only to physicians.[59] Doctors, it was assumed, were sufficiently rational not to succumb to dishonest persuasion.

The art collecting and publicity activities of pharmaceutical manufacturers Abbott Laboratories and The Upjohn Company were outgrowths of these events. Their art patronage represented an effort to retain their high standing as responsible businesses and to convince the public that pharmaceutical companies complied with federal restrictions to provide products of distinction that served medical experts and the American public.

Abbott Laboratories followed a path similar to SONJ's. As early as 1936 the company had commissioned artists to illustrate monthly advertising fliers and a house organ, sent to doctors. In 1939 the firm hired Reeves Lewenthal and Associated American Artists as its consultants, and by the next year it had begun to sponsor a series of war-related public relations paintings. These included the Art for Bonds project, in which the company commissioned paintings and donated them to the Treasury Department, which in turn gave them to museums that had achieved big sales in war bonds. Abbott Laboratories also commissioned eight apocalyptic paintings on the "horrors of war" by Thomas Hart Benton, the 1942 "Year of Peril" series (of which 55 million reproductions were disseminated by the Office of War Information, along with stamps, stickers, and posters), and an additional five projects in which artists were sent to the front to record medical activity in wartime. Abbott Laboratories published these pictures in its house magazine *What's New,* distributed reproductions to clients, and sent the originals on tour around the country. Besides Benton, artists who painted for Abbott included Arnold Blanche, Alexander Brook, Peter Blume, Adolf Dehn, Julian Levi, Kerr Eby, Federico Castellon, Anton Refregier, and Marion Greenwood.[60]

Like CCA and SONJ, Abbott Laboratories geared much of its institutional advertising and public relations toward professionals. Abbott Laboratories initially turned to "fine artists" in order to appeal to doctors, their primary target, expecting them to identify with the exclusive and tasteful high cultural enterprise signified by "good painting." In addition, Abbott Laboratories executives claimed that fine artists were "more adept at capturing the spirit of the stories contained in the advertising copy."[61] Modern art advocate Ralph Pearson approved of this "new" practice of appealing to an audience presumed to be "civilized adults" rather than "morons." "They contradict the beliefs and practices of the mass-production industries, including those producing so-called 'high class' merchandise, that the only profitable appeal is to swank, snobbery, social fears, ignorance, and infantilism—all expressed pictorially by the trivialities and banalities of commercial artists [in] mass appeal magazines and newspapers."[62]

The Upjohn Company of Kalamazoo, Michigan, likewise sought to create a high-toned picture of the pharmaceutical industry. At the suggestion of its advertising agency, William Douglas McAdams, Upjohn used easel pictures for both institutional and product advertising, primarily in magazines, although like Abbott, SONJ, and IBM, it also sent its collections on touring exhibitions. Upjohn's advertisements appeared in 1944 and 1945 in magazines like *Fortune, Life,* and *Saturday Evening Post,* as well as in a book distributed to 100,000 doctors for their waiting rooms. The ads emphasized the expertise of doctors and of The Upjohn Company, their commitment to patients, and the close cooperation between responsible segments of the pharmaceutical industry and the American Medical Association in providing necessary services.[63] Since the law forbade promotion of certain drugs except to physicians, and since military needs precluded advertising to create consumer demand, the Upjohn advertisements were meant to promote name recognition and company reputation, and more generally, to counteract negative sentiments about pharmaceutical companies. In the words of one observer, company officials sought to "aid overworked physicians who would like to explain recent developments in the field of medicine to their patients but are prevented by lack of time" because of the war. Upjohn's advertisements would serve as helpful substitutes for the live family doctor, and as expressions of the company's dedication to the health and well-being of the community.

Each advertisement in the series, titled "Your Doctor Speaks," provided a message, "the equivalent of an informal deskside chat with a physician, [which] sums up the latest medical advances in the treatment of various ills."[64] Easel pictures (fig. 6.8) were the symbols of the company's expertise, commitment, quality, and integrity, signifying that it would scrupulously comply with government standards. The company also utilized procedures that, in contrast to those of American Tobacco, would show their commitment to painters and free creativity. Upjohn selected the themes, then had representatives from the Midtown Gallery in Manhattan scour galleries, studios, and exhibitions for suitable contemporary American paintings. Once a work of art had been purchased for the collection, the McAdams agency would prepare copy and color layout. The paintings, rendered in an "expressionist-realist" style, were clearly selected for their conservatism. Unlike Abbott Laboratories and Standard Oil, Upjohn did not go with the AAA and its now familiar talent roster. The company did, however, use the work of respected figurative artists familiar to visitors to midtown galleries and to readers of *Life,* for which several of the artists worked as art correspondents.[65] Fifteen percent of the artists were women—a high number for the time. Twenty percent were foreign-born—a low percentage, according to contemporary commentators.[66] Artists included Karl Anderson, Julien Binford, Paul Lewis Clemens, Wilford S. Conrow, Bernard Karfiol, Earl Kerkam, John Koch, Waldo Pierce, Simka Simkhovitch, Miron Sole, Margit Varga, Fletcher Martin, and Gladys Rockmore Davis.[67] Most of the paintings were

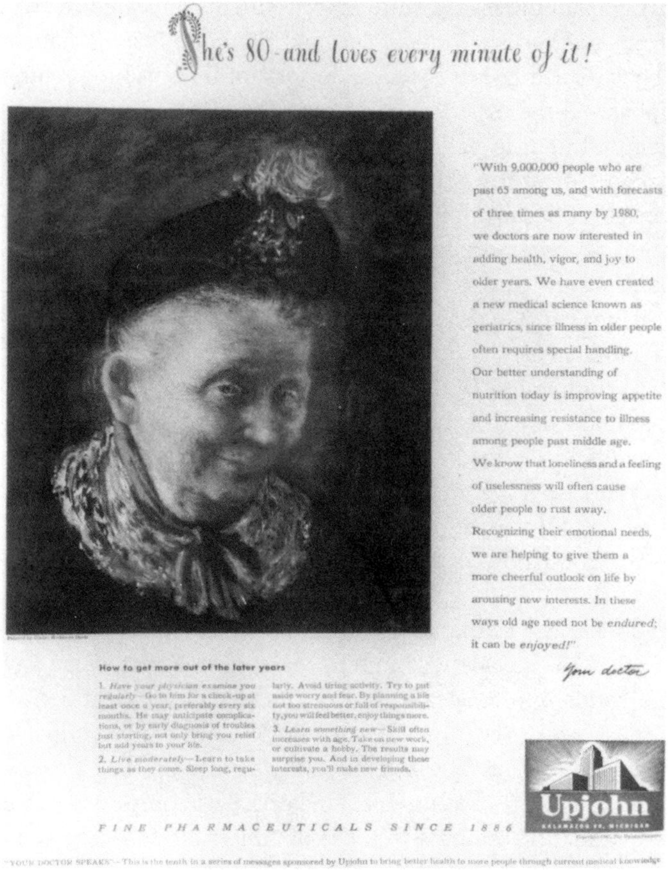

6.8. Advertisement for The Upjohn Company, illustration by Gladys Rockmore Davis, 1945.

sentimental "realist" portraits that could appeal to those with little education in art (fig. 6.8), who might well be sitting in doctors' waiting rooms.

The Upjohn campaign received a mixed response from art and advertising professionals. Michigan State art historian Walter Abell, for example, felt that the Upjohn system of selection had drawbacks. Abell objected to the poor aesthetic quality of the paintings and to the "pathological context" resulting from "using the paintings as illustrations to medical themes." The imposition of a succinct medical theme, such as the "hypothetical diagnosis 'Anemia?'" in Fletcher Martin's portrait (fig. 6.9), struck Abell as "humorous if not sacrilegious." In Abell's view, such

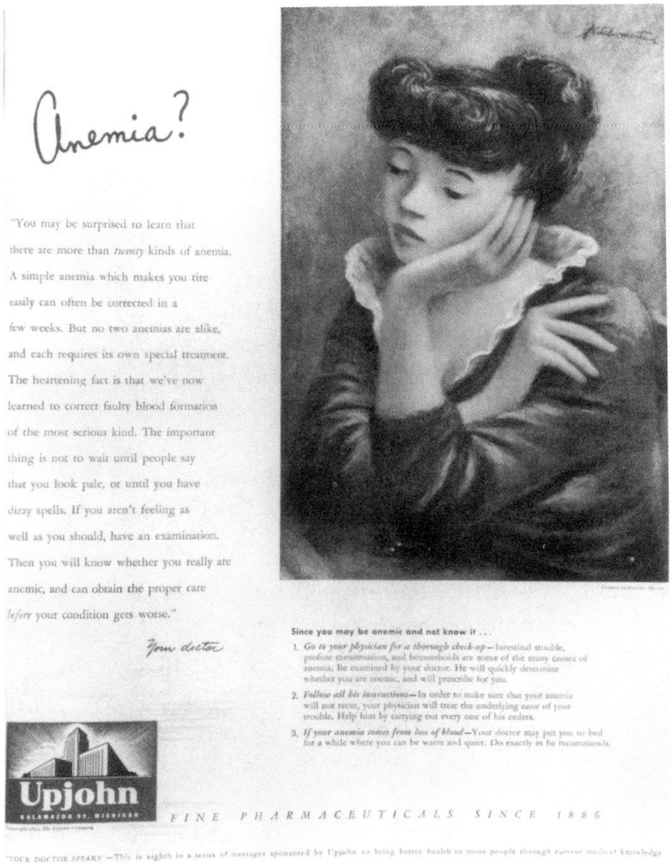

6.9. Advertisement for The Upjohn Company, illustration by Fletcher Martin, 1945.

applications ultimately lessened the impact and significance of works of fine art, whatever their aesthetic merits; they limited the possibilities for interpretation and encouraged the beholder to view the image from a single, narrow perspective, of which the painter had been unaware when creating the work.[68]

Despite his reservations about the Upjohn advertisements, Abell, as well as writers in *Life* and *Art Digest,* acknowledged the benefits of corporate support for American painting, and expressed approval that industry was using commercial means to distribute American art. For these observers, Upjohn's widespread dissemination of color reproductions through magazine advertisements and reprint portfolios, along with its traveling displays of original paintings, served as a valuable "stimulus to cultural and artistic growth."[69] Such activities exposed millions of Americans to the work of contemporary American painters and helped support these artists. "To have the work of some of our best painters in a dozen periodicals on every newsstand, in 100,000 doctors' offices, in the reading matter distributed by large corporations to their employees and business associates, is a leavening influence favorable to the understanding and enjoyment of art on an unprecedented scale."[70] Like radio broadcasters, wrote Abell, industries like Upjohn were making an important contribution as popularizers of the arts, drawing "into the orbit of the art world sections of the public not otherwise interested."[71] Such events, these writers hoped, could only result in more work for American artists.

Shifting Boundaries

Abell's mixed response to the Upjohn campaign reflected more than his own ambivalence about corporate patronage in the mid-1940s. It was also symptomatic of larger uncertainties on the part of artists, art critics, curators, and businessmen about what exactly art in advertising meant. Disagreement remained about the merits of corporate support of artists. And the relationship of occupational activity (self-expressive fine art versus advertising) to the quality and social status of the product, the image, had not been resolved.

Many observers believed that industry and the commercial print media, in providing gallery artists with the employment they had been calling for since the depression, were contributing to a breakdown of distinctions between commercial art and fine art (see fig. 6.7). For *Art Digest* editor Peyton Boswell, for example, "the point of demarcation between fine and commercial art" had been essentially eliminated, and that was a positive thing. Writing in 1942, he noted that hard financial times had forced painters to turn their attention to advertising. Yet even so, he claimed, illustrators like Rockwell or Stevan Dohanos, who painted for advertisers, were often "more talented than many who publicly display their fumbling brushwork [in galleries] on 57th Street. . . . commercial art has been elevated to such a position that the fine artists have to extend themselves to retain their adjective."[72] According to Boswell, then, the aesthetic quality of illustrators' advertising imagery was forcing easel painters to expand their occupational identities in order to maintain a fictive rhetorical and professional distinction. In his view, there were in fact no feasible grounds for drawing distinctions, professionally or aesthetically.[73]

Frederic Price, director of Ferargil Gallery in New York City, cast the argument differently in 1946. He contended that the distinction between fine and commercial art boiled down to a difference between good and bad art: an art that appealed to people versus one that did not. "It is a mistake to think that the great artist has to learn how to interest the public," he wrote. "The fine arts from the beginning were a part of the daily life of the people. Canterbury and Santiago were objects of pilgrimage for their art as well as for their miraculous relics." All the great old patrons of the arts were, moreover, comparable to today's advertisers.

> The Sistine Chapel was made to attract the multitude. The ornamentation of St. Marks was an advertisement. Kings and Popes were astute publicists, luring visitors to their cathedrals; new murals by Giotto for Our Lady of the Arena, marvelous stained glass windows at Notre Dame of Paris. People came from the hinterland to see towering campaniles quite as they do today when they come to see Rockefeller's towering Radio City. That is a cathedral of today, and so is the Empire State Building. Rockefeller employed Sert and Rivera to paint murals, the Pope Julius employed Michelangelo. Each wanted to sell the people a thrill.
>
> The ancient advertisers employed contemporary artists, whom we now call old masters, but many of whom were then on the make.[74]

As Price put it, crassly, the great "gallery artists" of the past knew as much about advertising as any present-day artist in advertising. Indeed, he insisted, the field of art was all-inclusive. The work of art's ultimate purpose (or presumably, its patron) did not matter except insofar as it did or did not lure an audience.[75]

Many painters, of course, held different views. Ideological disenchantment and frustration about disintegrating state support for serious painting were leading many artists to disavow the old populist urges and the ideal of service. Clement Greenberg articulated this disenchantment publicly as early as 1939 in his much-discussed tract "Avant-Garde and Kitsch."[76] Hilaire Hiler, a West Coast painter who had signed the 1936 call for the American Artists' Congress, expressed his distress privately in 1940. "You and I are not *entertainers* in the real american sense of the term," he wrote his colleague Abraham Rattner. "we're not journalistic and journalism in all its 'bright' superficiality is all that the public here cares for or will pay for." The "real entertainers," he claimed, were "journalistic illustrators" like "curry, benton, wood [*sic*] et al." The problem was that the "potentially literate American public" seemed incapable of understanding and discriminating between these artists and others.[77]

"There is a complete inability to recognize different very important premises and different *planes* upon which different sorts of endeavor and methods of expression are carried out," he continued.

> comic strip artists, cartoonists like disney, men who draw toilet paper or cotex [*sic*] advs. caricaturists, fashion illustrators, illustrators, etc. are all rigidly lumped together and comparisons made where no comparison is either useful or possible! . . .
>
> the psychological impossibility of being at one and the same time a careerist and an artist is not only not recognized or appreciated but because of the complete occupation of super-careerists of all key positions in the art world as in every other world of the american scene, only *arriviste* language is understood.[78]

Painter Ad Reinhardt also had his misgivings, and voiced his disillusionment through manifesto and satire. For example, in his "How to Look at Modern Art in America," a June 1946 cartoon in the newspaper *PM* (which tried to operate without advertising), Reinhardt provided a visual critique of contemporary art and its relation to business. The image ("the art world in a nutshell," according to Reinhardt) depicted a tree of modern art, with leaves inscribed with contemporary artists' names, arranged on branches of "pure (abstract) 'painting'" (up high) and "pure (illustrative) 'pictures'" (weighted down). Hanging off the tree was an old shoe with the words "Business as Art Patron." Bottle-like "flags" tied to various leaves signified "Pepsi-Cola Contest Winner."[79]

The artists on the tree's leaves appear to have grown organically from "roots" located in postimpressionism and a varied soil including both Monet and "Negro Sculpture." Yet the same soil also produces a cemetery-like cornfield with headstones representing other modern artists and organizations with more commercial or popular leanings, against whom Reinhardt counterposed his own artistic identity; these included Thomas Hart Benton, Norman Rockwell, Howard Chandler Christy, and Associated American Artists, Pepsi-Cola, IBM, Lucky Strike, Calendars, Pin-ups, and Oil. For Reinhardt, true ("pure") abstract art was defined not only against the more realistic, expressionist, and surrealist styles that had dominated easel painting for a decade and a half, but also against the commercial institutional and organizational frameworks within which art was also fabricated.[80] As he put it to his colleagues in 1950, "Does not one have to remove oneself from the business world in order to create 'fine' art to exist as a 'fine artist'?"[81]

Walter Abell did not share these antagonisms toward commercial art with Hiler and Reinhardt. Writing in the same year as Reinhardt, Abell concurred with Price and Boswell that industry was becoming so dominant a source of art patronage that the distinctions between fine and advertising art were irrelevant, both in their practices and their products. Nor did he take the stance that art for advertising and public relations was necessarily aesthetically inferior. Nevertheless, unlike Boswell and

Price, he regarded the arts' growing dependence on big business as disturbing, not liberating. The views of the Michigan State professor were undoubtedly colored by very nonaesthetic concerns about the automobile industry's ongoing domination of his own state's economy, politics, and social policies, circumstances that at that moment were breeding racial unrest in Detroit and labor strife between General Motors and the United Automobile Workers.[82]

Abell feared the ramifications if the corporation and commercial print media effectively claimed jurisdiction over all art. Whether an artist worked for himself or for others, he stated, industry commissions with ground rules set "by a handful of corporation executives" preimposed limitations and restraints that resulted in "fewer means through which the social will and the cultural impulse of the American people can freely formulate themselves, independent of all cultural bias. In a society faced with acute economic and social problems—problems which are not likely to be solved without strong opposition between conflicting interests—the potential dangers of an industry-controlled, rather than community-controlled culture are obvious."[83] In Abell's view, corporate patronage stifled the dissent and debate essential to a healthy society. The use and status of the object and the distinctions between fine art and commercial practice were of secondary importance compared with the long-term cultural and political implications of corporate sponsorship of art for advertising or public relations purposes.

The anonymous author of a later (1949) article in *American Artist* claimed that the activities and products of commercial and fine artists were equally legitimate. The commentator did not share Abell's worry about industry limiting art's function as an expression of the collective social will, but did voice concern about the implications of corporate sponsorship for individual artistic freedom. The argument was that art created as personal expression had to be differentiated from art created for advertising. Commercial artists, whether painters or illustrators, learned the techniques of working for industry, a process that did not preclude aesthetic status for their creations. The problems arose when a corporation mistakenly tried to emphasize "art," the product (created as the expression of an individual), instead of the "artist" (producer of a certain style and means of expression) in publicizing goods "otherwise unrelated to art." Such a move created difficulties because the artist might create differently for himself than for an industrial client. Although the distinctions between fine art and commercial art ought not to be assessed qualitatively, the two had to be differentiated. Occupational identity had to be connected with a work's purpose and methods.[84]

In arguing that there was a fundamental difference between art produced for advertising and art produced independently, in accord with the older romantic ideal of self-expression, the commentary in *American Artist* represented, both ideologically and chronologically, a point of transition. The dominant line among mid-1940s art observers, advertisers, and businessmen was that fine art and commercial art were merging. By 1950, they were beginning to retreat from this point of view. This shift is apparent in one last prominent advertising campaign of the 1940s, the Pepsi-Cola competition, whose demise was the subject of the anonymous article just cited in *American Artist.*

Pepsi-Cola

Executives like CCA's Walter Paepcke, as committed to cultural as to industrial advancement, had sought to give artists as much autonomy as possible in the hope that the end result would serve his company's business goals. Yet businesses were unconvinced that CCA's approach to advertising was effective. George Washington Hill represented the opposite pole, closely controlling the execution as well as the theme. SONJ, Abbott Laboratories, and Upjohn forged a middle position. Abbott Laboratories and SONJ commissioned artists to document preselected topics for public relations but gave them relative (though not unlimited) freedom of interpretation. Upjohn appropriated already completed paintings that were congruent with the company's specific interests. From the standpoint of many painters, none of these solutions was entirely satisfactory, if Thomas Hart Benton's experiences were typical. Either clients placed too many constraints on what artists could depict, or they transformed the artists' original visions in order to hawk the product. Advertisers were demanding too much control, and consequently, quality and the artists' reputations suffered.

Walter Staunton Mack Jr. (1895–1990), chief executive of the Pepsi-Cola Company, experimented with a different way of utilizing art for advertising and public relations. His Pepsi-Cola "Portrait of America" competitions represented a sincere and calculated effort to promote artists and their interests. Held annually between 1944 and 1948, the Pepsi competitions were intended to serve as a model for corporate support of contemporary art, of the sort that many artists had hoped would come from the federal government. As a sign of Pepsi's commitment to artists as professionals, Mack brought them into the administrative process, giving them primary responsibility for the competition. Corporate financing and more autonomy for artists could not ensure success, however, and the publicity project collapsed.

Pepsi-Cola's art calendars and art competitions were an offshoot of the company's long-standing attempts to surpass its rival, Coca-Cola. The Pepsi beverage dated back to the 1890s, but the company had filed for bankruptcy twice, and had suffered through a series of lawsuits and changes of ownership. The corporation began to experience a turnaround in the late 1930s when owner Charles C. Guth decided to price Pepsi in a way that gave retail customers twice as much soda for the same price as Coke. In the midst of the depression such a move proved highly effective, and the company emerged as a serious challenger.[85]

In 1939, the year Mack succeeded Guth as chief executive, Pepsi's profits before taxes were up 50 percent. A Harvard graduate, cultivated and involved in civic affairs, Mack, like Thomas Watson of IBM and Walter Paepcke of CCA, regarded support of culture as a part of corporate responsibility to the community, a means of contributing to the public welfare. His interests meshed with the older liberal ideal of "public relations" as promoted by Theodore Vail of AT&T.[86] A shrewd, pragmatic, and up-to-date businessman, Mack had big plans for Pepsi. Wartime sugar rationing had cut supplies, and constraints on advertisers would have made a large and aggressively self-serving ad campaign seem inappropriate.[87] Art was one of the methods Mack used to try to outdistance Coke. He surmised that corporate support of art could perform multiple roles that would serve artists, the soda-drinking public, and, of course, the company. As with CCA and IBM, Pepsi's venture into art resulted from the influence of a company president who was both "culturally astute" and civic-minded.[88]

In 1941 Pepsi officials decided to "do a real public service" by publishing an art calendar that would double as advertising. Its first, for the year 1942, reproduced older American paintings from the Metropolitan Museum of Art; this approach was a departure from that of Coca-Cola, which had relied primarily on illustrators' images of "pretty girls" drinking the soda. It was also a way of identifying Pepsi with national pride during wartime without ostentatiously broadcasting such concerns.[89] The 1943 calendar reproduced American paintings from the Corcoran Gallery of Art in Washington, D.C. Over 500,000 copies were distributed. The third year's calendar included works by the usual group of AAA American scene painters: Benton, John Steuart Curry, Adolf Dehn, Earnest Fiene, Peter Hurd, Grant Wood, and Paul Sample, along with five other AAA affiliates: Frances Criss, Gordon Grant, James Perrin, John Costigan, and Edna Reindel. According to Mack, however, this calendar "did not turn out to be as satisfactory as we hoped." The quality of work by some artists apparently "fell short" of what company officials had anticipated.[90]

At the suggestion of *New York World Telegram* art critic Emily Genauer, a friend, Mack and his colleagues decided to hold a competition for new American paintings; the best submissions would then be used for calendar images. Following Genauer's recommendation, Mack approached Artists for Victory, the organization of artists' groups working on behalf of the war effort, to help Pepsi-Cola launch its "Portrait of America" competition and exhibition. Incorporated in New York City in January 1942, Artists for Victory was composed primarily of delegates from the major national and New York art societies and unions, ranging politically from far left to right, and including the Allied Artists of America, American Society of Miniature Painters, the Mural Artists Guild of the United Scenic Artists, National Academy of Design, American Abstract Artists, New York Society of Women Artists, Sculptors' Guild, Municipal Art Society, New York Chapter of the American Institute of Architects, the American Society of Landscape Architects, and the Architectural League of New York. The group's primary purpose was to serve the nation's war effort. It also sought to promote contemporary American art, sponsoring numerous competitive exhibitions, including the one for war posters at the Museum of Modern Art. "Portrait of America"'s immediate purposes were to expose people to contemporary American art, provide artists financial assistance through prize money, and offer artists a chance to compete and compare their works. The exhibition also offered painters a valuable opportunity to acquire a reputation and perhaps even future commissions.[91]

Under an arrangement with Pepsi, negotiated despite disagreement among the group's members, Artists for Victory selected the judges and administered the "Portrait of America" competition. Pepsi provided the prize money and funded expenses.[92] Artists were solicited to paint pictures in keeping with the broad theme "Portrait of America." It was a vast undertaking. As of late March 1944, 11,000 artists had requested entry cards. Over 5,000 pictures were submitted, including works by servicemen. In May a jury of selection headed by the prominent social realist painter Reginald Marsh narrowed down the entries to 150 pictures. A separate jury of awards then made its selections.[93] The exhibition of the best pictures was held at the Metropolitan Museum of Art, then traveled to museums around the country. Pepsi purchased the four top prizewinners, plus fourteen other paintings; nineteen additional paintings were sold to other buyers. The company printed 650,000 calendars reproducing twelve winning paintings. Altogether, Pepsi distributed $11,000 in prize money that year.[94]

Through this first competition, Mack and Pepsi-Cola won praise for their "cultural hands off policy," for allowing experts to control the artistic procedures, and especially for lending so much support for contemporary painting.[95] Yet for all involved, the 1944 competition had proved to be risky. According to *Art Digest* editor Peyton Boswell, "General opinion among the critics and along 57th Street is that it is a pretty depressing picture of both life and art in America that this show gives."[96]

Even members of Artists for Victory panned the show. Some complained that too many New York-based artists had been chosen. Some simply criticized poor work that revealed the bankruptcy of American art, still inspired by the Ashcan school, social and magic realism, and surrealism.[97] Others, notably Ernest Watson of *American Artist,* thought the exhibition contained too many dreary, sordid pictures of American life (fig. 6.10) that failed to represent the positive along with the negative, or to do justice to the industrial patron. The identity of this particular client, after all, was synonymous with the light and bubbly. The gloomy images many of the artists presented clearly did not resonate with the effervescent good feelings that Pepsi marketers strove to identify with their product.

For Watson (known for his upbeat articles on the practices of promi-

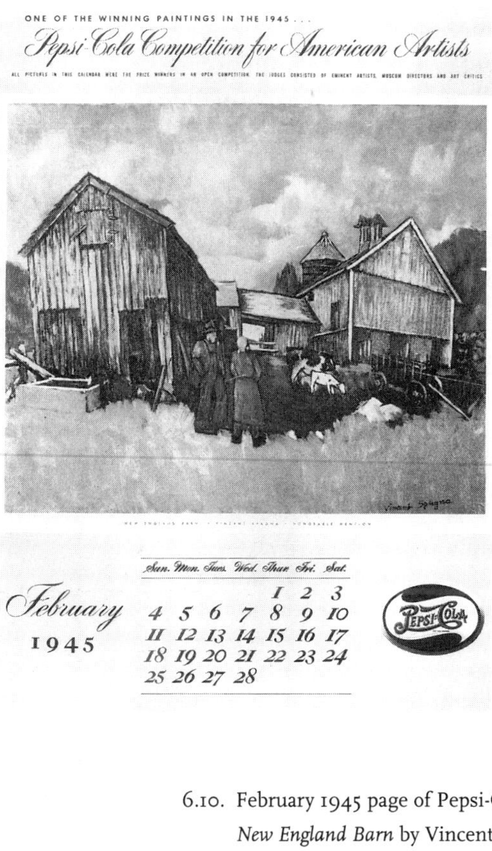

6.10. February 1945 page of Pepsi-Cola calendar, with painting *New England Barn* by Vincent Spagna.

nent contemporary illustrators), the matter of patronage was crucial. Artists had to be responsible both to their clients and to their audiences. Artists for Victory was misguided in emphasizing self-expression and sitting passively by while second-tier artists showcased their wares. Watson insisted that artists could not be self-indulgent, or ignore the fact that industry was footing the bill and trying to appeal to a broad clientele. "Painter groups" thus had "to discover a formula for handling such a project in successful competition with buyers whose profession is catering to public taste. Let us not think we can thumb our noses at Mr. and Mrs. John Q. Public when we address ourselves to them."[98] Artists for Victory had to meet its obligations to Pepsi by working out better procedures for obtaining the best art available, the kind of popular art, for example, that advertising agencies were already buying.[99]

Watson conceived of the Pepsi competitions as "art for industry." Clearly, many members of Artists for Victory did not feel the same way. They believed that the purpose of the contest was to serve art and artists, not the corporation, although they acknowledged a need to revamp competition procedures to obtain a better and wider range of paintings. Thus for the second go-around in 1945, Artists for Victory, in consultation with Mack, worked out a new set of procedures that still focused on accommodating artists, not helping Pepsi. The most notable of the new procedures was a two-pronged jury, made up of an "advanced" segment, whose sympathies lay with modern art and a "traditional jury." Artists themselves would decide which jury would judge their submissions.[100]

Although he did nothing to obstruct its implementation, Mack disapproved of Artists for Victory's decision, and he was not alone. Prominent artists refused to enter the competition, and the reviews of the next exhibition were little better than those of the first.[101] Pepsi-Cola again sought modifications. In 1946 a frustrated Mack hired former Los Angeles County Museum director Roland McKinney to administer the competitions. Jury types and procedures shifted several more times, and the competition title was changed from "Portrait of America" to the less restrictive "Paintings of the Year." The change in title served several purposes. First, it represented a shift from the concern for unity and nationalism of wartime to an emphasis on the individual, thus reflecting the broader cultural preferences of the late 1940s. Second, by removing the mandate to depict a specific theme, the new title was intended to give painters more creative independence and to encourage a broader range of artists to participate. Finally, such an open-ended theme served as an incentive for viewers to approach the results without specific expectations. Freed from the need to assess artists' interpretations of a specific theme, beholders might be less likely to be disappointed in the results. The company also decided to make its own selections for the Pepsi-Cola calendar, instead of automatically choosing from the preselected pool of paintings—hardly a vote of confidence in the jury. By 1948, every painting in the show also received some small monetary award, in effect a rental fee of the sort Rockwell Kent had called for twenty years earlier. Still, from Mack's perspective, the results and the publicity did not improve.[102]

As early as 1945, moreover, the Pepsi-Cola competition had become a cause of division and strife over organizational structure and policy within Artists for Victory. The undertaking was perhaps bound to fail, partly because of the still highly charged political atmosphere in which the competitions were conducted. Some artists, like the leftist Hugo Gellert, were concerned that Artists for Victory was shilling for industry, and did not approve of artists going into the "advertising business."[103] Neither, ostensibly, did IBM president Thomas Watson, who had been on the verge of making a monetary donation to Artists for Victory until he learned of its involvement with Pepsi-Cola. Asserting that commercial companies should not be using the "work of artists to further their own advertising interests," he withdrew his commitment.[104] In contrast to Ernest Watson (who was no relation to IBM's leader), Hugo Gellert and others insisted that if such competitions were to continue, equal opportunity and democratic methods of selection always had to take higher priority than the quality of the artistic product.[105] No special treatment should be afforded to prominent artists just to get them to participate. Work and affirmation of creative activity were more important than obtaining the best art through elitist practices. Gellert's point of view prevailed.

If, as many of its members acknowledged, the Pepsi-Cola competition was the only enterprise keeping Artists for Victory afloat, the contests were also a primary cause of the group's demise. To be sure, the war had served as Artists for Victory's reason for existence, but the organization had hoped to continue its work on an ongoing basis. In December 1945 it appeared that Mack had dropped Artists for Victory as competition administrators. Two months later, the body disbanded.[106]

Pepsi-Cola continued the competition and calendar through 1948, then suspended them entirely, preferring to pump its publicity money into more popular enterprises like sweepstakes. The competition results clearly were not contributing to the company's hoped-for victory in the "Great Cola War" in which Mack was embroiled during this period. Moreover, in 1948, Pepsi-Cola's profits disappeared. Its losses continued, making continued outlays on art ($41,500 in 1948) simply unfeasible.[107] Reeling from the negative response to the competition, Mack and Pepsi officials had finally reached the limits of their willingness to provide work for painters' sake. The competitions may have been intended to help support American art, but the bottom line had always been publicity.[108] If the paintings produced even under these favorable conditions were only going to embarrass the sponsoring company, they were clearly not worth the bother. Perhaps fine art really did have its limitations as a corporate promotion strategy.

Increasing numbers of businessmen and advertising people concurred. "Art in Advertising," a McCann-Erikson researcher and art director reminded *Printer's Ink* readers in 1948, "must justify itself today in terms of the cash register." Defining "fine-art artists" as "the men who paint for their own self expression," the authors commented, "There are times when the self-expression of the artist can perform advertising functions," such as associating a product with quality. "But examples of success should not lead to indiscriminate use of fine art in advertising." Indeed, they observed, "inclusion of illustration of the fine arts variety" could often "lower the effectiveness of an advertisement."[109]

The Demise of "Fine Art" Advertising

These were just opinions, but they clearly affected advertising practice. "Fine art" had never constituted more than a single-digit percentage of magazine advertising, even during the peak of its popularity among clients during the mid-1940s. In the late 1940s, even clients like the United States Brewers Foundation, who had experimented with "fine-art artists," turned to more old-fashioned illustrators.[110] Ralph Pearson, who had been compiling his own informal survey on the "art content" in *Life* "advertising pictures," cited in 1950 a noticeable drop over a five-year period in the number of advertisements with "genuine works of art" ("designed creation," as he also characterized it) rather than factual or naturalistic pictures.[111]

While there are differences of opinion about what type of illustration might fit into the "fine art" category, a review of a sampling of full-page advertisements in mass-market magazines from the 1940s and 1950s corroborates Pearson's observations. In an average of several issues of the *Saturday Evening Post* from 1942, for example, 2 percent of the advertising imagery in full-page advertisements was of the "fine arts" kind. This percentage includes images rendered in a loosely painted style, or with imagery that bore no obvious relation to the accompanying text and that served as a metaphor for independent self-expression, as well as images that were "framed" as "paintings" or that were explicitly described as such in the copy. By contrast, 48 percent of the full-page advertising images were painted or drawn illustrations, 38 percent were photographs, 10 percent were a combination of illustration and photography, and 3 percent were cartoons. In 1946 the percentage of "fine art" rose to 7 percent as opposed to 53 percent illustrations and 33 percent photographs. (Illustration remained prominent in the *Saturday Evening Post* because advertisers desired to maintain consistency between their images and those of the many illustrated stories.) In 1952 "fine art" had declined to 3 percent, compared with 45 percent illustrations and 34 percent photographs. And in 1959, anything remotely approximating "fine art" had dropped to 1 percent; illustrations dropped to 20 percent, while photographs rose to 71 percent. In an average 1942 issue of *Vogue,* "fine art" represented 3 percent of the total number of full-page advertisements, illustrations 41 percent, and photographs 50 percent. By 1946, "fine art" had risen to 5 percent, but by 1952 was back down to 1 percent of all full-page ads, with photographs rising to over 70 percent. "Fine art" imagery represented 3 percent of the full-page advertising in the November issue of *Ladies' Home Journal* in 1942, 1 percent in 1952, and zero percent in 1959. In 1942, 45 percent of the full-page images were photographs and 32 percent were illustrations. In 1952, photographs represented 66 percent and illustration 16 percent. In 1959, illustration had dropped to 10 percent and photographs had risen to 80 percent. The percentages for *Life* Magazine were similar.[112]

The evidence is clear. "Fine art" had never been a major component of advertising imagery. Although several companies used the services of reputable painters in the 1950s (Ben Shahn's print advertisements for the Columbia Broadcasting System are a notable example), and Container Corporation of America continued its "Great Ideas" series until 1980, these were exceptions. By the end of the 1950s, advertising commissions for "fine-art artists" had all but dried up. Corporate clients left painters to go their own way.

This shift suited some painters and art supporters just fine. As we have seen, politically disillusioned painters, following Clement Greenberg, were seeking to redefine the boundaries of fine art in the narrowest possible manner—even more so than earlier, espousing an ideal of non-service, non-work, nonprofessionalism, and in the case of Ad Reinhardt, even non-art [referring to art as conventionally conceived].[113] They insisted that artists should not attempt to serve an ignorant mass public. Satisfaction would be found not in earning a living, but through the act of creation. The responsibility of the artist was to represent himself on canvas, revealing the only truth knowable through that creative process.[114] These self-professed avant-garde painters spurned the conventional ideal of professionals as an autonomous occupational group that controlled a body of abstract knowledge, standards, and techniques, sought to provide socially useful services, enforced vocational boundaries through training, and established bureaucracies and hierarchies.[115] In theory, at least, professional status was no longer necessary or even desirable; in privileging individual expression over conventional shareable meanings and values, every artist became an expert.

The new anti-conception of artistic activity also covered art for advertising. As Russell Lynes put it, the aims of artists and businessmen were basically incompatible when it came to advertising in the postwar culture of abundance:

> The problem of industrial patronage cannot be solved by telling the artist to get wise to himself and the ways of the world. He is a man who knows that there are greater pleasures than owning a refrigerator and he is confident that he is in a position to provide such pleasures. The artist is a producer of delectation, not of utility and, furthermore, does not want to be the bait on someone else's hook; he wants to be the hook itself.[116]

Lynes, along with adman David Ogilvy, recommended that businessmen patronize artists in a more indirect fashion than through advertising commissions, by purchasing their art. Use photographs in advertising, Ogilvy urged readers, "and your clients will prosper sufficiently to buy paintings and drawings and present them to public galleries."[117]

Many corporate executives now preferred to follow this advice. Many of them, like artists, embraced the notion that avant-garde art was "nonwork." Through their presence on boards of major corporations and art institutions they played a reinvigorated role in shaping the dominant cultural hierarchies from the late 1950s onward. Rather than presenting pictures to public galleries, the chief executive officers of Chase Manhattan Bank, Hallmark Cards, Miller Company, and Metamold Aluminum followed the example of Thomas Watson of IBM and established corporate art collections, whose contents often reflected their personal tastes and visions.[118]

Yet these events, far from resolving artists' dilemmas, produced even greater confusion about the cultural positions of "fine-art painters" and commercial artists. The situation was complicated by the resurgence of the illustrator, the emergence of the "Sunday painter," and the effect of television.

Challenges to Art-Art

Corporate managers might agree that fine art and advertising imagery should be distinct. But in another sphere, through a profit-making company operating as an educational institution, magazine illustrators and career advertising artists were constructing an alternative framework within which they, too, could be fine artists in postwar America. During the late 1940s, illustrators, like painters, were on the defensive. Both photographers and what *Business Week* described as the "fine-arts boys" were making significant inroads into advertising.[119] At the same time, cultural highbrows, especially proponents of avant-gardism, were condemning illustrators for catering to philistine tastes (although avant-garde artists themselves were certainly not immune to the lure of the commercial media).[120] Attacked on two fronts, big-name illustrators decided to defend their turf. The Famous Artists Schools, Inc., was their attempt to prove that illustration was alive and well, and that it was truly art.

The correspondence-based Famous Artists Schools was founded as the Institute of Commercial Art in Westport, Connecticut, in 1947. Initially the Institute was set up by illustrator Albert Dorne as an enterprise separate and distinct from what sociologist Herbert Gans termed "creator-oriented" fine art.[121] Intended to train students for art careers in business and fashion, it espoused an artistic ideal structured in terms of popular appeal and commercial values. This implied that illustrators no longer aspired to reputations in the exclusive world of high art, as defined by painters, intellectuals, museum curators, and elite corporate executives. The school's founders, stockholders, and advisory faculty were twelve of the country's leading illustrators and advertising artists, and included Norman Rockwell, John Atherton, and Jon Whitcomb. They contributed material for the step-by-step lesson textbooks, such as "How I Make a Picture," distributed in huge leatherlike notebooks.[122] Its students, who included "doctors, dentists, lumberjacks, mechanics, butchers . . . nuns, bartenders, and truckdrivers," learned about the school from ads in popular and art magazines and, later, comics. The school would have also been an attractive option for veterans, for whom correspondence schools qualified for benefits under the GI Bill of Rights.[123] The ICA was thus very much an outgrowth of American social life of the late 1940s. Its very existence was made possible by the postwar economic boom, with its resulting expansion of the job market, rise in household income and leisure time, faith in expertise, and explosion of consumer spending among a growing middle class.[124]

The idea of a correspondence school in art was not new; there were commercial art schools and correspondence courses in the first decades of the century. But the popular success of this commercial art school revolved paradoxically around the prestige of its faculty, its "Twelve Famous Artists." The phrase connoted a certain fine art status, but these were men who in sophisticated fine art circles would have been classed as commercial illustrators, advertising artists, or perhaps even hacks. Dorne and his staff just ignored such elitist views. Banking on their faculty's popular cachet, they soon began to pursue a course that challenged the world of high culture as the exclusive domain of fine art activity (and by implication attempted to challenge photography as an illustrative tool). In 1952 the school, having changed its name to Famous Artists Schools, Inc., broadened its scope to include a fine arts course in painting. It was geared toward the amateur, "who doesn't care about making money but wants to satisfy some inner urge."[125]

The school's new orientation toward the amateur acknowledged the rise of the so-called "Sunday painter" (fig. 6.11), whose emergence was another postwar phenomenon, one that expressed the anxieties and tensions that coexisted with the prevailing optimism and consensus. Dabbling in paint in one's leisure time was of course not new. As observers were quick to point out, the Douannier Rousseau had been a Sunday painter. Winston Churchill expounded on the joys of painting as a hobby in his 1932 autobiography. But since the nightmares of the war, Churchill's aristocratic pastime for restoring "psychic equilibrium" had gained ground with ordinary people. Painting to kill time, to escape routine and numbing fears, to fill a spiritual void, became a major popular fad. Dwight D. Eisenhower and Grandma Moses became America's Sunday painter "heroes," and art supply sales soared from $4 million in 1939 to $40 million by about 1950.[126]

Amateur painters longed for a sense of technical mastery, and for their friends to recognize their abilities. Many believed that to achieve these goals they had to learn to paint in the *proper* manner, that such a method existed, and that the Famous Artists Schools provided the means to acquire it. Small business executives, truck drivers, waitresses, football players, housewives, and even "uranium mogul" Joseph Hirshhorn looked to the explicitly audience-oriented *commercial* realm—to illustrators like the Twelve Famous Artists—to learn not only how to become an artist, but also the definitions, standards, and meanings of art itself.[127]

The school was hugely successful. Ten thousand students were reportedly enrolled in 1954, and ten times that many ten years later.[128] With the Famous Artists Schools, illustrators had established an institutional framework within which they could be identified as true artists—if not by the art world, then at least by the general public, whose values and

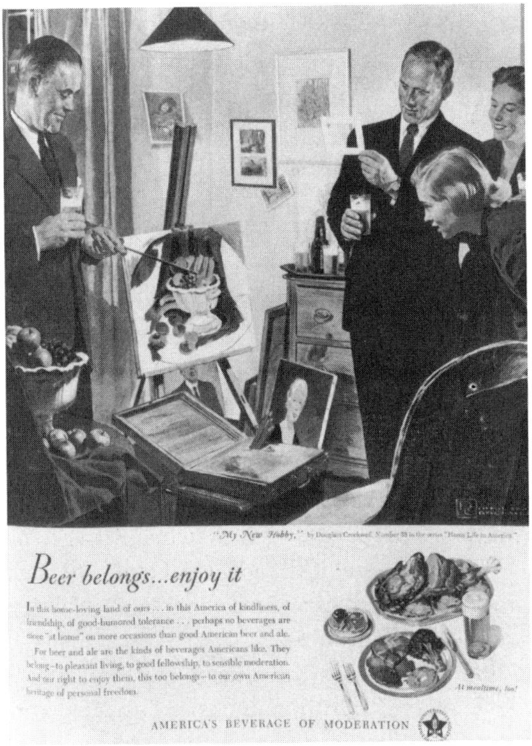

6.11. Advertisement for United States Brewers Foundation, illustration by Douglas Crockwell, 1950.

attitudes were, perhaps, more overtly shaped by mass media, national advertising, and mass-market publishing than by their high-culture counterparts. With its dual emphases and its blatantly commercial orientation and practices, the school represented an alternative to the artistic ideals, myths, standards, and definitions structured by the elite world of urban artistic culture. Supporters of the avant-garde tried their best to exclude this "other" art world from artistic discourse. As a consequence of its influence on Sunday painters, however, the Famous Artists Schools had an impact whose broader ramifications could not be ignored.

Sunday painters helped to revitalize the status of the illustrator, but their presence on the scene proved problematic for the "fine-arts painter," especially when television emerged as a mass communication medium. Television contributed further to the rising influence of the Sunday painter and challenged the privileged status of the fine artist.

The program *You Are an Artist,* hosted by a former advertising art director, Jon Gnagy (1907–1981), was an indicator of the effect television could have on conceptions of art and the artist. Sponsored by Gulf Oil and aired weekly on NBC over a twenty-five-year period beginning in 1946, the program (later syndicated as *Draw With Me* and *Learn To Draw*) was a televised counterpart of the Famous Artists Schools. Inspiring viewers with the reassuring words "you are an artist," the goateed and plaid-shirted Gnagy urged viewers to express themselves by learning a method of "putting on paper what the beholder sees in such simple basic forms as ball, cone, cube, and cylinder," and working up images from there.[129] A committee of art educators headed by Museum of Modern Art education director Victor d'Amico protested to the network that the program stifled creativity and perpetuated "outmoded and authoritarian concepts of education." But in arousing confidence among would-be artists, Gnagy touched millions. The *New York Times* reported (and photographs corroborate) that even some bars aired the Thursday night broadcasts; customers brought sketchbooks and pencils and watched Gnagy together.[130] Andy Warhol reportedly was one of Gnagy's loyal fans. He later testified that "Jon Gnagy taught me how to draw. I watched his show every Saturday morning and I bought all of his books."[131]

It is hardly surprising that modernist sympathizers felt threatened. Programs like *You Are an Artist* were inspiring millions of Sunday painters whose ideals were antithetical to their own, and some of whom were indistinguishable from the same commercial artists from whom they were trying to distinguish themselves. At a time when avant-garde painters and critics, fearful of mass culture, were attempting to narrow conceptions of art, the newly emboldened "Sunday painters," inspired by *You Are an Artist* and the Famous Artists Schools, were undermining such efforts. The presence of the Sunday painter prevented rigid distinctions between artist and audience, producer and consumer, art-as-experience and art-as-commodity, commercial and noncommercial work, or high art and popular culture. The opposites often collapsed.

Sunday painters, after all, produced unique, authentic images, which were often sold at art shows.[132] In contrast, the work of the professionals might as easily be experienced through reproductions as through originals. These factors, along with the fact that many Sunday painters were genuinely talented, challenged the idea that art as an *activity* could be conceived in terms of differences between amateurs and experts. For distinctions between true artists and others to hold up, differences would have to be conceived in terms of vocation. Here again, clear-cut boundaries were elusive. Few painters or illustrators were people of independent means; as earlier, most had to work at jobs that were not art-related.

There was thus little to distinguish them from Sunday painters, who likewise earned their keep through non-art employment and were equally devoted to their painting. Under these circumstances, self-perceived "fine artists" were also Sunday painters.

There was one difference, however. Unlike Sunday painters, both artists and illustrators were also employed doing advertising and other commercial tasks—when they could get the work. For, indeed, aspiring painters competed with illustrators for agency jobs, such as lettering, layout, and graphics. In the 1940s illustration still prevailed over fine art in advertising, maintaining a presence despite significant encroachment by photography. By the late 1950s, advertisers had largely abandoned illustration in favor of photography.[133] Illustrators thus did not benefit greatly from advertisers' rejection of "fine-art artists." As with the phenomenon of the Sunday painter, the reasons had much to do with the ascendancy of television.

Television's importance for illustrators went far beyond Jon Gnagy's program. Initially television held out promise as a new medium for aesthetic experimentation. CBS commissioned illustrators, graphic designers, and painters (like Ben Shahn) to create print advertisements and public relations materials. Continuing the practices established by Hollywood, art and creative directors for all the networks, for producers, and for sponsors (or their agencies) hired artists to design title cards, backgrounds, station break identification images, and storyboards.[134]

From the standpoint of artists, however, television's most significant impact was undoubtedly its negative influence on their occupation. As early as 1956, sociologist Leo Bogart concluded that television was replacing magazines and books as a source of fantasy and of dramatic entertainment. Reduced circulation produced a "striking decrease" in magazine fiction and, in turn, fewer opportunities for illustrators in this area.[135] Magazine advertising gravitated toward photography in order to maintain consistency with the growing proportion of nonfiction editorial content. The circulation of the photographic picture magazines *Life* and *Look* rose 33 percent during the 1960s, but the decade saw the demise of the *Saturday Evening Post,* the magazine that heretofore had relied most heavily on illustrators.[136] Specialized-interest magazine and paperback book publishers filled the void somewhat, but their effect was limited. "When I got out of art school there was an aura of glamour surrounding the top illustrators," reminisced illustrator Bernard Fuchs (born in 1932). "No more."[137]

Toward Separate Spheres

With government and advertiser support so scarce, and artists so eager to do work in their métier, illustrators and painters found themselves competing for and employed in the same kinds of jobs, and faced with professional uncertainty. Sociologist Mason Griff proclaimed in 1960 that commercial artists were experiencing a crisis of identity, and commented on the inconsistency between society's encouragement of children's artistic talents and its discouragement of those who pursued art as a career.[138] This incongruity, he observed, was rooted in the stereotype of the artist as Bohemian—a notion that clashed with the middle-class emphasis on conformity and financial success. In the face of such social pressure, an artist might stick to his brushes and thus likely become marginal to society, or he could become a commercial artist, earning some social approval and a decent living.

Many of those who took the commercial path adapted to this situation, Griff noted, relinquishing their former fine art aspirations to varying degrees. Some took on "identifications" as "commercial role" artists, who "organize their role on the basis that both fine art and commercial art are utilitarian," and whose activities were geared toward advancing their careers and pleasing clients. Some became "compromise-role artists," refusing to be "passive agents." While they tried to accommodate advertising clients, they also sought to persuade them to do things their way. Their goals of improving the art of advertising and raising public taste in the process served as rationalizations for not doing more "pure painting."[139] A third group, whom Griff described as "traditional-role artists," clung to Bohemian ideals and experienced tremendous conflict. Believing that their commercial work was a "*betrayal to the cause of fine art and the prostitution of a God-given talent*," they had difficulty achieving a stable identity in a society in which identity was defined by work.[140]

Griff's discussion reflected the concerns of many intellectuals and artists of the period, including the volume's other contributors. These included psychologist Erik Erikson, whose *Childhood and Identity* (1950) was a seminal text in formulating "identity" as a psychosocial phenomenon.[141] Erikson, the popularizer of the "identity crisis," was coincidently providing therapy to Norman Rockwell, who was trying to resolve his own identity problems. Indeed, 1960 was the year Rockwell published his autobiography and painted his *Triple Self-Portrait*.[142]

Griff's description of multiple and confused identities was borne out in the art and career not only of Rockwell but also of Andy Warhol. If Rockwell represented the older predicament, stemming from the disjunction between the romantic fine arts ideal and the demands of a culture dominated by commercial mass media, Warhol, of a younger generation, found a new way around the old contradictions. Warhol was a successful commercial illustrator in the 1950s. His agitated, idiosyncratic, easily reproducible "line art" style appealed to art directors searching for a non-photographic fantasy look, and he was reliable and prompt.[143] Warhol aspired to be a painter, but he evidently believed it futile to try to cast off his "other" commercial identity and the expectations and practices linked with it. He thus brought a different trajectory to the fine artist's career. The expectations and values of most artists, including Norman Rockwell, remained influenced by romantic ideologies absorbed in art school and the culture at large. By contrast, Warhol brought to his work an outlook and values absorbed through his successful commercial art practice and through the mass media; he and his painting seemed egoless, deadpan, impersonal, unemotional, inauthentic, contradictory.[144]

A typical Warhol painting from the early 1960s, *Green Coca-Cola Bottles* (1962, fig. 6.12), expressed the contradictions bound up with the

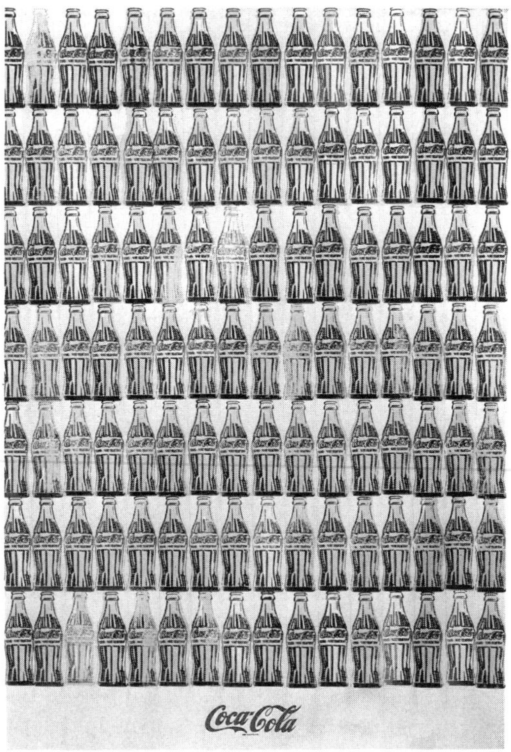

6.12. Andy Warhol, *Green Coca-Cola Bottles,* 1962.

question of artistic identity. In the painting, Warhol rendered multiple versions of a photographically "realistic" image, ordinarily seen individually but repeatedly in the soft drink's illustrated advertisements. In so doing, he alluded to the ubiquitous presence of the impersonal mass reproduction technology on which the work of the advertising artist depended. Yet Warhol's technique was inseparably linked to what, echoing John Hylan some forty years earlier, he called "Art Art." Each of the multiple images was individually produced (possibly stamped with a single balsa wood carving).[145] Each was rendered unique, as was the painting itself. The final product was not a reproduction, nor an advertisement, but a single canvas, a scintillating configuration of vibrating color and shape patterns. The image confirmed the persistence and force of "fine art" ideology even as it mocked these elite and transcendental ideals.

From the perspective of this study, Warhol's art represented the culmination of dilemmas about the relationship of art, media, and advertising that artists had confronted since the turn of the century. Warhol's art and career also represented a shrewd and effective public articulation of those dilemmas as they affected artists circa 1960. He forged an art and an artistic persona predicated on the clash of traditional but persistent romantic ideals with the equally persistent collapse of distinctions between "Art Art" and "Business Art."[146] Embracing the contradictions of being an artist in commerce, Warhol's practices were an effective personal resolution of a sort that had eluded his predecessors. His actions, along with those of other pop artists, helped to make the tension between fine art and commercial art a central aesthetic issue in the 1960s and onward.[147]

Yet there was a certain irony to all of this. The issue of art corrupted by advertising was being raised just at the point when advertisers themselves were largely turning their backs on art, when debates over the artist's relationship to commerce were becoming, from the advertiser's perspective, a dead issue. To be sure, there was corporate collecting, which used art (ever more pervasively) for public relations and to boost employee morale. Yet there the relationship between artist and client was more impersonal and indirect, and simply extended a tradition of patronage that had existed since the Renaissance. Relinquishing their efforts to claim fine art for advertising, advertisers and businessmen were now only too willing to accept a separate category of fine art. The creative opportunities, tensions, and exchanges that characterized advertising and publishing enterprises at the turn of the century had largely dissipated, except where photography was concerned. As we have seen throughout this book, those challenges and possibilities were once issues of central *professional* concern for illustrators and painters—matters around which they had organized their practices, work, and self-images. By 1960, with the realization that art for advertising was no longer an obvious or conceivable representation or option, artists and critics began heatedly to discuss the relationship of fine art and commercial art, epitomized by Warhol, as an *aesthetic* problem. By the time this discussion was absorbed into aesthetic discourse, however, it had already ceased to be a matter of pressing professional interest, identity, or action.

Throughout the first half of the century, artists strove to relate purposefully to the corporate presence, to explore possibilities offered by new media and centers of cultural power. As this book has shown, adjustment to the new market-oriented frameworks presented technical, aesthetic, and professional challenges. Romantic ideals remained a persistent influence on image production and artistic identity. The 1950s marked a period of notable reconfiguration in which romantic high-art values, privileging autonomous creation and reception, emerged triumphant. The shift in emphasis from occupational to aesthetic debate signaled a resolution of the question regarding the borders of art: "Fine" art was clearly separate from other artistic enterprises. This shift was manifest in the rising interest in contemporary American painting and the explosion of its market value. For artists to accept these conditions appeared to be a good solution, with the question of maintaining creative autonomy resolved to their benefit. As connoisseurs and collectors, businessmen, who acquired great leverage in the art world through patronage, accepted artists on the latter's terms and prized artistic productions as worthy in their own right. The endorsement of art as an aesthetic category rather than as a social undertaking may also have had less beneficial consequences, however. Such sanctions were symptomatic of artists' decreasing ability to shape the cultural economy in which they were enmeshed.

In recent years many have argued, with varying degrees of enthusiasm, that the boundaries between fine art and commercial art have relaxed once again. Much of the discussion has centered around the work of postmodern artists like Barbara Kruger and Jeff Koons, as well as the notorious Museum of Modern Art exhibition "High and Low" (1990), which focused on the impact of (low) popular culture—like advertising—on (high) modern art. But those fearful of an imminent collapse of distinctions have little to fear. For all the hoopla about the breakdown of borders, the notion of "fine" art continues to structure some formidable intellectual hierarchies. The integrity of art-art remains very much a given. It remains a common assumption that a discrete category, "fine art," has always existed but that the last one hundred years have seen its broadening or demise. Yet as we have seen, the broadening of fine art's parameters on a wide cultural scale occurred only after commercial art's challenge to fine art had been contained, and its producers marginalized. This alternative history of artists in commerce resituates these individuals in their proper place—alongside the art-artists. It suggests a more inclusive, egalitarian way to picture the artistic enterprise—not as unrivaled creators and works but as artistic activity.

Notes

abbreviations

AAA	Archives of American Art, Smithsonian Institution
ACNY	Art Commission of the City of New York
AV	Artists for Victory Papers, Archives of American Art
Calkins/Geohagen Papers	Earnest Elmo Calkins/Walter B. Geohagen Papers, Seymour Library, Archives and Manuscript Collection, Knox College, Galesburg, Illinois
CCNY	City College of New York Archives
JWTA	J. Walter Thompson Company Archives, Special Collections Library, Duke University
MAS	Municipal Art Society Papers, Archives of American Art
MMAA	The Metropolitan Museum of Art Archives
MPP	Maxfield Parrish Papers, Dartmouth College Library, Hanover, New Hampshire
NYHS	New-York Historical Society, New York City
RK	Rockwell Kent Papers, Archives of American Art
SI	Society of Illustrators, New York City

introduction

1. For "Common Man," see Jack Alexander's "Biographical Introduction," in Arthur R. Guptill, *Norman Rockwell: Illustrator* (New York: Watson-Guptill, 1946), xxi, and 3. See also Thomas S. Buechner, *Norman Rockwell: Artist and Illustrator* (New York: Harry N. Abrams, 1970).

2. See, for example, Norman Rockwell, *My Adventures as an Illustrator,* as told to Thomas Rockwell (New York: Doubleday, 1960), 236–59, 322, 328–31; Norman Rockwell, *How I Make a Picture* (Westport, Conn.: Institute of Commercial Art, 1949); Guptill, *Norman Rockwell: Illustrator.*

3. One of the most recent examples of this cultural hierarchicalization is Kirk Varnedoe and Adam Gopnik, *High and Low: Modern Art and Popular Culture* (New York: Harry N. Abrams, 1990). See also its excellent bibliography, compiled by Matthew Armstrong and Fereshteh Daftari, 429–31; and Kirk Varnedoe and Adam Gopnik, eds., *Modern Art and Popular Culture: Readings in High and Low* (New York: Harry N. Abrams, 1990). Feminist scholars have challenged the assumptions, categories, and priorities of modern art history, pointing to its marginalization of women and women's activities. See, for example, Lisa Tickner, *The Spectacle of Women: Imagery of the Suffrage Campaign, 1907–14* (Chicago: University of Chicago Press, 1988), ix–xii; idem, "Feminism, Art History, and Sexual Difference,"

Genders 1, no. 3 (Fall 1988): 93–98. Similar modernist biases have colored the historical analyses of other forms of material culture, including art for advertising. Other important recent studies that contribute—implicitly and explicitly—to this debate over cultural hierarchies include: Pierre Bourdieu, *Distinction: A Social Critique of the Judgement of Taste* (Cambridge, Mass.: Harvard University Press, 1984); T. J. Clark, "Jackson Pollock's Abstraction," in Serge Guilbaut, ed., *Reconstructing Modernism: Art in New York, Paris, and Montreal 1945–1964* (Cambridge, Mass.: MIT Press, 1990), 172–243; John Clarke, "Pessimism vs. Populism: The Problematic Politics of Popular Culture," in Richard Butsch, ed., *For Fun and Profit: The Transformation of Leisure into Consumption* (Philadelphia: Temple University Press, 1990), 28–44; Thomas Crow, "Modernism and Mass Culture in the Visual Arts," in Francis Frascina, ed., *Pollock and After: The Critical Debate* (New York: Harper and Row, 1985), 233–66; David Freedberg, *The Power of Images: Studies in the History and Theory of Response* (Chicago: University of Chicago Press, 1989); Herbert Gans, *Popular Culture and High Culture: An Analysis and Evaluation of Taste* (New York: Basic Books, 1974); idem, "American Popular Culture and High Culture in a Changing Class Structure," *Prospects* 10 (1985): 17–37; Clement Greenberg, "Avant Garde and Kitsch," in Clement Greenberg, *The Collected Essays and Criticism*, vol. 1, *Perceptions and Judgments 1939–1944* (Chicago: University of Chicago Press, 1986), 5–22; Andreas Huyssen, "Mass Culture as Woman: Modernism's Other," in *After the Great Divide: Modernism, Mass Culture, Postmodernism* (Bloomington: Indiana University Press, 1986), 44–62; John F. Kasson, *Amusing the Million: Coney Island at the Turn of the Century* (New York: Hill and Wang, 1978); Jackson Lears, "A Matter of Taste: Corporate Cultural Hegemony in a Mass-Consumption Society," in Lary May, ed., *Recasting America: Culture and Politics in the Age of Cold War* (Chicago: University of Chicago Press, 1989), 38–57; Lawrence W. Levine, *Highbrow/Lowbrow: The Emergence of Cultural Hierarchy in America* (Cambridge, Mass.: Harvard University Press, 1988); Russell Lynes, *The Tastemakers* (New York: Harper and Brothers, 1949); Kathleen D. McCarthy, *Women's Culture: American Philanthropy and Art, 1830–1930* (Chicago: University of Chicago Press, 1991); Grant McCracken, *Culture and Consumption: New Approaches to the Symbolic Character of Consumer Goods and Activities* (Bloomington: Indiana University Press, 1990); Karal Ann Marling, "Disneyland, 1955," *American Art* 5 (Winter/Spring 1991): 169–207; Karal Ann Marling and John Wetenhall, *Iwo Jima: Monuments, Memories, and the American Hero* (Cambridge, Mass.: Harvard University Press, 1991); Chandra Mukerji and Michael Schudson, *Rethinking Popular Culture: Contemporary Perspectives in Cultural Studies* (Berkeley: University of California Press, 1991); Anne Norton, *Republic of Signs: Liberal Theory and American Popular Culture* (Chicago: University of Chicago Press, 1993), 47–86; Janice Radway, *Reading the Romance: Women, Patriarchy, and Popular Literature* (Chapel Hill: University of North Carolina Press, 1984); idem, "Mail-Order Culture and Its Critics: The Book-of-the-Month-Club, Commodification and Consumption, and the Problem of Cultural Authority," in Lawrence Grossberg, Cary Nelson, and Paula A. Treichler, eds., *Cultural Studies* (New York and London: Routledge, 1992), 512–30; Andrew Ross, *No Respect: Intellectuals and Popular Culture* (New York and London: Routledge, 1989); Joan Shelley Rubin, *The Making of Middlebrow Culture* (Chapel Hill: University of North Carolina Press, 1992); Barbara Herrnstein

Smith, "Contingencies of Value," in Robert von Hallberg, ed., *Canons* (Chicago: University of Chicago Press, 1984), 3–39.

4. This consumer culture, described by T. J. Jackson Lears and Richard Wightman Fox as a system of values, standards of living, and power structure, was an expression and outgrowth of the shift from a production economy, in which goods were produced locally and in response to specific market needs, to a national economy structured by large, hierarchically organized business enterprises and administered by a new class of salaried managers. The new economy functioned on the principle of continuous output that both created and necessitated growth of national markets and of an ethos of consumption to stoke the fires of demand and insure ongoing production. See Richard Wightman Fox and T. J. Jackson Lears, "Introduction," in Richard Wightman Fox and T. J. Jackson Lears, eds., *The Culture of Consumption: Critical Essays in American History, 1880–1980* (New York: Pantheon, 1983), xii; T. J. Jackson Lears, "Beyond Veblen: Rethinking American Consumer Culture," in Simon J. Bronner, ed., *Consuming Visions: The Accumulation and Display of Goods in America, 1880–1920* (New York: W. W. Norton, 1989), 73–98; Stuart Ewen, *Captains of Consciousness: Advertising and the Social Roots of Consumer Culture* (New York: McGraw-Hill, 1976); Stuart Ewen and Elizabeth Ewen, *Channels of Desire: Mass Images and the Shaping of American Consciousness* (Minneapolis: University of Minnesota Press, 1992; first published 1982), chapters 1–3; William Leach, *Land of Desire: Merchants, Power, and the Rise of a New American Culture* (New York: Pantheon, 1993); Warren Susman, *Culture as History: The Transformation of American Society in the Twentieth Century* (New York: Pantheon, 1984), xi–xxx; Alan Trachtenberg, *The Incorporation of America: Culture and Society in the Gilded Age* (New York: Hill and Wang, 1982), 130–39, 150–51; Alfred D. Chandler, *The Visible Hand: The Managerial Revolution in American Business* (Cambridge, Mass.: Harvard University Press, 1977), 10–12; Olivier Zunz, *Making America Corporate: 1870–1920* (Chicago: University of Chicago Press, 1990).

5. Concerning Pollock, see Erika Doss, *Benton, Pollock, and the Politics of Modernism* (Chicago: University of Chicago Press, 1991), 363–416; Christin J. Mamiya, *Pop Art and Consumer Culture: American Super Market* (Austin: University of Texas Press, 1992); Clark, "Jackson Pollock's Abstraction;" Bradford R. Collins, "*Life* Magazine and the Abstract Expressionists, 1948–51: A Historiographic Study of a Late Bohemian Enterprise," *Art Bulletin* 73 (June 1991): 283–307. On de Kooning, see Richard Shiff, "Water and Lipstick," in Marla Prather, Richard Shiff, and David Sylvester, *Willem De Kooning: Paintings* (New Haven: Yale University Press, 1994), 48–49, 68–69. For references to Warhol, see chapter 6, n. 145, 147.

6. On magazines, see Frank Luther Mott, *A History of American Magazines, 1885–1905*, vol. 4 (Cambridge, Mass.: Harvard University Press, 1957), 1–70; Judy L. Larson, *American Illustration, 1890–1925: Romance, Adventure, and Suspense* (Calgary, Alberta: Glenbow Museum, 1986), 19–20, 39–49; Neil Harris, *Cultural Excursions: Marketing Appetites and Cultural Tastes in Modern America* (Chicago: University of Chicago Press, 1990), 304–48.

7. T. J. Jackson Lears, "Some Versions of Fantasy: Toward A Cultural History of American Advertising, 1880–1930," *Prospects* 9 (1984): 355; Charles Goodrum and Helen Dalrymple, *Advertising in America: The First Two Hundred Years* (New York: Harry N. Abrams, 1990), 13–22; Daniel Pope, *The Making of Modern Advertising* (New York: Basic Books, 1983),

108–9; Stephen Fox, *The Mirror Makers: A History of American Advertising and Its Creators* (New York: William Morrow, 1984), 40.

8. Pope, *Making of Modern Advertising,* 108–9; Lears, "Some Versions of Fantasy," 355–57.

9. Neil Harris, *Cultural Excursions,* 307; Harris charts responses to the innovations in color printing on 318–40.

10. Sociologist Joseph Gusfield makes this clear in his discussion of the construction of "social problems." See his introduction to *The Culture of Public Problems: Drinking-Driving and the Symbolic Order* (Chicago: University of Chicago Press, 1981), 1–23.

11. On the importance of background, experience, and expectations in governing identity and practice, see Robert R. Faulkner, *Hollywood Studio Musicians* (Chicago: Aldine, 1971); and idem, *Music on Demand: Composers and Careers in the Hollywood Film Industry* (New Brunswick: Transaction Books, 1983).

12. Sociological studies of culture and the professions have provided helpful models and insights. See Andrew Abbott, *The System of Professions: An Essay on the Division of Expert Labor* (Chicago: University of Chicago Press, 1988); Faulkner, *Music on Demand;* Howard Becker, *Art Worlds* (Berkeley: University of California Press, 1982); Howard Becker and Michal M. McCall, *Symbolic Interaction and Cultural Studies* (Chicago: University of Chicago Press, 1990); Paul J. DiMaggio, "Constructing an Organizational Field as a Professional Project: U.S. Art Museums, 1920–1940," in Walter W. Powell and Paul J. DiMaggio, eds., *The New Institutionalism in Organizational Analysis* (Chicago: University of Chicago Press, 1991); Janet Wolff, *The Social Production of Art* (New York: New York University Press, 1984; first published 1981); Vera L. Zolberg, *Constructing a Sociology of the Arts* (Cambridge: Cambridge University Press, 1990). See also Samuel Haber, *The Quest for Authority and Honor in the American Professions, 1750–1900* (Chicago: University of Chicago Press, 1991); Charles Rosenberg, "Toward an Ecology of Knowledge: On Discipline, Context, and History," in Alexandra Oleson and John Voss, *The Organization of Knowledge in Modern America* (Baltimore: Johns Hopkins University Press, 1979), 440–54; Radway, "Mail-Order Culture," 512–26.

13. For discussions of the relationship among professional jurisdiction, cultural authority, and taste hierarchies, see Michele H. Bogart, *Public Sculpture and the Civic Ideal in New York City, 1890–1930* (Chicago: University of Chicago Press, 1989), 61–66, 221–57; Bourdieu, *Distinction;* Paul DiMaggio, "Cultural Entrepreneurship in Nineteenth Century Boston: The Creation of an Organizational Base for High Culture in America," in Mukerji and Schudson, *Rethinking Popular Culture,* 374–97; McCarthy, *Women's Culture,* 59–79; Radway, "Mail Order Culture," 512–30; idem, "The Scandal of the Middlebrow: The Book-of-the-Month-Club, Class Fracture, and Cultural Authority," *South Atlantic Quarterly,* Fall 1990, 703–37.

14. For discussion of these ideals as they developed within the discourse of nineteenth-century art, see Hugh Honour, *Romanticism* (New York: Harper and Row, 1979), 14–26, 245–75; Richard Shiff, *Cézanne and the End of Impressionism: A Study of the Theory, Technique, and Critical Evaluation of Modern Art* (Chicago: University of Chicago Press, 1984). On con-

cerns about autonomy, see T. J. Jackson Lears, *No Place of Grace: Antimodernism and the Transformation of American Culture 1880–1920* (New York: Pantheon Books, 1981), 34–35; idem, "Beyond Veblen," 81–84; Rubin, *The Making of Middlebrow Culture*, 22–26.

15. The neologism "art-artists" is said to have been coined by New York City mayor John Hylan. I will periodically use my own variation, "art-art" (often described by period observers as "Art with a capital A"), to characterize "fine" art production at the culturally specific moment when commentators used the term "art-artists." I will also be using the more inclusive term "art" to connote an ideal of serious quality: creation of a high moral tenor, executed in accord with romantic standards of authenticity and originality and privileging the artist. "Art" (small a) may refer to any medium or mode of expression. For "art-artists," see Joseph Cummings Chase, "What Is This Art Game?" *Saturday Evening Post*, 15 October 1927, 17; Edward Alden Jewell, "In the Realm of Art," *New York Times*, 26 April 1942, sec. 6, 5. For "Art with a capital A," see Harford Powel Jr., "Pictures vs. 'Art,'" *Advertising and Selling*, 26 January 1928, 26; Frank Caspers, "Advertising Art," *Art Digest*, 1 June 1941, 31.

16. On this "professional-managerial 'class,'" see Fox and Lears, "Introduction," and Christopher Wilson, "The Rhetoric of Consumption: Mass-Market Magazines and the Demise of the Gentle Reader, 1880–1920," in Fox and Lears, *The Culture of Consumption*, xi, 40–64; Leach, *Land of Desire*, 3–12; Michele H. Bogart, *Public Sculpture and the Civic Ideal*, 5–7.

17. Fox and Lears, "Introduction," x–xii; Lears, "Beyond Veblen," 73–78. On modernity and modernization, see Gwendolyn Wright, *The Politics of French Colonial Urbanism* (Chicago: University of Chicago Press, 1991), 8–10; Chandler, *The Visible Hand*, 1–12. See also essays in Daniel Joseph Singal, ed., "Modernist Culture in America," *American Quarterly* 39 (Summer 1987). One additional strain of modernity recently highlighted by scholars is the relationship between the rise of urban commercial culture and "ocularcentrism" or "visuality"—the dominance of a visual paradigm for thought, knowledge, representation, and power. This perspective focuses on the privileging of surfaces, spectacles, and the pleasure of looking at the expense of an awareness of the social relations of production. For a good summary of these issues, see James Donald, "Metropolis: The City as Text," in Robert Bocock and Kenneth Thompson, eds., *Social and Cultural Forms of Modernity* (Cambridge: Polity Press, 1992), 434–36. See also Susan Buck-Morss, *The Dialectics of Seeing: Walter Benjamin and the Arcades Project* (Cambridge, Mass.: MIT Press, 1989), 83–86, 253–54. For two different perspectives that specifically address the American context, see Neil Harris, *Cultural Excursions*, chapters 14–17, and forthcoming work on John Sloan by Rebecca Zurier.

18. See Paul Boyer, *Urban Masses and Moral Order in America, 1890–1930* (Cambridge, Mass.: Harvard University Press, 1978); Lears, *No Place of Grace;* Robert H. Wiebe, *The Search for Order 1877–1920* (New York: Hill and Wang, 1967); Cecilia Tichi, *Shifting Gears: Technology, Literature, Culture in Modernist America* (Chapel Hill: University of North Caro- Press, 1987); Raymond Williams, *The Politics of Modernism: Against the New Conformists* (New York: Verso, 1989).

19. Depending on the actors and the context of the discussion, the word *modern* can refer to works as diverse as those by Edwin Howland Blashfield, Thomas Hart Benton, and

Pablo Picasso. On "the modern" and art, see Doss, *Benton, Pollock, and the Politics of Modernism,* 1–65; George H. Roeder, *Forum of Uncertainty: Confrontations with Modern Painting in Twentieth-Century American Thought* (Ann Arbor: UMI Research Press, 1980); T. J. Clark, *The Painting of Modern Life: Paris in the Art of Manet and His Followers* (Princeton: Princeton University Press, 1984); Francis Frascina and Charles Harrison, *Modern Art and Modernism: A Critical Anthology* (New York: Harper and Row, 1982); Daniel Joseph Singal, "Towards a Definition of American Modernism," George H. Roeder Jr., "What Have Modernists Looked At? Experiential Roots of Twentieth Century American Painting"; Jackson Lears, "Uneasy Courtship: Modern Art and Modern Advertising," all in *American Quarterly* 39 (Spring 1987): 7–26, 56–83, 133–54; and Ruth E. Iskin, "Selling, Seduction, and Soliciting the Eye: Manet's *Bar at the Folies-Bergère,*" *Art Bulletin* 77 (March 1995): 25–44.

20. The Art Directors Club set the standard, establishing separate categories for packaging for their annual exhibitions of advertising art. See their publication, *Annual of Advertising Art,* beginning in the late 1920s; see also "Art Directors Hold Fifth Exhibition of Advertising Art," *Printer's Ink,* 13 May 1926, 44. Important recent discussions of modernism, packaging, and display include James Sloan Allen, *The Romance of Commerce and Culture: Capitalism, Modernism, and the Chicago-Aspen Crusade for Cultural Reform* (Chicago: University of Chicago Press, 1983), 1–34; Stuart Ewen, *All Consuming Images: The Politics of Style in Contemporary Culture* (New York: Basic Books, 1988), 45–47, 241–58; Leach, *Land of Desire;* Roland Marchand, "The Designers Go to the Fair: Walter Dorwin Teague and the Professionalization of Corporate Industrial Exhibits, 1933–1940," *Design Issues* 8 (Fall 1991): 4–17; Jeffrey L. Meikle, *Twentieth Century Limited: Industrial Design in America, 1925–1939* (Philadelphia: Temple University Press, 1979); Terry Smith, *Making the Modern: Industry, Art, and Design in America* (Chicago: University of Chicago Press, 1993), 353–84; Sally Stein, "The Contested Value of Word and Image in the Discourse of American Advertising, 1900–1925," unpublished lecture, American Studies Association, 1991, 11–17; Susan Strasser, *Satisfaction Guaranteed: The Making of the American Mass Market* (New York: Pantheon, 1989).

21. Important critiques of advertising and consumerism include Ewen, *Captains of Consciousness;* Christopher Lasch, *The Culture of Narcissism* (New York: W. W. Norton, 1978), 72; Thomas Richards, *The Commodity Culture of Victorian England: Advertising and Spectacle, 1851–1914* (Stanford: Stanford University Press, 1990); Judith Williamson, *Decoding Advertisements: Ideology and Meaning in Advertising* (London: Marion Boyers, 1978). Alternative perspectives include Karal Ann Marling on Disney; Lears, "Some Versions of Fantasy," 349–405; idem, "Uneasy Courtship"; Leach, *Land of Desire;* Roland Marchand, *Advertising the American Dream: Making Way for Modernity, 1920–1940* (Berkeley: University of California Press, 1985); Michael Schudson, *Advertising: The Uneasy Persuasion* (New York: Basic Books, 1984), 1–11; Smith, "Contingencies of Value," 5–39; Susman, *Culture as History,* xix–xxx; Neil Harris, *Cultural Excursions,* 349–78.

chapter one

1. For a discussion of such values, see Daniel Joseph Singal, "Towards a Definition of American Modernism," *American Quarterly* 39 (Spring 1987): 7–26. For theorization of the

cultural process whereby something increases or decreases in value, see Michael Thompson, *Rubbish Theory: The Creation and Destruction of Value* (New York: Oxford University Press, 1979), especially chapters 1, 2, and 6.

2. Sid Hydeman, *How to Illustrate for Money* (New York: Harper and Brothers, 1936), 2.

3. The easel was a support device that paradoxically connoted creative autonomy. According to the *Compact Edition of the Oxford English Dictionary* (Oxford: Oxford University Press, 1971), the term "easel picture" was used as early as 1841, before the period in which illustration would have been rendered as painting. Although illustrators painted with oils on canvas by the turn of the century, critics employed the term "easel picture" to refer to "fine" art production, and distinguished it from illustration. See Royal Cortissoz, "Introduction," in Society of Illustrators, *Annual of the Society of Illustrators* (New York: Charles Scribner's Sons, 1911), viii; "A Declaration of Art in Advertising," *Arts and Decoration* 14 (April 1921): 464. My use of the term "easel painters" alludes to painters of easel pictures who: regarded their creations as autonomous, unique objects meant to be appreciated in their own right; did not paint pictures for reproduction or as an accompaniment to a verbal text; and imagined themselves as ideologically and/or professionally aloof from practices that entailed aesthetic compromise in exchange for money or popular approval. The term "easel artist" is used in "Fine Art in Ads," *Business Week*, 20 May 1944, 76–80.

4. The notion of status utilized in this chapter derives from the classic Weberian definition of the term as "every typical component of the life fate of men that is determined by a specific, positive or negative, social estimation of *honor*." Sociologist Edward A. Shils qualified the definition, calling it "deference-position" to highlight "the fact that status is not a substantial property of the person arising automatically from the possession of certain entitlements but is in fact an element in a relationship between the person deferred to and the deferent person." Such entitlements could include "occupational role and accomplishment, wealth . . . income, and the mode of its acquisition, style of life, level of educational attainment, political or corporate power, proximity or roles exercising political or corporate power, kinship connections, ethnicity, performance on behalf of the community or society in relation to external communities or societies, and the possession of 'objective acknowledgements' of deference such as titles or ranks." See Max Weber, "Class, Status, Party," and Edward A. Shils, "Deference," in Edward O. Laumann, Paul M. Siegel, and Robert W. Hodge, eds., *The Logic of Social Hierarchies* (Chicago: Markham Publishing Company, 1970), 73–75, 422, 431–32. See also Andrew Abbott, *The System of Professions: An Essay on the Division of Organized Labor* (Chicago: University of Chicago Press, 1988), 118–24. Abbott links status within a given profession to the "degree of involvement" with the system of knowledge that that profession applies. The highest-status professions are those that employ that knowledge alone, without need to compromise that erudition in order to accommodate to a client.

5. See discussion and bibliography in Herbert L. Kessler, "On the State of Medieval Art History," *Art Bulletin* 70 (June 1988): 172, 178–86.

6. Art historian Rowland Elzea defines illustration as "a picture which makes visual an event or passage in a written text." The text is enhanced by illustration, but illustration requires the text to complete its meaning. Rowland Elzea, "The Golden Age of American

Illustration and Its Sources," in Delaware Art Museum, *The Golden Age of American Illustration 1880–1914* (Wilmington: Delaware Art Museum, 1972), 8.

7. Kathleen Foster, "John La Farge and the American Watercolor Movement: Art for the 'Decorative Age,'" in Henry Adams et al., *John La Farge* (New York: Abbeville Press, 1987), 133; Henry Adams, "The Mind of John La Farge," in ibid., 31–36; Helene Barbara Weinberg, "John La Farge: The Relation of His Illustrations to His Ideal Art," *American Art Journal* 5, no. 1 (May 1973): 54–73; Lucas, *Edwin Austin Abbey, Royal Academician: A Record of His Life and Work* (London: Methuen, 1921), 17, 22–59; Henry C. Pitz, *Howard Pyle: Writer, Illustrator, Founder of the Brandywine School* (New York: Clarkson N. Potter, 1975), 23–35; David Tatham, *Winslow Homer and the Illustrated Book* (Syracuse: Syracuse University Press, 1992). Homer's formative years as an artist-reporter were outgrowths of the rise of the American weekly illustrated press in the 1850s. See Joshua Emmett Brown, "*Frank Leslie's Illustrated Newspaper:* The Pictorial Press and the Representation of America, 1855–1889" (Ph.D. dissertation, Columbia University, 1993), chapter 1.

8. Lucas, *Edwin Austin Abbey,* 59; Pitz, *Howard Pyle,* 34–35. In his essay on the golden age of American illustration, Rowland Elzea argues that Abbey approached his easel and mural painting with the same frame of mind as his illustrations: both relied upon text. He makes this point, however, in order to substantiate his larger argument concerning the aesthetic validity of illustration. Elzea, "The Golden Age of American Illustration and Its Sources," 9.

9. La Farge, for example, asserted at the time that the oil painter did not tread "some higher path," and that the illustrator's "task calls upon all the powers of the artist." Foster, "John La Farge and the American Watercolor Movement," 133; Adams, "The Mind of John La Farge," 31–36; Weinberg, "John La Farge," 56; T. J. Jackson Lears, *No Place of Grace: Antimodernism and the Transformation of American Culture, 1880–1920* (New York: Pantheon, 1981), 164–65.

The painter-etcher movement, which flourished in the 1880s, was another aspect of this ideal in the realm of draftsmanship. See Maureen C. O'Brien and Patricia F. Mandel, *The Painter-Etcher Movement* (Southampton, N.Y.: The Parrish Art Museum, 1984), 8–17.

Such concerns for artistic unity also had political underpinnings that went beyond the altruistic desire to discourage alienated labor and preserve the handicrafts in a modern industrial society. American artists' appropriation of other types of creative endeavor was part of a larger effort to assert occupational expertise and attain more status and professional authority in late-nineteenth-century American society. See Sarah Burns, "Old Maverick to Old Master: Whistler in the Public Eye in Turn-of-the-Century America," *American Art Journal* 22, no. 1 (1990): 29–47; Brooklyn Museum, *American Renaissance 1876–1917* (New York: Brooklyn Museum, 1979); Kathleen D. McCarthy, *Women's Culture: American Philanthropy and Art 1830–1930* (Chicago: University of Chicago Press, 1991), 65–67.

10. On the international copyright and publishing, see Christopher Wilson, *The Labor of Words: Literary Professionalism in the Progressive Era* (Athens: University of Georgia Press, 1985), 63–91.

11. John William Tebbel, *A History of Book Publishing in the United States,* vol. 2, *The*

Expansion of an Industry 1865–1919 (New York: R. R. Bowker, 1975), 508, 640–44; Jo Ann Early Levin, "The Golden Age of American Illustration" (Ph.D. dissertation, University of Pennsylvania, 1980), 41–75; Michael Leja, "The Illustrated Magazines and Print Connoisseurship in the Late 19th Century," *BlockPoints* (1993): 54–73.

12. Bennard B. Perlman, *The Golden Age of American Illustration: F. R. Gruger and His Circle* (Westport, Conn.: North Light Publishers, 1978), 25, 34; E. John Bullard, "John Sloan: His Graphics," in *John Sloan 1871–1951* (Boston: Boston Book and Art, 1971), 27.

13. "The work here was peculiar in that it included not only pen and ink but the chalk plate process which was a method of drawing with a steel point upon a zinc plate covered with a deposit of chalk, which left a design which was easily reproduced. . . . [Eugene] found it hard on his lungs, for he had constantly to keep blowing the chalk away as he scratched the surface of the plate, and sometimes the dust went up into his nostrils." Theodore Dreiser, *The "Genius"* (New York: New American Library, 1981; first published 1915), 83.

14. Elzea, "The Golden Age of American Illustration and Its Sources," 8.

15. See Theodore Greene, *America's Heroes: The Changing Models of Success in American Magazines* (New York: Oxford University Press, 1970), 64–66; Frank Luther Mott, *A History of American Magazines, 1885–1905*, vol. 4 (Cambridge, Mass.: Harvard University Press, 1957), 15–24; Levin, "The Golden Age of American Illustration," 105–8; Elzea, "The Golden Age of American Illustration and Its Sources," 8.

16. The *Ladies' Home Journal* was first published in 1883 as *Ladies' Home Journal and Practical Housekeeper.* The *Saturday Evening Post* began publication under Curtis in 1897. On Curtis, Bok, and Lorimer, see John William Tebbel, *The American Magazine: A Compact History* (New York: Hawthorne Books, 1969), 181–202; Salme Harju Steinberg, *Reformer in the Marketplace: Edward W. Bok and the Ladies' Home Journal* (Baton Rouge: Louisiana State University Press, 1979); Jan Cohn, *Creating America: George Horace Lorimer and the Saturday Evening Post* (Pittsburgh: University of Pittsburgh Press, 1989); Christopher Wilson, "The Rhetoric of Consumption: Mass Market Magazines and the Demise of the Gentle Reader, 1880–1920," in Richard Wightman Fox and T. J. Jackson Lears, eds., *The Culture of Consumption: Critical Essays in American History, 1880–1980* (New York: Pantheon, 1983), 44–50; Judy L. Larson, *American Illustration 1890–1925: Romance, Adventure, and Suspense* (Calgary, Alberta: Glenbow Museum, 1986), 42, 45.

17. Cohn, *Creating America,* 28, 83–86. See also Steinberg, *Reformer in the Marketplace,* 53–54.

18. Of course, these criticisms were not directed solely toward the *Journal* or the *Post.* See Neil Harris, "Iconography and Intellectual History: The Halftone Effect," and "Pictorial Perils: The Rise of American Illustration," in *Cultural Excursions: Marketing Appetites and Cultural Tastes in Modern America* (Chicago: University of Chicago Press, 1990), 312–13, 337–43.

19. On Bok's and Lorimer's concern for cultural edification and reform, see Steinberg, *Reformer in the Marketplace,* especially xv–xix, 42–79; Cohn, *Creating America,* 28–39, 64–65. On the ramifications of such reform concerns for the emergence of consumer culture, see Wilson, "The Rhetoric of Consumption," 60–64.

20. Norman Rockwell, *My Adventures as an Illustrator,* as told to Thomas Rockwell (Garden City: Doubleday, 1960), 177–79; Cohn, *Creating America,* 29, 272–76.

21. See *Ladies' Home Journal,* January 1901, 31.

22. See, for example, the diary entries of fledgling children's book illustrator Wanda Gág, in Wanda Gág, *Growing Pains: Diaries and Drawings 1908–1917* (Saint Paul: Minnesota Historical Society, 1984; first published 1940), 48, 51. See also Cohn, *Creating America,* 81–83.

23. Judy L. Larson, *American Illustration,* 42; Cohn, *Creating America,* 81, 87.

24. Cohn, *Creating America,* 47, 79–83; Gág, *Growing Pains,* 48, 51, 57, 59, 86. See also Maxfield Parrish's later discussion of such blurring of boundaries with reference to prints, calendar pictures, and framed images, in Parrish to A. E. Reinthal, 15 February 1929, box 3, file 1; Parrish to Stephen Newman, 20 December 1935, box 3, file 3, Maxfield Parrish Papers, Dartmouth College Library, Hanover, N. H. (hereafter MPP).

25. Cohn, *Creating America,* 10, 65, 81, 83; Tebbel, *The American Magazine,* 192–93, 196; Judy L. Larson, *American Illustration,* 28–29.

26. Cohn, *Creating America,* 81. Cohn argues that the *Saturday Evening Post's* early pretty girl covers in particular represented "fetishes of consumerism" that meshed more with the concerns of the magazine's advertisers than with those of its editorial writers.

27. Tebbel, *The American Magazine,* 186, 191–92; Cohn, *Creating America,* 65–71; Steinberg, *Reformer in the Marketplace,* 22–23, 60–63, 65.

28. See, for example, Arthur Hoeber, "A Century of American Illustration," *Bookman* 8, no. 6 (February 1899): 542.

29. Dreiser, *The "Genius,"* 102–3.

30. Hoeber, "A Century of American Illustration," 542.

31. See Judy L. Larson, *American Illustration,* 20; Elzea, "The Golden Age of American Illustration and Its Sources," 9; Paul H. Douglas, *Real Wages in the United States 1890–1926* (New York: Augustus M. Kelley, 1966), 364, 382, 386, and appendix E.

32. Fairfax Downey, *Portrait of an Era as Drawn by Charles Dana Gibson* (New York: Charles Scribner's Sons, 1936); Susan E. Meyer, *America's Great Illustrators* (New York: Harry N. Abrams, 1978), 211–31; Collier's Weekly, *Charles Dana Gibson: The Man and His Art* (New York: Collier's Weekly, 1903).

33. Harrison Fisher, for example, could earn $3,000 for a single magazine cover. In 1910 the *New York Times* published a list of "approximate estimates of the yearly earnings of the leading illustrators." According to this source, Fisher earned $75,000, Howard Chandler Christy made $50,000, and Howard Pyle $20,000. Flagg and Parrish supposedly earned $15,000 (although Susan E. Meyer reports that Flagg earned $75,000 in 1909); the Leyendecker brothers, Orsen Lowell, and Jessie Willcox Smith made $12,000; Sarah Stillwell Weber, Elizabeth Shippen Green, and Frank L. Schoonover all made $10,000; Lucius Hitchcock, C. Allen Gilbert, Henry Hutt, Albert Wenzell, and A. I. Keller earned $8,000; Sloan, on the other hand, earned $2,750 in 1908, which to him was satisfactory. See "A Latter Day Industry and Its Rewards," *New York Times,* 6 February 1910, sec. 5, 9; Susan E. Meyer, *James Montgomery Flagg* (New York: Watson-Guptill, 1974), 16; idem, *Great American Illus-*

trators, 31; Judy L. Larson, *American Illustration,* 31; E. John Bullard, "John Sloan," 100, 115; Amos Stote, "The Illustrator and his Income," *Bookman* 28 (September 1908): 25–26.

34. Helen Goodman, "Women Illustrators of the Golden Age of Illustration," *Women's Art Journal* 8, no. 1 (Spring/Summer 1981): 13–22; Catherine Connell Stryker, *The Studios at Cogslea* (Wilmington: Delaware Art Museum, 1976), 4–5; on Smith, see S. Michael Schnessel, *Jessie Willcox Smith* (New York: Thomas Crowell, n.d.). Compare the circumstances of their careers with Pnina G. Abir-am and Dorinda Outram, eds., *Uneasy Careers and Intimate Lives: Women in Science, 1789–1979* (New Brunswick: Rutgers University Press, 1987), 9–15; Penina Midgal Glazer and Miriam Slater, *Unequal Colleagues: The Entry of Women into the Professions, 1890–1940* (New Brunswick: Rutgers University Press, 1987), 6–7, 11–16; Shelley Armitage, *Kewpies and Beyond: The World of Rose O'Neill* (Jackson: University of Missouri Press, 1994).

35. Marshall Landgren, *Years of Art: The Story of the Art Students League of New York* (New York: Robert M. McBride, 1940), 43–44; C. M. Fairbanks, "Illustration and Our Illustrators," *Chautauquan* 13, no. 5 (August 1891): 599.

36. Cooper Union for the Advancement of Science and Art, *31st Annual Report* (New York: Edward N. Brokaw, 1890), 15; idem, *41st Annual Report, 1900* (New York: n. p., 1900), 46.

The New York School of Applied Design course was taught by Ernest Knaufft in 1894, by Daniel Beard in 1895. See New York School of Applied Design for Women, *2nd Annual Report, 1894* (New York: New York School of Applied Design for Women, 1894); idem, *3rd Annual Report, 1895* (New York: New York School of Applied Design for Women, 1895).

37. According to his biographers Peggy and Harold Samuels, this sum was just double Remington's actual salary. In 1903, a contract signed with Collier's brought him $500 per month for a minimum of $6,000 per year. Remington could choose his own subjects, with the painting published in color. This sum was later increased to $1,000 per painting for a total of $12,000 per year, with a four-year contract.

However, Remington's financial success and his boisterous personality estranged him from the artistic establishment at the National Academy of Design. Its members objected to his popularity, wealth, and commercialism (he had carried out commercial auctions of his own work and made money). As a result he was not elected an Academician, the sign of artistic accomplishment. See Peggy and Harold Samuels, *Frederic Remington: A Biography* (Garden City, N.Y.: Doubleday, 1982), 122, 168, 209, 238, 345, 360.

38. By 1890, Abbey was working in England. Although he continued to take on illustration assignments for such publications as *Harper's Monthly* and *Scribner's,* he was detached from the American illustration scene, centered in New York. He had achieved a reputation as an easel painter, and his closest associates were painters, such as Edward Alma Tadema. Indeed, in 1896 Abbey was elected an Associate of the Royal Academy of Arts, an institution noted for upholding staunch professional distinctions between the fine arts (painting and sculpture) and other artistic endeavors; he also received the official commission to paint the coronation of Edward VII. La Farge remained at the forefront of efforts to acquire more artistic control over the production of decorative art. He continued to do some illustration

under limited, utilitarian circumstances: as accompaniments to his own writings and in conjunction with the work of his friend Henry James. La Farge focused on the creation of oils, watercolors, and stained glass. Illustrations were a minor part of his overall production. Peter Stansky, *Redesigning the World: William Morris, the 1880s, and the Arts and Crafts* (Princeton: Princeton University Press, 1985), 140–41; see the essays by Kathleen Foster and Michael Quick in Yale University Art Gallery, *Edwin Austin Abbey (1852–1911)* (New Haven: Yale University Art Gallery, 1973), esp. iii, 26. In 1889 La Farge illustrated ten of his own articles, published in *Century* from 1890 to 1893 as "An Artist's Letters from Japan," and in 1897 as a book, published by *Century*. He provided some of the illustrations for James's *Turn of the Screw* when it was serialized in *McClure's* in 1899. And in 1900–1901, his illustrations accompanied three of his articles in *Scribner's*, "Passages from a Diary in the Pacific." Information provided in conversation by James Yarnall, 18 January 1989; to be published in Henry Adams La Farge and James Yarnall, *Catalogue Raisonné of the Work of John La Farge* (forthcoming).

39. See Elizabeth H. Hawkes, "Drawn in Ink: Book Illustrations by Howard Pyle," in Gerald W. R. Ward, ed., *The American Illustrated Book in the Nineteenth Century* (Charlottesville: University Press of Virginia, 1987), 201–32.

40. William A. Coffin, "American Illustration of Today," *Scribner's Magazine* 11, January 1892, 106–17; February 1892, 197–205; March 1892, 333–49; Hoeber, "A Century of American Illustration," *Bookman* 8 (1898–1899): 213–19, 316–24, 429–39, 540–48; James B. Carrington, "The Illustrator and the Artist," *Independent* 51 (December 1899), 3352; Joseph Pennell, "A New Profession Wanting Professors," *Contemporary Review* 58 (July 1890): 121–32; Francis Hopkinson Smith, *American Illustrators* (New York: Charles Scribner's Sons, 1894).

41. Pitz, *Howard Pyle*, 132; Lois Fink and Joshua Taylor, *Academy: The Academic Tradition in American Art* (Washington, D.C.: Smithsonian Institution Press, 1975), 60, 64.

42. New York School of Applied Design for Women, *2nd Annual Report, 1894*; idem, *3rd Annual Report, 1895*. The Cooper Union course was geared toward "such work as is necessary for newspaper sketches, etc. This branch is expanding rapidly and seems to furnish a good field for employment." Cooper Union for the Advancement of Science and Art, *31st Annual Report*, 15; idem, *41st Annual Report, 1900*, 46. Cooper Union offered no comparable illustration course in its Night School for Men.

43. Such pictures certainly had an impact on the young Minnesotan Wanda Gág, who noted in her diary: "Went over to Fern's last night and read in some magazines, and saw some of the cutest pictures by Jessie Wilcox [*sic*] Smith. Rose O'Neil—whoever that is—seems to be getting awfully popular there is an illustrated poem of hers in the Ladies' Home Journal, called the Kewpies. Oh hum! don't I wish I could have those magazines and fine pictures? Really, some people don't know how lucky they are." Diary entry for 29 November 1909 in Gág, *Growing Pains*, 48. On the Kewpies, see Armitage, *Kewpies and Beyond*, 106–44.

On the training of women illustrators, see Cooper Union for the Advancement of Science and Art, *41st Annual Report*, 47; idem, *President's Annual Report, 1902* (New York: n. p., 1902), 44; Elizabeth Lore North, "Women Illustrators of Child Life," *Outlook* 78

(October 1904), 271–80; Stryker, *The Studios at Cogslea,* 4–5; Goodman, "Women Illustrators," 13–22.

44. The impact of women artists upon prevailing notions of professional authority in the visual arts in America merits further study. On the problematic relationship between professional identity and female participation in other disciplines, specifically, science, medicine, education, and social work, see Margaret W. Rossiter, *Women Scientists in America: Struggles and Strategies to 1940* (Baltimore: Johns Hopkins University Press, 1982), 72–99; Abir-am and Outram, *Uneasy Careers,* 1–16; Glazer and Slater, *Unequal Colleagues,* 5, 11–13.

Concerns about feminization were representative of a larger and much discussed "crisis of masculinity" at the turn of the century. George Chauncey's explorations of the challenges posed by gay men to notions of middle-class manhood add a new dimension to this complex issue. Chauncey has shown how the increased visibility and influence of both effeminate "fairies" and seemingly more masculine "queers" were instrumental in precipitating the construction of more rigidly bifurcated conceptual categories—"heterosexual" and "homosexual"—based on choice of sexual preference. The efforts to assert professional identity in masculine terms might be considered as one aspect of the transformation Chauncey describes. See George Chauncey, *Gay New York: Gender, Urban Culture, and the Making of the Gay Male World, 1890–1940* (New York: Basic Books, 1994), 111–27. See also E. Anthony Rotundo, *American Manhood: Transformations in Masculinity from the Revolution to the Modern Era* (New York: Basic Books, 1993), 247–62.

45. See, for example, Burns, "Old Maverick to Old Master," 29–47; idem, "The Artist as Expert in America's Gilded Age," unpublished paper delivered at the meeting of the American Studies Association, 1991, and part of her forthcoming book *The Modernization of the Artist in America's Gilded Age* (New Haven: Yale University Press); Randall C. Griffin, "Thomas Anschutz's *The Ironworkers' Noontime:* Remythologizing the Industrial Worker," *Smithsonian Studies in American Art* 4 (Summer/Fall 1990): 138–43.

46. Twenty percent of women students dropped out from 1897 to 1898, probably discouraged by Pyle. See Pitz, *Howard Pyle,* 133–34; Jean Henry, "Drexel's Great School of American Illustration," in Drexel University Museum, *Drexel's Great School of Illustration: Violet Oakley and Her Contemporaries* (Philadelphia: Drexel University Museum, 1984), 6–7; Rowland Elzea, "The Teacher and His School," unpublished lecture, Delaware Art Museum, 1987. See also Jean Henry, "Introduction," in Drexel University Museum, *Frank Schoonover at Drexel: Illustration and the Academic Tradition, 1892–1903* (Philadelphia: Drexel University Museum, 1986), 5–6; Rowland Elzea and Elizabeth H. Hawkes, eds., *A Small School of Art: The Students of Howard Pyle* (Wilmington: Delaware Art Museum, 1980); Richard Wayne Lykes, "Howard Pyle: Teacher of Illustration," *The Pennsylvania Magazine* 80, no. 3 (July 1956): 344–49.

47. Charles D. Abbott, *Howard Pyle: A Chronicle* (New York and London: Harper and Brothers, 1925), 213–17; Pitz, *Howard Pyle,* 135.

48. Elzea, "A Teacher and his School," 10.

49. Pitz, *Howard Pyle,* 135.

50. Pyle dissolved the school in 1905 when he became art editor for *McClure's;* he of-

fered informal critiques until his departure for Italy in 1910. Pitz, *Howard Pyle,* 141; see also Elzea's introduction in Elzea and Hawkes, *A Small School of Art,* 3–4.

51. Judy L. Larson, *American Illustration,* 25, points out the advantages of hiring freelancers. The temporary exceptions were illustrators on the staffs of the daily newspapers, but these, too, eliminated most of their artists shortly after the turn of the century. E. John Bullard, "John Sloan," 35–42, 49; Perlman, *The Golden Age of American Illustration,* 25, 34.

52. Judy L. Larson, *American Illustration,* 25.

53. Bruce St. John, ed., *John Sloan's New York Scene* (New York: Harper and Row, 1965), 245. (hereafter cited as Sloan diaries).

Animal illustrator and future American Museum of Natural History muralist Charles Robert Knight made similar rounds, "going back again and again to see editors, sub-editors, and just office boys." Knight, quoted in Robert McCracken Peck, "The Artist Who Saw Through Time," *Natural History,* August 1992, 61. See also Dreiser, *The "Genius,"* 106–7, 130–31.

54. Judy L. Larson, *American Illustration,* 25–26; Rockwell, *My Adventures as an Illustrator,* 174–75; August F. Jaccaci to Bertha Corson Day, 23 February 1900, Bertha Corson Day Collection, box 4, Business Correspondence, file M-2, Helen Farr Sloan Library, Delaware Art Museum. See also the fictional account of this process in Dreiser's *The "Genius,"* 101.

55. Dreiser, a former editor at Butterick, recounted the experience of the younger artist. Eugene Witla, a talented young illustrator, brought his drawings to the art director of *Truth.* Taken by them, the art director brought one of the drawings in to the editor.

> "How much does he want for this?" [asked the editor].
> "Oh, he doesn't know. He'll take almost anything. I'll give him seventy-five dollars."
> "That's all right," said the Editor as the Art Director took the drawing down. "There's something new there. You ought to hang on to him."
> "I will," replied his associate. "He's young yet. He doesn't want to be encouraged too much."

Dreiser, *The "Genius,"* 106.

John Sloan complained of being kept waiting for assignments, then of having to complete them on short notice. See Sloan diaries, 21 March 1908, in *John Sloan's New York Scene,* 207. See also "Asked by Art Students: A Department Conducted by William Martin Johnson," *Ladies' Home Journal* 28, 1 February 1911, 33.

Frederic Remington represented the flip side of the coin. In 1899, at the height of his career as an illustrator, *Harper's* reduced the level of his payments because of their own financial difficulties. Ultimately they had to drop him altogether. Remington wrote to his friend Owen Wister in 1900, "As to Harpers—They are hard up and employ cheap men. Also Harpers wants new men. New and cheap lets you out along with all the other old men. They dropped me out of the window but I find a way to get printed." Samuels and Samuels, *Frederic Remington,* 290–91, 295.

56. The National Sculpture Society was founded in 1893 and the National Society of Mural Painters incorporated in 1895. See Michele H. Bogart, *Public Sculpture and the Civic Ideal in New York City, 1890–1930* (Chicago: University of Chicago Press, 1989), 44–55; Rich-

ard N. Murray, "Painting and Sculpture," in Brooklyn Museum, *American Renaissance,* 181.

57. See Society of Illustrators, *Constitution, 1901; List of Members* (adopted 5 January 1903, amended 21 April 1906), pamphlet, n.d., Society of Illustrators, New York City (hereafter SI).

58. Ibid., 3.

59. Society of Illustrators, *Society of Illustrators 1901–1928* (New York: Society of Illustrators, 1928), 7–8.

60. Society of Illustrators, *Constitution, 1901,* 10.

61. Society of Illustrators, *Constitution, 1901;* Society of Illustrators, *Society of Illustrators,* 8. Compare with Rossiter, *Women Scientists,* 76–84.

62. Their early efforts culminated in the publication of a tenth anniversary illustrated annual. The introduction, by critic Royal Cortissoz, a somewhat lackluster commendation, concentrated on discussion of the aesthetic tradition of American illustration. Cortissoz, "Introduction," in *Annual of the Society of Illustrators* (1911), vii–xiii.

63. Sculptors, who were even more dependent upon outside support and connections for professional advancement, encountered a similar situation. See Michele H. Bogart, *Public Sculpture and the Civic Ideal,* 49–52.

64. Michele H. Bogart, *Public Sculpture and the Civic Ideal,* 49, 52–55.

65. Quoted in Samuels and Samuels, *Frederic Remington,* 336.

66. "Sent $5 (which I can ill afford) to the Secretary of the Society of Illustrators to which I have recently been elected (oh joy!!?)" Sloan diaries, 26 April 1907, in *John Sloan's New York Scene,* 124.

67. Sloan diaries, 22 May 1907, in *John Sloan's New York Scene,* 130.

68. Sloan diaries, 6 January 1908, 25 January 1908, 28 January 1908, in *John Sloan's New York Scene,* 180, 188–89.

69. See Burns, "Old Maverick to Old Master," 39–41, for discussion of the shifting orientation toward an ostensibly uncommercial, autonomous art; on painters' uncertain identities, see idem, *The Modernization of the Artist,* chapters 2 and 3.

70. Society of Illustrators, *Society of Illustrators,* 9–10.

71. See Burns, "Old Maverick to Old Master," 36–39.

72. Rowland Elzea estimates that periodicals used over 100,000 illustrations per year, and that some illustrators produced 200–300 illustrations per year for weeklies like *Life.* Elzea, "The Golden Age of American Illustration and Its Sources," 9. Reporters experienced similar competitive pressures. For an instructive comparison, see Wilson, *The Labor of Words,* 30–33; and Robert R. Faulkner, *Music on Demand: Composers and Careers in the Hollywood Film Industry* (New Brunswick: Transaction Books, 1983), 69–87, 101–19, 168, 221, 240–67.

73. Dreiser, *"The Genius,"* 107, chapter xvii, 141, chapter xxii; Sloan diaries, 2 February 1907, 18 February 1907, in *John Sloan's New York Scene,* 102, 104. See also Donald Pizer, *The Novels of Theodore Dreiser: A Critical Study* (Minneapolis: University of Minnesota Press, 1976), 139; T. J. Jackson Lears, *Fables of Abundance: A Cultural History of Advertising in America* (New York: Basic Books, 1994), 274–82.

Dreiser's novel vividly conveys the extent to which the self-image of the New York artist was bound up with issues of status, money, and business success that were associated with the commercial side of illustration.

74. "Incomes of Illustrators," New York Times, 11 May 1910, 8.

75. Knight, quoted in Peck, "The Artist Who Saw Through Time," 61.

76. Dreiser, *The "Genius,"* 141–42. Dollar calculations based on data provided in John J. McCusker, *How Much Is That Worth in Real Money: A Historical Price Index for Use as a Deflator of Money Values in the Economy of the United States* (Worcester: American Antiquarian Society, 1992), 328–32; David B. Johnson, *Finding and Using Economic Information: A Guide to Sources and Interpretation* (London: Bristlecone Books, 1993), 90–91.

77. "Asked by Art Students," 33. See also "Illustrations in Museum Galleries," *New York Herald,* 8 December 1907, Literature and Art section, 3.

78. "A Latter Day Industry and Its Rewards," 9. See also Stote, "The Illustrator and his Income," 25–26.

79. Daniel Chester French, annual expenses, box 28, reel 22, fr. 655, 663, 672, 710, French Family Papers, Library of Congress Manuscript Division, Washington, D.C. French's gross income was considerably higher, but like those of any sculptor, his working costs were extremely high.

80. "A Latter Day Industry and Its Rewards," 9.

81. "A Latter Day Industry and Its Rewards," 9. In 1911, when a reader wrote to William Martin Johnson in the *Ladies' Home Journal* for advice on how much one could make as an illustrator, he responded acerbically: "If you strike the popular fancy—and, by the way, no one can foretell the verdict—publishers will pay liberally for technically inferior work." Johnson informed the reader that it was certainly possible to create works of merit, but that doing so posed many challenges. She need not be discouraged, he reassured her; a great many bad artists accomplished their goals and made a lot of money. "Asked By Art Students," 33.

82. See, for example, Max Eastman, *Journalism versus Art* (New York: Knopf, 1916), 42. See also Neil Harris, "Pictorial Perils," in *Cultural Excursions,* 337–43.

Max Weber would also later (1946) note that "very frequently every rational economic pursuit, and especially 'entrepreneurial activity,' is looked upon as a disqualification of status. Artistic and literary activity is also considered as degrading work as soon as it is exploited for income." Weber, "Class, Status, Party," 78.

83. The closest anyone came to an explanation was that of author/illustrator George Gibbs, who noted that "the great mass of drawings illustrating the fiction of the day (as everyone knows) is done for an especial clientele, surrounded by a hundred restrictions as to space, color, character, and medium, to which the commercial processes of reproduction and printing only are adequate." Under these circumstances, he admitted, few of these pictures could live up to the high standards of excellence required even for *consideration* for exhibition at the Metropolitan. "Should Museums Form Collections of Illustrations?" *New York Herald,* 1 December 1907, Literature and Art section, 5. See also Neil Harris, "Pictorial Perils," in *Cultural Excursions,* 337–43.

84. "Should Museums Form Collections?" 5.

85. Glackens stated that "considering the gross commercialism of present day illustrators, one shrinks from indorsing the permanency of such a collection." "Should Museums Form Collections?" 5.

86. "Should Museums Form Collections?" 5.

87. The Trustees of the New York Public Library established a department of prints in 1899. The Samuel Avery collection of mostly nineteenth-century French etchings formed the basis of the department's holdings, but curator Frank Weitenkampf also encouraged American artists to submit "specimens" of their work: etchings, lithographs, original drawings, or photographs of the drawings. Frank Weitenkampf, *New York Public Library. Print Division. Report on the Print Room 1899–1909* (New York: New York Public Library, 1910), 1, 3, 7.

88. Arthur W. Little to The Metropolitan Museum of Art, 30 November 1907, The Metropolitan Museum of Art Archives (hereafter MMAA). On the Metropolitan Museum and its mission, see Calvin Tomkins, *Merchants and Masterpieces: The Story of the Metropolitan Museum of Art* (New York: E. Dutton, 1973; first published 1970), 99.

89. Little to Metropolitan Museum of Art, 30 November 1907, MMAA.

90. Caspar Purdon Clarke to Robert de Forest, 6 December 1907, MMAA.

91. Roger Fry, report on letter from Mr. Arthur W. Little of *Pearson's Magazine* dated 30 November 1907 [n.d. on report], MMAA.

92. Although the museum never implemented this accession policy, its officials did establish classes in metalwork, drawing, modeling, carriage drafting, and plumbing. Tomkins, Merchants and Masterpieces, 62.

93. Tomkins, *Merchants and Masterpieces,* 102.

94. Sociologist Paul DiMaggio has called this process the "sacralization of art." See Paul DiMaggio, "Cultural Entrepreneurship in Nineteenth Century Boston: The Creation of an Organizational Base for High Culture in America," in Chandra Mukerji and Michael Schudson, eds., *Rethinking Popular Culture: Contemporary Perspectives in Cultural Studies* (Berkeley: University of California Press, 1991), 376–77; McCarthy, *Women's Culture,* 112.

95. The observations in this paragraph are indebted to Michael Leja, in correspondence with the author, 2 July 1992.

96. Caspar Purdon Clarke to Frank S. Guild, 31 January 1908, MMAA. For more on the poor relations between Fry and Morgan, see Tomkins, Merchants and Masterpieces, 108–10.

97. Frank S. Guild to Robert W. de Forest, 30 January 1908; Frank S. Guild to Caspar Purdon Clarke, 7 February 1908, both in MMAA.

98. Caspar Purdon Clarke to Frank S. Guild, 31 January 1908, MMAA. In this correspondence, it is clear that the publishers were trying to coax the museum into agreeing to set up a department. Guild phrased his statement to make it sound as if the Museum were in fact planning such an arrangement. The response provided no such indication.

A department of prints was established in 1916, but in 1924 illustrators were still trying to convince the museum to develop a permanent exhibit of the work of major American illustrators. Norman Price, notes of meetings taken while Secretary of the Society of Illustrators, 11 March 1925, SI; Tomkins, *Merchants and Masterpieces,* 238.

99. Dreiser, *The "Genius,"* 387.

100. T. J. Jackson Lears, "Some Versions of Fantasy: Toward a Cultural History of American Advertising, 1880–1930," *Prospects* 9 (1984): 355; Daniel Pope, *The Making of Modern Advertising,* (New York: Basic Books, 1983), 185–92; Victor Margolin and Ira and Vivian Brichta, *The Promise and the Product: 200 Years of American Advertising Posters* (New York: Macmillan, 1979), 29–30, 38–41; Calkins, quoted in Frank H. Young, *Modern Advertising Art* (New York: Covici, Friede, Inc., 1930), 9; Charles Goodrum and Helen Dalrymple, *Advertising in America: The First Two Hundred Years* (New York: Harry N. Abrams, 1990), 7–29.

101. Ralph M. Hower, *The History of an Advertising Agency: N. W. Ayer and Son at Work, 1869–1939* (Cambridge, Mass.: Harvard University Press, 1939), 315–29; Walter Dill Scott, *The Psychology of Advertising: A Simple Exposition of the Principles of Psychology in their Relation to Successful Advertising* (1913; New York: Arno Press, 1976), 11–21, 77, 128; Lears, "Some Versions of Fantasy," 379.

102. Margolin, Brichta, and Brichta, *The Promise and the Product,* 31–41.

103. Dreiser, *The "Genius,"* 388.

104. James Montgomery Flagg, for example, created advertisements for Edison Phono and for Adler Rochester Overcoats. Yet according to Earnest Elmo Calkins, Flagg agreed to take on such commissions only on the condition that his name not be associated with the campaign. See introduction in Young, *Modern Advertising Art,* 10. For an illustration of the Flagg ad for overcoats, see Herbert W. Hess, *Productive Advertising* (Philadelphia and London: J. B. Lippincott, 1915), 45. See also Rockwell, *My Adventures as an Illustrator,* 68.

On the Truth in Advertising movement, see Pope, *Making of Modern Advertising,* 196–208; Lears, "Some Versions of Fantasy," 366–68. See also Rockwell, *My Adventures as an Illustrator,* 70–71; Hower, *History of an Advertising Agency,* 330; Leon Barritt, "Illustrations in Advertising," *Printer's Ink,* 5 August 1891, 101; Jessie McDermut, "Artistic Advertising," *Printer's Ink,* 30 July 1890, 107; "Exceptional German Advertising Poster Work," *Printer's Ink,* 6 April 1910, 85; George Ethridge, "Commercial Art," *Printer's Ink,* 21 July 1910, 74; "Multiplying the Value of High Grade Art Work," *Printer's Ink,* 27 April 1910, 29–31.

105. Earnest Elmo Calkins, *"And Hearing Not—"* (New York: Charles Scribner's Sons, 1946), 168–69.

106. Earnest Elmo Calkins, "Exhibition of Advertising Art," *International Studio* 34 (May 1908): cix. On the importance of the National Arts Club, see Elizabeth Milroy, *Painters of a New Century: The Eight and American Art* (Milwaukee: Milwaukee Art Museum, 1991), 34–35.

107. Advertising agents and artists were invited to submit "magazine advertising designs, newspaper advertising designs, posters, covers of catalogues, booklets, folders or pamphlets, covers of magazines, entire booklets, and any other specimens of art applied to advertising." See Earnest Elmo Calkins, "The First Time on any Stage," in Art Directors Club of New York, *Fourth Annual of Advertising Art* (New York: Art Directors Club, 1925), unpaginated.

108. Calkins, "The First Time on any Stage."

109. Ibid.

110. "Advertising Art Shown," *New York Times*, 10 January 1909, 12; Calkins, "Exhibition of Advertising Art," cix.

111. On print advertisers' methods at the turn of the century, see Susan Strasser, *Satisfaction Guaranteed: The Making of an American Mass Market* (New York: Pantheon, 1989), 90.

112. Art Directors Club of New York, *Fourth Annual of Advertising Art.*

113. J. Nilsen Laurvik, "The Third Annual Exhibition of Advertising Art in the Galleries of the National Arts Club," *International Studio* 42 (November 1910): xli. Calkins omitted cover designs from the 1909 exhibition, but, he observed, advertisers and designers of advertising "do not seem to be ready to take advantage of this exhibition so fully as the committee thought, so that the exhibition was not as large as it was last year." Earnest Elmo Calkins, "Second Annual Exhibition of Advertising Art," *International Studio* 36 (February 1909): cxlvi.

114. Art Directors Club of New York, *Fourth Annual of Advertising Art.*

115. "You printed the other day an automobile cover of Mr. J. C. Leyendecker's entitled "The Speed God" [a nude Mercury figure perched on an automobile]. . . . Mr. Leyendecker's genius was never more triumphantly shown. . . . To be sure, the artistic mugwump might complain that this was not really the Speed God at all, that the most cursory glance would reveal him as merely the familiar Hart, Schaeffenbaum, and Marxheimer ready-to-wear gentleman of the advertising section, who has removed his clothes and attached to his ankles a pair of property wings." "A Letter to the Editor," *Collier's Weekly* 37 (23 March 1907): 17. See also Will A. Bradley, "The Art of Illustration," *Nation* 97 (10 July 1913), 42–43; Judy L. Larson, *American Illustration*, 28.

116. Eastman, *Journalism versus Art*, 42.

117. Rebecca Zurier, *Art for the Masses: A Radical Magazine and Its Graphics, 1911–1917* (Philadelphia: Temple University Press, 1988), 46–50, 104, 129, 139, 145.

118. Eastman, *Journalism versus Art*, 42, quoted in Judy L. Larson, *American Illustration*, 28.

119. Noting a general dissatisfaction with contemporary illustration, Will Bradley commented that the present-day illustrators were less interested in art "than by the promise of large and prompt profits." If illustration was inferior to what it was ten to fifteen years earlier it was because honest men in the field were swamped by "hordes of half trained, and, worse still, unscrupulous illustrators whose sole ambition is to make money easily, spend it freely, and ride around in big motor cars. . . . Thus illustration forms today merely a transition stage for most artists who practice it. And instead of painters becoming illustrators as before, we have now the spectacle of the ablest men starting into paint as soon as they are pecuniarily able to do so." Bradley, "The Art of Illustration," 42–43.

For discussion of the cultural underpinnings of the negative responses to commercial art, see Lears, *Fables of Abundance*, chapter 9.

120. Pitz, *Howard Pyle*, 186–88.

121. Ibid., 175, 178.

122. Pyle had begun such work in 1905, but only in 1906 did he receive commissions, the first for the Battle of Nashville for the Minnesota State Capitol, the second for the Landing of Carteret for the Essex County Courthouse in Newark, New Jersey (completed 1907), and a third for the panels for the Hudson County Courthouse in Jersey City, New Jersey (1910). Pitz, *Howard Pyle,* 186–88, 193.

123. Betsy James Wyeth, ed., *The Wyeths. The Letters of N. C. Wyeth, 1901–1945* (Boston: Gambit Press, 1971), 144, 145, 176, 189, 202, 211, 244, 258, 277, 290, 292, 293, 299, 300, 315, 368, 389, 502, 561, 619, 830 (hereafter cited as *The Wyeths*).

124. N. C. Wyeth to Henriette Wyeth, 25 January 1907, in *The Wyeths,* 202.

125. N. C. Wyeth to Sidney M. Chase, 15 April 1914, in *The Wyeths,* 459.

126. N. C. Wyeth to Henriette Wyeth, 17 February 1916, in *The Wyeths,* 521; see also Rockwell, *My Adventures as an Illustrator,* 215.

127. N. C. Wyeth, "On Illustrations," *New York Times Book Review,* 13 October 1912, 574.

128. N. C. Wyeth to Henriette Wyeth, 7 June 1907, in *The Wyeths,* 211.

129. N. C. Wyeth to Edwin Rudolph Wyeth, 5 December 1943, in *The Wyeths,* 830. One might profitably compare Wyeth with author Sherwood Anderson, who worked for many years as a copywriter. See T. J. Jackson Lears, "Sherwood Anderson: Looking for the White Spot," in Richard Wightman Fox and T. J. Jackson Lears, *The Power of Culture: Critical Essays in American History* (Chicago: University of Chicago Press, 1993), esp. 23–36.

130. Downey, *Portrait of an Era,* 1, 5–20.

131. Ibid., 94–106, 184, 196–204, 278–82.

132. Ibid., 150, 166, 204–12; Robert Bridges, "Charles Dana Gibson: An Appreciation," *Collier's Weekly* 34 (15 October 1904), 12–13.

133. Downey, *Portrait of an Era,* 287, 289, 303.

134. Ibid., 269, 303; Meyer, *America's Great Illustrators,* 230. Gibson had also served as the society's president from 1904 to 1907, but his role was probably honorific during his years away from illustration.

135. James R. Mock and Cedric Larson, *Words That Won the War: The Story of the Committee on Public Information, 1917–1919* (Princeton: Princeton University Press, 1939), 4.

136. Mock and Larson, *Words That Won the War,* 101–2; "Report of the Work Accomplished by the Society of Illustrators in Helping the Government to Obtain Pictorial Publicity," 1 October 1917 (New York: Society of Illustrators).

137. George Creel, *How We Advertised America: The First Telling of the Amazing Story of the Committee of Public Information that Carried the Gospel of Americanism to Every Corner of the Globe* (New York: Arno Press, 1972; first published 1920), 103; Honoré Willsie, "Charles Dana Gibson Mobilizes American Illustrators," *The Delineator* 93, no. 5 (November 1918): 16. On the Committee of Public Information, see also Stephen Vaughn, *Holding Fast the Inner Lines: Democracy, Nationalism, and the Committee on Public Information* (Chapel Hill: University of North Carolina Press, 1980).

138. Mock and Larson, *Words That Won the War,* 105; Creel, *How We Advertised America,* 138; Society of Illustrators, "Report," 1–6; F. A. Vanderlip to Charles Dana Gibson, 18 October 1917; Oscar A. Price to Charles Dana Gibson, 16 October 1917; C. E. Raymond to Charles

Dana Gibson, 9 November 1917, SI. See also Walton Rawls, *Wake Up America! World War I and the American Poster* (New York: Abbeville Publishers, 1988), 149–69.

139. Mock and Larson, *Words That Won the War,* 103. For illustrations of these posters, see Rawls, *Wake Up, America!* Rawls discusses the work of the Division of Pictorial Publicity on 149–69.

140. Creel, *How We Advertised America,* 136; Willsie, "Charles Dana Gibson," 16; Mock and Larson, *Words That Won the War,* 105.

141. Creel, *How We Advertised America,* 160; Mock and Larson, *Words That Won the War,* 105.

142. Levin, "The Golden Age of American Illustration," 115; Creel, *How We Advertised America,* 156–64; see Rawls, *Wake Up, America!* for pictures.

143. On the working procedures of one advertising illustrator, see the contract between Covici, Friede, Inc. and Rockwell Kent, 4 February 1929, box 12, file 37; N. W. Ayer correspondence in box 5, file 18; Egmont Arens to Rockwell Kent, 3 May 1930, box 8, file 31; J. M. Daiger to Rockwell Kent, 24 May 1929, box 15, file 23, all in Rockwell Kent Papers, Archives of American Art, Smithsonian Institution, Washington, D.C. (hereafter RK, AAA).

144. This and the ensuing discussion have benefited from the models provided by Robert R. Faulkner in his studies *Hollywood Studio Musicians* (Chicago: Aldine Publishing, 1971) and *Music on Demand.*

145. Gordon C. Aymar, *An Introduction to Advertising Illustration* (New York: Harper and Brothers, 1929), 223.

146. Ernest W. Watson, *Forty Illustrators and How They Work* (New York: Watson-Guptill, 1946), x. Also see Joseph Cummings Chase, "What is This Art Game?" *Saturday Evening Post,* 15 October 1927, 17; Aymar, *An Introduction to Advertising Illustration,* 15–16; Carl Richard Greer, *Advertising and Its Mechanical Reproduction* (New York: Tudor Publishing, 1931), 303–6; Hydeman, *How to Illustrate for Money,* 136–38; "Charles E. Cooper," *Design* 51 (January 1950): 21–22; "The Artist's Career in Advertising," *Design* 53 (March 1952): 136–37, 147.

147. On newspaper advertising, see Strasser, *Satisfaction Guaranteed,* 210; Truman A. DeWeese, *The Principles of Practical Publicity* (Philadelphia: George W. Jacobs and Co., 1908, first published 1906), 102–17; Roy Durstine, *Making Advertisements and Making Them Pay* (New York: Charles Scribner's Sons, 1920), 157, 244; John Caples, *Advertising for Immediate Sales* (New York: Harper and Brothers, 1936), 20–30; Aymar, *An Introduction to Advertising Illustration,* 53, 103–8, 179.

148. Watson, *Forty Illustrators and How They Work,* x. Although writing in 1946, Watson dated the practice back to the Ethridge Company, which was in operation during the first decade of the century.

149. Faulkner, *Music on Demand,* 164.

150. In this sense the career of the advertising artist had much in common with that of painters, as well as musicians. See Faulkner's *Music on Demand,* 240–64, for comparison.

These more marginal artists were undoubtedly those toward whom art directors Aymar and Hydeman directed their "how-to" books. See Aymar, *An Introduction to Advertising Illustration,* and Hydeman, *How to Illustrate for Money,* as well as Heyworth Campbell, "Suggestions for the Ambitious Young Commercial Artist," *Industrial-Arts Magazine* 8 (March 1919): 81–84. For background on some of these illustrators, see Walt and Roger Reed, *The Illustrator in America 1880–1980: A Century of Illustration* (New York: Society of Illustrators, 1984; first published 1966).

151. For information on this core group, see Reed and Reed, *The Illustrator in America;* Watson, *Forty Illustrators and How They Work,* and vertical files, SI.

152. Aymar, *An Introduction to Advertising Illustration,* 2, 17–19, 54; Hydeman, *How to Illustrate for Money,* 24, 123; M. Rusling Wood to John Darnall, 11 August 1915, box 3, file 54, MPP. On selectivity, see Rockwell, *My Adventures as an Illustrator,* 218–19, and next note below.

153. See, for example, Maxfield Parrish to M. Rusling Wood, 30 November 1914, 30 September 1915, 28 July 1915, 11 February 1918, box 3, file 54; M. Rusling Wood to John Darnall, 11 August 1915, box 3, file 54; Parrish to George Von Bernuth, 5 November 1930, box 3, file 38; Parrish to Celia Mendelsohn, 12 January 1935, box 1, file 6; all in MPP; Rockwell Kent to Vaughn Flannery, 6 May 1929, box 5, file 18; Theodore Weicker to Kent, 22 November 1928, box 37, file 20; Kent to René Clarke, 11 January 1930, 3 May 1930, box 8, file 31; Kent to Sidney Mendelsohn, 15 September 1930, box 1, file 42, all in RK, AAA; and Rockwell, *My Adventures as an Illustrator,* 215–20; Arthur R. Guptill, *Norman Rockwell: Illustrator* (New York: Watson-Guptill, 1946), 129–30.

154. One of the solutions that some established middle- and top-tier artists found was to minimize contact with clients. Some artists hired representatives who acted as middlemen and took 25 percent of the profits. In 1921 a group of illustrators established the Guild of Free Lance Artists, which maintained files of the work of its members for potential "art buyers" to consult. In concert with the Art Directors Club, the guild developed a code of ethics, proper practices, and grievance procedures that would help alleviate misunderstandings among illustrators, art directors, publishers, and advertising agencies. Guild members included Charles Dana Gibson, Harvey Dunn, and James Montgomery Flagg. See "The Best Advertising Art Always Comes from the Studios of Free Lance Artists," pamphlet, n.d. [ca. 1927]; "The Guild of Free Lance Artists: A Group with a Constructive Purpose," *Arts and Decoration* 14, no. 5 (March 1921): 362–63; Aymar, *An Introduction to Advertising Illustration,* 32–34. On balancing egos, see Hydeman, *How to Illustrate for Money,* 24, 123.

155. Rockwell, for example, worked for a number of smaller outfits, mostly in the 1920s and after 1960. See Laurie Norton Moffatt, *Norman Rockwell: A Definitive Catalogue,* 2 vols. (Hanover, N.H.: University Press of New England, 1986): 1: 252–575, for illustrations of his advertising commissions.

156. Society of Illustrators, *Constitution and List of Members, 1922,* pamphlet, SI.

157. Norman Price, "Notes of meetings, rough suggestions from letters herewith, 1921," Norman Price file box, Society of Illustrators. John Sloan had objected to the Society's emphasis on entertainment as early as 1908. He noted in his diary that his election as chairman of the entertainment committee was "a mistake, a joke on me. I can't want to entertain them." Sloan diaries, 6 January 1908, in *John Sloan's New York Scene,* 180.

158. During the early 1920s the society contracted with Lee and J. J. Shubert to allow the Shuberts to incorporate select numbers from the illustrators' annual shows into Shubert revues, with the society receiving a small percentage of the royalties. One of them, the famous "Artists and Models," reportedly grossed the Shuberts over $400,000. See "Flagg Creates Stir at Show of Artists," *New York Times*, 23 May 1924, 9; "Reply to Artist Flagg," *New York Times*, 25 May 1924, 18; James Montgomery Flagg, *Roses and Buckshot* (New York: G. Putnam's Sons, 1946), 129.

159. Police arrested five female dancers on indecency charges for their seminude performances in numbers called "Welcome Pilgrims" and "The Warming of the Bastille." The *New York Times* reported that the audience, five to eight hundred men "in evening dress," and who included prominent writers, businessmen, and city magistrates, "laughed heartily" during the raid because they mistook it for part of the show. They remained in their seats for twenty minutes before learning what had actually happened. See "Charity Benefit Raided by the Police," *New York Times*, 9 November 1935, 18; "Valentine Backs Raid on Artists," *New York Times*, 10 November 1935, 3; "Complaint Detailed in Attack on Artists," *New York Times*, 12 November 1935, 25; "Girls in Show Raid Freed at Hearing," *New York Times*, 15 November 1935, 21.

160. During the depression these benefits raised funds for illustrators on the dole. See card from Women's Committee, Society of Illustrators, 3 December 1932. R. H. Reilly to Society of Illustrators, 12 December 1932, General Correspondence files, 1933–1934, SI, is an example of one artist's request for financial assistance.

161. Tebbel, *A History of Book Publishing in the United States*, vol. 3, *The Golden Age between Two Wars, 1920–1940* (New York: R. R. Bowker, 1978), 376–77; Levin, "The Golden Age of American Illustration," 132–34; Judy L. Larson, *American Illustration*, 37; Leon Whipple, "The Revolution on Quality Street," *The Survey* 57, no. 3 (1 November 1926): 119, 121; no. 7 (1 January 1927): 430–31; Joseph Pennell, *The Adventures of an Illustrator* (Boston: Little, Brown and Company, 1925), 358; Thomas Craven, "The Decline of Illustration," *American Mercury* 12, no. 46 (October 1927): 204–7.

162. Roland Marchand, *Advertising the American Dream: Making Way for Modernity, 1920–1940* (Berkeley: University of California Press, 1985), 104–5, 110–16, 121–22; see also Moffatt, *Norman Rockwell*, vol. 1.

163. During this decade even Wyeth executed commissions for Aunt Jemima Pancake Flour, N. W. Ayer, Interwoven Stocking Company, New York Telephone, and Steinway and Sons. His younger colleagues took on advertising assignments much more readily. Although Norman Rockwell, for example, preferred to do magazine illustration, especially covers for the *Saturday Evening Post*, he was not at all troubled about accepting commercial assignments, so long as they did not involve long-term contracts. Douglas Allen and Douglas Allen Jr., *N. C. Wyeth: The Collected Paintings, Illustrations, and Murals* (New York: Bonanza Books, 1972), 141–72, 293–95; Flagg, *Roses and Buckshot*, 102; Rockwell, *My Adventures as an Illustrator*, 373, 374. See also E. John Bullard, "John Sloan," 134, for the comments of George Luks on commercial art.

164. Rockwell, *My Adventures as an Illustrator*, 67–71. Unfortunately, the Norman Rock-

well Archives, housed in the Norman Rockwell Museum, were not yet accessible at the time of this writing.

165. Rockwell, *My Adventures as an Illustrator,* 70–71.

166. Ibid., 218–19. Once having become an established artist for the Saturday Evening Post, Rockwell, on the advice of his editor George Horace Lorimer, made a policy of charging advertisers double his magazine fees.

167. Guptill, *Norman Rockwell, Illustrator,* x.

168. On this ideology of "producerism" and artistic work, see Erika Doss, *Benton, Pollock, and the Politics of Modernism: From Regionalism to Abstract Expressionism* (Chicago: University of Chicago Press, 1991), 14–15, 272.

169. "There was (I hope it's changed; it's a nasty, stupid business) a lot of racial prejudice in New York City in those days—we called Italians wops, Frenchmen frogs, Jews kikes—and class feeling was strong." Rockwell, *My Adventures as an Illustrator,* 32–33.

170. Ibid., 37–39, 60.

171. Ibid., 38.

172. Ibid., 46–47.

173. Ibid., 44.

174. Ibid., 46–47. On antimodernism, see Lears, *No Place of Grace.*

175. Rockwell, *My Adventures as an Illustrator,* 47, 126.

176. Ibid., 22–23, 26–27, 50–51.

177. Ibid., 26–28.

178. Ibid., 29, 126.

179. Ibid., 171.

180. Ibid., 136, 325.

181. Ibid., 220–21, 301, 326.

182. Norman Rockwell, "Artist's Forward," in Moffatt, *Norman Rockwell,* 1: xi.

183. Rockwell, *My Adventures as an Illustrator,* 289.

184. Ibid., 126, 221, 288–89, 301, 386–87.

185. Ibid., 115.

186. Ibid., 221, 289, 301. For more on Rockwell's role as producer, see Thomas Buechner, *Norman Rockwell: Artist and Illustrator* (New York: Harry N. Abrams, 1970), 41–49.

187. Guptill, *Norman Rockwell, Illustrator,* 35.

188. Rockwell, *My Adventures as an Illustrator,* 301.

189. See discussions of his marriage in Rockwell, *My Adventures as an Illustrator,* 135–36, 288, 301, 388.

chapter two

1. Strictly speaking, the word *billboard* refers to the structure on which a billboard-sized poster is placed, also known as a hoarding. In common parlance, the word *billboard* typically refers to the poster itself, and I am using the word in this sense. See also William H. Wilson, "The Billboard: Bane of the City Beautiful," *Journal of Urban History* 13 (August

1987): 395; James Fraser, *The American Billboard: 100 Years* (New York: Harry N. Abrams, 1991), 8–9.

2. On early posters, see Victor Margolin, *American Poster Renaissance* (New York: Watson-Guptill, 1975), 17–18. See also Herbert Cecil Duce, *Poster Advertising* (Chicago: Blakely Printing Company, 1912), 17–19; Jacqueline Days Serwer, "The American Artistic Poster of the 1890s" (Ph.D. dissertation, City University of New York, 1980), 6–11.

3. The first association, the International Billposters Association of the United States and Canada, was formed in 1872. The International Distributors Association of the United States and Canada was formed in 1899. This organization merged with the Associated Billposters in 1906 to become the Associated Billposters and Distributors of the United States and Canada. See Duce, *Poster Advertising,* 9, 17; George W. Kleiser, "The Story of the National Association," in Outdoor Advertising Association, *Outdoor Advertising Association 1891–1941* (U.S.A.: Outdoor Advertising Association, 1941), 14, 57; Hugh E. Agnew, *Outdoor Advertising* (New York: McGraw-Hill, 1938), 29–35; Fraser, *American Billboard,* 10–16.

4. "The American Poster," *Billboard Advertising* 5 (April 1896): 8.

5. Discussions of French posters constitute four of the six chapters in Charles Hiatt, *Picture Posters* (London: George Bell and Sons, 1896). See also Duce, *Poster Advertising,* 139; Phillip Dennis Cate, "The French Poster, 1868–1900," in Metropolitan Museum of Art, *American Art Posters of the 1890s* (New York: Harry N. Abrams, 1987), 57–72; Margolin, *American Poster Renaissance,* 12–15; Jack Rennert, *100 Years of Bicycle Posters* (New York: Darien House/Harper and Row, 1973); Kirk Varnedoe, "Advertising," in Kirk Varnedoe and Adam Gopnik, *High and Low: Modern Art and Popular Culture* (New York: Harry N. Abrams, 1990), 232–43, 247–49; Charles Knowles Bolton, *The Reign of the Poster: Being Comments and Criticisms* (Boston: Winthrop B. Jones, 1895), 4.

6. Editorial, *Billboard Advertising* 2 (January 1895): 5; 2 (March 1895): 4.

7. See David W. Kiehl, "American Art Posters of the 1890s," and Nancy Finlay, "American Posters and Advertising in the 1890s," in Metropolitan Museum of Art, *American Art Posters of the 1890s,* 11–20, 45–55; Serwer, "The American Artistic Poster," 12–14, 60–63.

8. Kiehl, "American Art Posters," 12–14; Finlay, "American Posters and Advertising," 45–46. With the exception of Bradley, most poster artists usually sold their drawings directly to the publishers, who took charge of reproduction.

9. See, for example, *Catalogue of an Exhibition of Original Posters by Louis I. Rhead,* reel N44, fr. 546, AAA; Bolton, *The Reign of the Poster,* 5–12.

10. In the early pages of Dreiser's *The "Genius,"* for example, to be *au courant* was to be "aware of Steinlen and Cheret and Mucha and the whole rising young school of French poster workers." Theodore Dreiser, *The "Genius"* (New York: New American Library, 1981; first published 1915), 85.

11. *Catalogue of an Exhibition of Original Posters,* 12.

Rhead, for example, lectured on "The Moral Indifference of the Artistic Poster," criticizing Cheret's work as "lewd." See Margolin, *American Poster Renaissance,* 22. The larger companies implemented strict moral censorship policies, but this hardly checked production of offensive posters.

Later viewers such as Louis Baury also admired such images for their detachment. "Their artistic significance as advertising lay in the fact that they were abstract—detached. To be sure the titles of the publications they proclaimed had to be emblazoned upon them. But there the connection with the thing advertised ceased. . . . They were not in any sense of the word illustrations of a commodity offered. They were pictorial designs expressing absolutely nothing save the sweet pleasure of the men who created them." Louis Baury, "Art in Publicity," *Bookman* 36 (October 1912): 129–30.

For debates about the imaging of women as passive, decorative objects, see Martha Banta, *Imaging American Women: Idea and Ideals in Cultural History* (New York: Columbia University Press, 1987), 339–73; Bailey Van Hook, "Decorative Images of American Women," *Smithsonian Studies in American Art* 4 (Winter 1990): 45–69.

Victor Margolin has observed that the monied people shown in the posters of these years reflected the limited clientele for expensive magazines during the years of depression. While this is certainly true, they are also indicative of a longer-lasting and fairly common tendency to image exclusively upper- and upper-middle-class Americans both as an ideal and as "fact." See Margolin, *American Poster Renaissance,* 5, 29.

The works of Maxfield Parrish may have appealed for somewhat different reasons than those of his contemporaries. Parrish's images usually depicted nursery rhyme figures and nude prepubescents. On one level these appealed to a sense of nostalgia, a desire to return to the primitive innocence of youth, the age just preceding physical and psychological transformation. Parrish presented his youths as objects of desire. His advertising images of altered nursery rhymes served a similar purpose. In the ads, however, phrases were added to jog the memory, with the familiar phrase replaced by one related to the product advertised. Parrish advertisements created a memorable image of a product with positive connotations because of its association with unsullied, innocent times of youth.

Parrish's pictures formed part of a broader pool of fetishized images of children at the turn of the century. See Bram Dijkstra, *Idols of Perversity: Images of Feminine Evil in Fin de Siècle Culture* (New York: Oxford University Press, 1986), 190–91. See also T. J. Jackson Lears, *No Place of Grace: Antimodernism and the Transformation of American Culture 1880–1920* (New York: Pantheon Books, 1981), 170–71. In *Poster Advertising,* 117–20, Herbert Cecil Duce of the Poster Advertising Association argued that the image of the child attracts attention because it "represents everything that is best in the nature of each one of us, . . . carrying a message of cheer, or hope, or perhaps shame, into many a benighted heart."

12. Finlay, "American Posters and Advertising," 50.

13. Margolin, *American Poster Renaissance,* 20–22; Serwer, "American Artistic Posters," 61–63.

14. Still other small and specialized firms cropped up to meet the rising demand for the new posters. Kiehl, "American Art Posters," 20; "Posters," *The Billboard* 12, no. 1 (November 1899): 3. See also "Vulgarity not yet Downed by the Poster," letter to the editor, *New York Times,* 12 August 1899, Saturday Review of Literature and Art, 544.

15. Editorial, *Billboard Advertising* 2 (March 1895): 4. See also *Billboard Advertising* 2 (January 1895): 5; 4 (September 1895): 9; 4 (October 1895): 8; 5 (May 1895): 8; 8 (January 1897):

4; Charles Paddock, "Some Notable Posters," *Printer's Ink*, 7 July 1897, 8; "Vulgarity not yet Downed by the Poster," 544.

16. Duce, *Poster Advertising*, 129; Paddock, "Some Notable Posters," 8; editorial, Billboard Advertising 4 (October 1895): 8; 5 (May 1895): 8; and 2 (March 1895): 4. See also Fraser, *American Billboard*, 16.

17. Finlay, "American Posters and Advertising," 50–53; Serwer, "The American Artistic Poster," 188–201. Serwer also contends that the decline of advertising posters for newspapers such as William Randolph Hearst's *Journal* can be attributed to the publisher's successful publicity tactics and yellow journalism in the late 1890s, which rendered promotional advertising unnecessary. See also "The Passing of the Poster Craze," *New York Times*, 8 July 1899, Saturday Review of Literature and Art, 456.

18. Finlay, "American Posters and Advertising," 50–53; Earnest Elmo Calkins, "The Psychology of the Poster," *International Studio* 45, no. 178 (December 1911): xlix.

19. On foreign regulations, see *Report of the Mayor's Billboard Advertising Commission of the City of New York, August 1913* (New York: M. B. Brown, 1913), 76–80; William H. Wilson, "The Billboard," 397; Charles Mulford Robinson, The Improvement of Towns and Cities: or, The Practical Basis of Civic Aesthetics (New York: G. Putnam's Sons, 1909, first published 1901), 76–91; Varnedoe and Gopnik, *High and Low*, 232–35.

20. *Report of the Mayor's Billboard Advertising Commission*, 103. See also New York City Commissioner of Accounts, *Report on an Investigation of Billboard Advertising in New York City* (New York: M. B. Brown, 1912), 12; William H. Wilson, "The Billboard," 414.

21. Harvey A. Kantor, "Modern Urban Planning in New York City, Origins and Evolution 1890–1935" (Ph.D. dissertation, New York University, 1971), 148–49. See also "Report of the Secretary as to the Legislative Work of the [City] Club for 1906," 13 June 1906, Albert Sprague Bard Papers, box 11, New York Public Library, Manuscript Division (hereafter Bard Papers); City Club, "Report on Record of Activities, 1892–1922," City Club Papers, box 2, New York Public Library, Manuscript Division.

22. Kantor, "Modern Urban Planning," 148–49.

23. See Robinson, *The Improvement of Towns and Cities*, 196–99, 216–20. On Robinson, see *Dictionary of American Biography*, vol. 8 (New York: Charles Scribner's Sons, 1935), 36–37, and William H. Wilson, *The City Beautiful Movement* (Baltimore: Johns Hopkins University Press, 1989), 45–48, 71–74, 86–95. For discussion of the European impulses that contributed to Robinson's aesthetic, see Donald J. Olsen, *The City as a Work of Art: London, Paris, Vienna* (New Haven: Yale University Press, 1987).

24. Charles Mulford Robinson, "Abuses of Public Advertising," *Atlantic Monthly* 93 (March 1904): 289–90.

25. Charles Mulford Robinson, "The Artistic Possibilities of Advertising," *Atlantic Monthly* 94 (July 1904): 54.

26. Ibid., 58.

27. Ibid.

28. Robinson, *The Improvement of Towns and Cities*, 91–92.

29. "Report of Committee on Private Advertising," Municipal Art Society Minutes

(hereafter Minutes), 1905, reel 15, fr. 395, Municipal Art Society Papers (hereafter MAS), AAA. See also Minutes, 1 February 1902, 26 March 1902, 27 April 1903, reel 15, frs. 50, 66, 201, MAS, AAA. Gregory F. Gilmartin, *Shaping the City: New York and the Municipal Art Society* (New York: Clarkson N. Potter, 1995) appeared when this book was in press.

30. On these broader efforts, see David Ward and Olivier Zunz, "Between Rationalism and Pluralism: Creating the Modern City"; Keith D. Revell, "Regulating the Landscape: Real Estate Values, City Planning, and the 1916 Zoning Ordinance"; Marc A. Weiss, "Density and Intervention: New York's Planning Traditions"; Daniel Bluestone, "The Pushcart Evil"; all in David Ward and Olivier Zunz, eds., *The Landscape of Modernity: Essays on New York City, 1900–1940* (New York: Russell Sage Foundation, 1992), 2–75, 287–312; Elizabeth Blackmar, "Uptown Real Estate and the Invention of Times Square," in William R. Taylor, ed., *Inventing Times Square: Commerce and Culture at the Crossroads of the World* (New York: Russell Sage Foundation, 1991), 51–65.

31. William R. Taylor, "Introduction," in Taylor, *Inventing Times Square,* xiii.

32. Paradoxically, the MAS argument depended upon a challenge to the newfound status of the electric light, to which urban reformers like themselves were contributing. New types of electric lighting and light furnishings were appearing in the metropolis during this very period, much to the praise of civic art and planning advocates. The latter regarded the new lights as a powerful vehicle for deterring crime, promoting beautification, and enhancing property values. Using a similar argument, editors at the *New York Times* (whose own building stood at Broadway and Forty-second Street) defended the signs, emphasizing further how they contributed to the lively spirit of the place. Within the year, however, even they had decided that the situation was out of control, and joined the outcry against the proliferating signs. "Report of the Committee on Private Signs for the Year 1906–1907," MAS, AAA; "Have given the Great White Way its Name," *New York Times,* 20 July 1910, 8; John Allen Corcoran, "The City Light and Beautiful," *American City* 7 (July 1912): 46–49; C. Lacombe, "Street Lighting Systems and Fixtures in New York City," *American City* 8 (May 1913): 516–19; Editorial, *New York Times,* 9 January 1909, 6; "Illumination that is Running Wild," *New York Times,* 7 July 1910, 6; "Ugly Electric Signs Mar Fifth Avenue," *New York Times,* 8 July 1910, 6. For accounts of the effect of the electrical spectacular, and of electric light more generally upon the American built environment, especially the development and experience of the Great White Way, see David E. Nye, *Electrifying America: Social Meanings of a New Technology* (Cambridge, Mass.: MIT Press, 1990), 28–84; David Nasaw, "Cities of Light: Landscapes of Pleasure," in Ward and Zunz, *Landscape of Modernity,* 272–86; William Leach, "Introductory Essay: Commercial Aesthetics," in Taylor, *Inventing Times Square,* 234–42; William Leach, *Land of Desire: Merchants, Power, and the Rise of a New American Culture* (New York: Pantheon, 1993), 46–49.

33. "Fifth Avenue Merchants Fight Ugly 'Ad' Signs," *World,* 8 July 1919, 16; "Ugly Electric Signs Mar Fifth Avenue," 6; Minutes, 26 September 1910, reel 16, fr. 91, MAS, AAA. On American Civic Association activities, see William H. Wilson, "The Billboard," 395.

34. Civic Association president Horace MacFarlane called night signs "electrical hysterics"—fast becoming a "jerking, pulling, worrying, jarring public nuisance"—that were a

"form of special privilege and a violation of property rights." "Ugly Electric Signs Mar Fifth Avenue," 6; "Fifth Avenue Merchants Fight Ugly 'Ad' Signs," 16.

35. "Arguments against Big Signs," *New York Times,* 9 July 1910, 6; Minutes, 27 December 1909, 26 December 1910, reel 16, frs. 31, 91, MAS, AAA.

36. Minutes, 27 March 1911, 31 July 1911, reel 16, frs. 178, 190, MAS, AAA; "Fighting Public Sentiment," *New York Times,* 25 March 1911, 10; "Favor License Fee to Regulate Signs," *New York Times,* 9 April 1911, 8.

37. Minutes, 14 October 1912, reel 16, frs. 415–16, MAS, AAA.

38. "Favor License Fee to Regulate Signs," 8; Minutes, 27 March 1911, 31 July 1911, 3 October 1912, 14 October 1912, reel 16, fr. 178, 190, 371, 374, 415–16, MAS, AAA; *New York Times,* 24 April 1911, 7.

39. Henry Collins Brown, *Fifth Avenue Old and New, 1824–1924* (New York: The Fifth Avenue Association, 1924), 14.

40. "At a Loss to Bar 5th Avenue Signs," *New York Times,* 9 July 1910, 6; "Ugly Electric Signs Mar Fifth Avenue," 6; Minutes, 26 September 1910, reel 16, fr. 91, MAS, AAA. Midways were the commercial entertainment strips at the major world's fairs of 1876, 1893, 1901, and 1904. Bustling, chaotic, undidactic, and ethnically varied, they stood in sharp contrast to the more refined official portions of the fairs. See John F. Kasson, *Amusing the Million: Coney Island at the Turn of the Century* (New York: Hill and Wang, 1978), 23; Michele H. Bogart, *Public Sculpture and the Civic Ideal in New York City, 1890–1930* (Chicago: University of Chicago Press, 1989), 243.

41. "Fighting Public Sentiment," 10. The Fifth Avenue Association determined to regulate signs within the broader context of zoning and controlling development. The association became the lobbying force behind a proposed zoning bill, and helped ensure its successful passage in 1916. As we shall see, it was zoning legislation that ultimately prevented erection of billboards in residential areas. The association's involvement with billboard issues was simply one aspect of its members' concern with this larger planning picture. Weiss, "Density and Intervention," 51–56.

42. A member of the City Club, McAneny traveled in many of the same social circles as members of the MAS, the Fifth Avenue Association, and other civic groups. He had long been sympathetic to the idea that direct government intervention on behalf of the public welfare had priority over individual property rights. In 1912 he was appointed by Mayor William J. Gaynor to a commission studying problems affecting Fifth Avenue and developing plans for zoning. Fosdick, educated at Princeton and New York Law School, had worked at the Henry Street Settlement and was rapidly on the way up. As Commissioner of Accounts (1910–1912), he gained renown for his investigations of graft and waste in city government. See Kantor, "Modern Urban Planning," 148, 179, and the *National Cyclopedia of American Biography* (New York: James T. White, 1922). See also "War on Electric Signs," *New York Times,* 10 October 1911, 1; New York City Commissioner of Accounts, *Report;* Raymond B. Fosdick, "Big Billboards in Big Cities," *American City* 7, no. 6 (December 1912): 511–17.

43. "Mayor's Billboard Commission to Probe Sign Evil," *New York Times,* 12 January

1913, 12. The other members of the commission were engineer Reginald Bottom, publisher Ingals Kimbell, lawyer Henry W. Sackett, insurance executive Walter Stabler, and Edmund B. Wells. In pre-report public hearings, the civic organizations spoke against billboards, the advertising men spoke in favor, and in the end, the commission heard selectively what it wanted to hear. For further information on events leading up to the report, see Official Transcripts, Public Hearing of the Mayor's Billboard Commission, box 25, Bard Papers.

44. *Report of the Mayor's Billboard Advertising Commission,* 37.

45. Ibid., 25–43; William H. Wilson, "The Billboard," 414–19.

46. *Report of the Mayor's Billboard Advertising Commission,* 6.

47. See Allan M. Brandt, *No Magic Bullet: A Social History of Venereal Disease in the United States since 1880* (New York: Oxford University Press, 1985), 31–47, 53. On efforts to control prostitution and vice in the Times Square area, see Timothy J. Gilfoyle, "Policing of Sexuality," in Taylor, *Inventing Times Square,* 297–314.

48. *Report of the Mayor's Billboard Advertising Commission,* 7.

49. Ibid., 15, 19.

50. Ibid., 39.

51. Ibid., 7.

52. Ibid., 18.

53. Ibid.

54. Ibid., 24.

55. Ibid., 37.

56. Ibid., 40.

57. Quotation and argument from Bluestone, "The Pushcart Evil," 287–89, 292–95, 308–9. Such a City Beautiful ideal was analogous to what the late Michel de Certeau described as "concept city," a falsely pervasive vision of the city as organic, cohesive unit. De Certeau regarded such an image as repressive because it could not readily represent or imagine the "mythical" element of human life—"superstitions: supererogatory semantic overlays that insert themselves 'over and above' and 'in excess.'" See Michel de Certeau, *The Practice of Everyday Life,* trans. Steven Randall (Berkeley: University of California Press, 1984), 106.

58. *Report of the Mayor's Billboard Advertising Commission,* 8, 49.

59. Mayor's Billboard Commission, Official Transcripts, 9, 38. For illustrations of Sixth Avenue at about this time, see 0377, E2 (April 1909) and F5 (ca. 1901), microfiche collection of photographs of New York in the Local History and Genealogy Division of the New York Public Library.

According to historian Andrew Dolkart, Andrew Carnegie did not own the land near his mansion on which the billboards were posted, but purchased it in 1917 from big landowner Charles A. Gould. See Conveyance Books, 1917, 1925, Surrogates Court, New York City.

60. Minutes, 22 December 1913, 23 February 1914, reel 16, frs. 536–37, 545, MAS, AAA; "Plan to Control Billboards Here," New York Times, 28 January 1914, 7; Albert S. Bard to B. de Cruger, 5 March 1914, John Purroy Mitchel Mayoral Papers, New York City Municipal Archives.

61. "Billboard Commission Advises Drastic Reforms," *New York Times,* 5 April 1914, sec. 5, 10.

62. Mayor's Billboard Commission, *Official Transcripts,* 24; "One Big Billboard an Aid to Burglers," *New York Times,* 2 April 1914, 8; "Billboard Men Start an 'Uplift' of Their Own," *World,* 9 April 1914, 20. At the hearing, outdoor advertiser O. J. Gude provided his own form of dissent. A large poster depicting children led to church and inscribed "Take your children to church, give them the right start," was unfurled from the chamber balcony. As Gude put it ironically, the billboard men were "doing a little 'uplift' work of their own even while they were being attacked by uplifters."

63. "Curran Withdraws Billboard Act," *New York Times,* 9 April 1914, 5.

64. "Municipal Art," *Signs of the Times,* 1 November 1913, 14.

65. "Curran Withdraws Billboard Act," 5. See also "Gaynor's 'Impartial' Billboard Commission Reports," *Signs of the Times,* 1 September 1913, 11, 36; "Look at this Pink Tea Conclusion from the Committee of Seven," *Signs of the Times,* 1 September 1913, 11.

66. Woman's Municipal League, "Beauty and the Beast," undated leaflet [ca. 1916], New York Public Library. The league was essentially the female counterpart of the all-male City Club. Its purpose was to "promote among women an intelligent interest in municipal affairs and to aid in securing good government for the city of New York without regard to party or sectional lines." Woman's Municipal League, *Bulletin* 2, no. 5 (December 1903): 3.

67. The bill established height restrictions (thirty-one feet as opposed to the ten-foot limit proposed by the commission), and prohibited triple-decker (but not double-decker) billboards. It also required that future sign builders obtain permits from the Department of Buildings. "All Now in Accord on Billboard Rules," *New York Times,* 11 May 1914, 7; "Billboard Commission Advises Drastic Reforms," 10; Minutes, 25 May 1914, reel 16, fr. 557, MAS, AAA. For the outdoor advertising industry's response, see K. O. Renaud, "On Both Sides of Broadway—New York News," and "Not Today, Says N. Y. Aldermen," *Signs of the Times,* 15 April 1914, 6, 8.

68. Minutes, 25 May 1914, reel 16, fr. 558, MAS, AAA.

69. "All Now in Accord on Billboard Rules," 7; Minutes, 10 May 1914, reel 16, fr. 562, MAS, AAA. Cass Gilbert, as representative of the Architectural League, refused to take part in such a commission so long as it included members who had financial interests in the outdoor advertising business. Cass Gilbert to Laurel Harris, 29 June 1914, reel 16, fr. 569–70, MAS, AAA.

70. Minutes, 27 September 1915, reel 16, fr. 732, MAS, AAA.

71. On Gude's involvement, see Minutes, 24 February 1913, 24 March 1913, 21 October 1913, 22 December 1913, reel 16, frs. 465, 468, 505, 537, MAS, AAA.

72. Minutes, 25 October 1915, 22 November 1915, 27 March 1916, 1 May 1916, 22 May 1916; *Bulletin of the Municipal Art Society* 9 (1917), reel 16, frs. 739, 753, 781, 824–25, 830–31, 935, MAS, AAA; National Highways Association, *The Billboard Nuisance in New York,* pamphlet no. 1, #829333, Division of Municipal Art, 1916, New York Public Library. Other associations allied with the MAS included the Citizen's Union, the City Club, the Fifth Avenue, the

Broadway, and the Forty-second Street Associations, and the American Scenic and Historic Preservation Society.

73. "Art Fight on Sky Signs," *New York Times,* 30 November 1916, 15; Robert Whitten, Secretary of the Committee on City Plan to Samuel L. Martin, Executive Secretary to the Mayor, 18 December 1916, Mitchel Mayoral Papers. On zoning, see Kantor, "Modern Urban Planning," 165–230; Weiss, "Density and Intervention," 48–68; Emanuel Tobier, "Manhattan's Business District in the Industrial Age," in John Hull Mollenkopf, ed., *Power, Culture, and Place: Essays on New York City* (New York: Russell Sage Foundation, 1988), 92–96; Carol Willis, "Zoning and Zeitgeist: The Skyscraper City in the 1920s," *Journal of the Society of Architectural Historians* 45 (March 1986): 47–59.

74. In 1917, moreover, the Fifth Avenue Association helped push through an ordinance preventing projecting and illuminated signs on the avenue. "Zoning the Billboard," *New York Times,* 5 October 1919, 12: 1; Albert S. Bard, "Editorial Notes," *Bulletin of the Municipal Art Society,* no. 14 (1918), unpaginated, reel 16, fr. 1065, MAS, AAA.

75. Minutes, 28 May 1917, reel 16, fr. 966, MAS, AAA.

76. Minutes, 24 September 1917, 22 October 1917, 26 November 1917, 17 December 1917, reel 16, frs. 977, 984, 1009, 1019, MAS, AAA.

77. See, for example, Susan Gilbert's interpretation of Christy's Red Cross poster "The Greatest Mother in the World," in "Soldier's Heart: Literary Men, Literary Women, and the Great War," in Margaret Randolph Higgonet, Jane Jenson, Sonya Michel, Margaret Collins Weitz, eds., *Behind the Lines: Gender and the Two World Wars* (New Haven: Yale University Press, 1987), 197–226. For a differing interpretation, see Banta, *Imaging American Women,* 556.

78. Minutes, 21 October 1913, reel 16, fr. 505, MAS, AAA; Fraser, *American Billboard,* 16, 48.

In 1913 outdoor advertisers sponsored the production and display of 5,000 multicolored posters of the Nativity, with accompanying text urging viewers to "Ask Your Sunday School Teacher to Tell You the Story." For illustration, see "The Poster Directory Meeting," *Signs of the Times,* 1 December 1913, 16. See also "Billboard Men Start an 'Uplift' of Their Own," 20.

79. Fraser, *American Billboard,* 24.

80. Link, quoted in Fraser, *American Billboard,* 28.

81. Fraser, *American Billboard,* 28.

82. Minutes, 26 January 1918, reel 16, fr. 1028, MAS, AAA. A sampling of poster sizes is provided in Walton Rawls, *Wake Up America! World War I and the American Poster* (New York: Abbeville Press, 1988), 105–20.

83. Minutes, 26 January 1918, 25 February 1918, reel 16, frs. 1028, 1036, MAS, AAA.

84. Advertisers like Wrigley's promoted Liberty Bonds and chewing gum in their 24-sheet posters. "BUY LIBERTY BONDS AND Be Patient Here," the copy stated, "They're Getting WRIGLEY'S Over There." The image depicted the Wrigley's Spearman firing a cannon from which exploded three packs of gum. Fraser, *American Billboard,* 30.

85. Lee Simonson, "Mobilizing the Billboards," *New Republic* (10 November 1917): 42; Montrose J. Moses, "Making Posters Fight," *Bookman* 47 (July 1918): 504–13. See also Har-

old R. Willoughby, "What the Advertising Man can Learn from Propaganda Posters," *The Poster* 14, no. 2 (February 1922): 9–11; W. Livingston Larned, "The New Tendencies in Poster Art," *The Poster* 10, no. 9 (September 1919): 28. See also Neil Harris, "Graphic Art for the Public Welfare," in Walker Art Center, *Graphic Design in America: A Visual Language History* (New York: Harry N. Abrams, 1989), 77, 93.

86. MAS to Committee of the Near East Relief, 24 March 1920; Minutes, 25 November 1918, 27 October 1919, 3 June 1920, 16 May 1921, 17 January 1922, reel 16, frs. 2141, 1140, 2059–60, 2186, 2295, 2372, MAS, AAA.

87. Fraser, *American Billboard,* 46.

88. This is not to say that there was no concern about billboards in poorer areas. In an article in its 1922 *Bulletin,* the MAS attacked the inequities of billboards, pointing out that the manufacturers and advertisers responsible for posting billboards in the poorer and more industrial areas would likely never agree to the presence of signs in their own residential neighborhoods. "The Billboard Blight and What to Do About It," *Bulletin of the Municipal Art Society,* no. 22 (1922); Albert S. Bard, "The Outdoor Advertiser As He Appears to a Citizen," unpublished manuscript, Billboard Meeting, 29 March 1922, box 19, Bard Papers. Advocates countered by claiming that it was the wives of the big corporate moguls most responsible for billboard pollution who were involved in the anti-billboard campaigns. See G. F. Scotson-Clark, "Billboard War," letter to the editor, *New York Times,* 20 January 1924, 8.

Albert S. Bard continued to be a leader in this effort. The MAS and City Club member now carried on his anti-billboard vigils as a member of the National and New York State Roadside Councils. See boxes 20–28, Bard Papers; Woman's Municipal League of New York, *Annual Report 1921* (New York: Woman's Municipal League of New York, 1921), 2. On "roadside blight," see Daniel M. Bluestone, "Roadside Blight and the Reform of Commercial Architecture," in Jan Jennings, ed., *Roadside America: The Automobile in Design and Culture* (Ames: Iowa State University Press, 1990), 170–84.

89. "Chesterfield Poster Wins Cup," *The Poster* 10, no. 1 (January 1919): 5–8; "Boycott Suggested in Billboard War," *New York Times,* 7 May 1922, sec. 2, 14.

90. The first trade association, the Poster Advertising Association, was founded in 1891 to regulate the industry. It began the process of size and type standardization and established procedures for leasing locations, listing locations, and protecting outdoor displays. In 1925 the industry consolidated its power when the Poster Advertising Association and the Painted Outdoor Advertising Association joined to form the Outdoor Advertising Association of America, Inc., "to provide for the American business community an efficient and economical instrument of distribution; to insure thorough standardization of practice and structure a scientific advertising medium; and to advance the common interests of those engaged in the business of advertising." Outdoor Advertising Association of America, *Manual of the Outdoor Advertising Association of America* (U.S.A.: The Outdoor Advertising Association of America, 1926), 217; and Outdoor Advertising Association, *Outdoor Advertising: The Modern Marketing Force* (U.S.A.: The Outdoor Advertising Association of America, 1928), 200; Charles R. Frazier, "The ABC of Poster Advertising," *The Poster* 3, no. 3 (November 1912): 44; F. W. Nye, "What is Poster Advertising?" *The Poster* 14, no. 2

(February 1922): 29; Robinson, "Abuses of Public Advertising," 293; Fraser, *American Billboard,* 14.

91. "Organization is Watchword," *The Poster* 10, no. 4 (April 1919): 6.

92. "The Outdoor Medium has been attacked from the beginning of its existence and has had to fight for its life almost every minute. It has been reformed by professional reformers; attempts have been made to tax it out of existence, but all that the reformers and all that the other attacks have succeeded in doing has been to improve the medium." Outdoor men simply addressed whatever problems anyone complained about. Minutes of Representatives Meeting, 13 June 1928, 1/5, RG2, J. Walter Thompson Company Archives, Special Collections Library, Duke University (hereafter JWTA). See also "Legislative and Voluntary Restrictions for Outdoor Advertising," *J. Walter Thompson Newsletter* 10, no. 12 (15 June 1928): 233, 26/1, RG11, JWTA.

93. Outdoor Advertising Association, *Outdoor Advertising,* 201, 210; John Donnelly and Sons, *Advertising in Public 1850–1950* (U.S.A.: John Donnelly and Sons, 1950), unpaginated.

94. See Amos Stote, "The Purpose of the Poster," *The Printing Art* 25, no. 2 (April 1915): 102–7; Arthur Wiener, "Bernhard," *The Poster* 4, no. 1 (September 1913): 27–29; idem, "Julius Klinger," *The Poster* 4, no. 2 (October 1913): 31–36; idem, "Willy Sesser," *The Poster* 4, no. 3 (November 1913): 22–28; "Making Plans to Advertise Poster Advertising," *The Poster* 3, no. 12 (August 1913): 40. The enthusiastic articles on German design diminished with the onset of World War I.

95. "Convention Celebrates Greatest Year in Poster Advertising," *The Poster* 10, no. 8 (August 1919): 2–15, 73; M. Rusling Wood to Maxfield Parrish, 26 October 1917, 30 August 1916, 29 September 1916, 2 June 1917, 17 August 1917, 31 August 1917, 5 December 1917, 7 February 1918, 2 July 1919, 23 July 1919, 31 December 1919; Parrish to Wood, 1 September 1916, 8 January 1917, 1 February 1917, 16 July 1917, 27 December 1919; M. G. Webber to Parrish, 6 October 1916, 7 January 1918, all in box 3, file 54, MPP; Fraser, *American Billboard,* 38–39, 46.

96. Minutes, 23 December 1912, 27 January 1913, reel 16, frs. 456, 462, MAS, AAA.

97. Laurel Harris, MAS president, would give the first talk. A second would be given by eminent muralist Edwin Blashfield. Minutes, 24 March 1913, 26 May 1913, 21 October 1913, reel 16, frs. 468, 474–75, 505, MAS, AAA. For more on Gude, especially with reference to electric signs, see Leach, *Land of Desire,* 46–49; idem, "Introductory Essay," 235–42.

98. Such work was to serve as an instructive example of the artistic lessons and possibilities attainable through posters. (After all, how could anyone object to the display of masterpieces, even in double-decker format?) Gude also indicated that his and several other New York–based advertising companies were voluntarily implementing plans to "beautify and improve every sign board and structure" they controlled and making efforts to remove signs along Riverside Drive. Such cooperative and voluntary measures by outdoor advertisers—not "coercive measures"—were the means to improve the city's appearance. Minutes, 21 October 1913, reel 16, fr. 505, MAS, AAA.

99. "The reflex of the Life Beautiful . . . must precede the City Beautiful," he was quoted

as saying. See "This Ten Year Old Argument Still Potent and Powerful," *Signs of the Times,* 1 November 1914, 14.

100. Earnest Elmo Calkins to Robert Grier Cooke, 7 December 1917, reel 16, fr. 1022, MAS, AAA.

101. Outdoor Advertising Association, *Outdoor Advertising,* 192. See also the articles in *The Poster* from about 1910 through the early 1920s.

102. Outdoor Advertising Association, *Outdoor Advertising,* 190.

103. Indeed, car cards and smaller posters do not seem to have become commodified as did the earlier art posters. Several factors may account for this: the banality of the imagery and the products advertised, the ubiquity of the posters and their cheapness and reproducibility (which made for easy replacement), and the stricter standards placed upon markets by the outdoor advertisers and clients.

One measure of the impact of the billboard and the outdoor advertisers' perspective on "art" could be seen in contemporary painting, where artists like Charles Demuth celebrated the billboard in "poster portraits" like *I Saw the Figure Five in Gold* (1928). For eloquent discussion of this work in the context of the debates, on the one hand, over billboards, and on the other hand, over the nature of modern American art, see Wanda M. Corn, *In The American Grain: The Billboard Poetics of Charles Demuth* (Poughkeepsie: Vassar College Art Gallery, 1991).

104. Outdoor Advertising Association, *Outdoor Advertising,* 196.

105. Minutes of Representatives Meeting, 20 June 1928, 1/5, RG2, JWTA.

106. Illustrated in Fraser, *American Billboard,* 53.

107. Agnew, *Outdoor Advertising,* 34, 38, 40–41; M. Rusling Wood to Maxfield Parrish, 21 February 1921, box 3, file 55, MPP. Wood asked Parrish's opinion of the "Mural Advertising" slogan, noting that one colleague called it too highbrow, but that Wood saw murals as a "dignified and highly thought of field of art." Parrish provided no written response.

It should be noted, of course, that the shift from long lines of double-decker billboard displays to single images also was a response to changing opinions about the psychology of advertising effectiveness.

108. Outdoor Advertising Association, *Outdoor Advertising,* 197.

109. Outdoor Advertising Association, *100 Best Posters* (New York: Outdoor Advertising Association, 1938); Fraser, *American Billboard,* 44–68.

110. Outdoor Advertising Association, *Outdoor Advertising,* 192; Minutes of Representatives' Meeting, 20 June 1928, 1/5, RG 2, JWTA.

111. See John Donnelly and Sons, *Advertising in Public.*

112. See Willoughby, "What the Advertising Men Can Learn from Propaganda Posters," 9–11. American design standards made significant inroads into European poster advertising during this period. See Victoria de Grazia, "The Arts of Purchase: How American Publicity Subverted the European Poster, 1920–1940," in Barbara Kruger and Phil Mariani, eds., *Remaking History* (Dia Art Foundation Discussions in Contemporary Culture, no. 4) (Seattle: Bay Press, 1989), 220–57.

113. On the differences between the East and West Coasts and the industry's general conservatism, see Fraser, *American Billboard,* 48–54, 71, 75, 79, 91. On Shepard, see Steve Strauss, *Moving Images: The Transportation Poster in America* (Boston and San Francisco: Fullcourt Press, 1984): 67–81; Otis Shepard, "Posters in the United States of America," *Commercial Art and Industry* 15 (December 1933): 226–30; for examples of typical posters of the late 1920s see Annual Design Issue, *The Poster* (1926).

114. Minutes of Representatives Meeting, 20 June 1928, 10, JWTA. This tendency was corroborated in 1930 by a writer for the art directors' magazine *PM,* who noted that art directors were loath to use the work of Bernhard because it was too "modern." Percy Seitlen, "Lucien Bernhard: Master of Applied Art," *PM* 2, no. 7 (March 1930): unpaginated. See also Fraser, *American Billboard,* 52, 79.

115. See Outdoor Advertising Association, *100 Best Posters.* Cartoons and realistic close-ups of food products were also popular. Minutes of Staff Meeting, J. Walter Thompson Forum, December 1936, 7/2, RG5, JWTA; Shepard, "Posters in the United States of America," 226–30.

116. Minutes of J. Walter Thompson Forum, 1 December 1936, 4–5, 7/2, RG5, JWTA.

117. Bernhard wrote, "I have never heard of a lithographer in this country who would not consent to a customer's tampering with a good design" just to save money. The result, he asserted, was many bad posters. "Instead of enjoying posters," people "often regard them as a nuisance, as witness the women's clubs and other organizations which are constantly fighting them. . . . Why so many proud companies who spend hundreds of thousands on advertising yearly still leave their poster problems to the ingenuity of a litho salesman is one of the riddles that, in my spare time, you will find me brooding over."

Bernhard's comments, along with others made earlier, suggest that the tensions between lithographer and artist that arose in the 1890s had never disappeared. See Lucien Bernhard, "What's Wrong with the American Poster?" *PM* 2, no. 7 (March 1936): 9–10; W. Livingston Larned, "Intimate Studies of Poster Artists," *The Poster* 10, no. 11 (November 1919): 11; Arthur Wiener, "Applying Poster Art to Commercial Needs in America," *The Poster* 3, no. 12 (August 1913): 53, 55. See also Minutes of J. Walter Thompson Forum, 1 December 1936, 6–7, JWTA.

118. Outdoor Advertising Association, *1946 Poster Annual* (U.S.A.: Outdoor Advertising Association, 1946), unpaginated.

119. A key figure in the project, Anthony Velonis, was a graduate of New York University School of Fine Arts who had worked for Stern Brothers making show cards for window displays. On the WPA poster, see Christopher DeNoon, *Posters of the WPA* (Seattle: Wheatley Press, 1987), 17–18, 72–79. See also Holger Cahill to C. E. Triggs, "Report on Accomplishments of the WPA Art Program," 18 June 1940, Record Group 69, Records of the Works Progress Administration, Central Files, General (1935–1944), box 0458, file 211.52–211.53, and "Records of Work Done by the Poster Project for Periods February 21–March 5 and March 6–20, 1937," RG 69, Records of the Works Progress Administration, Records of the Federal Art Project, State and Regional Correspondence, 1935–1940, New York City, box 40, National Archives, Washington, D.C.

120. Barbara Melosh, *Engendering Culture: Manhood and Womanhood in New Deal Public Art and Theater* (Washington, D.C.: Smithsonian Institution Press, 1991), 184, 192–94.

121. Praise came from T. J. Maloney, Incorporated, as well as from the press. See Arthur G. Burdett to Richard Floethe, 20 January 1938, RG 69, Records of the Works Progress Administration, Records of the Federal Art Project, Regional and State Correspondence 1935–1940, New York City 1938–1940, box 56, file Posters 1938–1940. See also DeNoon, *Posters of the WPA,* 26, 72–75, 78–79.

122. DeNoon, *Posters of the WPA,* 31.

123. Fraser, *American Billboard,* 84–91. The Treasury Department, for example, used posters such as Norman Rockwell's *Four Freedoms* series as part of its War Bond Drives. The OWI also circulated the Rockwell images. Arthur Guptill, *Norman Rockwell: Illustrator* (New York: Watson-Guptill, 1946), 140.

124. Barr's ideal would include all the visual arts. Such a notion was consistent with Barr's vision, soon written into the museum's charter, that the museum was to encourage and develop the study of modern art and "the application of such art to manufacture and the practical life." See Helaine Ruth Messer, "MoMA, Museum in Search of an Image" (Ph.D. dissertation, Columbia University, 1979), 93. See also Russell Lynes, *Good Old Modern: An Intimate Portrait of the Museum of Modern Art* (New York: Atheneum, 1973), 73.

125. Lynes, *Good Old Modern,* 84, 323.

126. Huxley observed that while many advertising artists used symbols to represent "something different from the commodity they are advertising" (such as sex), Kauffer was more direct, using symbols that "stand for the particular things which are at the moment under consideration." The reference is "never to extraneous matters." Museum of Modern Art, *Posters by E. MacKnight Kauffer* (New York: Museum of Modern Art, 1937), unpaginated. See also Museum of Modern Art, *Posters by A. M. Cassandre* (New York: Museum of Modern Art, 1936). See also Lynes, *Good Old Modern,* 136, and Edgar J. Kauffman Jr., "What is Industrial Design?" *Museum of Modern Art Bulletin* 14, no. 1 (Fall 1946): 3, 13.

127. As an example, see the essay by department curator Ernestine M. Fantl in Museum of Modern Art, *Posters by A. M. Cassandre,* 1–3.

128. Sizes are listed in Museum of Modern Art, *Posters by A. M. Cassandre.*

129. Incorporated in New York City in January 1942, Artists for Victory was dedicated to providing "patriotic service" to assist the nation's war effort. The group cosponsored the MoMA exhibition of war posters, sending out calls for submissions to over 75,000 artists. Out of 2,200 submissions, 216 were exhibited, and 9 were prize winners. The winners were E. B. Greenhaw ("War Bonds"), Karl Koehler and Victor Ancona ("Nature of the Enemy" and "People on the March"), Henry Koerner ("Loose Talk" and "Sacrifice"), N. Schottenstein ("Sacrifice"), Seymour Fogel ("Deliver Us From Evil"), and George Maas ("Slave World or Free World" and "Production"). The Office of War Information bought three posters (two of which were designed by Anton Otto Fischer, an illustrator popular since World War I but not one of the prizewinners) on the theme of "Loose Talk." The Office of Civilian Defense distributed the prizewinning images. See "Posters for Victory," *New York Times Magazine,* 29 November 1942, 20. Spanish and U.S. government poster exhibition listed in Museum

of Modern Art, Department of Industrial Design, "What is Modern Industrial Design?" *Bulletin of the Museum of Modern Art* 14, no. 1 (Fall 1946): 13. See also Certificate of Incorporation of Artists for Victory, n. d. [1941]; Minutes, 18 January 1942, 28 October 1942, 4 November 1942, 11 November 1942, 27 January 1943, all in Artists for Victory Papers, reel 115, no frame numbers; and Minutes, 16 February 1945, reel 116, all in AAA. See also Publicity notice, n.d. [ca. 10 December 1943], box 4, file 1; and National War Poster Competition Circular, box 42, file 11, both in RK, AAA.

130. See Lynes, *Good Old Modern*, 136. Comments on Christy in "Defense Posters for Two Wars," *Bulletin of the Museum of Modern Art* 8, no. 6 (September 1941): 6–7. The museum's priorities can also be gauged by its acquisition policies. Of the 281 posters by American artists acquired by the Museum of Modern Art between 1930 and 1947, 150 were by American expatriate MacKnight Kauffer, renowned for his modernist advertising and theater poster designs. Most had been produced for English clients. Of the remaining 121 posters, 30 were advertising posters. 15 of these were by Otis Shepard, and 11 of the other 15 were travel advertisements rather than product advertisements. The other 81 posters were WPA and war posters, mostly from World War II. This computerized list of posters was provided by Matilda McQuaid, Assistant Curator, Department of Architecture and Design, Museum of Modern Art.

chapter three

1. Although this chapter focuses on agency art directors, art directors for the big retail stores (which placed their advertising directly) also had an effect on the world of advertising art, helping to create a distinctive visual idiom for their business. As store employees, however, they worked in a very different sort of institutional environment from that of the agency art directors, and experienced a different type of company loyalty. For a comprehensive examination of department stores, see William Leach, *Land of Desire: Merchants, Power, and the Rise of a New American Culture* (New York: Pantheon, 1993).

2. On shopping as a "female activity," see William Leach, "Transformations in a Culture of Consumption: Women and Department Stores, 1890–1925," *Journal of American History* 71 (September 1984): 333; Joseph Siry, *Carson Pirie Scott: Louis Sullivan and the Chicago Department Store* (Chicago: University of Chicago Press, 1988), 127–39. On nineteenth-century women as consumers, see Kathleen D. McCarthy, *Women's Culture: American Philanthropy and Art, 1830–1930* (Chicago: University of Chicago Press, 1991), 53–54. On the "New Woman" and artistic representation, see Ellen Wiley Todd, *The New Woman Revised: Painting and Gender on Fourteenth Street* (Berkeley: University of California Press, 1993), 4–39. On the targeting of women by advertisers and social scientists in the 1920s, see Nancy Cott, *The Grounding of Modern Feminism* (New Haven: Yale University Press, 1987), 145–74. For more discussion of the importance of department stores, but without the focus on gender, see Simon Bronner, "Reading Consumer Culture," in Simon Bronner, ed., *Consuming Visions: Accumulation and Display of Goods in America 1880–1920* (New York: W. W. Norton, 1989), 25–32; Alan Trachtenberg, *The Incorporation of America: Culture and Society in the Gilded Age* (New York: Hill and Wang, 1982), 130–36.

3. Theodore Dreiser, *The "Genius"* (New York: New American Library, 1981; first published 1915), 394–408.

4. Art Directors Club, *Annual of Advertising Art in the United States, 1921* (New York: Publishers' Printing Company, 1921), iv; see also Nathaniel Pousette-Dart, "The Evolution of American Advertising Art," in Art Directors Club, *Twentieth Annual of Advertising Art* (New York: Watson-Guptill, 1941), 11–12; "Art Directors Hold Fifth Exhibition of Advertising Art," *Printers' Ink*, 13 May 1926, 44.

5. Art Directors Club, *Annual of Advertising Art* (1921), vii.

6. The term "modernist" here refers to those artistic styles and sensibilities that broke from the academic tradition of representation in an effort both to express the truths and complexities of contemporary life and to restore a sense of order to what otherwise seemed like a chaotic, contradictory world. "Modernism" and "modernist" art were inspired by European movements (including impressionism, cubism, futurism, and constructivism) that searched for originality in an attempt to articulate fundamental epistemological shifts in late-nineteenth- and early-twentieth-century experience. Some early-twentieth-century American critics used the term "modernistic" interchangeably with "modern" and "modernist." Others distinguished "modernist" from "modernistic" art, especially when discussing advertising art. From their perspective, "modernistic" art exploited the stylistic features and techniques of "modernist" art, but ignored its deeper, transcendent vision. I will maintain this distinction where it seems appropriate. On modernism, see Daniel Joseph Singal, "Towards a Definition of American Modernism," *American Quarterly* 39 (Spring 1987): 7–26. On "modernist" versus "modernistic," see George H. Roeder Jr., *Forum of Uncertainty: Confrontations with Modern Painting in Twentieth Century American Thought* (Ann Arbor: UMI Research Press, 1980). Jackson Lears, contrasting modern art and advertising, draws essentially the same distinctions, although he does not use the term "modernistic." See Jackson Lears, "Uneasy Courtship: Modern Art and Modern Advertising," *American Quarterly* 39 (Spring 1987): 133–54. For additional perspectives, see also Richard Shiff, *Cézanne and the End of Impressionism: A Study of the Theory, Technique, and Critical Evaluation of Modern Art* (Chicago: University of Chicago Press, 1984), 65; T. J. Clark, *The Painting of Modern Life: Paris in the Art of Manet and His Followers* (Princeton: Princeton University Press, 1984), 1–22; Griselda Pollock, *Vision and Difference: Femininity, Feminism, and Histories of Art* (London and New York: Routledge, 1988), 50–90; David Michael Levin, ed., *Modernity and the Hegemony of Vision* (Berkeley: University of California Press, 1993). For illustrations of advertisements, see Art Directors Club, *Annual of Advertising Art* (1921), xii, 6, 10, 39, 82. On Odorono and the body, see T. J. Jackson Lears, "American Advertising and the Reconstruction of the Body, 1880–1930," in Kathryn Grover, ed., *Fitness in American Culture: Images of Health, Sport, and the Body, 1830–1940* (Rochester: Margaret Woodbury Strong Museum, 1989), 47–66.

7. J. Walter Thompson Company, *News Bulletin*, 22 March 1921, RG 11, 8–9, JWTA.

8. Art Directors Club, *Annual of Advertising Art* (1921), iv; "A Declaration of Art in Advertising," *Arts and Decoration* 14 (April 1921): 464–65, 498; "The World of Art: Advertising Art," *New York Times*, 20 March 1921, sec. 3, 220–21; "The World of Art: Industrial and

Advertising Art and the Fine Arts," *New York Times Magazine,* 22 October 1922, 10; "Art Directors Hold Fifth Exhibition of Advertising Art."

9. On advertising men's perceptions of women as consumers, see Roland Marchand, *Advertising the American Dream: Making Way for Modernity 1920–1940* (Berkeley: University of California Press, 1985), 63–72, 188–89; Frederick Chr. Brøgger, "Grinding the Gears of Production and Consumption: Representational versus Nonrepresentational Advertising for Automobiles in the Mid 1920s," *Prospects* 15 (1990): 206.

10. John F. Arndt, "Why *Should* a Copywriter Sign His Work? *Printer's Ink,* 6 February 1930, 52.

11. Art Directors Club, *Second Annual of Illustration for Advertisements in the United States* (New York: Art Directors Club, 1923), 9. The second year's jury consisted of Frederick Suhr, Cass Gilbert, Edward Penfield, Jules Guerin, and William J. Boardman. Although art directors played an increased role on subsequent juries, artists and other distinguished art professionals continued to have input. Henri, for example, returned to the jury in 1926. See Art Directors Club, *Fifth Annual of Advertising Art* (New York: Art Directors Club, 1926), unpaginaged.

12. Art Directors Club, *Second Annual,* 9.

13. Gordon C. Aymar, "The Third Exhibition," Art Directors Club, *Third Annual of Advertising Art* (New York: Art Directors Club, 1924), unpaginated.

14. Hitchcock, whose ancestors were noted as being among the first New England settlers, was the wife of author Ripley Hitchcock. See "Helen Sargent Hitchcock," *National Cyclopedia of American Biography* (New York: James T. White, 1922), 18: 174; "Helen Hitchcock, Clubwoman, Dies," *New York Times,* 31 December 1958, 38. On club members and activities, see "Greetings!" *Bulletin of the Art Center* 1 (July 1922): 1; Art Center, Inc., *Prospectus 1920* (New York: Art Center, 1920), unpaginated; Art Center, Inc., "To Develop Art in Use," pamphlet, 1926, 11 (found at the New York Public Library, New York City); Bonnie Yochelson, "Clarence H. White Reconsidered: An Alternative to the Modernist Aesthetic of Straight Photography," *Studies in Visual Communication* 9 (Fall 1983): 28, 31.

15. Edward L. Bernays, *Biography of an Idea: Memoirs of a Public Relations Counsel* (New York: Simon and Schuster, 1962), 196; "Greens and Art," *Bulletin of the Art Center* 5 (March 1927): 127–28.

16. See *Bulletin of the Art Center* 4 (February and March 1926), 183, 216; 7 (December 1928): 33–35.

17. Building upon her activities with the Art Workers Club, Hitchcock had organized the Vocational League for Art Workers. In 1914, joined by another arts organizer, Emily V. Hammond (president of the Three Arts Club and wife of prominent lawyer John Henry Hammond), Hitchcock expanded operations into the Art Alliance of America "to connect" creators of art with those who "appreciate and use it," and to form an educational center to spur on the "industrial, decorative and graphic arts." The Alliance set up a placement bureau, thus establishing a means for artists, especially women, to forge respectable connections with wealthy female patrons and with the male world of business. The alliance thus served as a kind of vocational clearinghouse and as a benevolent organization for unmarried

women seeking occupational status within the sphere of the crafts. It was an extension of the older social welfare activities into a more public sphere—a move from guidance to actual intervention through establishment of institutional structures and services.

On the Art Workers Club, see "Helen Sargent Hitchcock," *National Cyclopedia of American Biography;* "Helen Hitchcock, Clubwoman, Dies." On the Vocational League and the Art Alliance, see "Art Centre Has Greater Plans," *New York Times,* 28 February 1926, sec. 9, 9; Helen Sargent Hitchcock, "The Origin and Development of the Art Center," *Bulletin of the Art Center* 8 (May 1930): 95–96. The role of elite and working women in the development of craft and commercial training, ideals and practices in the applied arts, and the emergence of industrial design merits additional investigation. Kathleen D. McCarthy has begun this task in her important study *Women's Culture.* For more on the larger "arts in industry" movement of which the Art Alliance and Art Center were part, see Leach, *Land of Desire,* 156–57.

On the nineteenth-century women's political culture (termed "domestic feminism") and its transformations, see Paula Baker, "The Domestication of Politics: Women and American Political Society, 1780–1920," *American Historical Review* 89 (June 1984): 625–47; William Chafe, *The Paradox of Change: American Women in the Twentieth Century* (New York: Oxford University Press, 1991), 9–12; Suzanne Lebsock, "Women and American Politics, 1880–1920," in Louise A. Tilly and Patricia Gurin, eds., *Women, Politics, and Change* (New York: Russell Sage, 1990), 35–50; Cott, *The Grounding of Modern Feminism,* 22–23. On efforts to protect unmarried working women from sexual exploitation, see Joanne J. Meyerowitz, *Women Adrift: Independent Wage Earners in Chicago, 1880–1920* (Chicago: University of Chicago Press, 1988), 44–45. For an examination of the culture of working-class women and the role of social clubs in general, see Kathy Peiss, *Cheap Amusements: Working Women and Leisure in Turn of the Century New York* (Philadelphia: Temple University Press, 1986), 59–62.

18. Hitchcock was so closely associated with the Art Center that she was elected its president, but the center's Board of Directors remained primarily male. The first Board of Directors included Hitchcock and Hammond. Charles Dana Gibson was vice president, Col. Wade H. Hayes, treasurer, and Condé Nast art director Heyworth Campbell, secretary. Also on the board were Walter Ehrlich, W. Frank Purdy, Ray Greenleaf, Charles E. Pellew, Clarence White, and Richard Marwede. Gertrude Vanderbilt Whitney, Mrs. Leonard K. Elmhirst, Mrs. E. H. Harriman, and Mrs. Walter Ladd were principal bondholders. Whitney, Harriman, and Mrs. Howard Mansfield served on the Advisory Council. Florence N. Levy, Blanch Byerley, Katherine Audley, and Etta Sardy were among the important members of the center's staff. See Hitchcock, "Origin and Development of the Art Center," 97–99; Art Center, *Prospectus.*

19. These circumstances were consistent with trends in the sphere of politics as well. See Estelle Freedman, "Separatism as Strategy: Female Institution Building and American Feminism, 1870–1930," *Feminist Studies* 5 (1979): 524; Chafe, *Paradox of Change,* 42–44; Cott, *Grounding of Modern Feminism,* 95–96; Lebsock, "Women and American Politics," 56.

20. On Campbell, see Heyworth Campbell Letterbooks, Illustration House, New York City; Caroline Seebohm, *The Man Who Was Vogue: The Life and Times of Condé Nast* (New

York: Viking Press, 1982), 175, 224–25. On melding reformism and capitalism, see Lebsock, "Women and American Politics," 46–49.

21. *Bulletin of the Art Center* 1 (October 1922): 36–37; 1 (December 1922): 78; 2 (June 1924): 317–18; 7 (February 1929): 64.

22. "V. Flannery, 57, A Noted Painter," *New York Times*, 28 December 1955, 24; "Gordon Christian Aymar," *Darien News-Review*, 16 February 1989, clipping, Darien Historical Society; "René Clarke," in Walt and Roger Reed, *The Illustrator in America 1880–1980: A Century of Illustration* (New York: The Society of Illustrators, 1984; first published 1966), 120; J. D. Tarcher, "Will There be Commercial Artists in 1950?" *Advertising and Selling* n.s. 12 (3 October 1928): 32.

One key difference between art directors and the illustrators and painters of this period, however, was that some of the advertising men had also attended college. Flannery had gone to the University of Illinois, Calkins to Knox College, and Aymar to Yale. This distinction was crucial: the majority of upper-level creative staff in advertising agencies were college men of Anglo-Saxon Protestant descent. For art directors, the degree, even college attendance, was crucial for acceptance among other advertising professionals, signaling a level of class and refinement (as sociologist Pierre Bourdieu would characterize it, "cultural capital") that distinguished them from other artsy types: the degree gave the art director a tie with other professional men who might under other circumstances take art directors' aesthetic proclivities less seriously. On cultural capital in relation to the activity of distinction, see Pierre Bourdieu, *Distinction: A Social Critique of the Judgement of Taste* (Cambridge, Mass.: Harvard University Press, 1984), 1–96, especially 12, 53–54.

23. Dreiser, *The "Genius,"* 395.

24. Earnest Elmo Calkins, *The Advertising Man* (New York: Charles Scribner's Sons, 1922), 83.

25. Ralph M. Hower, *The History of an Advertising Agency: N. W. Ayer and Son at Work* (Cambridge, Mass.: Harvard University Press, 1949), 313, 316, 491; Calkins, *The Advertising Man*, 84–85; Sid Hydeman, *How to Illustrate for Money* (New York: Harper and Brothers, 1936), 141–49; Gordon C. Aymar, *An Introduction to Advertising Illustration* (New York: Harper and Brothers, 1929), 15.

The term "generative phase" is derived from Albert Boime's discussion of French academic painting. See Albert Boime, *The Academy and French Painting in the Nineteenth Century* (London and New York: Phaidon Press, 1971), 87.

26. See, for example, Gordon M. Wilbur to Rockwell Kent, 1 February 1930, box 5, file 18; René Clarke to Kent, 1 May 1930, 3 May 1930, box 8, file 30; John T. Harman to Frances L. Kent, 10 January 1930, 24 February 1930, 8 April 1930, box 15, file 23, all in RK, AAA.

27. Hydeman, *How to Illustrate for Money;* Aymar, *An Introduction to Advertising Illustration;* A. J. Aylward, "Advertising Art at Home and Abroad," *Bulletin of the Art Center* 4 (November 1925): 77. N. W. Ayer art director Vaughn Flannery's defense of Rockwell Kent's solicited introduction for the Seventh Annual of the Art Directors Club—an essay that in effect condemned advertising and was never published—exemplifies art directors' identification with artists. See Secretary to Vaughn Flannery to Rockwell Kent, 13 September 1928;

Flannery to Stuart Campbell, 26 November 1928, box 5, file 18; Sanford Gerard to Kent, 23 May 1945, box 6, file 18, RK, AAA.

28. George French, *Twentieth Century Advertising* (New York: D. Van Nostrand Company, 1926), 240; Joseph Cummings Chase, "What Is This Art Game?" *Saturday Evening Post,* 15 October 1927, 16, 206, 209; "Art Directors' Notes," *Bulletin of the Art Center* 4 (March 1926): 216–17; 4 (May 1926): 270–72; Aylward, "Advertising Art at Home and Abroad," 77; A. Rowden King, "Art vs. Commercial Art," *Advertising and Selling* 26 (October 1911): 53; Aymar, *Introduction to Advertising Illustration,* 6, 17–19; Hydeman, *How to Illustrate for Money,* 145–49.

29. Important recent discussions of modernism in advertising include: Jeffrey L. Meikle, *Twentieth Century Limited: Industrial Design in America, 1925–1939* (Philadelphia: Temple University Press, 1979), 10–18; James Sloan Allen, *The Romance of Commerce and Culture: Capitalism, Modernism, and the Chicago-Aspen Crusade for Cultural Reform* (Chicago: University of Chicago Press, 1983), 3–34; Marchand, *Advertising the American Dream,* 140–48; Lears, "Uneasy Courtship," 132–54; Neil Harris, "Designs on Demand: Art and the Modern Corporation," in *Cultural Excursions: Marketing Appetites and Cultural Tastes in Modern America* (Chicago: University of Chicago Press, 1990), 355–63; Terry Smith, *Making the Modern: Industry, Art, and Design in America* (Chicago: University of Chicago Press, 1993), 101–11, 159–89. For a view that focuses primarily on European art, see Kirk Varnedoe and Adam Gopnik, *High and Low: Modern Art and Popular Culture* (New York: Harry N. Abrams, 1990), 231–304.

30. Marchand, *Advertising the American Dream,* 144–47, 181–84; W. Livingston Larned, "Merry-Go-Round Art Compositions," *Printer's Ink,* 11 September 1930, 42–50; Varnedoe and Gopnik, *High and Low,* 286–99. For examples of such images, see Art Directors Club, *Annual of Advertising Art* (New York: Art Directors Club, 1928), especially 37, 38, 66.

31. Contrast, for example, Nathaniel Pousette-Dart, "Modern Art—Its Genesis and Destination," *Printer's Ink,* 23 October 1930, 150, 152; Earnest Elmo Calkins, "Beauty in the Machine Age," *Printer's Ink,* 25 September 1930, 78; "Pictures in Advertising," *New York Times,* 3 October 1926, sec. 2, 8; French, *Twentieth Century Advertising,* 236; Ernest Knaufft, "Art in Advertising," *Review of Reviews* 65 (June 1922): 625–34; A Commercial Art Manager, "The Allegory as An Advertising Asset," *Printer's Ink,* 15 June 1922, 139–43; Commercial Art Manager, "Putting the Human Element in 'Human Interest' Illustrations," *Printer's Ink,* 10 August 1922, 73–76; Thomas Erwin, "What Has Happened to Advertising Art?" *Printer's Ink Monthly* 16 (June 1928): 37–39, 143; Carl Richard Greer, *Advertising and Its Mechanical Reproduction* (New York: Thomas Y. Crowell, 1931), 291; C. K. Morris, "In Defense of American Advertising Art," *Printer's Ink,* 5 November 1931, 101, 104–5.

32. See, for example, Commercial Art Manager, "Futuristic Monstrosities Are All the Rage," *Printer's Ink,* 12 November 1925, 57–60; Commercial Art Manager, "Advertising Art," *Printer's Ink,* 18 November 1925, 145–50; Don Gridley, "Is Modern Advertising Art Modern Enough?" *Printer's Ink,* 2 April 1925, 81–82; Hiram Blaufelt, "When the Modernist Invades Advertising," *Printer's Ink Monthly* 10 (May 1925): 65–66; Milton Towne, "Is the Trend of Advertising Art Toward Over-Sophistication?" *Advertising and Selling* 8 (December 1926): 32;

Lloyd Goodrich, "A Note on Advertising Art," *The Arts* 9 (June 1926): 338–41; Don Gridley, "A Statistical Glass Applied to Modernism," *Printer's Ink Monthly* 17 (December 1928): 44–46, 130, 133; Thomas Erwin, "What Has Happened to Advertising Art?" 37–39, 143; Pousette-Dart, "Modern Art," 150, 152; Marchand, *Advertising the American Dream*, 142–43.

33. Marchand, *Advertising the American Dream*, 140–48, 181–82; Alyward, "Advertising Art at Home and Abroad," 77; Towne, "Is the Trend of Advertising Toward Over-Sophistication?" 32, 52, 54; Brøgger, "Grinding the Gears of Production and Consumption," 197–224. Brøgger makes a similar point about advertisers' views of women as consumers, but is concerned primarily with the relationship of what he calls "representational" and "nonrepresentational" styles as expressions of the shift from a more traditional, production-oriented society to a consumer society. He does not focus on the adoption of "modernistic" styles but on the relationship between straightforward, "factual," and narrative imagery and more metaphorical devices used to trigger desire.

34. On modernism as masculinity in painting, see Pollock, *Vision and Difference*, 50; Carol Duncan, "Virility and Domination in Early Twentieth Century Vanguard Painting," in Norma Broude and Mary Garrard, *Feminism and Art History: Questioning the Litany* (New York: Harper and Row, 1982), 292–313.

35. J. Walter Thompson Company, *News Letter*, 15 August 1927, RG 11, JWTA.

36. "Is Art Always Advertising Art?" J. Walter Thompson Company, *News Letter*, 14 April 1927, RG 11, JWTA.

37. According to historian Roland Marchand, advertisers regarded the "masses" as the lower-income segment of a preselected "Able-to-Buy" class. Hence "the term mass audience thus referred primarily to those Americans with higher than average incomes," those who could afford magazines like the *Saturday Evening Post*. "Class" referred to the narrower group of high-income people, although the boundaries between the two categories, "mass" and "class," were fluid and often confused. Marchand, *Advertising the American Dream*, 63–66, 77–80.

38. Art Deerson, "Should the Magazine Covers Be Our Criterion of Advertising Art?" J. Walter Thompson Company, *News Letter*, 1 August 1927, RG 11, JWTA.

39. Ibid.

40. Kenneth M. Goode, "The Art Director in an Iron Mask," *Advertising and Selling*, 10 July 1929, 19–20; W. Livingston Larned, "Choosing a Pictorial Atmosphere for the Entire Campaign," *Printer's Ink*, 25 July 1929, 104–9; French, *Twentieth Century Advertising*, 239; "Art in Advertising," *New York Times*, 7 February 1928, 26; E. T. Grundlach, "Art versus Advertising," *Advertising and Selling*, 29 December 1926, 27; Harford Powell, "Pictures versus Art," *Advertising and Selling*, 26 January 1928, 26.

41. Erwin, "What Has Happened to Advertising Art?" 143.

42. Hiram Blauvelt, "When the Modernist Invades Advertising," *Printer's Ink Monthly* 10 (May 1925): 66; Gridley, "Is Modern Advertising Art Modern Enough?" 81–82; Towne, "Is the Trend of Advertising Art Toward Over-Sophistication?" 32, 52–54; Erwin, "What Has Happened to Advertising Art?" 37, 143.

43. Commercial Art Manager, "Advertising Art," 145–50; Commercial Art Manager, "Futuristic Monstrosities Are All the Rage," 57–58.

44. Gridley, "A Statistical Glass Applied to Modernism," 44–46; Pousette-Dart, "Modern Art," 150–52; Nathaniel Pousette-Dart, "Art Directors Club," *Bulletin of the Art Center* 7 (May 1929): 91.

45. On professional authority, see Andrew Abbott, *The System of Professions: An Essay on the Division of Expert Labor* (Chicago: University of Chicago Press, 1988), 8–9, 35–113.

46. J. Walter Thompson *News Bulletin*, 12 February 1917, RG 11, JWTA.

47. For discussion of copywriters' dissatisfactions, see Helen Woodward, *Through Many Windows* (New York: Harper, 1926), 357–61; T. J. Jackson Lears, "Some Versions of Fantasy: Toward a Cultural History of American Advertising," *Prospects* 9 (1984): 358–63; Marchand, *Advertising the American Dream*, 42–44, 153–54.

48. Edward Prager, "Millions for Artwork, But Not One Cent for Copy," *Printer's Ink*, 3 April 1930, 84; Lears, "Some Versions of Fantasy," 359–63.

49. Arndt, "Why Should a Copywriter Sign His Work?" 52. Like some art directors and advertising artists, many copywriters were ambivalent about their commercial work. Tensions were greatest when the copywriter aspired to be an independent author, as was the case with Sherwood Anderson, for example. See T. J. Jackson Lears, "Sherwood Anderson: Looking for the White Spot," in Richard Wightman Fox and T. J. Jackson Lears, eds., *The Power of Culture: Critical Essays in American History* (Chicago: University of Chicago Press, 1993), 12–37.

50. G. W. Freeman, "Let Copywriters Sign Copy? I Should Say Not!" *Printer's Ink*, 27 February 1930, 84.

51. Lloyd Goodrich, *Richard Pousette-Dart* (New York: Whitney Museum of Art, 1963), 7.

52. On the Cunard Building, see Robert A. M. Stern, Gregory Gilmartin, and Thomas Mellins, *New York 1930: Architecture and Urbanism Between the Two World Wars* (New York: Rizzoli, 1987), 528.

53. Until the late 1930s, the Art Directors Club annuals of advertising art listed artist and agency, but not art director. Since Pousette-Dart's service worked for advertising agencies and not as an agency, it is not surprising that his name does not come up.

54. Edward Alden Jewell, "Further Comment on Art," *New York Times*, 7 October 1928, and "Nathaniel Pousette-Dart, 79, Artist and Lecturer," *Herald Tribune*, 20 October 1965, clippings in vertical files, National Museum of American Art; "Nathaniel Pousette-Dart Dead; Artist, 79, Also Wrote on Art," *New York Times*, 18 October 1965, 35; *Who Was Who in America* (Chicago: Who Was Who, Inc., 1968), vol. 4, 762; Tarcher, "Will There Be "Commercial" Art in 1950?" 30, 32; Judith Higgins, "To the Point of Vision: A Profile of Richard Pousette-Dart," in *Transcending Abstraction: Richard Pousette-Dart, Paintings, 1939–1985* (Fort Lauderdale: Museum of Art, Fort Lauderdale, 1986), 13.

55. Nathaniel Pousette-Dart, "Art Directors Club," *Bulletin of the Art Center* 7 (February 1929): 64.

56. Higgins, "To the Point of Vision," 15.

57. Tarcher, "Will There Be "Commercial" Art in 1950?" 30.

58. Ibid.; Lears, "Some Versions of Fantasy," 360–61.

59. Pousette-Dart, "Modern Art," 152.

60. Ibid., 150; Nathaniel Pousette-Dart, "Art Directors Club," *Bulletin of the Art Center* 7 (April 1929): 88.

61. R. D. Dunn, "Art Directors Club," *Bulletin of the Art Center* 2 (May 1924): 283; Nathaniel Pousette-Dart, "Art Directors Club," *Bulletin of the Art Center* 7 (February 1929): 64. One of the standard signals of professionalization (if not always an indication of success) was the establishment of schools controlled by the experts in question. See Laurence Veysey, "The Plural Organized Worlds of the Humanities," in Alexandra Oleson and John Voss, *The Organization of Knowledge in Modern America, 1860–1920* (Baltimore: Johns Hopkins University Press, 1979), 58–59.

62. Nathaniel Pousette-Dart, "Art Directors Club," *Bulletin of the Art Center* 7 (February 1929): 64.

63. Nathaniel Pousette-Dart, "Art Directors Club, 8th Annual Exhibition of Advertising Art," *Bulletin of the Art Center* 7 (May 1929): 91–96; idem, "The Artist Comes Down to Earth," *Printer's Ink Monthly* 25 (December 1932): 37–38; idem, "The Evolution of Advertising Art," in Art Directors Club, *Twentieth Annual of Advertising Art,* 9–15.

64. See, for example, Artists for Victory Papers, 31 January 1944 and 16 February 1944; and "Report from Mr. Pousette d'art [*sic*], Artists for Victory, Post-War Planning Committee, n.d. [ca. August 1944], all on reel 116, no frame numbers, AAA.

65. "Nathaniel Pousette-Dart Dead," 35.

66. Thomas Erwin, "The 11th Art Directors Show," *Printer's Ink Monthly* 24 (May 1932): 33; Marchand, *Advertising the American Dream,* 286–89, 300–306; W. K. Nield, "The Disloyal Art Director," *Advertising and Selling* 19 (18 August 1932): 21. For an additional indication of advertisers' cautiousness, see E. W. Power to Rockwell Kent, 12 August 1930, box 15, file 23, RK, AAA.

67. Erwin, "11th Art Directors Show," 33. See also "New Art Publications," *New York Times,* 8 December 1935, sec. 10, 15; Minutes of the Creative Organization Staff Meeting, J. Walter Thompson Company, 12 March 1932, 11 October 1932, 23 March 1933, RG 5, JWTA; Otis Pease, *The Responsibilities of American Advertising, 1920–1940* (New Haven: Yale University Press, 1958), 181–92.

According to Roland Marchand, comic strip advertising combined the "best techniques learned from other sources." "From the movies came the ideas of continuity of action, quick cutting from scene to scene, and focusing attention through the occasional close-up. From the confession magazines came the power of personal testimony and the intimate drama. From the tabloids came an emphasis on brevity and pictorial imagery. And from radio came the persuasiveness of a conversational style and the seductiveness of eavesdropping." Marchand, *Advertising the American Dream,* 112. See also 111–16.

On the concern for lifelikeness, see W. Livingston Larned, "Facial Expression—An Advertising Language," *Printer's Ink,* 20 November 1930, 116, 120, 125–26; idem, "Make Your Portrait Illustrations 'Real People,'" *Printer's Ink,* 13 February 1930, 96, 100, 104; idem,

"Animating the Inanimate," *Printer's Ink,* 27 November 1930, 89–92; Sohn, "Misbehaviorism in Advertising Art," *Printer's Ink Monthly* 24 (January 1932): 21–22; M. F. Agha, "Leave European Art in Europe," *Advertising and Selling* (January 1932): 17–18; Lears, "Some Versions of Fantasy," 383–85.

68. Charles Elliott, "Is Art Moderne Passé?" J. Walter Thompson Company, *News Letter,* 1 January 1929, RG 11, JWTA.

69. Monte W. Sohn, "Misbehaviorism in Advertising Art," *Printer's Ink Monthly* 24 (January 1932): 21. See also Goode, "The Art Director in an Iron Mask," 19–20; "Minority Report," *Advertising Arts* (September 1932): 14–15; Dale Nichols, "Wake Up Michelangelo!" *Printer's Ink Monthly* 45 (October 1941): 15, 61; and Val Pianka and Richard Giles, "Go Back to Sleep, Michelangelo!" *Printer's Ink Monthly* 42 (June 1941): 31.

70. Nield, "The Disloyal Art Director," 21.

71. C. B. Larrabee, "They Still Like Grandma," *Printer's Ink Monthly* 30 (June 1935): 19, 61; Goode, "The Art Director in an Iron Mask," 19–20; Nield, "The Disloyal Art Director," 21; Sohn, "Misbehaviorism in Advertising Art," 21; Erwin, "11th Art Directors Show," 32. The "Grandma" picture is illustrated in both the Larrabee and Nield articles and on the back cover of the City College *Alumnus* 31 (February 1935).

72. Nield, "The Disloyal Art Director," 21. See also Thomas Erwin, "Forward," in Art Directors Club, *Eleventh Annual of Advertising Art* (New York: Art Directors Club, 1932), unpaginated.

73. Pianka and Giles, "Go Back to Sleep, Michelangelo!" 31.

74. See, for example, Pianka and Giles, "Go Back to Sleep, Michelangelo!" 31; "To Survey Consumer Likes," *New York Times,* 11 May 1937, 46.

75. See Jean M. Converse, *Survey Research in the United States: Roots and Emergence 1860–1960* (Berkeley: University of California Press, 1987), 87–161; Marchand, *Advertising the American Dream,* 75–76; Gordon White, *John Caples: Adman* (Chicago: Crain Books, 1977), 1–55; Earnest Elmo Calkins, *Modern Advertising* (New York: D. Appleton and Company, 1912; first published 1905), 270; Lears, "Some Versions of Fantasy," 380–81; Daniel J. Boorstin, *The Americans: The Democratic Experience* (New York: Random House, 1973), 148–56; Sanford Gerard to Rockwell Kent, 23 May 1945, box 6, file 18, RK, AAA; author's interview with Leo Bogart (former Executive Vice President and General Manager of the Newspaper Advertising Bureau), 21 July 1993. On the limitations of public opinion polling, see Leo Bogart, *Silent Politics: Polls and the Awareness of Public Opinion* (New York: John Wiley and Sons, 1972).

76. Deane Uptegrove, "The Four Million Picks Its Pictures," *Advertising and Selling,* 6 June 1935, 28. Magazine art directors also resorted to polling to determine which illustrators produced sales. See Hydeman, *How to Illustrate for Money,* 150–58.

77. Larabee, "They Still Like Grandma," 61; "quaint" cited in Uptegrove, "The Four Million Picks Its Pictures," 28. Selections and winners are listed in Art Directors Club, *Fourteenth Annual of Advertising Art* (New York: Book Service Company, 1935).

78. Larabee, "They Still Like Grandma," 19, 61. See also "Talks on Advertising Art," *New York Times,* 21 April 1937, 21; Pianka and Giles, "Go Back to Sleep, Michelangelo!" 31.

79. "National Alliance of Art and Industry," *American Art Annual* (Washington, D.C.: American Federation of Arts, 1937), 244 and (1941–1943), 334; "Art Center Changes," *Bulletin of the Art Center* 9 (November-December 1931): 131–33.

80. Henry M. Lester, "Evaluating Reader's Interest in Pictures," in Art Directors Club, *Nineteenth Annual of Advertising Art* (New York: Longman's Green and Company, 1940), 78, 82, 85, 88, 95; Pease, *The Responsibilities of American Advertising*, 185–88; Marchand, *Advertising the American Dream*, 110–15, 304.

81. Uptegrove, "The Four Million Picks Its Pictures," 42–44; Erwin, "Forward," in Art Directors Club, *Eleventh Annual*, unpaginated; M. F. Agha, "Forward," in Art Directors Club, *Fourteenth Annual of Advertising Art*, 7–8; William H. Schneider, "What is an Art Director?" in Art Directors Club, *Eighteenth Annual of Advertising Art* (New York: Longman's, Green and Company, 1939), 14; Sanford Gerard, "The Purpose of Advertising Art," in Art Directors Club, *Nineteenth Annual*, 55, 59.

The publication *Advertising Arts*, published by Frederick G. Kendall, was one such effort at resistance. *Advertising Arts* began in 1929 as a supplement to the trade journal *Advertising and Selling*, and soon expanded into a separate quarterly publication; Earnest Elmo Calkins served as a contributing editor. Intended to stir up among advertising people and clients a "greater consciousness of beauty, both in the design of merchandise, and in the physical appearance of advertising," *Advertising Arts* showcased the latest in "quality," modern advertising, packaging, industrial design, paper, and typography. Leading art directors and designers linked with modern art in design—Charles Coiner, René Clarke, Mehemed Fehmy Agha, Joseph Sinel, Faber Birren, and Norman Bel Geddes—wrote articles on these developments, which in advertising contrasted markedly with dominant trends. *Advertising Arts* could not survive the depression; after the May 1935 issue, it appeared irregularly only as a ten-page glossy insert in *Advertising and Selling*, consisting of pictures of award-winning ads and package designs, but no articles. *Advertising Arts* ceased entirely after the 9 April 1936 issue.

82. Uptegrove, "The Four Million Picks Its Pictures," 42–44. See also Pousette-Dart, "The Artist Comes Down to Earth," 37–38; Agha, "Leave European Art in Europe," 14–18; G. Lynn Summer, "Return of the Artist," *Advertising and Selling*, n.s. 34 (January 1941): 28. Although Uptegrove justified artistic variety in advertising by highlighting market segmentation and class and taste distinctions, he ignored racial and ethnic differences as much as advertisers had ever done.

83. See Art Directors Club, *Fourteenth Annual*, 9; Art Directors Club, *Sixteenth Annual of Advertising Art* (New York: Book Service Company, 1937); Art Directors Club, *Eighteenth Annual*; "Medals Awarded for Advertising Art," *New York Times*, 10 April 1937, 22; "Honors Awarded to Advertising Art," *New York Times*, 29 March 1939, 40. From the outset, the Art Directors Club annuals had included, at the end of the volume, a sampling of complete advertisements in miniature. The art director was not credited, however.

84. "New Art Publications," 15. "Lowbrow" is referred to in William H. Schneider, "What is an Art Director?" in Art Directors Club, *Eighteenth Annual*, 14. According to historian Lawrence W. Levine, the term "lowbrow" was "first used shortly after 1900" to refer to

a person or thing "neither highly intellectual" nor "aesthetically refined." Along with the term "highbrow," "lowbrow" derived from phrenology, "the nineteenth-century practice of determining racial types and intelligence by measuring cranial shapes and capacities." The term was popularized by Van Wyck Brooks in *America's Coming of Age* (New York, 1915), 6–7. See Lawrence W. Levine, *Highbrow/Lowbrow: The Emergence of Cultural Hierarchy in America* (Cambridge, Mass.: Harvard University Press, 1988), 221–22; idem, "William Shakespeare and the American People," in Chandra Mukerji and Michael Schudson, *Rethinking Popular Culture: Contemporary Perspectives in Cultural Studies* (Berkeley: University of California Press, 1991), 196, n. 73.

85. Agha, "Forward," *Fourteenth Annual*, 7.

86. Born in Santa Clara, California, Coiner decided at age seventeen to become a commercial artist. Two years later he left for Chicago to study at the Chicago Academy of Fine Arts and the Art Institute. In 1919 he joined the art department of the Chicago branch of the advertising agency Erwin and Wasey, where he spent the next "six uneventful years." Coiner joined the staff of N. W. Ayer in 1924, and in 1929 became art director. Quote from "Charles Coiner, Art Director," *Portfolio* 1, no. 2 (Summer 1950): unpaginated. See also R. Roger Remington and Barbara J. Hodik, *Nine Pioneers in Modern American Graphic Design* (Cambridge, Mass.: MIT Press, 1989), 55; obituary in *New York Times*, 16 August 1989, sec. 2, 9.

87. Phrase comes from Charles T. Coiner, "Art with a Capital 'A,'" in *Nineteenth Annual*, 46.

88. Hower, *History of an Advertising Agency*, 318. See also Mitchell Douglas Kahn, *Art, Inc.: American Paintings in Corporate Collections* (Montgomery: Montgomery Museum of Fine Arts, 1979), 10.

89. Between 1921 and 1948, for example, Ayer received a total of 93 awards in the Art Directors Club annual exhibitions, rivaled only by J. Walter Thompson, which received 61. Hower, *History of an Advertising Agency*, 326–28.

90. Remington and Hodik, *Nine Pioneers of American Graphic Design*, 56–59.

91. The Hawaiian Pineapple Company, for example, had been founded in 1901 by James Dole, Harvard-educated scion of an old New England family involved with the development of Hawaii since the early missionary days of the nineteenth century; in 1932 the company had come under the control of Castle and Cooke, Ltd., an even larger corporation whose activities became synonymous with the growth, development, politics, and even ownership of Hawaii. See Henry A. White, *James D. Dole, Industrial Pioneer of the Pacific. Founder of Hawaii's Pineapple Industry* (New York: Newcomen Society, 1957); Castle and Cooke, Ltd., *The First 100 Years. A Report on the Operations of Castle and Cooke for the Years 1851–1951* (Honolulu: Castle and Cooke, 1951).

De Beers Consolidated Mines founder and chairman of the board Cecil John Rhodes (1853–1902) had been the central figure in the "founding" of Rhodesia. A successor, Sir Ernest Oppenheimer (1880–1957), successfully extended Rhodes's efforts to consolidate control over production of South African diamonds. Indeed, the history of De Beers Consolidated Mines was inseparable from British imperialism in South Africa and Rhodesia, a fact of which company officials were well aware. Their sense of destiny led them to identify their activities with the highest of human endeavors. Rhodes founded the Rhodes scholarships at Oxford University; the company historian praised its leaders' devotion to "great 'public acts,' and the furtherance of education, social welfare, and science." See Hedley A. Chilvers, *The Story of De Beers* (London: Cassell and Co., 1939), 260.

Container Corporation of America, too, was a family business, a split-off division of Walter Paepcke's father's Chicago Mill and Lumber Company. Paepcke's father Hermann, a German immigrant, was very self-conscious about his cultural standing, and impressed the ideal of *Kultur* on his children. See Allen, *The Romance of Commerce and Culture,* 17–23.

92. Cultural "capital" refers to the accumulation of class and ideologically defined forms of knowledge about "high" cultural enterprises such as modern art, dance, music, and theater. Such knowledge serves to enhance the social status of the individuals and groups who acquire such erudition by virtue of class background or education. Bourdieu, *Distinction,* 1–96.

93. Charles T. Coiner, "Atelier to Advertising," *Advertising Arts* (March 1934): 9. See also Charles T. Coiner, taped interview with Martina Norelli, 1985, AAA, Washington, D.C.

94. White, *James D. Dole,* 23, 25–27.

95. Robert Goldwater, *Primitivism in Modern Art* (New York: Random House, 1967; first published 1938); reviewed in *Art in America* 27 (January 1939): 41; also see J. A. Porter in *Magazine of Art* 32 (February 1939): 110–11, and A. McMahon in *Parnassus* 10 (December 1938): 34.

96. Castle and Cooke in particular was heavily committed to the promotion of tourism; among other things, the company was a co-owner of the Royal Hawaiian Hotel. Castle and Cooke, *The First 100 Years,* 30.

97. "O'Keeffe in Review," *Art Digest* 17, 15 February 1943, 14; Laurie Lisle, *Portrait of an Artist: A Biography of Georgia O'Keeffe* (Albuquerque: University of New Mexico Press, 1986), 242–44; Roxanna Robinson, *Georgia O'Keeffe: A Life* (New York: Harper and Row, 1989), 426–27; Coiner interview, AAA.

98. "O'Keeffe's Pineapple," *Art Digest,* 15 February 1940, 23; "O'Keeffe's Pineapple," *Art Digest,* 1 March 1943, 17.

99. Coiner himself stated that the Art Directors Club exhibition offered an "opportunity to justify the art directors' career and do a little missionary work at the same time." Coiner, "Art with a Capital 'A,'" 48.

100. "Charles Coiner, Art Director."

101. Lorraine Wild, "Europeans in America," in Walker Art Center, *Graphic Design in America: A Visual Language History* (New York: Harry N. Abrams, 1989), 157–69; Allen, *The Romance of Commerce and Culture,* 25–34; 53–77.

102. In carving out a position of respect for art and the artist, Coiner held a singular position among art directors in the agencies. He was not, however, alone in attaining an association of modern art and commerce. Mehemed Fehmy Agha (1896–1978), art director for Condé Nast Publications, Inc., from 1929 to 1943, and Alexey Brodovich (1898–1971), art director for *Harper's Bazaar* from 1934 to 1958, also were influential in asserting the

presence of the art director as an influential artistic figure and in establishing viable links between the organizational structures of avant-garde art and the commercial print media. Together, Agha and Brodovich significantly transformed the look and conception of American magazine design. Their work, along with the contributions of such graphic designers as Will Burtin (art director for *Fortune* from 1945–1949), Herbert Bayer, Paul Rand, Lester Beall, Alvin Lustig, and Bradbury Thompson would have a marked influence on advertising in the same class magazines and other corporate venues in the early 1950s and onward.

European modernism, especially constructivism, provided Agha and Brodovich with a stable of inventive, attention-getting principles and devices: their innovations lay in emphasizing as both art and as advertising the artistic design of the printed page as a whole, rather than just the illustration upon it. While page layout and advertising illustration had always been a crucial component of an advertisement, the art of the printed page had rarely been foregrounded as bearing meaning in and of itself. Such methods helped to highlight the creativity and artistry of the art director, whose role, as earlier, was to coordinate, and even conceptualize, the layout and imagery. This totalizing strategy in effect made it possible for the art director to respond to critics who had contended that the art director was too concerned with the art of the images within individual advertisements and not enough with the persuasive power of the advertisement as a whole. From the perspective of art directors like Agha, Brodovich, and Coiner, the effect of the publicity could not be separated from its art, which now constituted the entire page or advertisement. So, too, the effectiveness of any individual advertisement was inseparable from the work of the art director (with the help of assistants) as an artist. Agha and Brodovich's integrative aesthetics tended to rely heavily on photography. Further consideration of their activities will thus be deferred to chapter 4. On these designers, see Remington and Hodik, *Nine Pioneers*, 8–53, 86–135, 151–69; Seebohm, *The Man Who Was Vogue*, 228–29, 254–57; Wild, "Europeans in America," 153–69; Paul Rand, *Thoughts on Design* (New York: Wittenborn, 1947), 1–2.

103. The agency paid the artist for the sketch, and, if the art directors approved it, commissioned a finished painting. On working procedures, see Edward W. Warwick, interview with Martina Norelli, 8 July 1985, AAA.

104. The importance of such institutional backing was underscored by the Useful Objects (1938), Good Design (1950–1955), and Modern Art in Your Life (1949) exhibitions at the Museum of Modern Art. Their curator linked art, graphic design, packaging, and print advertising, arguing that the same principles applied to all types of representation. See Ellen Lupton and J. Abbott Miller, "A Time Line of American Graphic Design, 1829–1989," in Walker Art Center, *Graphic Design in America*, 50–51; Robert Goldwater in collaboration with René d'Harnoncourt, *Modern Art in Your Life* (New York: Museum of Modern Art and Doubleday, 1953); Rand, *Thoughts on Design*, 1–2.

105. Ralph Steiner, *A Point of View* (Middletown: Wesleyan University Press, 1978), 22.

106. See, for example, K. Thomajan, "Introducing the Art Director," *Design* (March 1941): 19; Paul Gropman, "Why Artists Shouldn't Be Art Directors," *Advertising Agency* 45 (September 1952): 87, 164, 166.

107. Designer Paul Rand himself wrote: "That which makes for good *advertising* is one

thing, and that which makes for good *art* another; but that which makes for *advertising art* is a harmonious resolution of both, integrating as a whole the utilitarian and formal requirements of the problem." Rand, *Thoughts on Design,* 1. See also Will Burtin, "Interrelations," *Graphis* 4 (1948): 108–11. Paul Smith, "Win, Place, or Show," in Art Directors Club, *27th Annual of Advertising and Editorial Art* (New York: Pitman Publishing, 1948), unpaginated, discusses the diminished interest in "fine art" advertising; the breakdown of categories and contents of the Art Directors Club *33rd Annual of Advertising and Editorial Art and Design* (New York: Farrar, Strauss, and Young, 1954) demonstrates the rising influence of the graphic designer.

108. Rosser Reeves, *Reality in Advertising* (New York: Alfred A. Knopf, 1961); David Ogilvy, *Confessions of an Advertising Man* (New York: Atheneum, 1966). On the Ogilvy/Reeves rivalry, see Philip Gold, *Advertising, Politics, and American Culture: From Salesmanship to Therapy* (New York: Paragon House, 1987), 57–61.

109. Reeves, *Reality in Advertising,* 117–18.

110. Ibid., 122; Ogilvy, *Confessions of an Advertising Man,* 118.

111. Coiner evidently found this development sufficiently discouraging that he decided to take his retirement. Coiner interview, AAA.

chapter four

1. Recent historical discussions of the problematic nature of photographic realism include Rosalind Krauss, "Photography's Discursive Spaces: Landscape/View," *Art Journal* 42 (Winter 1982): 311–19; Richard Shiff, "Phototropism: (Figuring the Proper)," *Studies in the History of Art* 20 (1989): 161–80; Alan Trachtenberg, *Reading American Photographs: Images as History, Matthew Brady to Walter Evans* (New York: Hill and Wang, 1989), 12–20; John Szarkowski, *Photography Until Now* (New York: Museum of Modern Art, 1989), 35–64; Miles Orvell, *The Real Thing: Imitation and Authenticity in America, 1880–1940* (Chapel Hill: University of North Carolina Press, 1989), 198–211; and essays by Bernard Marbot, André Rouillé, Anne McCauley, and Marc Melon in Jean-Claude Lemagny and Andre Rouillé, eds., *A History of Photography: Social and Cultural Perspectives* (Cambridge: Cambridge University Press, 1987), 13–17, 23–27, 31–36, 44.

2. My use of the terms "social worlds" and "camera world" derives from Howard S. Becker, *Art Worlds* (Berkeley: University of California Press, 1982); Michal M. McCall and Howard S. Becker, "Introduction," and Samuel Gilmore, "Art Worlds: Developing the Interactionist Approach to Social Organization," in Howard S. Becker and Michal M. McCall, eds., *Symbolic Interaction and Cultural Studies* (Chicago: University of Chicago Press, 1991), 1–15, 148–78. This "production-of-culture" perspective is also discussed in Janet Wolff, *The Social Production of Art* (New York: New York University Press, 1984), 31–34, and Chandra Mukerji and Michael Schudson, eds., *Rethinking Popular Culture: Contemporary Perspectives in Cultural Studies* (Berkeley: University of California Press, 1991), 28–33. See also Elizabeth Anne McCauley's important *Industrial Madness: Commercial Photography in Paris, 1848–1871* (New Haven: Yale University Press, 1994), 3–7.

3. On Pirie MacDonald, known as the foremost photographer of men, see obituary, *New York Times*, 23 April 1941, 23, and Allan Harding, "The Story of a Famous Photographer," *American Magazine* 94 (October 1922): 37–39, 94–96.

4. On the varieties of amateurs, and amateurs versus professionals, see Sarah Greenough, "'Of Charming Glens, Graceful Glades, and Frowning Cliffs': The Economic Incentives, Social Inducements, and Aesthetic Issues of American Pictorial Photography, 1880–1902," in Martha A. Sandweiss, ed., *Photography in Nineteenth Century America* (Fort Worth: Amon Carter Museum, 1991), 260–81; Rune Hassner, "Amateur Photography," in Lemagny and Rouillé, *History of Photography*, 80; Szarkowski, *Photography Until Now*, 71, 76–92; Peter C. Bunnell, ed., "Introduction," *A Photographic Vision: Pictorial Photography, 1889–1923* (Salt Lake City: Peregrine Smith, 1980), 4–5.

5. Marketed beginning in 1888, Eastman's little box camera had revolutionized the field by simplifying the photographic process such that the average person could ostensibly become a photographer. "You push the button," read the company slogan, "we do the rest." The Kodak consisted of a small box camera with film. The enthusiast would shoot the roll of 100 pictures, send the entire camera back to the factory for processing and reloading, and begin again.

The pictorialists, "serious" amateurs who always did their own printing, found the Kodak craze and its followers a threat to their own status and cause: from their vantage point, the Kodakers reinforced photography's reputation as a mere mechanical procedure, democratizing and trivializing the image. The Kodak allowed anyone to photograph anything; hence it made a mockery of the pictorialists' craftsmanship, artistry, and discriminating taste. On the Kodak craze and snapshot enthusiasts, see Szarkowski, *Photography Until Now*, 144; Hassner, "Amateur Photography," 80; Sarah Greenough, "The Curious Contagion of the Camera," in Sarah Greenough et al., *The Art of Fixing a Shadow: One Hundred and Fifty Years of Photography* (Washington, D.C.: National Gallery of Art, 1989), 129–35; Greenough, "'Of Charming Glens,'" 260–78; Brian Coe and Paul Gates, *The Snapshot Photograph. The Rise of Popular Photography 1888–1939* (London: Ash and Grant, 1977), 8–29; C. Jane Gover, *The Positive Image: Women Photographers in Turn of the Century America* (Albany: State University of New York Press, 1988), 2, 4, 12–14; Barbara L. Michaels, *Gertrude Käsebier: The Photographer and Her Photographs* (New York: Harry N. Abrams, 1992), 20. On the pictorialists' efforts to distinguish themselves from other amateurs, see Ulrich Keller, "The Myth of Art Photography: A Sociological Analysis," *History of Photography* 8, no. 4 (October–December 1984): 249–50; Richard John Kent, "Alfred Stieglitz and the Maturation of American Culture" (Ph.D. dissertation, Johns Hopkins University, 1974), 234. For comparison with circumstances in France, see Molly Nesbit, *Atget's Seven Albums* (New Haven: Yale University Press, 1989), 80, 222, 223, n. 124.

6. Kent, "Alfred Stieglitz," 231–95; Marc Melon, "Beyond Reality: Art Photography," in Lemagny and Rouillé, *History of Photography*, 98; Greenough, "'Of Charming Glens,'" 275–78; Mary Panzer, *Philadelphia Naturalistic Photography, 1865–1908* (New Haven: Yale University Press, 1982), 16–22. On other pictorialist groups, see Gillian B. Greenhill Han-

num, "The Salon Club and the Popularization of Pictorial Photography," in Kathleen Collins, ed., *Shadow and Substance: Essays on the History of Photography* (Bloomfield Hills: Amorphous Press, 1990), 255–60.

7. Keller, "The Myth of Art Photography," 256.

8. Keller, "The Myth of Art Photography," 254; Szarkowski, Photography Until Now, 86. On professionalism, see Andrew Abbott, *The System of Professions: An Essay on the Division of Expert Labor* (Chicago: University of Chicago Press, 1988), 8–9, 102–13.

9. In 1908 *Abel's Photographic Weekly* estimated an active membership of 1,000 photographers against an approximate 14,000 active professional photographers. See "Does the P. A. of A. Live Up to Its Constitution?" *Abel's Photographic Weekly,* 10 October 1908, 411. On the absence of national organizational cohesion and the greater orientation toward local activity, see "The Professional Photographers' Society of New York," *Wilson's Photographic Journal* 44 (March 1907): 122–23; "The New York Convention and Its Lessons," *Wilson's Photographic Journal* 44 (May 1907): 193–94; "The Professional and the Amateur," *Abel's Photographic Weekly,* 16 January 1907, 71; "Does the P. A. of A. Live Up to Its Constitution?" *Abel's Photographic Weekly,* 10 October 1908, 417 and 21 November 1908, 459; "Editorial Comment, Why Photographers, Generally, Avoid the Conventions," *Abel's Photographic Weekly,* 22 August 1908, 355; "Suggestions for Increasing the Membership In and Adding to the General Usefulness of the PA of A," *Abel's Photographic Weekly,* 28 August 1918, 198–201.

10. According to Abel, the ethics of a profession demanded a certain standard of "outward behavior" to which photographers could not conform because of the need for self-promotion. He also observed that photographers lacked an enforceable code of ethics or standard of practice—a hallmark of professionalism. To make his point, Abel reprinted an article in the *British Journal of Photography:* "Our good friends among portrait photographers . . . are convinced that there is 'more in' portrait photography when it is regarded as a profession than when it is conducted on the common principle of buying and selling. . . . The question is—and apparently it is not definitely asked and answered by those who prescribe professional dignity as a panacea for the ills of the portrait business—can the so-called 'professional photographer's' business be profitably reconstituted on the lines of the professions proper, such as the dentist's, the doctor's, the lawyer's. There are photographers who are quite professional in their methods, who announce their habitation as formally as the brass plate of 'Messrs. Silk and Stuff, Attorneys,' who never resort to a solitary line of advertisement, and whose other procedure is in accordance with the canons of 'professional conduct.' But such men would never pay a quarter's rent if their work was not so distinctive that people . . . sought them out to commission them. . . . [A] photographer is a tradesman just as an author is a tradesman, and both get on in precise proportion as they produce a saleable article and take the best means to secure the best price for it." "Should the Photographer Pose as a Professional Man?" *Abel's Photographic Weekly,* 15 February 1908, 96; phrase "outward behavior" from "Photography Not a Profession, Editorial Comment," *Abel's Photographic Weekly,* 9 May 1908, 1. See also "Talks to One-Horse Photographers," *Abel's Photographic Weekly,* 25 January 1907, 71; Sidney Allan, "An Open Letter from Sidney Allan," *Wilson's Photographic Journal* 44 (June 1907): 243–45; "Business Method, Newspaper Adver-

tising," *Abel's Photographic Weekly,* 12 December 1908, 16–17; "The Time to Advertise—Is All the Time," *Abel's Photographic Weekly,* 20 November 1909, 197; "Etiquette among Professional Photographers," *Abel's Photographic Weekly,* 15 February 1908, 96, 104–5; "Photographers as Professional Men," *Abel's Photographic Weekly,* 29 February 1908, 25, 28; "In Passing By," *Abel's Photographic Weekly,* 1 May 1915, 412 and 20 November 1915, 484.

11. "Photographers as Professional Men," 25, 28; "National Academy of Photography," in "Official Report P. A. of A. Convention," *Abel's Photographic Weekly,* 16 July 1910, 18–21; "In Passing By," *Abel's Photographic Weekly,* 10 April 1915, 340–43 and 1 May 1915, 412.

12. "Talks to One-Horse Photographers," 77; "Business Method, Newspaper Advertising," 16–17; "The Time to Advertise—Is All the Time," 197; "Etiquette Among Professional Photographers," 104–5; "Photographers as Professional Men," 25, 28; "Photography Not a Profession," 1; "In Passing By," *Abel's Photographic Weekly,* 1 May 1915, 412 and 20 November 1915, 484.

13. Stieglitz sought to draw a line between a truly modern photographic art and the more popular style of art photography that emulated academic painting. Stieglitz's ideal corresponds to those characterized by critic Miles Orvell as expressive of the "culture of authenticity." The culture of authenticity, essentially modernism, esteemed directness, sincerity, immediacy, and originality as paths to truth. The approaches to photographic truth that Stieglitz opposed could be described as representative of Orvell's "culture of imitation," in which truth and meaning were rooted in a mere simulation of appearances and a confounding of nature and artifice. For Orvell, the cultures of imitation and authenticity were both contemporaneous outgrowths of commercial culture, with the culture of imitation embracing a consumption ethos, the culture of authenticity rejecting it. On the cultures of imitation and authenticity as related to photography, see Orvell, *The Real Thing,* 198–211.

Two of the most eminent members of the Photo-Secession, Clarence White and Gertrude Käsebier, worked commercially as studio portraitists and editorial photographers; their activities ultimately resulted in a break with Stieglitz. It was less their commercial work that caused the schism than Stieglitz's perception that they did not have the right attitude. See Alfred Stieglitz to Heinrich Kühn, 1 March 1909, Kühn folder, Stieglitz Archive, Beinecke Rare Book and Manuscript Library, Yale University (hereafter Stieglitz Archive); University Art Museum, California State University at Long Beach, *A Collective Vision: Clarence H. White and His Students* (Long Beach: University Art Museum, 1985), 13–14; Gover, *The Positive Image,* 71.

Richard John Kent has suggested that Stieglitz's convictions about the incompatibility of true art and commercial practice were a form of denial—an attempt to overcome his sense of ambivalence and inferiority about his failure to succeed in a respectable business career and to justify his own commitment to photography by endowing financially disinterested work with status. Kent, "Alfred Stieglitz," 196. See also Keller, "The Myth of Art Photography."

14. On class and status, see "Photographers as Professional Men," 25, 28; Keller, "Myth of Art Photography"; "Talks to One-Horse Photographers," 77; Allan, "An Open Letter from Sidney Allan," 243–45; "Replies to Sidney Allan's Open Letter," *Wilson's Photographic Journal*

44 (June 1907): 245–48. Cosmopolitan snobbery is conveyed in Stieglitz's characterization of Clarence White as a "small-towner." See Stieglitz to Heinrich Kühn, 25 August 1925, Kühn file, Stieglitz Archive. Perusal of *Abel's Photographic Weekly* between 1905 and 1920 indicates that a good proportion of the PA of A membership and leadership came from smaller towns and cities. As an example, see "Why Photographers, Generally, Avoid the Conventions," 315–16; "Official Report, PA of A Convention," *Abel's Photographic Weekly*, 16 July 1910 and 23 July 1919, 16–25, 32–39.

15. Important developments that improved the reproduction of images included the use of machine-driven presses, advances in the gelatin dry-plate process and the manufacture of papers and inks, and the emergence of an expert photo-finishing industry. Szarkowski, *Photography Until Now*, 184–89; Neil Harris, "Iconography and Intellectual History: The Half-Tone Effect," in *Cultural Excursions: Marketing Appetites and Cultural Tastes in Modern America* (Chicago: University of Chicago Press, 1990), 304–17; John William Tebbel, *The American Magazine: A Compact History* (New York: Hawthorne Books, 1969), 157, 165–202. Halftone reproductions had been used in weekly magazines since 1867 and since 1880 in newspapers. See Ulrich Keller, "Photojournalism around 1900: The Institutionalization of a Mass Medium," in Collins, ed., *Shadow and Substance*, 285.

16. Hassner, "Photography and the Press," in Lemagny and Rouillé, *History of Photography*, 77; "Showing the Real Thing," *Fame* 18 (January 1909): 12. My assessments of these images are based on an unscientific sampling of issues of *Ladies' Home Journal, Collier's, Vogue, Saturday Evening Post*, and *Woman's Home Companion* between 1898 and 1925.

The prevalence of reworked halftones can be seen in the tiny advertisements that lined the side columns of the *Ladies' Home Journal*. As Ralph Bogardus has argued, there was a clear-cut rise in the number of advertisements that used photographic elements as part of the image at the turn of the century. Based on his survey of original magazines and microfilm, Bogardus states that 9 percent of all ads in an average 1896 issue of the journal utilized photographs, and that this figure rose to 25 percent by 1898. These figures may be a bit high. As Bogardus notes, it is often difficult to tell when the images are truly photographic and when they just look so, especially on microfilm, which Bogardus used for part of his sample. My own assessment of some of the same images differs from Bogardus's. For example, it is not apparent that the Whitely Exerciser advertisement, *Ladies' Home Journal* 15 (December 1897): 43, is based on a photograph. See Ralph F. Bogardus, "Tea Wars: Advertising Photography and Ideology in the *Ladies' Home Journal*," *Prospects* 16 (1991): 297–321. Of those images that did appear to use photographs, most displayed a photographed person or object in isolation, with no illustrated background. These images were used to draw attention to the text and away from the clutter of competing advertisements (sometimes five or six in one vertical column). Images of this type persisted on into the second decade of the century. The initial rise in the use of tiny photographic elements in *Ladies' Home Journal* advertisements also predated the point when advertisers began to make a concerted effort to illustrate their images more attractively.

17. Earnest Elmo Calkins, "Is the Lens Ousting the Brush?" *Commercial Photographer* 6 (September 1931): 699.

18. "There is an old saying that the 'camera never lies,'" wrote the author of a 1903 article in *Photo-Era*. "It depicts people, places, and things as they are, and by so doing it tells a story that is sincere and convincing. . . . Many advertisers realize that this method of illustrating their announcements has advantages worth considering." A true-to-life photograph of an object could help people imagine what it might be like to own one. A truthful rendering of the object, enhanced through a knowledge of design, artistic lighting, and composition derived from illustration to create attraction and interest, could be a "valuable factor" in selling a product. "Photography in Advertising," *Photo-Era* 10 (February 1903): 73–74, 114–15. See also Harvey S. Lewis, "Commercial Photography, Lesson No. 16: Arranging Special Scenes and Advertising Groups," *Western Camera Notes* no. 5 (May 1905): 127–29; "Showing the Real Thing," 12.

19. Untitled note in *American Photography* 2, no. 4 (April 1908): 233; "Prize Contest for Professional Photographers," *American Photography*, 1, no. 1 (July 1907): 50. The contest was juried by portrait photographer Pirie MacDonald, one Colonel Marceau, and the advertising managers of *Saturday Evening Post* and *Century*, thus suggesting the support of both mass market and "class" publications.

Eastman Kodak continued to be a pioneer in efforts to promote photography in advertising. It established the Eastman School of Professional Photography in Rochester, New York, a move Abel observed was premised on the idea that "the better photographer you are and the better a businessman, the more money you will make for yourself and for the manufacturer of which the Eastman Kodak Company figures it will get its due share." "In Passing By," *Abel's Photographic Weekly*, 13 February 1915, 147. Kodak used large, well-reproduced, illustrative photographs in its ads during this time. One of its leading photographers, William Shewell Ellis (1876–1931), who produced many of the company's famous "Kodak Girl" advertisements before 1917, ran a successful commercial and advertising photography studio during the 1920s. Ellis illustrated ads for Corbin Hardware, Ivory Soap, Ireland Gloves, Milano Pipe, and Gorham Silver as well as for Kodak. Art Directors Club annuals for the years 1923 to 1929 illustrate examples of this work. See also biography compiled by Jeanne W. Verhulst in Robert Sobieszek, *The Art of Persuasion: A History of Advertising Photography* (New York: Harry N. Abrams, 1988), 194.

20. "Showing the Real Thing," 12; "Photography in Advertising," *Photo-Era* 10 (February 1903): 73.

21. Manson Gibson, "Commerce and the Camera," *Abel's Photographic Weekly*, 25 December 1915, 605. See also L. M. Maynard, "Photography in Advertising," *American Photography* 9 (November 1915): 626–28.

Photographs were used for illustrating fiction, but only on a limited basis. Lejaren à Hiller (born John Hiller, 1880–1969) was one of these photographic illustrators. Hiller started his career as a conventional illustrator. In the second decade of the twentieth century, however, he created some elaborately staged photographic illustrations for fiction for *Cosmopolitan Magazine*, often working them over with oil paint. Extrapolating from her study of Hiller, cultural historian Mary Panzer has suggested that at least some of "the dramatic tableaux with characters in scenic settings" rendered by other artists to illustrate fiction may also have been based on photographs that were "heavily retouched, recombined, and rephotographed." In the 1920s and 1930s, Hiller would adapt the same narrative devices and retouching techniques to advertising photography. Hence, according to Panzer, such photographic illustration represents one of the routes to advertising photography, a path that ran alongside that of photographic portraiture. Mary Panzer, in correspondence with the author, 28 August 1993; idem, unpublished paper delivered at the American Studies Association meeting, Baltimore, 1991; *Lejaren à Hiller: A Half Century of Photographic Illustration* (Rochester: Visual Studies Workshop, n.d.).

22. J. B. Schriever, *Complete Self Instructing Library of Practical Photography*, vol. 9, *Commercial, Press, Scientific Photography* (Scranton, Pa.: American School of Art and Photography, 1909), 8. For insights into corporate use of photographs of factory workers, see David Nye, *Image Worlds: Corporate Identities at General Electric, 1890–1930* (Cambridge, Mass.: MIT Press, 1985).

23. Maynard, "Photography in Advertising," 628; untitled note in *American Photography* 2 (April 1908): 233; Lewis, "Commercial Photography," 129; Gibson, "Commerce and the Camera," 605.

24. Edward Steichen, *A Life in Photography* (New York: Museum of Modern Art and Doubleday, 1963), unpaginated.

25. Steichen, *A Life in Photography.*

26. Morgan reportedly paid Steichen the unprecedented sum of $500 for his portrait. *Everybody's Magazine* matched that amount for reproduction rights for his 1907 portrait of President Theodore Roosevelt and his 1908 picture of cabinet member and presidential hopeful William Howard Taft. Steichen, *A Life in Photography.*

27. Steichen, *A Life in Photography.*

28. Käsebier exhibited at the turn of the century in such artistic venues as the Philadelphia Photographic Salon, sponsored by the Photographic Society of Philadelphia and the Pennsylvania Academy of Fine Arts. Käsebier's ongoing activities as an aggressive and successful professional photographer ultimately became a point of contention between her and Stieglitz. During 1908 and 1909, she "increasingly cast her lot" with the professionals; in 1912 she resigned from the Photo-Secession. See Michaels, *Gertrude Käsebier*, 28, 45–60, 118–28 (quote), 138; Gover, *The Positive Image*, 40–41, 94–95.

There were also nineteenth-century precedents for such efforts to elevate the social and professional standing of the photographer of celebrities and affluent clients by promoting the superior artistry of their portraits. See, for example, Barbara McCandless, "The Portrait Studio and the Celebrity: Promoting the Art," in Sandweiss, *Photography in Nineteenth Century America*, 48–75.

29. Frank Crowninshield, the worldly editor of *Vanity Fair*, was intrigued by the aesthetics of photography, and included the work of pictorialists and other artistic photographers in the editorial sections of the magazine. For Nast, pictorialist photography had an additional attraction: it was more informative and legible than painting or drawing, yet at the same time could signify art, hence also connoting "high class," distinction from the ordinary. As Nast biographer Caroline Seebohm has observed, photography did not come fully into its

own as an advertising medium in the pages of *Vogue* until the 1930s, under art editor Mehemed Fehmy Agha. Nevertheless, Nast's patronage of artistic photography in his publications helped significantly not only to acquaint Americans with European artistic modernism, but also to accelerate the "acceptance of the [photographic] medium," providing photographers with a "wider audience" and "social acceptability." See Caroline Seebohm, *The Man Who Was Vogue: The Life and Times of Condé Nast* (New York: Alfred Knopf, 1982), 30–39, 70–82, 184–85, 193–203, 223–45, 254–58; R. Roger Remington and Barbara J. Hodik, *Nine Pioneers in Modern Graphic Design* (Cambridge, Mass.: Cambridge University Press, 1989), 8–28.

30. Increasingly dissatisfied with his "lucrative but stultifying portrait business," Steichen had in 1906 begun to travel back and forth to France to drum up more satisfying portrait commissions and to line up avant-garde paintings and sculptures for exhibitions at the 291 Gallery. He became a regular in the social circle of Gertrude and Leo Stein, and in 1911 began to concentrate more on painting. Steichen, *A Life in Photography.*

31. On the differences between Steichen and Stieglitz, see Lowe, *Stieglitz,* 186–89; Stieglitz to Heinrich Kühn, 30 September 1930, Kühn folder, Stieglitz Archive.

32. Edouard Steichen to Alfred Stieglitz, 27 August 1914, Steichen folder, Stieglitz Archive.

33. Steichen, *A Life in Photography.* According to Stieglitz biographer Sue Davidson Lowe, Stieglitz was sympathetic to Germany because he saw its actions as a battle for "moral independence in a degenerate world." After 1917 he evidently changed his mind and considered seeking war work. Lowe, *Stieglitz,* 191–92.

34. Steichen, *A Life in Photography;* Christopher Phillips, *Steichen at War* (New York: Harry N. Abrams, 1985), 11, 14.

35. See Patricia Johnston, "Romance, Class, Strategy and Style: Edward Steichen's Photographs for Jergens Lotion," *Exposure* 26, no. 4 (1989): 11.

36. Seebohm, *The Man Who Was Vogue,* 201; Steichen, *A Life in Photography.* On Steichen's work for J. Walter Thompson, see Johnston, "Romance, Class, Strategy, and Style," 4–22.

37. On Steichen's celebrity testimonial advertisements, see Patricia Johnston, "The Personal Touch: Edward Steichen's Testimonial Advertisements," *Views: The Journal of Photography in New England* 13 (Spring 1992): 11–16. On the Jergens Lotion advertisements, see Johnston, "Romance, Class, Strategy, and Style."

38. G[ordon] A[ymar], "Steichen—An Artist," J. Walter Thompson Company, *News Letter,* no. 187, 1 September 1927, 374–75, 26/6, RG 11, Publications, Company Newsletters, JWTA.

39. Minutes of Representatives Meeting, 31 January 1928, 2, 1/4, RG 2, U.S.A. and International Offices: New York, Minutes of Representatives Meetings, 1928, January 5–April 18, JWTA; "Artist or Photographer?" *Printer's Ink,* 26 November 1931, 64.

40. Minutes of Representatives Meeting, 31 January 1928, 2, JWTA. "Why worry?" cited in Bonnie Yochelson, "Clarence H. White Reconsidered: An Alternative to the Modernist Aesthetic of Straight Photography," *Studies in Visual Communication* 9 (Fall 1983): 46.

41. Minutes of Representatives Meeting, 31 January 1928, JWTA.

42. Ibid., 2; "Artist or Photographer?" 64.

43. Minutes of Representatives Meeting, 31 January 1928, 7, JWTA.

44. Ibid., 3.

45. Ibid., 3, 6.

46. J. Walter Thompson Company, *News Letter,* 15 February 1928; see also Minutes of Representatives Meeting, 31 January 1928, 3–6, JWTA.

47. Minutes of Representatives Meeting, 31 January 1928, 5, JWTA.

48. Ibid., 10.

49. Lillian Sabine, "Edward J. Steichen," *Commercial Photographer* 7 (May 1932): 307.

50. Johnston, "Romance, Class, Strategy, and Style," 17.

51. Sabine, "Edward J. Steichen," 312; Minutes of Representatives Meeting, 31 January 1928, 5, 6, 11, JWTA.

52. Roland Marchand, *Advertising the American Dream: Making Way for Modernity 1920–1940* (Berkeley: University of California Press, 1985), 16–18.

53. White's activities in this vein have been discussed in Yochelson's important article "Clarence H. White Reconsidered," 25–44.

54. On White's early years, see Peter C. Bunnell, *Clarence H. White: The Reverence for Beauty* (Athens: Ohio University Art Gallery, 1986). For more on White, see Maynard Pressley White Jr., "Clarence H. White, A Personal Portrait" (Ph.D. dissertation, University of Delaware, 1975).

55. Bunnell, *Clarence H. White,* 24; White Jr., "Clarence H. White," 79–80, 166–67, 172, 183; Maynard White Jr., "Clarence H. White: 'Artist in Life and Photography,'" in Delaware Art Museum, *Symbolism of Light: The Photographs of Clarence H. White* (Newark: University of Delaware Art Museum, 1977), 18–20; Clarence H. White to Alfred Stieglitz, 14 June 1907, 1 September 1907, 8 August 1908, 15 May 1912, White folder (1902–1923); Stieglitz to Heinrich Kühn, 14 October 1912, 25 August 1925, Kühn folder, Stieglitz Archive.

56. Susan Doniger, "The Clarence H. White Schools of Photography," in University Art Museum, *A Collective Vision,* 20–21.

57. On the school, see Yochelson, "Clarence H. White Reconsidered," 28. On these photographers, see Vicki Goldberg, *Margaret Bourke-White: A Biography* (New York: Harper and Row, 1986); Jonathan Silverman, *For All the World to See: The Life of Margaret Bourke-White* (New York: Viking Press, 1983), 8, 11, 56–57; Elaine Dines, *Paul Outerbridge: A Singular Aesthetic* (Santa Barbara: Arabesque Books, 1981); Graham Howe and G. Ray Hawkins, eds., *Paul Outerbridge Jr.: Photographs* (New York: Rizzoli, 1980), 7–21; University Art Museum, *A Collective Vision,* 36–37, 52–53 (Anton Breuhl and Ralph Steiner); Charles Abel, "Commercial Prices," *Commercial Photographer* 4 (May 1929): 381. On Arthur Wesley Dow, see Frederick C. Moffatt, *Arthur Wesley Dow (1857–1922)* (Washington, D.C.: National Collection of Fine Arts, 1977), 104–11.

58. Michele A. Barnack and Terry Joanis, with Lucinda Barnes, "The Clarence H. White Aesthetic in Context," Ralph Steiner and Donna Sandrock, "An Interview with Ralph Steiner," and Terry Joanis, "Anton Bruehl," all in University Art Museum, *A Collective Vision,*

23–28, 36–37; Ralph Steiner, *A Point of View* (Middletown: Wesleyan University Press, 1978), 4–6; Goldberg, *Margaret Bourke-White*, 25–26, 67.

59. Pictorialist Photographers of America, *Yearbook* (New York: Pictorialist Photographers of America, 1917); Yochelson, "Clarence H. White Reconsidered," 27.

60. Pictorialist Photographers of America, *Yearbook*, 12; Yochelson, "Clarence H. White Reconsidered," 33.

61. Yochelson, "Clarence H. White Reconsidered," 33, 41; Susan Doniger, "The Clarence H. White Schools of Photography"; Barnack, Joanis, and Barnes, "The Clarence H. White Aesthetic in Context," 19, 23–26.

62. Lillian Sabine, "Ralph Steiner, New York City," *Commercial Photographer* 8 (March 1933): 167; Steiner, *A Point of View*, 3; "The Marketplace," *American Photography* 28 (September 1934): 586; Goldberg, *Margaret Bourke-White*, 59–63.

Steiner and Bourke-White were both college graduates—Steiner from Dartmouth and Bourke-White from Cornell. The Australian-born Bruehl was trained as an electrical engineer.

63. Walter Livingston Larned, "The Camera Goes in for Extraordinary New Devices," *Printer's Ink*, 18 August 1927, 158, 161–62. See also Walter Livingston Larned, "The Camera Plays a Few Tricks," *Commercial Photographer* 4 (August 1929): 546–47; idem, "Simple Art Ideas That Make Ordinary Photographs Unusual," *Printer's Ink*, 16 May 1929, 88–93; Christopher Phillips, "The United States," in Lemagny and Rouillé, *History of Photography*, 158–60; Yochelson, "Clarence H. White Reconsidered," 33–34; John Pultz and Catherine B. Scallen, *Cubism and American Photography, 1910–1930* (Williamstown: Sterling and Francine Clark Art Institute, 1981); Marchand, *Advertising the American Dream*, 149; J. Walter Thompson Company, *News Letter*, 15 July 1927, 326–27, JWTA; Thomas F. Walsh, "Giving the Still Life the Modern Touch," *Commercial Photographer* 4 (January 1929): 171–77; Richard Guy Wilson, "Machine Aesthetics," and "Selling the Machine Age," in Brooklyn Museum, *The Machine Age in America* (New York: Harry N. Abrams, 1986), 45–51, 65–68.

For examples, see Steiner's *Typewriter Keys* for Oxford Paper, illustrated in Art Directors Club, *Eighth Annual of Advertising Art* (New York: Art Directors Club, 1929), and Bruehl's Weber and Heilbroner advertisements in *The New Yorker* for 1929 (30 March, 40; 20 April, 44; 27 April, 43; 15 June, 44; 29 June, 41; 5 October, 43; 2 November, 43; 9 November, 51).

64. Lejaren à Hiller was a leading photographer for Underwood and Underwood Commercial, a "colossus" in the field of commercial photography. In the mid-1920s he photographed for clients such as Western Electric, Hot Water Installation, Sunmaid Raisins, Fatima Cigarettes, Royal Typewriter, Oshkosh Trunks, and Davis and Geck Pharmaceuticals.

Little is known about Horace W. Scandlin, who had a successful commercial practice, then fell into obscurity. In a 1933 interview, he claimed to have had neither art training nor formal education. Scandlin entered commercial photography after World War I and worked for a time for Wanamaker and Company in New York. He traveled much abroad, but clearly was doing advertising work in the early 1920s. Art Directors Club annuals of the mid-1920s show several Scandlin images in each exhibition. He himself submitted many of them, indicating that he was making a concerted effort to promote his business. Scandlin shot advertising photographs for Hampton Shops, New York Shipbuilding Corporation, Weber Piano, Colgate Toothpaste, and Bien Jolie Corsets.

On Hiller as advertising photographer, see Arnold Sorvari, "Operating Theater," *Camera Arts* 2 (December 1982): 23–25; Mary Panzer, note 21 above. On Scandlin, see Lillian Sabine, "Horace Scandlin, New York City," *Commercial Photographer* 8 (January 1933): 98–102. See Art Directors Club annuals, 1923–1929, for images by these photographers. Capsule biographies of Hiller, Ellis, and other advertising photographers can be found in Sobieszek, *The Art of Persuasion*, 194–99. References to Underwood and Underwood as a "colossus" in Berti Lon, "How Do You Advertise for Business?" *Commercial Photographer* 1 (December 1925): 21.

65. The various ways in which this photograph plays with the contradictions between sincerity and artifice, art and advertising, are especially evident when the image is interpreted in relation to the copy. The photograph represents a group of artists, presumably students, in the act of painting from the live model. The advertisement thus seems to be about art. It addresses issues of truth inherent to prevailing notions of art; at the same time, however, it calls them into question.

For starters, the photograph is a masterfully staged representation, composed through a careful arrangement of figures, shape and space, and light and shade. The centerpoint of the composition is a void of light. The eye is drawn up to the canvas through the legs of the easel, a visual path encouraged by the parallel lines defined by the arms of the standing painter. His right arm points directly to the model in the foreground. The line established by the shadow cast across her right leg leads the eye back to the grouping of painters on the right, and around again. The composition is unified through this harmonious oval. Through such devices, the image itself is an expression of the artifice of photography, its unique ability to simulate life itself. The photograph, in other words, is a representation of art. Indeed, it depicts the artists drawing and painting from life, in the process of trying to capture life, much like the photographer.

The image allies itself with art in other ways. It draws upon gendered themes of male artist and female model found in the works of well-known modern masters such as Matisse and Picasso, a relationship also parodied by illustrators in pictures and theatrical revues. Connecting with familiar associations and contrasts commonly linked with art, it plays upon the heroic contrast of nature (traditionally signified by feminity and nudity) and sincerity, symbolizing culture (the masculine artist), but also the contrast between inspiration (the model as muse) and truth, connoted by the *act* of painting. This correlation of art and sincerity was highlighted by the copy: "When you ask of an artist, 'Is his work sincere?' you need not go much further." The answer, implied the copy, if taken at face value, was "of course!" But "of course" was not the answer. For the image was an advertisement, and this factor added a necessary twist that was borne out in the copy.

Bruehl's image has affinities with painted images of artist and model. Bruehl's nude is objectified by and for the male gaze; like Art, the advertisement's effectiveness hinged on the gendered relations of power inherent to painting. Indeed, its effectiveness as an advertisement for men's clothing also depended upon such renderings of the female body as the manifestation and visualization of desire. Yet in contrast to most painted nudes, the face and sex of the model in Bruehl's image are obscured. Unlike "real" art, nudity was impossible in this context. The advertising photograph could not offend; hence the circuit of meaning imbued in the production of art necessarily remained incomplete.

This photograph could not feign to be art. Its necessary failure of nerve was addressed head on in the copy, whose disingenuous honesty was so devastatingly ironic (highlighting the disparity between the purported sincerity of the artist and the insincerity of the advertising presentation) as to render the statement entirely sincere. From this perspective, the "tailoring of a suit" became a metaphor for the practice of advertising artists—represented photographically by their alter egos, the painters.

The bottom line, of course, was that the Weber and Heilbroner image was an image of persuasion. But it was also an artfully crafted exploration of the meanings of art and its relation to advertising, and an image of professional self-scrutiny. Like the painters, the advertising artists represented the model and thereby controlled the images presented to the consumer. They might not always mean what they said, but like the tailors, they strove to have pride in their work and to do it well. It might be impossible to produce good work with tongue in cheek, but that was exactly what Bruehl and the copywriters were seeking to do. The results might not be "an art," ("we do not say"), but if carried out with pride, produced laudable results, even marked by "beauty of execution."

See Joanis, "Anton Bruehl," 36–37; Robert S. Mann, "Anton Bruehl Sees Advance in Photography," *Commercial Photographer* 7 (April 1937): 263, 265.

66. Orvell, *The Real Thing*, 144–45; Jackson Lears, "Uneasy Courtship: Modern Art and Modern Advertising," *American Quarterly* 39 (Spring 1987): 135–36. See also Michael Schudson's discussion of "capitalist realism" in *Advertising: The Uneasy Persuasion* (New York: Basic Books, 1984), 204–13.

67. William Clive Duncan, "Photographing the Appetite Appeal," *Commercial Photographer* 4 (April 1929): 329–33; "Looking Around in New York Commercial Studios," *Commercial Photographer* 11 (October 1935): 23–26.

68. The phrase "truth of surface" and subsequent quotation are from Phillips, "The United States," 158–60, quote, 160. See also Marchand, *Advertising the American Dream*, 149; Orvell, *The Real Thing*, 144–45; Larned, "The Camera Plays a Few Tricks," 546–47; J. Walter Thompson Company, *News Letter*, 15 July 1927, 326–27, JWTA.

69. "Now for Business," *Abel's Photographic Weekly*, 31 October 1908, 435; "In Passing By," *Abel's Photographic Weekly*, 20 November 1915, 484; Alva C. Townsend, "The Business End of Photography," *Wilson's Photographic Journal* 44 (July 1907): 315–18; "Words from the Watchtower," *American Photography* 2 (January 1908): 34; "Photographers as Professional Men," 25, 28; "Why Photographers, Generally, Avoid the Conventions," 355; "The Professional and His Relations to the Amateur," *Abel's Photographic Weekly*, 16 January 1909, 71.

70. On the history of the commercial section, see Charles Abel, "Looking Backward," *Commercial Photographer* 21 (October 1945): 11–14; Charles Howson, "A Message to all Commercial Photographers," *Commercial Photographer* 4 (December 1928): 113–44. See also Leon G. Rose, *The Commercial Photographer* (Philadelphia: Frank V. Chambers, 1920).

71. "The Camera in Advertising," *Abel's Photographic Weekly*, 13 May 1922, 526–29; "Two Hundred Dollars for a Picture!" *Commercial Photographer* 1 (October 1925): 18–19; J. C. Abel, "Telling It in Photography," *Commercial Photographer* 1 (July 1926): 341–47.

72. Arthur Hammond, "Hints for Beginners: Making Money By Photography," *American Photography* 14 (May 1920): 274.

73. Frederick C. Davis, "Selling Your Photographs," *Photo-Era* 47 (May 1922): 254.

74. W. J. Turnbull, "Making Money with the Camera: Opportunities That Knock at Our Door," *American Photography* 14 (November 1920): 618–20. See Hammond, "Hints for Beginners," 268–74; Davis, "Selling Your Photographs," *Photo-Era* 47 (May 1922): 254, (June 1922): 313–15.

75. Hammond, "Hints for Beginners," 274.

76. "In Passing By," *Abel's Photographic Weekly*, 18 February 1922, 171; Gilbert H. Montague, "Portraits that are Permissible in Advertising," *Abel's Photographic Weekly*, 3 April 1920, 326, 328–30; C. W. Millis, "Commercial Photography," *American Photography* 14 (July 1920): 388–95; William Shewell Ellis, "Photographs for Advertisements," *Abel's Photographic Weekly*, 22 April 1922, 426.

77. Montague, "Portraits that Are Permissible in Advertising," 326–30; Frank H. Williams, "Boosting Commercial Business by Showing How Photographs Will Get Publicity for Users," *Abel's Photographic Weekly*, 7 August 1920, 133–35; J. E. Bullard, "Photographs and Selling," *Abel's Photographic Weekly*, 11 February 1922, 140–42; Ellis, "Photographs for Advertisements," 426; "In Passing By," *Abel's Photographic Weekly*, 1 April 1922, 331 and 4 July 1925, 3; "National Biscuit Company Offers $250.00 Cash For Best Still Life Photograph of Uneeda Biscuit," *Abel's Photographic Weekly*, 1 April 1922, 337–38.

78. "Some Kind Words from the British Journal of Photography," *Commercial Photographer* 1 (December 1925): 98; "The Big City Fetish," and "Hats—And Photographs That Sell Them," *Commercial Photographer* 1 (November 1925): 42–47; "In Passing By," *Abel's Photographic Weekly*, 16 June 1928, 619.

79. Begun in 1925, the class was held at Winona Lake, Indiana. In 1928, for fifty dollars apiece, forty aspiring photographers could spend two weeks in July working on their techniques and attending lectures "by prominent photographers and artists" who spoke on negatives, composition, color plates, lenses, photochemistry, advertising and publicity, and "the Business of being a photographer." The school's speakers included William A. Towles of Washington, D. C., Charles Kanarian of New York City, H. L. Corey, Eva Hale, Charles Aylett, and representatives from the Cramer Dry Plate Company, Agfa-Ansco Company, Eastman Kodak, Millis Advertising Company, and Defender Photo Supply Company. Although a provincial and small-time operation, the Winona School helped to enhance the association's reputation and visibility. "PA of A Summer School, Association News," *Abel's Photographic Weekly*, 16 May 1925, 492; "Winona School," *Abel's Photographic Weekly*, 23 June 1928, 644; "Winona School," *Abel's Photographic Weekly*, 16 June 1928, 620; "A Real Commercial School This Year," *Commercial Photographer* 4 (February 1929): 216.

80. Abel, "Looking Backward," 13; Lon, "How Do You Advertise for Business?" 15–21; Ralph Young, "Photographs: Creations of Effective Advertising," *Commercial Photographer* 3

(May 1928): 363–67; George W. Harris, "Business Looks to the Camera," *Commercial Photographer* 3 (April 1928): 310–14; "Sparkling," advertisement in *Printer's Ink*, 16 May 1929, 137; Ralph Young, "Proving to Business That the Photographer is a Businessman," *Commercial Photographer* 5 (January 1930): 194–201; Ellis, "Photographs for Advertisements," 426; "Folders—One of the Helps Offered to Subscribers of the National Advertising Campaign," *Commercial Photographer* 4 (July 1929): 495–500.

81. George Winemiller, "Photographers as Advertising Artists," *Abel's Photographic Weekly*, 7 February 1925, 135–36. See also "Two Hundred Dollars for a Picture!" 18–19; Abel, "Telling It in Photography," 344–47; Gordon Aymar, "The Third Exhibition," in Art Directors Club, *Third Annual of Advertising Art* (New York: Art Directors Club, 1924), unpaginated. J. Walter Thompson art director Aymar, who insisted that "the place of the photograph in advertising is unquestioned," had of course a vested interest in asserting the new authority of the photograph. Three years earlier his agency had just made a significant financial commitment to photography by hiring Steichen.

82. For examples of this earlier downplay of art, see "Talks to One-Horse Photographers," 77; "An Open Letter from Sidney Allan," 243–45; "Business Methods, Newspaper Advertising," 16–17; "Why Photographers, Generally, Avoid the Conventions," 355.

83. "The Camera in Advertising," 526. For other references to the camera's art, see William Shewell Ellis, "The Advertising Photograph," *Commercial Photographer* 4 (November 1928): 61; Walsh, "Giving the Still Life a Modern Touch," 172; Roberta K. Bushnell, "The Making of Advertising Photographs," *Abel's Photographic Weekly*, 30 May 1925, 536.

Paradoxically, one practice that later commentators associated with the earlier photograph's mechanicalism was retouching. The new trend toward a greater individualism was typified for some by unretouched images. Steichen insisted on no retouching. Not surprisingly, J. Walter Thompson art director Gordon Aymar wrote that the key to successful photographs was good composition and the "proper selection of material, photographed in a direct and honest way." Sincerity of intent and compositional arrangement of materials made for more compelling, memorable pictures. Aymar, "The Third Exhibition;" see also Sabine, "Horace Scandlin," 100.

84. "The Camera in Advertising," 526.

85. "The Camera in Advertising," 526. Similar points would be echoed a decade later in Calkins, "Is the Lens Ousting the Brush?" 699; Sabine, "Horace Scandlin," 100.

86. "The Camera In Advertising," 526–28. The same writer likened the photographer's studio to a motion picture studio. It is no coincidence that photographers were inspired to create fictional tableaux at the time when sound entered motion pictures. Advertising photographs became frozen imitations of silent picture film stills. Representatives of the J. Walter Thompson advertising agency even noted that they wanted a photographer with motion picture experience. J. Walter Thompson Company, *News Letter*, no. 184, 15 July 1927, 326, JWTA; "honest" used by Aymar in "The Third Exhibition."

See also Bushnell, "The Making of Advertising Photographs," 536–38; Ralph Young, "The Illustrative Photograph in Advertising," *Commercial Photographer* 3 (September 1928): 548–51; Ellis, "Photographs for Advertisements," 426, 560–61; "The Illustrative Field," *Com-*

mercial Photographer 4 (January 1929): 163–64; Lejaren à Hiller, "Illustrating Magazine Articles and Advertising By the Use of the Camera," *Commercial Photographer* 3 (October 1926): 17–20, 26; Lou Ingwerson, "Yes the Lens Lends a Hand!" J. Walter Thompson Company, *News Letter,* no. 186, 15 August 1927, 357, JWTA; Minutes of Meeting of Representatives, 31 January 1928, 4, JWTA.

87. Temple Scott, "The Use of Photography in Advertising," *Abel's Photographic Weekly,* 18 April 1925, 20. See also Bushnell, "The Making of Advertising Photographs," 536; George W. Harris, "Business Looks to the Camera," 310–15; and debates on photography in J. Walter Thompson Company, *News Letter,* 15 August 1927, JWTA. See Shiff, "Phototropism," 164; Christopher Phillips, "The United States," 160.

88. Scott, "The Use of Photography in Advertising," 18.

89. Ibid., 18–19.

90. Ibid., 19. This argument would be constantly reiterated. See "Artist or Photographer?" 64; Young, "The Illustrative Photograph in Advertising," 548; Bushnell, "The Making of Advertising Photographs," 35; Walsh, "Giving the Still Life the Modern Touch," 171–77; R. F. Field, "Photography in Advertising—Why Not More?" *Commercial Photographer* 6 (November 1930): 84–88; "Put Sanity Into Photographic Illustrations," *Commercial Photographer* 8 (February 1933): 128–30; Geoffry Gilbert, "Advertising Photography," *American Photography* 26 (October 1932): 588–91.

91. *Printer's Ink,* 16 May 1929, 137. Also see Marchand, *Advertising the American Dream,* 150.

92. Aymar, "$500 for a Photograph," *Commercial Photographer* 7 (February 1932): 182–89; J. Walter Thompson Company, *News Letter,* no. 184, 15 July 1928; Lon, "How Do You Advertise for Business?" 20, noted the challenge of trying to drum up business for advertising photography in small towns.

93. Young, "Proving to Business that the Photographer is a Businessman," 195. See also Young, "The Illustrative Photograph in Advertising," 548–51; Abel, "Commercial Prices," 381–89; Jerome B. Gray, "Photographers—Creators of Effective Advertising," *Commercial Photographer* 3 (May 1928): 363–69; Frank Williams, "Cooperating with the Commercial Artist," *Commercial Photographer* 4 (September 1929): 617; Aymar, "$500 for a Photograph," 182–89; Paul Newman, "General Advertising Illustration," *Commercial Photographer* 6 (February 1931): 275–79; Field, "Photography in Advertising—Why Not More?" 84–93; David Charles, "The Future of Photography in Advertising," *Commercial Photographer* 4 (March 1929): 282–84; Ingwerson, "Yes, the Lens Lends a Hand!" 358.

94. "First Reports of the Nationwide Survey," *Abel's Photographic Weekly,* 6 September 1930, 282.

95. The two publications also began to utilize asymmetrical juxtapositions of word and image, sans serif typeface, extensive use of white space, and, after April 1932, full-color photography. On Agha's and Brodovich's use of photography, see Remington and Hodik, *Nine Pioneers,* 8–53, 86–135, 151–69; Seebohm, *The Man Who Was Vogue,* 228–29, 254–57.

96. "Commercial Artist vs. Photographic Illustrator," *Commercial Photographer* 10 (June 1935): 275–76. Reference to "artiness" in William Engle, "Steichen the Photographer," *Com-*

mercial Photographer 5 (September 1930): 618–20. See also Calkins, "Is the Lens Ousting the Brush?" 699; Sabine, "Horace Scandlin," 100; Gilbert, "Advertising Photography," *American Photography* 26 (October 1932): 588–91; "Put Sanity Into Photographic Illustrations," 128–30; Seebohm, *The Man Who Was Vogue,* 238–45; Marchand, *Advertising the American Dream,* 149, 300–303. On photomontage and modernism, see also Stanley A. Brady, "'Photomontage'—A New Art From Europe," *Commercial Photographer* 8 (February 1933): 124–30; Sally Stein, "'Good Fences Make Good Neighbors': American Resistance to Photomontage Between the Wars," in Matthew Teitelbaum, ed., *Montage and Modern Life, 1919–1942* (Cambridge, Mass.: MIT Press, 1992), 129–89.

97. Phillips, "The United States," 161–62.

98. Edward C. Buxbaum, "Modernism in Photography," *American Photography* 26 (November 1932): 620; Charles Abel, "Commercial Prices," 381–89; Marchand, *Advertising the American Dream,* 149; Phillips, "The United States," 161–62; Young, "The Illustrative Photograph in Advertising," 548; "The Section in Buffalo," *Commercial Photographer* 4 (July 1929): 495; Gilbert, "Advertising Photography," 588–91; Arthur Hammond, "Questions and Answers," *American Photography* 28 (July 1934): 449–50; "Commercial Artist vs. Photographic Illustrator," 275–76.

Much-touted photographers like Margaret Bourke-White, still in a position to claim the best of both worlds, referred to the photographer as a "camera artist," and to photography as a direct and honest medium. See Minutes of Meeting of the Creative Staff, 1 February 1933, 5/10 RG 5, U.S.A. and International Offices: New York, JWTA.

99. Abel, "Commercial Prices," 381–89; Marchand, *Advertising the American Dream,* 149. On the complexities of producing such images, see Minutes of Meeting of the Creative Staff, 15 February 1933, JWTA.

100. Both photographers and illustrators were paid per image, however, not per hour. An article on Steichen claimed that he used to spend weeks on a single photograph, but that he usually would work on one per day, with a sitting taking about ten minutes. Lejaren à Hiller took 125 photographs for the J. Walter Thompson agency in four days. Maxfield Parrish received $5,000 for one painting for an advertising calendar for General Electric in 1921. In 1928 Steinway and Sons paid Rockwell Kent $3,500 for a painting, ordered in mid-March and due on 1 June. Medium made a difference, however. At the same time Kent received only $400 each for pen and ink drawings for the jewelers Marcus and Company. He usually was given anywhere from one week to a month to complete these assignments. Minutes of the Representatives' Meeting, 31 January 1928, 5; J. Walter Thompson Company, *News Letter,* no. 184, 15 July 1927, JWTA; Sabine, "Edward J. Steichen," 308, 312; Maxfield Parrish to M. Rusling Wood, 16 February 1921, box 3, file 55, MPP; N. W. Ayer assignment sheets to Rockwell Kent, no. 6192, 18 June 1927 and no. 736, 12 April 1928, box 5, file 18, RK, AAA.

101. See Minutes of Staff Meeting, Research Department, J. Walter Thompson Company, March 1931, 3/5, RG 2, JWTA.

102. The Eight Minute Egg, "Who Will Emerge Winner in the Photographer-Artist Imbroglio?" *Commercial Photographer* 8 (November 1932): 43–46; Edwin Birnbaum, "Modern-

ism in Photography," *American Photography* 26 (November 1932): 611–12; "The Commercial Section in Buffalo," 495; Young, "The Illustrative Photograph in Advertising," 548; "Commercial Artist vs. Photographic Illustrator," 275; Gilbert, "Advertising Photography," 588. Gallup poll cited in Marchand, *Advertising the American Dream,* 149.

A count of images in an average issue of the *Ladies' Home Journal* for 1928 showed 61 percent of all ads using illustration and 36 percent using photography. Most large advertisements used illustration. In contrast, by 1935 the averages had been reversed, with 61 percent of all advertisements using photographs and 29 percent illustration. Five percent used cartoons. Fashion photography followed a similar development. Condé Nast spent $101,000 on art and $40,000 on photography in 1930, $73,000 on art and $60,000 on photography in 1933; by the end of the decade his editorial use of photography far surpassed that of illustration: Seebohm, *The Man Who Was Vogue,* 187. During the World War II period, as we shall see in chapter 6, the percentage of advertising photographs in the mass-market magazines declined slightly, then rose again immediately after the war.

103. Szarkowski, *Photography Until Now,* 219–28; Seebohm, *The Man Who Was Vogue,* 241–45; Colin Osman and Jean-Claude Lemagny, "Photography Sure of Itself (1930–1950)," in Lemagny and Rouillé, *History of Photography,* 166–68; Marianne Fulton, *Eyes of Time: Photojournalism in America* (New York: New York Graphic Society, 1988); Seebohm, *The Man Who Was Vogue,* 240–45.

Conversely, because photography was so closely associated with realism, photographs did not so readily replace illustration in retail apparel advertisements, where the objective was to create a fantasy about the merchandise.

104. Discussion of the widespread publication of FSA photography is found in Maren Stange, *Symbols of Ideal Life: Social Documentary Photography in America 1890–1950* (New York: Cambridge University Press, 1989), 108–11, and idem, "'The Record Itself': Farm Security Administration Photography and the Transformation of Rural Life," in Pete Daniel, Merry A. Foresta, Maren Stange, and Sally Stein, *Official Images: New Deal Photography* (Washington, D.C.: Smithsonian Institution Press, 1987), 1; Terry Smith, *Making the Modern: Industry, Art, and Design in America* (Chicago: University of Chicago Press, 1993), 340–50.

105. Historian David Nye has argued that General Electric used similar "visual vocabularies" decades prior to the government projects. On this, and on the relationship between documentary photography and advertising and public relations photography, see David Nye, *Electrifying America: Social Meanings of a New Technology* (Cambridge, Mass.: MIT Press, 1990), 328–37; William Stott, *Documentary Expression and Thirties America* (New York: Oxford University Press, 1973), 5–18, 129–30. Stott cites advertisements for Lucky Strike and General Electric (*Life,* 18 September 1939 and 19 February 1940) as examples of "documentary expression." On the problematic nature of documentary photography, see Stange, *Symbols of Ideal Life,* 89–148; idem, "'The Record Itself,'" 1–5; Sally Stein, "Figures of the Future: Photography of the National Youth Administration," in *Official Images,* 92–107. See also Trachtenberg, *Reading American Photographs,* 231–85; Phillips, "The United States," 158, 160–62; James C. Curtis, "Dorothea Lange, Migrant Mother, and the Culture of the Depres-

sion," *Winterthur Portfolio* 21 (Spring 1986): 1–20; John Tagg, *The Burden of Representation: Essays on Photographies and Histories* (Amherst: University of Massachusetts Press, 1988), 153–83; F. Jack Hurley, *Portrait of a Decade: Roy Stryker and the Development of Documentary Photography in the Thirties* (Baton Rouge: Louisiana State University Press, 1972); Steven W. Plattner, *Roy Stryker, U.S.A. 1943–1950: The Standard Oil (New Jersey) Photography Project* (Austin: University of Texas Press, 1983); Ulrich Keller, *The Highway as Habitat: A Roy Stryker Documentation* (Santa Barbara: University Art Museum, 1986); Margaret Olin, "'It is Not Going to be Easy to Look into Their Eyes': Privilege of Perception in *Let Us Now Praise Famous Men*," *Art History* 14 (March 1991): 92–112; Smith, *Making the Modern*, 283–340.

106. Paul Rosenfeld, "Carl Sandburg and Photography," *New Republic*, 22 January 1930, 251–53; Paul Strand, "Steichen and Commercial Photography," *New Republic*, 19 February 1930, 21; Walker Evans, "The Reappearance of Photography," *Hound and Horn* 6 (October-December 1931): 125–28.

107. Sabine, "Edward J. Steichen," 307–12; "'Photography as I Know It.' A Talk by Edward Steichen at the Chicago Convention of the Photographers' Association of America," *Abel's Photographic Weekly*, 7 January 1928, 7–9; Engle, "Steichen the Photographer," 618–20.

108. Phillips, "The United States," and idem, "The Judgement Seat of Photography," *October* 22 (Fall 1982): 29–38, 40, 45, 53–63.

109. "Arty" and "drivel" from William Engle, "Steichen the Photographer," 618–20; "hoot in hell" quoted in Phillips, "The Judgement Seat of Photography," 41.

110. Phillips, "The Judgement Seat of Photography," 45; Stange, *Symbols of Ideal Life*, 133–40.

111. By the mid-1940s, articles in the two magazines tended to be short, technical "how-to" discussions focusing on specific kinds of materials and objects; appreciative descriptions of small commercial studios; or "what's wrong with this picture" critiques of images—all pitched to small-time operators in a no-nonsense style.

On professionalism and expertise, see "All Past Records Broken By Chicago Convention," *Commercial Photographer* 12 (September 1937): 469–71, 497; "Our Own New Deal," *Professional Photographer*, 5 February 1934, 77; "Wisconsin Association Insures Photographers Their Due Share of CWA Expenditures," *Professional Photographer*, 20 February 1934, 106.

Articles like "How to Light Commercial Photographs" and "What's Wrong with This Photograph" (*Commercial Photographer* 1944–1945), and "Catalog Photographs of Trailer Interiors," (*Commercial Photographer* 1948–1949) were typical. See also Charles Tunnell, "Start Going After That 'Post-War Business' Now," *Commercial Photographer* 20 (March 1945): 183–88.

112. Charles Abel, "And Now—We Go Places!" *Professional Photographer* 77 (March 1950): 155. These circumstances may be attributed in part to the fact that photographers still faced competition. Mass-market magazines and major national advertisers still tended to hire the leading names, such as Bruehl, Margaret Bourke-White, Nickolas Muray, Grancel Fitz, Louise Dahl-Wolfe, and Irving Penn. To break in and survive, a photographer had to

be versatile. Thus although the question of whether advertising photography was art had become essentially inconsequential, there remained certain de facto distinctions between center and periphery; those whose work art directors found *aesthetically* compelling were the ones who got the jobs. As such, art directors and advertising executives were central in deciding, if not which photography was art, then which artistic aspects of photography were appropriately commercial.

chapter five

1. Daniel Pope, *The Making of Modern Advertising* (New York: Basic Books, 1983), 108–9; T. J. Jackson Lears, "Some Versions of Fantasy: Toward a Cultural History of American Advertising, 1880–1930," *Prospects* 9 (1984:) 355–57. See also Charles Goodrum and Helen Dalrymple, *Advertising in America: The First Two Hundred Years* (New York: Harry N. Abrams, 1990), 24–33.

2. Earnest Elmo Calkins, *"Louder Please!" The Autobiography of a Deaf Man* (Boston: Atlantic Monthly Press, 1924), 120–21, 132–35, 147, 155–56, 164–65, 191, 208–9; Stephen Fox, *The Mirror Makers: A History of American Advertising and Its Creators* (New York: William Morrow, 1984), 41.

3. Stephen Fox, *Mirror Makers,* 40–43.

4. Calkins, *"Louder Please!"* 165.

5. Ibid., 166–67; Stephen Fox, *Mirror Makers,* 42–43.

6. Stephen Fox, *Mirror Makers,* 44.

7. On trademarks and trade images, see Susan Strasser, *Satisfaction Guaranteed: The Story of Mass Marketing in America* (New York: Pantheon Books, 1989); on Leyendecker and Cluett-Peabody, see Michael Schau, *J. C. Leyendecker* (New York: Watson-Guptill, 1974), 27–30, 47; James Morske, "And it all began with one woman," in Russell Sage College Gallery, *The Arrow Man: Collar City Chic* (Troy: Russell Sage Art Gallery, 1987), 8. Information on Leyendecker and Calkins was also provided by James Morske of Latham, New York, author of a forthcoming Leyendecker biography; see also "Earnest Elmo Calkins," *National Cyclopedia of American Biography* (New York: James T. White, 1960), I: 327.

8. Schau, *J. C. Leyendecker,* 18–20.

9. Hopkins favored a textually oriented, explanatory "reason-why" approach to salesmanship to create consumer desire among average Americans. "Fine art work, like fine language," wrote Hopkins, "merely makes buyers wary." Claude C. Hopkins, *My Life in Advertising* (New York: Harper and Brothers, 1927), 151–57, 183 (quote), 185. See also Stephen Fox, *Mirror Makers,* 49–55; T. J. Jackson Lears, "From Salvation to Self Realization: Advertising and the Therapeutic Roots of the Consumer Culture, 1880–1930," in Richard Wightman Fox and T. J. Jackson Lears, eds., *The Culture of Consumption: Critical Essays in American History: 1880–1925* (New York: Pantheon Books, 1983), 18; Earnest Elmo Calkins, "Exhibition of Advertising Art," *International Studio* 34 (May 1908): cix; idem, *Business the Civilizer* (New York: Little, Brown and Company, 1928), 21–36; idem, "Beauty in the Machine Age," *Printer's Ink,* 25 September 1930, 72–83; idem, "Commercialism in Art," *American Magazine of Art* 15 (February 1924): 92; Walter B. Geohagen to Earnest Elmo Calkins, 28 April 1952,

press release, 22 November 1960, Earnest Elmo Calkins/Walter B. Geohagen Papers, Seymour Library, Archives and Manuscript Collection, Knox College, Galesburg, Illinois (hereafter Calkins/Geohagen Papers).

10. Other noteworthy advertisements included those for Fisk Tire (with illustrations by Maxfield Parrish and N. C. Wyeth); Crane Paper and Wesson Oil (illustrated by René Clarke); and Fine Art Coffee (with photographs by Lejaren à Hiller and Anton Bruehl).

11. Calkins, "Exhibition of Advertising Art," cix; idem, "Commercialism in Art," 92; idem, *Business the Civilizer,* 21–36; idem, "Beauty in the Machine Age," 72–83; Walter B. Geohagen to Earnest Elmo Calkins, 28 April 1952, press release, 22 November 1960, Calkins/Geohagen Papers.

12. Earnest Elmo Calkins, *The Advertising Man* (New York: Charles Scribner's Sons, 1922), 26–29, 34–35, 193, 200. Calkins's arguments represented what historian Jackson Lears characterized as a shift "from a Protestant ethos of salvation through self denial toward a therapeutic ethos of self realization in this world." From this perspective, consumables were the means to achieving a satisfying, meaningful life. Lears, "From Salvation to Self Realization," 9.

13. Calkins, "Beauty the New Business Tool," 153. Discussions of advertising as a force of uplift are found in Calkins, *The Advertising Man,* 26–29, 34–35, 193, 200.

14. Calkins, "Beauty the New Business Tool," 153; idem, "Beauty in the Machine Age," 78; idem, *Business the Civilizer,* 22.

15. Calkins, *Business the Civilizer,* 21; idem, "Beauty the New Business Tool," 145–54; idem, "Commercialism in Art," 92. Indeed, Calkins specifically sought out those individuals whom he considered to be good artists, as opposed to advertising art specialists. "The actual art work is produced by artists who have no special training in advertising and need none," he wrote in 1929. "It is required only that they should be exceedingly proficient as artists in whatever medium they work." Earnest Elmo Calkins to F. K. W. Drury, 11 January 1929, box 8, file 85, Calkins/Geohagen Papers.

16. Stuart Ewen, *All Consuming Images: The Politics of Style in Contemporary Culture* (New York: Basic Books, 1988), 45.

17. Lears, "From Salvation to Self Realization," 22.

18. Calkins, "Beauty the New Business Tool," 151, 153, 154–56.

19. Calkins, "Exhibition of Advertising Art," cxi.

20. Calkins, *The Advertising Man,* 17, 26.

21. In 1895 a group of painters and cultural advocates incorporated the National Society of Mural Painters to establish standards of professional practice, hold exhibitions, and publicize the purpose and value of mural painting. Among the founders were John La Farge, Frederic Crowninshield, Charles M. Shean, Otto Heinigke, Frederick Lamb, Francis Jones, Will Low, Maitland Armstrong, George Maynard, and Charles Lamb. "Certificate of Incorporation of The Mural Painters," National Society of Mural Painters Papers, reel D250, fr. 1186–97. For more on murals, see Pauline King, *American Mural Painting: A Study of the Important Decorations by Distinguished Artists in the United States* (Boston: Noyes, Platt, and Company, 1902), 15, 72–74; "Mural Painting: An Art for the People and a Record of the

Nation's Development," *The Craftsman* 10 (April 1906): 54–56; Charles M. Shean, "Mural Painting from the American Point of View," *The Craftsman* 7 (October 1904): 18–27; Irene Sargent, "Comment upon Mr. Shean's 'Mural Painting,'" *The Craftsman* 7 (October 1904): 28–34; William Walton, "Mural Painting in This Country since 1898," *Scribner's* 40 (November 1906), 637–40; "Art at Home and Abroad," *New York Times*, 29 May 1910, sec. 6, 15; Richard Murray, Mural Database, National Museum of American Art (in progress); Education Building Guide, *A Guide to the Education Building of the State of New York* (Albany: n.p., n.d.); The University of the State of New York, *Mural Paintings in the Rotunda of the State Education Building, Albany, New York* (Albany: The University of the State of New York, The State Education Department, 1958). See also Minutes of the Municipal Art Society (hereafter Minutes), 14 April 1904, 30 April 1906, 1 May 1906, reel 15, frs. 289–92, 451, 463–64, 490–94, MAS, AAA; Municipal Art Society, *Adopt-A-Mural* (New York: Municipal Art Society and the Art Commission of the City of New York, 1991), 8–9, 20–21, 28–29; William A. Coffin, "Decorations in the Congressional Library," *Century Magazine* 53 (March 1897): 694–711; Harper Small, *The Library of Congress: Its Architecture and Decoration* (New York: W. W. Norton, 1982; first published 1896); Sarah J. Moore, "In Search of an American Iconography: Critical Reaction to the Murals at the Library of Congress," *Winterthur Portfolio* 25 (Winter 1990): 230–39; Janet Marstine, "Working History: Images of Labor and Industry in American Mural Painting, 1893–1903" (Ph.D. dissertation, University of Pittsburgh, 1993); H. Wayne Morgan, *Kenyon Cox 1856–1919: A Life in American Art* (Kent, Ohio: Kent State University Press, 1994), 132–78. On the American Renaissance and the ideals of its artists, see, for example, Richard Guy Wilson, "Statements of Identity," "Cultural Conditions," "Expressions of Identity," and "Presence of the Past," and Richard Murray, "Painting and Sculpture," in Brooklyn Museum, *American Renaissance 1876–1917* (New York: Pantheon, 1979), 11–32, 34–41, 178–81; Michele H. Bogart, *Public Sculpture and the Civic Ideal in New York City, 1890–1930* (Chicago: University of Chicago Press, 1989), 40, 57–58. See also Jeanne Weimann, *The Fair Women* (Chicago: Academy Chicago, 1981), 194, 214, 313–19.

22. "Mural Painting: An Art for the People," 60; Shean, "Mural Painting from the American Point of View," 19–26. On service and the professions, see Lawrence Veysey, "The Plural Organized Worlds of the Humanities," in Alexandra Oleson and John Voss, eds., *The Organization of Knowledge in Modern America* (Baltimore: Johns Hopkins University Press, 1979), 58–59; Andrew Abbott, *The System of Professions: An Essay on The Division of Expert Labor* (Chicago: University of Chicago Press, 1988), 59–61.

23. Shean, "Mural Painting From the American Point of View," 18; "Mural Painting: An Art for the People," 60. See also Sargent, "Comment upon Mr. Shean's 'Mural Painting,'" 29; Edwin Howland Blashfield, *Mural Painting in America* (New York: Charles Scribner's Sons, 1913), 79, 82–85, 93, 98; idem, "A Word for Municipal Art," *Municipal Affairs* 3 (September-December 1899): 582–83.

24. "Mural art," or "mural decoration," as it was often called, relied on several methods of communication to reach these viewers. The primary means of signification was through color and composition. Indeed, for muralists, the word "decoration" generally meant more than just "embellishment." Derived from contemporary European theory and practice, the

idea of "decoration" connoted a unified composition of line, form, and color that harmonized with its architectural surroundings and reinforced and enhanced the meanings of the images. Such images had to contribute to the significance of the totality. "Decorative art must be architectonic and help to build up the architectural effect," stated Edwin Blashfield. "All good art implies selection, but good decorative art implies that selection which is peculiarly limited by the architectural character of the entire scheme which the painter is supposed to enhance by his contribution." The whole had to be greater than the sum of its parts. Yet those parts, from the standpoint of their creators, had to be significant in their own right, even as they contributed to a larger end. Thus iconography operated as a second key mode of signification. In general, mural painters' narrative subjects, with historical figures or allegorical personification, derived from antiquity or the Renaissance. Some artists depicted classically garbed allegorical figures modified to convey up-to-date messages. Others viewed the historical, the classical, and the allegorical as perfectly reconcilable, and used a combination of all three. Murals such as Henry Siddons Mowbray's *Transmission of the Law* for the New York State Supreme Court, Appellate Division Courthouse (entrance hall, north wall) were updated versions of what many regarded as a transcendent, universal, classical tradition that formed the essential basis of American culture. On the link between the classical tradition and late-nineteenth-century American culture, see Richard Guy Wilson, "Presence of the Past," and Murray, "Painting and Sculpture," in *American Renaissance*, 39–40; 156–70; Blashfield, "A Word for Municipal Art," 588–89. See also King, *American Mural Painting*, 4–5.

The idea of mural decoration was also linked to the artists' efforts to acquire greater control over artistic work, in part through ostensibly shattering artistic hierarchies by transforming all objects into works of "decorative art." This tendency, linked to English Pre-Raphaelitism and the Aesthetic movement as well as to the French academics, is discussed in chapter 1. See Doreen Bolger Burke, "Painters and Sculptors in a Decorative Age," in Metropolitan Museum of Art, *In Pursuit of Beauty: Americans and the Aesthetic Movement* (New York: Metropolitan Museum of Art and Rizzoli, 1987), 295–339; Marie Jeannine Acquilino, "The Decorating Campaigns at the Salon du Champ-de-Mars and the Salon des Champs-Elysées in the 1890s," *Art Journal* 48, no. 1 (Spring 1989): 78–84.

25. Kathleen A. Pyne, "Edwin Howland Blashfield," in Detroit Institute of Arts, *The Quest for Unity: American Art Between World's Fairs 1876–1893* (Detroit: Detroit Institute of Arts, 1983), 87.

26. "Edwin Blashfield, Noted Artist, Dies," *New York Times*, 13 October 1936, clipping in National Society of Mural Painters Papers, reel D250, fr. 1149, AAA; Doreen Bolger Burke, *American Paintings in the Metropolitan Museum of Art*, 3 vols. (New York: Metropolitan Museum of Art, 1980), 3: 68; Henry Hope Reed, "Edwin Howland Blashfield," *Dictionary of American Biography* (New York: Charles Scribner's Sons, 1981), suppl. 2: 42.

27. "Edwin Blashfield, Noted Artist, Dies."

28. Blashfield, *Mural Painting in America*, 126.

29. Ibid., 3.

30. Ibid., 24–30; Blashfield, address, 26 April 1910, reel D250, fr. 1168, AAA.

31. Blashfield, *Mural Painting in America,* 30–32. See also idem, "A Word for Municipal Art," 582–83, 585–86.

32. Exhibit 319A, 10 March 1908, Art Commission of the City of New York (hereafter ACNY); Contract, Edwin H. Blashfield and the Trustees of the City College of New York, 24 March 1906, box 3, Misc. file, Edwin Howland Blashfield Papers, New-York Historical Society (hereafter NYHS); William Walton, "Mr. Blashfield's Mural Painting in the College of the City of New York," *Scribner's* 44 (July 1908), 125–26; Leonard N. Amicco, *The Mural Decorations of Edwin Howland Blashfield* (Williamstown: Sterling and Francine Clark Institute, 1978), 32.

33. Exhibit 319 A, ACNY; Walton, "Mr. Blashfield's Mural Painting," 127.

34. Exhibit 319 A, ACNY.

35. Information on the predominantly Jewish composition of the student body at City College can be found in Willis Rudy, *The College of the City of New York, A History* (New York: City College Press, 1949), 292.

36. Blashfield referred to the "indifference" of the public's "attitude" in *Mural Painting in America,* 21. For other displays of this ambivalence, see 7–8, 20, 81–82, 98, 140. Blashfield's charitable didactic rhetoric glossed over an urgent concern for immigrant socialization, and intimated that such socializing methods and goals might in fact not be effective. "I say again that we must be modern, and we must be American," he exclaimed. Artists had to "learn to treat decoratively the marking events of our history, past or contemporaneous, of our puritans and Dutch, our Revolutionary heroes, our argonauts of '49, our pioneers and colonizers and soldiers of the Civil War, our inventors and organizers, our men in the streets and in the fields of today" (*Mural Painting in America,* 198–99).

Who was that "we" to be? In an earlier statement referring to artists and patrons, "we" meant "Americans, French, Italians, men of occidental race and inheritors of Greek tradition," (Blashfield, "A Word for Municipal Art," 590). In references to a public or audience for mural art, Blashfield broadened his definition somewhat. Judging from his statements, his audience included the upper middle classes. "Clients" included businessmen and building commissioners, patrons and therefore publics (81–82). Blashfield's conception of public also permitted some ethnic diversity and allowed select groups of assimilatable immigrants (Irish, Swedes, Italians, and Germans) who could rightly and reasonably claim "our" Puritan and Dutch history as part of their own. These immigrants had a will and a capacity to learn the lessons of the images. "The artist is teaching the lesson of intellectual development; teaching it with brush and chisel to the child who has not learned to read and the peasant who is too old to learn," Blashfield wrote. "It is a common thing to say: "How intelligent the French workman is; how he understands pictures!" But a great deal of this quickness comes from the fact that he has been learning from them all his life. And if this is good for the uneducated Frenchman, it is good, too, for the uneducated Irishman, German, Swede, Italian, who may stroll into some new city hall in our own country. This is the strongest appeal which can be made for public and municipal art, that it is a public and municipal educator." (*Mural Painting in America,* 7–8).

37. Lewis Sayre Burchard to Edwin Howland Blashfield, 4 December 1907 and 7 December 1907, box 4, Misc. file, Blashfield Papers, NYHS.

38. Burchard to Blashfield, 4 December 1907, Blashfield Papers, NYHS.

39. *College Mercury* 29 (1908): 155, Dedication of Building Files (1908), City College of New York Archives (hereafter CCNY).

40. William Couper to Blashfield, 10 March 1908, Misc. file, Blashfield Papers, NYHS.

41. Eliza Couper to Blashfield, 11 March 1908, Blashfield Papers, NYHS.

42. See, for example, Charles Planick to Blashfield, 31 January 1915, Blashfield Papers, NYHS. References to *The Graduate* are found in an address by Edward M. Shepard of 11 February 1908, cited in *City College of New York Quarterly* 4 (1908): 9–10; and "Sons of the City," a Bacchalaureate address by John Finley, reprinted in *City College of New York Quarterly* 5 (1909), reprint, CCNY.

For an analogous problem in architecture, see William B. Rhoads, "The Colonial Revival and the Americanization of Immigrants," in Alan Axelrod, ed., *The Colonial Revival in America* (New York: W. W. Norton: 1985), 340–61.

43. See Minutes, 22 December 1913, reel 16, frs. 536–37, MAS, AAA.

44. Minutes, 21 October 1913, reel 16, fr. 505, MAS, AAA.

45. Earnest Elmo Calkins, "Artist into Advertising Man," in Elizabeth McCausland, ed., *Work for Artists: What? Where? How?* (New York: American Artists Group, 1947), 17.

46. Earnest Elmo Calkins to Robert Grier Cooke, 7 December 1917, reel 16, fr. 1023, MAS, AAA. Calkins and Holden had the Fisk Tire account.

47. Calkins to Cooke, 7 December 1917, reel 16, frs. 1022–25, MAS, AAA.

48. Blashfield's Scammon Lectures are a good indication of his influence. See, for example, Blashfield, *Mural Painting in America,* 82–85.

49. Quotation from undated manuscript autobiography written by Walter Pach, Walter Pach 1903 file, Walter Pach 1903 box, CCNY; Milton Brown, "Walt Kuhn's Armory Show," *Archives of American Art Journal* 27 (1987): 9; William Agee, "Walter Pach: An Introduction," and Nancy Malloy, "Selections from the Walter Pach Papers," in "Discovering Modernism: Selections from the Walter Pach Papers," pamphlet, AAA, 1991.

50. Brown, "Walt Kuhn's Armory Show," 4–9.

51. Its early members included Gutzon Borglum, Arthur B. Davies, Leon Dabo, William Glackens, Kuhn, Ernest Lawson, Jonas Lie, George B. Luks, MacRae, Myers, Taylor, James Earle Fraser, and J. Alden Weir. Alliances of the more cautious, tradition-minded affiliates may have clashed with those who had nothing to lose by challenging the status quo. Henry Fitch Taylor memo, 2 January 1912, memo, 14 December 1911, reel D72, fr. 80, Walt Kuhn Papers, AAA; Milton Brown, *The Story of the Armory Show* (New York: Abbeville Press, 1988), 5, 48–49, 52–55. See also Walt Kuhn, "The Story of the Armory Show," *Art News Annual* 37 (1939): 63–64, 168–73.

The idea that an organization could help to cultivate and improve the taste of the country dated back to the nineteenth century. The notion of leading public taste assumed a newer, more activist stance that was consistent with the growing corporate concern for controlling information and shaping public opinion, whose implications will be discussed below.

52. Henry Fitch Taylor, statement, 14 December 1911, reel D72, fr. 80, Kuhn Papers, AAA.

53. Brown, *Story of the Armory Show*, 50–55.

54. Ibid., 77–98, 131–33.

55. Quoted in Brown, *Story of the Armory Show*, 82; see also 56–57, 61, 80; Walt Kuhn to Roland Knoedler, 1 February 1913, reel D72, fr. 779, Kuhn Papers, AAA.

Indeed, as historian Kathleen D. McCarthy has observed, the support of women was central to the enterprise, although they received little credit for their contributions. See Kathleen D. McCarthy, *Women's Culture: American Philanthropy and Art, 1830–1930* (Chicago: University of Chicago Press, 1991), 184–88.

56. The press agent was an established, if somewhat suspect, presence on the urban scene at this time, when press agentry was distinguished from public relations. In the second decade of the twentieth century, the phrase "public relations" still had civic connotations, and was not yet in wide circulation. Corporate presidents like Theodore Vail of American Telephone and Telegraph used the term "public relations" to refer to the company's responsibility to inform the community about its responsibilities, actions, and contributions. It has subsequently been defined by historian Richard Tedlow as, among other things, "the controlling of news about an individual or organization by planned and organized effort through informing and cultivating the press and through encouraging the corporation itself to alter its policies in accord with perceived public desires." Historian Eric Goldman contended in 1946 that the early press agent "operated on the principle of the public be fooled." "Ordinarily," he cited one anonymous press agent as saying, "the business of the press agent is not the decimation of truth, but the avoidance of its inopportune discovery." By the early 1920s, the new publicity men, "counsels on public relations," had shifted the emphasis to "the public be informed." Former press agent Edward Bernays (often cited as the father of public relations) drew a comparable distinction between press agent and counsel on public relations. "From a one-way street of information and persuasion from client to public, it became a two-way street with the element of adjustment added to the other two elements."

See Richard Tedlow, *Keeping the Corporate Image: Public Relations and Business, 1900–1950* (Greenwich: JAI Press, 1979), xviii, 18, 12–13, 34, 50; Eric Goldman, *Two Way Street: The Emergence of the Public Relations Counsel* (Boston: Bellman Publishing Company, 1948), 1–12; Edward Bernays, *Biography of an Idea: Memoirs of a Public Relations Counsel* (New York: Simon and Schuster, 1965), 53–62, 287.

57. "Beginning the first of January, I am going to organize a new society," Kuhn wrote his wife. "The plans are still in embryo state but clear enough in my mind to spell positive success. . . . As soon as I have it thoroughly planned we are going to give it to all the papers and they'll jump on it." Three days later he stated, "We may not be able to have a show this year [1911] but . . . I feel absolutely certain that the thing can be done and just think of the publicity!" Walt Kuhn to Vera Kuhn, 12 December 1911 and 15 December 1911, in Brown, "Walt Kuhn's Armory Show," 5; Kuhn, "Story of the Armory Show," 169.

58. Brown, *Story of the Armory Show,* 92–93.

59. Sarah Burns, "Old Maverick to Old Master: Whistler in the Public Eye," *American Art Journal* 22, no. 1 (1990): 228–47. See also idem, "The Price of Beauty: Art, Commerce, and the Nineteenth Century American Studio Interior," in David C. Miller, ed., *American Iconology: New Approaches to Nineteenth Century Art and Literature* (New Haven: Yale University Press, 1993), 209–38.

60. See Elizabeth Milroy, "Introduction," and "Modernist Ritual and the Politics of Display," in Elizabeth Milroy, *Painters of a New Century: The Eight and American Art* (Milwaukee: Milwaukee Art Museum, 1991), 17–18, 44–51.

61. Brown, *Story of the Armory Show,* 92–93.

62. Walt Kuhn to Edward Goewy, 31 January 1913, reel D72, fr. 774, Kuhn Papers, AAA (italics added). For other examples of publicity, see reel D72, frs. 752–854, Kuhn Papers; Brown, *Story of the Armory Show,* 90–93; Kuhn, "Story of the Armory Show," 169.

63. On "American methods" and their internationalization, see Victoria de Grazia, "The Arts of Purchase: How American Publicity Subverted the European Poster, 1920–1940," in Barbara Kruger and Phil Mariani, eds., *Remaking History: DIA Foundation Discussions in Contemporary Art no. 4* (Seattle: Bay Press, 1978), 222–25. See also Daniel Pope, "French Advertising Men and America's 'Promised Land,'" *Historical Reflections* 5 (Summer 1978): 117–39.

64. Unintelligible [Swenson?] to Kuhn, 28 December 1912, reel D72, fr. 253, Kuhn Papers, AAA.

65. Brown, *Story of the Armory Show,* 223.

66. George H. Roeder Jr., *Forum of Uncertainty: Confrontations with Modern Painting in Twentieth-Century American Thought* (Ann Arbor: UMI Press, 1980), 71.

67. Brown, *Story of the Armory Show,* 133; "The Armory Show: A Selection of Primary Documents," *Archives of American Art Journal* 27 (1987): 12–33; Kuhn, "Story of the Armory Show," 172.

68. Roeder, *Forum of Uncertainty,* 8–16, 19.

69. Brown, *Story of the Armory Show,* 136; Roeder, *Forum of Uncertainty,* 32–33, 64–65.

70. Brown, *Story of the Armory Show,* 223–33.

71. See, for example, Milton Brown, *American Painting from the Armory Show to the Depression* (Princeton: Princeton University Press, 1955), 55, 57–59.

72. Walter Pach, *Ananais, Or the False Artist* (New York: Harper and Brothers, 1928), 34–37.

73. Ibid., 41.

74. Ibid., 44.

75. Ibid., 44–45.

76. Ibid., 42–43.

77. On these two paintings, see Burke, *American Paintings in the Metropolitan Museum of Art,* 3: 313–14.

78. Pach, *Ananais,* 124.

79. "[I]f the better kind of home still retains the tradition of having pictures, and an

effort is made to place before the family a finer thing than it gets from the advertisements, no such loving care presides over the decoration of public buildings. There are large sums of money to expend for these, and so they are a very favored matter of attention for Ananais." Pach, *Ananais,* 42.

80. Ibid., 43.

81. Although neither Pach nor his family was especially religious, any Jewish intellectual involved in the predominantly elite Anglo-American culture of the period would have been conscious of his ethnicity. Indeed, there is evidence to suggest that Pach worked hard to avoid being stereotyped as a Jew by men like Walt Kuhn. In his correspondence, Kuhn on several occasions remarked on Jewish colleagues (like Jo Davidson) acting too "jewy." Pach, he remarked, was "easier to handle." Even so, he claimed, "they all have their ax to grind." Pach's own efforts to assimilate may have made him all the more conscious of the denials on view in *The Graduate.*

Information on Pach's background was provided to the author in a telephone conversation with Nancy Malloy, Archives of American Art, 25 January 1991. On Kuhn's anti-Semitism, see Brown, "Walt Kuhn's Armory Show," 9. Significantly, Kuhn and Blashfield, but not Pach, are listed in the *Dictionary of American Biography* and the *National Cyclopedia of American Biography.*

82. William C. Agee, "Walter Pach and Modernism: A Sampler from New York, Paris, and Mexico City," *Archives of American Art Journal* 28 (1988): 2–10.

83. Pach, *Ananais,* 38

84. Pach himself acknowledged his stronger reputation as a critic in an unpublished autobiographical manuscript, presently in the Walter Pach 1903 file, Walter Pach box, CCNY. See also biographical notes to finder's aid, Walter Pach Papers, AAA. "Drearily static" in Edward Alden Jewell, "New Pach Fresco on Public View," *New York Times,* 21 May 1935, 17; "disappointing," "halting if not niggly" quoted from untitled newspaper clipping, 26 May 1935, Walter Pach clipping file, Walter Pach box, CCNY. The mural is illustrated (no text) in "Mural for City College Given by the Class of 1903," *New York Times,* 5 May 1935, sec. 2, 2.

85. "The Modern Point of View," he wrote, "Means overthrow of childhood's romantic ideals. Means the end of imitation and an epoch of fearless experimentation." Stuart Davis Notebooks, 1920–1922, entries of 20 November 1921, 63, reel 3842, Stuart Davis Papers, AAA (hereafter cited as Davis Notebooks).

86. Entries of 29 May 1921, 39, and May 1921 (undated), 35, Davis Notebooks, AAA.

In embracing commercial culture in this fashion, Davis's interests were congruent with those of such painters and writers as Charles Demuth, Joseph Stella, Robert Coady, Malcolm Cowley, Matthew Josephson, Harold A. Loeb, and Gilbert Seldes, all of whom, as Wanda Corn has shown, "promoted the new vernacular 'arts' of advertising and jazz as indigenous American products" and embraced the ideal of an American art inspired by the "culture of materialism." Corn has characterized this group as the "new vulgarians." One camp of the New York avant-garde, the "new vulgarians" were embroiled in debates with a second camp, described by Corn as "the soil spirit school" (represented by Alfred Stieglitz, Waldo Frank, and Paul Rosenfeld), which spurned the vulgarian stance in favor of a purer and more unmediated vision. Hence Davis's concerns were part of a larger disputation within the avant-garde over the nature of, and proper inspiration for, an authentically American art. See Wanda M. Corn, *In the American Grain: The Billboard Poetics of Charles Demuth* (Poughkeepsie: Vassar College Art Gallery, 1991), 22–27.

87. Barbara Zabel, "Stuart Davis's Appropriation of Advertising," *American Art* 5 (Fall 1991): 57–67.

88. This discussion is entirely indebted to Zabel, "Stuart Davis's Appropriation of Advertising."

89. Entry of April 1921, 28; see also May 1920, 7; 28 May 1922, 113; November 1921, 51; 28 October 1922, 174, Davis Notebooks, AAA. On Davis's background and experiences as an illustrator, see Elise K. Kenney and Earl Davis, "Stuart Davis," in Rebecca Zurier, *Art for the Masses: A Radical Magazine and Its Graphics* (Philadelphia: Temple University Press, 1988), 177.

90. Entry of November 1921, 51, 55–56, Davis Notebooks, AAA.

91. Entry of 29 May 1921, 39, Davis Notebooks, AAA.

92. Entry of November 1921, 51, Davis Notebooks, AAA; Kenney and Davis, "Stuart Davis," 177. As M. Sue Kendall has observed, however, corporations were not beyond appropriating Davis's art for public relations purposes. In May 1951 the American Tobacco Company purchased Davis's other version of *Lucky Strike* (1921) from the Downtown Gallery and donated it to the Museum of Modern Art. See M. Sue Kendall, review of *Benton, Pollock, and the Politics of Modernism* by Erika Doss, in *Winterthur Portfolio* 27 (Summer/Autumn 1992): 203. Information on provenance from files of the Office of the Registrar, Museum of Modern Art.

93. Entries of May 1921, 35; 28 May 1921, 113; 29 May 1921, 38–39; 1 June 1921, 41, Davis Notebooks, AAA.

94. Parrish graduated from Haverford, class of 1892. His ancestor, Edward Parrish, captain of a trading vessel that sailed between England and the Chesapeake Bay, was one of the country's early settlers. He owned 3,000 acres of land and served as surveyor general of Baltimore. Another forefather was Caleb Pusey, an eminent Quaker author who was closely connected with William Penn in his colonization of Philadelphia. Parrish's father was an amateur, one who by avocation must have believed in art as an activity defined in broad and democratic terms. On Parrish's background, see Coy Ludwig, *Maxfield Parrish* (New York: Watson-Guptill, 1973), 11.

Rockwell Kent entered Columbia University School of Architecture in 1900. An ancestor on one side, William Rockwell, was a deacon in the Congregational Church who settled in Dorchester, Massachusetts, and then in Windsor, Connecticut. Another relative, Thomas Kent, had settled in Massachusetts before 1643. See Fridolf Johnson, "Introduction," in Fridolf Johnson, ed., *Rockwell Kent: An Anthology of His Works* (New York: Alfred Knopf, 1982), 15.

95. Lists of income and expenses, 1925, box 6, file 15, MPP. Calculations based on John

J. McCusker, *How Much Is That in Real Money? A Historical Price Index for Use as a Deflator of Money Values in the Economy of the United States* (Worcester: American Antiquarian Society, 1992), 328–32.

96. Ludwig, *Maxfield Parrish,* 7.

97. Parrish rarely used allegorical personification, focusing on images of childlike fantasy rather than didactic subjects. Allegorical personifications "are all very well in their way, but not for me," he wrote. Maxfield Parrish to Clarence Crane, 7 January 1917, box 1, file 45, MPP. See also Ludwig, *Maxfield Parrish,* 14, 22, 55. On Parrish's use of nursery rhymes in advertisements, see Maxfield Parrish to M. Rusling Wood, 1 February 1917, 6 August 1917; M. G. Webber to Parrish, 2 July 1919, all in box 3, file 54, MPP. See also William Leach, *Land of Desire: Merchants, Power, and the Rise of a New American Culture* (New York: Pantheon, 1993), 52–55.

98. Ludwig, *Maxfield Parrish,* 104.

99. For correspondence related to the Fisk Tire commissions, see M. G. Webber to Parrish, 30 August 1916, 7 January 1918; Parrish to Wood, 1 September 1916, 8 January 1917, 1 February 1917, 28 July 1917; Wood to Parrish, 29 September 1916, 12 January 1917, 3 February 1917, 2 June 1917, 26 October 1917, 5 December 1917, 12 December 1917, 23 July 1919, all in box 3, file 54, MPP. See also Calkins to Cooke, 7 December 1917, reel 16, fr. 1923, MAS, AAA; Ludwig, *Maxfield Parrish,* 106.

100. The artist, who kept strict control of his business, was a fastidious letter writer and bookkeeper, and even simple transactions were frequently chatty and lengthy. See Parrish to Wood, 16 February 1921, box 3, file 54; Parrish to Crane, 28 May 1916, box 1, file 45, MPP. Ludwig, *Maxfield Parrish,* 122.

101. Parrish to Wood, 5 February 1923, box 3, file 54; H. S. Morgan to Parrish, 21 December 1922, 30 January 1924, box 2, file 9; Morgan to Parrish, 13 February 1925, box 2, file 10; Parrish to T. J. McMannis, 20 February 1926 and General Electric to Parrish, 1 November 1932, both in box 2, file 11, MPP. See also Ludwig, *Maxfield Parrish,* 126–27.

102. On art reproductions, see Harry T. Peters, *Currier and Ives: Printmakers to the American People* (Garden City, N.Y.: Doubleday, Doran, and Co., 1929); Katharine Martinez, "Images of Love, Tokens of Friendship: Gift Book Illustration by John Sartain," in Gerald W. R. Ward, ed., *The American Illustrated Book in the Nineteenth Century* (Charlottesville: University Press of Virginia, 1987) 89–112; Peter C. Marzio, *Chromolithography 1840–1900: The Democratic Art; Pictures for a Nineteenth Century America* (Boston: David R. Godine and Amon Carter Museum of Art, 1979), 49–63, 94–129; Judy L. Larson, *American Illustration 1890–1925: Romance, Adventure, and Suspense* (Calgary, Alberta: Glenbow Museum, 1986), 24; Patricia Hills, "Picturing Progress in the Era of Westward Expansion," in William Truettner, ed., *The West as America: Reinterpreting Images of the Frontier 1820–1920* (Washington, D.C.: Smithsonian Institution Press, 1991), 97–110; Scott Casper, "Politics, Art, and the Contradictions of a Market Culture," *American Art* 5 (Summer 1991): 40–44; McCarthy, *Women's Culture,* 5–6, 17–18.

103. Ludwig, *Maxfield Parrish,* 130–38. See also box 1, files 45 and 46 for correspondence between Crane and Parrish, especially Crane to Parrish, 10 February 1917, box 1, file 45;

Parrish to Crane, 25 May 1917, 1 December 1919, 22 December 1919, box 1, file 45; and 16 February 1921, 26 February 1921, box 2, file 46, MPP. After his experience with Crane, Parrish became much more adamant on the question of artists' copyrights.

I have been unable to find any published material on House of Art. Additional research may uncover yet unknown sources of information about this and other elusive art publishing businesses.

104. Ludwig, *Maxfield Parrish*, 138–39.

105. Stephen Newman, Parrish's associate at the House of Art, told Parrish in 1924 that "the popularity of Daybreak is ever on the increase." Newman to Parrish, 9 October 1923, box 2, file 70, MPP. For figures on sales, see royalty statement, 31 December 1925, box 6, file 36, MPP.

On the fascination with youth, see T. J. Jackson Lears, *No Place of Grace: Antimodernism and the Transformation of American Culture, 1880–1920* (New York: Pantheon Books, 1981), 249–50. See also Michele H. Bogart, "American Garden Sculpture: A New Perspective," in Parrish Art Museum, *Fauns and Fountains: American Garden Statuary, 1890–1930* (Southampton, N.Y.: Parrish Art Museum, 1985), unpaginated; Bram Dijkstra, *Idols of Perversity: Fantasies of Feminine Evil in Fin-de-Siècle Culture* (New York: Oxford University Press, 1986), 190–98.

106. Parrish to Charles Dana Gibson, 1 February 1922, box 2, file 31; Parrish to A. M. Reinthal, 15 February 1929, box 3, file 1, MPP.

107. Describing a nude painting that he thought might be popular (possibly *The Beach*), Parrish told House of Art president Stephen Newman that "the appeal is 98% pure and chaste and impersonal, though I never considered nudes of this kind very seriously as prints, as they seemed to excite the Anti-Vice Society unduly." Parrish to Newman, 11 February 1924, box 2, file 70. On Parrish's problems with models, see Parrish to Newman, 30 August 1923, box 2, file 70; Parrish to Reinthal, 23 September 1926, box 2, file 71; all in MPP.

108. Parrish to Newman, 30 August 1923. See also 11 February 1924, box 2, file 70; Parrish to Reinthal, 15 February 1929, box 3, file 1, MPP.

The original painting for *Daybreak* sold for $10,000 in 1925.

109. Reinthal to Parrish, 30 June 1927, box 2, file 71, MPP.

110. Parrish to Newman, 15 February 1929, box 3, file 1, MPP.

111. Parrish to Reinthal, 15 February 1929, box 3, file 1, MPP.

112. Ibid.

113. Ibid.

114. "Maxfield Parrish Will Discard 'Girl on Rock' Idea in Art," Associated Press, 27 April 1931, in Ludwig, *Maxfield Parrish*, 129; Maxfield Parrish to R. E. Harrington, 8 November 1932, box 2, file 11, MPP.

115. On landscape as self-expression, see, for example, Richard Shiff, *Cézanne and the End of Impressionism: A Study of the Theory, Technique, and Critical Evaluation of Modern Art* (Chicago: University of Chicago Press, 1984), 99–123.

116. Harrington to Parrish, 15 January 1934; Parrish to Harrington, 22 January 1934, both in box 2, file 11; Parrish to Newman, 12 March 1923, box 2, file 70; Parrish to Reinthal,

15 February 1929, box 3, file 1; Orion Winford to Parrish, 4 November 1930, box 1, file 22; Parrish to Brown and Bigelow, 22 August 1934, box 1, file 22; Brown and Bigelow to Parrish, 22 June 1936, box 1, file 22; all in MPP; Ludwig, *Maxfield Parrish,* 174–77.

117. Reinthal to Parrish, 10 September 1930, 28 April 1931, 2 July 1931, 2 July 1932, box 3, file 2; Parrish to Newman, 26 December 1935, box 3, file 3; Newman to Parrish, 24 December 1935, box 3, file 3, all in MPP.

118. Parrish to Celia Mendelsohn, 2 February 1935, box 1, file 6, MPP.

119. Parrish to Reinthal, 15 February 1929, box 3, file 1, MPP.

120. Parrish to Maxfield Parrish Jr., 1 March 1930, box 6, file 8, MPP.

121. Ludwig, *Maxfield Parrish,* 201–2; Clement Greenberg, "Avant-Garde and Kitsch," in Clement Greenberg, *The Collected Essays and Criticism,* vol. 1, *Perceptions and Judgments, 1939–1944* (Chicago: University of Chicago Press, 1986), 15. The erotic appeal of Parrish's work would be worth considering further in light of arguments provided by David Freedberg, *The Power of Images: Studies in the History and Theory of Response* (Chicago: University of Chicago Press, 1989), 1–26, 317–44, 429–40.

122. Prints might be a "low down form of art," he had written, but they had "many advantages." They brought in "enormous sums of money, a commodity real good artists are supposed to shun, but money with me means opportunity, and opportunity means being able to paint exactly what I please, so that in the end I feel the net result is very high, pure, and lofty." Parrish to Martin Birnbaum, 1 April 1925, box 3, file 15, MPP. See also Parrish to Harrington, 12 July 1933, box 2, file 11; Parrish to W. O. Chessman, 27 March 1936, box 1, file 40, MPP. On Parrish's technique, see Ludwig, *Maxfield Parrish,* 189–200; Parrish to Wood, 5 February 1923, box 3, file 55, MPP.

123. Rockwell Kent, *It's Me O Lord: The Autobiography of Rockwell Kent* (New York: Da Capo Press, 1977; first published 1955), 52; Johnson, "Introduction," 20–21.

124. "'Knavery?'" *Time,* 1 April 1929, 55, in box 39, file 19; Charles Caffin to Kent, 27 April 1917, box 8, file 21; summary of arguments, undated, box 39, file 18; Gordon Aymar to Kent, 2 July 1928, box 5, file 22; Kent to editors of the *New York Times,* 30 March 1927, box 12, file 21, all in RK, AAA; Alden Whitman, "Rockwell Kent, Artist, Is Dead; Championed Left Wing Causes," *New York Times,* 14 March 1971, 73.

125. Johnson, "Introduction," 22.

126. Indeed, Kent was to write Pach that *Ananais* was "the worst of the few books on art he had ever read." Walter Pach, "Ananais: Two Years After," undated typescript, Pach Papers, AAA; Kent to T. J. Mahoney, 3 May 1934, box 39, file 12, RK, AAA.

127. A. D. F. Hamlin to Kent, n.d., box 12, file 14, RK, AAA; Johnson, "Introduction," 18–21.

128. Like Parrish, who lived in Cornish, New Hampshire, and avoided New York, Kent found refuge in the country at Monhegan Island off the coast of Maine, in Au Sable Forks, New York, where he bought a home in 1927, and in Tierra del Fuego, Alaska, and Greenland. But whereas Parrish was fundamentally a homebody, a family man, Kent's distant sojourns were attempts to escape the constrictions and obligations of his familial and extramarital relationships. The virile, rugged, outdoorsy image Kent crafted for himself and his

work were expressions of a cult of masculinity of which his philandering and his escapism were also symptomatic. See Johnson, "Introduction," 14–76.

129. On Kent's political commitments and activism, see Frances K. Pohl, "Rockwell Kent and the Vermont Marble Workers' Strike," *Archives of American Art Journal* 29 (1989): 50–60; Johnson, "Introduction," 65–67.

130. Johnson, "Introduction," 25; Alan Wallach, "Rockwell Kent," *Arts* 54, no. 2 (October 1979): 15.

131. "This is not in any sense an attack upon the general worthlessness of Academy shows," Kent wrote the *Times*, "for their cheap banality has reaped it's [*sic*] own reward of public indifference, but it is an attack upon the National Academy as an organized power in the politics of Art affairs, and is based upon the conduct of those men whom the Academy has elevated to leadership and who, by that leadership, are ex-officio privileged to exercise a strong influence on the culture of America. We who are outside of the Academy, we artists who are contributors to that American culture, out of contempt for the academic standard and the professional ability of the Academy's spokesmen, resent their influence as tending to degrade the public taste." Kent to editors of the *New York Times*, 16 March 1927. See also Kent to editors of the *New York Times*, 30 March 1927; Kent to *New York World*, 9 March 1927; Kent to Henry [McBride?], 21 February 1927; *Commercial Advertiser* to Kent, 21 March 1927; Pompeo Coppini to Kent, 21 March 1927, all in box 12, file 21, RK, AAA; Rockwell Kent, "The Academy Cachet," *New York Times*, 30 March 1927, clipping; idem, "The Academy," *World*, 27 March 1927, clipping; "Artists Open War on Design Academy," clipping, 20 March 1927. All clippings in box 12, file 21, RK, AAA.

132. "Academy of Design Opens 102nd Annual Exhibition Today," clipping, 23 March 1927, in box 12, file 21, RK, AAA.

133. Kent to George Bridges, 26 May 1927; James Rosenberg to Kent, 14 June 1927, box 12, file 23, RK, AAA. See also "Millionaires and Art," *Philadelphia Public Ledger*, clipping, 3 July 1927; "Proposed Constitution and By-Laws of the International Gallery of Contemporary Art, Inc.," 30 May 1927; "Preamble and Prospectus of the International Gallery of Contemporary Art," 30 May 1927, all in box 43, file 12, RK, AAA; Kent to Adeline Lobdell Atwater, 7 July 1927, box 12, file 22, RK, AAA; Kent to Artists Guild, 7 February 1936; Kent to Joseph Sinel, 28 March 1936, both in box 4, file 2, RK, AAA; Stuart Davis to Kent, 11 January 1936; Kent to Margaret Bourke-White, 31 January 1936; Kent, address to American Artists' Congress, 1 February 1936, all in box 1, file 43, RK, AAA; Johnson, "Introduction," 64–72.

In undated personal notes from the 1930s, Edwin Blashfield lamented the tactics of the artistic "radicals": "call aggression experiment and advertise, advertise, advertise—. Advertisement say some of the experts, is always triumphant if persistent. This thank heaven is *not* true but superficially it is nearly true." It is tempting to wonder whether Blashfield had in mind (among others) his old adversary Kent. Undated, unpaginated manuscripts, box 1A, Blashfield Papers, NYHS.

134. See Johnson, "Introduction," 14–76.

135. Kent to Ordway Tead, 1 April 1928 and 29 August 1928, box 5, file 22, RK, AAA; Rockwell Kent, "A Solicited Introduction for 'The Art Directors Annual,'" and "A Solicited

Introduction to a Book on Advertising," in Rockwell Kent, *Rockwellkentiana* (New York: Harcourt Brace, 1933), 21–22, 25. Neither introduction was published in the volume for which it was solicited.

136. "The artist displays his work before the general public free," Kent wrote in a letter to the editors of the *New York Times*. "If he is popular his exhibitions are attended by crowds. This should profit him, it should mean success. It doesn't. Dealers in art will tell you—I am stating facts—that crowds do not mean sales. . . . The American public does not buy art." Kent to *New York Times*, 30 March 1927, box 12, file 21, RK, AAA. See also "The National Gallery of Contemporary Art—A Declaration," n.d. [1927], box 12, file 22, RK, AAA; Kent, *It's Me O Lord*, 304–5.

137. See Kent to Sinel, 28 January 1936 and 19 November 1935; Kent to Artists Guild, 7 February 1936, all in box 4, file 2, RK, AAA.

138. Kent, "Solicited Introduction for 'The Art Directors Annual,'" 22. See also Kent to René Clarke, 11 January 1930, box 8, file 31; Kent to Sidney Mendelsohn, 15 September 1930, box 1, file 42; Sanford Gerard to Kent, 23 May 1945, box 6, file 18, all in RK, AAA.

139. See, for example, order forms from N. W. Ayer to Kent, 13 August 1926, 28 April 1927, 26 May 1927, 10 June 1927, 27 October 1927, 10 March 1928, 5 July 1928, 8 August 1928, 26 December 1928, 3 January 1929, in box 5, file 18, RK, AAA.

140. See, for example, R. Schmuck memo to Art Bureau, N. W. Ayer, 30 October 1928, box 5, file 18; and "Summary of Relations with Marcus and Company," n.d., 1–4, box 39, file 18, RK, AAA.

141. Harvard University, Graduate School of Business Administration, *The Harvard Advertising Awards, 1928* (Cambridge, Mass.: Harvard University Graduate School of Business, 1929), 7 (quotation); The Harvard Graduate School of Business Administration, *Harvard Advertising Awards: First Five Years 1924–1928* (New York: McGraw-Hill Book Company, 1930), 4–6; "Aim of the Harvard Advertising Awards," *Advertising and Selling*, 28 May 1930, 29. On the importance of the Harvard Business School in the context of 1920s consumer culture, see Leach, *Land of Desire*, 286–92.

142. "'Knavery?'" 55.

143. "Summary of Relations," 4.

144. Kent, *It's Me O Lord*, 436; "Summary of Relations"; James Rosenberg to Kent, 20 March 1929; Kent to Thomas Cleland, 20 March 1929; Kent to Rosenberg, 18 March 1929, 22 March 1929, 27 March 1929; Kent to Chapin Marcus, 23 March 1929; Marcus to Kent, 26 March 1929; Kent to Mr. Spitzer, 21 April 1929; Kent to Flannery, 30 March 1929; Philip Lowry to Rosenberg, 30 March 1929; Rockwell Kent, "Thoughts for additions to the complaint," typescript, n.d., all in box 39, file 18, RK, AAA; Johnson, "Introduction," 14.

145. Kent to Rosenberg, 18 March 1929, box 39, file 18, RK, AAA.

146. "The enclosed [grievance] explains itself," Kent wrote *New Yorker* editor Harold Ross. "Isn't that the kind of thing worth mentioning editorially? I would appreciate it very much if you might make mention of it as you feel worth while, for that is about the only action I can hope for in a matter that involves a principle and precedent that is of some public importance." Ross did not follow up. See Kent to Harold Ross, 18 March 1929, box

39, file 18, RK, AAA. See also Kent to Geoffry Parsons, 16 March 1929; Kent to editor, *New York American,* 16 March 1929; Kent to Lee Simonson, 18 March 1929; Kent to Artists Guild, 20 March 1929; Kent to Spitzer, 21 April 1929; "Ethics Committee Takes Up Rockwell Kent Case against Marcus and Company," *Guild News* 2 (March 1929), unpaginated, all in box 39, file 18, RK, AAA. Kent's artistic reputation is noted in "'Knavery?'" 55.

147. Kent to Flannery, 30 March 1929, box 39, file 18, RK, AAA.

148. Rockwell Kent, typed notes, undated, box 39, file 18, RK, AAA.

149. "Summary of Relations," 1.

150. Kent to Artists Guild, 20 March 1929, box 39, file 18, RK, AAA.

151. Kent to Artists Guild, 20 March 1929; "Thoughts for Addition to the Complaint," both in box 39, file 18, RK, AAA.

152. See undated typescript of notes for possible court case, box 39, file 18; Kent to T. J. Mahoney, 3 May 1934, box 39, file 12, both in RK, AAA.

153. "A Solicited Introduction to a Book on Advertising"; "A Solicited Introduction for 'The Art Directors' Annual,'" 21–25.

154. Chapin Marcus to Kent, 26 March 1929, box 39, file 18, RK, AAA (italics in original). For debates concerning priorities of art versus selling, the nature of professionalism in advertising, and the Harvard Awards, see Roland Marchand, *Advertising the American Dream: Making Way for Modernity 1920–1940* (Berkeley: University of California Press, 1985), 26, 28, 29; Clarence Wagner, "Don't Give Advertising Professional Status," *Printer's Ink,* 30 June 1927, 121–24; Gerald B. Lamber, "Lessons for Listerine's Success," *Printer's Ink,* 10 November 1927, 3; advertisement for the Erikson Company, *Printer's Ink,* 20 December 1928, 98; "Aim of the Harvard Advertising Awards," 29; "My Dear Mr. Kendall," *Advertising and Selling,* 20 August 1930, 54; Kenneth Groesbeck, "Are You a Member of the Advertising Profession?" *Advertising and Selling,* 15 October 1930, 28, 72, 74; "The Harvard Advertising Awards Should Not be Allowed to Go," *Advertising and Selling,* 27 May 1931, 31.

155. Neil Borden to Edward Wilson, 17 April 1929 and 16 October 1929, box 39, file 18, RK, AAA.

156. Philip Lowry to James Rosenberg, 30 March 1929; Marcus to Kent, 26 March 1929, box 39, file 18, RK, AAA.

157. Harvard University, Graduate School of Business, *Harvard Advertising Awards, 1928,* 11.

158. Kent, *It's Me O Lord,* 436; Johnson, "Introduction," 14.

159. Kent to Margaret Bourke-White, 31 January 1936, box 1, file 43, RK, AAA.

160. Wallach, "Rockwell Kent," 15. Terry Smith has proposed a political reading of Kent's art, suggesting that his "neoclassical critique" may represent "resistance to brutal inequities which underlay modernity's visible progress." Smith's brief hypothesis is certainly plausible. As he himself observed, however, it needs to be investigated further. Terry Smith, *Making the Modern: Industry, Art, and Design in America* (Chicago: University of Chicago Press, 1993), 381.

161. Carl Zigrosser to Kent, 4 April 1936, box 2, file 2, RK, AAA.

162. Samuel Golden to Kent, 20 December 1935, 14 January 1936, 7 August 1936, 25

November 1936; Kent to Golden, 1 December 1936; Zigrosser to Kent, 24 January 1936, 15 February 1936, 11 April 1936, 9 June 1936, 10 July 1936; Kent to Zigrosser, 18 February 1936, 28 March 1936, all in box 2, file 1, RK, AAA.

Kent also suggested marketing these artists' prints as "Hotel room art." Kent to Golden, 13 September 1940, box 2, file 3, RK, AAA.

163. See also Charles Boni to Kent, 23 March 1937, 6 April 1937, box 37, file 36, RK, AAA; Living American Art, Inc. to Kent, 9 June 1941; Advertising prospectus, Living American Art, Inc.; Zigrosser to Kent, 11 February 1940; Kent to L. C. Guthman, 23 February 1940, 26 February 1940, all in box 21, file 9, RK, AAA.

164. Kent, "A Solicited Introduction to a Book on Advertising," 25.

chapter 6

1. On agency travails, see Roland Marchand, *Advertising the American Dream: Making Way for Modernity, 1920–1940* (Berkeley: University of California Press, 1985), 285–87.

2. The Emergency Work Bureau (later the Emergency Relief Bureau) was financed first by a private agency and subsequently by the Temporary Emergency Relief Administration (a New York State agency).

Other programs included the Public Works of Art Project, (established in 1933 as a non-relief program employing over 3,700 artists), and the Treasury Section of Painting and Sculpture (1934–1939), later known as the Section of Fine Arts of the Public Buildings Administration of the Federal Works Agency (1939–1943). The Section commissioned mural paintings and sculptures for the nation's post offices and for federal buildings in the District of Columbia. Artists were selected through competition, not on the basis of need. In 1935, the government also established the Federal Art Project of the Works Progress Administration and the Treasury Relief Art Project, funded by the Works Progress Administration. These programs awarded financial assistance to artists in need by providing them stipends to paint murals and easel pictures. The paintings were placed in offices, schools, hospitals, and other public buildings. See Patricia Hills, *Social Concern and Urban Realism: American Painting of the 1930s* (Boston: Boston University Art Gallery, 1983), 10; Karal Ann Marling, *Wall-to-Wall America: A Cultural History of Post Office Murals in the Great Depression* (Minneapolis: University of Minnesota Press, 1982); Edith Tonelli, "'By the People, For the People,'" in De Cordova Museum, *"By the People, For the People: New England* (Lincoln, Ma.: De Cordova Museum, 1977), 24–29; Marlene Park and Gerald Markowitz, *Democratic Vistas: Post Offices and Public Art in the New Deal* (Philadelphia: Temple University Press, 1984); Francis V. O'Connor, ed., *The New Deal Art Projects: An Anthology of Memoirs* (Washington, D.C.: Smithsonian Institution Press, 1972), 3–4; Gerald M. Monroe, "Artists on the Barricades: The Militant Artists Union Treats with the New Deal," *Archives of American Art Journal* 18 (1978): 20.

3. See Harold Rosenberg's highly critical reminiscence, "The Profession of Art: The WPA Art Project," in Harold Rosenberg, *Art on the Edge: Creators and Situations* (New York: Macmillan, 1975), 195–205; Alexander B. Stavenitz, "Economic Problems of the American Artist," in Matthew Baigell and Julia Williams, eds., *Artists against War and Fascism: Papers*

of the First American Artists' Congress (New Brunswick: Rutgers University Press, 1986), 176–79.

4. The Artists' Union, an offshoot of the John Reed Clubs, began in 1933 as the militant "Unemployed Artists Group." After getting support from some non-Communist liberals, it changed its name in 1934 to Artists' Union. The union was active in pressuring the federal government to implement a comprehensive jobs program, which ultimately became the Federal Art Project. It then served as "bargaining agent" for artists working on federal art projects, although the organization also aspired to represent all employed artists and to have a more general influence in the private sector. From November 1934 to December 1937 it published *Art Front*, which, in addition to published reviews and membership information, included essays on significant issues of art and society.

Championing the Marxist idea that every artist is a cultural worker, the union believed in parity between painters and artists engaged in other enterprises. It included locals, such as the Commercial Artists Section, which sought minimum salaries and rates (to be determined for a range of different classifications of artist—layout, lettering, illustration, still life, retouching, fashion, furniture, and poster), opposed speculation (creation of designs on demand from potential clients without compensation if they were not used), and called for minimums on overtime, improved working conditions, and sick leave.

The union, along with the Artists Guild (the former Guild of Free Lance Artists), mediated between artists and patrons. The Artists Guild represented freelancers in their dealings with art directors and businesses. The Artists' Union negotiated between artists and the government on the various art projects, while the guild tended to serve the already established painters, graphic artists, and illustrators with successful careers in editorial illustration and advertising. It promoted standards of ethics and mediated in business disputes, but it also served as a clearinghouse for artists' work. Its most prominent members, if not apolitical, sought to give the appearance of being so.

Like the Artists' Union, the American Artists' Congress sought to come to terms with the role of art and the artist in society. Organized in May 1935, the Congress became aligned with the strategies of the Communist Party's Popular Front, formed later that year. In keeping with this alliance, the Artists' Congress assumed a cooperative rather than a combative stance, and sought to tap into mainstream liberal concerns set in motion by the rise of European fascism. Comprising mostly established artists, the Congress served as a forum for discussion of immediate political concerns like racial discrimination and fascism, as well as longer-term internal issues like the future of American art and its audiences. Between 1936 and 1942 the Congress held exhibitions and generally served as artists' advocates on a range of matters, including the unsuccessful congressional Coffee-Pepper Bill, which sought to establish a permanent federal arts program. The organization was also concerned with expanding the audience for art.

On the Artists' Union, see David Shapiro and Cecile Shapiro, "Abstract Expressionism: The Politics of Apolitical Painting," *Prospects* 3 (1977): 176; David Shapiro, "Social Realism Reconsidered," in David Shapiro, ed., *Social Realism: Art as a Weapon* (New York: Frederick Ungar, 1973), 18–21; Francine Tyler, "Artists Respond to the Great Depression and the

Threat of Fascism: The New York Artists' Union and Its Magazine *Art Front*," (Ph.D. dissertation, New York University, 1991); "Prevailing Wages for Artists," *Art Front* 2 (September-October 1936): 3–4; "Full Report of the Eastern District Conventions of the Artists' Unions," *Art Front* 2 (June 1936): 5–7; "National Organization," *Art Front* 2 (March 1936): 2, 15; Meyer Schapiro, "The Public Use of Art," *Art Front* 2 (November 1936): 4–6; Monroe, "Artists on the Barricades," 20–23; "Commercial Artists: Don't Speculate with Your Future!" undated leaflet, box 4, file 2; Ben Lassen to Rockwell Kent, 26 March 1936, box 4, file 21; The Artists' Union (Commercial Artists Section), "Resolutions to be submitted and voted upon at a symposium on 'Speculation and the Free Lance Artist,'" 1936, in box 4, file 21, all in RK, AAA. On the Artists Guild, see Pamphlet Box, Art Division, New York Public Library; "The Artists Guild: Its Purpose and Function," pamphlet 1941, both on reel N122, fr. 310–13, 319–24, AAA; *American Art Annual* (Washington, D.C.: American Federation of Arts, 1934). See also Joseph Sinel to Rockwell Kent, 15 November 1935, 27 November 1935; Kent to Sinel, 19 November 1935, 28 January 1936; Kent to Artists Guild, 7 February 1936, box 4, file 2, RK, AAA.

On the American Artists' Congress, see Matthew Baigell and Julia Williams, "Introduction," in Baigell and Williams, eds., *Artists against War and Fascism*, 3–44; Serge Guilbaut, *How New York Stole the Idea of Modern Art: Abstract Expressionism, Freedom, and the Second World War*, trans. by Arthur Goldhammer (Chicago: University of Chicago Press, 1983), 18–21; Cécile Whiting, *Antifascism in American Art* (New Haven: Yale University Press, 1989), 34–64; Report of the American Artists' Congress to the Membership by the Editorial Committee, 15 March 1936, box 1, file 44; Stuart Davis to Rockwell Kent, box 1, file 43; letter to American Artists' Congress members from Stuart Davis, n.d. [1936], box 1, file 43, all in RK, AAA.

5. The John Reed Clubs, established in 1929, were made up of artist members of the American Communist Party seeking to build a mass movement of "new working class writers and artists." The clubs dissipated in 1935 when the earlier rhetoric of class struggle was shelved with the creation of the Popular Front. The Popular Front, which emerged in August 1935, was a Comintern (Communist International) strategy aimed at creating an alliance between the Soviet Union and the Western democratic nations to combat fascism. By arguing that leftist unity was required to protect democracy, the Popular Front succeeded, during the impassioned period of the Spanish Civil War, in enlisting large numbers of non-Communists in organizations under Communist Party control. Quotation cited in Hills, *Social Concern*, 15–16. See also Shapiro and Shapiro, "Abstract Expressionism," 176; Shapiro, "Social Realism Reconsidered," 18–21; Whiting, *Antifascism in American Art*, 8–33; Tyler, "Artists Respond to the Great Depression," 2–60; Irving Howe and Louis Coser, *The American Communist Party: A Critical History (1919–1957)* (Boston: Beacon Press, 1957), 273–386; Andrew Ross, *No Respect: Intellectuals and Popular Culture* (New York: Routledge, 1989), 15–41; Guilbaut, *How New York Stole the Idea of Modern Art*, 17–27; Andrew Hemingway, "Fictional Unities: 'Antifascism' and 'Antifascist Art' in 30s America," *Oxford Art Journal* 14 (1991): 107–17.

6. The Artists' Union and the American Artists' Congress suffered amid mounting

charges that the organization was dominated by the Communist Party, at a time when even the most ardent supporters of the Soviet Union were hard-pressed to defend party tactics. In the wake of the Moscow treason trials (1936–1938) and the Nazi-Soviet pact (1939), many intellectuals and artists on the left disavowed the Soviet Communist Party. These events, followed by the Soviet invasion of Finland in 1940, resulted in widespread defections from the Congress and a breakdown of support for the union. Individuals like Stuart Davis, Harold Rosenberg, and Meyer Schapiro rejected the Popular Front, and the idea of mass culture associated with it, as dangerous expressions of middlebrow aesthetics and politics that provided fertile ground for totalitarianism. On this political fragmentation, see Florence S. Berryman, "Eighteen Months in Art," *American Art Annual* 34 (1937–1938): 24; Monroe, "Artists on the Barricades," 23; Guilbaut, *How New York Stole the Idea of Modern Art,* 25, 37–40; Ross, *No Respect,* 15–41; Howe and Coser, *The American Communist Party,* 387–405, 500–554; Erika Doss, *Benton, Pollock, and the Politics of Modernism: From Regionalism to Abstract Expressionism* (Chicago: University of Chicago Press, 1991), 275–79, 370–73; "Looking Toward 1939," American Artists' Congress, box 1, file 48, RK, AAA; Tyler, "Artists Respond to the Great Depression," 69–75, 125.

7. On Artists for Victory, see Minutes of the Artists for Victory, 19 January 1942, Artists for Victory Papers, reels 115–16, no frame numbers, AAA (hereafter AV, AAA); Ellen G. Landau, "America in the War," in *Artists for Victory: An Exhibition Catalogue* (Washington, D.C.: Library of Congress, 1983), 2–5; idem, "'A Certain Rightness': Artists for Victory's America in the War," *Arts* 60 (February 1986): 43–55; press release, n.d. [January 1942], box 4, file 1, RK, AAA.

8. See, for example, Elizabeth McCausland, "The Use of Art in America," and Charles Coiner, "Full Employment and the Artist," in Elizabeth McCausland, *Work for Artists: What? Where? How?* (New York: American Artists Group, 1947), 3–13, 36–41; Rosenberg, "The Profession of Art," 195–97.

9. Erika Doss, "Catering to Consumerism: Associated American Artists and the Marketing of American Art, 1934–1958," *Winterthur Portfolio* 26 (Summer/Autumn 1991): 149.

10. Doss, "Catering to Consumerism," 143–54 (quote). See also Wanda M. Corn, *Grant Wood: The Regionalist Vision* (New Haven: Yale University Press, 1983), 49–51.

AAA published large editions (100–250 impressions), although they were more limited than the editions of Parrish prints published by House of Art. House of Art paid Parrish on a royalty basis, whereas AAA paid its artists a flat fee of $200 per edition.

11. Guilbaut, *How New York Stole the Idea of Modern Art,* 17–47; Ross, *No Respect,* 64; Doss, *Benton, Pollock, and the Politics of Modernism,* 125–26 and chapters 4, 5, and 6.

12. In the early 1940s, AAA began selling higher-priced paintings and drawings and cheap color reproductions in addition to its black-and-white prints. In 1943–1944 the AAA "handled 107 American artists and sold 62,374 prints and 1736 paintings, netting an income of more than $1 million per month." Lewenthal was reportedly sending some artists monthly checks of $25,000 to $75,000. Doss, "Catering to Consumerism," 151.

13. Ibid., 152–56; "Money in Pictures," *Time,* 21 April 1941, 71–72.

14. The discussion in the following section is largely indebted to James Sloan Allen, *The*

Romance of Commerce and Culture: Capitalism, Modernism, and the Chicago-Aspen Crusade for Cultural Reform (Chicago: University of Chicago Press, 1983), chapter 1, and Neil Harris and Martina Roudabush Norelli, *Art, Design, and the Modern Corporation* (Washington, D.C.: Smithsonian Institution Press, 1985).

15. See "Container Kraft," *Time*, 1 June 1936, 58–59; Arthur Van Vlissingen, "He Knows How to Kill Price Wars," *Forbes*, 15 September 1937, 14–15, 38.

16. Martina Norelli, interview with Elizabeth Nitze Paepcke, 20 November 1984, AAA; Allen, *Romance of Commerce and Culture*, 20–24; Neil Harris, "Designs on Demand: Art and the Modern Corporation," in Harris and Norelli, *Art, Design, and the Modern Corporation*, 16–17. Harris's essay is reprinted in Neil Harris, *Cultural Excursions: Marketing Appetites and Cultural Tastes in Modern America* (Chicago: University of Chicago Press, 1990), 349–78.

17. Allen, *Romance of Commerce and Culture*, 17–21, 25–27.

18. Ibid., 27; Elizabeth Paepcke interview, AAA.

19. Allen, *Romance of Commerce and Culture*, 27–29; Neil Harris, "Designs on Demand," 17–18.

20. Allen, *Romance of Commerce and Culture*, 29.

21. Several of the artists, including Bayer, joined László Moholy-Nagy in establishing a new school of design in Chicago. Walter Paepcke became one of Moholy-Nagy's closest friends and one of the school's primary allies, providing it with crucial financial support and thus strengthening the ties between the CCA image and Bauhaus aesthetic ideals. Martina Norelli, "Early Series," in Harris and Norelli, *Art, Design, and the Modern Corporation*, 34; Allen, *Romance of Commerce and Culture*, 34–77; "Charles Coiner, Art Director," *Portfolio* 1, no. 2 (Summer 1950): unpaginated.

22. Allen, *Romance of Commerce and Culture*, 29; Norelli, "Early Series," 32.

23. "Container's ads tell nothing specific about the product," wrote Rosamund Frost admiringly in *Art News* in 1945, "they merely suggest, strike the eye, stick in the memory, and make the reader come to the advertiser to find out what it's all about." Form and function were also connected. The original images for the entire first series were rendered on paperboard. Hence the medium became part of the message. The literal substance of the advertisements became proof of the value and versatility of the product, and of the sincerity of the artists' creation (although this aspect of the work was inevitably lost in reproduction). Rosamund Frost, "This Business Ties Art Into a Neat Package," *Art News* 44 (15–31 May 1945), 13. See also "Charles Coiner, Art Director."

24. Allen, *Romance of Commerce and Culture*, 58–59; Gwen Finkel Chanzit, *Herbert Bayer and Modernist Design in America* (Ann Arbor: UMI Research Press, 1987), 18, 51–85.

25. On wartime advertising, see Mark H. Leff, "The Politics of Sacrifice on the American Home Front in World War II," *Journal of American History* 77 (March 1991): 1312–13; Robert Griffith, "The Selling of America: The Advertising Council and American Politics, 1942–1960," *Business History Review* 57 (Autumn 1983): 3388–90; Frank W. Fox, *Madison Avenue Goes to War: The Strange Military Career of American Advertising, 1941–1945* (Provo: Brigham Young University Press, 1975), 25–35, 92. Robert Westbrook explores the popular political

philosophies underlying some wartime advertising; see Robert B. Westbrook, "'I Want a Girl, Just like the Girl that Married Harry James': American Women and the Problem of Political Obligation in World War II," *American Quarterly* 42 (1990): 587–614; idem, "Fighting for the American Family: Private Interests and Political Obligations in World War II," in Richard Wightman Fox and T. J. Jackson Lears, eds., *The Power of Culture: Critical Essays in American History* (Chicago: University of Chicago Press, 1993), 194–221. See also Norelli, "Early Series," 34.

26. Norelli, "Early Series," 34.

27. Martina Norelli, "The United Nations Series," in Harris and Norelli, *Art, Design, and the Modern Corporation,* 48–57.

28. Norelli, "The United Nations Series," 48.

29. N. W. Ayer art buyer Edward Warwick had previously been with Radio Corporation of America as art director. He himself had been a painter before developing eye problems that led him to take up administrative work. Usually, primary responsibility for selecting and commissioning advertising pictures lay with the art director. Ayer's system of delegating authority to a special art buyer was unusual for the time. Having decided upon certain artists, Warwick would commission sketches, at rates of $150 to $250, depending on the prominence of the artist. If the Paepckes, Jacobson, and Coiner approved of the image, Warwick would contract with the artist for a finished work of art. Warwick recalled that the Ayer approach worked well for Coiner, allowing him to concentrate more efficiently on overall supervision of an account. Coiner still had to give the final approval on any work of art. Martina Norelli, interview with Edward W. Warwick, 8 July 1985, AAA.

30. Allen, *Romance of Commerce and Culture,* 78–109, 213–14. The series up to 1976 is illustrated in Container Corporation of America, *Great Ideas* (United States: Container Corporation of America, 1976).

31. Allen, *Romance of Commerce and Culture,* 213–14.

32. "Fine Art for an Institutional Series," *American Artist* 30 (September 1966): 36–47, 66–67.

33. Paepcke noted that "Among some businessmen and some professional advertising people it evoked a reaction bordering on shock." Quoted in Allen, *Romance of Commerce and Culture,* 30, 31.

34. Ralph M. Pearson, *Experiencing American Pictures* (New York: Harper and Brothers, 1943), 78; Rosamund Frost, "Has Advertising Art Improved?" *Art News* 43 (1–30 September 1944): 10; Walter Abell, "Industry and Painting," *Magazine of Art* 39 (March 1946): 89.

35. Advertising man David Ogilvy considered CCA an anomaly. He noted in 1976—as he had earlier in *Confessions of an Advertising Man* (New York: Atheneum, 1966), 118 (see chapter 3, n. 110)—that CCA ads were "unique." "I must admit," he added, "that I have yet to read the *copy* in a Container Corporation advertisement, and in this I may not be alone; like many businessmen I have little interest in philosophy. What's more, the copy is often laid out in a way which defies readership. But even if I don't *read* the advertisements, once a month for almost forty years I have *seen* one of them, and I always recognize the sponsor and admire him." David Ogilvy, in Container Corporation, *Great Ideas,* x.

36. Robert Sobel, *They Satisfy: The Cigarette in American Life* (New York: Anchor Books, 1978), 127, 131.

37. On the American Tobacco advertisements, see Erika Doss, "Borrowing Regionalism: Advertising's Use of American Art in the 1930s and 40s," *Journal of American Culture* 5 (Winter 1982): 15; Doss, "Catering to Consumerism"; "Money in Pictures," 71–72. On the antitrust charges, see Nannie M. Tilley, *The R. J. Reynolds Tobacco Company* (Chapel Hill: University of North Carolina Press, 1985), 414–26. For a view of the larger post-NRA efforts to regulate industry, see Ellis W. Hawley, *The New Deal and the Problem of Monopoly* (Princeton: Princeton University Press, 1966), 149–68, 439, 445.

38. Doss, *Benton, Pollock, and the Politics of Modernism,* 235; Sobel, *They Satisfy,* 135.

39. Doss, "Borrowing Regionalism," 15; Sobel, *They Satisfy,* 135, 141. Artists included Arnold Blanch, Aaron Bohrod, James Chapin, John Steuart Curry, Ernest Fiene, Joe Jones, Doris Lee, David Stone Martin, Fletcher Martin, Robert Philipp, Paul Sample, George Schreiber, Lawrence Beall Smith, and Frederic Taubes. See Associated American Artists Papers, reel D256, AAA.

Just as the tobacco companies anticipated, cigarette sales rose considerably during the war. Demand increased in large part because of the large number of soldiers who took up or increased the habit. Tobacco companies and well-meaning citizens provided encouragement, offering free cigarettes to soldiers. See Sobel, *They Satisfy,* 131–41; R. J. Reynolds Company, *Golden Leaves: R. J. Reynolds Tobacco Company and the Art of Advertising* (Winston-Salem: R. J. Reynolds Tobacco Company, 1986), 54.

40. Thomas Hart Benton, quoted in Doss, "Catering to Consumerism," 158.

41. Doss, *Benton, Pollock, and the Politics of Modernism,* 229–40.

42. Otis Pease, *The Responsibilities of American Advertising: Private Control and Public Influence, 1920–1940* (New Haven: Yale University Press, 1958), 60–64; Marchand, *Advertising the American Dream,* 96–102; American Tobacco Company, *"Sold American!"—The First Fifty Years* (U.S.A.: American Tobacco Company, 1954), 75–77. On testimonial advertising, see also Patricia Johnston, "The Personal Touch: Edward Steichen's Testimonial Advertisements," *Views: The Journal of Photography in New England* 13, no. 2 (Spring 1992): 11–16.

43. Frank Caspars, "Patrons at a Profit—Business Discovers Art as a Selling Force," *Art Digest,* 1 May 1943, 17; Peyton Boswell, "Portrait of America," *Art Digest,* 1 April 1944, 3; Reeves Lewenthal, "The Artist Has Never Been So Busy," in McCausland, ed., *Work for Artists,* 125–26; Abell, "Industry and Painting," 85, 114.

44. Thomas Hart Benton, "Business and Art," in McCausland, ed., *Work for Artists,* 25–26.

45. Jo Gibbs, "I.B.M.: 1936–1946," in McCausland, ed., *Work for Artists,* 107–9. See also Mitchell Douglass Kahan, *Art, Inc.: American Paintings from Corporate Collections* (Montgomery: Montgomery Museum of Art, 1979), 11. On IBM's profitability during the depression, see Katharine Davis Fishman, *The Computer Establishment* (New York: Harper and Row, 1981), 34–35, 61; David Mercer, *IBM: How the World's Most Successful Corporation is Managed* (London: Kogan Page, 1987), 33–34.

46. The New York fair exhibit reportedly drew 3,000,000 people—16.5 percent of the fair's total attendance—and the corporation naturally received a great deal of publicity. The corporation also funded a catalog of the exhibition. In his 1990 memoir, Watson's son and IBM chief executive officer Thomas J. Watson Jr. described the World's Fair exhibit and his father's orchestration of a special IBM day a "public relations coup." Thomas J. Watson Jr., *Father, Son & Company: My Life at IBM and Beyond* (New York: Bantam Books, 1990), 84. See also Gibbs, "I.B.M.," 109.

47. Gibbs, "I.B.M.," 107–17.

48. See, for example, Terry Smith's discussion of Rivera's murals *Detroit Industry* for the Detroit Institute of Arts. Terry Smith, *Making the Modern: Industry, Art, and Design in America* (Chicago: University of Chicago Press, 1993), 199–206.

49. On Watson Sr. and IBM policies, see Watson Jr., *Father, Son & Company*, 33, 83–84, 150–51; Fishman, *The Computer Establishment*, 61, 74–75; Mercer, *IBM*, 26–35; William Rogers, *Think: A Biography of the Watsons and IBM* (New York: Stein and Day, 1969); Robert Sobel, *IBM, A Colossus in Transition* (New York: New York Times Books, 1981). See also Smith, *Making the Modern*, 208.

50. Gibbs, "I.B.M.," 107–9. See also Kahan, *Art, Inc.*, 11; Abell, "Industry and Painting," 84. Abell wrote that "the International Business Machines Corporation appears to have been the first industrial organization to separate its use of art from ordinary advertising and lift it to the level of public relations." Abell's characterization of public relations as being somehow more uplifting than advertising was subject to differences of opinion. Richard Tedlow has observed that many advertising men regarded "publicity as reprehensible because it involved getting something for nothing and took people by surprise, while advertising helped to support the medium that carried it and included a frank declaration of its source." Others, like Abell, regarded public relations as the more justifiable practice because it was not so obviously tainted with the commercial aura, operated at a more rarefied level, and related to the larger purpose of a corporation. See Richard S. Tedlow, *Keeping the Corporate Image: Public Relations and Business, 1900–1950* (Greenwich: JAI Press, 1975), 171.

51. Phrase "sponsor-related interest" comes from Rosanne Martorella, *Corporate Art* (New Brunswick: Rutgers University Press, 1990), 22.

52. The Encyclopaedia Britannica was one of those inspired to start collecting to avoid excess profits. The corporation amassed a large collection of contemporary art, both commissioned and purchased, to illustrate its volumes, to highlight its educational mission, and to promote the fact that Britannica was an American company and no longer British owned. Painters included Grant Wood and Thomas Hart Benton (whose painting *Boom Town* illustrated the Britannica article on petroleum). In addition, the company sent out a questionnaire to 200 prominent critics, art dealers, museum directors, and artists, asking them to nominate painters whose work would best "sell American Art to Americans." The organization owned 121 paintings by 1945, and it exhibited the collection in 45 cities around the country. See Sidney Hyman, *The Lives of William Benton* (Chicago: University of Chicago Press, 1969), 284–85 (quote); Grace Pagano, *Catalog of the Encyclopaedia Britannica Collection of Contemporary American Painting* (Chicago: Encyclopaedia Britannica, Inc., 1945);

E. H. Powell, "The Britannica Collection," in McCausland, ed., *Work for Artists,* 146–52; Glenn Price to Gladys Rockmore Davis, 28 January 1944, Gladys Rockmore Davis Papers, reel D288, fr. 215, AAA. On incentives for corporate collecting, see Kahan, *Art Inc.,* 14; Martorella, *Corporate Art,* 26; Leff, "The Politics of Sacrifice," 1312; "Fine Art in Ads," *Business Week,* 20 May 1949, 78.

53. See, for example, Robert Griffith, "The Selling of America: The Advertising Council and American Politics, 1942–1960," *Business History Review* 57 (Autumn 1983): 388–91; Leff, "The Politics of Sacrifice," 1296–1313; James Harvey Young, *The Medical Messiahs: A Social History of Health Quackery in Twentieth Century America* (Princeton: Princeton University Press, 1967): 151–216.

54. Steven Wright Plattner, "How the Other Half Lived: The Standard Oil Company (New Jersey) Photographic Project, 1943–1950" (M.A. thesis, George Washington University, 1981), 19.

55. Jo Gibbs, "Artists Recount the Story of Oil," *Art Digest,* 15 January 1946, 5. See also "Oil at War," *Art News,* 44 (15–31 January 1946): 5–7.

56. See "Oil at War," 5–7; Gibbs, "Artists Recount the Story of Oil," 5–7; "Art for Prestige's Sake," *Business Week,* 18 December 1948, 38–46; Maren Stange, *Symbols of Ideal Life: Social Documentary Photography in America, 1890–1950* (New York: Cambridge University Press, 1989), 141–42; Plattner, "How the Other Half Lived," 6–69.

57. Thomas Hart Benton, "Business and Art from the Artists Angle," *Art Digest,* 15 January 1946, 8.

58. Young, *Medical Messiahs,* 1–190; Harvey Levenstein, *Paradox of Plenty: A Social History of Eating in America* (New York: Oxford University Press, 1993), 17–19.

59. Young, *Medical Messiahs,* 191–216, 260–81, 296–305.

60. Several of these artists had signed the 1936 call for the American Artists' Congress. On "Year of Peril," see Doss, *Benton, Pollock, and the Politics of Modernism,* 282–89; on Abbott Laboratories, see Abell, "Industry and Painting," 85; Pearson, *Experiencing American Pictures,* 78–81; "Fine Art in Ads," 79; "Art for Prestige's Sake," 44; Kahan, *Art Inc.,* 13.

61. Pearson, *Experiencing American Pictures,* 78.

62. Pearson, *Experiencing American Pictures,* 75, 78–79.

63. "Upjohn Collection Brings Art to an Audience of Ten Million," *Art Digest,* 15 November 1947, 17–20.

64. Ibid., 18.

65. On *Life* publisher Henry Luce's support of American art, see Doss, *Benton, Pollock, and the Politics of Modernism,* 174–93.

66. "Upjohn Collection Brings Fine Art to an Audience of Ten Million," 18–20; "Art in Advertising," *Life,* 14 May 1945, 75–77.

67. Davis's correspondence includes a large number of fan letters that allow glimpses of the responses to the artist's work. "I am trying to understand your picture "The Pink Skirt," wrote Mrs. J. S. MacRae Jr. of Maxton, South Carolina. "I know you are trying to say something that my little mind will not comprehend. If you will help me I will appreciate it very much." For Private Joseph Jankowski of Sheppard Field, Texas, Davis was very much

more than an artist. She was a "Goddess . . . whom we aspirants look up to for encouragement and inspiration. George Charney of Plainfield, New Jersey, wrote, "you sure do wonderful nice work of art, which I have seen." "Hello Gladys Rockmore Davis," wrote one. "There are lots of things that make a soldier think of home. Some 'GI Johns' think of home and mother when they see a picture of a luscious roast chicken; others get a 'condition' to see love scenes in the movies,—and still others get a bang out of watching some civilians superconvertible coupe roll through the streets of some strange town. As for me, well, it may not enter your mind when you sit down at your drawing board and do your next sketch for the Munsingwear ads, that somewhere deep in the heart of Texas, there's a soldier waiting to see a reproduction of that drawing in *Life* Magazine, that to see your work lifts him out of his Army world and takes him home to his wife." Frank B. Potter to Davis, 25 May 1944; Mrs. J. S. MacRae to Davis, 14 February 1939; Henry R. Luce to Davis, 13 October 1939; Adele Chase to Davis, 2 January 1942; Joseph Jankowski to Davis, 18 October 1942, 3 November 1942, 27 November 1942; George Charney to Davis, 28 February 1944; H. W. Pier to Davis, 26 March 1944, all on reel D288, frs. 75, 80, 174, 182–86, 288, 224, 243, Gladys Rockmore Davis Papers, AAA. See also Robert Westbrook, "'I Want a Girl, Just Like the Girl That Married Harry James,'" 587–614.

68. Abell, "Industry and Painting," 88.

69. "Upjohn Collection Brings Art to an Audience of Ten Million," 20; "Art in Advertising," 75, 77.

70. Abell, "Industry and Painting," 91. See also "Upjohn Collection Brings Fine Art to an Audience of Ten Million," 17.

71. Abell, "Industry and Painting," 92. See also "Upjohn Collection Brings Fine Art to an Audience of Ten Million," 19–20.

72. Peyton Boswell, "Broken Boundaries," *Art Digest,* 1 May 1942, 3.

73. Boswell, "Broken Boundaries," 3. See also Ernest W. Watson, *Forty Illustrators and How They Work* (New York: Watson-Guptill Publications, 1946), ix.

74. Frederic Newlin Price, "Society of Illustrators, Inc.," *Art Digest,* 1 May 1946, 20, 31.

75. Price, "Society of Illustrators," 20, 31.

76. Published in 1939 in *Partisan Review,* but especially influential when reprinted in 1961, "Avant-Garde and Kitsch" warned against the threat inherent in the popularity of artists like Parrish and Rockwell, and decried the aspiration to serve either a mass audience or a more limited one of "cultivated spectators." An early expression of anti-Stalinist sentiment, it theorized and codified the moral imperative of an adversarial stance toward nonelite popular taste and cultures. Clement Greenberg, "Avant Garde and Kitsch," in Clement Greenberg, *The Collected Essays and Criticism,* vol. 1, *Perceptions and Judgments 1939–1944* (Chicago: University of Chicago Press, 1986; first published 1939), 5–22. On the political implications of this essay, see Guilbaut, *How New York Stole the Idea of Modern Art,* 33–38; Ross, *No Respect,* 43–45; Robert Storr, "No Joy in Mudville: Greenberg's Modernism Then and Now," in Kirk Varnedoe and Adam Gopnik, eds., *Modern Art and Popular Culture: Readings in High and Low* (New York: Harry N. Abrams, 1990), 161–90; Doss, *Benton, Pollock, and the Politics of Modernism,* 370–79. See also T. J. Clark, "Clement Greenberg's Theory of

Art," in Francis Frascina, ed., *Pollock and After: The Critical Debate* (New York: Harper and Row, 1985), 47–63.

77. Hilaire Hiler to Abraham Rattner, 17/18 May 1940, box 1, Abraham Rattner Papers, AAA.

78. Ibid.

79. Paradoxically, the tree was inspired by a 1938 "Gestaltian Chart of American Art" diagram of art styles depicted by art director Nathaniel Pousette-Dart in his book *Art and Artists of Today*. For an illustration and discussion of this tree see Doss, *Benton, Pollock, and the Politics of Modernism*, 260.

80. For a discussion of the organizational nebulousness of the avant-garde with which Reinhardt is associated, see Michael Leja, *Reframing Abstract Expressionism: Subjectivity and Painting in the 1940s* (New Haven: Yale University Press, 1993), 18–48.

81. Robert Goodnough, ed., "Artists' Session at Studio 35 (1950)," in Robert Motherwell and Ad Reinhardt, eds., *Modern Artists in America* (New York: Wittenborn Schultz, 1951), 21, quoted in David Craven, "Abstract Expressionism, Autonomism, and the Age of Automation," *Art History* 13 (March 1990): 85. For an additional sampling of Reinhardt's writings, see Barbara Rose, ed., *Art-as-Art: The Selected Writings of Ad Reinhardt* (Berkeley: University of California Press, 1991, first published 1975); Museum of Modern Art, *Ad Reinhardt* (New York: Rizzoli, 1991).

82. For an overview of this context, see the American Social History Project, *Who Built America?: Working People and the Nation's Economy, Politics, Culture, and Society*, 2 vols. (New York: Pantheon Books, 1992), 2: 472–75.

83. Abell, "Industry and Painting," 118.

84. "Editorial," *American Artist* 13 (March 1949): 3, 63.

85. Richard S. Tedlow, *New and Improved: The Story of Mass Marketing in America* (New York: Basic Books, 1990), 22–23, 70–79.

86. Tedlow, *New and Improved*, 79; Walter S. Mack Jr., "Pepsi-Cola's Competition-Exhibition," in McCausland, ed., *Work for Artists*, 139; Walter S. Mack Jr., "Viewpoints: A New Step in Art Patronage," *Magazine of Art* 37 (October 1944): 228; idem, with Peter Buckley, *No Time Lost* (New York: Athenaeum, 1982), 20, 117–83.

87. Tedlow, *New and Improved*, 90–92.

88. "Culturally astute," from Martorella, *Corporate Art*, 22–23.

89. Mack, "Pepsi-Cola's Competition-Exhibition," 139; Kahan, *Art, Inc.*, 12.

Some advertising executives were criticized for exploiting patriotism for selling purposes during the war. Overall, however, business, especially big business, regained public favor. On wartime advertising, see Frank W. Fox, *Madison Avenue Goes to War*, 34; on big business, see Barton J. Bernstein, "America in War and Peace," in Barton J. Bernstein, ed., *Towards a New Past: Essays in American History* (New York: Random House, 1968), 290–91.

Coca-Cola calendars in the 1930s also included quaint "American" subjects, also by illustrators, such as the rugged old salt and young girl relaxing with their soft drinks painted by N. C. Wyeth for the 1936 calendar. The image, located in the Coca-Cola Archives in Atlanta,

Georgia, is now reproduced on a postcard sold at "Coca-Cola Fifth Avenue," a store in New York City.

90. Mack, "Pepsi-Cola's Competition-Exhibition," 240.

91. Mack, "Pepsi-Cola's Competition-Exhibition," 142–43; Boswell, "Portrait of America," 3; Minutes, Artists for Victory, 31 January 1944, reel 116, no frame numbers, AV, AAA.

Significantly, illustrators, more economically secure and politically middle-of-the-road, were not invited to join Artists for Victory. They in turn successfully volunteered their services much as they had in the World War I, creating posters, instructional pamphlets, and animated films. The Red Cross arranged for illustrators to visit veterans' hospitals, sketch convalescents, and teach. Many illustrators also became artist war correspondents. On illustrators' war activities, see Al Parker, "The Decade: 1940–1950," in Walt and Roger Reed, *The Illustrator in America 1880–1980: A Century of Illustration* (New York: The Society of Illustrators, 1984; first published 1966), 206; Melissa Dabakis, "Gendered Labor: Norman Rockwell's *Rosie the Riveter* and the Discourses of Wartime Womanhood," in Barbara Melosh, ed., *Gender and American History since 1890* (New York: Routledge, 1993), 182–204. Painter Ad Reinhardt challenged the wisdom of excluding the illustrators. See Ad Reinhardt ["The Fine Artist and the War Effort"] in Rose, *Art-as-Art*, 173–77.

92. Minutes, Artists for Victory, 16 February 1944, 18 March 1944, 31 March 1944, reel 116, AV, AAA.

93. The jury of awards consisted of painters Leon Kroll, Peter Blume, Raphael Soyer, Franklin Watkins, and Fernand Léger; John Abbott of the Museum of Modern Art; Henri Marceau of the Philadelphia Museum; Emily Genauer; and Peyton Boswell of *Art Digest*. See Minutes, Artists for Victory, 31 March 1944, 26 May 1944, 7 June 1944, 14 June 1944, reel 116, AV, AAA; "Pepsi-Cola Response," *Art News* 43 (1–31 August 1944): 9.

94. The first prize winner, Waldo Pierce's *Maine Swimming Hole* (1939), won $2,500. Philip Evergood's *Wheels of Victory* won the second prize of $2,000. Louis Bosa's *Sidewalk Market* won the third prize of $1,500, and Joseph De Martini's *Summer's Day* won the fourth prize of $1,000. The remaining eight winners, including Stuart Davis's *The Terminal*, took $500 each. "12 Americans Hit the Spot!" *Art News* 44 (1–31 August 1944): 13–14, 27; "Pepsi-Cola Buys 14 More Paintings," *Art Digest*, 15 November 1944, 8. See also Minutes, Artists for Victory, 27 June 1944, and Report, Artists for Victory, 16 February 1945, both on reel 116, AV, AAA.

95. Minutes, Artists for Victory, 27 June 1944, reel 116, AV, AAA; "12 Americans Hit the Spot!" 27; Boswell, "Portrait of America," 3; "Story of a Modern Calendar," *Design* 48 (November 1946): 8.

96. Peyton Boswell, "Portrait of America?" *Art Digest*, 15 October 1944, 3.

97. Ernest W. Watson, "Portrait of America: Comment on the Pepsi-Cola Competition," *American Artist* 8 (October 1944): 25–27; Mack, "Pepsi-Cola's Competition-Exhibition," 143; Minutes, Artists for Victory, 15 November 1944, reel 116, AV, AAA.

98. Watson, "Portrait of America," 25.

99. Ibid.

100. The "modern" jurists were Henry Schnakenberg, Henry Varnum Poor, and Joseph Stella, with Hugo Gellert, Katherine Schmidt, and Robert Gwathmey as alternates. The "traditional" jurists were Hobart Nichols, Wayman Adams, and Alexander Brook; alternates were Gladys Rockmore Davis, Leon Kroll, and Adolf Dehn. See "Next Year's Calendar Competition," 2 November 1944; Minutes, Artists for Victory, 9 December 1944, both on reel 116, AV, AAA; Mack, "Pepsi-Cola's Competition-Exhibition," 144; "Calendars," *Life*, 1 January 1945, 41–44.

101. Mack, "Pepsi-Cola's Competition-Exhibition," 144; Peyton Boswell, "Another Portrait of America," *Art Digest*, 15 January 1945, 3; idem, "To Jury or Not to Jury No. 2," *Art Digest*, 1 November 1947, 7; "Pepsi-Cola Plans," *Art Digest*, 15 February 1946, 11; "The Pepsi-Cola Competition," *Art Digest*, 1 December 1945, 32; "Boston and California View with Alarm," *Art Digest*, 15 September 1945, 16; "Story of a Modern Calendar," 9; Minutes, Artists for Victory, 15 February 1945, 7 March 1945, 26 April 1945, reel 116, AV, AAA.

102. "Story of a Modern Calendar," 9; "Pepsi-Cola Plans," 11; Peyton Boswell, "Changes for the Better," *Art Digest*, 15 February 1948, 7.

103. Minutes, Artists for Victory, 26 July 1945, reel 116, AV, AAA.

104. Minutes, Artists for Victory, 14 June 1944, reel 116, AV, AAA. One cannot discount the possibility that Watson simply did not like the idea that another corporation should be successfully garnering such publicity.

105. Minutes, Artists for Victory, 14 June 1944, 26 June 1944, 7 March 1945, 26 April 1945, reel 116, AV, AAA.

106. Minutes, Artists for Victory, 26 July 1944, 29 November 1944, 12 December 1945, 4 April 1945, 19 February 1946, reel 116, AV, AAA.

107. "Pepsi-Cola, R.I.P.," *American Artist* 13 (March 1949): 3; Tedlow, *New and Improved*, 81–93, 103. For Pepsi sweepstakes advertisement, see *Life*, 17 May 1948, 137.

108. Russell Lynes, "Whose Business is Art?" *Art in America*, Spring 1956, 12.

109. Franklin Baker and Gladys Hinnus, "Does Fine Art Pay?" *Printer's Ink*, 2 January 1948, 30–31.

"The philosophy of art for art's sake has no standing in the field of advertising," wrote Paul Gropman of Allied Advertising Artists in Los Angeles in 1952. "Since advertising has the responsibility of achieving specific aims, it must impose limitations upon art which is created to serve the end desired. Under this constraint the artist chafes. Artists now working in the field may, and I am sure, will reject this statement with vigor, but they cannot, with much success, repudiate it." Paul Gropman, "Why Artists Shouldn't Be Art Directors," *Advertising Agency* 45 (September 1952): 166. See also Ralph Pearson, "Is There Art in Commercial Art?" *Design* 51 (January 1950): 6, 30; Rosser Reeves, *Reality in Advertising* (New York: Alfred A. Knopf, 1961), 117–18.

110. According to Baker and Hinnus, market research showed the United States Brewers Foundation's newer advertisements increasing "observation by men" by 33 percent and "by women by over 20 percent." Baker and Hinnus, "Does Fine Art Pay?" 31. The sort of

people who paid attention to beer advertisements were evidently not the most appropriate audience for art.

111. Pearson, "Is There Art in Commercial Art?" 6.

112. This limited sampling was based on counting full-page advertisements because "fine art" advertisements were always full page. The percentage of "fine art" images would be much lower were full-, half-, and quarter-page ads to be counted. The percentage of "fine art" was slightly higher in *Life* in 1942, closer to 8 percent; the percentage of "fine art" advertisements dropped to about 3 percent by 1947. The ratio of illustrations to photographs was actually slightly higher during the war years, averaging 32 percent for illustrations to 28 percent for photographs in 1942 and 47 percent to 40 percent in 1947.

Karal Ann Marling describes an alternative aesthetic that advertisers were developing primarily for food advertising and packaging, one that relied on color photography and virtuoso culinary concoctions. See Karal Ann Marling, *As Seen on TV: The Visual Culture of Everyday Life in the 1950s* (Cambridge, Mass.: Harvard University Press, 1994), 202–240.

113. Craven, "Abstract Expressionism," 84–92. See also Ad Reinhardt, "Art-as-Art," in Richard Kostelantz, *Esthetics Contemporary* (Buffalo: Prometheus Books, 1978), 213–16; Harold Rosenberg, "Pop-Culture: Kitsch Criticism," in *Tradition of the New* (New York: McGraw Hill, 1965; first published 1959), 266–67.

114. As Reinhardt wrote in 1952, ". . . today many artists like myself refuse to be involved in some ideas. In painting, for me no fooling-the-eye, no window-hole-in-the-wall, no illusions, no representations, no associations, no distortions, no paint-caricaturings, no cream pictures or drippings, no delirium trimmings, no sadism or slashings, no therapy, no kicking-the-effigy, no clowning, no acrobatics, no heroics, no self-pity, no guilt, no anguish, no supernaturalism or subhumanism, no divine inspiration or daily perspiration, no personality-picturesqueness, no romantic bait, no gallery gimmicks, no neo-religious or neo-architectural hocuspocus, no poetry or drama or theater, no entertainment business, no vested interests, no Sunday hobby, no drug-store museums, no free-for-all history, no art history in America of ashcan-regional-WPA-Pepsi-Cola styles, no professionalism, no equity, no cultural enterprises, no bargain-art commodity, no juries, no contests, no masterpieces, no prizes, no mannerisms or techniques, no communication or information, no magic tools, no bag of tricks-of-the-trade . . . no confusing painting with everything that is not painting." Ad Reinhardt, "Abstract Art Refuses" (1950), in Rose, *Art-as-Art,* 50–51.

In the words of critic Harold Rosenberg, "the best art of our time restricts its appeal to other artists, a group that has neither money nor social glamor to bestow and whose members are for the most part bitter and miserly in handclapping." Rosenberg, "Pop Culture, Kitsch Criticism," 267. See also Rosenberg, "The American Action Painters," in *Tradition of the New,* 25–32; Michael Leja, "The Formation of an Avant-Garde in New York," and Richard Shiff, "Performing an Appearance: On the Surface of Abstract Expressionism," in Michael Auping, ed., *Abstract Expressionism: The Critical Developments* (New York: Harry N. Abrams, 1987), 20–30, 94–95; Judith Higgins, "To the Point of Vision: A Profile of Richard Pousette-Dart," in *Transcending Abstraction: Richard Pousette-Dart, Paintings, 1939–1985* (Fort Lauderdale: Museum of Art, Fort Lauderdale, 1986), 14. Recent scholarship has refuted the myth of the avant-garde artist as bohemian outsider. See Leja, *Reframing Abstract Expressionism,* 46–48; T. J. Clark, "Jackson Pollock's Abstraction," and Serge Guilbaut, "Post War Painting Games," in Serge Guilbaut, ed., *Reconstructing Modernism: Art in New York, Paris, and Montreal, 1945–1964* (Cambridge, Mass.: MIT Press, 1990), 30–83, 172–243; Guilbaut, *How New York Stole the Idea of Modern Art;* Doss, *Benton, Pollock, and the Politics of Modernism,* chapter 6; Bradford R. Collins, "*Life* Magazine and the Abstract Expressionists, 1948–51: A Historiographic Study of a Late Bohemian Enterprise," *Art Bulletin* 73 (June 1991): 283–307.

115. By "self-professed" avant-garde, I am referring to those artists who saw themselves as part of a collectivity committed to extending the modernist aesthetic project (initiated in Europe some 75 years earlier) and opposing prevailing artistic standards and methods through radical, innovative means of expression or subject matter. In mentioning the artists' concepts of an avant-garde as an "aesthetic phenomenon" I am drawing upon Michael Leja's fine-tuned discussion of "avant-garde" in *Reframing Abstract Expressionism,* 20–24. On ideals of professionalism, see Laurence Veysey, "The Plural Organized World of the Professions," in Alexandra Oleson and John Voss, eds., *The Organization of Knowledge in Modern America 1870–1930* (Baltimore: Johns Hopkins University Press, 1979), 50–60; Andrew Abbott, *The System of Professions: An Essay on the Division of Expert Labor* (Chicago: University of Chicago Press, 1988), 8–9; Howard Becker, *Art Worlds* (Berkeley: University of California Press, 1982), 228–32.

116. Lynes, "Whose Business is Art?" 60.

117. David Ogilvy, *Confessions of an Advertising Man,* 118.

118. On corporate collections, see Neil Harris, "Designs on Demand," 376–78; Kahan, *Art, Inc.;* Martorella, *Corporate Art,* 104–19; Richard Ells, *The Corporation and the Arts* (New York: Macmillan, 1967); Eloise Spaeth, "Art and Industry," *Art in America* (Spring 1956): 8–9.

119. The phrase "fine-arts boys" comes from "Fine Art in Ads," *Business Week,* 20 May 1944, 76–80. On illustrators' problems, see Al Parker, "The Decade, 1940–1950," in Walt and Roger Reed, *The Illustrator in America, 1880–1980: A Century of Illustration* (New York: Society of Illustrators, 1984; first published 1966), 206; Watson, *Forty Illustrators and How They Work,* x.

120. Greenberg, "Avant Garde and Kitsch," 16. On "highbrows" and their distinction from middle- and lowbrows, see Russell Lynes, *The Tastemakers* (New York: Harper and Brothers, 1949), 310–33. On the relationship between the avant-garde and commercial culture, see Clark, "Jackson Pollock's Abstraction," 30–83; Doss, *Benton, Pollock, and the Politics of Modernism,* chapter 6; Collins, "*Life* Magazine and the Abstract Expressionists," 283–307.

121. Gans distinguished between "creator-oriented" and "user-oriented" culture in Herbert Gans, *Popular Culture and High Culture* (New York: Basic Books, 1974), 20–27, 75–89.

122. The earliest courses were lessons taught by specific well-known illustrators. However, these books proved too advanced for students, and the organizers soon went back to the drawing board to develop new approaches. The new program began with basics: materials and their use, form, anatomy, figures in motion, perspective, composition, costumes,

and interiors. Students then moved on to line drawing, tone painting, research files, and use of color. After mastering these fundamentals, students would turn to the more advanced lessons in design, lettering, layout, advertising, editorial illustration, and other subjects. The full course consisted of 24 lessons. The school spurned theory: so-called "non-essentials" were kept to a minimum so that students could dive right in and draw pictures. The school, reasoned one commentator, was designed to turn out good *artists,* not art critics—and not everyone had "this theoretical desire to learn esoteric badinage and what can only be described as high-level double talk. They would rather be taught sound, basic fundamentals." Gerry A. Turner, "Institute of Commercial Art: If You'd Like to be an Illustrator," *Design* 51 (January 1950): 12–14. Students learned through copying famous artists' drawings, photographs, and actual objects. Lessons delegated compositional assignments with deadlines, similar to those one might get in a commercial art job. Students would send in completed work; the instructors would make comments and overdrawings and return them to the students. John Atherton, *How I Make a Picture* (Westport, Conn.: Institute of Commercial Art, 1949); Rockwell, *How I Make a Picture;* Jon Whitcomb, *How I Make a Picture* (Westport, Conn.: Institute of Commercial Art, 1949); Famous Artists Schools, *Famous Artists Course* (Westport, Conn.: Famous Artists Schools, 1960). Information on courses also relayed to author by Walt Reed, president of Illustration House and a former instructor at the school. See also Arthur D. Morse, "Twelve Famous Artists, C.O.D.," *Collier's* 125 (25 March 1950): 40–42; "Art as a Career for Women," pamphlet, Famous Artists Schools, 1951; M. B. Ray, "The Story of an Artists' School," *Coronet* 35 (March 1954): 101–2; "The Case of the Practical Artist," *Fortune* 60 (November 1959): 290.

123. Morse, "Twelve Famous Artists, C.O.D.," 30–31, 40. For an example of an advertisement, see *Design* 52 (June 1951): 3. Confirmation that the school would have qualified under the GI Bill of Rights was provided to the author by a representative of the United States Veterans' Administration, phone conversation of 10 August 1993.

124. Famous Artists Schools, "Catalog," n.d. [ca. 1955–1960], 11. On the postwar cultural context, see Frederick Lewis Allen, *The Big Change: America Transforms Itself 1900–1950* (New York: Harper and Brothers, 1952), 221; William E. Leuchtenberg, *A Troubled Feast: American Society since 1945* (Boston: Little, Brown and Company, 1973), 10, 38–64; Thomas Hine, *Populuxe* (New York: Alfred E. Knopf, 1986), 10–17; Warren Susman, with the assistance of Edward Griffen, "Did Success Spoil the United States?: Dual Representations in Postwar America," in Lary May, ed., *Recasting America: Culture and Politics in the Age of Cold War* (Chicago: University of Chicago Press, 1989), 21–22.

125. Ray, "The Story of an Artists' School," 101–2; Famous Artists Schools, "Historical Backgrounds," typescript, Famous Artists Schools. For an earlier example of advertising for a correspondence school in art, see "We Teach Commercial Art," *Vogue,* 1 April 1923, 38.

126. Winston Churchill, *Amid These Storms: Thoughts and Adventures* (New York: Charles Scribner's Sons, 1932), 297–302; 305–20. On Sunday painters, see Eric Newton, "Diagnosis of a New Disease: Amateur Painters," *New York Times Magazine,* 25 September 1949, 17, 34–35; Ray, "The Story of an Artists' School," 101–2; "Executive Grabs His Paints," *Business Week,* 14 April 1951, 22–23; "Amateur Big League," *Life,* 16 April 1951, 71–75; H. J.

Wechsler, "Blessed be the Sunday Painter, May His Tribe Increase," *House and Garden* 102 (August 1952): 69, 85; "Look Out Rembrandt," *American Magazine* 153 (May 1952): 38–39. Statistics found in Allen, *The Big Change*, 274. On postwar malaise, see Leuchtenberg, *A Troubled Feast*, 6, 10; Susman and Griffen, "Did Success Spoil the United States?" 19–37; Elaine Tyler May, *Homeward Bound: American Families in the Cold War Era* (New York: Basic Books, 1988), 92–113.

127. Ironically, by the mid-1950s, the Famous themselves played a limited role in teaching because of the growing numbers of students. The *real* famous artists basically just prepared lesson texts and played a part-time supervisory role—a fact brochure copy indicated, if downplayed. School president Albert Dorne wrote in the catalog, "I want to introduce you to my world-famous colleagues, who, with me, founded the Famous Artists Schools—to our distinguished Guiding Faculties—to our dedicated and experienced instructors." "Catalog," 1. An illustrated section showed artists like Adolph Dehn and Ben Shahn demonstrating their techniques to instructors, with accompanying blurbs. The promotional copy itself was more misleading, however, using phrases like "each of the great creators of your course lends his golden touch of genius to your training. They not only tell you how to be a successful artist—they show you how." "Catalog," 11. Such statements circumvented the fact that the student's actual *correspondence* was with the "artist-instructor," not with the Famous Artist. Art educator Ralph Pearson attacked such tactics and other even more blatant come-ons in correspondence school advertising, without referring specifically to the Famous Artists Schools. See his "Commercial Art School Racketeers," *Design* 51 (April 1950): 7–8. More straightforward discussions of instructors' activities are Ray, "The Story of An Artists' School," 101–2; "The Case of the Practical Artist," 290; "Famous Money-Makers Hit Gold at Westport," *Business Week*, 28 December 1963, 39.

By the mid-1950s, the school was so popular that it not only confronted the realm of high art, it could even subsume part of it. For in addition to its famous illustrators, the school hired some "real" artists, including Stuart Davis and Will Barnet, as Guiding Faculty for its painting course. See "Catalog," pictorial section; Famous Artists Schools, Inc., *Famous Artists Schools Painting Course* (Westport, Conn.: Famous Artists Schools, 1965), sec. 5, lists Guiding Faculty as including Ben Shahn, Stuart Davis, Doris Lee, Will Barnet, Ernest Fiene, Syd Solomon, Doug Kingman, Arnold Blanch, and Adolf Dehn. In 1960 a group of businessmen launched a parallel Famous Writers School, whose training faculty included Bennett Cerf, Faith Baldwin, Berrian Evans, Bruce Catton, Mignon Eberhart, John Caples, Red Smith, and Rod Serling. See Gordon White, *John Caples: Adman* (Chicago: Crain Books, 1977), 100–102.

128. "The Case of the Practical Artist," 290; "Famous Money-Makers Hit Gold at Westport," 38.

129. "Instruction in Art," *New York Times*, 28 March 1948, sec. 2, 11; Val Adams, "Art Instruction for the Masses," *New York Times*, 20 January 1952, sec. 2, 11; Jon Gnagy, *Learn to Draw* (Philadelphia: Martin F. Weber, n.d.). See also Noel Holston, "The Unfinished Work of Jon Gnagy," clipping, *Orlando Sun*, 1986; Liz Seymour, "Jon Gnagy's Big Break," *Art and*

Antiques (May 1991): 17. Both clippings in collection of Greg Etchison, Brownstone Gallery, Brooklyn, N.Y.

130. Adams, "Instruction in Art," 11.

131. Quoted in Holston, "The Unfinished Work of Jon Gnagy."

132. The Washington Square Outdoor Art Exhibit was one of the largest and best known of these exhibitions. Informal exhibitions began in Washington Square in 1931, but the Washington Square Outdoor Art Exhibit was incorporated in 1950. See Janet Summer, "Washington Square Outdoor Art Exhibit, Past and Present," in *Washington Square Outdoor Art Exhibit, 61st Year,* Fall 1992, pamphlet, (New York: Washington Square Outdoor Art Exhibit, 1992), unpaginated. See also "Winner is Repeater in Outdoor Art Show," *New York Times,* 23 May 1950, 62; "Part-Time Artists Put Work on View," *New York Times,* 9 June 1950, 21. See also Marling, *As Seen on TV,* 50–84.

For an intriguing example of the threat posed to the art professionals by a Sunday painter-celebrity, see "Churchill Art Rejected in Chicago as 'Amateur,'" *New York Times,* 22 April 1958, 35. The cultural importance of the Sunday artist was also conveyed in children's picture books. In Don Freeman's 1959 *Norman the Doorman,* for example, mouse Norman, who acts as a doorman/docent in the "Majestic Museum of Art" (enabling his rodent friends to enter safely and admire the "masterpieces"), enters a tiny Calderesque sculpture, fabricated from a mousetrap, in an art contest, "OPEN TO ALL ARTISTS, GREAT AND SMALL!" The tuxedoed and begowned judges (complete with lorgnettes) award his work a first prize, and are shocked to learn that the winner is a mouse. Nevertheless, they treat him quite civilly ("What is your name, my good fellow") and allow him in effect to have the run of the museum. The Sunday artist thus makes himself at home in the established art world. Don Freeman, *Norman the Doorman* (New York: Puffin Books, 1987; first published 1959).

133. By the late 1950s, advertising illustrations were 75 to 80 percent photographs. In an effort to discourage this, some artists and art directors cultivated a distinctive linear style that was easily reproducible and was described as "creative" and "personal," in contradistinction to photography. See Ellen Lupton and J. Abbott Miller, "Line Art: Andy Warhol and the Commercial Art World of the 1950s," in Grey Art Gallery, *"Success is a Job in New York . . .": The Early Art and Business of Andy Warhol* (New York: Grey Art Gallery, 1989), 29–41.

Willem de Kooning was one of the "fine art" painters who competed with illustrators for advertising jobs. See Marla Prather, "Catalogue," in Marla Prather, David Sylvester, and Richard Shiff, *Willem De Kooning: Paintings* (New Haven: Yale University Press, 1994), 80 (illustration), 81.

134. Attempting to establish the image of CBS as a cultivated network, CBS director of graphic arts Georg Olden, for example, commissioned, among others, Howard Mandel, Burton Freud, John Groth, Richard Lindner, and a young Andrew Warhol to paint title cards for its live drama program Studio One, sponsored by Westinghouse. The drama and immediacy of the painting would serve as the artistic counterpart to the excitement of the live programming.

Television advertising storyboards were often done by former Hollywood animators, the primary creators of the animated and live-action commercials favored by clients in the 1950s. As filmed and video commercials and programming began to supplant live advertising and programming after 1956, cinematic models gradually reigned over painted or cartoon animation. Ironically, as programming became one more step removed from "live experience," television advertisers sought increasingly to simulate the "real" in commercials. The shift to cinematic models in television thus paralleled that from illustration to photography in print advertising. The animator's work was no longer highlighted onscreen as conspicuous creation in the ways that it had been earlier in the decade. In the late 1950s, articles on art in television emphasized opportunities in creative departments, such as storyboard design, or as "graphics men," as opposed to work in animation. Judging by the number of listings on the subject in *Art Index,* the number of articles on "art" in television had dropped considerably by the mid-1960s.

On the rise of television and its broader cultural impact, see Leo Bogart, *The Age of Television: A Study of Viewing Habits and the Impact of Television on American Life* (New York: Frederick Ungar, 1956); Lynn Spigel, *Make Room for TV: Television and the Family Ideal in Postwar America* (Chicago: University of Chicago Press, 1992); Cecilia Tichi, *Electronic Hearth: Creating an American Television Culture* (New York: Oxford University Press, 1991). On artists in television, see Lionel Naum, "Television as an Art Career," *American Artist* 15 (February 1951): 31, 67–68; Lawrence Berger, "Requirements for a Career in TV Advertising Art," *American Artist* 17 (February 1953): 42–46, 67–68; Robert J. Wade, "Graphic Art for TV," *Design* 57 (March 1956): 146–47, 155; Lawrence Berger, "The Storyboard," *Design* 59 (May 1958): 198–99; Guy Fraumeni, "Graphics for Television," *American Artist* 25 (February 1961): 34–39. On CBS and the arts, see Georg Olden, "Graphic Arts in TV," *Design* 54 (June 1953): 217, 224; "Illustrating for Television," *American Artist* 18 (September 1954): 42–45; Jules Perel, "Lou Dorfsman: Creative Director of Advertising, CBS Television Network," *American Artist* 25 (June 1961): 42–47; R. Roger Remington and Barbara J. Hodik, *Nine Pioneers in American Graphic Design* (Cambridge, Mass.: MIT Press, 1989), 70–85. Although animators' work for advertisers is certainly part of the story of commercial art, it is beyond the scope of this study. For some introductory material, see Lincoln Diament, *Television's Classic Commercials: The Golden Years 1948–1958* (New York: Hastings House, 1971); Shamus Culhane, *Talking Animals and Other People* (New York: St. Martin's Press, 1986), 280–335; Norman M. Klein, *Seven Minutes: The Life and Death of the American Animated Cartoon* (London: Verso, 1993), 216–17. On Studio One and live programming, see William Boddy, *Fifties Television: The Industry and Its Critics* (Urbana: University of Illinois Press, 1990), 80–92; Eric Barnouw, *Tube of Plenty: The Evolution of American Television* (New York: Oxford University Press, 1990), 154–67.

135. Leo Bogart, *Age of Television,* 140–41.

136. Leo Bogart, *Age of Television* (rev. ed., 1972), note 9, 410; A. J. van Zuilen, *The Life Cycle of Magazines: A Historical Study of the Decline and Fall of the General Interest Mass Audience Magazine in the United States during the Period 1946–1972* (Uithoorn: Graduate Press, 1977).

137. Bernard Fuchs, "The Decade: 1960–1970," and Murray Tinkelman, "The Decade: 1970–1980" in Reed and Reed, *The Illustrator in America*, 282, 312.

138. Mason Griff, "The Commercial Artist," in Maurice R. Stein, Arthur J. Vidich, and David Manning White, eds., *Identity and Anxiety: Survival of the Person in Mass Society* (Illinois: Free Press of Glencoe, 1960), 220–26.

139. Ibid., 231–36.

140. Ibid., 230; italics in original.

141. Erik H. Erikson, "The Problem of Ego Identity," in Stein, Vidich, and White, *Identity and Anxiety*, 37–87; idem, *Childhood and Society* (New York: W. W. Norton, 1963, first published 1950). On the search for identity, see Lary May, "Introduction," and Susman and Griffen, "Did Success Spoil the United States?" 6–7, 23–24; William S. Graebner, *The Age of Doubt: American Thought and Culture in the 1940's* (Boston: Twayne Publishers, 1991), 105–20. See also Leja, *Reframing Abstract Expressionism*, 203–74.

142. Norman Rockwell, *My Adventures as an Illustrator*, as told to Thomas Rockwell (New York: Doubleday, 1960), 301, 386–87.

143. On Warhol's reliability, see Donna M. DeSalvo, "Learning the Ropes: Some Notes About the Early Work of Andy Warhol," in Grey Art Gallery, "*Success is a Job in New York*," 4.

144. The good commercial artist had to be totally malleable, Warhol told an interviewer in 1963. "If they told me to correct it [a drawing of a shoe], I would—I'd do anything they told me to, correct it and do it right." Yet commercial art also demanded creativity and emotion. "I'd have to invent and now I don't; after all that 'correction,' those commercial drawings would have feelings, they would have a style. The attitude of those who hired me had feeling or something to it; they know what they wanted, they insisted; sometimes they got very emotional. The process of doing work in commercial art was machine-like, but the attitude had feeling to it." Andy Warhol, interview with G. R. Swenson, 1963; see also Larry Bell, "Andy Warhol," 1963, both in John Russell and Suzie Gablik, eds., *Pop Art Redefined* (New York: Frederick A. Praeger, 1969), 115–19, quote in Swenson interview, 117.

145. "Art Art," in Andy Warhol, *The Philosophy of Andy Warhol (From A to B and Back Again)* (New York: Harcourt Brace Jovanovich, 1975), 144. Technique of *Coca-Cola Bottles* described by Marco Livingstone, "Do It Yourself: Notes on Warhol's Techniques," in Kynaston McShine, ed., *Andy Warhol, A Retrospective* (New York: Museum of Modern Art, 1989), 68–69.

146. Warhol later wrote, "An artist is somebody who produces things that people don't need to have but that he—for *some reason*—thinks it would be a good idea to give them. Business Art is a much better thing to be making than Art Art, because Art Art doesn't support the space it takes up, whereas Business Art does. If Business Art doesn't support its own space it goes out-of-business." Warhol, *The Philosophy of Andy Warhol*, 144.

147. See Warhol, *The Philosophy of Andy Warhol*, 92. The literature on Warhol is voluminous. Recent discussions include McShine, *Andy Warhol, A Retrospective;* Fred Lawrence Guiles, *Loner at the Ball: The Life of Andy Warhol* (London and New York: Bantam Press, 1989); Victor Bokris, *The Life and Death of Andy Warhol* (London and New York: Bantam

Press, 1989); on Warhol and pop art, see Kirk Varnedoe and Adam Gopnik, *High and Low: Modern Art and Popular Culture* (New York: Harry N. Abrams, 1990), 324–67; Max Kozloff, "American Painting During the Cold War," in Frascina, *Pollock and After*, 117–19; Sidra Stich, *Made in U.S.A.: An Americanization in Modern Art, The '50s and '60s* (Berkeley: University of California Press, 1987); Christen J. Mamiya, *Pop Art and Consumer Culture: American Super Market* (Austin: University of Texas Press, 1992), 131–42.

Illustration Credits

1. Cover, *Saturday Evening Post*, with *Triple Self-Portrait* by Norman Rockwell, 13 February 1960. (Printed by permission of the Norman Rockwell Family Trust. Copyright ©1960 by the Norman Rockwell Family Trust.)

1.1. John Sloan, *Snake Charmer Puzzle*, 1901, *Philadelphia Press*, ink on board. (Delaware Art Museum, Wilmington. Gift of Helen Farr Sloan.)

1.2. Albert Herter, cover for *Ladies' Home Journal* (October 1901). (General Research Division, The New York Public Library, Astor, Lenox and Tilden Foundations.)

1.3. Elizabeth Shippen Green, *The Library*, 1905, watercolor, oil, and charcoal on illustration board. For "The Mistress of the House," *Harper's Monthly Magazine*. (Delaware Art Museum, Wilmington. Samuel and Mary R. Bancroft Memorial, 1935.)

1.4. Howard Pyle, *Peterkin, with ye help of the Hare, carries off the Giant's goose*, ca. 1885, ink, for "Peterkin and the Little Gray Hare," *Harper's Young People*. (Delaware Art Museum, Wilmington.)

1.5. Howard Pyle with his students in studio, ca. 1903 (shows George Harding, Gordon McConik, Thornton Oakley, N. C. Wyeth, and Allen True). (Delaware Art Museum, Wilmington, Howard Pyle Collection.)

1.6. John Sloan, *"Don't you want—th'umbrella?"* 1904, crayon on board. (Delaware Art Museum, Wilmington. Gift of Helen Farr Sloan.)

1.7. Illustrators at Play, 19 February 1914. (Courtesy of the Library of Congress.)

1.8. Thomas Fogarty, *Wee Annie*, drawing, 1907. (All rights reserved, The Metropolitan Museum of Art, Gift of Pearson's Magazine, 1907.)

1.9. Louis Rhead, Poster for the *Morning Journal*, 1895, Liebler and Maass. Lith. N.Y., commercial lithography, 44 9/16 by 58 11/16 inches. (All rights reserved, The Metropolitan Museum of Art, Purchase, The Lauder Foundation, Leonard and Evelyn Lauder Fund Gift, 1986 [1986.1005.15]. Photograph by Bobbie Hansson.)

1.10. Advertisement for *The Adlake Camera*, illustration by Maxfield Parrish, 1897. (Dartmouth College Library.)

1.11. Stuart Davis, *"Gee Mag, Think of Us Bein' on a Magazine Cover,"* cover illustration for *The Masses* 4 (June 1913). (Yale Collection of American Literature, Beinecke Rare Book and Manuscript Library, Yale University.)

1.12. Joseph C. Leyendecker, *Vacation*, cover for *Collier's*, 17 August 1907. (General Research Division, The New York Public Library, Astor, Lenox and Tilden Foundations.)

1.13. Harrison Fisher, *Armour's Harrison Fisher Girl*. (Courtesy of the Library of Congress.)

1.14. N. C. Wyeth, *Where the Mail Goes, Cream of Wheat Goes*, 1906. (Minneapolis Institute of Arts.)

1.15. Charles Dana Gibson, *The Weaker Sex I, Collier's*, 27 June 1903. (General Research Division, The New York Public Library, Astor, Lenox and Tilden Foundations.)

1.16. Charles Dana Gibson, 1916. W. S. Ellis, photographer. (Courtesy National Archives, photo no. 165-WW-61-6.)

1.17. Howard Chandler Christy, *I Want You for the Navy,* 1917. (Courtesy of the Library of Congress.)

1.18. Francis Xavier Leyendecker, *These Men Have Come Across,* 1917. (Courtesy of the Library of Congress.)

1.19. R. F. Babcock, *Join the Navy,* 1917. (Courtesy of the Library of Congress.)

1.20. Henry Reuterdahl and N. C. Wyeth putting last touches on giant battle picture at the Subtreasury Building, Third Liberty Loan Campaign, April 1918. Paul Thompson, photographer (Courtesy National Archives, photo no. 165-WW-61-62.)

1.21. Advertisement for Lux, illustration by McClelland Barclay, 1927. (J. Walter Thompson Company Archives, Special Collections Library, Duke University, Durham, N. C. Courtesy of Lever Brothers Company.)

1.22. Advertisment for Adams® Black Jack Gum®, illustration by Norman Rockwell, *Saturday Evening Post,* 20 March 1920, 18. (Courtesy of Warner-Lambert Company.)

1.23. Page from Norman Rockwell, "My Adventures as an Illustrator," in *Saturday Evening Post,* 13 February 1960, 19. (Printed by permission of the Norman Rockwell Family Trust. Copyright ©1960 by the Norman Rockwell Family Trust.)

2.1. Billboards, Broadway at Forty-second Street, 1905. (Courtesy of the Library of Congress.)

2.2. Joseph Christian Leyendecker, Poster for the August *Century* Midsummer Holiday Number, 1896, published by the Century Company, commercial lithography, 21 5/6 by 15 15/16 inches. (All rights reserved, The Metropolitan Museum of Art, Gift of Bessie Potter Vonnoh, 1941 [41.12.98]. Photograph by Bobbie Hansson.)

2.3. Will H. Bradley, Poster for Victor Bicycles, 1896, J. Ottmann, Lith., commercial lithography, 40 9/16 by 13 1/8 inches. (All rights reserved, The Metropolitan Museum of Art, Leonard A. Lauder Collection of American Posters. Gift of Leonard A. Lauder, 1984 [1984.1202.12]. Photograph by Bobbie Hansson.)

2.4. "Up and Going," Excelsior Ginger Ale, lithograph. (Courtesy of the Library of Congress.)

2.5. Riverside Drive at 119th Street, from New York City, Commissioner of Accounts, *Report on an Investigation of Billboard Advertising in the City of New York* (New York: M. B. Brown, 1912), 2.

2.6. Central Park West, Sixtieth Street and Broadway, from New York City, Commissioner of Accounts, *Report on an Investigation of Billboard Advertising in the City of New York* (New York: M. B. Brown, 1912), 29.

2.7. Guy Carlton Wiggins, *Columbus Circle,* 1911, oil on canvas, 33 1/2 by 40 1/4 inches. (National Museum of American Art, Smithsonian Institution, Gift of William T. Evans.)

2.8. Fifth Avenue, ca. 1910–1915. (Courtesy of the Library of Congress.)

2.9. Ninety-sixth Street and Riverside Drive, from New York City, Mayor's Billboard Advertising Commission, *Report,* 1 August 1913, 128. (General Research Division, The New York Public Library, Astor, Lenox and Tilden Foundations.)

2.10. Rear of sign on Riverside Drive, ca. 1912, from New York City, Commissioner of Accounts, *Report on an Investigation of Billboard Advertising in the City of New York* (New York: M. B. Brown, 1912), 9.

2.11. View of Pennsylvania Station and Eighth Avenue at Thirty-fourth Street, ca. 1916, from National Highways Association, "The Billboard Nuisance in New York City," pamphlet no. 1, 829333, Division of Municipal Art, 2. (Science & Technology Research Center, The New York Public Library, Astor, Lenox and Tilden Foundations.)

2.12. Fifth Avenue at Eighty-ninth Street and Ninetieth Street opposite the Carnegie Mansion, from New York City, Commissioner of Accounts, *Report on an Investigation of Billboard Advertising in the City of New York* (New York: M. B. Brown, 1912), 16.

2.13. Nassau Street, North at Liberty, 25 July 1916. (Courtesy of the Library of Congress.)

2.14. James Montgomery Flagg painting Belgium at New York Public Library for Fourth Liberty Loan Campaign, Underwood & Underwood, photographers. (Courtesy National Archives, photo no. 165-WW-61-4.)

2.15. "Fatty Arbuckle, the movie star, putting up a Liberty Loan poster at Times Square," n.d. [1918], Paul Thompson, photographer. (Courtesy National Archives, photo no. 165-WW-232 B-13.)

2.16. Lucien Bernhard, *Bosch,* 1914. Lithograph, printed in color, 17 7/8 by 25 1/4 inches. (Collection, The Museum of Modern Art, New York. Gift of The Lauder Foundation, Leonard and Evelyn Lauder Fund.)

2.17. Advertisement for poster advertising, featuring billboard for Honey Scotch Candy, in *The Poster* 17 (January 1926): 13. (General Research Division, The New York Public Library, Astor, Lenox and Tilden Foundations.)

2.18. Otis Shepard, *Wrigley's Spearmint Gum,* 1936. Lithograph, 42 by 28 inches. (Collection, The Museum of Modern Art. Gift of the Wrigley Company.)

2.19. Margaret Bourke-White, *At the Time of the Louisville Flood,* 1937, gelatin-silver print, 9 3/4 by 13 1/8 inches. (Collection, The Museum of Modern Art, New York. Gift of the photographer.)

2.20. Anonymous, *Don't Wait,* WPA poster, ca. 1936, 22 by 28 inches. (Courtesy of the Library of Congress.)

2.21. A. M. Cassandre, *Watch the Fords Go By,* 1937. Offset lithograph, printed in color, 8 feet 11 inches by 19 feet 6 1/2 inches. (Collection, The Museum of Modern Art, New York. Gift of the designer.)

3.1. *Carmen,* advertisement for Columbia Graphophone Company, illustration by W. E. Heitland, in Art Directors Club, *Annual of Advertising Art* (New York: Art Directors Club, 1921), frontispiece. (Art & Architecture Collection, Miriam & Ira D. Wallach Division of Art, Prints and Photographs, The New York Public Library, Astor, Lenox and Tilden Foundations.

3.2. Advertisements for Snowdrift and Wesson Oil, illustration by René Clarke, from Art Directors Club, *Annual of Advertising Art* (New York: Art Directors Club, 1921), 82. (General Research Division, New York Public Library, Astor, Lenox and Tilden Foundations. Reprinted by permission of Hunt-Wesson, Inc.)

136 **3.3.** Advertisement for Cheney Silks, illustration by Kees Van Dongen, *Vogue,* 15 November

1927, 141. (General Research Division, The New York Public Library, Astor, Lenox and Tilden Foundations.)

3.4. Advertisement for Lux, 1927. (J. Walter Thompson Company Archives, Special Collections Library, Duke University, Durham, N.C. Courtesy of Lever Brothers Company.)

3.5. Advertisement for Kelly-Springfield Tires, 1923. (Courtesy Kelly-Springfield Tires.)

3.6. Advertisement for Lux, 1936. (J. Walter Thompson Company Archives, Special Collections Library, Duke University, Durham, N.C. Courtesy of Lever Brothers Company.)

3.7. Advertisement for French Line, illustration by Marie Laurencin, 1933. (N. W. Ayer Archive, Warshaw Collection, Archives Center, NMAH, Smithsonian Institution.)

3.8. Advertisement for De Beers Consolidated Mines, Ltd., illustration by Pablo Picasso, 1940. (N. W. Ayer Archive, Warshaw Collection, Archives Center, NMAH, Smithsonian Institution. Photograph: De Beers.)

3.9. Advertisment for Steinway Piano, illustration by Rockwell Kent, in *Vogue,* 1 December 1927, 129. (General Research Division, The New York Public Library, Astor, Lenox and Tilden Foundations. Courtesy of Steinway & Sons New York.)

3.10. Advertisement for Dole Pineapple Juice, illustration by Miguel Covarrubias and Anton Bruehl, 1937. (O/S box 260, N. W. Ayer Archive, Archives Center, NMAH, Smithsonian Institution. Reprinted with permission of Dole Packaged Foods Company.)

3.11. Advertisement for Dole Pineapple Juice, illustration by A. M. Cassandre, 1938. (N. W. Ayer Archive, Archives Center, NMAH, Smithsonian Institution. Reprinted with permission of Dole Packaged Foods Company.)

3.12. Advertisement for Hawaiian Pineapple, illustration by Georgia O'Keeffe, in *Saturday Evening Post,* 15 April 1940, 115. (Columbia University Libraries. Reprinted with permission of Dole Packaged Foods Company.)

4.1. Pirie MacDonald, portrait of Theodore Vail, gelatin silver print, NPG.77.315. (The National Portrait Gallery, Smithsonian Institution.)

4.2. Advertisement for Wade photographic studio, *Abel's Photographic Weekly,* 3 July 1915, 79. (Photograph Collection, Miriam & Ira D. Wallach Division of Art, Prints and Photographs, The New York Public Library, Astor, Lenox and Tilden Foundations.)

4.3. Advertisement for Pond's® Extract Company, Edward Steichen, photographer, in *Vogue,* 15 March 1927, 11. (General Research Division, The New York Public Library, Astor, Lenox and Tilden Foundations. Chesebrough-Pond's Inc. is owner of the registered trademark POND'S.)

4.4. Advertisement for Jergens Lotion, photograph by Edward Steichen, in *Ladies' Home Journal,* November 1924, 95. (General Research Division, The New York Public Library, Astor, Lenox and Tilden Foundations.)

4.5. Clarence White, *Self Portrait,* Collotype, NPG.82.153. (The National Portrait Gallery, Smithsonian Institution.)

4.6. Paul Outerbridge, *Collar.* 1922, gelatin silver print, 4 ½ by 3 ⅝ inches. (Collection, The Museum of Modern Art, New York. Gift of the photographer.)

4.7. "Fabric Group Suits," advertisement for Weber and Heilbroner, Anton Bruehl, photographer, 1927, in Art Directors Club, *Annual of Advertising Art* (New York: Art Directors

Club, 1928), 25. (General Research Division, New York Public Library, Astor, Lenox and Tilden Foundations.)

4.8. Advertisement for Douglass Lighters, Edward Steichen, photographer, in *The New Yorker,* 7 December 1929, 112. (Columbia University Libraries.)

4.9. Advertisement for Weber and Heilbroner Shops, Anton Bruehl, photographer, in *The New Yorker,* 16 November 1929, 83. (Columbia University Libraries.)

4.10. Advertisement for Fostoria Glass, Grancel Fitz, photographer, 1927, in Art Directors Club, *Annual of Advertising Art* (New York: Art Directors Club, 1928), 91. (Art & Architecture Collection, Miriam & Ira D. Wallach Division of Art, Prints and Photographs, The New York Public Library, Astor, Lenox and Tilden Foundations.)

4.11. Advertisement for Julius Keyser and Company, Anton Bruehl, photographer, in *Commercial Photographer* 11 (1936): 435. (Photograph Collection, Miriam & Ira D. Wallach Division of Art, Prints and Photographs, The New York Public Library, Astor, Lenox and Tilden Foundations.)

4.12. Advertisement for Cannon Towels, 1938. (N. W. Ayer Archive, Warshaw Collection, Archives Center, NMAH, Smithsonian Institution. Reprinted with permission from Fieldcrest Cannon, Inc.)

4.13. Advertisement for Scott Tissue, *Ladies' Home Journal,* February 1931, 145. (General Research Division, The New York Public Library, Astor, Lenox and Tilden Foundations.)

5.1. Advertisement for Arrow shirt, ca. 1912, illustration by Joseph C. Leyendecker. (Courtesy of The Arrow Shirt Company.)

5.2. Edwin Howland Blashfield, *The Graduate,* 1907–1908, College of the City of New York, oil on canvas, 264 by 516 inches. (Collection of the City of New York. Courtesy of the Art Commission of the City of New York, Exhibition File 319.)

5.3. Walt Kuhn, *The Publicity Man* (Frederick James Gregg), 1912–1913, pen-and-ink and collage on paper, 5 ¾ by 3 ¾ inches. (Hirshhorn Museum and Sculpture Garden, Smithsonian Institution, Gift of the Joseph H. Hirshhorn Foundation, 1966. Photographer, Lee Stalsworth.)

5.4. Frederick Carl Frieseke, *The Toilet,* oil on canvas, 31 ⅞ by 31 ¾ inches. (All rights reserved, The Metropolitan Museum of Art, Gift of Rodman Wanamaker, 1912 [12.42].)

5.5. Harry W. Watrous, *The Passing of Summer,* 1912, oil on canvas, 36 3/16 by 30 inches (91.9 by 76.2 cm.). (All rights reserved, The Metropolitan Museum of Art, George A. Hearn Fund, 1912 [12.105.3].)

5.6. Stuart Davis, *Lucky Strike,* 1924, oil on paperboard, 18 by 24 inches. (©1995 Estate of Stuart Davis, Licensed by VAGA, New York, N.Y. Hirshhorn Museum and Sculpture Garden, Smithsonian Institution, Museum Purchase, 1974. Photographer, Lee Stalsworth.)

5.7. Maxfield Parrish. (Dartmouth College Library.)

5.8. Advertisement for Fisk Tire, illustration by Maxfield Parrish, 1920. (Dartmouth College Library.)

5.9. Maxfield Parrish, *Daybreak,* 1923, Reinthal and Newman lithograph. (Dartmouth College Library.)

5.10. Rockwell Kent, *Self Portrait (It's Me O Lord)*, 1934, 13 7/16 by 9 3/4 inches. (National Museum of American Art, Smithsonian Institution.)

5.11. "Delectable Crescent," advertisement for Marcus and Company Jewelers, 1928, illustration by Rockwell Kent. (N. W. Ayer Archive, Warshaw Collection, Archives Center, NMAH, Smithsonian Institution.)

5.12. Advertisement for American Export Lines, illustration by Rockwell Kent, 1946. (N. W. Ayer Archive, Warshaw Collection, Archives Center, NMAH, Smithsonian Institution.)

6.1. "Concentration," advertisement for Container Corporation of America, illustration by A. M. Cassandre, 1938. (N. W. Ayer Archive, Warshaw Collection, Archives Center, NMAH, Smithsonian Institution.)

6.2. "Responsibility," advertisement for Container Corporation of America, illustration by Gyorgy Kepes, 1938. (N. W. Ayer Archive, Warshaw Collection, Archives Center, NMAH, Smithsonian Institution.)

6.3. Jean Carlu, *Gift Packages for Hitler*, 1943, ink, gouache, photomontage, and airbrush, 23 1/2 by 18 3/4 inches. (National Museum of American Art, Smithsonian Institution, Gift of Container Corporation of America.)

6.4. *The Netherlands*, advertisement for Container Corporation of America, United Nations series, illustration by Willem de Kooning, 1944. (N. W. Ayer Archive, Warshaw Collection, Archives Center, NMAH, Smithsonian Institution.)

6.5. Charlotte J. Sternberg, *Connecticut*, 1946, gouache on prepared paperboard, 18 1/16 by 15 inches. (National Museum of American Art, Smithsonian Institution, Gift of Container Corporation of America.)

6.6. Jacob Lawrence, *New Jersey*, 1946, watercolor, gouache, and pencil on paper, 24 1/8 by 20 1/6 inches. (National Museum of American Art, Smithsonian Institution, Gift of Container Corporation of America.)

6.7. Corporate advertisement for Young and Rubicam, in *Fortune* 32 (November 1945): 177. (Columbia University Libraries.)

6.8. Advertisement for The Upjohn Company, illustration by Gladys Rockmore Davis, in *Fortune* 32 (December 1945): 98. (Columbia University Libraries. Courtesy of The Upjohn Company.)

6.9. Advertisement for The Upjohn Company, illustration by Fletcher Martin, in *Fortune* 32 (October 1945): 45. (Columbia University Libraries. Courtesy of The Upjohn Company.)

6.10. February 1945 page of Pepsi-Cola calendar, with painting *New England Barn* by Vincent Spagna. (Picture provided courtesy of Pepsi-Cola Co., registered trademark of Pepsico, Inc.)

6.11. Advertisement for United States Brewers Foundation, illustration by Douglas Crockwell, in *Women's Home Companion*, February 1950, 99. (Columbia University Libraries.)

6.12. Andy Warhol, *Green Coca-Cola Bottles*, 1962, oil on canvas, 82 1/2 by 57 inches (209.6 by 144.8 cm.). (Collection of Whitney Museum of American Art, New York. Purchase, with funds from the Friends of the Whitney Museum of American Art, 68.25. © 1995 Andy Warhol Foundation for the Visual Arts/ARS, New York.)

Index

Page numbers in italics refer to illustrations.